Living Trusts

Third Edition

Doug H. Moy

WILEY

John Wiley & Sons, Inc.

This book is printed on acid-free paper. ∞

Copyright © 2003 by Doug H. Moy. All rights reserved.

Published by John Wiley & Sons, Inc., Hoboken, New Jersey
Published simultaneously in Canada

For general information on our other products and services, or technical support, please contact our Customer Care Department within the United States at 800-762-2974, outside the United States at 317-572-3993 or fax 317-572-4002.

Wiley also publishes its books in a variety of electronic formats. Some content that appears in print may not be available in electronic books.

For more information about Wiley products, visit our web site at *www.wiley.com*.

Library of Congress Cataloging-in-Publication Data:

Moy, Doug H.
    Living trusts / Doug H. Moy. — 3rd ed.
        p. cm.
    Includes bibliographical references and index
    ISBN 0–471–26380–X (PAPER / WEBSITE)
    1. Living trusts—United States. I. Title.
    KF734.M69   2003
    343.7305'3—dc21   200215695

Printed in the United States of America

10 9 8 7 6 5 4 3 2 1

About the Website

INTRODUCTION

A website accompanying this book contains an appendix of forms that can be adapted in funding a revocable living trust. The website address is *www.wiley.com/go/livingtrusts*. The password is: moy.

Many of these forms have been universally accepted by financial institutions and other interested parties. Throughout this book, the symbol 📠 appears to identify an appendix on the website. The forms contain information in brackets ([ ]) that may be changed to accommodate a particular situation. Also, the brackets may contain commentary on the use of certain information in the forms or suggestions for completing them. For example, [name of trust] indicates that the name of the living trust agreement should be inserted; that is, the [CURTIS FAMILY] REVOCABLE LIVING TRUST AGREEMENT. Before using the forms, they should be copied to the hard drive of the user's computer. Then open the file on the hard drive and make the appropriate substitutions in brackets or elsewhere in the form.

The forms are believed to be reliable and have been tested and applied in many real-life situations, but they cannot be guaranteed to comply with local law and practice. Because each person's situation may be different, a particular form may need to be modified to comply with the requirements and practice of local law. When legal questions arise in connection with the design of a revocable living trust and with the forms used to fund the trust, the advice of qualified legal counsel should be obtained. *Living Trusts* is not intended as a substitute for qualified legal counsel. In this regard, the advice of a qualified attorney is essential regarding the information, opinions, observations, and recommendations in *Living Trusts*.

About the Author

Doug H. Moy is a consultant to attorneys, accountants, and tax practitioners within his field of specialization—namely, estate/gift taxation and planning, with special expertise in living trusts, community property, lottery-prize winnings, structured settlement trusts, extricating clients from abusive trust tax shelters, and preparation of Form 706 Estate Tax Returns and Form 709 Gift Tax Returns. He offers particular assistance and exceptional skill in designing creative, practical solutions to challenging and difficult estate planning situations, as well as assisting practitioners representing clients before the IRS Conference of Right and Appeals Division.

As a nationally recognized author, seminar speaker, and tax conference lecturer, Mr. Moy has frequently taught CPE for both the National Association of Tax Professionals and the National Society of Accountants. He is an active member of both organizations and has also served on NSA's Federal Taxation Committee. Mr. Moy is a two-time recipient of the "Golden Quill Award," presented by NSA in recognition of his outstanding contributions to the education offerings of the Society. Additionally, he is a past recipient of NSA's "Speaker of the Year Award." A cofounder and charter member of NSA's Institute for Business, Financial & Estate Planning, he designed and coordinated the First Annual Business, Financial & Estate Planning Symposium. Mr. Moy is also an instructor in the Continuing Professional Education Department of Portland Community College. He has frequently been published in *Tax Management Estates Gifts and Trusts Journal* and the *National Public Accountant* and is the author of *Wealth Preservation: How to Start and Develop an Estate Planning Practice*, published by John Wiley & Sons, Inc., and *A Practitioner's Guide to Estate Planning: Guidance and Planning Strategies*, 2 vols., published by Aspen Publishers, Inc. Both native Oregonians, Mr. Moy and his wife, Sharon, reside in Lake Oswego, Oregon. They have two children and two grandchildren.

Craig and Judy, this book is dedicated to you.
Your unwavering friendship and support I value
more than words can ever express.

Contents

Preface

Now in its third edition, *Living Trusts* has been written for three groups of people: those who already have revocable living trusts; those already working with attorneys in the design of revocable living trusts; and those contemplating revocable living trusts. For those people who already have revocable living trusts, odds are they will not operate as they should!

Each chapter of this third edition has been completely revised and updated, and a new chapter on the continuing need for estate planning has been added. Four complete sample revocable living trusts and pour-over wills are included in the appendices. Additional suggested language has been included to guide the reader and his or her attorney on such issues as: business partners serving as co-trustees; surviving spouse and decedent's business partner serving as co-trustees; how to compensate a trustee so that compensation is income tax-free to the trustee, and so forth. Seventeen new appendices have been added. Because of finalized Treasury Regulations issued by the Internal Revenue Service relative to required minimum distributions from qualified plans, a new Chapter 15 has been added just to address Qualified and Nonqualified Plans. In view of these Treasury Regulations, all revocable living trusts named beneficiaries of qualified plans should be reviewed and, if necessary, amended to be in compliance with the new rules regarding required minimum distributions. Such amendments are especially critical if estate tax marital deduction and credit shelter trusts are involved for the trust estates of married trustors. Complete in-depth discussion of the requirements for naming the trustee of a revocable living trust beneficiary of qualified plans is included.

A revocable living trust cannot operate as it should unless legal title to the trustor's assets is correctly conveyed to the trustee; in other words, the trust must be funded. Use of a revocable living trust in estate planning has gained much deserved recognition and acceptance. Local newspapers regularly advertise seminars extolling the advantages of the revocable living trust as an estate planning wonder. Interest in it, as an integral part of a person's estate plan, has skyrocketed. Advertisements hail the revocable living trust as enabling a person to "save thousands in unnecessary conservatorship and probate costs; save thousands in unnecessary estate taxes; and protect children's inheritances from divorces, lawsuits, and from being squandered."

A revocable living trust is a marvelous legal document. When properly designed by a qualified attorney and correctly funded, it can provide all of the estate tax-saving benefits available under a decedent's Last Will. Moreover, it can eliminate a lifetime court-supervised financial guardianship of a person's financial affairs in the event of physical or mental incapacity. Upon the trustor's death, it can facilitate estate administration without the necessity of a court-supervised process known as probate. Unfortunately, though, many times the revocable living trust fails to carry out the trustor's goals of avoiding lifetime court-supervised financial guardianship, avoiding probate at death, and ensuring the privacy of settling one's estate because the trust was either incorrectly funded or not funded at all. All of the legitimate advertised benefits of the revocable living trust are obtainable but only if the trust is correctly funded during the trustor's lifetime.

Unfortunately, some of this author's clients have died; and some of them either became physically disabled or mentally incapacitated before their deaths. Right up to the moment of death, their financial affairs were managed by the successor trustees of their revocable living trusts without the necessity of humiliating court-supervised competency proceedings followed by expensive court-supervised financial guardianships. Similarly, at death, not one estate of those clients who died with a properly funded living trust was probated. These dignity-saving and wealth-preserving results did not occur by accident; they occurred intentionally by design and because each revocable living trust was correctly funded with the trustor's property. *Living Trusts* explains how to avoid an unnecessary lifetime court-supervised financial guardianship and probate at death.

Funding a revocable living trust is usually not a one-time event. That's why *Living Trusts* has been written. Since the successful operation of a revocable living trust depends on it being properly funded during the trustor's lifetime, *Living Trusts* should be read by anyone seeking information and guidance about the funding and day-to-day operation of a revocable living trust. Its purpose is to inform the reader about how a revocable living trust operates, how to correctly convey the legal ownership of property to the trustee of a revocable living trust, how to manage the day-to-day operation of the trust, and what to ask an attorney about designing and funding a revocable living trust agreement. Whether the reader has just recently executed a revocable living trust or has had a revocable living trust for some time, *Living Trusts* provides essential guidance for the reader in working with his or her attorney in designing, funding, and managing a revocable living trust.

In the business of estate planning, degrees of ignorance are more plentiful than experts. Most people don't know how to ask what they don't know. Throughout *Living Trusts* are questions for the reader to ask his or her attorney, together with the answers. These questions appear as **Ask Your Attorney**, followed by the **Answer**. The reader may also find these questions and answers helpful to evaluate whether an attorney is qualified to practice estate planning and to advise the reader about the use and operation of a revocable living trust. Every effort has been made to make *Living Trusts* user-friendly and provide the reader, his or her attorney, tax adviser, and other financial advisers involved in the design, implementation, and funding of a revocable living trust with accurate, objective information based on reliable authority.

Every effort has been made to ensure the accuracy and reliability of the information imparted in *Living Trusts*, but the accuracy of the information is not guaranteed. *Living Trusts* has been written with the understanding that the author, the author's corporation, and the author's employees are not engaged in rendering legal, accounting, or trust services. Finally, if a question arises about conveying to the trustee of a revocable living trust ownership of a particular kind of property not addressed in *Living Trusts*, it does not mean that the title to such property cannot be conveyed. Rather, what it does mean is that this author has yet to consult to a client's attorney with regard to that particular kind of property.

Doug H. Moy
dougmoy@msn.com
Lake Oswego, OR
June 2003

Acknowledgments

Although writing a book is a team effort, I am solely responsible for the information imparted to the reader. To my executive editor, John DeRemigis, for knowing the importance of keeping *Living Trusts* alive with a completely revised and updated third edition and to my associate editor, Judith Howarth, for her unflappable demeanor and undying patience with me in meeting deadlines; thank you both for being such enjoyable professionals with whom to work and associate—both of you are greatly respected and appreciated.

To all of the other members of the publishing team at John Wiley & Sons, Inc. whose names I do not know and have not enjoyed the privilege of meeting and whose skills and expertise have contributed to the publication of this title, I offer you my sincerest appreciation and gratitude for a job well done.

For more than twenty-eight years, Thomas P. Joseph, Jr. has been my friend, confidant, and personal attorney. Tom, you are appreciated so much; and your continued support of my writing projects and your unselfish willingness to brainstorm technical estate planning challenges are extremely valuable; thank you for continuing to share your valuable insight and practical legal knowledge and experience with me and for your continued confidence in my skills as a consultant to attorneys.

Since the use of revocable living trusts continues to grow, the issue of property insurance is of paramount importance to the trustor and trustee. My thanks to Jim Nelson of State Farm Insurance and his legal staff for their assistance and interest in answering my questions regarding the underwriting of homeowner policies when a revocable living trust is involved.

To Robert St. Marie, Ph.D., my deepest gratitude for helping me to focus on the enjoyment of writing and not the outcome.

William F. Nessly, Jr., Assistant Attorney General, Oregon Department of Justice, understands the legal issues of assigning a lottery winner's interest in a lottery annuity to the trustee of a revocable living trust. Your patience, genuine interest, and willingness to brainstorm these issues with me are sincerely appreciated. Also, thank you for your invaluable assistance in procuring the Oregon Department of Revenue Administrative Rules on Declaratory Rulings.

Last, to my wife, Sharon, whose command of the English language and editing skills are second to none and who is primarily responsible for a very clean manuscript: Thank you for your love, undying devotion, strength, continuing encouragement (even in the face of seemingly overwhelming deadlines), and most of all for being the most important person in my life—I love you.

Abbreviations, Acronyms, and Synonyms

adjusted gross estate (AGE)

Annual Summary and Transmittal of U.S. Information Returns (Form 1096)

applicable credit amount (unified credit)

applicable exclusion amount (exemption amount)

applicable federal rate (APR)

Bureau of Land Management (BLM)

certificate of beneficial interest (CBI)

certificate of deposit (C.D.)

Committee on Uniform Security Identification Procedure (CUSIP)

Community Property Rights at Death Act (CPRDA)

Economic Recovery Tax Act of 1981 (ERTA '81)

Employee Stock Ownership Plan (ESOP)

employer identification number (EIN)

estate tax credit (applicable credit amount)

Exclusive Economic Zone (EEZ)

fair market value (FMV)

family limited partnership (FLP)

Federal Aviation Administration (FAA)

Federal Deposit Insurance Corporation (FDIC)

Federal Employee's Group Life Insurance (FEGLI)

Financial Institution Letter (FIL)

for and on behalf of; or for the benefit of (F/B/O)

General Counsel Memorandum (GCM)

generation-skipping transfer (GST)

generation-skipping transfer tax (GSTT)

grantor retained annuity trust (GRAT)

grantor retained unitrust (GRUT)

growers cooperative (co-op)

income in respect of a decedent (IRD)

Individual Retirement Account (IRA)

Internal Revenue Code (IRC; the Code)

Internal Revenue Service ("IRS" or "the Service")

joint tenants with right of survivorship (JTWROS)

limited liability company (LLC)

National Service Life Insurance (NSLI)

nonsocial security equivalent benefit (NSSEB)

out-of-state probate (ancillary probate)

payable on death (POD)

Private Letter Ruling (Priv. Ltr. Rul.)

qualified domestic trust (QDOT)

qualified family-owned business interest (QFOBI)

qualified personal residence trust (QPRT)

qualified revocable trust (QRT)

qualified subchapter S trust (QSST)

qualified terminable interest property (QTIP)

Revenue Ruling (Rev. Rul.)

revocable living trust (RLT; living trust; living trust agreement)

Secretary of the Treasury (Secretary)

Simplified Employee Pensions (SEP)

social security equivalent benefit (SSEB)

supplemental disability income (SDI)

supplemental security income (SSI)

Tax Reform Act of 1986 (TRA '86)

Tax Reform Act of 1976 (TRA '76)

tax-deferred annuity (TDA)

tax-sheltered annuity (TSA)

taxpayer identification number (TIN)

Technical Advice Memorandum (Tech. Adv. Mem.)

Technical and Miscellaneous Revenue Act of 1988 (TAMRA '88)

transfer on death (TOD)

Treasury Regulations (Regulations)

Under Declaration of Trust (U/D/T)

United States Estate (and Generation-Skipping Transfer) Tax Return (Form 706)

United States Fiduciary Income Tax Return (Form 1041)

United States Gift (and Generation-Skipping Transfer) Tax Return (Form 709)

U.S. Individual Income Tax Return (Form 1040)

U.S. Office of Personnel Management (OPM)

United States Securities & Exchange Commission (SEC)

units of beneficial interest (UBI)

PART I

The Revocable Living Trust in Perspective

CHAPTER 1

Continuing Need for Estate Planning

TRANSFER TAX SYSTEM

For decades, estate planning has been significantly impacted by the federal transfer tax system; namely, estate tax, gift tax, and the generation-skipping transfer tax.

Federal Estate Tax

The U.S. government imposes an indirect progressive estate tax on the privilege of transferring property upon one's death.[1] The property to be valued for estate tax purposes is that which the decedent actually transfers at death, rather than the interest held by the decedent before death or that held by the legatee after death.[2] An estate tax credit (*applicable credit amount*) is allowed against the estate tax imposed by Internal Revenue Code (I.R.C.; Code) Section 2001 on the estate of every decedent who is a citizen or resident of the United States.[3] Because the estate tax is levied upon the "happening of an event" (death) and not on the "tangible fruits" of that event, it is an indirect excise tax. Furthermore, as an indirect tax, the U.S. Constitution does not prohibit Congress from imposing the estate tax. In fact, courts have upheld its constitutionality.[4] Furthermore, it has been held that the imposition of the estate tax is not a deprivation of equal protection under the law in violation of the U. S. Constitution.[5]

There exists a subtle dichotomy in the definition of the estate tax. On the one hand, the Treasury Regulations say that the estate tax is "neither a property tax nor an inheritance tax" but, rather, "is a tax imposed upon the transfer of the entire taxable estate and not upon any particular . . . distributive share." On the other hand, the Treasury Regulations say that the purpose of the federal estate tax is to tax the privilege of transferring the value of the estate owner's property at death.[6] In a way, this is all very interesting but quite academic. Not so academic, however, is the fact that, even though the estate tax is not levied

---

[1] *United States v. Manufacturers Natl. Bank of Detroit,* 363 U.S. 194, 198 (1960); *see* discussion in Chapter 8, sections on "Federal Estate Tax" and "Federal Estate Tax and Revocable Living Trust."

[2] *Propstra v. United States,* 680 F.2d 1248, 1250 (9th Cir. 1982); *see also Ahmanson Found. v. United States,* 674 F.2d 761, 769 (9th Cir. 1981); *Estate of Nowell v. Comm'r,* T.C. Memo 1999-15.

[3] I.R.C. § 2010(a). All section references herein are to the Internal Revenue Code of 1986, as amended, and the regulations thereunder, unless otherwise specified.

[4] Treas. Reg. § 20.0-2(a) and 20.0-2(b)(2); *N.Y. Trust Co. (Purdy Est.) v. Eisner,* 256 U.S. 345, 65 L.Ed. 963 (1921); *Heitsch v. Kavanagh,* 200 F.2d 178 (6th Cir. 1952).

[5] *Estate of Koester v. Comm'r,* T.C. Memo 2002-82.

[6] Treas. Reg. § 20.0-2(a) and 20.0-2(b)(2).

on a particular asset or a beneficiary's distributive share, it generally is payable before the asset is distributed to a beneficiary.

State law creates taxable legal interests and property rights in estates. The ultimate impact of the federal estate tax is controlled by state law. The federal estate tax is merely a tax imposed upon the *transfer of the value of property* at death; it does not control the method of distribution of that property to the decedent's beneficiary's or heirs.

Federal Gift Tax

Code Section 2501 imposes a progressive excise tax on the value of lifetime transfers of property by individual citizens or residents of the United States.[7] The first federal gift tax was imposed by the Revenue Act of 1924. Repealed by the Revenue Act of 1926, the gift tax was reinstituted by the Revenue Act of 1932. With modifications, it has remained part of the Code ever since.

The gift tax is not a property tax but, like the estate tax, is a progressive excise tax on the value of lifetime property transfers by individual citizens or residents of the United States.[8] The gift tax is an excise tax upon the donor's act of making the transfer and is measured by the value of the property passing from the donor to the donee. The gift tax is not imposed upon the receipt of the property by the donee, nor is it necessarily determined by the measure of enrichment resulting to the donee from the transfer.[9]

In the case of a gift by a nonresident alien, the gift tax applies only if the gift consisted of real property or tangible personal property situated within the United States at the time of the transfer.[10] As a general rule, except for shares of stock issued by a domestic corporation or debt obligations,[11] gifts of intangible personal property made by nonresident aliens on or after January 1, 1967, are not subject to the gift tax.[12] However, the gift tax does apply to the transfer of all property (whether real or personal, tangible, or intangible) situated in the United States at the time of the transfer, if either (1) the gift was made on or after January 1, 1967, by a nonresident alien who was an expatriate to whom I.R.C. Section 2501(a)(2) was inapplicable on the date of the gift by reason of I.R.C. Section 2501(a)(3) and Treasury Regulation Section 25.2501-1(a)(3) or (2) the gift was made before January 1, 1967, by a nonresident alien who was engaged in business in the United States during the calendar year in which the gift was made.[13]

Observation

A donor's parents were born in Puerto Rico in 1895 and 1896, respectively, and never filed a declaration of allegiance to Spain. The donor's parents were domiciled in Puerto Rico their entire lives, except for one period from 1924 through 1935. From 1924 through 1926, they resided in another country, where, in 1926, the donor was born. From 1927 to 1935, the donor and the donor's parents resided in yet another country. The donor has resided in Puerto Rico at all times since 1935.

---

[7] Treas. Reg. § 25.2511-2(a); *see* discussion in the "Federal Gift Tax" and "State Gift Tax" sections in Chapter 8.

[8] Treas. Reg. § 25.2511-2(a).

[9] Rev. Rul. 77-378, 1977-2 C.B. 348. *See* Treas. Reg. § 25.2511-2(a).

[10] Treas. Reg. § 25.2511-1(b).

[11] I.R.C. § 2511(b).

[12] I.R.C. § 2501(a)(2); Treas. Reg. §§ 25.2501-1(a)(3)(i), 25.2511-1(b), 25.2511-3(a)(i).

[13] Treas. Reg. § 25.2511-3(a)(2).

The donor's citizenship was derived from Puerto Rican citizenship by operation of the Foraker Act and the donor's U.S. citizenship under the Jones Act by virtue of Puerto Rican citizenship or under 8 U.S.C. 1401(c) and its predecessor statutes. Under these circumstances, the donor's citizenship is derived solely from the donor's citizenship with respect to a United States possession for purposes of applying I.R.C. Sections 2209 and 2501(c). Thus, for purposes of the U.S. gift tax, the donor is considered a *nonresident—not a citizen of the United States*.[14] Such a donor will continue to be considered a nonresident—not a citizen of the United States—for such time as the donor remains a resident of Puerto Rico or another outlying United States possession.[15]

The gift tax is based upon the amount of the gift; and, if the gift is made in property, its *value* on the date of the gift is considered the amount of the gift.[16] An alternate valuation date is not available with respect to determining the amount of gift tax, as is the case with I.R.C. Section 2032 for estate tax valuation. The value of the property gifted is the price at which such property would change hands between a willing buyer and a willing seller, neither being under any compulsion to buy or to sell and both having reasonable knowledge of relevant facts.[17]

Five types of transfers are not subject to the gift tax: (1) transfers to political organizations;[18] (2) transfers to charitable organizations;[19] (3) gifts that qualify for the unlimited gift tax marital deduction;[20] (4) gifts that qualify for the gift tax annual exclusion;[21] and (5) gifts that qualify for the educational and medical expenses exclusion.[22] Gifts that qualify for the gift tax annual exclusion are indexed for inflation.[23] Finally, the gift tax is not imposed upon the receipt of property by the donee; nor is it necessarily determined by the donee's enrichment or benefit from the gift.[24]

Generation-Skipping Transfer Tax

Before the Tax Reform Act of 1976 (TRA '76), successive estate tax could be avoided from one generation to another by placing property in trust for beneficiaries of two or more generations younger than the grantor (transferor). For example, a grandparent could establish a trust for the benefit of his or her children and grandchildren and avoid estate tax at the children's generation. In other words, for gift and estate tax purposes, the trust property skipped one generation (children of the grantor) on its way from the grandparent to the child and then to the grandchild.

In an effort to reduce lost revenue from this planning technique, Congress enacted, as part of TRA '76, the generation-skipping transfer tax (GSTT) into the Code as Chapter 13. The GSTT was designed to be substantially equivalent to the tax that would have been imposed if the property had actually been transferred outright to each successive

---

[14] *See* Treas. Reg. § 25.2501-1(d), examples 2 and 5, and Treas. Reg. § 20.2209-1, examples 2 and 5.

[15] *See* Rev. Rul. 74-25, 1974-1 C.B. 284; Priv. Ltr. Rul. 9720029 (February 13, 1997).

[16] Treas. Reg. § 25.2512(a).

[17] Treas. Reg. § 25.2512-1.

[18] I.R.C. § 2522(a)(1).

[19] I.R.C. § 2522(a)(2).

[20] I.R.C. § 2523(a).

[21] I.R.C. § 2503(b).

[22] I.R.C. § 2503(e).

[23] I.R.C. § 2503(b)(2).

[24] Treas. Reg. § 25.2511-2(a), (b).

generation.[25] The GSTT is imposed in addition to any federal gift tax on lifetime transfers or estate tax imposed at death.

Observation

Certain interests are disregarded if the primary purpose of the interest is to avoid any GSTT. For example, if a transferor placed property in a trust that is to pay income to a great-grandchild for a relatively short period then income to a grandchild for life, with the remainder going back to a great-grandchild, in order to avoid a second imposition of the GSTT, the income interest of the great-grandchild would be disregarded so that GSTT would be imposed upon the death of the grandchild. Such an interest would be disregarded, even though distributions to the great-grandchild are taxable distributions.[26]

Furthermore, parental support obligations may be disregarded in determining a parent's interest in a generation-skipping transfer (GST) trust. Provided the parent's use of trust principal or income to satisfy support obligations is discretionary or pursuant to any state law substantially equivalent to the Uniform Gifts to Minors Act, the parent will not be considered to have an *interest* in the trust for GST purposes. Thus, a parent is not treated as having an interest in a trust by reason of powers the parent may have as guardian for the child. On the other hand, a parent will be treated as having an interest in a trust if the trust instrument requires that trust assets be used to discharge the parent's support obligation.[27]

Example

Grandparent establishes an irrevocable trust for the benefit of grandparent's grandchild. The trustee has discretion to distribute property for the grandchild's support without regard to the duty or ability of the grandchild's parent to support the grandchild. Because the grandchild is a permissible current recipient of trust property, the grandchild has an interest in the trust. The grandchild's parent does not have an interest in the trust because the potential use of the trust property to satisfy the parent's support obligation is within the discretion of a fiduciary. The grandchild's parent would be treated as having an interest in the trust if the trustee was required to distribute trust property for the grandchild's support.[28]

Under the Tax Reform Act of 1986 (TRA '86),[29] a GST means a *taxable distribution*, a *taxable termination* and a *direct skip*.[30] In each case, a GST of *income* or *principal* to a beneficiary who is at least two generations younger than the transferor (grantor) is subject to the GSTT. The term *generation-skipping transfer* does not include:

---

[25] Lloyd Leva Plaine, "The Proposed Generation-Skipping Transfer Tax in the House-Passed Tax Reform Bill," *Tax Management Estates, Gifts and Trusts Journal* 63-64 (May-June 1986) (hereafter, Plaine, *The Proposed Generation-Skipping Transfer Tax*).

[26] *Technical and Miscellaneous Revenue Act of 1988*, Pub. L. No. 100-647, 100th Cong., 2d Sess. (10 November 1988), 1988-3 C.B. 1, S. Rep. at 1173 (hereafter TAMRA '88).

[27] I.R.C. §§ 2652(c)(3) and 2642(c)(2).

[28] Treas. Reg. § 26.2612-1(f), example (15).

[29] *Tax Reform Act of 1986*, Pub. L. No. 99-514, 99th Cong., 2d Sess. (22 October 1986), 1986-3 C.B. 1 (hereafter TRA '86).

[30] I.R.C. §§ 2601 and 2611(a).

- A property transfer, subject to estate or gift tax, to a person in the first generation below the grantor's (transferor's) generation.[31] For example, grandparent transfers property valued at $50,000 outright to grandparent's child; this is not a GST. Or an aunt or an uncle transfers property valued at $100,000 to a nephew or a niece; this is not a GST.

- Any lifetime gift that qualifies for the gift tax annual exclusion under I.R.C. Section 2503(b) or qualified transfers under I.R.C. Section 2503(e) for educational or medical expenses.[32] Similarly, a GST does not include such gifts made in trust after March 31, 1988, provided: (a) during the life of the beneficiary, no portion of the principal or income of the trust may be distributed to or for the benefit of anyone other than such beneficiary; and (b) if the beneficiary dies before the trust is terminated, the assets of the trust will be includable in the gross estate of the beneficiary.[33]

- Any property transfer to the extent the property transferred was subject to a prior GSTT.[34]

- Any GST under a trust [as defined in I.R.C. Section 2652(b)] that was irrevocable on September 25, 1985. This rule does not apply to a pro rata portion of any GST under an irrevocable trust if additions are made to the trust after September 25, 1985.[35]

- Any GST under a trust that is a direct skip, occurring by reason of a decedent's death, is not subject to the GSTT if the decedent was legally incompetent on October 22, 1986, and at all times thereafter until death.[36] However, the incompetency exemption does not apply to property received by the transferor from another person by lifetime gift or testamentary transfer after August 3, 1990.[37]

Proceeds from the settlement of a wrongful death lawsuit (other than the amounts attributable to pain and suffering and reimbursements for medical expenses) not included in decedent's gross estate are not subject to the GSTT.[38]

Examples

1. Grandparent transfers property valued at $50,000 outright to a grandchild. If the grandchild's parent is alive at the time of the transfer, the transfer of the property to the grandchild is a GST. The taxable amount of the gift for purposes of the GST tax is $39,000 [$50,000 − $11,000 gift tax annual exclusion for a gift of a present interest (2002) = $39,000]. Whether grandparent pays any GST tax depends on the extent of the grandparent's unused GST tax exemption.

---

[31] I.R.C. § 2611(b)(2)(B).

[32] I.R.C. §§ 2611(b)(1), 2642(c)(3). *See also* Priv. Ltr. Rul. 9124018 (March 14, 1991) (the merger of two trusts will not result in an addition to corpus for GST purposes and will not result in a taxable gift within the meaning of I.R.C. § 2501).

[33] I.R.C. § 2642(c); Treas. Reg. § 26.2642-1(c)(3). *See also* Priv. Ltr. Rul. 9124018 (March 14, 1991) (the merger of two trusts will not result in an addition to corpus for GST purposes and will not result in a taxable gift within the meaning of I.R.C. § 2501).

[34] I.R.C. § 2611(b)(2)(A).

[35] Treas. Reg. § 26.2601-1(b)(1)(i).

[36] TRA '86 § 1433(b)(2)(C).

[37] *Revenue Reconciliation Act of 1990 (H.R. 5835) Law and Explanation* [Extra Edition No. 48], Stand. Fed. Tax Rep. (CCH) § 11703(c)(3) amending § 1433(b)(2)(C) of the Tax Reform Act of 1986 and § 11703(c)(4) (hereafter RRA '90 Law and Explanation).

[38] Priv. Ltr. Rul. 9622035 (March 4, 1996).

2. Grandparent creates a trust for grandparent's child and grandchild. If the trustee distributes income or principal to the grandchild during the life of the child, that distribution is a GST.

3. Grandparent creates a testamentary trust and provides a life estate for grandparent's child with remainder to grandchild. Child receives income only from the life estate and has no power over the beneficial enjoyment of the life estate trust assets. In the event of the child's death, because the value of the assets composing the life estate trust is not includable in the child's gross estate, it is not subject to estate tax. In effect, for estate tax purposes, the assets of the life estate trust have skipped the child's generation on their way to the grandchild. Such an arrangement constitutes a GST.

With respect to the exemption from GSTT for a decedent who was mentally incompetent on October 22, 1986, and at all times thereafter until death, if a court has not adjudicated the decedent mentally incompetent on or before October 22, 1986, the executor must file, with Form 706, either: A certification from a qualified physician stating that the decedent was mentally incompetent at all times on and after October 22, 1986, and did not regain competence to modify or revoke the terms of the trust or will prior to his or her death; or sufficient other evidence demonstrating that the decedent was mentally incompetent at all times on and after October 22, 1986, as well as a statement explaining why no certification is available from a physician; and any judgment or decree relating to the decedent's incompetency which was made after October 22, 1986. Such items will be considered relevant but not determinative in establishing the decedent's state of competency. If the decedent has been adjudged mentally incompetent on or before October 22, 1986, a copy of the judgment or decree, and any modification thereof, must be filed with the Form 706.[39] The term *mental disability* means mental incompetence to execute an instrument governing the disposition of the individual's property, whether or not there was an adjudication of incompetence and regardless of whether there has been an appointment of a guardian, fiduciary, or other person charged with either the care of the individual or the care of the individual's property.[40] However, where the decedent's executor did not file the required certification with the Form 706 and the decedent's physician and records were currently available, the Internal Revenue Service (IRS or the Service) ruled that the government's interest was not jeopardized by the delay in filing the required information on the decedent's mental condition. Accordingly, a GST trust was not disqualified from eligibility for the mental incompetency exemption contained in the transitional rule solely as a result of the late filing of the necessary documents relating to the decedent's mental condition.[41]

Since a decedent was mentally incompetent on October 22, 1986, until the time of his death, the IRS ruled that the reverse qualified terminable interest property (QTIP) election had been made by the decedent and that the inclusion of the value of QTIP marital trust in the surviving spouse's gross estate pursuant to I.R.C. Section 2044 would not affect the exempt status of the trust for GSTT purposes. The decedent executed his will in 1982 and died in 1992. The decedent's Form 706 contained the statement and the physician's certification regarding the decedent's mental incompetency as required by Treasury Regulations Section 26.2601-1(b)(3)(iii). The Service accepted the return as filed, and the federal estate tax closing letter was issued by the Service on April 29, 1994. Therefore, because the Service agreed that the decedent was under a mental disability to change the disposition of his property continuously from October 22, 1986, until the date of his death, the GSTT did not

---

[39] Treas. Reg. § 26.2601-1(b)(3)(iii), (iv).

[40] Treas. Reg. § 26.2601-1(b)(3)(ii).

[41] Priv. Ltr. Rul. 9535039 (June 2, 1995).

apply to any GST under a QTIP marital trust established under the decedent's will. In addition, because the decedent could not, by reason of incompetency, change his will as of October 22, 1986, the provisions of the will would have been on that date, and dating back to September 25, 1985, as a practical matter, irrevocable. Consequently, the Service concluded that the provisions applicable to the grandfathering of irrevocable trusts[42] were applicable to the QTIP marital trust and that the decedent's estate would be deemed to have made a reverse QTIP election[43] with respect to the marital trust.[44]

IMPACT OF TAX LEGISLATION

Tax Reform Act of 1976

The Tax Reform Act of 1976 (TRA '76)[45] changed significantly the strategies and planning techniques used by estate owners to plan their estates. Before 1977, two separate tax rate schedules applied to lifetime gifts and transfers of property at death. Congress viewed the two-tax-rate system as a way for people to avoid paying the higher tax on the real value of property at death. Furthermore, Congress viewed lifetime transfers as a tax-reducing vehicle afforded to only the wealthy and generally unavailable for those of small and moderate wealth. These estate owners generally want to retain their property until death to assure financial security during lifetime. TRA '76 consolidated the gift and estate tax rates to create a single unified transfer tax and credit system. This unified rate schedule provides progressive rates and applies to decedents dying after December 31, 1976, and to cumulative lifetime gifts made after that date.

For federal estate tax purposes, TRA '76 introduced special use valuation as a new method for the valuation of real property used as a farm for farming purposes or in a trade or business other than the trade or business of farming.[46] Additionally, with the introduction of the generation-skipping transfer tax, estate planning can no longer be undertaken just once every other generation. No longer can the attorney simply design a trust with the income to the estate owner's children for life and the principal to his or her grandchildren without taking into account the impact of the generation-skipping transfer tax. Changes in the federal estate tax marital deduction further complicated the use of formulas in order to ensure effective use of the marital deduction for property passing under the decedent's will and for property passing outside the will to the decedent's surviving spouse.

Economic Recovery Tax Act of 1981

The new planning strategies and techniques brought about by TRA '76 were followed and further influenced by the complex rules found in the Economic Recovery Tax Act of 1981 (ERTA '81).[47] Perhaps the most profound and significant change introduced by ERTA '81

---

[42] TRA '86 § 1433(b)(2)(A) and Treas. Reg. § 26.2601-1(b)(1)(i).

[43] I.R.C. § 2652(a)(3).

[44] Priv. Ltr. Rul. 9639015 (June 14, 1996). *See also* Priv. Ltr. Rul. 9741025 (July 11, 1997) (because decedent could not by reason of incompetency change her will as of October 22, 1986, the provisions of the will would have been, on that date, and dating back to September 25, 1985, as a practical matter, irrevocable).

[45] *Tax Reform Act of 1976*, Pub. L. No. 94-455, 94th Cong., 2d Sess. (24 October 1976), 1976-3 (Vol. 1) C.B. 1 (hereafter TRA '76).

[46] I.R.C. § 2032A(a)(1) and (b)(2).

[47] *Economic Recovery Tax Act of 1981*, Pub. L. No. 97-34, 97th Cong., 1st Sess. (13 August 1981), 1981-2 C.B. 256 (hereafter ERTA '81).

was the unlimited federal estate tax marital deduction. No single estate and gift tax planning benefit has been more misunderstood and misused by married persons than the unlimited estate tax marital deduction. Its misuse, in conjunction with the federal estate tax exemption amount, has done more than any other single factor to cause the payment of additional and unnecessary federal estate tax upon the subsequent death of the surviving spouse.

Even before ERTA '81 became law, someone created the absurd notion that it would eventually eliminate approximately "99.6 percent of all estates from estate and gift taxes!" Unfortunately, many people believed this—probably because it was what they wanted to hear. Apparently, though, because of the increased amounts exempt from estate and gift tax, the new unlimited estate and gift tax marital deduction, and the reduction in estate and gift tax rates, many people erroneously dismissed the importance of estate planning. Similar inertia to engage in estate planning is affecting many people in view of The Economic Growth and Tax Relief Reconciliation Act of 2001 (the 2001 Act).[48] Indeed, it is absurd to think that estate planning is no longer necessary just because the 2001 Act has increased the amount exempt[49] from federal estate tax.

Tax Reform Act of 1986

The Tax Reform Act of 1986 (TRA' 86)[50] substituted the Code of 1986 for the Code of 1954. TRA '86 replaced the generation-skipping transfer tax rules established under TRA '76 by imposing a completely new set of rules. Gone also were many of the loopholes upon which generations of practitioners and estate owners had come to rely for the avoidance of transfer tax on their wealth. President Ronald Reagan hailed TRA '86 as the "most sweeping overhaul of our tax code in our nation's history."

Revenue Reconciliation Act of 1990

In yet another attempt to feed its insatiable spending appetite and wring more revenue out of the already overburdened American taxpayer, Congress passed the Revenue Reconciliation Act of 1990 (RRA '90).[51] The provisions of RRA '90 significantly impacted the use of retained life estates as a technique for reducing the value of the gross estate subject to federal estate tax. In addition, the special valuation rules of I.R.C. Sections 2701-2704 were added to the Code, which severely curtailed the so-called *estate-freezing* technique previously used by many closely-held business owners. This technique was used as a means of shifting to their children the appreciation in value on closely-held stock owned by parents, thereby reducing the value of the stock included in the parents' gross estate for federal estate tax purposes. Moreover, I.R.C. Sections 2701-2702 and 2704 have rendered it more difficult for older family members to transfer interests in closely-held businesses to younger family members without incurring gift tax.

The decade of the eighties may very well be remembered as producing more tax legislation than any other in twentieth-century American history. Practitioners and estate owners

---

[48] *The Economic Growth and Tax Relief Reconciliation Act of 2001*, Pub. L. No. 107-16, 107th Cong., 1st Sess. (7 June 2001) (hereafter the 2001 Act).

[49] The amount exempt from federal estate tax is the *applicable exclusion amount*, which is commonly referred to as the *exemption amount*.

[50] *Tax Reform Act of 1986*, Pub. L. No. 99-514, 99th Cong., 2d Sess. (22 October 1986), 1986-3 C.B. 1 (hereafter TRA '86).

[51] *Revenue Reconciliation Act of 1990* in *Omnibus Budget Reconciliation Act of 1990*, Pub. L. No. 101-508, 101st Cong., 2d Sess. (1990), 1991-2 C.B. 481 (hereafter RRA '90).

must continue to deal with complexities in the myriad tax laws enacted since TRA '76. In its continuing effort to "simplify" the tax laws, Congress continues to rely on its members and their aides whose theoretical abilities overshadow their practical and real-life experiences in designing comprehensive and simplified tax laws. At the other extreme, the irony of politicians, lawyers, and accountants discussing ways to reduce the complexity of the tax laws is, in the words of former Joint Committee on Taxation Chief of Staff David H. Brockway, "like going to a Hell's Angels Conference on the decline of social graces in America. . . . We *are* the problem." It seems that one tax act is only replaced by new legislation as esoteric and confusing to estate owners as the already unmanageable law it modified or replaced. Additional complexity and confusion have been created because some of the tax acts themselves have amended previous tax acts, the provisions of which have not become part of the Code. Overall, much of the legislation resulting in the myriad tax acts was poorly conceived, poorly drafted, and leaned more heavily for implementation on regulations,[52] many of which have not yet been drafted.

Taxpayer Relief Act of 1997

The Taxpayer Relief Act of 1997 ("the 1997 Act")[53] enacted several changes that move trusts and estates toward closer tax parity and effected myriad other technical changes to the Code with respect to estate, gift, and generation-skipping transfer taxes. All of these changes add further complexity to the estate-planning process. The federal estate tax exemption amount was to have increased from $600,000 in 1997 to $1 million in 2006 and thereafter.[54] After 1998, the $10,000 gift tax annual exclusion, the $750,000 ceiling on special use valuation, the $1 million generation-skipping transfer tax exemption, and the $1 million ceiling on the value of closely-held business interests eligible for the special low interest rate for deferred payment of federal estate tax are all indexed annually for inflation.[55] In addition, under the 1997 Act, the executor of a decedent's estate may elect special estate tax treatment for qualified family-owned business interests, if such interests comprise more than 50 percent of a decedent's estate and certain other requirements are met. In general, the provision excludes the first $1 million of value in qualified family-owned business interests from a decedent's taxable estate.[56] With respect to the deferred payment of federal estate tax attributable to the value of closely-held business interests included in the decedent's estate, the 1997 Act reduces the 4 percent interest rate to 2 percent and makes the interest paid on estate tax deferred under I.R.C. Section 6166 nondeductible for estate and income tax purposes. Finally, as a general rule, the Service cannot revalue a gift for estate tax purposes after expiration of the statute of limitations, provided the gift is adequately disclosed on a gift tax return.

---

[52] Commerce Clearing House Tax Advisory Board, "The Changing Practice of Tax Law for Lawyers and Accountants," 72 *Taxes* 190, 207 (April 1994) (hereafter, CCH Tax Advisory Board, "Practice of Tax Law for Lawyers and Accountants").

[53] *Taxpayer Relief Act of 1997*, Pub. L. No. 105-34, 105th Cong., 1st Sess. (1997), 111 Stat. 788 (hereafter "the 1997 Act").

[54] *But see* discussion under "Federal Estate Tax Exempt Amount Increased" section, *infra* for changes made to the exemption amount by *The Economic Growth and Tax Relief Reconciliation Act of 2001*, Pub. L. No. 107-16, 107th Cong., 1st Sess. (7 June 2001) (hereafter "the 2001 Act").

[55] *But see* discussion under "Federal Estate Tax Exempt Amount Increased" section, *infra* for changes made to generation-skipping transfer exemption amount beginning in 2002 under the 2001 Act.

[56] *But see* discussion under "Family-Owned Business Interest Deduction" section, *infra* regarding repeal of the qualified family-owned business interest deduction after December 31, 2003, I.R.C. § 2057(j).

THE ECONOMIC GROWTH AND TAX RELIEF RECONCILIATION ACT OF 2001

Overview

Congress added more unnecessary complexity to the Code by enacting the 2001 Act. Congress added new rules that will significantly impact estate planning for the next several years. The 2001 Act is truly unique in that never before has Congress enacted a tax act based on ten-year revenue projections. Estate planners must now address clients' estate planning needs and objectives by employing the rules promulgated under TRA '76, ERTA '81, TRA '86, the 1997 Act, and what may well prove to be nonpermanent rules under the 2001 Act.

Repeal of the Federal Estate and Generation-Skipping Transfer Tax

Perhaps the most significant impact of the 2001 Act is the scheduled repeal of the federal estate and generation-skipping transfer tax after December 31, 2009.[57] However, the federal gift tax is not repealed; and the maximum federal gift tax exemption amount is $1 million in 2002 and thereafter.[58]

Federal Estate Tax Exemption Amount Increased

The 2001 Act phases in a new applicable exclusion amount (exemption amount) and applicable credit amount,[59] which is gradually increased to shelter from federal estate tax $3.5 million of the value of property transferred at death. The exemption, referred to as the *applicable exclusion amount*[60] (exemption amount), and the unified credit, referred to as the *applicable credit amount*[61] (unified credit), is $1,000,000 and $345,800, respectively, in 2003.[62] In the case of estates of decedents dying in calendar years after 2002 and before 2010, the tentative federal estate tax will be determined by using a table prescribed by the IRS [in lieu of using the table contained in I.R.C. Section 2001(c)(1) which will be the same table, except that the maximum rate of tax for any calendar year will be the rate discussed below; and the marginal federal estate tax brackets and the amounts setting forth the tax will be adjusted to the extent necessary to reflect the adjustments made by the reduction in the maximum federal estate tax rate].[63] From 2002 through 2009, the maximum federal estate tax rates and the exemption amount are shown in Exhibit 1.1 :[64]

The exemption amount is reduced (but not below zero) by the sum of (1) the amount of decedent's taxable gifts (adjusted taxable gifts) made after December 31, 1976, which are not includable in the decedent's gross estate and (2) the aggregate amount of the pre-TRA '76 $30,000 specific gift tax exemption allowed for gifts made by the decedent after September 8, 1976. In effect, the *exemption amount* is the reciprocal of the unified credit. The *exemption* is the amount of the gross estate exempt from (not subject to) federal estate tax or

---

[57] I.R.C. §§ 2210(a); 2664 flush language and (d).

[58] I.R.C. § 2505(a)(1); the 2001 Act, § 521(b), (e)(2).

[59] In effect, the unified credit is the tax credit equivalent of the exemption amount.

[60] I.R.C. § 2010(c).

[61] I.R.C. § 2010(a).

[62] I.R.C. §§ 2001(c)(1), 2010(c).

[63] I.R.C. § 2001(c)(2)(A).

[64] I.R.C. §§ 2001(c)(2) and 2010(c).

Exhibit 1.1   Maximum Federal Estate Tax Rates And The Exemption Amount

Calendar Year	Estate and GST Tax Deathtime Transfer Exemption Amount	Highest Estate and Gift Tax Rates
2002	$1 million	50 percent
2003	$1 million	49 percent
2004	$1.5 million	48 percent
2005	$1.5 million	47 percent
2006	$2 million	46 percent
2007	$2 million	45 percent
2008	$2 million	45 percent
2009	$3.5 million	45 percent
2010	N/A (taxes repealed)	Top individual income tax rate

gift tax on lifetime gifts in excess of the gift tax annual exclusion amount or gift tax marital deduction. Conversely, the *unified credit* is a tax credit equivalent to the amount that is exempt from federal estate (or gift) tax and is subtracted from the tentative tax due (estate or gift tax). The applicable exclusion amount of the unified credit is not indexed for inflation.

With respect to the generation-skipping transfer tax, for estates of decedents dying, and generation-skipping transfers, *before* January 1, 2004, the GST exemption amount is $1 million subject to an inflation adjustment.[65] This adjustment is obtained by multiplying $1 million by the cost-of-living adjustment determined under I.R.C. Section 1(f)(3) for such calendar year by substituting "calendar year 1997" for "calendar year 1992" in subparagraph (B) thereof.[66] The generation-skipping transfer tax exemption amount for the year 2003 is $1,120,000.[67] For decedents dying, and generation-skipping transfers, *after* December 31, 2003, the GSTT exemption amount for any calendar year will not be indexed for inflation but will be equal to the applicable exclusion amount under I.R.C. Section 2010(c) for such calendar year.[68] Thus, in 2004 and 2005, the GSTT exemption amount is $1.5 million; in 2006, 2007, and 2008, the GSTT exemption amount is $2 million; and, in 2009, the GSTT exemption amount is $3.5 million.[69]

Payment of Federal Gift Tax on Transfer of Property to Trust

After December 31, 2009, the top federal gift tax rate will be the top individual income tax rate (35 percent);[70] and, except as provided in regulations, the transfer to a trust will be treated as a taxable gift, unless the trust is treated as wholly owned by the donor or the donor's spouse under the grantor trust provision of I.R.C. Sections 671-678.[71] Since the revocable living trust (RLT) is governed for tax purposes by I.R.C. Sections 671-678, the conveyance of title to assets to a revocable living trust is not a gift taxable event. Thus, as a general rule, none of the trustor's exemption amount is used up in effecting such conveyances.

---

[65] I.R.C. § 2631(a) and (c).

[66] I.R.C. § 2631(c)(1).

[67] Rev. Proc. 2002-70, 2002-46, I.R.B. 1 at .25.

[68] I.R.C. § 2631(c) applicable to estates of decedents dying, and generation-skipping transfers after December 31, 2003.

[69] I.R.C. §§ 2010(c); 2631(a) and (c).

[70] I.R.C. § 2502(a)(2).

[71] I.R.C. § 2511(c).

Federal Estate and Gift Tax Rates Reduced

The 2001 Act reduces the federal estate and gift tax rates. The maximum federal estate and gift tax rate for taxable estates and gifts in excess of $2.5 million in 2003 is 49 percent; 2004, 48 percent; 2005, 47 percent; 2006, 46 percent; and, in 2007, 2008, and 2009, 45 percent.[72] In 2002, the 5 percent surtax (which phased out the benefit of the graduated rates) was repealed.[73] As previously mentioned, the maximum federal gift tax rate after 2009 is scheduled to be 35 percent.[74]

Family-Owned Business Interest Deduction

In 2004, the qualified family-owned business interest deduction is repealed.[75]

State Death Tax Credit

Under the 2001 Act, from 2002 through 2004, the state death tax credit rate is, in effect, decreased from a maximum of 16 percent as follows: to 12 percent in 2002, to 8 percent in 2003, and to 4 percent in 2004. The amount of state death tax credit shown in the table in I.R.C. Section 2011(b) is reduced by 25 percent in 2002, 50 percent for the estates of decedents dying in 2003, and 75 percent for the estates of decedents dying in 2004.[76] The state death tax credit is repealed for estates of decedents dying after December 31, 2004.[77] In 2005, after the state death tax credit is repealed, there will be a deduction for death taxes (e.g., any estate, inheritance, legacy, or succession taxes) actually paid to any state or the District of Columbia in respect of property included in the decedent's gross estate.[78]

REPEAL OF STEPPED-UP BASIS

Another significant change under the 2001 Act affecting estate plans now and after 2009 is the repeal of stepped-up basis for property in the hands of a beneficiary received from a decedent's estate after December 31, 2009.[79]

Modified Carryover Basis

After repeal of the federal estate and generation-skipping transfer tax,[80] the basis of assets acquired from a decedent for income tax reporting purposes, generally, will equal *the lesser of* the basis of the decedent (i.e., carryover basis) at death or the fair market value of the property at the date of the decedent's death.[81] However, a decedent's estate is permitted to increase the basis of appreciated assets transferred to any beneficiary by up to a total of $1.3 million (i.e., the basis of the asset(s) may be *modified*).[82] The basis of appreciated property

---

[72] I.R.C. § 2001(c)(2)(B).
[73] The 2001 Act, § 511(b) and (f)(1).
[74] I.R.C. § 2502(a)(2).
[75] I.R.C. § 2057(j).
[76] I.R.C. § 2011(b)(2); the 2001 Act, § 531(b).
[77] I.R.C. § 2011(g).
[78] I.R.C. § 2058(a).
[79] I.R.C. § 1014(f).
[80] I.R.C. § 1022(a)(1).
[81] I.R.C. § 1022(a)(2).
[82] I.R.C. § 1022(b)(2)(B).

transferred to a surviving spouse can be increased (i.e., stepped-up) by an additional $3 million.[83] Thus, the basis of property transferred to a surviving spouse can be increased (i.e., stepped-up) by a total of $4.3 million.[84] With respect to the $1.3 million and $3 million amounts, the decedent (e.g., the trustor) will be treated as owning property transferred by the decedent during his or her lifetime to a qualified revocable trust, as defined in I.R.C. Section 645(b)(1).[85] In no case can the basis of an asset be adjusted above its fair market value.[86] For these purposes, the decedent's personal representative will determine which assets and to what extent each asset receives a basis increase.[87] The $1.3 million and $3 million amounts are adjusted annually for inflation occurring after 2010.[88]

New Reporting Requirements for Large Transfers

Under the 2001 Act, new reporting requirements are imposed with respect to carryover basis. For transfers at death *after* December 31, 2009, of *noncash* assets in excess of $1.3 million[89] (so-called *large transfers*), and for appreciated property, the value of which exceeds $25,000 (except for gifts to charitable organizations)[90] received by a decedent within three years of death,[91] the decedent's personal representative (or the trustee of a revocable trust) would report[92] to the IRS:[93]

- The name and taxpayer identification number of the recipient of the property;
- An accurate description of the property;
- The adjusted basis of the property in the hands of the decedent and its fair market value at the time of death;
- The decedent's holding period for the property;
- Sufficient information to determine whether any gain on the sale of the property would be treated as ordinary income;
- The amount of basis increase allocated to the property; and
- Any other information as the Treasury Secretary may prescribe by regulation.

Information Furnished to Recipient of Property

In addition, every person required to report *large transfers* to the IRS is required to furnish not later than 30 days after the date the return is filed[94] to each person (i.e., beneficiary, heir, or property recipient) whose name is required to be listed in such return (other than the

---

[83] I.R.C. § 1022(c)(2)(B).

[84] I.R.C. § 1022(c)(1).

[85] I.R.C. § 1022(d)(1)(B)(ii).

[86] I.R.C. § 1022(d)(2).

[87] I.R.C. § 1022(d)(3)(A).

[88] I.R.C. § 1022(d)(4)(A).

[89] I.R.C. § 6018(b)(1).

[90] *Economic Growth and Tax Relief Reconciliation Bill 2001 (H.R.. 1836), Descriptions Contained in the Conference Committee Report on H.R. 1836, the Economic Growth and Tax Relief Reconciliation Bill of 2001,* as released on May 30, 2001, Fed. Est & Gift Tax Rep. (CCH), ¶ 29,056, 44,145, 44,151 (hereafter *Conference Committee Report on H.R. 1836*).

[91] I.R.C. § 6018(b)(2).

[92] I.R.C. § 6018(b)(4).

[93] I.R.C. § 6018(c).

[94] I.R.C. § 6018(e) flush language.

person required to make such return) a written statement showing: the name, address, and phone number of the person required to make such return and the information described above which is reportable to the IRS on the return.[95]

Penalties

The required return is to be filed with the decedent's income tax return for the decedent's last taxable year or such later date specified in regulations prescribed by the secretary of the treasury.[96] Any person required to furnish such information is subject to a penalty of $10,000 for each failure to do so.[97] Any person who must report to the IRS the receipt by a decedent within three years of death of appreciated property valued in excess of $25,000 within three years of death and who fails to do so is liable for a penalty of $500 for the failure to report such information to the IRS.[98] A penalty of $50 is imposed for each failure to report such information to a beneficiary.[99] No penalty is imposed with respect to any failure that is due to reasonable cause.[100] If any failure to report to the IRS or a beneficiary is due to intentional disregard of the rules, then the penalty is 5 percent of the fair market value of the property for which reporting was required, determined at the date of the decedent's death (for property passing at death) or determined at the time of gift (for a lifetime gift).[101]

Lifetime Gifts

For lifetime gifts required to be reported on a gift tax return for the calendar year, the donor must provide each donee (property recipients) listed on the return: (1) the name, address, and phone number of the person required to make such a return, and (2) the information specified in the gift tax return with respect to property received by the donee.[102] The written statement must be furnished to the donee not later than 30 days after the date that the gift tax return is filed.[103]

OTHER CHANGES UNDER THE 2001 ACT AND SUNSET PROVISION

Other changes under the 2001 Act, but less significant as far as their impact on estate planning is concerned, are those with respect to the repeal of certain restrictions on where land is located with respect to conservation easements under I.R.C. Section 2031(c)(8)(A)(i); various amendments to the generation-skipping transfer tax under I.R.C. Sections 2632 and 2642;[104] amendments to I.R.C. Section 6166 for the installment payment of federal estate tax;[105] and waiver of statute of limitations for taxes on certain farm valuations.

---

[95] I.R.C. § 6018(e).

[96] I.R.C. § 6075(a).

[97] I.R.C. § 6716(a).

[98] I.R.C. § 6716(a).

[99] I.R.C. § 6716(b).

[100] I.R.C. § 6716(c).

[101] I.R.C. § 6716(d).

[102] I.R.C. § 6019(b).

[103] I.R.C. § 6019(b) flush language.

[104] *See* discussion in Chapter 8.

[105] *See* discussion in Chapter 12.

The 2001 Act is subject to a sunset provision. In this regard, all provisions of, and amendments made by, the 2001 Act do not apply to estates of decedents dying, gifts made, or generation-skipping transfers, after December 31, 2010. Whether the sunset provision of the 2001 Act is set aside by future legislation remains to be seen. Based on this author's more than 30 years of estate planning experience, it is unlikely that the federal estate and generation-skipping transfer tax will be repealed after December 31, 2009, as scheduled. The sunset provision provides that all provisions of, and amendments made by, the 2001 Act will not apply to estates of decedents dying, gifts made, or generation-skipping transfers, after December 31, 2010.[106] In effect, the Code of 1986 will apply as if the provisions and amendments made by the 2001 Act had never been enacted.[107]

CONTINUING NEED FOR ESTATE PLANNING

Prior to the enactment by Congress of TRA '76, estate planning was relatively simple and straightforward. The family attorney was usually quite adept at designing a will and trust to administer and distribute an estate owner's property at death. Furthermore, the preparation of wills used to be a loss leader—the theory being that such client services led to other business, including a profitable fee for probating the testator's estate.[108] The tax laws were relatively understandable and contained many loopholes; creative and ingenious planning opportunities abounded.

However, with the promulgation of TRA '76, estate planning became complicated. The tax laws are no longer rational, and they are unnecessarily complex. It has become a real challenge for practitioners just to communicate the effect of particular estate, gift, and generation-skipping transfer tax provisions of the Code to estate owners. Today, the family attorney and accountant find themselves bewildered by estate planning as we have come to know it. Gone are the days of preparing a will as a loss leader for other more profitable legal services.

Estate Planning without Estate Tax

Some years ago, the National Association of Estate Planning Councils observed that nearly 5 percent of those persons who have estates to plan do any significant estate planning. Although many people perceive estate planning as dealing only with taxes and the purchase of life insurance, ample evidence suggests that most people need advice and guidance in the preservation and disposition of the estates they have created. Unfortunately, for many decades, estate owners have allowed tax planning to become the tail that wags the dog. Even if the federal estate tax and generation-skipping transfer taxes are, in fact, repealed in 2010, estate planning is still necessary. Trust planning for a surviving spouse will still be necessary to provide financial security and efficient management of assets, particularly for a surviving spouse who does not have a penchant for asset management. Divorces will still occur; children with special needs will still be born; protection for spendthrifts will still be necessary; trusts for education funds will still be desirable; cautionary advice will continue to be needed about the perils of abusive trust tax shelters; and business succession planning will still be of vital concern to business owners. People will still need to know their planning options regarding a variety of needs and objectives to ensure family wealth

---

[106] The 2001 Act, Sec. 901(a)(2).

[107] The 2001 Act, Sec. 901(b).

[108] Nicholas U. Sommerfeld, "Techniques That Can Help Professionals Develop A More Successful Practice," 10 *Estate Planning* 330, 333 (November 1983).

preservation. The revocable living trust can effectively serve as the primary instrument for the lifetime management of a person's assets and for the orderly and cost effective disposition of those assets upon the death of the trustor. To this end, will and trust planning will continue for totally nontaxable reasons.

In retrospect, starting with TRA '76 all tax laws enacted by Congress have brought unprecedented complexity into the estate and gift tax planning arena. Today practitioners and estate owners are faced with new challenges as a direct result of post-TRA '76 legislation, case law, IRS rulings, and regulations. Thus, in view of all of the tax law changes that have occurred, anyone who is seriously interested in keeping together and transferring to their loved ones, with the least amount of emotional trauma and financial cost, that which they have worked so hard to create needs estate planning. With the exemption amount scheduled to increase to $3.5 million in 2009, persons whose estates are valued at less than $3.5 million will tend to dismiss the value and need for comprehensive estate planning, since such an amount will not be subject to federal estate tax. Yet, $3.5 million represents a substantial estate that deserves to be afforded every nontax estate planning strategy available to ensure its preservation.

The need for comprehensive and effective estate planning is greater than ever. Some married estate owners will say, "If my wife and I can each leave an amount equal to the federal estate tax exemption amount free of estate tax to our children, I don't have anything to worry about because our total estate is not worth two times the exemption amount." Or, "Since I can leave the entire value of my estate to my spouse estate tax free, why should I worry about planning my estate?" The reality is that, even for smaller estates, estate planning is essential to lifetime financial security.[109] In view of the 2001 Act, wills and trusts should be designed to accommodate the three phases of the 2001 Act, namely, "rate reduction/exclusion increase, repeal, and revival."[110]

Following the enactment by Congress of ERTA '81, estate-planning inertia befell many estate owners. Like untreated depression, similar inertia will challenge estate owners in view of the 2001 Act. As the exemption amount increases, estate owners will have more to protect—not necessarily from federal estate and state death tax but for the economic, social, educational, health care, and special needs of beneficiaries. Marital deduction trust plan-

---

[109] *See* Jonathan G. Blattmachr, Georgiana J. Slade, and Bridget J. Crawford, "Selected Estate Planning Strategies for Persons With Less Than $3 Million," *Estate Planning* 243 (July 1999).

[110] Sidney Kess and Lee Slavutin, "Planning Techniques and Tips: Important Considerations in Drafting the Will," *Estate Planning Review* in 4 *Financial and Estate Planning* 60, 62, Commerce Clearing House, Inc., Chicago, Ill (July 19, 2001); for additional reading, *see* Ronald D. Aucutt, "An A-to-Z 'To Do' List Following EGTRRA," 28 *Estate Planning* 606 (December 2001); Jonathan G. Blattmachr and Lauren Y. Detzel, "Estate Planning Changes in the 2001 Tax Act—More Than You Can Count," 95 *Journal of Taxation* 74 (August 2001); David Frees, "Marketing Estate Planning After The 2001 Act: Interview With David Frees," interview by editors of Commerce Clearing House, Inc., *Estate Planning Review* in 4 *Financial and Estate Planning*, issue 521 (August 20, 2001): 89; James F. Gulecas and Alan S. Gassman, "The Economic Growth and Tax Relief Reconciliation Act of 2001: Practical Estate Planning," 15 *Practical Tax Lawyer.* 35 (Summer 2001); Philip Marcovici, Teresa Lewis, Marnin J. Michaels, Victoria A. Dalmas and Christine Hsieh-Kammerlander, "New U.S. Tax Act: Dramatic Consequences for Estate, Gift, GST Regime in the Foreign Context: Part 1," 26 *Estate Planner's Alert* 2 (September 2001), Part 2 (October 2001) 2 in Research Institute of America *Estate Planning & Taxation Coordinator*; Charles F. Newlin and Andrea C. Chomakos, "The 2001 Tax Act: Uncharted Waters for Estate Planners," 15 *Probate & Property* 32 (September-October 2001); Northern Trust Company, "The Economic Growth and Tax Relief Reconciliation Act of 2001," in 3 *Financial and Estate Planning*, Commerce Clearing House, Chicago, IL, ¶ 32,351, at 27,171; Sanford J. Schlesinger, "Estate and Gift Tax—Update 2001," *Estate Planning Review*, in 4 *Financial and Estate Planning* 1, Commerce Clearing House, Chicago, IL (January 22, 2002); Edward Spacapan, Jr., "2001 Tax Act Substantially Improve Retirement and Savings Plans," 29 *Estate Planning* 16 (January 2002).

ning to minimize estate tax, for example, may no longer be necessary for many estate owners; nevertheless, these same estate owners may be duly concerned about providing a surviving spouse with financial security and protection of assets from mismanagement. Trusts for a surviving spouse which bear some resemblance to marital and nonmarital deduction planning trusts may still be employed but not necessarily for the purposes of minimizing or entirely eliminating federal estate tax in both the decedent spouse's and surviving spouse's respective estates. Or an estate owner may be concerned about the impact of divorce on the ultimate disposition of his or her estate in the event of remarriage and how such an event, such as divorce, might affect his or her children. Likewise, an estate owner may be concerned about the potential for a child to divorce his or her spouse and the impact that such a marriage termination would have on the share of the estate owner's estate in the hands of the divorcing child. TRA '76 and all of the tax laws enacted since TRA '76 demand that anyone with an estate make a financial and time investment in properly planning his or her estate.

Furthermore, even if under the 2001 Act the estate and generation-skipping transfer taxes are permanently repealed, the gift tax remains in effect. Moreover, after December 31, 2009, except as provided in Treasury Regulations, the transfer of property to a trust will be treated as a taxable gift, unless the trust is wholly owned by the donor or the donor's spouse under the grantor trust provisions of I.R.C. Sections 671 through 678.[111] Conceivably, a transfer of property in trust for charitable purposes could reduce the donor's available gift tax exemption amount, if the trust is not wholly owned by the donor or the donor's spouse.[112] As a general rule, a charitable remainder trust is not a grantor trust; but a revocable living trust is a grantor trust.

Definition of an Estate

At the risk of oversimplification, all of a person's property or interests in property comprises his or her gross estate.[113] Legally speaking, an estate is the degree, quantity, nature, and extent of a person's interest in real and personal property.[114] Thus, in the broadest terms, anyone who owns property or has an interest in property has an estate.

Property Included in the Gross Estate

As a general rule, the gross estate includes the value of all property to the extent of the decedent's interest in the property at the time of death.[115] It is the decedent's possession of the economic benefits of property that determines whether the value of the property is included in the decedent's gross estate.[116] Accordingly, the gross estate includes property owned by a decedent at the time of death which can be transferred in accordance with the terms of a will, under the provisions of a revocable living trust, by right of survivorship, by beneficiary designation in a contract, or by the law of intestate distribution (i.e., to die

---

[111] I.R.C. § 2511(c).

[112] *See* Commerce Clearing House, ed., *2001 Tax Legislation: Law, Explanation and Analysis (Economic Growth and Tax Relief Reconciliation Act of 2001)*, Commerce Clearing House, Chicago, IL, 2001, Practical Analysis at 105 (hereafter CCH, *2001 Tax Legislation: Law, Explanation and Analysis*).

[113] I.R.C. §§ 2031 and 2033.

[114] Henry Campbell Black, M.A., *Black's Law Dictionary* (West Publishing, 5th ed. 1979), 490 (hereafter Black, *Black's Law Dictionary*).

[115] I.R.C. § 2033.

[116] *Burnet v. Wells*, 289 U.S. 670, 678 (1933); *Helvering v. Safe Deposit & Trust Co. of Baltimore*, 316 U.S. 56, 56 n. 1 (1942).

without a will).[117] Hence, a decedent's estate may include probate assets (probate estate), as well as property passing to a decedent's beneficiaries outside of probate (nonprobate estate).

The gross estate may also include other property interests that the decedent did not own at death. Such interests may include: dower or courtesy interests (I.R.C. Section 2034); transfers of property for insufficient consideration (I.R.C. Section 2043); qualified terminable interest property (QTIP) for which the marital deduction was previously claimed (I.R.C. Section 2044); prior interests (I.R.C. Section 2045); disclaimed property (I.R.C. Section 2046); income in respect of a decedent (IRD) (I.R.C. Section 691); gifts of property made within three years of death (I.R.C. Section 2035); transfers of property with retained life estate (I.R.C. Section 2036); transfers of property taking effect at death (I.R.C. Section 2037); revocable transfers of property (I.R.C. Section 2038); property subject to a grantor retained annuity or income trust (I.R.C. Section 2702); property subject to a general power of appointment (I.R.C. Section 2041); and annuities, including retirement plan benefits (I.R.C. Section 2039). The gross estate does not include property that the decedent owned at death that could not be transferred by a will or by intestate distribution, such as a life estate created by another person.

Transfer Taxes Imposed upon the Estate

The value of a decedent's estate may be subject to federal estate tax and state death taxes (transfer taxes).[118] For both tax and nontax planning purposes, the federal estate tax exemption amount may be used to determine whether a person's estate is small, medium, or large. An estate valued at the federal estate tax exemption amount or less may be a small estate; an estate valued in excess of the federal estate tax exemption amount, but less than two times the federal estate tax exemption amount, may be a medium-size estate; and an estate valued in excess of two times the federal estate tax exemption amount may be a large estate. However, a husband and wife might each have a small to medium-size estate; but, combined, they might have one large estate for the survivor of them. Regardless of value, effective and efficient estate planning begins and ends with the correct form of property ownership and the proper beneficiary designations of contract benefits.

UNDERSTANDING THE FIVE ESTATES IN ESTATE PLANNING

A person's estate consists of the *gross estate, adjusted gross estate* (AGE), and *taxable estate*. The gross estate, however, consists of assets that compose the *probate estate* and the *nonprobate estate*. Certain deductions are allowed to be taken from the value of the *gross estate* to determine the value of the AGE, which, in turn, leads to determining the value of the *taxable estate*. Taxes levied on the taxable estate can be reduced by certain tax credits. Thus, five different estates must be taken into account in the estate planning process.

Developing an effective estate plan depends on the practitioner's and estate owner's ability to understand the interrelationship of the probate and nonprobate estates to the gross estate, together with their relation to the AGE, and the taxable estate. Remember, the gross estate includes the decedent's probate estate and nonprobate estate.

Probate Estate

What is the probate estate? A person's probate estate consists of all property passing to beneficiaries under the terms of a will; or, if the estate owner dies without a will (to die *intestate*), the probate estate includes property passing to the decedent's heirs by state law of

---

[117] Black, *Black's Law Dictionary*, 490.

[118] I.R.C. § 2001(a).

intestate distribution. Probate property includes all property a person owns individually as tenants in common and, in certain cases, as community property. Any property that is payable to or distributable to the decedent's estate at death is part of the decedent's probate estate. For example, an insured decedent's estate may have been designated beneficiary of life insurance proceeds. In such case, the value of the life insurance proceeds is includable in the decedent's gross estate for purposes of the federal estate tax and is also part of the decedent's probate estate. Accordingly, the life insurance proceeds are subject to the court-supervised procedure known as *probate* before the proceeds are distributable to the decedent's beneficiaries under a will or, if the decedent died without a will, to the decedent's heirs under state law of intestate succession.

Example

Neville B. Johnson is the owner of a life insurance policy insuring his life for $200,000. When his insurance agent asked him to whom he wanted the insurance proceeds paid upon his death, Neville replied, "To my estate." Accordingly, the insurance agent wrote on the insurance application in the space provided for designating the beneficiary the following: "Beneficiary: to the estate of the insured Neville B. Johnson." Thus, in the event of Neville's death, and assuming this beneficiary designation is not revoked prior to Neville's death, the insurance company will pay the insurance proceeds "to the estate of Neville B. Johnson." Accordingly, the life insurance proceeds will become part of Neville's probate estate and will be subject to the court-supervised process known as probate.

Property Directed to Decedent's Estate

Any property that is payable or distributable to the decedent's estate is part of the probate estate (e.g., payable-on-death (POD) bank accounts, qualified plan benefits, any type of contractual benefit wherein the decedent's estate can be designated beneficiary). Remember: if the decedent's estate is the beneficiary of any property, then the value of such property is part of the decedent's probate estate; if property owned by the decedent passes to a beneficiary by the terms of the decedent's will, the value of the property is part of the decedent's probate estate; and, if the decedent dies without a will, the value of property in the decedent's own individual name or property that is payable to the decedent's estate is part of the probate estate and passes to the decedent's heirs under the laws of intestate distribution.

Community Property

If property is owned by a husband and wife as community property, the surviving spouse's one-half interest may or may not be subject to probate, depending on state community property law. This may be the case if the spouses entered into a community property agreement that contains a survivorship provision. Even if the decedent spouse's one-half interest in the community property need not be probated because it passes outright to the surviving spouse, it may be necessary for a probate court to determine that the property is, in fact, community property. Absent such a determination, a title company may be unwilling to insure the title to real property.

Necessity of Probate Estate

Along with the correct form of property ownership and beneficiary designation of contract benefits, the probate estate is the next most important consideration in the estate planning process. This is particularly true when a revocable living trust is not used in the estate plan. A decedent's will cannot carry out its purpose unless there is a probate estate. Generally, a will cannot distribute property that is not part of the probate estate.

For example, if the decedent spouse owns property with the other spouse as joint tenants with right of survivorship (JTWROS), or the surviving spouse is designated beneficiary of the decedent spouse's contract benefits (e.g., qualified plan benefits, 401(k) plans, Simplified Employee Pensions (SEP), Individual Retirement Accounts (IRA), Keogh plans, qualified or nonqualified deferred compensation plans, salary continuation benefits, survivor benefits, individual life insurance, group term life insurance, and so forth), then, upon the decedent spouse's death, those assets pass directly to the surviving spouse and not by the terms of the decedent spouse's will. Hence, trusts for the surviving spouse, minor and adult children, or beneficiaries with special needs cannot be funded. Likewise, special bequests not in trust to specific beneficiaries, such as individuals and charities, cannot be funded.

Pour-Over Will

The only exception to this rule is a pour-over will that directs property in the decedent's probate estate to be distributed under the terms of a revocable living trust (RLT) created before a person's death. Such assets may be subject to a probate proceeding before being distributed to the RLT. Under the small estate statutes of most states, depending on the value of such probate estate assets, a formal probate proceeding may or may not be required to clear title to such assets before being distributed to the RLT. In other words, the will recognizes the existence of the RLT and provides that any property discovered after the decedent's death which was not conveyed to the trustee of the RLT before the decedent's death is to be distributed (*poured over*) to the RLT and administered according to the terms of the RLT. Property conveyed (titled in the name of the RLT trustee) to the RLT during the decedent's lifetime is not part of the decedent's probate estate because legal title or ownership of the property vests by law in the trustee, thereby obviating the need to clear title to such property in a probate proceeding.

Nonprobate Estate

What is the nonprobate estate? Generally, all property passing outside the decedent's will is not subject to the probate process. Accordingly, such property is not part of the decedent's probate estate.

Life Insurance

Life insurance proceeds paid to a designated beneficiary other than the insured decedent's estate are included in the nonprobate estate. In other words, if the life insurance proceeds are payable to a named beneficiary other than the decedent's estate (e.g., a surviving spouse, to any person, or to the trustee of a trust), then, such proceeds are not part of the probate estate. Rather, such proceeds are part of the decedent's nonprobate estate. However, if the insured decedent possessed an incidents of ownership in the life insurance policy at death, then, the proceeds are includable in the value of the decedent's gross estate.

Property Received by Right of Survivorship

Property owned by the decedent as JTWROS (including tenancy by the entirety) with any other person, whether such person is related or unrelated to the decedent or is the decedent's spouse, is includable in the value of the decedent's gross estate and is part of the decedent's nonprobate estate. Perhaps the most popular and celebrated reason for joint ownership with right of survivorship is the avoidance of probate. Since the surviving co-tenant (joint owner) acquires ownership of the entire property automatically by right of survivorship upon the death of the other co-tenant, the decedent co-tenant's interest in the property is not part of the decedent's court-administered probate estate. Likewise, out-of-state probate (ancillary probate) can be avoided on property located in another state that is owned as JTWROS. Finally, the absence of probate may also prevent publicity and ensure privacy about the nature and value of the property passing to the surviving co-tenant.

Bank Trust Accounts and Contract Benefits

Bank accounts and contract benefits may be part of the decedent's nonprobate estate. Bank accounts held *in trust for* (so-called Totten trust) a person who survives the decedent are included in the nonprobate estate. Qualified retirement plan benefits, including IRAs, Keogh plans and 401(k) plans, SEPs, qualified and nonqualified deferred compensation plan benefits, salary continuation benefits, annuity contracts, and individual and group life insurance proceeds payable to a designated beneficiary other than the decedent's estate are part of the nonprobate estate.

Other Nonprobate Property

Other property interests included in the nonprobate estate are: property gifted by the estate owner during lifetime, the value of which may be included in the decedent's gross estate solely for computing the federal estate tax, and property interests given in trust by someone else to the decedent which pass upon the decedent's death by a general power of appointment exercised by the decedent in favor of another beneficiary. However, if the decedent exercised a general power of appointment over such property in favor of the decedent's estate, then such property is included in the decedent's probate estate. Finally, property conveyed to a revocable (or irrevocable) living trust by the decedent before death is not subject to probate. Accordingly, such property may be includable in the value of the decedent's gross estate and is part of the decedent's nonprobate estate. Not only is such property not subject to probate but the trustor can also control the ultimate disposition of the property; whereas, if the decedent had continued to own the property as JTWROS, or if the property passed by beneficiary designation, then trusts would not be funded with the property as they could be if the property were distributable under the provisions of a RLT.

Coordination of Beneficiaries with Property Ownership

Regardless of whether transfer taxes are of concern to the estate owner, distributions of property to a surviving spouse and to other beneficiaries of the decedent require careful coordination. In second marriage situations, aside from the matter of taxes, the more important objective may be to provide for the surviving spouse's financial needs while ensuring that, upon the surviving spouse's subsequent death, the property set aside for the surviving spouse's financial support will pass to the first decedent spouse's children by a former marriage. Alternatively, one spouse may be at least a generation (25 years or more) older than the other spouse; the older spouse may have (by a former marriage) adult children who are older than the present younger spouse and minor children of the present marriage. In such a situation, the older spouse may want to leave one-eighth of his or her estate to each of the four adult children, one-eighth to each of the two minor children, and one-quarter to his or her present spouse with the assurance that, upon the subsequent death of the surviving spouse, at least one-half of that spouse's one-quarter share of the first decedent spouse's estate will be distributable to the minor children of the marriage. In such a case, special attention must be given to the surviving spouse's right under state law to elect against the decedent spouse's estate. Many states provide that, when a spouse dies with surviving children of the present marriage, the surviving spouse is entitled to at least one-half of the decedent spouse's estate (in some states, the elective share is one-third). Thus, leaving the surviving spouse a one-quarter interest in the decedent spouse's estate may not satisfy a surviving spouse's right to elect against the decedent spouse's estate under state law.

Situations such as these are increasingly prevalent among senior citizens who have adult children by former divorced or deceased spouses. Closely associated with these considerations may be the matter of transfer taxes as they relate to both spouses' estates. The proper use of marital and nonmarital deduction estate planning can enable the estate owner to designate the ultimate beneficiaries of the estate while providing lifetime financial security for the surviving spouse and still minimize or eliminate transfer taxes.

Probate and Nonprobate Estate Assets

Strict attention must be paid to the assets composing the first decedent spouse's probate and nonprobate estates in order to achieve effective results from marital and nonmarital deduction planning. In order to determine whether and to what extent the marital deduction should be used, property that will pass to the surviving spouse under the first decedent spouse's will (probate estate), as well as outside the will (nonprobate estate), must be identified. Furthermore, in determining the amount of property necessary to provide for the surviving spouse's financial support and the approximate value of the surviving spouse's resulting taxable estate, it is important to consider the value of property the surviving spouse may have available which is not includable in the first decedent spouse's gross estate and which will not be includable in the surviving spouse's estate (e.g., life insurance proceeds on the life of the first decedent spouse from a policy owned by and payable to an irrevocable trust that provides a life estate for the surviving spouse).

Gross Estate

As previously discussed, a decedent's gross estate includes the value, at the time of death, of all property, real or personal, tangible or intangible, wherever situated.[119] In this regard, specific types of property come to mind, such as the family home, stocks, bonds, cash, jewelry, automobiles, and so forth, as being includable in the gross estate. Such property certainly is includable, but other considerations identified as interests in property are also includable in the gross estate. These considerations are: I.R.C. Sections 2033 and 2034 interests in property; I.R.C. Sections 2035, 2036, 2037, and 2038 transfers during lifetime; I.R.C. Sections 2039, 2040, 2041, and 2042 specific properties; I.R.C. Section 2043 lifetime transfers for insufficient consideration; I.R.C. Sections 2044 and 2045 preexisting transfers or interests; and I.R.C. Section 2046 disclaimers.

Adjusted Gross Estate

The value of the decedent's adjusted gross estate (AGE) is extremely important in qualifying the estate for the following tax-favored benefits: redemption of stock in a closely-held corporation under I.R.C. Section 303; special use valuation under I.R.C. Section 2032A; qualified family-owned business interest deduction under I.R.C. Section 2057;[120] determination of the allowable marital deduction under I.R.C. Section 2056 for wills and trusts effected before September 12, 1981, containing maximum marital deduction formula provisions; and deferred installment payment of estate taxes under I.R.C. Section 6166.

The AGE is determined by subtracting from the value of the gross estate those deductions allowable under I.R.C. Sections 2053 and 2054. Deductions from the value of the gross

---

[119] I.R.C. § 2031.

[120] The qualified family-owned business interest deduction is repealed after December 31, 2003, by I.R.C. § 2057(j).

estate are generally of three types: those allowed for costs actually incurred (e.g., administration fees, funeral costs, and so forth); those that reduce to its net fair market value the value of property (e.g., mortgages); and those bona fide losses incurred through casualty or theft.

Taxable Estate

Two possible definitions may be used to describe the taxable estate, depending on one's point of view. On the one hand, the Code and Treasury Regulations (Regulations) provide that the taxable estate of a decedent who was a citizen or resident of the United States at the time of death is determined by subtracting from the total value of the decedent's gross estate the total amount of the deductions allowable by I.R.C. Sections 2053-2056. As previously mentioned, these deductions are:[121] funeral and administration expenses and claims against the estate (including certain taxes and charitable pledges);[122] losses from casualty or theft during the administration of the estate;[123] charitable transfers;[124] and the estate tax marital deduction.[125]

On the other hand, the taxable estate may be defined as the adjusted gross estate, less any charitable and marital deductions available to the decedent's estate. In fact, computing the federal estate tax is a six-step process:

1. Value of the gross estate is determined;
2. AGE is determined;
3. Depending on whether the charitable or the marital deduction applies, the taxable estate is determined;
4. Tentative tax base is determined by adding to the taxable estate any adjusted taxable gifts. Adjusted taxable gifts are the total amount of taxable gifts made by the decedent after December 31, 1976, other than charitable gifts, gifts that are includable in the value of the decedent's gross estate, and gifts to a spouse after 1981.[126] Gifts qualifying for the gift tax annual exclusion are not includable as adjusted taxable gifts in the decedent's taxable estate because they are not taxable gifts. Thus, a decedent's adjusted taxable gifts do not include the one-half value of gifts made by the decedent attributable to his or her spouse because of gift-splitting, provided the one-half value per gift does not exceed the gift tax annual exclusion amount.[127] Apart from these exceptions, even if no gift tax was paid on a gift because the unified credit was used to offset any gift tax otherwise due, the gift is still considered a taxable gift. For this reason, the value of the gift must be added to the taxable estate as a taxable gift;
5. Tentative tax is computed on the tentative tax base;
6. Certain allowable tax credits are subtracted from the tentative tax to arrive at the net federal estate tax due.

---

[121] I.R.C. § 2051; Treas. Reg. § 20.2051-1.

[122] I.R.C. § 2053; Treas. Reg. §§ 20.2053-1 through 20.2053-10.

[123] I.R.C. § 2054; Treas. Reg. § 20.2054-1.

[124] I.R.C. § 2055; Treas. Reg. §§ 20.2055-1 through 20.2055-5; § 24.1.

[125] I.R.C. § 2056; Treas. Reg. §§ 20.2056(a)-1 through 20.2056(e)-3; 22.2056-1.

[126] I.R.C. §§ 2001(b); 2503(a); 2522(a); and 2523(a).

[127] I.R.C. § 2503(b).

EFFECTIVE ESTATE PLANNING DEFINED

Estate planning is a branch of the law[128] that involves the design and implementation of a written plan for the lifetime and testamentary management of a person's estate. Effective estate planning depends upon a careful examination of the estate owner's assets. In this regard, are the assets income producing or nonincome producing? How will the assets be managed for the estate owner's benefit during his or her lifetime in the event of physical or mental incapacity? How will the assets be transferred at death? What are the needs of the estate owner's beneficiaries? For the estate owner, these and many other questions will be asked and answered for the fist time during the fact-finding process.

A written estate plan is to an attorney who designs and prepares the legal documents required to implement a person's estate plan what an architect's blueprints are to the contractor constructing a building. In other words, a formal written plan is necessary to guide the person responsible for building the end product; namely, the legal documents required to implement and carry out the estate plan. Contrary to popular belief, a will and trust by themselves are not an estate plan. These are only legal documents that carry out a person's estate plan. Unless the issues of property ownership and beneficiary designations of contract benefits are properly coordinated, the will and trust may not carry out a person's estate plan as intended. Accordingly, an estate plan is an indispensable formal written report that describes the operation of a person's present estate plan and offers recommendations for implementing a person's estate planning goals and objectives.

Properly designed, prepared, and executed legal documents are required to implement a well-designed estate plan. The primary operative documents are the last will and testament (will) and trust (testamentary or living trust). A testamentary trust may either be included in the will or may be a separate document. A living (*inter vivos*) trust, whether revocable or irrevocable, is never part of the will.

In addition, business agreements and other legal documents may supplement the will and trust. Such agreements and documents may include a buy-sell agreement or stock-redemption agreement, a living will (directive to physicians), a general or special durable power of attorney, and a durable power of attorney for health care.

Finally, conveyance documents may be needed to supplement the will and trust. These documents may include deeds, an assignment of contract, an assignment of lease, an assignment of personal property, an assignment of installment note, an assignment of stock and stock power, and a memorandum of trust. Other specially designed conveyance documents may be required, depending on the assets composing the estate and the estate owner's objectives.

Estate Planning and Tax Law

Of all the areas of tax law, estate planning is one of the most complex. For example, of all tax returns filed, the Form 706 has the highest probability of audit at the rate of approximately 20 percent, which is almost ten times the audit rate of an income tax return. For estates valued in excess of $1 million, the audit rate exceeds 50 percent. Faced with these audit probabilities, it is critically important that Form 706 be prepared carefully and correctly so as to minimize or entirely avoid an audit and to prevent assessment of tax deficiencies and penalties, even if the Form 706 is audited. A well-planned estate, coupled with a correctly prepared Form 706, greatly reduce the odds that the decedent estate owner's Form 706 will be audited.

To be a good estate planner, the practitioner needs to know how to correctly complete Form 706; conversely, to correctly complete Form 706, the practitioner must be a good estate planner. In order to complete the Form 706 correctly, the practitioner must possess not

---

[128] Black, *Black's Law Dictionary*, 493.

only knowledge of relevant Code provisions but also knowledge and understanding of the law of wills, trusts, life insurance, forms of property ownership, interests in property, and how these areas of the law are affected by income, estate, and gift taxes. Just to complete the first three pages of Form 706, the practitioner must thoroughly understand twenty-six essential areas of the federal tax system as embodied in Subtitle B of the Internal Revenue Code. Throughout this book, "Ask Your Attorney" questions and "Answers" are designed to assist the reader in determining whether his or her attorney is qualified to practice estate planning.

Purposes of Estate Planning

As a general rule, estate planning has at least three purposes: (1) eliminate an unnecessary court-supervised financial guardianship (conservatorship) of the estate owner's financial affairs during lifetime in the event of physical or mental incapacity; (2) carry out the estate owner's wishes and directions regarding the transfer of property to intended beneficiaries in the event of death; and (3) accomplish these objectives at a minimum financial cost and with the least amount of emotional distress.

Effective estate planning should not be limited strictly to tax considerations. In other words, the matter of taxes should not become the tail that wags the dog in the process of carrying out the purposes of estate planning. The estate owner's nontax estate planning objectives should be considered before tax-planning objectives. The tax impact of those objectives should then be compared. If the tax impact on nontax objectives is acceptable to the estate owner, fine; if not compatible, then the estate owner's adviser should present and recommend alternate planning arrangements closest to satisfying those objectives.

Lifetime Management Plan

A comprehensive estate plan includes a lifetime estate management plan that addresses the issue of how a person's estate is to be managed for the estate owner's benefit in the event of physical or mental incapacity. In this regard, if the estate owner does not have a plan in the event of physical or mental incapacity, a proper court of jurisdiction will appoint a guardian or conservator to manage the estate owner's personal and financial affairs. On the other hand, the estate owner may choose not to involve the courts, in which case only the following four options are available for the protection and management of property and financial affairs: (1) own property jointly with right of survivorship with another person; (2) designate an immediate family member or close trusted friend as attorney-in-fact under a durable general or special power of attorney; (3) create a funded revocable (or irrevocable) living trust; or (4) implement a combination of these options. In discussing each of these options, a qualified practitioner will identify a soft spot in the estate owner's present estate plan where improvement may be necessary or, conversely, identify a subject about which the estate owner wants to know more. In this regard, the practitioner should provide the estate owner with accurate, objective information that he or she may use to make an intelligent decision about his or her overall estate planning.

Plan to Transfer Property at Death

A comprehensive estate plan must also include a plan for the transfer and management of a person's estate in the event of death by identifying the intended beneficiaries and the manner in which property is distributable to them. Each beneficiary's age, maturity, educational needs, medical requirements, social and vocational opportunities, present financial status, and physical and emotional needs must be recognized in view of the methods that may be employed to transfer property to him or her. In this regard, only five ways exist to transfer property at the estate owner's death:

1. Last will and testament (which may or may not incorporate a testamentary trust);
2. Contract (e.g., a life insurance policy). Designation of a beneficiary in a life insurance contract takes precedence over any beneficiary of the same insurance proceeds named in the decedent's will. The sole exception to this rule is when the estate of the insured decedent is designated primary beneficiary of the insurance proceeds. By such a designation, the insurance proceeds are payable to the insured decedent's estate (or trust estate, in the case of a living trust) and are distributable, along with all of the decedent's other assets, to the beneficiaries named under the decedent's will (or living trust). This same rule applies with regard to an IRA, SEP, 401(k) plan, Keogh plan, salary continuation plan, deferred compensation (qualified and nonqualified), qualified retirement plan benefits, group life insurance, or any other contract benefit;
3. Survivorship [i.e., JTWROS; tenants by the entirety (with right of survivorship); tenants in common with right of survivorship; survivorship in a community property agreement];
4. Operation of law [i.e., dying without a will (intestate succession)]; and
5. Revocable or irrevocable living trust created and funded during the estate owner's lifetime. *Funded* means that the estate owner's property (assets) is properly registered (titled) in the name of the trustee of the living trust.

Observation

A grantor retained annuity trust (GRAT), a grantor retained unitrust (GRUT), and a qualified personal residence trust (QPRT) are irrevocable living trusts that may be used to transfer the decedent grantor's property to his or her intended beneficiaries.

MISCONCEPTIONS ABOUT ESTATE PLANNING

Many estate owners do not understand the process of estate planning. This is due in large part to the inability of the practitioner to communicate to the estate owner exactly what is involved in the estate planning process. Further, because estate planning involves more than just effecting a will or trust, many estate owners have misconceptions about estate planning. These misconceptions, when not addressed by practitioners, are some of the primary reasons why so many so-called estate plans fail to operate as the estate owners intended.

Misconception: Will and Trust Are an Estate Plan

One misconception is that a will and trust constitute an estate plan. As previously discussed, these legal documents only carry out the decedent's estate plan. Unless the practitioner conducts a thorough fact-finding interview and designs a formal, written estate plan based on the estate owner's goals and objectives, the resulting estate plan will look much like a Rube Goldberg cartoon—the end result achieved solely by chance.

Misconception: Probate and Taxes Are Related

Another misconception is that, if estate taxes (federal and state) are not imposed on an estate, probate of the estate is unnecessary. Of course, transfer taxes and probate have absolutely nothing to do with one another. They are completely unrelated matters. On the one hand, as a general rule, if estate taxes are due, property comprising the probate estate will not be released from the probate process to be distributed by the personal representative (or administrator, if the decedent dies intestate) to those beneficiaries (or heirs) of the decedent entitled to receive such property until the taxes are paid or arrangements have been made to pay the taxes. On the other hand, an estate may be subject to probate when income or transfer taxes are not imposed.

Misconception: Having a Will Eliminates Probate

Many people also operate under the misconception that, if a person has a will, probate is unnecessary. Having a will does not guarantee that probate can be avoided. The truth is that a person's estate may be probated whether or not a will is involved. If the decedent's estate includes probate estate property, probate may be required. Generally, the value of such property determines whether a formal probate proceeding is required or if the property can be administered under a state's small estate statute.

Misconception: Probate Is Determined by Federal Estate Tax Exemption Amount

A fourth misconception is that, if the value of a person's estate is less than the federal estate tax exemption amount, probate is unnecessary. The federal estate tax exemption amount relates to federal estate tax; it has nothing to do with whether a decedent's estate is required to be probated. Also, the federal estate tax exemption amount should not be used as a guide to determine whether a person's estate is large enough to warrant the use of a revocable living trust. The use of a revocable living trust should not be determined by the value for federal estate tax purposes of a person's estate.

COMMON MISTAKES MADE IN ESTATE PLANNING

Misconceptions about estate planning contribute to mistakes made in estate planning. Since 1979, as a fee-paid specialist in estate/gift taxation and planning, this author has yet to review in the initial get-acquainted interview a person's existing will and trust that would carry out the person's estate plan as intended. Many reasons exist for this truism; yet, the majority of the reasons can be attributed to often-repeated common mistakes.

Updating

The most frequent mistake people make is not updating their estate plans, wills, or trusts. People simply do not realize that their estate plans are dynamic, rather than static. People forget that marriages and divorces; deaths and births; changes of domicile, residencies, or jobs; illnesses in families; changes in the tax laws; and other myriad factors influence estate plans. Often, modifications made to estate plans necessitate amendments to existing wills and trusts.

Incorrect Form of Property Ownership

Incorrect form of property ownership in relation to the terms of the estate owner's will and trust agreement can compromise the estate owner's intentions for how the property should pass to intended beneficiaries. Owning property as JTWROS is the single most common mistake that causes estate plans of married persons to fail. As previously mentioned, a will cannot distribute property that is owned by the decedent and another person as JTWROS. Likewise, a trust under a will, or as a separate legal document, cannot be funded when property is owned by two or more persons as JTWROS. Consequently, the estate tax marital deduction taken in the decedent spouse's gross estate may be more than necessary (overqualified marital deduction) to reduce or eliminate estate tax in relation to the decedent spouse's federal estate tax exemption amount; and the surviving spouse's estate may be subject to unnecessary estate tax because too much property received by right of survivorship is included in the surviving spouse's gross estate.

Incorrect Beneficiary Designations of Contract Benefits

Incorrect beneficiary designations of employer-provided contract benefits are another common mistake. Designating the wrong beneficiary of a contract benefit (e.g., qualified plan benefits, 401(k) plans, SEPs, IRAs, Keogh plans, nonqualified deferred compensation plans, salary continuation benefits, survivor benefits, group term life insurance) can have the same effect as owning property jointly with right of survivorship. In situations involving married persons, too much property may be eligible for the estate tax marital deduction in the estate of the first decedent spouse, resulting in overexposure of this property to estate tax in the estate of the surviving spouse. Moreover, the Service's new rules limit the circumstances under which a trust will qualify as a designated beneficiary for minimum distribution purposes of qualified retirement plan benefits, which, in turn, may cause unintended income tax consequences upon the death of a plan participant.[129]

Life Insurance Ownership

Life insurance is one of the most valuable assets available to the estate owner. Yet, its importance in providing liquidity and a source of funds for a variety of purposes is greatly misunderstood and disregarded. Mistakes are frequently made regarding the ownership and beneficiary designations of life insurance policies in relation to other assets composing a person's estate. Furthermore, violating the life insurance policy transfer-for-value rules can subject the beneficiary of the life insurance proceeds to unnecessary income tax.

Use of Investment Assets to Provide Estate Liquidity

Overreliance on investment property to provide liquidity in an estate is also a common mistake. It makes no sense to sell income-producing real property, long-term growth stocks, highly appreciated securities, or property that produces tax-free income just to pay transfer costs and estate administration expenses. The use of income-tax-free life insurance proceeds to provide needed liquidity may be more prudent. It would be the exception, rather than the rule, for a person to pay total premiums on a life insurance policy equal to the death proceeds. This is why life insurance proceeds are called "dollars for pennies apiece" or "discounted dollars."

Absence of Closely-Held Business Planning

Absence of planning for closely-held business interests accounts for many mistakes. Often the matter of preserving business ownership and continuity of management is not given adequate attention in the estate planning process. Such oversight in a family business operated as a sole proprietorship may cause the business to die with the owner. Moreover, many family-operated businesses fail to develop plans to mitigate divisiveness or promote equity of participation among family members or nonfamily key employees. Finally, many

---

[129] *See* discussion in Chapter 15.

an estate owner makes the mistake of not providing adequate operating funds for the daily operation of the business upon his or her death.

Numerous mistakes are made in the planning of buy-sell agreements. In view of I.R.C. Section 2703, particular attention must be paid to any buy-sell agreement entered into or substantially modified after October 8, 1990.[130] Despite the attention that must be paid to I.R.C. Section 2703 when a buy-sell agreement is contemplated, the following questions and concerns should also be addressed to avoid unnecessary mistakes:

- What method is used to determine the value of the business?
- Are provisions made to periodically adjust the value of the business?
- Are the terms and conditions for a lifetime purchase of a shareholder's business interest the same as those terms and conditions for purchase of the shareholder's interest in the event of death?
- Will a shareholder's interest in the business be acquired in the event of long-term disability? If yes, is the agreement funded with long-term disability insurance?
- To avoid costly mistakes that can arise when buy-sell agreements are funded with life insurance, consideration must be given to the identity of the beneficiary of the insurance proceeds; [i.e., whether the decedent-shareholder's estate (or surviving spouse) or the surviving shareholder is the beneficiary];
- The rules of attribution under I.R.C. Section 318 must be carefully observed in relation to the rules covering distributions in redemption of stock under I.R.C. Section 302. These sections of the Code are traps for the unsuspecting estate planner and business owner when lifetime redemptions of stock are contemplated;
- If an I.R.C. Section 303 stock redemption is contemplated under a stock-redemption arrangement, will the shareholder's interest in the shares to be redeemed be directly reduced by transfer taxes and funeral and administration expenses?

Selection of Fiduciaries

Mistakes are often made in the selection of a personal representative to administer a person's estate or in selecting a trustee to administer and manage the property in a trust. A will or trust cannot fail to operate for want of a personal representative or trustee, but it can fail to operate as the estate owner intended because the wrong fiduciary was chosen. Provision can be made in a will or trust agreement for the replacement of a fiduciary by the decedent's beneficiaries; or, absent their agreement, a proper court of jurisdiction can remove a fiduciary for cause or on the grounds cited in the will or trust agreement.

Unequivocally, the most important attributes of a good fiduciary are honesty and integrity. Acumen in business and investment matters is not absolutely essential to the question of whether an individual can be an effective fiduciary. This is because many of the tasks that a fiduciary is called upon to perform can be delegated to persons skilled in particular occupations. Other considerations in the selection of a fiduciary are whether: the trustee's interests might be adverse to the beneficiary's interests; the trustee will have the time and desire to administer the estate; the trustee will get along well with the beneficiary; and the trustee's interests as a beneficiary will be above the interests of any other beneficiary. To be a fiduciary is not an honor; it is a serious and responsible endeavor that should not be undertaken lightly or in a cavalier fashion.

---

[130] *Omnibus Budget Reconciliation Act of 1990*, Pub. L. No. 101-508, 101st Cong., 2d Sess. (5 November 1990), 1991-2 C.B.481, § 11602(e)(1)(A)(ii).

Design of Wills and Trusts

Too many mistakes are made in the design of wills and trusts. Coupled with these errors are the mistakes made in not coordinating the form of property ownership and beneficiary designations of contract benefits with the provisions of the will and trust. Also, when a RLT is involved, legal title to property is either not conveyed to the trust during the trustor's lifetime or the conveyance documents are incorrectly prepared, thereby rendering the trust partially funded or completely unfunded. Furthermore, in this regard, it is not uncommon for a person with more than one state residence not to convey all of his or her property to a RLT. Most often, such a mistake is made because the person's focus is only on the property in the state of current residence. Even people who reside in only one state make the same error with real property that they own in other states.

Other errors made relative to the design and execution of wills and trusts include:

- Improper provisions for the apportionment of taxes and expenses. Tax apportionment clauses are critical to the proper allocation of taxes and expenses among beneficiaries when the decedent's estate includes property eligible for the tax-favored benefits of I.R.C. Section 303 (distributions in redemption of stock to pay death taxes) or when the I.R.C. Section 2055 charitable estate tax deduction is used for property passing to charity. Moreover, when a decedent's property is distributable by will (probate estate) and outside the will (nonprobate estate), unless attention is paid to tax-apportionment provisions, property in the probate estate may be used to pay taxes at the expense of the beneficiaries under the decedent's will. If such an arrangement is the estate owner's objective, fine; but, if the estate owner wants the beneficiaries under the will, and those persons receiving property from the decedent's nonprobate estate, to share in the taxes, then appropriate tax-apportionment provisions must be designed to accomplish the estate owner's purpose.

- Divorce can partially revoke the provisions of a will or trust which pertain to the decedent spouse's former spouse. The mistake made is in the identification of the spouse in the decedent's will or trust. A person can remarry, not change the will or trust, and then die; and the new spouse becomes the spouse mentioned in the will or trust. This can occur if the former spouse is not identified by name but is referred to only as *my spouse*. The decedent spouse's estate could be denied the estate tax marital deduction if it cannot be determined which spouse the decedent had in mind—the former spouse or the new spouse. On the other hand, the new spouse may receive all of the decedent's estate at the expense of the decedent's children by the former spouse. In such case, the estate tax marital deduction would be available to the decedent spouse's estate.

- Absence of successor personal representative or trustee. As previously mentioned, a will or trust cannot fail for want of a fiduciary. However, by not providing for a successor fiduciary, the decedent's beneficiaries may have to incur the unnecessary expense of petitioning a court to appoint a successor fiduciary.

- A person may lack testamentary capacity or may be under undue influence to effect a will or trust.

- Occasionally, drafting errors are made in the preparation of codicils to wills and amendments to trusts.

- Although rare, a will or trust can be rendered inoperative because of an insufficient number of witnesses to the testator's or trustor's execution of the instrument.

From the foregoing, it should be apparent that effective estate planning involves more than just transfer tax considerations. Even if the federal estate and generation-skipping transfer tax is, in fact, repealed after 2009, myriad reasons exist for the continued need to plan a person's estate.

CHAPTER 2

Framework of a Revocable Living Trust

DEFINITION OF A REVOCABLE LIVING TRUST

The term *living trust*, as used in this book, means a written revocable living trust instrument that an individual creates during his or her lifetime; that is, an *inter vivos* trust.[1] As used in this book, the term *living trust* does not include: a grantor retained annuity trust (or grantor retained unitrust) (GRAT or GRUT); a qualified personal residence trust (QPRT); a *Crummey* trust; or an I.R.C. Section 2503(c) trust (so-called gifts to minors trust)—all of which are *living trusts* but are *irrevocable living trusts.* A living or *inter vivos* trust agreement becomes operational during the trustor's lifetime as contrasted with a testamentary trust, which takes effect on the death of the testator. Of all the forms of property ownership, property owned by a trustee of a living trust is perhaps the most interesting. Knowing the cast of characters involved in the ownership of trust property is essential to understanding how a revocable living trust operates.

In simple language, a valid trust agreement exists when one person, the *trustor* (settlor or grantor), creates a declaration of trust in which the legal title to property and its management is vested in a *trustee*; and the beneficial (or equitable) interest in the same property is vested in a person known as a *beneficiary.* Thus, the *trustee* acquires legal title to the trust property; and the *beneficiary* of the trust acquires equitable title.

REQUIREMENTS TO CREATE A LIVING TRUST

For estate planning purposes, a revocable living trust is created by a written declaration and must satisfy eight requirements:

1. The trustor must express an intention to create a trust for the benefit of a beneficiary;
2. Legal title to any property that the trustor intends the trust to hold must be transferred to the trustee. In other words, the trustor must vest legal title to the property transferred to the trust in the name of the trustee;
3. The primary beneficiary of the trust is usually identified in the preamble of the trust agreement. Generally, the contingent beneficiaries are identified in Article I (see file "APP0201.DOC");

---

[1]Throughout this book, the term *revocable living trust* includes the terms *living trust* and *living trust agreement,* and such terms may be used interchangeably.

4. Duties and powers of the trustee must be expressed (see file "APP0201.DOC" Article IX) . In addition, any miscellaneous provisions relating to the Trustee are also described (see file "APP0201.DOC" Articles VIII and X);

5. Property transferred to the trust is described in schedules that are attached to the trust agreement following the signature pages. These schedules are referenced in the article of the trust agreement acknowledging that the trustor has acquired real property, tangible personal property and intangible personal property and has transferred to or is in the process of transferring the legal title of such property to the trustee without consideration (see file "APP0201.DOC" Article III). Property (assets) titled in the name of the trustee is called the *trust estate*.

6. The extent of a beneficiary's interest in the trust estate, the manner in which the beneficiary's interest is to be distributed to the beneficiary and any conditions limiting the beneficiary's interest in the trust estate should be thoroughly described in the living trust agreement (see file "APP0201.DOC" Article VI).

7. The purpose for which the living trust is created should be clearly expressed (see file "APP0201.DOC" Articles III, IV, V, VI, VII, X, XI, and XII); and

8. The duration of the trust which cannot be longer than allowed under local law must be expressed (see file "APP0201.DOC" Article IV).

COMPONENTS OF A REVOCABLE LIVING TRUST

As previously mentioned, for estate planning purposes, a revocable living trust is created by a written declaration. Four complete sample revocable living trusts are included in the Appendices (see file "APP0201.DOC": Revocable Living Trust Agreement for a Single Person; file "APP0202.DOC": Revocable Living Trust Agreement for a Husband; file "APP0203.DOC": Revocable Living Trust Agreement for a Wife; and file "APP0204.DOC": Joint Revocable Living Trust for a Husband and Wife). The following discussion of the components of a revocable living trust is based on the revocable living trust for a single person (see file "APP0201.DOC"). As a general rule, a trust, whether revocable or irrevocable, living or testamentary, must contain at least five of six components in order to be a valid legal trust: (1) trustor; (2) trustee; (3) beneficiary; (4) trust property (trust estate); (5) terms of the trust; and (6) legal jurisdiction (*situs*).

Preamble

The Preamble, though not titled as such on page one of the trust agreement, includes three of the six components necessary to create a valid legal trust; namely, the identity of the *trustor*, *trustee,* and *beneficiary* of the trust agreement and includes the effective date of the trust agreement (see Preambles in files "APP0201.DOC," "APP0202.DOC," "APP0203.DOC," and "APP0204.DOC").

Explanation

Two of the most important of the eight requirements necessary to create a revocable living trust, namely, intention to create a trust and identification of the beneficiaries, are expressed in the Preamble of the revocable living trust agreement, as illustrated in the previously mentioned Appendices. In the Preamble, the trustor expresses his or her intention to create a trust (see file "APP0201.DOC") :

"**This Trust Agreement** is entered into by and between **Evelyn M.** _____
of the County of _____, State of _____, hereinafter called "Trustor,"
and **Evelyn M.** _____ of the County of _____, State of _____,
hereinafter referred to as "Trustee," and shall be known as the **Evelyn M.**
_____ **Revocable Living Trust Agreement (Trust Agreement)."**

Beneficiaries other than the trustor-trustee, as the primary beneficiary, are also identified: "The contingent beneficiaries of the Trust Estate shall be those persons designated in
Article I." Although the living trust cannot fail if the trustee is not identified, in most trusts,
the trustee is identified:

"**Evelyn M.** _____, hereinafter referred to as Trustee." The Preamble
concludes by stating the effective date of the trust agreement: "September 1, 2000."
The date identifies this living trust as being distinct from any other trust (living or testamentary) that the trustor(s) may establish. If, for some reason, the trustor creates
more than one living trust containing similar provisions on the same day, then the
trusts are time dated to give them separate identity. The remaining six requirements
are embodied in the living trust agreement.

Trustor

The *trustor* of a revocable living trust is the person who creates the trust. Technically, if the
person creating a trust does so through a Last Will, such person is called the *testator*, if
male—*testatrix*, if female. If the trust is created through a living trust agreement to operate
during lifetime (*inter vivos*), the creator of the trust is called the *trustor, settlor,* or *grantor*. In
reality, these terms are interchangeable. The trustor must express an intention to create a
trust for the benefit of a beneficiary. As a rule, the trustor of a revocable living trust retains
the right to revoke and amend the trust, either alone or in conjunction with another person
(see file "APP0201.DOC" Article V). 🖾 Ordinarily, upon revocation or termination of the
trust, the trust property reverts to the trustor, unless the trustor directs some other disposition. Though not commonly used, a living trust can be a valid legal entity without the
identity or existence of a trustor. This may occur for instance when an irrevocable living
trust is used to manage the proceeds in a structured settlement case for the benefit of minor
children. In such case, it might be inappropriate for the parent of the minor children to be
the trustor or settlor of the trust agreement.

Ask Your Attorney

Even though I am a citizen of another country, could I effect a living trust in the United States?

Answer

Yes.

Trustee

The *trustee* is the entity (e.g., corporation or other business entity recognized by state law),
person or individual in legal title to the trust property (assets, corpus, trust estate) who ad-
ministers or manages the property of the trust. The trustee is in legal title to the trust assets.
The trustor can also be the trustee of a living trust. If the living trust has no trustee (as a
result of death, incapacity, resignation, or for any other reason) and the trust agreement

does not provide for the appointment of a successor trustee, a proper court of jurisdiction will appoint a successor trustee. Remember, a valid living trust cannot fail for want of a trustee; but the purpose of the trust can fail because of the wrong trustee. As previously mentioned, the assets of the trust agreement (living or testamentary) are called the *trust estate*.

Beneficiary

The primary *beneficiary* of a living trust is the individual for whom the trust is established. The primary beneficiary is in equitable title to the trust property. In other words, the beneficiary does not possess legal title to the trust property but rather a beneficial interest in the property. In most cases, the *trustor, trustee,* and *primary beneficiary* of the living trust are all one and the same person. This does not mean that other persons cannot also be primary beneficiaries during the trustor's lifetime. Upon the trustor's death, persons designated to receive the trust property are known as contingent beneficiaries.

In order for a revocable living trust to be legally valid and effective, a trustor-trustee should not be the sole beneficiary of the trust agreement. This is because, under common law, legal title and equitable title in the property conveyed to the trust would merge; and the trust would no longer exist.[2] If such a merger occurred, a declaration of trust would have no legal effect, unless a beneficiary other than the person (trustor-trustee) in legal title to the trust estate is in existence at the time of the trustor-trustee-beneficiary's death. Whenever the trustor is also the trustee and the primary beneficiary of a living trust, a contingent beneficiary must be designated to succeed to the primary beneficiary's equitable interest in the trust estate.

Identification of Family: Article I

Other than for the purpose of identifying the contingent beneficiaries as provided in the Preamble, the information in Article I (see, e.g., file "APP0201.DOC") is intended solely to assist the successor trustee in identifying members of the Trustor's immediate family. In this regard, it may be helpful to the successor trustee to know whether the contingent beneficiaries are adults or minors and their whereabouts, at least at the time the trust was effected.

Initial and Successor Trustees: Article II

Article II (see, e.g., file "APP0201.DOC") provides that the trustor is the initial trustee and that, during the trustor's lifetime, he or she may for any reason instruct in writing the successor trustee to assume the duties as trustee. This provision is essential to initiate, in effect, the management provisions of the trust in the event the trustor becomes physically or mentally incapacitated and the services of the successor trustee are required to administer the trust estate for the benefit of the trustor without the necessity of court intervention. Notice, too, that the trustor retains the right to discharge any trustee and to designate additional trustees or successor trustees.

Provision is included with respect to the death, resignation, or incapacity of the initial individual trustee. In these regards, the inability of the individual trustee to serve is addressed along with how the trust is to be handled if a trustee resigns and who is to serve as trustee upon the trustor's death. While it may seem obvious that the designated successor

---

[2] *Blades v. Norfolk S. Ry.*, 224 N.C. 32, 29 S.E. 141, 151 (1944).

trustee would serve as trustee upon the trustor's death, in some cases, the trustor may want to designate one of the successor trustees to serve as the trustee of a particular subtrust under the trust agreement or of a beneficiary's share and another designated trustee to serve as the successor trustee of the remainder of the trust estate. This part of Article II is the place where such an alternate designation would be made (see, e.g., file "APP0201 .DOC").

The determination of the trustor's or the trustee's physical or mental capacity is basically a medical determination. Court-supervised competency proceedings are financially expensive and emotionally traumatic. Judges alone are not qualified to determine whether a person possesses the mental capacity to handle his or her affairs. Hence, judges rely on the qualifications and expertise of physicians, psychiatrists, psychologists, and social workers to advise them as to a person's mental capacity. In view of this fact, it seems more prudent and cost effective in both monetary expenditure and minimization of emotional trauma to provide for the determination of the trustor's or individual trustee's mental capacity within the confines of the trust agreement, thus allowing the decision to be made within the privacy of the family unit, rather than in a court of law. Accordingly, a well-designed and thoughtful revocable living trust agreement will include a provision for the determination of incapacity (see, e.g., file "APP0201.DOC" Article II (D)).

An alternate provision to that in Article II (D) might read as follows:

(E) **Determination of Incapacity.** The Trustor or individual Trustee shall be considered "incapacitated" (1) if and as long as such person is adjudicated disabled because he or she is unable to manage his or her estate or affairs; or (2) if two doctors familiar with such person's physical and mental condition certify to the Trustee in writing that such person is unable to transact ordinary business and until there is a like certification to the Trustee that such incapacity has ended.

Under no circumstances should the trust agreement contain a provision that requires the trustor's or individual trustee's capacity be determined by a court of law. To include such a provision is to defeat one of the primary purposes and advantages of creating a revocable living trust; namely, to ensure privacy of the trustor's health and financial affairs and to prevent the same from becoming a matter of public record through a court-supervised financial guardianship.

The revocable living trust should include a provision for the appointment of a successor trustee in the event the trust is without a trustee (see, e.g., file "APP0201.DOC"). In this regard, the trust cannot fail for want of a trustee; but it can fail if the wrong individual or corporate trustee is entrusted with the trust estate. Provision can be made for the appointment of a successor trustee, for example, by "a majority in interest of those beneficiaries of such trust to whom income and/or principal may then be paid or who may be entitled to a distributable share of the trust estate may appoint a successor trustee or trustees" (see file "APP0201.DOC" Article II (E) (1)). A backup provision for the appointment of a successor trustee by a court of proper jurisdiction should be included in the event "a majority in interest of those beneficiaries . . ." cannot, will not, or are incapable of appointing a successor trustee (see file "APP0201.DOC" Article II (E) (2)). Finally, every revocable living trust should provide for the discharge or replacement of the trustee by the beneficiaries of the trust (see, e.g., file "APP0201.DOC" Article II (F)).

Finally, provision can be made for both a corporate trustee and an individual person to serve as co-trustees. In such a case, the responsibilities, duties, and powers of both trustees need to be very carefully expressed to avoid duplication of services and unnecessary expense.

When a corporate trustee (e.g., a bank or an independent trust company) and an individual person are designated co-trustees, it is absolutely essential to provide which of them will have the ultimate decision-making responsibility. Often, the decision-making authority is divided—the corporate trustee being responsible for the care and management of the trust estate, while the individual trustee oversees the day-to-day needs of the beneficiary(ies). These roles, however, may be reversed. In any event, each trustee has clearly delineated areas of responsibility and authority for making decisions affecting both the trust estate and the beneficiary entitled to those assets. Moreover, as previously mentioned, every trust should provide the beneficiaries the authority and power to replace a trustee, whether the trustee is a bank, independent trust company or an individual, and to select a successor trustee. Further, thought should be given to the matter of fees paid to the trustees. In this regard, neither a corporate trustee nor an individual trustee should receive fees for exercising duties and responsibilities not granted to the particular trustee. In other words, *double-dipping* should not be allowed to occur.

Examples[3]

1. "Management and Investment Counsel of Trust Assets.

With respect to securities comprising the trust assets, the Trustee (corporate or individual) is requested, without being required, to consult with **Steve K**_____, presently of **Thompson and Smith Investment Advisers, Inc.**, Gresham, Oregon, regarding those securities (investments) of the trust estate of which **Steve** is particularly knowledgeable and competent. Such consultation shall be made only when practicable; and any recommendations of **Steve** should be seriously considered and followed by the Trustee(s) to whatever extent, if any, the Trustee(s) deems advisable."

2. "Management and Investment Counsel of Trust Assets.

With respect to securities comprising the trust estate, the individual Trustee(s) shall employ a reputable independent professional investment adviser of his or her choice to manage and invest the securities that are part of or that may be added to and become part of the trust estate.

"(A) The decision of said independent investment adviser shall control the actions of the corporate and individual Trustee(s) with respect to the sale, investment, and reinvestment of the securities of the trust estate managed by the investment adviser.

"(B) The Trustees (corporate and individual) shall not be held liable or otherwise surcharged for any loss directly attributable to the investment advice of said investment adviser.

"(C) Among other professional standards to be considered, the individual Trustee should take into account the investment adviser's academic qualifications, previous professional experience as an investment adviser, past and current performance with similar investment portfolios, diversification of assets under management, and total value of all client asset portfolios under management, whether the adviser is registered under the Investment Advisers Act of 1940 (its successor or as amended), and investment philosophy regarding the selection of prudent investment vehicles that will best serve and benefit my goals, objectives, and wishes, as hereinbefore stated for trustor's children.

[3] Doug H. Moy, *A Practitioner's Guide to Estate Planning: Guidance and Planning Strategies*, 2 vols. (New York: Aspen Publishers, 2002, § 30.03[J], at 30-49 (hereafter Moy, *A Practitioner's Guide to Estate Planning*).

"(D) The investment adviser's fee shall be a charge against the trust estate as a whole and not against any distributable share. Trustor is most hopeful that the corporate Trustee will appreciate and respect Trustor's thoughts regarding the value of independent investment counsel to manage and invest the securities of the trust estate and will respect Trustor's request that the compensation of the investment adviser be paid from the whole of the trust estate assets and also by allocating to him, her or it a proportionate amount of the fees payable to the corporate Trustee with respect to the securities managed and invested by the adviser. This reduction of the corporate Trustee's compensation is to reflect the shift of investment responsibility in respect to the securities assets of the trust estate.

"(E) The investment adviser's authority herein granted, except with respect to the sale, investment, and reinvestment of securities comprising part of the trust estate assets, shall not abridge, compromise, or in any manner whatsoever alienate the Trustee's (corporate or individual) power to sell, exchange, transfer, assign, grant options to buy, lease, including leases extending beyond the terms of the trust, encumber, or otherwise alienate an or any other part of property of the trust estate in such manner and upon such terms as the Trustee may deem most beneficial to the trust estate."

Trust Property: Article III

A valid legal trust cannot exist without property being titled in the trustee.[4] Property owned by the trustee is called the trust *res* (pronounced race), trust principal, trust property, corpus, or trust estate. The trust estate can be tangible or intangible, but it must be both ascertainable and presently transferable.[5] All states and the District of Columbia have adopted the Uniform Testamentary Additions to Trusts Act or comparable legislation so that a trust is valid "regardless of the existence, size or character of the corpus."[6]

A revocable living trust does not own property; the trustee is in legal title to the property comprising the trust estate. A revocable living trust cannot operate unless the trustor conveys legal title to property to the trustee (or, upon the trustor's death, his or her Will transfers [pours over] property comprising the decedent trustor's probate estate to the revocable living trust). This process of conveying legal title is called *funding the trust*.[7] In other words, legal title to the trust property must be in the name of the trustee. This is the meaning of the expressions: "The trustee is in-title to the property," and "The trust is funded."

Property transferred to a revocable living trust is described in schedules that are attached to the trust agreement following the signature pages. These schedules are referenced in the article of the trust agreement acknowledging that the trustor has transferred and delivered to the trustee the legal title to the property described in the schedule or schedules [see, e.g. file "APP0201.DOC" Article III (A); "APP0202.DOC" Article III (A); "APP0203.DOC" Article III (A); and "APP0204.DOC" Article III (A)].

For trustors residing in community property states, care must be exercised to ensure that separate property of the spouses is not inadvertently commingled with community property when legal title to property is conveyed to the trustee of a joint revocable living

[4] *See* American Law Institute, *Restatement (Second) of Trusts* (1959) § 74 (hereafter *Restatement (Second) of Trusts*); Austin Wakeman Scott, 1 *Scott On Trusts* (3d ed., Boston, MA: Little, Brown, 1967 and Supp. 1987) § 17.1 (hereafter *Scott on Trusts*).

[5] 1 *Scott on Trusts*, §§ 74.1, 76.

[6] Uniform Testamentary Additions to Trust Act § 1, 8A U.L.A. 603 (West 1983).

[7] Lifetime funding of a revocable living trust is discussed in Chapters 9 through 15.

trust (or to the trustee of each spouse's own revocable living trust). Eight states are considered traditional community property states: Arizona, California, Idaho, Louisiana, Nevada, New Mexico, Texas, and Washington. The State of Wisconsin is a marital property state, but it does recognize the concept of community property between married individuals. In this regard, Wisconsin recognizes marital property as a form of community property.[8] Furthermore, the IRS has ruled that, unless the rights of the spouses are altered by agreement, the Wisconsin Marital Property Reform Act (the Act) automatically vests a 50 percent interest in the marital property in each spouse. Accordingly, under the Act, the rights of spouses in Wisconsin are community property rights.[9] The State of Alaska recognizes community property by consent, in that it allows married persons to classify their property as community property in a community property agreement.[10]

Example

Joint living trust, husband and wife, community property:

ARTICLE III

TRUST PROPERTY

(A) **Original Trust Estate.** The Trustors acknowledge that they have transferred to the Trustee the property set forth in Schedule "A," Schedule "B," Schedule "C," and Schedule "D" hereunto attached and by reference made part hereof.

(B) **Additions to Trust Estate.** Additional property may be added to the Trust Estate at any time by the Trustors, or either of them, or by any person or persons, by inter vivos or testamentary transfer; and the same may designate the trust to which the property shall be added. All such initial and additional property is referred to herein collectively as the Trust Estate and shall be held, managed, and distributed as herein provided.

(C) **Character of Property Unchanged.** During the joint life of the Trustors, any property transferred to this Trust Agreement shall retain its original character; and, in the event of revocation, the Trustee shall distribute such property to the Trustors based upon the same property rights they had prior to transfer to the Trust Agreement.

(D) **Schedule "A" Property.** The property described in Schedule "A" is the Trustors' community property, which shall remain such after its transfer to the Trustee hereunder, subject to the terms and conditions of this Trust Agreement. While both Trustors live, each reserves the right to direct the distribution of all income from, and principal of, the community property held under this Trust Agreement. Directions given hereunder shall be given orally or in writing but, if given orally, shall be confirmed in writing by such Trustor, if the Trustee so requests.

(E) **Schedule "B" Property.** The property described in Schedule "B" is the Trustors' property that was owned by Trustors as joint tenants with right of survivorship and/or as tenants by the entirety with right of survivorship prior to the execution of this Trust Agreement. Such property shall retain its character only with respect to the determination of the proportionate value of such property to be included

[8] Wisconsin. *Wisconsin Statutes Annotated* (Wis. Stat. Ann.). § 766.001(2) (Loislaw 2001).

[9] Rev. Rul. 87-13, 1987-1 C.B. 20.

[10] Alaska. *Alaska Statutes*. (Alaska Stat.) § 34.77.060(a) (Loislaw 2001); Moy, 1, *A Practitioner's Guide to Estate Planning*, § 7.01[A], at 7-5.

in the gross estate of the DECEDENT TRUSTOR as provided under I.R.C. Section 2040(b) and [name of state] State law. This limitation shall terminate on the death of the DECEDENT TRUSTOR. The initial Trustees shall have no more extensive power over such property than either of the Trustors would have had under [name of state] State law.

(F) **Schedule "C" Property.** The property described in Schedule "C" is the separate property of Trustor-Husband. Such property may include separate property and quasi-community property. For convenience, all such property shall be referred to in this Trust Agreement as "separate property." Trustor-Husband does not intend to change the character of his separate property, if any, included in the Trust Estate.

(G) **Schedule "D" Property.** The property described in Schedule "D" is the separate property of Trustor-Wife. Such property may include separate property and quasi-community property. For convenience, all such property shall be referred to in this Trust Agreement as "separate property." Trustor-Wife does not intend to change the character of her separate property, if any, included in the Trust Estate.

(H) **Additional Property.** Following the decease of either Trustor, property received by Trustee from the probate estate of the DECEDENT TRUSTOR or by other transfer by reason of the decease of such Trustor shall be allocated to the SURVIVOR'S TRUST or to the DECEDENT'S TRUST as hereinafter provided. Unless Trustee is otherwise instructed in writing, property received as an addition to any trust hereunder created from a source other than the probate estate of the DECEDENT TRUSTOR or by transfer attributable to the death of such Trustor shall be allocated among the SURVIVOR'S TRUST and the DECEDENT'S TRUST as hereinafter provided.

Information describing the property listed in the schedules should be sufficiently detailed so the reader of the living trust agreement can readily identify and locate the property of the trust estate (see file "APP0205.DOC"). Full legal descriptions of real property should be provided—not just a street address or tax lot number. Tax lot numbers can be changed over the years by the taxing authorities. Securities should be identified by company name, number of shares held by the trustor, the certificate number representing the shares, and the Committee on Uniform Security Identification Procedure (CUSIP) number—a nine-digit number that is assigned to all stocks and bonds traded on major exchanges and many unlisted securities. Usually, the CUSIP number is printed on the face of the stock certificate. If the CUSIP number is not printed on the certificate, it may be obtained through the company's transfer agent. Bank accounts, mutual funds, and credit union accounts should all be identified by name and account number and, if appropriate, by branch name. Similar descriptive thoroughness should be provided for other assets transferred to a revocable living trust, including tangible personal property. Remember, though, just because property is listed on the schedules does not mean that it has been actually conveyed to the trustee of the revocable living trust and that the trustee is in legal title to the property.

Assuming the revocable living trust is properly funded, the schedules serve multiple purposes. First, they inform interested parties to the revocable living trust of the identity of property comprising the trust estate. Second, when married individuals are the trustors of a joint revocable living trust or separate living trust agreements, the schedules serve as a means of classifying the trustors' property for federal estate and income tax purposes. In this regard, if the trustors owned property as joint tenants with right of survivorship, as tenants by the entirety, as community property, as quasi-community property (see discussion in Chapter 9, Overview of the Funding Process) or as separate property before the revocable living trust was effected, it may be important for them to preserve the identity of such property for federal estate and income tax purposes. And, third, if the revocable living trust is revoked, married trustors may want the trustee to reconvey title to the property which comprised the trust estate to them in exactly the same way the property was titled before it was transferred to the revocable living trust.

Disposition of Income and Principal during Lifetime of Trustor: Article IV

Provision is made for the payment of income and principal of the trust estate to or for the trustor's benefit during his or her lifetime. In other words, either in the event the trustor becomes incapacitated during the trustor's lifetime to the extent that the trustor cannot manage his or her affairs, becomes incompetent (whether or not a proper court of jurisdiction has declared trustor incompetent), mentally ill, or in need of a conservator—all as determined by doctors as provided for the testing of the capacity of the trustor and individual trustee—the trustee will distribute to or apply for the benefit of the trustor such amounts of net income and principal from the trust estate as trustee deems necessary for the proper health care (including but not limited to psychological, psychiatric, medical, dental, hospital, nursing expenses, and expenses of invalidism and long-term care [including the payment or premiums for long-term care insurance]), maintenance and support of the trustor; and to meet, in the judgment of the trustee, any catastrophic or emergency needs of trustor to enable trustor to maintain the standard of living to which trustor is accustomed, until trustor is again capable, if ever, to manage trustor's affairs, as determined by doctors as provided for the testing of the capacity of the trustor and individual trustee, or until the death of trustor, without the intervention or consent of any of the contingent beneficiaries or their representatives. Similarly, the same provisions would apply if the trustor simply chooses to turn management of his or her affairs (i.e., the trust estate) over to the successor trustee (see, e.g., file "APP0201.DOC" Article IV (C)). 🖾 Since a revocable living trust is a grantor trust, all items of income, deductions, and credits attributable to the assets composing the trust estate are reportable by the trustor on his or her personal individual income tax return.[11]

Revocation and Amendment: Article V

During the trustor's lifetime, he or she may revoke (terminate; take back property in the trust) the revocable living trust agreement (see, e.g., file "APP0201.DOC" Article V (A)). 🖾 In addition, provision should be included which addresses making gifts of trust estate assets, insofar as that subject relates to a revocation of the revocable living trust agreement with respect to such gifted assets (see, e.g., file "APP0201.DOC" Article V (A) (2)). 🖾 Furthermore, during the trustor's lifetime, the trustor may amend (change; revise; modify) the revocable living trust agreement. The retained powers to alter, amend, modify, revoke, or terminate the revocable living trust cause the value of the assets composing the trust estate to be includable in the decedent trustor's gross estate for purposes of the federal estate tax.[12]

Generally, following the decease of the trustor, the trust agreement cannot be revoked or amended, except for the purposes specifically provided in the trust agreement (see, e.g., file "APP0201.DOC" Article V (C)). 🖾 Such specific provisions are desirable, since changes in federal and state laws may cause the provisions of the trust agreement to be uncertain or incomplete, undesirable and unintended, or obsolete as to the effectiveness of the trust in carrying out the trustor's intentions. Furthermore, it is not uncommon for financial institutions and governmental agencies to arbitrarily and periodically change their requirements as to the peculiar language for a particular institution or agency which may be

---

[11] I.R.C. § 671.

[12] I.R.C. § 2038(a)(1).

required to enable the trustee to effectively utilize the trustee powers. Hence, whether the trustor is incapacitated or is deceased, then, in order to carry out the trustor's intentions, the trustee is authorized to alter or modify language of the trust agreement provisions to avoid court interpretation or language; to adjust provisions to follow laws affecting the income, estate, and gift tax treatment afforded the trust; to meet any unique requirements of any financial institution or governmental agency which may be required; and to otherwise modify the powers of the trustee to help the trustee to efficiently and effectively carry out the purposes of the trust agreement.

Finally, the rights of revocation, withdrawal, alteration, and amendment are reserved by the trustor (i.e., such rights are personal to the trustor) and may not be exercised by any other person, including any agent (e.g., attorney-in-fact under a power of attorney), guardian, or conservator. This provision is essential so as to prevent, for example, a guardian or an attorney-in-fact from misrepresenting the trustor's intentions by having the power to revoke, withdraw, alter, or amend the trust agreement without the trustor's knowledge or consent (see, e.g., file "APP0201.DOC" Article V (D)).

Distribution of Trust Property on Death of Trustor: Article VI

Upon the trustor's death, the trust estate may be held in an Administrative Trust. The Administrative Trust is intended to perform functions similar to those performed by a probate estate. The Administrative Trust terminates as soon as practicable after the trustor's death when the trustee has: gathered together the assets of the trust estate; determined, paid, and settled the expenses, liabilities, and taxes of the trustor's trust estate; and allocated all remaining administrative assets pursuant to the trustor's intentions regarding the disposition of the trust estate.

Observation

Some attorneys prefer not to include Administrative Trust provisions in a revocable living trust in the belief that the trust agreement itself serves as an administrative trust—this is okay. However, when married persons have a joint revocable living trust or when each spouse has his or her own revocable living trusts or a single trustor provides for one or more subtrusts under the revocable living trust, Administrative Trust provisions are helpful. In this regard, the Administrative Trust acts like a *private probate proceeding* and provides the trustee with a separate trust in which the trustee can gather and administer the decedent trustor's trust estate until the decedent trustor's trust estate can be distributed, for example, to a marital deduction trust and a nonmarital deduction trust, as well as other trusts (i.e., subtrusts) that the trustor may have created under the revocable living trust agreement (see files "APP0201.DOC," "APP0202.DOC," "APP0203.DOC," and "APP0204.DOC"). Furthermore, when the value of the decedent trustor's trust estate requires that a United States Estate (and Generation-Skipping Transfer) Tax Return (Form 706) be filed, the Administrative Trust can serve as a repository of trust estate assets until the trustee receives a closing letter from the IRS, at which time the trustee may proceed to fund the various subtrusts (e.g., general power of appointment marital deduction trust; qualified terminable interest property (QTIP) trust; qualified domestic trust (QDOT); nonmarital deduction trust, such as a credit shelter trust; and perhaps trusts for other family members).

Every trustor will have his or her own ideas about to whom and the manner in which the trust estate is to be distributed upon the trustor's death. For example, in file "APP0201.DOC" Article VI (C) , the trustor makes a specific distribution in the amount of five thousand and no one-hundredths dollars ($5,000.00) to close and devoted friends as joint tenants with right of survivorship. The remainder of the trustor's trust estate is to be divided in as nearly equal shares as may be practicable to the trustor's children and to the Joseph B. _____ Special Needs Trust for the benefit of her grandson (see file "APP0201.DOC" Article VI (D)). 📱 In this particular case, Joseph is the son of trustor's son, James, who is incarcerated in a state correctional institution for a period of 90 months. In acknowledging her son, James, and in view of the seriousness of the crimes for which he was convicted and incarcerated, the trustor determined that, due to the nature of the crimes committed by James, it would be inappropriate for him to share in the trust estate. Hence, and in view of the serious medical conditions affecting trustor's grandson, Joseph, trustor believes that Joseph would greatly benefit by the share of trustor's trust estate which would otherwise have been distributable to James but for his inability to adjust to the norms and laws of society. Designing the disposition provisions of a living trust to fulfill the trustor's goals and objectives requires the expertise and experience of a knowledgeable qualified attorney or estate planning practitioner experienced in advising attorneys in such matters.

Payment of Taxes, Debts, and Expenses after Death of Trustor: Article VII

This article in the trust agreement provides the trustee with rules and direction regarding the payment of taxes, debts, and expenses after the trustor's death. Every revocable living trust should contain a provision for the payment and apportionment of debts and taxes.[13] State law governs the manner in which a decedent's federal estate tax burden is allocated among estate assets.[14] In the cases involving revocable living trusts directing that federal estate tax be paid out of the residuary trust estate "without apportionment," courts have consistently held that the decedent used this language as an election out of an apportionment statute that otherwise would apply.[15] Furthermore, generally, if the revocable living trust is silent regarding the apportionment of the federal estate tax, the tax will be paid from the residuary trust estate. If the residuary trust estate has been exhausted, the remaining federal estate tax due will be apportioned among the beneficiaries' respective interests in the trust estate.[16]

The issue of tax apportionment is extremely important with respect to the value of any interest passing to the surviving spouse that qualifies for the marital deduction. This is so

---

[13] *See* Jonathan G. Blattmachr, "Are You Using the Wrong Tax Apportionment Clause?" 3 *Probate & Property* 23 (Nov./Dec. 1989); Jonathan G. Blattmachr, "Tax Apportionment: The Most Important Clause in Many Wills," 14 *American Law Institute–American Bar Association Course Materials J.* 107 (Dec. 1989); Stanley M. Johanson, "The Use of Tax-saving Clauses in Drafting Wills & Trusts," *The Fifteenth Annual Philip E. Heckerling Institute on Estate Planning.* (1981): Chapter 21; Trent S. Kiziah, "Estate Tax Apportionment: "'Except as Otherwise Directed,'" 64 *Florida Bar Journal* 52 (Nov. 1990).

[14] *Riggs v. Del Drago*, 317 U.S. 95, 100 (1942); *Estate of Wycoff v. Commissioner*, 506 F.2d 1144 (10th Cir. 1974), *aff'g* 59 T.C. 617, 622 (1973); *Thompson v. Thompson*, 149 Tex. 632, 236 S.W.2d 779, 789 (1951); *Estate of Swallen v. Commissioner*, 98 F.3d 919 (6th Cir. 1996), *rev'g* T.C. Memo 1993-149; *Estate of Vahlteich v. Commissioner*, 76 AFTR2d ¶ 95-5645, *rev'g and rem'g* T.C. Memo 1994-168; *Estate of Betty Pace Miller v. Commissioner*, T.C. Memo 1998-416.

[15] *Estate of Fine v. Commissioner*, 90 T.C. 1068 (1988), *affd.* without published opinion 885 F.2d 879 (11th Cir. 1989); *Estate of Brunetti v. Commissioner*, T.C. Memo 1988-517; *Estate of Betty Pace Miller v. Commissioner*, T.C. Memo 1998-416.

[16] *See Re Estate of Hawes*, 235 Kan 697, 683 P.2d 1252 (1984); Moy, 2, *A Practitioner's Guide to Estate Planning*, § 30.03 [C] at 30-19.

because the value of such interest is reduced by any encumbrance, obligation, federal estate tax, state estate, succession, legacy, or inheritance tax payable out of the property or required to be paid by the surviving spouse.[17] As a general rule, the marital deduction may be taken only with respect to the net value of any deductible interest that passed from the decedent to his or her surviving spouse.[18]

Equally important, the value of any property qualifying as a federal charitable estate tax deduction is reduced by the amount of any federal estate tax or any state estate, succession, legacy, or inheritance tax paid out of such property.[19] If the value of the charitable transfer is reduced by the amount of such taxes paid, the resulting decrease in the amount passing to charity further reduces the allowable charitable estate tax deduction. In such a case, the amount of the charitable deduction can only be obtained by a series of trial-and-error computations, or by a formula. If, in addition, interdependent state and federal taxes are involved, the computation becomes highly complicated.

Examples

1. If Frances bequeathed $50,000 to a charitable organization and the bequest is subject to a state inheritance tax of $5,000, payable out of the $50,000, then, the charitable deduction amount is $45,000.[20]

2. If a life estate is bequeathed to Mabel with the remainder to a charitable organization and local law of the decedent's domicile requires the inheritance tax (or state death tax) on the life estate to be paid out of the principal, thereby reducing the amount passing to charity, the federal estate tax charitable deduction is limited to the present value, as of the date of the decedent's death, of the remainder value of the reduced life estate.[21]

---

[17] I.R.C. § 2056(b)(4); Treas. Reg. § 20.2056(b)-4(b) and (c). *See Estate of Betty Pace Miller v. Commissioner,* T.C. Memo 1998-416 (Where decedent's will directed that all estate, inheritance, transfer, and succession taxes, including interest and penalties thereon, were to be borne by the decedent's residuary estate and that such payment was to be made as an expense of administration without apportionment and without contribution or reimbursement from anyone; the share of decedent's estate qualifying for the marital deduction and passing to the decedent's surviving spouse was reduced by that amount allocable to the surviving spouse's proportionate interest. By directing that there be no apportionment within the residuary estate, decedent expressed an intention that there be no discrimination between marital and nonmarital residual beneficiaries. Thus, the estate tax liability reduced the amount of the residuary available for distribution to decedent's surviving spouse and to the trust. Accordingly, the finding of the court was that, at the time of decedent's death, the property interests passing to decedent's surviving spouse, Mr. Miller, through the residuary estate were burdened with the federal estate tax and that the marital deduction should be reduced accordingly to reflect the net value of the interests passing to Mr. Miller). *But see McKeon v. United States,* 151 F.3d 1201 (9th Cir. 1998) (a decedent's estate properly calculated the amount of the marital deduction and federal estate tax was not payable out of the trust containing the marital deduction property even though decedent's will directed the executor to pay the federal estate tax out of the residue of the decedent's estate "without proration.")

[18] Treas. Reg. § 20.2056(b)-4(a); Moy, 2, *A Practitioner's Guide to Estate Planning,* § 30.03 [C] at 30-20.

[19] I.R.C. § 2055(c); Treas. Reg. § 20.2055-3(a)(1).

[20] Treas. Reg. § 20.2055-3(a)(1).

[21] Treas. Reg. § 20.2055-3(a)(1).

Recommendation/Planning Strategy:[22]

The following language may be included in a revocable living trust (or will) to avoid a circular arithmetic computation to determine the federal estate tax due when both charitable and noncharitable beneficiaries receive the decedent trustor's (or testator's) residuary estate:

> (A) Trustor directs trustee to pay all estate, inheritance, death, and succession taxes from trustor's residuary estate, except that the share of the Shriners Hospital in trustor's residuary trust estate shall be determined before such taxes are charged against the residuary trust estate, so that no part of such taxes shall be a charge against the charitable bequest.

To the extent that the decedent trustor's property passing to the surviving spouse does not qualify for the estate tax marital (or charitable) deduction or exceeds in value the exemption amount, such property is subject to federal estate tax. Likewise, the decedent trustor's state of residence may not have an unlimited estate tax marital deduction, thereby causing a state estate tax or inheritance tax to be levied against the decedent trustor's property passing to the surviving spouse and other beneficiaries. In addition, the decedent trustor's state of domicile may not be connected to federal law with respect to the phase-out of the federal state death tax credit.[23] In this regard, some states may still impose a state death tax equal to the federal state death tax credit computed under I.R.C. Section 2011 in effect before the 2001 Act became effective. In any event, when the decedent trustor fails to direct the source from which such taxes are to be paid, and state law apportions the payment of such taxes between the marital and nonmarital share of the decedent trustor's residuary trust estate, the marital share may be reduced by the amount of such tax paid by the surviving spouse. Such a result may be avoided by the trustor's direction that all taxes be paid out of the residuary trust estate or that portion of the residuary trust estate not qualifying for the marital (or charitable) deduction.[24]

Such a direction, however, may pose a disadvantage. Property subject to the decedent's will (e.g., specific bequests) may be reduced in value if a large part of the federal estate tax is caused by property passing outside the will (e.g., property owned as JTWROS, life insurance payable to named beneficiaries, qualified and nonqualified plan benefits payable to a named beneficiary, or property subject to transfer under a revocable living trust agreement). The ultimate decision regarding the source from which clearance and transfer costs are to be paid depends upon the value of the decedent's gross estate, the nature of the property in the gross estate, the kinds of bequests made under the testator's will, and the identity of the beneficiaries. One should remember, when a decedent's property passes by will, the Code and, generally, state law allows the testator to allocate the payment of expenses and taxes as he or she chooses. Absent the testator's (trustor's) directions regarding the apportionment of debts and taxes, state law will determine the property from which these items are to be satisfied.[25]

---

[22] Moy, 2, *A Practitioner's Guide to Estate Planning*, § 30.03 [C] at 30-22.

[23] Under the 2001 Act, the maximum credit will be reduced to 12 percent in 2002, 8 percent in 2003, and 4 percent in 2004. In 2005, the state death tax credit will be repealed and replaced with a deduction for death taxes actually paid to any state (or to the District of Columbia). Every trustor (or testator) should inquire of his or her attorney whether his or her state is coupled to federal law with respect to the maximum state death tax credit allowed his or her estate under state law when federal estate tax is due on the value of the decedent trustor's (or testator's) taxable estate.

[24] Moy, 2, *A Practitioner's Guide to Estate Planning*, § 30.03 [C] at 30-23.

[25] *See, e.g., Stickley v. Stickley*, 497 S.E.2d 862 (1998); Moy, 2, *A Practitioner's Guide to Estate Planning*, § 30.03 [C] at 30-23.

Not infrequently, the issue of federal estate tax apportionment arises with respect to the decedent trustor's probate estate and revocable living trust estate. In this regard, the question arises whether, under the terms of the decedent trustor's will and revocable living trust, the federal estate tax is to be equitably apportioned under state law.[26] Where the decedent trustor's will directs that federal estate tax is to be paid from the residue of the probate estate and further directs that, in no event, is the federal estate tax to be apportioned to any person holding any interest in the taxable estate, under the decedent's will and revocable living trust, the federal estate tax is payable from the probate estate without apportionment and before distribution from the estate to the revocable living trust.[27]

In view of the repeal of step-up in basis after 2009 by the 2001 Act of assets acquired from a decedent,[28] the revocable living trust should provide the trustee with the widest latitude in exercising the authority to allocate the available basis increases between or among the trustor's contingent beneficiaries. On the other hand, if the trustor has specific intentions about how the basis increases should be allocated between various trust estate assets and beneficiaries, these intentions should be described in the revocable living trust agreement. It may also be appropriate to include language in the revocable living trust agreement that, in effect, absolves the trustee from liability for basis decisions.[29]

Other Trustee Provisions: Article VIII

Other trustee provisions address the termination of trusts and the limitations concerning trustees, such as: delegation of trust administration; liability of third persons in dealing with the trustee; the actions of co-trustees; valuation of assets composing the trust estate; and that the trustee will be indemnified against liability (including liability for penalties) for valuation positions taken or settled if made in good faith and with reasonable basis; delivery of documents and instruments to the trustee; accounting of the trust estate to the beneficiaries; effect of notices to the trustee; compensation of the trustee; indemnity, receipts, payments to minors and incapacitated persons; merger, liquidation, or consolidation of a corporate trustee; exculpatory assurances given to a trustee by a successor trustee which, in effect, hold harmless the predecessor trustee from alleged fault or guilt if the predecessor trustee acted in good faith; trustee's discretions; trust merger and consolidation; and *situs*—the legal jurisdiction of the revocable living trust (see, e.g., file "APP0201.DOC" Article VIII).

Ask Your Attorney

If I effect a revocable living trust and later decide to move out-of-state, will the trust still work?

Answer

Yes.

---

[26] Moy, 2, *A Practitioner's Guide to Estate Planning*, § 30.03 [C] at 30-24.

[27] Ibid.

[28] *See* discussion in Chapter 1, Repeal of Stepped-up Basis.

[29] Commerce Clearing House, "Carryover Basis Redux," *Estate Planning Review*, in 4 *Financial and Estate Planning*, 46, 50, Commerce Clearing House, Inc., Chicago, IL (June 22, 2001).

All trusts must be subject to a legal jurisdiction. This jurisdiction is known as the *situs* of the trust. The situs of the trust is the legal jurisdiction that governs the trust; that is, state law (local law) (see, e.g., file "APP0201.DOC" Article VIII (M)). As a general rule, the situs of a trust can be changed from one jurisdiction to another, unless the trust instrument prohibits such a change. In most cases, even if the trust instrument prohibits a change in the trust situs, the trust can continue to operate, even though the law of the state where the trustor resided at the time he or she effected the trust governs its operation and the trustee's management of the trust estate.

Trustee Powers: Article IX

Trustee powers may also be called fiduciary powers. A living trust is a legal entity and a person for federal tax purposes.[30] Consequently, if the trust is to carry out the trustor's expectations and directions, the trust must have a code of conduct. Direction and guidance must be provided so the conduct can be performed in a manner expected by the trustor. This is why the trust agreement must state terms, the purpose of the trust agreement, and how the trust purposes are to be carried out by the trustee. Hence, the trust agreement must contain rules-of-the-game or a code of behavior for the trustee to follow (see, e.g., file "APP0201.DOC" Article IX, Article VIII, and Article X). The powers the trustor grants to the trustee need to be broad enough to cover many situations but also specific enough to effectively manage the trustor's particular assets composing the trust estate for special beneficiaries (see file "APP0201.DOC" Article VI (D)).[31]

A trustor may want to give the trustee a power not specifically addressed under local law.

Ask Your Attorney

If I want to give the trustee a power not specifically addressed under state statute (local law), does this mean that such a power is not permissible in the revocable living trust?

Answer

Not necessarily, unless the trustor resides in the state of Louisiana, whose laws are based on the Napoleonic Code. At the risk of oversimplification, in Louisiana, if the law is not written in the statutes, then it is illegal to do what is not covered by the law. This may be a flagrant interpretation, but it is done purposely to emphasize the caution needed when designing a revocable living trust for a trustor who resides in Louisiana. In most other states, however, any fiduciary power is probably acceptable, so long as it does not violate public policy.[32]

Even though fiduciary powers are established by state law (local law), a trustor may wish to provide the trustee special powers to handle a particular asset of the trust estate (e.g., a closely-held business interest) or to carry out a particular direction with regard to the management of the trust estate. A trustor may also want to give the trustee special directions regarding the use of trust estate assets for a particular beneficiary(ies).[33]

---

[30] I.R.C. § 7701(a)(1).

[31] Moy, 2, *A Practitioner's Guide to Estate Planning*, § 30.03 [I] at 30-47.

[32] Ibid., § 30.03 [I] 30-48.

[33] Ibid.

Examples

1. Jim and Karen, husband and wife, have each designated Karen's sister, Barbara, as successor trustee of their respective revocable living trusts for the benefit of their daughters, Carrie Ann and Renee Lynn. Barbara and her husband, Emanuel, reside in New York, where Emanuel successfully operates two restaurants. Jim has all the confidence and trust in the world in his sister-in-law Barbara's ability to successfully manage the trust estate for Carrie Ann and Renee in the event of both his and Karen's deaths. However, Jim does not want Emanuel tempted to exert influence on Barbara to use or invest any of the trust assets in any of his restaurant ventures. With this concern in mind, Jim provided in his revocable living trust that the "Trustee shall not have the power to invest any part of the property forming a part of the trust estate in closely-held business interests as defined by the Internal Revenue Code of 1986, as amended from time to time, and successor provisions thereto."[34]

2.

(F) **Administration of Ranch.** Trustor's entire interest in and to the certain real property tracts in Sections 28, 29, 32, and 33 and in the _____ Donation Land Claim, all in Township 4 South, Range 5 West of the _____ in _____ County, _____, together with all buildings and improvements thereon, all ground and farm equipment and implements, crops, animals, and livestock, or interests therein, commonly known as "the ranch," and all insurance policies relating thereto, shall continue in trust as a life estate for the lifetime benefit of Trustor's children under the following purposes, uses, and conditions:.

(1) **Beneficiaries.** The beneficiaries of the life estate shall be Trustor's surviving Children, **Crawford L.**_____, **Colleen S.** _____ and **Cynthia D.** _____, and shall be referred to in this Trust Agreement individually as Trustor's Child and collectively as Trustor's Children. The interests of Trustor's Children in the life estate shall be as follows: **Crawford L.** _____, as to a forty (40) percent interest; **Colleen S.** _____, as to a thirty (30) percent interest; **Cynthia D.** _____, as to a thirty (30) percent interest.

(2) **Purposes and Uses.** Subject to state, county, and local zoning building codes and ordinances, it is Trustor's intent and purpose that Trustor's Children shall have the rent-free use, benefit, and enjoyment of the ranch for their respective lifetimes. Trustor directs that, if a Child of Trustor should end his or her marriage by divorce, such Child shall retain possession of his or her separate interest in and to the life estate and that such interest shall not become part of any property settlement agreement. Further provided, **Cynthia** shall have the right to the rent-free use, benefit, enjoyment, and occupancy of Trustor's home and of Trustor's interest in and to any buildings and improvements on the ranch. Except, however, the immediate preceding provision shall not entitle **Cynthia** to the use, benefit, enjoyment, and occupancy of any buildings, improvements (including, but not limited to mobile homes or manufactured homes) erected or placed on the ranch by **Crawford L.** _____ and **Colleen S.** _____.

(3) **Conditions.** Except as otherwise provided under this paragraph, Trustee shall pay from income all real property taxes and assessments, insurance

---

[34] Ibid.

premiums, all necessary expenses for the maintenance (including but not limited to water and sewer charges [if any]), fuel, sanitation, and garbage collection charges, assessments, mortgage interest and amortization and repairs [including substantial repairs, alterations, and additions]), general upkeep, protection, and preservation of the ranch. In consultation with Trustor's surviving Children, Trustee is authorized to continue and carry on the operation of the ranch. Trustee may, only upon unanimous written consent of all of Trustor's Children and the surviving lineal descendants of a deceased Child of Trustor, effect a sale of the ranch. Trustee shall, in consultation with Trustor's Children and the surviving lineal descendants of a deceased Child of Trustor (a minor lineal descendant shall be represented by his or her Guardian [legal or natural]), determine the time, manner, and method for effecting such a sale. In making such sale, Trustee shall not be obligated either to obtain the authority, consent, or confirmation of any court therefore or thereof, either before or afterwards, or to make any report thereof. Trustee shall distribute the net proceeds from the sale in proportion to Trustor's Children's interest(s) in the life estate with the interest of a deceased Child of Trustor being distributable to the surviving lineal descendants of such deceased Child by right of representation, except as provided under this Article VI (H) (Beneficiary under Age Twenty-One).

(4) **Income.** Subject to the provisions of this Article VI (F) (3), Trustee shall distribute the net income from timber sales in excess of what is required to manage and perform reforestation to Trustor's Children in proportion to their separate interests in the life estate. Further provided, Trustee may accumulate the net income from ranching operations and leases, exclusive of timber sales, or so much thereof as Trustee shall deem advisable; or Trustee may, in Trustee's discretion, pay such net income, or so much thereof as Trustee deems advisable, to Trustor's Children in proportion to their interests in the life estate. Income otherwise distributable to a Child of Trustor who is deceased shall be distributable to such deceased Child's lineal descendants by right of representation in the same manner and under the same conditions as provided under this Article VI (F) for Trustor's Child.

(5) Duration.

   (a) **Trustor's Child Dies with Surviving Lineal Descendants.** Subject to the provisions of this Article VI (F) (5) (c), if Trustor's Child dies with surviving lineal descendants, the deceased Child's interest in the Ranch Trust shall be divided among the deceased Child's surviving lineal descendants by right of representation and shall continue in trust and be administered in the same manner and under the same conditions as provided for Trustor's Children under this Article VI (F).

   (b) **Trustor's Child Dies without Surviving Lineal Descendants.** If Trustor's Child dies and is not survived by lineal descendants, the interest of Trustor's deceased Child in the Ranch Trust shall be divided equally between Trustor's surviving Children.

   (c) **Trustor's Child Dies with Surviving Spouse.** If, at the time of the decease of Trustor's Child, such Child and his or her spouse are not legally separated or the marriage of Trustor's Child and his or her spouse has not been legally dissolved and/or a dissolution of marriage is not pending at the time of the Trustor's Child's decease and the Trustor's Child's spouse does not remarry or live with a partner, he or she may continue to reside on the Ranch.

Caution

Since fiduciary powers are governed by state—not federal—law, it is imperative that the trustor seek the advice and counsel of a qualified attorney in all matters involving the inclusion of trustee powers in a revocable living trust to be certain that such powers conform to state law. The trustee powers found in the appendices referred to in this chapter conform to the laws of the State of Oregon and should only be viewed as an illustration of what is possible, recognizing, of course, that certain powers may differ among the states.

Miscellaneous Provisions: Article X

These provisions are often referred to as *boilerplate*. They address such issues as the rights of creditors in a beneficiary's share of the testator's estate (so-called *spendthrift* provisions) (see file "APP0201.DOC" Article X (A)); the rule against perpetuities (see file "APP0201.DOC" Article X (B)); how accumulated and undistributed income of the trust estate is to be handled (see file "APP0201.DOC" Article X (C)); whether the fiduciary (trustee) should furnish a bond (in most states corporate trustees, if they are banks or independent trust companies, are not required to post a bond); distribution and taxation of income (see file "APP0201.DOC" Article X (D)); definitions, particularly, if the meanings of certain terms may be different from those provided by state law (e.g., the term *minor*) (see file "APP0201.DOC" Article X (E) (1)); direction to the trustee to make application to the proper court of jurisdiction if any dispute arises as to interpretation of the trust agreement or if there is need to obtain court approval of any accounting or any interpretation in regard to the trust agreement (see file "APP0201.DOC" Article X (F)); and how the trust agreement, as a whole, should be treated if a particular part or clause of the trust is declared void, invalid, or inoperative (see file "APP0201.DOC" Article X (G)). In sum, the miscellaneous provisions fill in any holes that may otherwise exist in the administration provisions of the revocable living trust. Lastly, these provisions can actually shorten the trust agreement by obviating the need to repeat the meaning of terms, conditions, and phrases throughout the document.[35]

Observation

The rule of perpetuities varies from state to state. Some states have repealed their rules against perpetuities. In general, the rule against perpetuities provides that no interest in property is good unless it vests, if at all, not later than: 21 years (plus the ordinary period of gestation) after the death of the last survivor of trustor's spouse and trustor's lineal descendants living on the date of trustor's death; or 90 years after the date of trustor's death, whichever period is later—at the end of which time, distribution of all principal and accrued, accumulated, and undistributed income must be made to the persons then entitled to distributions of income in the manner and proportions stated in the trust agreement (or, if not stated, then, equally) with respect to their attained ages. Accordingly, it is imperative that the trustor consult with qualified legal counsel to determine the rule of perpetuities in effect in the state that is to be the legal jurisdiction (*situs*) of the revocable living trust.

---

[35] Ibid., § 30.03 [H] 30-47.

Appointment of Guardian: Article XI

Some states recognize "any stated desire" of a person with respect to the appointment of a guardian for the person of an incapacitated individual.[36] Whether, and to what extent, a person's *desire* would be recognized by the proper court of jurisdiction may depend on whether the incapacitated person's desire was communicated before or after the onset of the incapacity. In this regard, the revocable living trust can serve as the legal instrument by which the trustor makes known in writing his or her desire with respect to the nomination and appointment of a guardian of the trustor's person in the event of physical or mental incapacity before the incapacity occurs (see file "APP0201.DOC" Article XI).

Cost to Beneficiary: Article XII

Some estate owners believe that no beneficiary who contests his or her revocable living trust should receive any share of his or her trust estate. Such *in terrorem* clauses are often frowned upon by the courts because they are viewed as effectively denying a trustor's beneficiary the right to bring an otherwise valid claim to the court's attention. Such intimidation clauses are usually viewed as being against public policy.

Use of a *cost-to-beneficiary* clause may be a more positive approach to dealing with a potentially difficult beneficiary. Such a clause may be appropriate in cases where the trustor is quite certain that a particular beneficiary may contest the pattern of distribution and become an irritant to the peaceful and orderly administration of his or her trust estate. The cost-to-beneficiary clause does not prevent a beneficiary from bringing a legitimate concern to the court's attention, but it should discourage frivolous claims[37] (see file "APP0201.DOC" Article XII).

Disposition of Remains

Certain states will honor requests made in a will or a revocable living trust if the testator or trustor has a particular philosophy, belief, or wish regarding a funeral service, place of burial, or other opinion regarding the disposition of his or her remains. A trustor may have definite ideas about the type of funeral service or memorial that he or she wishes performed. Furthermore, the trustor may direct that his or her remains or specific organs be donated for use in medical research or for possible transplant purposes. It should be noted that not all states give such wishes and directions legal effect. For example, in some states, statements in a will or revocable living trust regarding burial instructions may be respected but are not legally binding.[38]

Examples

1. "I direct that my body be cremated and the ashes scattered over the Crown Zellerbach tree farm east of Molalla, Oregon, and that no funeral service be conducted."
2. "I direct that my body be cremated and the ashes scattered over the Pacific Ocean off San Francisco Bay, California. I further direct that a modest memorial service be conducted in lieu of a traditional funeral service."

---

[36] *See, e.g.*, Oregon. *Oregon Revised Statutes* (Or. Rev. Stat.) 125.200 (Loislaw 2001).

[37] Moy, 2, *A Practitioner's Guide to Estate Planning*, § 30.03 [M] at 30-53; for additional reading, *see* Martin D. Begleiter, "Anti-contest Clauses: When You Care Enough to Send the Final Threat, 26 *Arizona State Law Journal* 629 (1994); John L. Carroll and Brian K. Carroll, "Avoiding the Will Contest," 8 *Property & Probate* 61 (May/June 1994).

[38] Moy, 2, *A Practitioner's Guide to Estate Planning*, § 30.03 [L] at 30-51.

3. "I wish my body to be donated to the UNIVERSITY OF OREGON HEALTH SCIENCES CEN-TER SCHOOL OF MEDICINE per instructions in my application dated February 1, 1996—'Donation of Body to the Department of Anatomy,' University of Oregon Health Sciences Center, Portland, Oregon 97201."

4. "I direct that my body shall be cremated and my ashes interred beside my former spouse, Bernice L. S_____ in Young Memorial Park, Portland, Oregon. I have ac-quired and paid for Grave(s) One and Two (1 and 2), Lot 111, Lilly Section in Young Memorial Park for said purpose. I direct that my memorial service be conducted in the Waters Funeral Chapel, 100 Boones Ferry Road, Woodburn, Oregon 97071, and that the minister from the Woodburn United Methodist Church officiate said memorial ser-vice. Finally, I suggest that family and friends make contributions to the charities of their choice in my memory."

5. "Upon my death, my Personal Representative or Trustee shall arrange with medical personnel or the appropriate authorities of the jurisdiction wherein my demise occurs to make use of whatever organs or parts of my body are medically acceptable. I also di-rect that an autopsy of my remains be performed for whatever reason. After compli-ance with the aforementioned directives, my body, without embalming, shall be cremated as immediately as possible, in view of the aforementioned directives, and the ashes scattered into the Pacific Ocean. I further direct there be no casket, no viewing of my body, no burial, no funeral service, and no unnecessary expense in connection with the disposition of my remains. I believe that the body without life is nothing to be immortalized. My Personal Representative or Trustee shall arrange for an upbeat memorial service in a church—not in a funeral home—valuing life and its continuity. Fi-nally, I believe that such a memorial service is to celebrate the graduation into a new adventure."[39]

6. "Trustor's body shall be cremated and the ashes scattered over Mt. Hood as near White River Glacier as possible or, if this is not possible, then over the general area of the Mt. Hood National Forest but not in the vicinity of Yokum Ridge." (Trustor did not want his ashes scattered in the vicinity of Yokum Ridge, because Yokum Ridge was in view of the kitchen window of trustor and his wife's mountain cabin.)

Signature Clause

The trustor should sign his or her revocable living trust exactly as his or her name appears in the preamble. The date of signature should be filled in so that there is absolutely no ques-tion which revocable living trust is the latest, if two or more such trusts are discovered upon the trustor's death. Though not mandatory, the formal requirements of state law for the execution and attestation of a will may be followed in the execution of a revocable liv-ing trust.

Attestation Clause

The signing of a revocable living trust by the trustor is an important event and must be done in accordance with procedures established by local law. Witnesses to a trustor's exe-cution of a revocable living trust are not required under most state jurisdictions. Even so, the signatures of both the trustor and trustee should be witnessed by at least the number of disinterested parties required for the witnessing of a Last Will; the witness should be at least the age of majority in the state governing (the *situs*) the revocable living trust; and, as a general rule, the witnesses should sign their names on the revocable living trust in the presence of the trustor and each other. Furthermore, the trustor's and trustee's signatures

---

[39] Ibid., § 30.03 [L] 30-52.

should be notarized (acknowledged). Such an acknowledgment may be required under local law if it should become necessary, for whatever reason, to admit the living trust agreement to a probate or any other legal proceeding. In addition, it may be a good idea to have the trustor's and trustee's signatures *guaranteed* by a commercial bank or by a member firm of the New York Stock Exchange in the event securities transactions must be executed by the trustee. Finally, documents conveying legal title to property to the trustee of a revocable living trust may require witnesses (e.g., deeds to real property, assignment of contracts, assignment of beneficiary's interest in a deed of trust, assignment of leases, bill of sale, assignment of notes, change of ownership/beneficiary designation of life insurance policies, and so forth).

Observation/Recommendation

If the trustor wants to be in substantial compliance with rules for the execution of a will, the trustor should sign the revocable living trust in the presence of the required number of witnesses and before the witnesses sign their names to the trust agreement.[40] The number of witnesses required depends upon local law; usually, two or more are required. The attorney conducting the signing *ceremony* should see to it that the witnesses clearly understand that the instrument being signed is, in fact, the trustor's revocable living trust.

As a rule, just as with the execution of a will, a beneficiary of the trustor should not sign the revocable living trust as a witness. This is because, if the beneficiary witness's testimony is required later to establish the validity of the trust agreement, local law may provide that the beneficiary must forfeit his or her interest under the trust, as can occur under a will.[41] The witnesses should add their addresses to the trust agreement (see file "APP0201.DOC" attestation of witnesses) so that they can be more easily located if the trust agreement is submitted to a proper court of jurisdiction for interpretation or administration. The inclusion of such information obviates the need to locate the witnesses at the time the trust agreement is admitted to a proper court of jurisdiction and, in effect, enables the trust agreement to be self-proving with respect to its execution.[42]

DETERMINING THE TRUSTEE OF A REVOCABLE LIVING TRUST

Who may and should be the trustee of a revocable living trust? First, state law should always be consulted regarding who may serve as a trustee. Consulting state law is important because some states forbid an out-of-state bank or trust company to hold or manage property as a trustee. As a rule, any person who is capable of taking legal or equitable title in property may do so as trustee for himself or herself or for the benefit of another person.[43] In all cases, while it should be obvious, it is advisable that an individual trustee be a person who is capable of managing his or her own personal affairs and is not under some disability.

---

[40] *See Burns v. Adamson,* 313 Ark. 281, 854 S.W.2d 723 (Ark., 1993); Moy, 2, *A Practitioner's Guide to Estate Planning,* § 30.03 [P] at 30-55.

[41] *See, e.g., Succession of Mitchell,* 524 So2d 150 (La. App. 1988) (will beneficiary who is also a witness cannot avoid invalidation of will by renouncing bequest).

[42] Moy, 2, *A Practitioner's Guide to Estate Planning,* § 30.03 [P] at 30-56.

[43] George M. Turner, M.S., J.D. *Revocable Trusts* (Colorado Springs: Shepard's/McGraw-Hill, 1983, at 102 (hereafter Turner, *Revocable Trusts*).

Trustor/Trustee

The trustor may serve as trustee. In some cases, a family member may serve as a co-trustee with the trustor as the other co-trustee. So long as the trustor is already managing his or her own financial affairs in a responsible manner and is otherwise capable of serving as trustee of his or her own revocable living trust, then there is absolutely no reason whatsoever why the trustor cannot serve in such a capacity.

Ask Your Attorney

Can my spouse and I name different trustees under our living trust agreement?

Answer

Yes.

Though not common, a husband and wife may be the trustees of their respective property interests under a joint living trust agreement but, for a variety of reasons, may not want to designate one another as successor trustees. Such may be the case in second-marriage situations where each spouse wants to designate his or her children as successor trustee as to that spouse's property interests in the revocable living trust. In families where the children by each spouse's former marriage have good relationships and are in accord as to their respective parents' estate planning objectives, such a trustee arrangement can work effectively. The same trustee arrangement can also be effective if each spouse has his or her own separate living trust.

Family Members as Trustees

Other family members or a beneficiary of the trustor may serve as co-trustee or as successor trustee. On the one hand, if a beneficiary is designated as a co-trustee or successor trustee, a potential conflict of interest could compromise the impartial administration of the trust estate. On the other hand, though, such a beneficiary or family member may be more sensitive to the trustor's needs and the needs of other beneficiaries of the trustor's trust estate. In turn, the trustor may feel more comfortable with a family member as successor trustee than if a bank or independent corporate trustee served in that role.

Ask Your Attorney

Do I have to use a bank as trustee of my living trust?

Answer

No.

In some cases, a bank or an independent trust company is named as the ultimate successor trustee in the event of the resignation or inability of an individual successor trustee to serve. By naming a bank or independent trust company as successor trustee, the beneficiaries do not have to turn to a proper court of jurisdiction to appoint a successor trustee in the event none of the individual successor trustees can serve. Moreover, a corporate trustee may be better able to interface and handle a difficult beneficiary, such as an *infamous* or *difficult* child. A corporate trustee can be a formidable opponent in the event a *difficult* beneficiary becomes bent on overturning a subtrust established under the revocable living trust agreement for that beneficiary.

Furthermore, the trustor may provide as many co-trustees as he or she wishes. However, practical considerations with regard to day-to-day trust administration may limit the number of co-trustees who should serve. Such consideration is particularly applicable if the persons designated as co-trustees reside in different cities or states. Delays can be experienced in obtaining signatures and in sending and receiving pertinent trust documents. Usually, whenever possible, the trustor may be well-advised to designate at least two or perhaps three individual successor trustees. The revocable living trust may provide that, if the trust is without a trustee, a majority of the beneficiaries of the trust can appoint a successor trustee. Or, in the absence of qualified family members to serve as trustee, provision can be made in the trust agreement for a designated corporate trustee (bank or independent trust company) to act as the ultimate successor trustee.

Ask Your Attorney

Could my son and my bank serve as co-trustees?

Answer

Yes.

If a corporate trustee and an individual person are designated co-trustees, it is absolutely essential that the trustor provide in the trust agreement which of them shall have the ultimate decision-making responsibility. In this regard, often the decision-making authority is divided—the corporate trustee being responsible for the safekeeping and management of the trust estate, while the individual trustee oversees the day-to-day needs of the primary beneficiary and ultimately the contingent beneficiary(ies). On the other hand, these roles may be reversed. In any event, each trustee should have clearly defined areas of responsibility and authority for making decisions affecting both the trust estate and the beneficiaries entitled to the property comprising the trust estate. Finally, every trust agreement should provide the grounds for the removal of a trustee and empower the beneficiaries to appoint a successor trustee to replace a trustee who has resigned, died, or been removed (see, e.g., file "APP0201.DOC" Article II (F)).

Ask Your Attorney

Can my daughter be the trustee of my revocable living trust though she lives in another state?

Answer

Yes.

Though, in many cases, it is not a legal requirement, ideally, when the trustor and trustee are different individuals, both should reside in the same state. As a practical matter, if for no other reason than for ease of administration, this rule should be followed, regardless of whether a particular state's laws require such an arrangement.

Ask Your Attorney

If, during my lifetime, my successor trustee assumes the role of managing my revocable living trust, would my trust estate be subject to the claims of my trustee's creditors if my trustee developed personal financial problems, were sued, or declared bankruptcy?

Answer

No.

A trustee is a fiduciary under state law. As a general rule, the trust estate entrusted to a trustee is not part of the trustee's personal assets. Therefore, the trust estate property cannot be subject to the claims of a third-party trustee's creditors. This rule is not applicable when the trustor and trustee are one and the same individual. In other words, a trustor cannot take title to his or her property as trustee for his or her own benefit and, by doing so, shelter the property from the claims of the trustor's creditors.

When multiple individuals are acting as co-trustees, the trustor may want to make provision for the delegation of authority. In this regard, caution must be observed. Some states do not permit a trustee to transfer responsibility to another or delegate the entire administration of the trust estate to a co-trustee or another person. Nevertheless, as a practical matter, the co-trustees may want to authorize just one of them signature authority on behalf of all the co-trustees. The following suggested language may accomplish such a purpose:

> (3) **Delegation of Trust Administration.** Except as herein specifically provided, the Trustee shall not transfer its office to another or delegate the entire administration of the trust estate to a co-Trustee or another. Further provided, no individual Trustee shall participate by delegation in the exercise of a power that was not initially granted to that individual Trustee. Provided, however, to the extent permitted under the laws of the State of _____, a co-Trustee may at any time, or from time-to-time, at co-Trustee's own election, either by power of attorney for that purpose or by an instrument to that effect, signed and acknowledged by co-Trustee and delivered to the other co-Trustees, delegate to one of the co-Trustees signature authority on behalf of all co-Trustees as Trustee in all matters affecting said trust in order to facilitate the administration of the trust. Such delegation of signature authority to another co-Trustee shall not constitute a transfer of said delegating co-Trustee's fiduciary responsibility or liability, nor shall such delegating co-Trustee be relieved from any and all obligation or duty as a co-Trustee under this Trust Agreement. The sole purpose of the aforementioned delegation of signature authority is to facilitate the effective and efficient administration of the trust.

Further, it is not uncommon for a trustor to have a bank account in his or her name with a child or other immediate family member. Most often, such an arrangement enables a family member to be listed on the account as an accommodation party to sign checks or to make deposits on behalf of the registered owner in the account owner's absence; for example, when the account owner is traveling. Unless the revocable living trust agreement empowers the trustor when acting as trustee to nominate an accommodation party, most banks and other financial institutions are reluctant to allow such an accommodation party to operate when the account is titled in the name of a trustee. The following suggested language in the living trust agreement can alleviate this concern:

> During the time Trustor is serving as Trustee and is not incapacitated, as determined under this Article V (D), Trustor, acting as Trustee, may nominate **Susan H.**

_____ and **Sharon M.** _____, or either of them, as signatories on any and all of Trustor's interest in and to (legal or equitable) bank accounts, including but not limited to savings, checking, money market, and credit union accounts held in the name of **Beverly A.** _____, Trustee under this the **Beverly A.** _____ Revocable Living Trust Agreement. Said signature authority in Susan or Sharon shall not confer upon either of them legal or equitable ownership in such accounts under this Trust Agreement; but rather said signature authority shall be for the sole purpose of accommodation to Trustor to enable **Susan** or **Sharon** to sign checks, execute bank drafts, and make deposits to such accounts as a convenience to Trustor. In the event of Trustor's incapacity, as determined under this Article V (D), or in the event of Trustor's death, the successor Trustee shall be empowered with the same nomination authority as the initial Trustee and may, in Trustee's discretion, nominate **Susan** and **Sharon**, or either of them, as signatories on any and all bank accounts, including but not limited to savings, checking, money market, and credit union accounts held in the name of the successor Trustee under the **Beverly A.** _____ Revocable Living Trust Agreement, including amendments thereto. The same conditions, limitations, and purposes shall apply to the nominee's signature authority granted by the successor Trustee as apply with respect to such authority granted by the initial Trustee to the nominee with respect to the accounts described herein.

Another approach that may be used to give an accommodation party signature authority on bank accounts is for the trustee to grant such authority in a letter to the financial institution (see file "APP0206.DOC"). 🖳 Obviously, whether the financial institution will accept such an arrangement by letter outside the parameters of the revocable living trust agreement is problematical. The better approach is to include in the revocable living trust agreement the above suggested language.

Ask Your Attorney

Could two or more of my children serve as co-trustees?

Answer

Yes.

For trustors with two adult children, it is not unusual for them to agonize about which child to designate as trustee or whether they should designate both children as co-trustees. Such a dilemma can be satisfactorily resolved if the trustor focuses on each child's special skills and abilities.

Example

Frances was uncertain about designating her son, William, and her daughter, Cheryl, co-trustees of her living trust. Her uncertainty was based on the fact that William is capable of making good investment and business decisions, while Cheryl, a registered nurse, is well-trained and quite skilled in providing care for senior citizens but has little interest in business and investment matters. Faced with these realities, Frances designated William and Cheryl, in the order named, as successor trustees of her living trust. Additionally, because of Cheryl's special skills, Frances nominated Cheryl as her guardian in the event Frances becomes physically or mentally incapacitated. Under this arrangement, William will serve as trustee in the event Frances can no longer act as trustee; and Cheryl will be responsible for Frances' day-to-day physical well-being as her guardian. Frances could have designated William and Cheryl as co-trustees and provided that William would be responsible for all of Frances' financial affairs with Cheryl being responsible for Frances' personal needs.

Ask Your Attorney

My son owes me hundreds of thousands of dollars, does not get along with my daughter who has successfully turned around our failing family business. He has attempted on several occasions to convince me that I should sell my ocean beach condominium to him which is to be included as part of the trust estate in my restated revocable living trust agreement. I do not want to sell the condominium to my son; but, because I am hearing-impaired and am becoming increasingly physically infirmed, I am concerned that due to my infirmities I may grow weary of his pressure for me to sell the condominium to him. How can I prevent a sale of the condominium to him if I reach the point where I may consider it easier to sell the condominium to him than to continue resisting his overtures?

Answer

In the restatement of your revocable living trust, you have three options—any of which can prevent a sale of the condominium if your better judgment is being compromised by your son's pressure to sell it to him: (1) you and your daughter can be the initial co-trustees of your revocable living trust agreement. Under this arrangement, your daughter would, in effect, be in an oversight position so that you are not unfairly taken advantage of by your son; (2) you could designate your daughter as the sole initial trustee; or (3) you could designate a corporate trustee as the initial trustee. Option (1) would require both you and your daughter to sign any documents effecting a sale of the condominium to your son. Similarly, Options (2) and (3) would require the trustee to effect any documents necessary to effect a sale of the condominium to your son. Under Options (2) and (3), you, as trustor, would be out-of-the-loop with respect to effecting a transfer of the legal title of the condominium to your son. By being out-of-the-loop, you would be relieved of the burden of having to say "no" to your son and could effectively transfer that responsibility to the trustee.

Regardless of whom the trustor selects as a co-trustee or successor trustee, this person must be absolutely trustworthy; and such person's integrity must be beyond reproach. The individual must also be financially responsible and, ideally, should have a basic understanding of business and financial subjects. This is not to imply that such a person must be a professional money manager or investment adviser or corporate mogul, but the prospective trustee should be comfortable dealing with business and financial matters. These same characteristics apply equally to a person designated as trustee of a testamentary trust. Remember, even in those states that do not permit a trustee to transfer responsibility to another or delegate the entire administration of the trust estate to a co-trustee or another person, the trustee can, nevertheless, be authorized to delegate to qualified and experienced persons duties of trust administration; for example, investing trust estate assets, accounting, bookkeeping, or filing income tax returns.

Contingent Beneficiary as Trustee

A contingent beneficiary of a revocable living trust can act as a trustee without adverse estate tax consequences to that beneficiary. For estate tax purposes, there is absolutely no reason why a contingent beneficiary, including the surviving spouse of the trustor, cannot serve as a co-trustee or sole trustee of a revocable living trust or of a nonmarital deduction trust (credit shelter trust; decedent's trust; Trust "B").[44] However, in order for the value of the property to be excluded from the gross estate over which the trustee-beneficiary has control, he or she must not have a general power of appointment over such property.

A power of appointment is a power given by one person (donor) to another (donee) to select and nominate (to appoint) a person who is to receive and enjoy an estate asset. Powers of appointment may be either general or limited. If the beneficiary of a trust is given the power to determine who is to receive the trust principal, the beneficiary holds a power of appointment. A beneficiary's power to consume or appropriate trust property is a power of appointment.[45] A beneficiary's power to affect the beneficial enjoyment of trust property or its income by altering, amending, revoking, or terminating the trust also constitutes a power of appointment.[46]

General Power of Appointment

As a rule, the term *general power of appointment* means any power of appointment exercisable in favor of the decedent, the decedent's estate, the decedent's creditors, or the creditors of the decedent's estate.[47] This general rule applies even if such a power is exercisable only in favor of one member of this group but not the others.[48] For example, if the contingent beneficiary (donee) was empowered to appoint trust property only to his or her creditors but not to himself or herself, to his or her estate, or to the creditors of his or her estate, the beneficiary would, nevertheless, hold a general power of appointment. The value of property subject to a general power of appointment is includable in the decedent-donee's gross estate for federal estate tax purposes.[49]

Further, a contingent beneficiary's power to remove or discharge a trustee and appoint himself or herself as trustee may constitute a general power of appointment. For example, if, under the terms of a revocable living trust, the trustee-beneficiary or successor trustee-beneficiary has the power to appoint the principal of the trust for the benefit of individuals, including the trustee, and the decedent has the unrestricted power to remove or discharge the trustee at any time and appoint any other person, including himself or herself, the decedent is considered to have a general power of appointment. However, a person does not have a general power of appointment if he or she only had the power to appoint a successor trustee, including himself or herself, *under limited conditions* that did not exist at the time of his or her death, without an accompanying unrestricted power of removal.[50] Furthermore, Revenue Ruling 95-58[51] and Revenue Ruling 81-51[52] conclude that an individual will not be treated as possessing the trustee's powers resulting in a general

---

[44] *See* Treas. Reg. § 25.2518-2(e)(2) and discussion in Chapter 16.

[45] Treas. Reg. § 20.2041-1(b)(1).

[46] Treas. Reg. §§ 20.2041-1(b)(1); 25.2514-1(b)(1); *Pittsburgh National Bank v. United States*, 319 F.Supp. 176 (W.D. Pa. 1970).

[47] I.R.C. § 2041(b)(1). Except, however, joint powers, to the extent provided in Treas. Reg. §§ 20.2041-2 and 20.2041-3, and certain powers limited by an ascertainable standard, to the extent provided in Treas. Reg. § 20.2041-1(c)(2) are not general powers of appointment.

[48] *Jenkins, Jr., exr. v. United States*, 428 F.2d 538 (5th Cir. 1970), *rev'g* (DC Ga) 296 F.Supp. 203, *cert. denied*, 400 U.S. 829, 27 L.Ed. 2d 59.

[49] I.R.C. § 2041(a)(1).

[50] Treas. Reg. § 20.2041-1(b)(1); *see also* Treas. Reg. § 25.2514-1(b); *Wilson v. Commissioner*, T.C.Memo 1992-479 (holding that, because Mrs. Wilson had the sole power to discharge any successor trustee and appoint the replacement trustee [including herself], the trustee's powers are attributed to her (including the power to appoint corpus to her); and, thus, Mrs. Wilson had a general power of appointment); Priv. Ltr. Rul. 8916032 (January 19, 1989); *cf. Wall Estate v. Commissioner*, 101 T.C. 300 (1993).

[51] Rev. Rul. 95-58, 1995-2 C.B. 191, *revoking* Rev. Rul. 79-353, 1979-2 C.B. 325.

[52] Rev. Rul. 81-51, 1981-1 C.B. 458.

power of appointment where the individual can remove and replace a trustee and appoint an individual or corporate successor trustee that is not related or subordinate to the individual within the meaning of I.R.C. Section 672(c).[53]

Similarly, a trustee-beneficiary who can remove and replace a co-trustee does not have a general power of appointment where the trustee-beneficiary does not have the discretionary power to make distributions to the trustee-beneficiary or to persons the trustee-beneficiary is legally obligated to support.[54] Moreover, in the case of a power that is exercisable by the decedent only in conjunction with another person, if the power is not exercisable by the decedent, except in conjunction with a person having a substantial interest in the property subject to the power that is adverse to the exercise of the power in favor of the decedent, such power is not a general power of appointment.[55]

Certain actions by a beneficiary may not constitute a general power of appointment. A power to amend only the administrative provisions of a trust instrument that cannot substantially affect the beneficial enjoyment of trust property or income is not a general power of appointment.[56] A trust beneficiary's agreement to a periodic accounting of the trust, thereby relieving the trustee from further accountability is not a power of appointment if the right to agree does not consist of any power or right to enlarge or shift the beneficial interest of any beneficiary in the trust.[57] The mere power of management, investment, custody of assets, or the power to allocate receipts and disbursements as between income and principal, exercisable in a fiduciary capacity, whereby, the trustee-beneficiary (donee) has no power to enlarge or shift any of the beneficial interests of the trust, except as an incidental consequence of the discharge of such fiduciary duties, is not a power of appointment.[58]

The critical determination as to the existence of a general power of appointment is whether the trustee-beneficiary may enlarge or shift the beneficial interests in the property via the administrative power.[59] To avoid the consequences of the IRS successfully arguing that such a power is not an *incidental consequence*, the trustee-beneficiary should be prohibited from participation in any decision concerning the allocation of receipts and disbursements of any principal and income. One commentator[60] suggests the following language be included in the trust agreement to avoid the trustee-beneficiary from holding a general power of appointment:

> No Trustee who is a beneficiary of any trust created hereunder or who is obligated to support a beneficiary of any trust created hereunder shall ever participate in, with respect to all trusts created hereunder, (i) the exercise of, or decision not to exercise, any discretion over payments, distributions, applications, uses, or accu-

---

[53] *See also* Priv. Ltr. Rul. 9607008 (November 9, 1995) (grandchildren appointed as co-trustees of trusts established by their decedent grandparent for their benefit not deemed to have a general power of appointment over the income and principal of their respective trusts by virtue of their power to remove and replace the corporate trustee of their respective trusts); Moy, 1 *A Practitioner's Guide to Estate Planning*, § 16.02 [B][1] at 16-5.

[54] Priv. Ltr. Rul. 9735023 (May 30, 1997).

[55] I.R.C. § 2041(b)(1)(C); Priv. Ltr. Rul. 8916032 (January 19, 1989); Moy, 1, *A Practitioner's Guide to Estate Planning*, § 16.02 [B][1] at 16-5.

[56] Treas. Reg. § 20.2041-1(b)(1).

[57] Ibid.

[58] Treas. Reg. §§ 20.2041-1(b)(1); 25.2514-1(b)(1).

[59] Tech. Adv. Mem. 8504011 (October 31, 1984); Priv. Ltr. Rul. 9038037 (June 26, 1990); Priv. Ltr. Rul. 9034031 (May 24, 1990).

[60] Georgiana J. Slade, "The Beneficiary as Trustee: A Pandora's Box," *Tax Management Estates, Gifts and Trusts Journal* 19 (November–December 1994): 197, 204.

mulations of income or principal by the Trustee, (ii) the exercise of discretion to allocate receipts or expenses between principal and income, (iii) the removal of any Trustee, (iv) the exercise of any power to amend or affect beneficiaries' powers of withdrawal over additions, or (v) the exercise of any general power of appointment described under sections 2041 or 2514 of the Internal Revenue Code of 1986, as amended. The determination of the remaining Trustee or Trustees shall be final and binding upon the beneficiaries of such trust.

Another technique that can be applied to thwart an unintentional general power of appointment in the trustee-beneficiary is to provide in the trust agreement that a trustee-beneficiary is prohibited from exercising any power of appointment which may be interpreted as a general power of appointment. This means that a trustee other than the trustee-beneficiary must make discretionary decisions affecting the trustee-beneficiary. The following language addresses this issue:

> (N) **Disinterested Trustee.** All powers given to the Trustee by this Trust Agreement are exercisable by the Trustee only in a fiduciary capacity. Notwithstanding any other provisions of this Trust Agreement and, except as provided for the initial Trustee and with respect to Trustee **Linda S. _____**'s power with regard to the Marital Trust and while the initial Trustee is incapacitated as determined for the testing of the capacity of the Trustor under Article V, all powers and discretions vested in the Trustee under this Trust Agreement, such as but not limited to powers, standards, and criteria for the determination to distribute income or principal, shall be vested in the disinterested Trustee. References in this Trust Agreement to "disinterested Trustee" mean the Trustee hereunder who has no interest in the trust property and who cannot be benefited by the exercise of the powers vested exclusively in the disinterested Trustee. In addition, the disinterested Trustee must be one who can possess the powers vested exclusively in the disinterested Trustee without causing trust income or principal to be attributable to a trust beneficiary for federal income, gift, or estate tax purposes prior to the distribution of the trust income or principal to the beneficiary.

Limited Power of Appointment

Generally, the value of property subject to a limited power of appointment (also referred to as a special power of appointment) is not included in the donee's gross estate for federal estate tax purposes. A power of appointment may be limited if it is exercisable only in favor of one or more persons or classes of beneficiaries (e.g., grandchildren, great-grandchildren, nieces, nephews, and so forth) other than the decedent-beneficiary (donee), his or her estate, his or her creditors, or the creditors of his or her estate.[61]

Example

Harry leaves property in trust for his wife, Margaret. Harry gives Margaret the right to appoint the trust remainder to her children or grandchildren. In this example, Margaret possesses a limited power of appointment in that she can only appoint the remainder property of the trust to her children or grandchildren, each constituting a separate class of beneficiary.[62]

---

[61] Treas. Reg. § 20.2041-1(c)(1).

[62] Ibid.

Ascertainable Standard

A power of appointment may also be limited by an ascertainable standard.[63] Strict adherence to limiting a power of appointment by an ascertainable standard is the key to a surviving spouse's (or other beneficiary of the decedent) continued use, benefit, and enjoyment of property in trust while acting as trustee of such property. The beneficiary (donee) of a limited power of appointment may have the power to consume, invade, or appropriate trust principal, income, or both, for his or her benefit if the power is limited by an ascertainable standard relating to the health, education, support, or maintenance of the donee without the value of the property subject to the power being includable in the trustee-beneficiary's gross estate.[64]

Although federal law controls the determination of how the powers and rights possessed by a decedent are taxed, state law prevails in determining the nature and extent of the powers and rights possessed by the decedent.[65] The issue of whether a decedent's power to invade the principal of a trust is limited by an ascertainable standard relating to health, education, support, and maintenance is a matter of state law.[66] State law is also determinative of whether a power of appointment is a general power of appointment or a special (limited) power of appointment.[67]

Special care must be exercised to effect a tax-wise limited power of appointment that qualifies under the ascertainable standard rule. The words *support* and *maintenance* are synonymous, and their meaning is not limited to the bare necessities of life.[68] Other words and phrases, such as *support; support in reasonable comfort; maintenance in health and reasonable comfort; support in his or her accustomed manner of living; care and comfort, considering his*

---

[63] Ibid.

[64] I.R.C. § 2041(b)(1)(A); Treas. Reg. § 20.2041-1(c)(2).

[65] *Morgan v. Commissioner*, 309 U.S. 78 (1940), 1940-1 C.B. 229.

[66] Tech. Adv. Mem. 9125002 (March 7, 1991); *see* Priv. Ltr. Rul. 9323028 (March 16, 1993) (Ohio Rev. Code § 1340.22 provides that a fiduciary cannot make discretionary distributions to himself or herself unless the power is limited by an ascertainable standard and that any such power authorizing discretionary distributions expressed in terms of "comfort (among other things) is limited by an ascertainable standard related to health, education, support, and maintenance." This statute was enacted effective October 8, 1992, but states it was the intention of the legislature that this rule be a codification of existing law. Stating that the statute was declaratory of existing Ohio law, the IRS held that a trust did not grant the surviving wife a general power of appointment over income or accumulated income).

[67] *See Duvall v. Commissioner*, T.C.Memo 1993-319 (Charles Duvall died testate on July 18, 1959. Under his Will, he left property in a life estate to his surviving wife, Jane H. Duvall, "to do as she pleases without bond as long as she lives and after her death the balance to be divided" among designated beneficiaries. The IRS successfully argued that this life estate bequest to Jane did not qualify for the federal estate tax marital deduction under I.R.C. Sec. 2056(b)(5) because it did not provide Jane a general power of appointment in the life estate property. However, when Jane died on February 25, 1983, the IRS attempted to include the value of the property comprising the life estate in Jane's gross estate, asserting that she had been given a general power of appointment over the property under her late husband's Will. The U.S. Tax Court held that under Kentucky state law, Jane possessed only a limited power of appointment in the assets comprising the life estate. Accordingly, the value of these assets was not includable in Jane's gross estate for purposes of the federal estate tax.); *Leach v. Hyatt*, 423 S.E.2d 165 (Va. 1992) (The Supreme Court of Virginia held that (1) a limited power of appointment under decedent's Will would not be struck down on the basis that it manifested uncertainty or indefiniteness in the donor's intent and (2) limited powers of appointment will be upheld when the donor's intent to establish the power is unambiguously expressed.)

[68] Treas. Reg. § 20.2041-1(c)(2).

standard of living; education, including college and professional education; health and medical, dental, hospital, and nursing expenses of invalidism are also considered ascertainable standards.[69] Under Illinois State law, the power to use any or all of the principal of a trust for the beneficiary's "care and comfort considering his standard of living as of the date of my death and considering his income, right to income and other property he may have, as known to the trustees" was held to be a power of appointment limited by an ascertainable standard.[70] The court reasoned, "What we have here is a limitation based on *care and comfort*, unlike *happiness*, which is obviously an open-ended, unascertainable standard."[71] In Straus, both parties (petitioner and respondent) agreed that a decision as to whether a standard is ascertainable must be based on how that standard would be interpreted under applicable state law.[72] Furthermore, both parties agreed that Illinois law governed the trust. Accordingly, it was the opinion of the court that the power of invasion, as it would be interpreted by the Illinois Supreme Court, was limited by an ascertainable standard.[73]

If modifying language accompanies the word *comfort*, then the phrase in which the word *comfort* is included may create a power limited by an ascertainable standard. In *Estate of Vissering v. Commissioner*,[74] the court opined that the Florida courts would hold that *comfort, in context*, does not permit an unlimited power of invasion. The court observed that the invasion of principal was permitted to the extent "REQUIRED for the CONTINUED comfort"[75] of the decedent was part of a clause referencing the support, maintenance, and education of the beneficiary. Invasion of the corpus was not permitted to the extent "determined" or "desired" for the beneficiary's comfort but only to the extent that it was "required." Furthermore, the court observed that the invasion must be for the beneficiary's "continued" comfort, implying more than the minimum necessary for survival, but nevertheless, reasonably necessary to maintain the beneficiary in his or her accustomed manner of living. According to the court, these words in context state a standard essentially no different from the examples in the Treasury Regulations, in which phrases, such as *support in reasonable comfort, maintenance in health and reasonable comfort*, and *support in his accustomed manner of living* are deemed to be limited by an ascertainable standard.[76] Similarly, the

---

[69] Treas. Reg. § 20.2041-1(c)(2); *Estate of Strauss v. Commissioner*, T.C.Memo 1995-248; *see also Estate of Vissering v. Commissioner*, 990 F.2d 578 (10th Cir. 1993), *rev'g and remanding* 96 T.C. 749 (1991).

[70] *Estate of Strauss v. Commissioner*, T.C.Memo 1995-248.

[71] *Estate of Strauss v. Commissioner*, T.C.Memo 1995-248; *cf. Merchants Nat'l Bank of Boston v. Commissioner*, 320 U.S. 256 (1943) (*happiness*); *Henslee v. Union Planters Nat'l Bank & Trust Co.*, 335 U.S. 595 (1949) (*pleasure*); *but see Ithaca Trust Co. v. United States*, 279 U.S. 151 (1929) (*comfort* found to be an ascertainable standard).

[72] *Morgan v. Commissioner*, 309 U.S. 78, 80 (1940); *Helvering v. Stuart*, 317 U.S. 154, 161 (1942).

[73] *Estate of Strauss v. Commissioner*, T.C.Memo 1995-248; Moy, 1 *A Practitioner's Guide to Estate Planning*, § 16.06 [B] at 16-17.

[74] *Estate of Vissering v. Commissioner*, 990 F.2d 578 (10th Cir. 1993), *rev'g and remanding* 96 T.C. 749 (1991).

[75] Emphasis in original.

[76] *Estate of Vissering v. Commissioner*, 990 F.2d 578 (10th Cir. 1993), *rev'g and remanding* 96 T.C. 749 (1991); Treas. Reg. § 20.2041-1(c)(2). *See, e.g., United States v. Powell*, 307 F.2d 821, 828 (10th Cir. 1962) (under Kansas law, invasion of the corpus if "it is necessary or advisable ... for the maintenance, welfare, comfort or happiness" of beneficiaries, and only if the need justifies the reduction in principal, is subject to ascertainable standard); *Hunter v. United States*, 597 F. Supp. 1293, 1295 (W.D. Pa. 1984) (power to invade for "comfortable support and maintenance" of beneficiaries is subject to ascertainable standard); *Best v. United States*, 79 AFTR2d ¶ 97-529 (D.C. Neb. 1995) (under Nebraska state law, a trust document permitting invasion of the trust's principal when "reasonably necessary for comfort, support, and maintenance," does not create a general power of appointment but does create an invasive power by an ascertainable standard relating to the health, education, support, or maintenance of the beneficiary consistent with I.R.C. § 2041(b)(1)(A)).

words *comfortable support and maintenance* are limited by an ascertainable standard in that the term *comfortable* modifies *support and maintenance*, rather than setting forth a separate standard for invasion. Accordingly, the standard for invasion based upon *comfortable support and maintenance* is similar in breadth to *support in reasonable comfort* as used in the Treasury Regulations.[77]

On the other hand, the use of certain words and phrases does not limit a power of appointment to an ascertainable standard. For example, a power to use property for the *comfort, welfare, or happiness* of the donee is not a limited power of appointment based on an ascertainable standard. In the absence of local law to the contrary, the IRS concluded that a standard of invasion based on *proper comfort and welfare;*[78] or for *health, support, and reasonable comfort; best interest and welfare;*[79] or for *support, comfort, happiness, and welfare;*[80] or for *health, maintenance, support, comfort, and welfare*[81] is not restricted by an ascertainable standard relating to health, maintenance, and support. Furthermore, the IRS has ruled that a standard of invasion of trust property based on *support, maintenance, comfort, emergencies, and serious illness* is not a limited power of appointment because *comfort* and *emergencies* do not constitute an ascertainable standard.[82]

However, when the word *comfort* is limited by an ascertainable standard, a limited power of appointment may exist. In this regard, a trustee's exercise of power "in its absolute discretion [that it] may consider necessary and advisable to adequately provide for said Surviving Trustor's maintenance, support, and comfort, in order to defray expenses incurred by reason of sickness, accidents, and disability and whether used for medical, dental, hospitals, nursing, and institutional costs during said surviving trustor's lifetime" constitutes a limited power of appointment. This is because, unlike other cases[83] in which the word *comfort* was used in an unqualified manner, in this case, the trustee's power to invade based on comfort is limited to amounts needed to defray health-related costs. Consequently, the power of invasion is limited by an ascertainable standard within the meaning of I.R.C. Section 2041.[84] Finally, a power to use property for the comfort, welfare, or happiness of the donee is not a limited power of appointment based upon an ascertainable standard.

In determining whether property subject to a power is limited by an ascertainable standard within the meaning of I.R.C. Section 2041, the test is the *measure of control* over the property by virtue of the grant of the power; that is, whether the exercise of the power is restricted by definite bounds.[85] In this regard, when the trustee-beneficiary has the power

---

[77] Priv. Ltr. Rul. 9728023 (April 11, 1997); Moy, 1, *A Practitioner's Guide to Estate Planning,* § 16.06 [B] at 16-18.

[78] *See* Rev. Ruls. 82-63, 1982-1 C.B. 135 and 77-194, 1977-1 C.B. 282 cited in Tech. Adv. Mem. 9125002 (March 7, 1991).

[79] Tech. Adv. Mem. 9125002 (March 7, 1991).

[80] Tech. Adv. Mem. 9318002 (January 15, 1993) (note, however, that Tech. Adv. Mem. 9510001[October 31, 1994] revokes, without explanation, Tech. Adv. Mem. 9318002).

[81] Tech. Adv. Mem. 9344004 (July 13, 1993).

[82] Priv. Ltr. Rul. 9235025 (May 29, 1992), citing Rev. Rul. 77-194, 1977-1 C.B. 283; *Estate of Sowell v. Commissioner*, 708 F.2d 1564 (10th Cir. 1983), *rev'g* 74 T.C. 1001 (1980); *contra Martin v. United States*, 780 F.2d 1147, 1150 n.10 (4th Cir. 1986); Priv. Ltr. Rul. 9012053 (December 27, 1989).

[83] A number of court cases have considered the word *comfort* when used as a standard of invasion of trust corpus. Some cases have held that, in appropriate circumstances, use of the word *comfort* creates a general power of appointment, rather than a power limited by the requisite ascertainable standard; *see e.g., In re Estate of Nunn*, 518 P.2d 1151, 112 Cal.Rptr. 199 (1974); *Estate of Allegeyer*, 60 Cal.App.3d, 169, 129 Cal.Rptr. 820 (1976); *Cory v. Ward*, 106 Cal.App.3d 631, 165 Cal.Rptr. 330 (1980). In all of these cases, however, the trustee's power to invade for the beneficiary's comfort was unqualified.

[84] Priv. Ltr. Rul. 9203047 (October 23, 1991).

[85] Rev. Rul. 77-60, 1977-1 C.B. 282.

to invade income and the corpus (principal) of the trust for the "maintenance, support, and care of the beneficiaries," such power is limited by an ascertainable standard and, thus, is not a general power of appointment.[86] According to the IRS, the word *care* denotes an ascertainable standard relating to health, education, support, or maintenance.[87] In other words, use of the word *care* exacts a measure of control and restricts the purpose for which the property may be used for the beneficiary.[88]

Planning Strategy

Married individuals, each with a taxable estate not exceeding the exemption amount, can transfer such amount for the lifetime use, benefit, and enjoyment of the surviving spouse entirely free of estate tax and GSTT to successive generations upon the subsequent death of the surviving spouse.[89] Thus, married individuals have the opportunity to transfer an amount equal to two times the exemption amount free of both estate tax and GSTT for as many generations as are in being at the time of the death of the first decedent spouse's death. A single individual whose taxable estate does not exceed the exemption amount can achieve similar estate and GSTT savings. For married individuals, such tax savings are achieved by the intentional use of a nonmarital deduction limited power of appointment trust (i.e., credit shelter trust; by-pass trust; Trust "B") for the benefit of the surviving spouse. As the trustee-beneficiary, the surviving spouse is given a lifetime limited power of appointment over the trust income and property. In this regard, the spouse's limited power of appointment is limited to distributions of the trust income and principal for his or her "health, maintenance, education, and support." The surviving spouse can also be given the limited power to appoint the remainder of the trust property to the beneficiary's children, grandchildren, great-grandchildren, or other class of beneficiaries. Or the first decedent spouse can direct the disposition of the trust property upon the death of the surviving spouse (e.g., to the first decedent spouse's children by a previous marriage; or to parents; or to charities).

Ask Your Attorney

Does this mean that the surviving spouse can only distribute income and principal to himself or herself strictly for his or her support and maintenance to the exclusion of anything else?

Answer

No. This is true because the words support and maintenance are synonymous, and their meaning is not limited to the bare necessities of life.[90] In other words, it is the presence of this language in the limited power of appointment nonmarital deduction trust (or any life estate trust) which prevents the value of the assets subject to the surviving spouse's authority as trustee-beneficiary of the trust to distribute income and principal to himself or

[86] Priv. Ltr. Rul. 9148036 (August 29, 1991); Rev. Rul. 76-547, 1976-2 C.B. 302.

[87] Priv. Ltr. Rul. 9148036 (August 29, 1991); Rev. Rul. 76-547, 1976-2 C.B. 302.

[88] Rev. Rul. 76-547, 1976-2 C.B. 302.

[89] See Chapter 1: Federal Estate Tax Exemption Increased regarding inflation adjustment for the GSTT exemption amount for estates of decedents dying *before* January 1, 2004.

[90] Treas. Reg. § 20.2041-1(c)(2).

herself from being included in the surviving spouse's gross estate—not whether the surviving spouse actually distributes income or principal to himself or herself as a beneficiary specifically for his or her health, maintenance, education, and support. Under present law, the IRS cannot monitor every trust in existence and the behavior of every trustee as to whether the ascertainable standard provisions are being followed to the letter of the law. Besides, the letter of the law specifically provides that the words support and maintenance are synonymous; and their meaning is not limited to the bare necessities of life.

The same strategy works for a single individual. In such case, the decedent would direct his or her trust estate to be held and administered in a life estate trust for the decedent's beneficiary. The beneficiary can be the trustee-beneficiary of the trust and possess a limited power of appointment to distribute income and principal to himself or herself according to an ascertainable standard. Upon the beneficiary's subsequent death, the value of the property in the trust is not included in the beneficiary's gross estate. The beneficiary can also be given the limited power to appoint the remainder of the trust property to the beneficiary's children, grandchildren, or other class of beneficiaries. Or the decedent trustor can direct the disposition of the property upon the death of the beneficiary, if the beneficiary does not survive the trustor as the beneficiary of the life estate.

With respect to the GSTT savings, upon the death of the first decedent spouse, or if a single individual is involved, the trustee will want to file a United States Estate (and Generation-Skipping Transfer) Tax Return (Form 706) in order to allocate the decedent spouse's GSTT exemption amount to the limited power of appointment nonmarital deduction trust (or, in the case of a single individual, to the limited power of appointment life estate trust). Any allocation by an individual of his or her GSTT exemption amount may be made at any time on or before the due date for filing Form 706, regardless of whether such a return is required to be filed.[91]

Once the GSTT exemption amount is applied to a transfer of property and the property (or a portion of it) is designated exempt, then all subsequent appreciation on the property is exempt in the same ratio the initially exempt property bore to the total property.[92] Accordingly, such an allocation can shelter the value of the trust assets from being subject to both federal estate tax and GSTT by continuing the assets in a life estate trust for the benefit of the decedent's children, grandchildren, and great-grandchildren.

Examples

(1) Ruth establishes a trust for her niece and great-nieces and funds the trust with her entire allowable GSTT exemption amount in the year the trust is funded. The assets in the trust appreciate to $4 million. None of the appreciation is subject to GSTT because the initial transfer was 100 percent exempt from GSTT.

(2) John establishes a trust for his children and grandchildren and funds the trust with $2 million. John allocates only 50 percent of his GSTT exemption amount to the trust. The value of the property in the trust appreciates to $8 million. Only one-quarter of the appreciation is exempt because, at the time of transfer, only one-quarter of the property was exempt from the GSTT.

---

[91] I.R.C. § 2632(a)(1).

[92] *Explanation of Tax Reform Act of 1986*, Fed. Tax Guide Rep. (CCH) 431 (1986) (hereafter *Explanation of Tax Reform Act of 1986*); I.R.C. § 2632(c)(2).

The IRS is resolute in its position with respect to the words or phraseology used to create a limited power of appointment through the use of an ascertainable standard. Given the fact that the words *support* and *maintenance* are synonymous and that their meaning is not limited to the bare necessities of life, the use of other words and phraseology is unnecessary to accomplish giving a beneficiary the use, benefit, and enjoyment of trust property without the value of such property being includable in the beneficiary's gross estate for federal estate tax purposes upon his or her subsequent death. With this caveat in mind, the trustor of a revocable living trust should not deviate from the use of the words, *health, maintenance, education, and support* to achieve an effective limited power of appointment.

REPLACING AN EXISTING REVOCABLE LIVING TRUST

If the trustor is replacing in its entirety an existing revocable living trust, the existing living trust should be revoked after the replacement living trust is effected. Such a revocation can be accomplished by the trustor informing the trustee of his or her intent to revoke the living trust (see file "APP0207. DOC"). 🔲 The letter informing the trustee of the revocation should be accompanied by a duly executed Revocation of Revocable Trust Agreement (see file "APP0208.DOC"). 🔲 If the existing revocable living trust agreement was recorded in the county of the trustor's domicile or residency, or if a Memorandum of Trust representing the revocable living trust agreement was recorded, it too should be revoked by recording a Revocation of Revocable Trust Agreement referencing the Memorandum of Trust, including recording information.

IS RECORDING A REVOCABLE LIVING TRUST NECESSARY?

Ask Your Attorney

Do I have to record my living trust?

Answer

Generally, no.

Unless otherwise required by local law,[93] the living trust agreement should not be recorded. In situations where recordation is required, usually a carefully designed Memorandum of Trust or Trust Abstract will suffice (see file "APP0210.DOC"). 🔲 Such a Memorandum ensures the trustor's privacy with respect to the confidential and detailed provisions of the revocable living trust agreement. Moreover, local law should always be consulted about the requirements for recording legal documents transferring property to a

---

[93] For example, § 15-7-101 of the Idaho Code requires the trustee of a revocable living trust, having its principal place of administration (i.e., situs) in the state of Idaho, to register the trust in the court of Idaho in the county that is the principal place of the administration of the trust. In effect, a Memorandum of Trust is filed with the court [§ 15-7-102 Idaho Code] (see "APP0209.DOC"). 🔲 It should be noted that the Registration of Trust must be filed with the *court*—not merely in the county wherein the trust has its principal place of administration. *See also, e.g.,* Colo. Rev. Stat. § 38-30-108.5 (Bradford Publishing Co. 2001) wherein a trust acquires title to real or personal property, a statement of authority may be effected by the trustee pursuant to § 38-30-172(2) (see related § 38-30-108); Mont. Code Ann. §§ 72-36-206(3) and 15-7-305 (Realty Transfer Certificate Required) (2001).

living trust, such as deeds, assignments of contracts, assignments of leases, bill of sale, assignments of notes, and other conveyance documents.

Furthermore, a Memorandum of Trust may be required with respect to the assignment of assets to a revocable living trust but recordation may not be required. For example, state law may require that the assignment of a lottery annuity to the trustee of a revocable living trust be "memorialized"[94] (see file "APP0211.DOC"). In the State of Oregon, a trustee may present a Certification of Trust (see file "APP0212.DOC") in lieu of providing a copy of the revocable living trust agreement and its amendments to banks, brokerage houses, and so forth; and, a person who proposes to deal with a trustee may require that the trustee execute and present to the person a Certification of Trust in lieu of providing a copy of the trust agreement and its amendments.[95] In lieu of utilizing a Certificate of Trust, the trustor may determine to provide persons relying on the efficacy of the living trust agreement with a copy of the preamble (page one of the living trust), Article II (Initial and Successor Trustees), Article V (Revocation and Amendment), Article IX (Trustee Powers), signature page, and attestation page.

Ask Your Attorney

Is the revocable living trust recorded after I die? Does it become a matter of public record?

Answer

Generally, no.

As a general rule, unlike a Last Will, most states do not require a revocable living trust itself to be *recorded*. However, this does not mean that a revocable living trust cannot become part of a probate court record. In cases involving legal challenges by the trustor's beneficiaries, or if the decedent trustor caused the wrongful death of another person, or if the decedent trustor's creditors file claims against the trust estate, the trustee may determine to submit the revocable living trust to the probate court's jurisdiction to toll the statute of limitations on creditors' claims or to render opinions and interpretations on behalf of the trustee and beneficiaries. Once the revocable living trust agreement is filed with the probate court, it becomes a matter of public record.

It is within this framework that the revocable living trust operates. For some people, the concept of owning property as a trustee when they are also the trustor and beneficiary is not easy to grasp. This is because most people are so used to owning property either in their individual names or as joint tenants with right of survivorship. Envision a tricorn embossed on each side with *trustor*, *trustee*, and *beneficiary*, respectively—"my hat it has three corners; three corners has my hat; and if it not three corners, it would not be my hat."

---

[94] *See* Or. Rev. Stat. § 461.253(4)(a) (Loislaw 2001).

[95] Or. Rev. Stat. § 128.234 (1999). The contents of a Certification of Trust are found at Or. Rev. Stat. § 128.236 (Loislaw 1999).

CHAPTER 3

Trustee's Powers, Duties, and Responsibilities

GENERAL POWERS

Day-to-day successful operation of a revocable living trust is directly related to the design of the trustee's powers. State law governs the powers given to a trustee. As a general rule, states empower a trustee to do anything appropriate for the orderly administration of the trust estate, subject to the trustee's power and control, unless otherwise specifically provided in the trust agreement. Powers given to a trustee should be broad enough to cover many situations but also specific enough so the trustee can effectively manage the trust estate. Moreover, the trustee should be given discretion to exercise those powers in order to carry out the purposes of the trust agreement so that the trust estate can be administered in the best interests of the beneficiaries. For example, from the time a revocable living trust is created until final distribution of the trust estate to the ultimate beneficiaries, the trustee can be empowered to perform, without court authorization, every act that a prudent person would perform for the purposes of the trust, including but not limited to any specific powers provided in the trust agreement.

Because most people are not well-acquainted with their state's specific laws regarding trustee powers and how to find them, the trustee's authority should be clearly defined in the living trust agreement so that the trustee has no doubt or hesitancy in exercising the powers granted. A trustee should not have to consult an attorney every time a question arises about whether the trustee possesses certain powers and discretions. Accordingly, without limiting the trustee's general power under state law, and without limitation of other powers granted or otherwise possessed by the trustee, the trustee should be authorized to exercise powers and discretions in a manner and upon such terms and conditions as the trustee deems necessary, desirable, or convenient for the administration of the trust estate.

EXPRESS TRUSTEE POWERS

Without limiting the authority of the trustee under state law or under provisions of the living trust agreement, the trustee may be given certain express powers over the trust estate with the same effect as might legally be done by an individual in absolute ownership and control of the trust estate without the approval of any court. In effect, this means that the trustee is authorized to exercise discretion, common sense, and fiscal responsibility in administering the trust estate for the use, benefit, and enjoyment of the beneficiaries.

Power to Retain Trust Estate Property

The trustee should be authorized to retain the original trust estate to minimize loss of value in the property acquired by the trustor. The trustee can use discretion to collect, hold, and retain trust assets received from the trustor until, in the judgment of the trustee, disposition of the assets should be made, independent of any requirement of diversification. Such assets may be retained by the trustee, even if the trustee has a personal interest in the asset being retained. Similarly, the trustee may receive property from any source, including other fiduciaries, and add it to the trust estate.

Except as provided in the living trust agreement for the division of the trust estate into separate trusts upon the death of the trustor, or some other designated event, the trustee may hold the trust estate as an undivided whole for any period the trustee considers expedient. However, the trustee should not be empowered to unilaterally defer or postpone vesting or distribution of a beneficiary's interest in the trust estate beyond those parameters or period provided in the trust agreement.

The trustee should be given the discretion to deposit trust estate funds at reasonable interest with an insured commercial or savings bank, an insured building and loan association, or an insured credit union, even if such financial institution is operated by, or is an affiliate of, the trustee. With regard to the deposit of trust estate funds, the trustee should not be prevented from holding an amount of the trust estate reasonably necessary for the orderly administration of the trust estate in the form of cash or in a checking account without interest, insured interest-bearing accounts, or short-term loan agreements.

If any stock of a corporate trustee is included in the trust estate, the trustee may be authorized to retain the stock. Such stock may include increases resulting from stock dividends or stock splits that result from exercising purchase rights or the purchase of fractional shares needed to round out fractional share holdings. In these regards, except as prohibited by law, the trustee may vote the stock either directly or by proxy. The trustee should be authorized to vote the stock in keeping with the purposes for which the trust is created and in the best interests of the beneficiaries. Furthermore, the IRS has ruled that a bank is an independent trustee under I.R.C. Section 672(c), even though a trustor owns some of the stock of the bank (less than 10 percent) and because neither the trustor nor beneficiary acting alone can control it.[1]

Closely-Held Business Interests

If the trustor owns an interest in a closely-held business, he or she may want to authorize the trustee to retain, terminate, continue, or participate in the operation of any business enterprise, including a corporation, a sole proprietorship, or a general or limited partnership (including a limited liability company). Such discretionary authority may also include the power to: effect any form of incorporation, dissolution, liquidation, reorganization, or other change in the form of the business enterprise; lend money or make a capital contribution to any such business enterprise; participate in any plan of reorganization, specifically including recapitalization, and to accept and retain new stock or other securities pursuant to any such plan; and exercise all voting and other rights pertaining to such property, including, without limitation, the right to enter into any shareholder agreements. If the trustor's closely-held business operates as a Subchapter S corporation, the foregoing authority in the trustee should also apply to any entity that may have succeeded to the business of a Subchapter S corporation or any other corporation electing Subchapter S corporation status.

If the trustor transfers his or her interest in a closely-held business to a revocable living trust, the trustee should be given the power to manage the business. In this regard, the trustee should be given discretionary authority to elect or employ directors, officers, employees, partners, or agents and to compensate such persons, whether or not any such person is a trustee, director, officer, partner, or agent of a trustee or beneficiary of the trust.

---

[1] Priv. Ltr. Ruls. 9841014 (July 2, 1998) and 9842007 (July 2, 1998).

Moreover, a special provision should be included in the living trust agreement if the trustee also holds an interest in the closely-held business. The following language should be considered to dispel any notion by a beneficiary that a conflict of interest exists in a trustee who may not be a beneficiary of the trust estate but does own an interest in the same business:

(1) **Retain Assets.** To collect, hold, and retain trust assets received from Trustor until, in the judgment of the Trustee, disposition of the assets should be made, independent of any requirement of diversification; and the assets may be retained even though they include an asset in which the Trustee is personally interested.

If, at the time of Trustor's death, Trustor shall own shares of stock of [name of business] or any entity that may have succeeded to its business, Trustor authorizes and empowers (but does not direct) Trustees, in their discretion, to continue such business for such period as Trustees, in their discretion, shall determine. Trustor realizes that a large portion of the assets of Trustor's estate or any trust created hereunder may be represented by Trustor's interest in [name of business] or any successor thereto, but Trustor expressly exonerates Trustees from any loss resulting from Trustee's failure to diversify the assets of Trustor's estate or any trust created hereunder. Trustees may invest additional assets of Trustor's estate or trust in [name of business], except to the extent prohibited under the provisions of Article IX (E) [name of marital deduction trust].

Trustor is aware that [name of trustee] and Trustor's spouse each have an interest in [name of business]. Trustor authorizes and empowers Trustees to act on behalf of any trust created hereunder as to all matters relating to [name of business], despite the possibility that there may be a conflict of interest between Trustor's estate, any trust created hereunder, or any beneficiary hereunder and any one of the Trustees. Subject to the express provisions of this Trust Agreement, Trustees shall have the same power to manage the business of [name of business] as they would have if they owned its stock in their own rights and not as Trustees; and they shall be absolved from any liability to any beneficiary hereunder in connection with any action or omission taken in good faith with respect to the business of [name of business].

If Trustees shall serve as officers, directors, or employees of [name of business], any salaries or other compensation paid to any of them shall be in addition to, and not in lieu of, any fiduciary commissions or fees receivable by them.

Real Property

With respect to real property, the trustee should be authorized to: subdivide, develop, or dedicate land to public use; make or obtain the vacation of plots and adjust boundaries; adjust differences in valuation on exchange or partition by giving or receiving consideration; dedicate easements to public use without consideration; and enter into a lease or arrangement, including a pooling or unitization agreement, for the exploration and removal of minerals or other natural resources. If farm or ranch property comprises part of the trustor's gross estate, he or she may want to authorize the trustee to participate in and operate any farm (including tree farm and aquaculture) or ranch operation personally or with hired labor, tenants, or sharecroppers. In support of this authorization, the trustee should be given license to: lease any farm for cash or for a share of crops under a lease that permits or precludes the material participation of the fiduciary; fertilize and improve the soil to employ conservation practices and to participate in government programs; and perform any other acts deemed necessary or desirable to operate the property. In making a decision whether to materially participate in farm or ranch operations, the trustee should be reminded to consider whether an election should be made or has been made under I.R.C.

Section 2032A to qualify the farm or ranch for special farm-use valuation. Additionally, if the trustor owns real property subject to development, the trustee may be empowered to use funds from the proceeds of life insurance comprising the trust estate upon the death of the trustor to fund development costs so that the trustee, in effect, acts as the general contractor, rather than turning over such development to outside contractors.

Contracts

The trustee should have the power to perform any contract or obligation that is an asset of the trust estate. In performing an enforceable contract to convey or lease, the trustee can be directed to execute and deliver a deed or conveyance for cash payment of all sums remaining due or for the note of the purchaser for the sum remaining due secured by a mortgage or deed of trust on the land, as the contract may provide.

With respect to life insurance policies owned by the trustor of which the trustee is the beneficiary, upon the trustor's death, the trustor may direct the trustee to collect the proceeds of all such policies held by the trustee as assets of the trust estate. Provision should be made in the trust agreement that payment to the trustee of the proceeds of any such policy of insurance is a full discharge of the insurance company with respect to such policy and that the insurance company is not responsible for the proper discharge of the trust estate. Furthermore, the trustee should not be required to enter into collection proceedings or institute any litigation to enforce payment of the policies until reasonable provision has been made for the indemnification of the trustee's anticipated expenses and liabilities related to such proceedings.

Life Insurance Policies

Additionally, the trustor may want to provide that the trustee retain for such periods as the trustee determines advisable any insurance policies owned by the trustor at the trustor's death on the life of any other person, including the trustor's spouse. In this regard, the trustee may have the discretion to:

- Pay the premiums on policies whenever they become due out of income and/or principal of the trust estate as the trustee determines necessary (except, however, income of a trust holding property that qualifies for the federal estate tax marital deduction[2] or that holds stock in a Subchapter S corporation[3] should not be used to pay the premiums);
- Designate the trustee as the beneficiary of the policies;
- Arrange for the automatic application of dividends in reduction of premium payments and effect automatic premium loans and repay such loans;
- Sell or assign the policies to the insured for the cash surrender value of the policies;
- Surrender the policies for their cash surrender value; and
- Convert the policies at any time into paid-up policies in whatever amounts may be provided by the terms of the policies.

---

[2] *See* I.R.C. § 2056(b)(5) and (b)(7)(B) for requirement that the surviving spouse must be entitled to all of the income from the property for life. If the income were used to pay insurance premiums, the surviving spouse would not receive all of the income.

[3] *See* I.R.C. § 1361(d)(3)(B) for the requirement that a qualified Subchapter S trust means a trust wherein all of the income is distributed currently to one individual. If income is used to pay insurance premiums, then not all of the income can be distributed currently to the beneficiary.

Caution is advised so that an *incident of ownership* in policies of life insurance owned by the trustor on another person's life (e.g., the trustor's surviving spouse) does not vest in the insured as an individual or as trustee of the trust agreement. In this regard, the ownership of such a policy should vest in a disinterested trustee. Moreover, except for policies insuring the life of the trustor of which the trustor is also the owner, the trustor, as trustee, should be expressly prohibited from exercising any of the incidents of ownership in life insurance policies in an individual capacity and from making any use, disposition, retention, or other control of the policies, either individually or as trustee, except as otherwise provided in the trust agreement. Finally, as the insured and primary beneficiary of the trust agreement, and to the extent permitted by the policies of insurance and the insuring companies, the trust agreement may provide that the trustor, as trustee, can elect a settlement option upon surrender or maturity of the insurance policy based upon the life of the trustor. Again, if the trustor is the insured but not the owner of the life insurance policy, to the extent the trustor does not want the value of the insurance proceeds included in his her gross estate for purposes of the federal estate tax, caution is advised so that ownership of the insurance policy does not vest in the insured trustor as an individual or as trustee.

Other Assets

With respect to all property comprising the trust estate, the trustee should be able to grant an option involving disposition of a trust estate asset or to take an option for the acquisition of any asset.

Power to Invest Trust Estate Assets

If the trustor invests in special classes of securities or in particular industries and wants the trustee to carry on such an investment plan in the event of the trustor's incapacity, death, or in the event the trustor goes missing, then the trustor should make his or her position in this regard unequivocally clear in the trust agreement. Absent a particular investment philosophy, the trustor may be well served by authorizing the trustee to invest and reinvest trust estate assets in accordance with the provisions of the trust agreement or as the trustee may determine to be in the best interests of the trust estate without limitation by any law applicable to investments by fiduciaries. The permitted investments and reinvestments may include securities, such as common or preferred stock, mortgages, notes, subordinated debentures, and warrants of any corporation and any common trust fund administered by a corporate fiduciary, or other property, real or personal, including savings accounts and deposits and interests in mutual or money market funds or investment trusts, annuities and insurance, whether or not such investments are unsecured or of a wasting nature. With regard to record keeping for investment transactions, the trustor may want to provide that the trustee need not provide confirmations or alternate reports. However, in this regard, the trustee should be required to report security transactions in the trustee's periodic accounting of the trust estate to the beneficiaries.

Perhaps, over the years, the trustor has relied on the investment counsel of a particular person. In this regard, the trustor may determine that, because of this person's qualifications, experience, and investment successes on the trustor's behalf, he or she should continue to manage the trustor's investment portfolio; but the trustor is concerned that, in the event of his incapacity, death, or missing status, the trustee might not follow this person's counsel. To remedy this concern in the living trust agreement, the trustor can either direct or request that the trustee consult with the trustor's investment advisor(s) with respect to securities composing the trust estate. The respective duties and responsibilities of the trustee and investment advisor should be clearly defined in the trust agreement. If a corporate trustee is involved, the trustor may want to discuss the role of the investment advisor with the trustee before such an arrangement is consummated to be certain that the corporate trustee is willing to accept such an arrangement.

Examples

1. **Management and Investment Counsel of Trust Assets.**

With respect to securities comprising the trust estate, the Trustee is requested, without being required, to consult with **Bertrand J.**, presently of **Investment Portfolio Management, Inc.**, Lake Oswego, OR, regarding those securities (investments) of the trust estate as to which **Bertrand** is particularly knowledgeable and competent. Such consultation shall be made only when practicable; and any recommendations of **Bertrand** should be seriously reviewed, considered, and followed by Trustee to whatever extent, if any, Trustee deems appropriate.

2. **Management and Investment Counsel of Trust Assets.**

With respect to securities composing the trust estate, the individual Trustee shall employ a reputable independent professional investment advisor of its choice to manage and invest the securities that are part of or which may be added to and become part of the trust estate.

(A) The decision of said independent investment adviser shall control the actions of the corporate and individual Trustee with respect to the sale, investment, and reinvestment of the securities of the trust estate managed by the investment adviser.

(B) The Trustees (corporate and individual) shall not be held liable or otherwise surcharged for any loss directly attributable to the investment advice of said investment adviser.

(C) Among other professional standards to be considered, the individual Trustee should take into account the investment adviser's academic qualifications; previous professional experience as an investment adviser; past and current performance with similar investment portfolios; diversification of assets under management, and total value of all client asset portfolios under management; whether the adviser is registered under the Investment Advisers Act of 1940 (its successor or as amended); and investment philosophy regarding the selection of prudent investment vehicles that will best serve and benefit Trustor's goals, objectives, and wishes as hereinbefore stated for Trustor's children.

(D) The investment adviser's fee shall be a charge against the trust estate as a whole and not against any distributable share. Trustor is most hopeful that the corporate Trustee will appreciate and respect Trustor's thoughts regarding the value of independent investment counsel to manage and invest the securities of the trust estate and will respect Trustor's request that the compensation of the investment adviser be paid from the whole of the trust estate assets and also by allocating to him a proportionate amount of the fees payable to the corporate Trustee with respect to the securities managed and invested by the investment adviser. This reduction of the corporate Trustee's compensation is to reflect the shift of investment responsibility in respect to the securities assets of the trust estate.

(E) The investment adviser's authority herein granted, except with respect to the sale, investment, and reinvestment of securities composing part of the trust estate, shall not abridge, compromise, or in any manner whatsoever alienate the Trustee's (corporate or individual) power to sell, exchange, transfer, assign, grant options to buy, lease, including leases extending beyond the terms of the trust, encumber, or otherwise alienate all or any other part of property of the trust estate in such manner and upon such terms as the Trustee may deem most beneficial to the trust estate.

The trustor may also want to authorize the trustee to invest in obligations of the United States Government. Such investments may be made directly or in the form of securities or other interests in an open-end or closed-end management-type investment company or investment trust registered under the Investment Company Act of 1940 or an investment vehicle authorized for the collective investment of trust funds if:

- The portfolio of the investment company, investment trust, or investment vehicle is limited to United States Government obligations and repurchase agreements fully collateralized by United States Government obligations; and
- The investment company, investment trust, or investment vehicle takes delivery of the collateral for any repurchase agreement, either directly or through an authorized custodian.

Stock brokerage firms carefully scrutinize revocable living trusts wherein the trustee is in legal title to securities. In this regard, confirmation is sought to determine if the trustee has the authority to vote a security, in person or by general or limited proxy, or enter into or participate in a voting trust or shareholder agreement, reorganization, dissolution, liquidation, or other action affecting any securities and to deposit securities with, and transfer title to, a protective or other committee. Additionally, the article enumerating the powers of the trustee is reviewed for authority in the trustee to pay calls, assessments, and any other sums chargeable or accruing against or on account of securities. The brokerage firm also wants to know if the trustee can sell or exercise stock subscriptions, conversion, or option rights, including options on stock owned by the trust estate, puts and calls, including maintaining margin accounts with brokers, and consent, directly or through a committee or other agent, to the reorganization, consolidation, merger, dissolution, or liquidation of a corporation or other business enterprise.

A convenient and efficient way for a living trust to hold securities is in a street name account. Each time a security in the account is traded, the trustor does not have to inquire if legal title to the new stock was conveyed to the trustee. This is because the account itself is titled (registered) in the name of the trustee of the living trust. Such is not the case if the trustor holds the stock certificate and requests reregistration through a transfer agent. With regard to street name accounts, the trustee should be authorized to hold securities and other property in negotiable form in the name of a nominee (including *street name* of a broker) or in other form or by deposit to a clearing corporation so that title to the security may pass by delivery. In these regards, the trustee should be liable for any act of the nominee or clearing corporation in connection with securities held by them.

Power to Sell Trust Estate Assets

The trustee should have no less power or authority to sell trust estate property than would the trustor if he or she owned the property as an individual. Such unequivocal power in the trustee relieves a purchaser of the property of the responsibility for seeing to the application of the sales proceeds. In other words, broad powers of sale in the trustee may give the purchaser greater assurance in dealing with the trustee. Accordingly, the trustee should be empowered to sell any and every kind of property, real or personal, for cash or credit, at public or private sale, without court order, upon such terms and conditions as the trustee may deem advisable and without liability on the part of the purchaser to see to the application of the sales proceeds.

Power to Lease Trust Estate Assets

A trustee should have the same authority to lease trust estate property as would the trustor in absolute ownership of the property as an individual. Since most trusts cannot operate in perpetuity,[4] and since many trusts terminate upon a beneficiary attaining a specified age or upon the beneficiary's death or the happening or nonhappening of an event, the trustee may be compromised in effecting long-term leases of real property comprising the trust estate, if not for the authority to effect leases extending beyond the duration of the trust agreement. A lessee may be willing to make extensive improvements and alterations to real property comprising the trust estate at his or her own expense but may not effect the lease if it cannot be long term. Such an express lease provision is advantageous to both the principal and income beneficiaries because it means that the property can be made income productive and maintained in good market condition, rather than be vacant and perhaps unrentable. Additionally, the trustee should be authorized to enter into, renew, or amend a lease as lessor or lessee with or without option to purchase or renew. Where appropriate, the trustee should be authorized to enter into a lease or an arrangement, including a pooling or unitization agreement for the exploration and removal of minerals or other natural resources for a term within or extending beyond the term of the trust agreement.

Power to Establish Reserves

The cost of maintaining real property improvements is not always the same from year to year. When improved real property is part of the trust estate, part of the principal and income of the trust estate should be set aside in reserve to satisfy unexpected and regular ongoing maintenance requirements of the real property to keep it in good marketable condition. A provision for setting up reserves for the upkeep and maintenance of real property and other trust estate property is advantageous to the trustee and the beneficiaries. In this regard, the trustee should be empowered to create reserves out of principal and income for depreciation, obsolescence, and amortization; for depletion in mineral or timber properties; for ordinary or extraordinary repairs or alterations in buildings or other structures; to demolish any improvements; to raze existing or erect new party walls or buildings; to pay taxes, insurance premiums, assessments, debts, claims, maintenance, repairs, management fees, and related costs with respect to property of the trust estate as the trustee considers necessary.

Power to Borrow

Regardless of the estate planning steps implemented during lifetime, some clearance (administration costs, debts, and so forth) and transfer costs (federal estate and state death taxes) usually remain to be paid at the trustor's death. Payment of these costs may require liquid dollars. The amount of liquidity in the trustor's trust estate depends on how rapidly the trustee can convert nonliquid assets into cash. It is well known that the availability of cash funds during periods of economic downturn has often helped avoid financial stress.

Moreover, a trustee often needs cash for cash bequests, a beneficiary's education expenses, to pay income and property taxes, and myriad other cash needs. If the trustee can distribute noncash trust estate assets in satisfaction of cash bequests, the cash needs of the trust estate will be reduced. This approach may be acceptable to satisfy what otherwise were to be cash bequests to the beneficiaries. But, if existing assets have to be sold to create

---

[4] In general, a trust cannot operate in perpetuity unless the legal jurisdiction of the trust has abolished its rule against perpetuity or permits a trustor, settlor or grantor to elect out of the rule against perpetuity.

cash, beneficiaries may suffer a potential loss of income. Also, if present assets must be sold, selling commissions and possible forced sale shrinkage could further reduce income flow.

The trustee could raise cash from closely-held business interests. If 35 percent or more of the value of the decedent trustor's adjusted gross estate (AGE) consists of an interest in a closely-held corporation, the trustee may use a tax-favored I.R.C. Section 303 stock redemption to obtain needed cash with which to satisfy clearance and transfer costs. Furthermore, if the trustor's business interest is not in the form of a closely-held corporation but, rather, is in the form of a sole proprietorship or partnership and the value of such business interest represents 35 percent or more of the value of the trustor's AGE, then an installment payment of estate tax liability under I.R.C. Section 6166 may be used to ease the liquidity problems of the trustor's estate. This same benefit is available if the trustor's business interest is in the form of a closely-held corporation.

Another source of liquid dollars to the trustee is life insurance proceeds. Ideally, the trustor should acquire sufficient amounts of life insurance during his or her lifetime to minimize or entirely eliminate the need to convert or liquidate estate property after death. In any event, whatever life insurance proceeds are available at death, they should be considered before all other estate property as a good source of funds with which to satisfy the cash needs of the trustor's estate. As a general rule, life insurance proceeds are received income tax-free by the beneficiary(ies)[5] and, with proper planning, can be exempt from federal estate tax, provided the trustor-insured does not have an incident of ownership in the life insurance policy(ies).

As a fallback position, the living trust agreement should authorize the trustee to borrow money. In this regard, the trustee should be authorized to borrow funds from any person, including the trustee, to be repaid from trust estate or other sources of repayment. In order to further protect the trust estate, the trustee may be authorized to advance money for the protection of the trust estate and for the payment of expenses, losses, and liabilities sustained in the administration of the trust. The trustee may also be authorized to guarantee indebtedness or indemnify others in the name of the trust estate and secure any such obligation by mortgage, pledge, security interest, or other encumbrance and renew, extend, or modify any such obligation for the life of the trust agreement or beyond the term of the trust agreement. With regard to funds borrowed by the trustee, lenders should not be responsible or liable for the application of the loan proceeds. As a general rule, the trustee is not personally liable for any such obligations.

Power to Compromise Claims

Events occur when the trustee must deal with claims against the trust estate. A trustee empowered to pay or contest any debt or claim; to settle a debt or claim by compromise; arbitration, or otherwise; and to release any claim belonging to the trust or adjust claims has an advantage over a trustee lacking this express power. The trustee should also be authorized to determine the procedure to be followed by claimants in presenting and perfecting claims. In this regard, the trustee may require claims to be perfected in probate proceedings; and the trustee may restrict payment of expenses, claims, and debts to only those certified by the decedent trustor's personal representative as due and owing.

Power to Vote by Proxy

Instances arise when shares of stock in a trust account need to be voted for one reason or another; yet, it may be impractical or not possible for the trustee to vote the shares in person. Under similar circumstances, the trustor, as an individual shareholder, would vote the

---

[5] I.R.C. § 101(a)(1).

stock by general proxy. Thus, it seems reasonable that a trustee should have the express power to vote a security, in person or by special, limited, or general proxy. Similarly, the trustee should be empowered to enter into or participate in a voting trust or shareholder agreement, reorganization, dissolution, liquidation, or other action affecting any securities composing the trust estate.

Power to Allocate and Apportion Income and Principal

A trust is administered with regard to the respective interests of income beneficiaries and remainder beneficiaries (i.e., remaindermen). Such administration may be carried out in accordance with the terms of the trust agreement, provided those terms do not violate the law of the jurisdiction governing the trust agreement. In the administration of the trust, the trustee may be authorized to credit receipts and charge expenditures to income or principal or partly to each. Generally, if the trust agreement gives the trustee discretion in crediting a receipt or charging an expenditure to income or principal or partly to each, no inference of imprudence or partiality arises from the fact that the trustee has made an allocation contrary to state law.

A trend involving changes in the types of available investments and investment philosophies has caused states to revise, or to consider revising, the traditional concepts of income and principal. With these changes in mind, the Service has recognized that the statutory definition of income and the regulatory provisions governing trust income date back to a time when, under state statutes, dividends and interest were considered income and were allocated to the income beneficiary while capital gains were allocated to the principal of the trust.[6]

As part of the investment changes taking place, the prudent investor standard for managing trust assets has been enacted by many states and encourages fiduciaries to adopt an investment strategy designed to maximize the total return on trust assets (i.e., a total return investment strategy).[7] Under this investment strategy, trust assets should be invested for total positive return—that is, ordinary income plus appreciation—in order to maximize the value of the trust. Thus, under certain economic circumstances, equities, rather than bonds, would constitute a greater portion of the trust assets than they would under traditional investment standards.[8]

One of the concerns with shifting trust investments toward equities and away from bonds is the potential adverse impact on the income beneficiary. Based on the traditional concepts of income and principal, the income beneficiary is entitled only to the dividends and interest earned by the trust assets. The dividend return on equities as a percentage of their value traditionally has been substantially less than the interest return on bonds.[9] To

---

[6] REG-106513-00 Feb. 14, 2001, ¶ [8].

[7] *See* Christopher P. Cline and Marcia L. Jory, "The Uniform Prudent Investor Act: Trust Drafting and Administration," 26 *Estate Planning* 451 (December 1999); Joel C. Dobris, "New Forms of Private Trusts for the Twenty-first Century—Principal and Income," 31 *Real Property, Probate & Trust Journal* 1 (1996); Jerold Horn, "Prudent Investor Rule, Modern Portfolio Theory, and Private Trusts: Drafting and Administration Including the Give-me-five Unitrust," 33 *Real Property, Probate & Trust Journal* 1 (Spring 1998); David W. Keister and William J. McCarthy, Jr., "1997 Principal and Income Act Reflects Modern Trust Investing," 26 *Estate Planning* 99 (Mar./Apr. 1999); John Train and Thomas A. Melfe, *Investing and Managing Trusts Under the New Prudent Investor Rule* (Harvard Business School Press 1999); Robert B. Wolf, "Total Return Trusts—Can Your Clients Afford Anything Less?" 33 *Real Property, Probate & Trust Journal* 131 (Spring 1998).

[8] REG-106513-00 Feb. 14, 2001, ¶ [9]; Moy, 2, *A Practitioner's Guide to Estate Planning*, § 27.05 [A][1] at 27-60.

[9] REG-106513-00 Feb. 14, 2001, ¶ [10].

ensure that the income beneficiary is not penalized if a trustee adopts a total return investment strategy, many states have made, or are considering making, revisions to the definitions of income and principal. Some state statutes permit the trustee to make an equitable adjustment between income and principal, if necessary, to ensure that both the income beneficiary and the remainder beneficiary are treated impartially based on what is fair and reasonable to all the beneficiaries.[10] Such an approach would eliminate the tug-of-war that historically has gone on between the income beneficiary, who wants the trustee to invest to produce the greatest amount of income, while the remainder beneficiary wants the trustee to invest so that the principal of the trust estate will increase for future distribution to the remainder beneficiary. Thus, a receipt of capital gains which previously would have been allocated to principal may be allocated by the trustee to income, if necessary, to treat both parties impartially. Conversely, a receipt of dividends or interest which previously would have been allocated to income may be allocated by the trustee to principal, if necessary, to treat both parties impartially.[11]

Other states are proposing legislation that would allow the trustee to pay a unitrust amount to the income beneficiary in satisfaction of that beneficiary's right to the income from the trust. This unitrust amount will be a fixed percentage, sometimes required to be within a range set by state statute, of the fair market value of the trust assets determined annually.[12] Accordingly, questions have arisen concerning how these state statutory changes affect the definition of income provided in I.R.C. Section 643(b) and the other Code provisions that rely on that section's definition of income. The I.R.C. Section 643(b) definition of income affects trusts including, but not limited to, grantor and testamentary trusts, irrevocable trusts, charitable remainder trusts, pooled income funds, and qualified Subchapter S trusts.[13]

In addition, trusts that qualify for the federal gift or estate tax marital deduction must pay to the spouse all the income from the property. All the income is considered paid to the spouse if the effect of the trust is to give the spouse substantially that degree of beneficial enjoyment of the trust property which the principles of trust law accord to a person who is unqualifiedly designated as the life beneficiary of a trust.[14] Questions have arisen whether the spouse is entitled to all the income from the property in a state that permits equitable adjustments or unitrust payments.[15] Similarly, there are questions as to whether an otherwise exempt trust that uses equitable adjustments or unitrust payments will be subject to the generation-skipping transfer tax.[16]

For federal income tax purposes, income of a trust estate, when not preceded by the words *taxable, distributable net, undistributed net,* or *gross,* means the amount of the income of the trust for the taxable year determined under the terms of the trust agreement and applicable state law. Items of gross income constituting extraordinary dividends or taxable stock dividends which the trustee, acting in good faith, determines to be allocable to principal under the terms of the trust agreement and applicable state law are not considered income.[17] Except as previously discussed with respect to the total investment return concept

[10] Moy, 2, *A Practitioner's Guide to Estate Planning,* § 27.05 [A][1] at 27-60.

[11] REG-106513-00 Feb. 14, 2001, ¶ [11]; Moy, 2, *A Practitioner's Guide to Estate Planning,* § 27.05 [A][1] at 27-60.

[12] REG-106513-00 Feb. 14, 2001, ¶ [12].

[13] REG-106513-00 Feb. 14, 2001, ¶ [13]; Moy, 2, *A Practitioner's Guide to Estate Planning,* § 27.05 [A][1] at 27-61.

[14] Treas. Reg. § 25.2523(e)-1(f) and Treas. Reg. § 20.2056(b)-5(f); REG-106513-00 Feb. 14, 2001, ¶ [14].

[15] REG-106513-00 Feb. 14, 2001, ¶ [14].

[16] REG-106513-00 Feb. 14, 2001, ¶ [15]; Moy, 2, *A Practitioner's Guide to Estate Planning,* § 27.05 [A][1] at 27-61.

[17] I.R.C. § 643(b).

and, as otherwise provided under a state's particular laws, income is the return in money or property derived from the use of principal, including return received as:

- Rent of real or personal property, including sums received for cancellation or renewal of a lease;
- Interest on money lent, including sums received as consideration for the privilege of prepayment of principal;
- Income earned during administration of a decedent's estate;
- Corporate distributions, except that corporate distributions of shares of stock, including distributions in the form of a stock split or stock dividend, are principal—not income. Furthermore, a right to subscribe to shares or other securities issued by the distributing corporation accruing to stockholders on account of their stock ownership and the proceeds of any sale of the right are principal—not income;
- Accrued increment on bonds or other obligations issued at a discount;
- Receipts from business and farming operations;
- Receipts from disposition of natural resources;
- Receipts from other principal of the trust estate subject to depletion; and
- Receipts from disposition of underproductive property.

Principal of a trust estate is the property held in the legal name of the trustee which eventually is delivered to a remainderman while the use, benefit, and enjoyment of the property in the meantime is held for an income beneficiary of the trust estate. Principal includes:

- Consideration received by the trustee on the sale or other transfer of principal or on repayment of a loan or as a refund or replacement or change in the form of principal;
- Proceeds of property taken in eminent domain proceedings;
- Proceeds of insurance upon property forming part of the principal, except proceeds of insurance upon a separate interest of an income beneficiary;
- Stock dividends, receipts on liquidation of a corporation, and other corporate distributions as provided under state law;
- Receipts from the disposition of corporate securities as provided under state law;
- Royalties and other receipts from disposition of natural resources as provided under state law;
- Receipts from principal subject to depletion as provided under state law;
- Any profit resulting from any change in the form of principal, except as otherwise provided under state law;
- Receipts from disposition of underproductive property as provided under state law; and
- Any allowances for depreciation established under state law.

After the trustee determines income and principal in accordance with the terms of the trust agreement, it allocates to income or principal expenses and other charges as provided under the terms of the trust agreement. Frequently, the trustee does not know and cannot ascertain with any degree of certainty whether an expense item should be charged against principal or income or divided between the two. For example, repairs to buildings may be required. These expenses may be partly for the benefit of the income beneficiaries and partly for the benefit of the principal beneficiaries, but it is impossible to determine with absolute accuracy the proportionate share chargeable to each. Granting the trustee the power to allocate or apportion gives the trustee authority to use its best judgment in dividing expenses equitably between principal and income.

Accordingly, a trustee should be given the power to allocate, in its absolute discretion, stock dividends and other extraordinary dividends to income or principal of the trust estate or to apportion them between income and principal. Additionally, the trustee should be authorized to charge, as the trustee deems advisable, the premiums on securities purchased at a premium either to principal or to income or partly to income and partly to principal. Finally, the trustee should be permitted, in the trustee's discretion, to determine what expenses, debts, and charges are to be charged against income and principal. With regard to this allocation and apportionment power, the trustee's decision should be conclusive and binding upon all persons interested in the trust estate.

Power to Distribute Trust Estate Property

The beneficiaries' best interests may be well served if the trustee is authorized to exercise its judgment in making distributions of the trust estate in cash or in kind. In the absence of such a provision, the trustee might have to sell trust estate property at less than fair market value in order to obtain funds with which to make distributions. The following suggested language may provide the trustee maximum flexibility with regard to such distributions:

> To make distributions in cash or in specific property, real or personal, or an undivided interest therein or partly in cash and partly in kind and to make pro-rata or nonpro-rata distributions of cash or property, or any combination thereof, among the beneficiaries without regard to any difference in tax basis on the assets and to adjust resulting differences in valuation, except as trustee, in Trustee's sole discretion, deems in the best interest of the beneficiaries; unless such property is otherwise specifically distributed under this Trust Agreement, Trustee shall have the specific authority to distribute any shares of the stock of a Subchapter S corporation passing under the terms of this Trust Agreement as Trustee, in its discretion, deems appropriate, taking into account all circumstances in existence at the time of Trustor's death, including the eligibility of such beneficiary to hold such stock under the provisions of Subchapter S of the Internal Revenue Code of 1986, as amended; Trustee shall have the sole discretionary power to determine whether or not to make the election as provided under I.R.C. Section 643(d), as amended by Section 81 of the Tax Reform Act of 1984 (TRA '84), to recognize gain or loss upon the distribution of property in kind. In addition, the Trustee is authorized to make this determination with or without making any adjustment between income and principal or among the beneficiaries. Any division, allocation, apportionment, or valuation of the property of the trust estate to distribute the assets to or among any of the trusts or beneficiaries herein shall be made by the Trustee without adjustment because of such distribution; and the good faith determination of the Trustee shall be binding and conclusive on all parties.

Power to Terminate Trusts

Circumstances can occur after the trustor's death that might render a trust unnecessary or undesirable. After the trustor's death, if the trustee determines that termination of a subtrust for a beneficiary, after considering the age and capacity of the beneficiary and the economic cost of maintaining such trust, is in the best interests of the beneficiary, the trustee should be empowered to distribute the property of such trust to the beneficiary or to the beneficiary's custodian, guardian, or conservator in the same proportion as the beneficiary would be entitled to receive at the designated time of termination. If any beneficiary is under legal disability, the trustee should give notice of such termination and distribution to the conservator of the beneficiary's estate or, if there is no conservator, to the person having the care or the legal custody of the beneficiary. The trustee should not be liable or responsible to any person for terminating a trust or in failing or refusing at any time to terminate such a trust. If such a trust is terminated, any property of the trust estate which is subject to a life estate interest in the beneficiary can be distributed to the beneficiary subject to the same uses, purposes, benefits, and conditions as were provided under the trust agreement for the beneficiary.

Other Express Trustee Powers

The express powers discussed above are by no means the only ones found in living trust agreements. The trustor may want to provide the trustee with special powers. Such powers may be provided to handle particular property of the trust estate (e.g., the trustor's interest in a closely-held business, a vacation home, and so forth) or to carry out a particular direction with regard to the management of the trust estate. The trustor may also want to give the trustee special directions regarding the use of trust property for a particular beneficiary (see file "APP0201.DOC" Article VI (D); see Chapter 2: Framework of a Revocable Living Trust, Trustee Powers: Article IX, Examples 1. and 2.). 📄

Likewise, the trustor may want the trustee to have a power that is not specifically addressed under local law.

Ask Your Attorney

If a power is not addressed under state law, does this mean it is not permitted in my living trust?

Answer

Not necessarily, unless the trustor resides in the State of Louisiana where laws are based on the Napoleonic Code. At the risk of oversimplification, in Louisiana, if the law is not written in the statutes, then it is illegal to do what is not covered by the law. This may be a flagrant interpretation, but it is done intentionally as a caution to beware when designing trustee powers in a living trust whose legal jurisdiction is the State of Louisiana. In all other states, however, any trustee power is probably acceptable, so long as it does not violate public policy.

An integral part of a trustor's estate plan may include a gifting program. In order to carry out this important part of the estate plan, the trustor may want to empower his or her trustee to make gifts of trust estate property on the trustor's behalf. The living trust can provide that, if the trust estate property is ample to provide for the trustor's health, support, education, and maintenance, the trustee can be authorized, on the trustor's behalf, to make gifts of the trust estate property to charity and other persons (including the trustor's spouse) as the trustor might make in amounts that do not exceed the gift tax annual exclusion amount under I.R.C. Sections 2503(b), 2503(e), or I.R.C. Section 2513 (in the case of split gifts between trustor and trustor's spouse). Or the trustor might direct the trustee to carry out gifting programs that the trustor has already established, including gifts by the trustor to his or her spouse as provided under I.R.C. Section 2523 in substantially the same amounts, manner, and form as the trustor previously made. In effecting such gifts, the trustee should be admonished to take into account and preserve insofar as possible the trustor's known estate plan, including any such plan under the trustor's Last Will, the living trust agreement itself, and any contract, transfer, or joint ownership arrangement with provisions for payment or transfer of benefits or property interests to other persons upon the trustor's death.

As a general rule, the value of property gifted by the trustee from a decedent trustor's revocable living trust within three years of the decedent trustor's death is not includable in the decedent trustor's gross estate. In this regard, such gifts are treated as a transfer made directly by the decedent.[18]

> ## Observation
>
> The transfer by the trustee of a revocable living trust of the incidents of ownership in a life insurance policy insuring the life of the trustor within three years of the insured trustor's death to a third party causes the value of the insurance proceeds to be included in the decedent insured trustor's gross estate for purposes of the federal estate tax.[19]

TRUSTEE DUTIES AND RESPONSIBILITIES

To whom is the trustee of a living trust responsible? The trustee's responsibility is foremost to the beneficiaries of the trust. This means that the trustee is responsible for the safekeeping of the trust estate property and management of the beneficiaries' interests in the trust estate. This responsibility includes, but is not limited to, prudently investing property comprising the trust estate and seeing to it that beneficiaries receive distributions of trust estate income and principal to which they are entitled. The trustee is also responsible for keeping accurate accounts and records of trust administration. Furthermore, the trustee has a duty to act with due regard to its obligation as a fiduciary, including a duty not to exercise any power under the laws of the state having legal jurisdiction of the trust agreement in such a way as to deprive the trust of an otherwise available tax exemption, deduction, or tax credit or deprive the trustor of a personal tax exemption, deduction, or credit, or operate to impose a tax upon a trustor or other person as owner of any portion of the trust estate.

Preserving and Safekeeping the Trust Estate

The trust estate may consist of cash, real property, intangible personal property (e.g., stocks, bonds, mutual funds, mortgages, notes receivable, installment contracts, patents, royalties, and copyrights), tangible personal property (e.g., art objects, hobby collections, jewelry, and household furnishings, and so forth), and the trustor's interest in a closely-held business. It is the trustee's duty and responsibility to protect and safeguard the trust estate property until such time as it is distributed to the designated beneficiaries. In carrying out this duty, the trustee is obligated to pay taxes, assessments, charges, commissions, reasonable compensation of the trustee, and other expenses (including legal and accounting fees) incurred in the collection, management, care, preservation, maintenance, admin-

---

[18] I.R.C. § 2035(e).

[19] *Estate of Kissling v. Commissioner*, 94-2 U.S. Tax Cas. (CCH) ¶ 60,176 (1994), *rev'g* T. C. Memo 1993-262.

istration, protection, and conservation of the trust estate. Furthermore, the trustee has a duty to insure property of the trust against any risk, damage, or loss and the trustee itself against liability with respect to third persons. Also, the trustee may need to institute or defend legal actions in order to protect the assets of the trust estate. Hence, the trustee should be empowered to prosecute, defend, or submit to arbitration any actions, suits, claims, or proceedings in any jurisdiction for the protection of the trust estate and of the trustee itself in the performance of the trustee's duties.

Cash

If large sums of cash are part of the trust estate, the trustee must give special attention to its preservation. If the cash is deposited in a financial institution, a trust account should be established separate from any account the individual trustee may have in the same financial institution in his or her own name. Attention must also be given to Federal Deposit Insurance Corporation (FDIC) insurance limits on trust accounts (see discussion in Chapter 13: Accounts in Banks, Savings Associations, and Credit Unions).

Real Property

Real property in the trust estate includes buildings and other improvements and must be handled in a manner commensurate with maintaining it in good marketable condition. The trustee should comply with existing tenants' requests concerning maintenance and repairs. Unless the beneficiary is obligated to pay real property taxes, the trustee should pay these taxes in a timely manner. Safeguarding the real property may include: perfecting title to the property in the name of the trustee (if title was not conveyed to the trustee during the trustor's lifetime); insuring title; executing documents affecting real property (e.g., deeds, contracts, and so forth); exchanging property; repairing property; settling disputes over boundaries; reviewing existing insurance coverage (fire, contents, liability, and so forth) for the property and improvements and seeing that the premiums are paid; developing or completing unfinished property, remodeling, or other unfinished projects affecting the property.

If real property is situated outside the state having jurisdiction over the living trust agreement, the trustee must determine if state law permits it to hold the property in the trust or whether a trustee who is a resident of the state in which the real property is situated must be appointed. Finally, if the trust agreement provides that real property is to be sold, the trustee should list the property with a qualified, experienced, and knowledgeable real estate agent. Even if the trustee is a licensed and qualified real estate agent, the property should be listed with an agent unrelated and unconnected to the trustee to avoid any real or imagined conflict of interest. This admonition is particularly applicable if the trustee is also a beneficiary of the trust estate.

Intangible Personal Property

Oftentimes, intangible personal property, such as stocks and bonds, creates the greatest challenge for a trustee. The trustee should pay particular attention to the preservation of the original investments comprising the trust estate. In this regard, the trustee must look to what powers have been granted to the trustee regarding a course of action for investing the original stocks and bonds comprising the trust estate. Regardless of the trustee's personal motivation and whether the trustee's powers under the trust agreement are broad or limited, the trustee must act in accordance with the trust agreement. If the trust agreement is silent as to a particular power, the trustee must turn to state law for guidance. Moreover, the trustee must act in the beneficiaries' best interests by diversifying the investments of the trust estate so as to minimize the risk of large losses, unless, under the circumstances, it is clearly prudent not to do so. Furthermore, the trustee must act with the care, skill, prudence, and diligence under the circumstances then prevailing that a prudent person acting in a like capacity and familiar with such matters would use in the conduct of an enterprise of a like character and with like aims. If the decision is to sell some or all of the original investment securities, then the time to sell them must be determined so as to obtain the highest price. Unless the trustee is knowledgeable, experienced, and skilled in the business of investments, the Trustee may be well advised to use the services of a qualified investment adviser—preferably one whose compensation is fee based, rather than based on commission.

Tangible Personal Property

A properly funded living trust includes tangible personal property. Where married individuals either create a joint living trust agreement or each spouse creates his and her own separate living trust agreement, if the surviving spouse is to be the beneficiary of the decedent spouse's tangible personal property, such property should continue in the living trust as part of the surviving spouse's own property. In other words, as a general rule, the surviving spouse should be given absolute unfettered control of such property. This approach eliminates the issue of whether the trustee should retain physical possession of the property. The beneficiary of the property should have physical possession of the property.

On the other hand, if the decedent trustor leaves tangible personal property for the benefit of a minor child, then provision should be made for the surviving parent, an immediate family member, or the child's guardian to take physical possession of such property until such time as the child is responsible enough to care for the property. The trustee may still retain legal ownership of the property and, unless required by the nature of the property to vest title in the trustee, does not have to take physical possession of the property.[20] If the trust agreement is silent regarding who is to take physical possession of such property, then the trustee and the child's guardian should reach an accommodation in the matter. Usually, in such situations, the trustee's authority is conclusive and binding on all interested parties. Particular care must be exercised in cases where the beneficiary is incapacitated and is receiving government assistance (e.g., supplemental security income, supplemental disability income, or Medicaid benefits) to ensure that the tangible personal property being held for such beneficiary does not become a *resource,* thereby, disqualifying the beneficiary from receiving such government assistance.

Business Interests

The trustor's interest in a closely-held business can be transferred to a living trust (see discussion in Chapter 12: Closely-Held Business Interests). Thoughtful planning is absolutely essential with regard to the matter of a trustee being in legal title to the trustor's interest in such a business. Assuming no impediments exist under state law, no special problems are created when the trustor is also the trustee of his or her living trust. However, the estate planning process must address both the legal and practical considerations involved when a successor trustee takes over as the legal owner of the trustor's interest in the business. State law must be reviewed to determine if any particular requirements apply to ownership of a business by a trustee.

Furthermore, the interpersonal relationships of other shareholders or partners must be taken into account. In this regard, the person succeeding as trustee may not be knowledgeable or experienced in the operation of the trustor's business enterprise. In such cases, it may be better for the trustor to provide that, with respect to the trustor's interest in the business and its operation, an advisory committee consisting of those persons intimately familiar

---

[20] See 89 *Corpus Juris Secundum* (C.J.S.) 841; 76 AmJur2d, Trusts, §§ 35, 62.

with and qualified to participate in the day-to-day operation of the business should manage the business operations. Such persons may include either the surviving or remaining shareholders or partners or the trustor's beneficiaries receiving the decedent trustor's interest in the business. The trustee may consult with the advisory committee or any member thereof and may be authorized to comply with and follow any advice or instructions given to the trustee by the advisory committee. The trustee can be absolved of all responsibility to any beneficiary for any action or omission relative to following the advisory committee's instructions as to the operation of the business (see file "APP0301.DOC").

Management of the Trust Estate

In effect, being a trustee is like acting as a manger of a business. In this regard, the trustee is responsible for the entire operation of the trust estate for the exclusive use, benefit, and enjoyment of the primary beneficiary and ultimately the contingent beneficiaries. In all matters of trust estate management, the trustee's decisions made in good faith should be binding and conclusive on all persons.

As an aid in executing management responsibilities, a well-designed living trust agreement empowers the trustee to perform ministerial functions. For example, the trustee should be authorized to employ for reasonable compensation persons, including attorneys, auditors, investment advisors, agents, or other persons with special skills, to advise or assist the trustee in the performance of its administrative duties, even if such persons are associated with the trustee. If state law requires the trustee to invest the trust estate property as a prudent investor, then the trustee is obligated to hire professional advisers if it is not sufficiently expert in investment matters.[21]

Oftentimes, a revocable living trust includes property (e.g., real property or securities) that is subject to the jurisdiction of a state other than the legal jurisdiction of the trust agreement. When the trustor conveys legal title to such property to the trustee, the trustee should be empowered, to the extent permitted under state law, to designate an ancillary fiduciary qualified to serve in the jurisdiction where the property is located and to delegate to the ancillary fiduciary those powers necessary to enable the fiduciary to perform its responsibilities relative to the property involved. The trustor may also want the trustee to determine whether any corporate fiduciary or any person or persons acting in an ancillary capacity should serve with or without bond.

Successful revocable living trust planning involves various *what-if* scenarios. Certainly, if a contingent beneficiary is disabled when the living trust agreement is being designed, provision should be made as to the method for making distributions of income and principal to such a beneficiary. Even if no contingent beneficiary(ies) is disabled when the living trust is being designed, nevertheless, provision should be made for such a possibility. With this in mind, provision can be made for payments from the trust estate directly to a disabled beneficiary or to a legal representative or relative of a disabled beneficiary without liability to the trustee for the application of any such payments made to the beneficiary.

The trustee can also be authorized to make loans to beneficiaries of the trust agreement. Such loans may be made to the beneficiary from the trust estate on terms and conditions that the trustee determines are fair and reasonable under the circumstances. The trustee may also guarantee loans to the beneficiary by encumbrances on assets composing the trust estate.

Certain duties of the trustee may also be expressed to eliminate uncertainty in the management of the trust estate. One such duty might include the power to grant an option

---

[21] See *O'Neill Irrevocable Trust v. Commissioner*, 994 F.2d 302 (6th Cir. 1993), *rev'g* 98 T.C. 227 (1992), *nonacq.*, 1994-38 I.R.B. 4.

involving disposition of a trust estate asset or to take an option for the acquisition of any asset. Additionally, the trustee may be given the power to exercise options, rights, and privileges contained in a life insurance policy, annuity, or endowment contract constituting property of the trust estate, including the right to obtain the cash surrender value, convert a policy to another type of policy, revoke any mode of settlement, and pay any or all of the premiums on the policy or contract.

If any assets of the trust estate are encumbered by a mortgage, pledge, lien, or other security interest, the trustee has a duty to pay the encumbrance or any part of it. Also, the trustee has a duty to renew or extend an obligation secured by such an encumbrance or convey or transfer the trust estate assets to the creditor in satisfaction of its security interest, if doing so is in the best interests of the trust estate. Similarly, the trustee is obligated to release or terminate any mortgage or security interest, if the obligation secured by the mortgage or security interest has been fully satisfied.

Distribution of Income and Principal to Trustor

During the trustor's lifetime, the trustee pays to or applies for the benefit of the trustor the income of the trust estate in convenient installments not less frequently than quarter-annually or as the trustor may from time-to-time request in writing (see file "APP0201.DOC" Article IV) 📄. Usually, the trust agreement provides that, if the trustee considers the net income of the trust estate insufficient, the trustee may pay to or apply for the benefit of the trustor as much of the principal of the trust estate as the trustor may from time-to-time request in writing or that the trustee considers necessary for the trustor's proper health care, maintenance, and support to enable the trustor to maintain the standard of living to which he or she is accustomed without the consent or approval of the contingent beneficiaries.

The trustor retains the right to direct the trustee in writing to pay to the trustor or apply for the trustor's benefit amounts from the principal of the trust estate as the trustor may designate. The trustee is obligated to comply with such written direction and has no responsibility to inquire into or determine for what purpose any such withdrawals are made. However, to the extent the trustor is not incapacitated, the trust agreement may provide that directions to the trustee need not be in writing when the trustor is acting as trustee. Furthermore, the trust agreement may provide that, in the event the trustor becomes incapacitated and cannot manage his or her financial and business affairs, becomes incompetent (whether or not a proper court of jurisdiction has declared trustor incompetent), mentally ill, or in need of a conservator, the trustee is obligated to pay to or apply for the trustor's benefit income and principal of the trust estate as the trustee considers necessary for the trustor's health care, maintenance, and support to enable trustor to maintain the standard of living to which trustor is accustomed, until the trustor is again able, if ever, to manage his or her business and financial affairs, or until trustor's death, without the consent or approval of any contingent beneficiary. In the year of any such incapacity, the trustee may exercise discretion whether to retain or distribute any portion of the net income of the trust estate (as defined in I.R.C. Section 643(b))[22] to or for the trustor's benefit in excess of the amounts applied for the trustor's benefit. In this regard, all amounts retained are added at least annually to the principal of the trust estate property. Generally, to the extent appropriate, in making distributions of income or principal of the trust estate, or both, to the trustor, the trustee is admonished to take into consideration all sources of income available to the trustor of which the trustee has actual knowledge.

---

[22] *See also* Treas. Reg. § 1.643-1 to be amended by REG-106513-00 Feb. 14, 2001, ¶s [16] and [17].

Accounting and Records of Administration

Generally, the trustee is required under the trust agreement to provide annually to each income beneficiary an itemized statement of all current receipts and disbursements of both income and principal of the trust estate. However, the trustee is not required to report information or to provide an annual statement to a beneficiary in any of the following circumstances:

- To the extent the trust agreement waives the report or annual statement;
- To the trustor who is a beneficiary of the trust agreement but only if the trustor is not incapacitated, as provided for the testing of the trustor's capacity in the trust agreement;
- As to a beneficiary who has waived in writing the right to a report or annual statement; or
- If the beneficiary and the trustee are the same person. In the event a current income beneficiary is a minor, the trustee may provide the accounting to the minor's parents or guardian (natural or legal).

Even though the trustor may not intend, upon his or her death, for the living trust agreement to be under court supervision, nevertheless, the trustee is required to keep complete and accurate records of its trust administration. These records must be sufficiently complete so as to be clearly understood by the beneficiaries, who are entitled to review the records at any time, and by the successor trustee. A beneficiary can petition a proper court of jurisdiction at any time to review, interpret, hear a beneficiary's complaint about the trustee or the administration of the trust estate, or give the trustee direction regarding matters affecting the trust estate or the beneficiaries. Moreover, such records may be subject to audit and, therefore, must be accurate and capable of independent verification. Lastly, since trusts often operate for many years, the trustee's accounts and records must be of sufficient thoroughness, permanence, and durability to justify and support the trustee's decisions and actions for the life of the trust agreement.

CHAPTER 4

Property Management and Other Benefits

IMPORTANCE OF THE TRUST ESTATE

As discussed in Chapter 2, Framework of a Revocable Living Trust, a legal trust cannot exist without the legal title to property being titled in the name of the trustee.[1] Furthermore, a revocable living trust cannot operate as intended unless the trustor conveys legal title to property to the trustee during the trustor's lifetime (or, upon the trustor's death, property comprising the decedent trustor's probate estate is conveyed to the trustee of the revocable living trust agreement under the trustor's Will). Of course, during the trustor's lifetime, he or she can also designate the revocable living trust as the beneficiary of contract benefits (e.g., personal and group life insurance, qualified and nonqualified deferred compensation, salary continuation payments, employee death benefits, qualified retirement plan benefits, and so forth), which then become part of the decedent trustor's nonprobate estate. It is the trustee's legal ownership of the property transferred to the revocable living trust agreement that enables the trustee to administer and manage the trust estate for the trustor as primary beneficiary during his or her lifetime. This ownership of property by the trustee can produce lifetime benefits for the trustor and, after the trustor's death, benefits for the trustor's beneficiaries which cannot otherwise be obtained or, at best, be achieved less effectively if the trustor continued to own property outside of a revocable living trust.

FINANCIAL GUARDIANSHIP UNNECESSARY

If a person becomes physically disabled or mentally incapacitated during lifetime, his or her personal and financial affairs may be subject to control by a court-appointed guardian. In most states, only a court has the power to appoint a person called a *guardian* who acts for another person called the *ward*, whom the law regards as incapable of managing his or her own personal and financial affairs.[2] As a general rule, to obtain a guardianship, it is sufficient to show only that a person is incapable of managing his or her personal or financial affairs in a manner indicating that he or she does not understand the consequences of his or her actions.[3] Thus, the primary purpose of a guardianship is for the physical protection of a person; however, in some states, a guardianship may be authorized for both a person's physical protection and for the management of his or her property (i.e., financial affairs; affairs).[4]

---

[1] *See Restatement (Second) of Trusts* § 74 (1959); 1 *Scott On Trusts* § 17.1 (3d ed. 1967 & Supp. 1987).

[2] 39 Am Jur2d, Guardian and Ward, §§ 1 and 45.

[3] 39 Am Jur2d, Guardian and Ward, § 20.

[4] 39 Am Jur2d, Guardian and Ward, § 18.

In such case, the guardian may be called a *conservator* (financial guardian). In effect, the guardian becomes a conservator of a disabled person's estate.[5] The court, under the guidelines of state law, has absolute discretion in the selection of the person to serve as guardian.[6] As an officer of the court, the guardian acts under the direction and judicial control of the court. Accordingly, the court can control the actions of the guardian with regard to the management and disposition of the ward's property. In reality, the court's control is more theoretical than real, in that the guardian is pretty much free to conduct the ward's personal and financial affairs as he or she deems best so long as such conduct is not detrimental to the ward. In effect, the guardian exercises his or her own judgment in managing the ward's property.[7] Unlike a trustee under a revocable living trust agreement, the guardian does not hold legal title to the ward's real, tangible, or intangible property. Thus, the guardian has no legal or beneficial interest in the ward's property. The guardian merely acts as a custodian or conservator of the ward's property.[8]

With regard to the appointment of a guardian for an incompetent or incapacitated adult, most state courts will appoint a close relative of the prospective ward. If possible, unless the welfare of the ward would be adversely affected, the court may prefer to appoint, over other family members seeking appointment,[9] the ward's spouse as guardian. Once appointed, the court retains jurisdiction for all purposes in connection with all activities of the guardian until the guardian is discharged of his or her responsibility by the court.[10]

The person seeking appointment as a guardian files a complaint or petition in the proper court of jurisdiction.[11] The petition, along with competent and relevant evidence that frequently includes, in open court, supporting testimony by physicians, psychiatrists, psychologists, and social workers is heard by the court on the alleged merits of the requested guardianship. Such a court proceeding can be financially expensive, emotionally upsetting to the prospective ward and to his or her immediate family members, and an unbelievably degrading and humiliating personal experience for the ward. Further, the guardian may be required to provide a bond in an amount determined by the court and with surety acceptable by the court for the execution of the guardianship.[12]

If a person becomes a ward of the court, any authority exercised by the guardian after the ward's death is void. Generally, in this regard, the guardian cannot collect debts due the ward, make contracts on the ward's behalf, or sell the ward's interest in real property. Nor can the guardian continue to prosecute actions on the ward's behalf that were initiated before the ward's death.[13] Thus, for all practical purposes, the guardian's authority to act on the ward's behalf terminates upon the ward's death. This is why a guardianship does not avoid probate of a ward's property in the event of his or her death and why the guardian cannot act in lieu of a personal representative of the ward's estate during the probate process, unless, of course, the guardian happens to also be the person designated in the ward's Will to serve as his or her personal representative under the terms of the ward's Will.

---

[5] 39 Am Jur2d, Guardian and Ward, § 1.

[6] 39 Am Jur2d, Guardian and Ward, § 27.

[7] 39 Am Jur2d, Guardian and Ward, § 62.

[8] 39 Am Jur2d, Guardian and Ward, § 111.

[9] 39 Am Jur2d, Guardian and Ward, § 29.

[10] 39 Am Jur2d, Guardian and Ward, § 24.

[11] 39 Am Jur2d, Guardian and Ward, § 46.

[12] 39 Am. Jur2d, Guardian and Ward, § 48.

[13] 39 Am Jur2d, Guardian and Ward, § 64.

Ask Your Attorney

Can a revocable living trust protect both the person and the person's financial affairs in the event he or she becomes physically disabled or mentally incapacitated?

Answer

Yes.

The necessity of a public competency proceeding for the appointment of a guardian of a person's personal and financial affairs and a court-supervised financial guardianship of a person's financial and business affairs in the event of physical or mental incapacity can be eliminated with a well-designed and correctly funded revocable living trust. In the event of physical or mental incapacity, or both, the successor trustee immediately assumes management of the trust estate for the benefit of the trustor.[14] Whether the trustee, as *guardian* of the trustor's personal affairs, must be court appointed depends entirely upon the acceptance of the trustor's nomination by those persons providing the trustor's personal care. Most care givers do not question the authority of the trustee in this regard. This is unquestionably the case when the trustor has designated the successor trustee as his or her attorney-in-fact under a durable power of attorney for health care. Upon the trustor's death, the successor trustee can administer, settle, and distribute the trust estate to the trustor's beneficiaries without the necessity of a probate proceeding. Or the trust estate may also continue in the revocable living trust for the trustor's beneficiaries (see e.g., files "APP0201.DOC" through "APP0203.DOC").

Most states allow a person to nominate, in writing, a guardian of his or her choice, if such nomination is made prior to the alleged incapacity.[15] As a rule, no specific written format is required to effect such a nomination. The trustor of a revocable living trust can designate a person (and successor persons) in his or her revocable living trust agreement to serve as guardian of the trustor's person in the event of physical disability or mental incapacity. The successor trustee or a trusted friend may serve as guardian of the trustor's person.[16]

Examples

1. Married trustor, single living trust agreement nominating guardian of trustor's person:

ARTICLE XV
APPOINTMENT OF GUARDIAN

If it becomes necessary to appoint a Guardian of the person of Trustor, Trustor hereby nominates and appoints one of the following in the order named to serve without bond or other undertaking: Trustor's husband, _____; Trustor's daughter, _____. If _____ and _____ are unable or unwilling to serve as Guardian, then, to the extent permitted under the governing law of this Trust Agreement, Trustor grants Trustee the option of appointing a Guardian for the person of Trustor. To the extent permitted under the governing law of this Trust Agreement, Trustee shall determine whether the person ap-

---

[14] Moy, 2, *A Practitioner's Guide to Estate Planning*, § 29.02 [A] at 29-14.

[15] 39 Am Jur2d, Guardian and Ward, § 30.

[16] Moy, 2, *A Practitioner's Guide to Estate Planning*, § 29.02 [A] at 29-14.

pointed by Trustee to serve as Guardian shall be required to serve with bond or other undertaking (see also file "APP0201.DOC" Article XI) .

2. Married trustors, joint living trust agreement nominating guardian for person of each trustor:

ARTICLE XIV
APPOINTMENT OF GUARDIANS FOR TRUSTORS

(A) **Trustor**_____. If it becomes necessary to appoint a Guardian of the person of Trustor _____, he hereby nominates and appoints his wife, _____, as Guardian of Trustor _____ to serve without bond or other undertaking. If _____ is unable or unwilling to serve, then Trustor _____ nominates and appoints one of the following in the order named to serve without bond or other undertaking: _____; _____; _____.

(B) **Trustor** _____. If it becomes necessary to appoint a Guardian of the person of Trustor _____, she hereby nominates and appoints her husband, _____, as Guardian of Trustor _____ to serve without bond or other undertaking. If _____ is unable or unwilling to serve, then Trustor _____ nominates and appoints one of the following in the order named to serve without bond or other undertaking: _____; _____; _____. (See also file "APP0204.DOC" Article XI.)

3. Married trustor, single trust nominating trustor's husband as guardian of trustor's person and nomination by trustor of guardian for trustor's incapacitated adult child:

ARTICLE XIV
APPOINTMENT OF GUARDIAN

(A) **Nomination and Appointment of Guardian for Trustor.** If it becomes necessary to appoint a Guardian of the person of Trustor, Trustor hereby nominates and appoints one of the following in the order named to serve as Guardian of Trustor without bond or other undertaking: Trustor's husband, _____; Trustor's daughter _____. If _____ and _____ are unable or unwilling to serve as Guardian, then, to the extent permitted under the governing law of this Trust Agreement, Trustor grants Trustee the option of appointing a Guardian for the person of Trustor. To the extent permitted under the governing law of this Trust Agreement, Trustee shall determine whether the person appointed by Trustee to serve as Guardian shall be required to serve with bond or other undertaking.

(B) **Nomination and Appointment of Guardian for (child's name here).** If it should become necessary to appoint a Guardian of the person of _____ and Trustor should die not having already obtained a Guardian for _____, then Trustor recommends that _____ petition the proper court of jurisdiction to be appointed as Guardian of _____.

Generally, the language used in the preceding examples satisfies the requirement that the nomination of a guardian be in writing. In many cases, the successor trustee or a trusted friend may serve as the guardian of the trustor's person. If the revocable living trust has been correctly funded, a court-appointed and supervised financial guardianship of the trustor's financial affairs is unnecessary. This is because the successor trustee is already in legal title to the property comprising the trust estate and is responsible for managing it for the benefit of the trustor as primary beneficiary of the revocable living trust.

Example

Paul, age 73, created a management revocable living trust with Wells Fargo Bank as trustee. Paul conveyed legal title to all of his property to the trustee. About two years after the trust was executed, Paul began to show signs of dementia. His increasing dementia demonstrated the need for a guardian of his person.

One of Paul's sons admitted that he could not wait for his father's death so that he could receive his "rightful share" of his father's estate that amounted to approximately $256,000. This particular son petitioned the probate court to be appointed as both his father's guardian and conservator. The conservatorship petition was denied because Paul had previously conveyed title to all of his property to the bank as trustee of his revocable living trust, thus rendering a court-appointed conservatorship of his property legally impossible and unnecessary. Furthermore, the son's petition to be appointed guardian of his father's person was denied because evidence was introduced at the hearing that convinced the court the son was unfit to serve as guardian of his father's person. The court ultimately appointed Paul's other son to serve as guardian of his father's person but not of his financial affairs, because Paul's property was already protected and managed by the bank as trustee under Paul's revocable living trust.

PROBATE UNNECESSARY

Regardless of whether a person dies with a Will, if the person owns property in his or her individual name or if the decedent's estate is the designated beneficiary of property comprising his or her estate, a court must supervise the administration of the decedent's estate. This court-supervised process is called *probate*. Technically, the purpose of probate is to prove the validity of the decedent's Will. In reality, however, probate has come to be a court-supervised procedure that oversees the administration of a decedent's entire probate estate.

Probate Estate

The probate estate consists of all property passing to the decedent's beneficiaries under the terms of his or her Will or, if a person dies without a Will, to such person's heirs by the local laws of intestate distribution. Probate property includes all property owned by a person in his or her individual name, as a tenant in common, or, in certain cases, community property. The probate estate may also include property payable to the decedent's estate; for example, personal and group life insurance proceeds, qualified or nonqualified deferred compensation, qualified retirement plan benefits (including 401(k) plans, SEPs, IRAs and tax sheltered annuities under I.R.C. Section 403(b)), and employee death benefits of which the decedent's estate is the designated beneficiary.

Nonprobate Estate

Generally, all property not distributable under the terms of a person's Will is not part of his or her probate estate and, therefore, is not subject to the probate process. Such property is part of the decedent's nonprobate estate and includes:

1. Personal and group life insurance proceeds paid to a beneficiary other than the decedent's estate;

2. Property that the decedent owned as joint tenants with right of survivorship (or as tenants by the entirety);

3. Bank accounts held *in trust for* a person who survives the decedent (Totten trust);

4. Individual retirement accounts (IRAs), Keogh plans, 401(k) plans, simplified employee pension plans, annuity contracts, including tax deferred annuities and tax sheltered annuities [I.R.C. Section 403(b) plans], payable to a beneficiary other than to the decedent's estate;

5. All other so-called contract benefits; for example, qualified and nonqualified deferred compensation, employee salary continuation benefits, personal and group life insurance, and employee death benefits, payable to a beneficiary other than to the decedent's estate;

6. Property gifted during lifetime, even if the value of such property is includable in the decedent's gross estate for purposes of computing the federal estate tax;

7. Any interests in property acquired in a trust created by someone else which terminate upon the decedent's death (i.e., a life estate), unless the decedent beneficiary exercises a general power of appointment over the property in the trust in favor of the beneficiary-donee's estate; and

8. Title to property which is correctly conveyed to the trustee of a revocable living trust agreement during the trustor's lifetime.

Ask Your Attorney

Why does property in a living trust avoid probate?

Answer

In general, probate of a person's estate is unnecessary for the administration of assets in a revocable living trust. When legal title to property is conveyed to the trustee of a revocable living trust, the trustee is in legal title to the property; while the trustor, as primary beneficiary of the trust estate during the trustor's lifetime, is in equitable title to the trust property. In other words, as beneficiary, the trustor does not possess legal title to the trust property but, rather, a beneficial (or equitable) interest in the property. Therefore, upon the death of the trustor, legal title to the property is not held in the trustor's individual name. Hence, it is not necessary to transfer the title to the property; the property is already titled in the name of the trustee for the benefit of the contingent beneficiaries of the revocable living trust. Generally, the probate system does not have jurisdiction over property to which a person does not possess legal title or which is not payable to the decedent's estate.

Ask Your Attorney

If I effect a revocable living trust, can I be assured that my estate will avoid probate?

Answer

As a general rule the answer is yes, provided the revocable living trust is properly designed and correctly funded during the trustor's lifetime. On the other hand, even though the trustor's revocable living trust may be correctly funded with all of his or her property comprising the trustor's gross estate, a probate proceeding may be initiated by the decedent trustor's personal representative. Initiating a probate proceeding may be desirable or necessary to toll the statute of limitations with respect to the claims of creditors, especially, if the trustor dies with significant amounts of indebtedness or if the trustor may have caused the wrongful death of another person or if a beneficiary of the trustor's trust estate files claims against the trustor's trust estate. In such events, the probate court is available to protect both the trustor's creditors and beneficiaries.

Probate Is a Requirement of State Law

Probate is strictly a requirement of state law; the federal government has absolutely nothing to do with the process of administering a decedent's estate. The process of proving the decedent's Will is supervised by a probate court, surrogate court, court of chancery, or orphans court. A probate court is a special court with general jurisdiction in law and equitable powers to make binding judgments in the administration of a decedent's estate, including matters concerning real and personal property (tangible and intangible), determination of heirs, and the distribution of the decedent's property. As a general rule, the location of probate is determined by the decedent's state of residence, the state (or county) where the decedent's property is located, or the county wherein the decedent's death occurs.

Ancillary Administration

If the decedent owns property in a state other than his or her state of legal residence, ancillary administration of such property may be required in the state having jurisdiction over such property. Generally, such an ancillary probate is only necessary for real property and tangible and intangible personal property coming under the jurisdiction of the state where the property is physically located. As a matter of practice, the attorney representing the personal representative of the decedent's estate would hire another attorney at the place where the out-of-state property is physically located.

Purposes of Probate

Probate has four primary purposes:

1. To clear and pass title to property titled in the individual name of the decedent to those persons designated as beneficiaries in the decedent's Will or to those persons entitled to inherit the decedent's property if the decedent dies intestate (i.e., to die without a Will);

Observation

A decedent's undivided interest in property as a tenant in common (without right of survivorship) would be considered property titled in the decedent's individual name; thus, it would be subject to probate.

2. To protect and preserve the decedent's property for his or her beneficiaries (or heirs if the decedent were to die intestate) and to protect the decedent's probate estate from unsubstantiated claims of other persons;
3. To protect the decedent's rightful creditors by providing them a forum to present their claims for bona fide debts and obligations owed by the decedent at the time of his or her death and to guarantee that all taxes and other legitimate expenses of administering and settling the decedent's estate are paid; and

4. To distribute property comprising the decedent's probate estate to the beneficiaries designated in his or her Will (or to the decedent's heirs if the decedent were to die intestate).

Prevalent Misconceptions Regarding Probate

Misconception: Transfer Taxes and Probate Are Related

One of the most difficult concepts for people to understand is that transfer taxes (i.e., federal estate, generation-skipping transfer tax, and state death taxes) and probate have absolutely nothing to do with one another. They are completely unrelated matters.

Misconception: Having a Will Avoids Probate

The most prevalent misconception is that, if a person has a Will, probate is unnecessary. Having a Will does not guarantee that probate can be avoided. The fact is, a decedent's estate may be probated whether or not he or she has a Will.

Misconception: Avoiding Probate Avoids Paying Transfer Taxes

Many people erroneously believe that, by avoiding probate, they can avoid paying transfer taxes. Again, the root of this belief is probably in the misconception that taxes and probate are somehow related. Strictly speaking, they are not. However, if a decedent's estate is probated, the court will see to it that income and transfer taxes, if any, are paid before the remaining assets of the probate estate are distributed to the decedent's beneficiaries or heirs. But probate avoidance should not be viewed as being synonymous with avoiding taxes.

The fact of the matter is a decedent may have an asset includable in his or her *gross estate* for federal estate tax purposes but not includable in the probate estate. For example, if a person has an interest in a bank account or a security (stock, bond, mutual fund, and so forth) as joint tenants with right of survivorship with another person, or has conveyed legal title to his or her property to the trustee of a revocable living trust, such property is includable in such person's *gross estate* for federal estate tax purposes; but it is not includable in the decedent's *probate estate*. Further, if a person retains any incidents of ownership in a life insurance policy on his or her own life or transfers such ownership within three years of his or her death to another person (including to the trustee of an irrevocable living trust), the proceeds will be includable in the value of the insured's *gross estate* for federal estate tax purposes but will not be includable in the insured decedent's *probate estate*. Finally, property that a person (donor) transfers to another person during lifetime as an incomplete gift may be includable in the value of the donor's *gross estate* for federal estate tax purposes; but it will not be subject to probate as part of the donor's *probate estate*.

Advantage of Probate

How can any court procedure that can be so time-consuming and expensive possibly be an advantage to a decedent's beneficiaries? Unequivocally, the disadvantages of probate far outweigh the advantage. Notice the word *advantage* is used in the singular and not in the plural. This is because probate may provide only one possible legitimate nontax advantage: the interests of the decedent's beneficiaries (or heirs) in the decedent's probate estate will be protected during the administration of the decedent's estate by the probate court's supervision. The probate court will ensure that the decedent's probate estate is, in fact, properly distributed and legal title to the property correctly conveyed to those beneficiaries who are entitled to a distributable share of it. In most states, the probate court enters a decree of distribution before the final distribution of property occurs and requires the beneficiaries (or heirs) to execute a receipt for the property received and the receipt to be filed with the court before the personal representative is discharged of his or her duties and responsibilities.

Observation

> Normally, a probate court does not supervise the administration of a revocable living trust. Thus, some practitioners attempt to dissuade their clients from using a revocable living trust by having them believe that their property and beneficiaries will not be protected by the probate court in the event such supervision is needed. Such advice is erroneous because the beneficiaries of the trust can always bring to the attention of a proper court of jurisdiction any matter within its jurisdiction, and most state courts have jurisdiction over revocable living trusts.[17]

Disadvantages of Probate

At least four major disadvantages of probate overshadow the single advantage just discussed: (1) probate can be expensive; (2) probate is time-consuming; (3) beneficiaries can experience detrimental psychological effects; and (4) probate is a matter of public record, thus inviting unwanted publicity.

Probate Can Be Expensive

The various costs associated with probate can make the process expensive. Such costs include personal representative fees; attorney's fees; and court-related costs, such as filing fees. Additionally, appraisal fees, tax return preparation fees, tax planning fees, and sales expenses and commissions can be imposed. The fees in this latter category may be incurred even if property is distributable under a revocable living trust. However, some sales expenses may be greater when probate is involved because certain statutory requirements and probate procedures must be followed in consummating the sale.

In many states, fees paid to the personal representative and attorney are established by statute. Generally, such fee schedules represent the maximum commissions and fees that may be legally charged by personal representatives and attorneys, respectively, for their services. However, in addition to these statutory commissions and fees, the probate court may award extraordinary commissions and fees for services considered to be "above and beyond the call of duty." In many states, the statutory compensation is the same for both the personal representative and his or her attorney.

In those states where attorney's fees are not fixed by statute, nevertheless, the fee must be reasonable and based upon the fair value of the lawyer's services actually rendered relative to the size of the decedent's estate. In most cases, the personal representative's commissions and the lawyer's fees are subject to approval of the probate court—a court presided over by none other than a judge who generally is also a lawyer. Nothing more need be said about the degree of *impartiality* likely to be exercised by the judge in rendering a decision about the *fair value* of the services performed by the attorney.

Finally, the overall cost of probate can range from 2 to 12 percent of the value of the decedent's gross estate. An analysis of local probate records indicates that the average cost of probating an estate is about 6 percent of the value of the decedent's gross estate. In some cases, this percentage includes both the commission paid to the personal representative and the attorney's fees; in other cases, it does not.

---

[17] Moy, 2, *A Practitioner's Guide to Estate Planning,* § 29.02 [B] at 29-15.

Observation

Many attorneys suggest that the monetary expense of avoiding probate may be more than the cost of probate itself. In certain cases, this may be true. Regardless, though, of any cost comparative analysis one might perform, the biggest unknown variable may be the cost of professional services rendered by an attorney, accountant, appraiser, or other professional adviser, whether a person's estate is probated or is administered under a revocable living trust.

Probate Is Time-Consuming

Another major disadvantage of probate is that it can be time-consuming. The initial step of admitting the decedent's Will to probate and the approval and appointment of the personal representative usually occurs within a relatively short period after filing the petition for admission of a decedent's Will with the probate court. However, a statutory delay occurs on behalf of creditors who generally may be allowed from four to six months, in most jurisdictions, to file claims, if any, against the decedent's probate estate. Hence, a partial distribution of assets, except for spousal and child support, usually cannot be made until the expiration of this period. Aside from the matter of creditor's claims, additional requirements may have to be satisfied before a partial distribution of assets can be made.

In most cases, a final distribution of assets cannot be made until all taxes are paid. The Form 706, if required, as well as the payment of any federal estate tax, is due nine months after the date of death, assuming an application on Form 4768 for an automatic six-month extension to file the Form 706 and a request to extend the time for payment of the federal estate tax is not filed. An estate will be allowed an automatic six-month extension of time beyond the date prescribed in I.R.C. Section 6075(a) to file Form 706, if Form 4768 is filed on or before the due date for filing Form 706 and in accordance with the procedures under Treasury Regulation Section 20.6081-1(a).[18] However, an extension of time to pay the federal estate tax is not automatic; and request must be made on Form 4768 to extend the time to pay the federal estate tax.[19]

Some states are connected to federal law with regard to the due date for filing state tax returns and for paying state death taxes, while others are not. Closing the probate estate may be further delayed due to tax complexities; time-consuming and inefficient supervision by the probate court regarding the sale, management, and investment of estate assets; cash problems; or unsettled lawsuits or other claims. Overall, the entire probate process can interrupt the continuity of property management which affects the timely performance of those persons involved in the administration process. It is not uncommon for the average probate procedure to run twelve to eighteen months or longer. Probably the primary reason why the cost of probating an estate "expands to consume the money available"[20] is because time and money are synonymous.

Observation

Even with a revocable living trust, the trustee should not effect a partial distribution of the trust estate until assurances are obtained that all claims, expenses of administration, and taxes have been paid. A trustee is personally liable for the payment of federal estate tax.[21]

---

[18] Treas. Reg. § 20.6081-1(b).

[19] Treas. Reg. § 20.6081-1(c).

[20] Turner, *Revocable Trusts*, at vii.

[21] I.R.C. § 6324(a)(2).

Beneficiaries Can Experience Detrimental Psychological Effects

Probate can be an emotionally upsetting experience for members of the decedent's family. Frustration associated with delays, seemingly endless expense, and unfamiliarity with the whole administration process can create an unhealthy situation. Beneficiaries' nerves can become frayed, and their otherwise friendly demeanors and relationships with one another can become unduly strained. Moreover, if extraordinary problems arise in the administration process (e.g., wrongful death claims against the decedent's estate and resulting lawsuits or other claims filed by family members for various reasons), the beneficiaries can be exposed to additional unwanted frustration, emotional stress, and financial pressure. All of these negative influences can leave permanent scars on beneficiaries' memories of the decedent. Probate of one's estate may be comparable to the battles waged in domestic relations courts. Oftentimes, the emotional cost of probate may be higher than the financial investment of working to avoid it.

Probate Is a Matter of Public Record

A visit to the local county courthouse can be an enlightening experience into the inner sanctum of the probate process. Some of the material for the best novels, movies, and soap operas is obtained from probate records. These records can be revealing and, for the most part, are interesting to read. Moreover, one may be horrified to learn that anybody can peruse a deceased person's probate file. It's all there—how much the decedent owned, whom the decedent owed, who owed the decedent, who got what, who got cheated, and so on. Unquestionably, probate records are the source of some good reading.

Thus, publicity is the fourth major disadvantage of probate. Since probate is a court proceeding, all of the documents filed in the administration process are a matter of public record. Believe it or not, probate records are the source of names for unscrupulous sales persons who prey on the elderly and other innocent and unsuspecting beneficiaries of the decedent's estate. Avoidance of such publicity is one of the major reasons why a person may want to avoid probate. Even when a transfer agent or a title insurance company requires a copy of a revocable living trust agreement to transfer legal title of the trustor's property to the trustee, generally they will accept an abstract or memorandum of trust that does not disclose the confidential provisions of the trust agreement (see files "APP0210.DOC" through "APP0212.DOC"). Unfortunately, and all too often, the probate process is what the late Senator Robert F. Kennedy called, "a political tollbooth exacting tribute from widows and orphans."[22]

Should Probate Be Avoided?

For some people, probating a deceased family member's estate is as horrid an experience as a contested divorce or child custody battle. Probate should be avoided whenever possible or practical, recognizing, of course, that situations do exist where probate may be appropriate.

Related Taxpayers Rule

As a reminder to practitioners, the trustee of a trust (living or testamentary) and the beneficiary of a trust are related taxpayers.[23] Similarly, except in the case of a sale or exchange in satisfaction of a pecuniary bequest, the personal representative of a decedent's estate and a beneficiary of such estate are also related taxpayers.[24] No income tax deduction is allowed

---

[22] Norman F. Dacey, *How to Avoid Probate* (New York: Crown Publishers, 1965), at 5.

[23] I.R.C. § 267(b)(6).

[24] I.R.C. § 267(b)(13).

for any loss from the sale or exchange of property between related taxpayers.[25] This rule also applies to losses incurred by the trust in satisfaction of fixed dollar (pecuniary) distributions from the trust to the beneficiaries of the trust. This rule has nothing to do with distributions of *in kind* property by estates or trusts to their respective beneficiaries.[26] In view of the related taxpayer rule, while it appears that it may be disadvantageous to convey title to property to a revocable living trust if such property may be subject to loss upon a sale, so too would it be a disadvantage with respect to such property being sold by the personal representative of the decedent's probate estate.

Sixty-Five Day Rule

A complex trust (i.e., a trust that accumulates income, that may or may not distribute income in the trustee's discretion, that distributes principal, or that makes charitable contributions) established under a revocable living trust, or a testamentary trust under the terms of the decedent's Will, can elect to treat distributions made in the first 65 days of a tax year as having been made in the previous tax year.[27] This rule applies with respect to any taxable year of an estate or a trust only if the personal representative of such estate or the trustee of such trust (as the case may be) elects, in such manner and at such time as prescribed in the treasury regulations, to have the sixty-five day rule apply for such taxable year.[28]

Elimination of Expense

Aside from what may be viewed as a disadvantage regarding the income tax treatment of losses from the sale or exchange of property between related taxpayers, a correctly funded revocable living trust can eliminate probate of the trustor's estate. Consequently, many costs associated with probate may be reduced or entirely eliminated. The elimination of these costs may be worth more than the potential loss of income tax deductions for losses that may or may not materialize on sales or exchanges of property between the trustee and a beneficiary.

Attorney Fees, Fiduciary Fees, and Miscellaneous Administration Costs

However, a revocable living trust should not be used with the belief that all attorney and fiduciary fees will be eliminated. Some attorney and fiduciary fees and other costs related to trust administration may still be incurred. For example, if a Form 706 is required to be filed because the value of the trustor's trust estate exceeds the exemption amount, estate and appraisal fees may be incurred in obtaining accurate valuations of real property, jewelry, works of art, closely-held business interests, and other assets that have subjective value. Likewise, fees will be incurred for the preparation of the Form 706. Moreover, the trustee may require the services of a qualified and knowledgeable attorney to assist in the titling of property distributed to the beneficiaries or for other legal services regarding the administration and protection of the trust estate. Administration expenses incurred by the trustee after the trustor's death are income tax deductible to the trust, except to the extent such deductions are taken as estate tax deductions for expenses, indebtedness, and taxes[29] or for certain losses sustained by the trustor's probate or trust estate.[30]

---

[25] I.R.C. § 267(a)(1).

[26] See I.R.C. § 643(e) for tax treatment of property distributed in kind.

[27] I.R.C. § 663(b)(1); Treas. Reg. §§ 1.663(b)-1(a)(1); 1.663(b)-2(a).

[28] I.R.C. § 663(b)(2).

[29] I.R.C. § 2053.

[30] I.R.C. § 2054.

Privacy

The elimination of probate assures more privacy for the administration of one's estate and for the decedent's beneficiaries. It may be more difficult for disgruntled beneficiaries to initiate unwarranted and frivolous legal actions against the decedent's estate. Trust distributions and the identity of trust beneficiaries remain private. Finally, ancillary probate proceedings can be eliminated when legal title to out-of-state property is conveyed to the trustee of a revocable living trust.

Example

Tony, a legal resident of Oregon, had commercial income-producing real property in California titled in his individual name. Tony was concerned that, upon his death, his family would have to institute ancillary probate proceedings in California before title to the property could be transferred according to the terms of his Will.

Tony decided that his estate plan should include the implementation of a revocable living trust wherein the trustee would be in title to all of his property, including the title to the real property in California. Prior to his death, Tony suffered debilitating strokes that rendered him incapable of managing his financial affairs. Because his revocable living trust was correctly funded, his wife, as successor trustee, was empowered to oversee the day-to-day management of his financial affairs and his personal care without the necessity of a court-appointed guardian. Upon Tony's death, because the trustee of Tony's living trust was in title to the real property in California before Tony died, no ancillary probate of this property was required. Thus, Tony's wife, as successor trustee-beneficiary, continued to receive the monthly rental income from the property without a California probate court administering what she had already been doing for years before she and Tony created the living trust; namely, receiving and depositing the monthly rental checks into their bank account titled in the joint revocable living trust and keeping the books relative to the property in California.

How Probate Is Avoided with a Revocable Living Trust

Ask Your Attorney

Exactly how can property transferred to a revocable living trust during the trustor's lifetime avoid probate upon the trustor's death?

Answer

During the trustor's lifetime, he or she creates and correctly funds a revocable living trust wherein the trustor designates himself or herself (or another person) the trustee with an immediate family member (or corporate trustee) as successor trustee. Then the trustor conveys legal title to property from the trustor, as an individual person, to the trustee of the living trust agreement. In effect, if the trustor is acting as the initial trustee, legal title to the property will be in the trustor's name, as trustee, under the provisions of the revocable living trust agreement for the benefit of the trustor as primary beneficiary of the living trust agreement.

Upon the trustor's death, under the provisions of the trust agreement, the successor trustee distributes the trust estate to the beneficiaries named by the trustor in the trust agreement. Upon the trustor's death, probate proceedings are not required to transfer title to the property distributable to the trustor's named beneficiaries. This is because the successor trustee succeeds as the legal title owner of the property under the terms of the trust agreement which provide that the successor trustee is to distribute the property to the trustor's designated beneficiaries.

In effect, the successor trustee acts as the probate court. Thus, there is no need for a court-supervised administration of the trust estate to transfer title to property (assets) comprising the trust estate to the trustor's designated beneficiaries. Overall, the revocable living trust can provide continuity of property management if the trustor becomes physically or mentally incapacitated during lifetime; and, upon the trustor's death, this continuity of property management can continue for the trustor's beneficiaries without the necessity of probate court proceedings.

CHALLENGES BY DISGRUNTLED BENEFICIARIES

The notion exists that difficult beneficiaries cannot challenge the provisions of a revocable living trust agreement. This belief is unfounded. Generally, a living trust agreement is not a matter of public record and does not become part of a probate proceeding. However, any beneficiary of a revocable living trust agreement is entitled under the law of most states to a copy of the trust agreement upon the death of the trustor. If the trustee refuses to provide a beneficiary with a copy of the trust agreement, the beneficiary can petition a proper court of jurisdiction (usually a probate court) for relief.

Since the trust estate under a revocable living trust agreement is not, as a rule, subject to probate proceedings and, thus, not a matter of public record, disgruntled and would-be beneficiaries may certainly have a more difficult time learning about the nature and value of the decedent trustor's trust estate. Accordingly, a disgruntled person—whether or not a beneficiary of the revocable living trust agreement—could have a more difficult time proceeding against the trust estate. Nevertheless, a beneficiary with a legitimate claim against the trust estate or a complaint about the manner in which the trust estate is being administered by the trustee for the beneficiary is just as entitled to a court hearing on the merits of his or her claim or complaint as he or she would be entitled to if the same claim or complaint arose as the result of the beneficiary's interest under the decedent's Will.

Of course, an assertive trustee could possibly defuse a potential unwarranted challenge by a disgruntled beneficiary by not providing that person information about the trust agreement in a timely manner or by not furnishing the beneficiary information about the nature of the property comprising the trust estate. In some cases, the trustee's posture in such circumstances may be justified, especially if the beneficiary is merely saber rattling, has no legitimate complaint, and really does not intend to initiate a legal challenge to the provisions of the revocable living trust agreement pertaining to the beneficiary. There is often the person who just likes to be a pain in the pin feathers. If a member of the trustor's immediate family has a propensity for such behavior, then the trustor may be well advised to make special provision in the revocable living trust agreement so, if such a person initiates what amounts to a frivolous legal action against the trust estate, the trustee will be empowered to deal with the action accordingly. In this regard, the trustor may want to include a cost to beneficiary provision in the revocable living trust agreement (see file "APP0201.DOC" Article XII) .

RECORD OF PROPERTY OWNERSHIP

A revocable living trust can provide all of the tax and nontax benefits of owning property as joint tenants with right of survivorship (including tenants by the entirety), tenants in common, community property, or as separate property in one's individual name (including quasi-community property) without many of the associated disadvantages. When the legal title to property is conveyed to the trustee of a revocable living trust agreement, the trustee becomes the legal owner of the property. Strictly speaking, this means that, in whatever form the trustor owned the property before it was transferred to the trustee, such form of ownership no longer exists. In other words, the trustor will no longer own property as joint tenants with right of survivorship (including tenants by the entirety), or as tenants in common, or as community property, or as separate property in the trustor's individual name (including quasi-community property). This does not mean, however, that the character of such property changes. For example, husband and wife trustors may still treat property formerly owned by them as joint tenants with right of survivorship (including real property formerly owned as tenants by the entirety) as being owned by them fifty-fifty, as provided under I.R.C. Section 2040(b), or in any other fractional interest of their choosing. Similarly, husband and wife trustors may still treat property owned by them as community property, separate property, or as quasi-community property before the conveyance of the legal title to such property to their respective revocable living trust agreements or joint revocable living trust agreement as community property, separate property, or quasi-community property after their joint revocable living trust agreements or respective revocable living trusts are effected (see file "APP0205.DOC").

Form of Property Ownership before Revocable Living Trust Effected

A properly designed revocable living trust agreement should describe the form in which property was owned prior to conveyance of legal title to the property to the trustee of the living trust agreement (see file "APP0204.DOC" Article III). By doing so, all of the tax and nontax benefits associated with a particular form of property ownership can be preserved under the living trust agreement (see discussion in Chapter 2: Framework of a Revocable Living Trust, Trust Property: Article III pertaining to listing property on schedules). Another reason for describing the form of property ownership is so, in the event the trustor revokes and terminates the trust agreement, the trustor will have a record of exactly how the property was owned before the living trust agreement was created.

Benefits to Married Trustors

Keeping track of how property was owned before legal title is transferred to the revocable living trust can result in significant income and estate tax savings. In this regard, married individuals can effectively equalize the value of their respective estates for federal estate tax purposes without the disadvantages associated with retaining title to the property in one of the forms previously mentioned. This is accomplished by using a joint revocable living trust agreement or by each spouse effecting his or her own revocable living trust agreement. Regardless of whether a joint trust agreement or separate trusts are effected, each spouse retains testamentary control over the disposition of his or her property upon death without a probate proceeding.

Controlling Disposition of Property

Before effecting a revocable living trust, the trustor may have owned his or her property in one of the forms described above. Generally, separate property that is owned in a person's individual name (including quasi-community property), or as a tenant in common, or as community property, may be subject to probate upon the property owner's death. Of course, testamentary disposition of such property can be controlled through a Will. On the other hand, property owned as joints tenant with right of survivorship (including tenants by the entirety) is not subject to probate upon the first co-tenant's death. However, the decedent co-tenant cannot control the testamentary disposition of such property through his or her Will. This is because title to the property is vested by right of survivorship in the surviving co-tenant(s). Hence, title cannot pass to the beneficiaries under the decedent co-tenant's Will. However, by conveying title to property once owned as joint tenants with right of survivorship to the trustee of a revocable living trust agreement and severing the survivorship feature, the trustor can control upon his or her death the disposition of such property without losing any of the income and estate tax benefits associated with that form of property ownership.

Remember, if property is owned as a joint tenant with right of survivorship with another person(s), then, upon the first co-tenant's death, leaving the other co-tenant(s) surviving, the decedent co-tenant's interest in such property is not subject to a probate proceeding. However, upon the subsequent death of the surviving co-tenant (assuming only two initial co-tenants in title to the property), the property is deemed owned by the surviving co-tenant in his or her individual name and may be subject to a probate proceeding. This would be true unless the surviving co-tenant retitled the property in his or her name and the name of another person as joint tenants with right of survivorship, or conveyed legal title to the property to the trustee of a revocable living trust agreement.

Repository for Estate Owner's Property

Whether one is married or single, a revocable living trust can be a repository for all of a person's property, regardless of the form in which title to the property was held before the revocable living trust agreement was effected. Accordingly, the revocable living trust agreement becomes a written record of how the trustor owned property before executing the trust agreement and enables the trustor to control upon his or her death the disposition of the property (trust estate) without a probate proceeding. Furthermore, whether one is married or single, by conveying legal title to property to the trustee of a revocable living trust, the unnecessary financial expense, emotional trauma, and socially degrading and humiliating experience of a court-appointed guardian managing one's personal and financial affairs in the event of physical disability or mental incapacity can be avoided.

FEDERAL ESTATE TAX SAVINGS

Advertisements hail the revocable living trust as a way to "save thousands in unnecessary estate taxes." Clearly, the implication is that estate tax savings can only be achieved with a revocable living trust. This is absolute nonsense. Any estate tax savings that can be obtained with a revocable living trust can also be obtained under a Will, provided the decedent testator's property is subject to the distribution provisions of his or her Will; that is, the decedent testator dies with a *probate* estate. As a rule, all of the federal estate tax savings obtainable through a properly and skillfully prepared revocable living trust agreement are equally available in a well-designed testamentary trust that is established under the provisions of a person's Will or as a separate trust instrument.

DISINHERITING A FAMILY MEMBER

Ask Your Attorney

Is it possible to disinherit a child with a revocable living trust?

Answer

Yes.

Unless a person dies intestate (without a Will), under the laws of most states, children, as well as other ascendants and descendants of the decedent, do not have a statutory right to share in his or her estate. Accordingly, one can intentionally not provide for a child or any other ascendant or descendant (family member, immediate or otherwise) to share in his or her estate, either under the provisions of a Will or a revocable living trust agreement. Because a revocable living trust is generally not admitted to probate and, therefore, does not become a matter of public record, it may be easier to intentionally exclude a person from sharing in the trust estate with a revocable living trust than with a Will, which does become a matter of public record.

Disinheriting a person should be accomplished by commission—not by omission. In other words, the person who is to be *disinherited* should be intentionally named in the revocable living trust agreement (or Will, if a revocable living trust is not part of one's estate plan). In addition, a positive, rather than negative, explanation should be given for why such person is not to share in the trustor's trust estate; for example, "For reasons known only to _____, . . ." A negative explanation may be construed as a libelous act on the trustor's part, giving the excluded person grounds for a lawsuit against the trustor's trust estate.

Example

Esther determined to exclude her adopted adult daughter, Alice, from sharing in her trust estate and gave the following explanation for doing so: "Further provided, in view of Alice's choosing to seek-out her birth mother and, thence, choosing to slight Trustor, the mother who adopted her, and, in view of her determination to no longer use the family name '_____,' knowing that this has offended and hurt her mother (Trustor), no distributions of Trustor's trust estate shall be made to Alice. The above provision has been adopted after threats and demands have been made by Alice to the Trustor which, in the opinion of the Trustor, have been damaging to the Trustor's family relationship, and after the Trustor has taken time to consider the motives and impact of such actions and the consequences of the provision set forth herein."[31]

Most states do not permit spouses to disinherit one another. Nevertheless, for either federal estate tax planning purposes or for other reasons, one spouse may not want the other spouse to receive directly any part of his or her estate. Rather than causing the surviving spouse to elect against the decedent spouse's trust estate (or probate estate under his or her Will), a surviving spouse can effectively be prevented from having any legal ownership of the decedent spouse's property. This can be accomplished if the decedent spouse directs in a revocable living trust (or Will) that his or her property be distributable to a qualified terminable interest property (QTIP) trust or to a credit shelter trust (nonmarital deduction trust; by-pass trust; Trust "B") for the lifetime benefit of the surviving spouse.

Under both the QTIP trust and credit shelter trust, the surviving spouse can be given the lifetime use, benefit, and enjoyment of the income and principal of the trust estate but not possess legal ownership of the property comprising the trust. This makes it possible for the decedent spouse to control the ultimate disposition of the property comprising these trusts upon the subsequent death of the surviving spouse. Remember, though, with the QTIP trust, the value of the property comprising the QTIP trust estate is includable in the surviving spouse's gross estate for federal estate tax purposes.[32] As a rule, the value of property in a credit shelter trust is not included in the beneficiary's gross estate for federal estate tax purposes. This is true whether the beneficiary is a surviving spouse or any other individual.[33]

---

[31] See also file "APP0201.DOC" Article VI (C) (2).

[32] I.R.C. § 2044(b)(1)(A).

[33] I.R.C. § 2041(b)(1)(A); Treas. Reg. § 20.2041-1(c)(1).

CHAPTER 5

Disadvantages, Reservations, and Limitations of a Revocable Living Trust

OVERVIEW

Most everything in life has its advantages and disadvantages. This is certainly true with a revocable living trust. The extent to which a revocable living trust is a panacea for one's estate planning needs depends entirely on a person's estate planning objectives and the property funding the trust agreement.

To say that a revocable living trust is not for everyone because of its alleged disadvantages is misleading. Moreover, it is prejudicial to claim, without qualification, that a revocable living trust has certain disadvantages compared with distributing property under the provisions of a Will. In these regards, it is prudent to identify the alleged disadvantage and focus on why it exists. Is the disadvantage perceived or real? Does the disadvantage exist because of certain property that may be transferred to the revocable living trust, or is it because the trust agreement does not address a particular contingency with respect to that property? Or is the alleged disadvantage because of a condition imposed upon the trustee by the trustor regarding the management of that property?

The majority of alleged disadvantages associated with a revocable living trust are nothing more than a quirk of the property being transferred to the trust. Or a disadvantage may result if a certain provision designed to carry out a particular objective of the trustor is included in the trust agreement. Or certain real disadvantages may result simply because the trustor does not play with a full deck and fails to impart important information to the practitioner responsible for designing the trust agreement.

Generally, though, perceived disadvantages can be eliminated through the creative and attentive design of the estate plan. It is the estate planning adviser's responsibility to present and discuss with the estate owner acceptable options and solutions so that a perceived disadvantage is nothing more than just that—perceived, rather than real. Lastly, in the design of an estate plan, the matter of taxes should not become the tail that wags the dog.

NONTAX DISADVANTAGES

Careful consideration must be given to whether an alleged disadvantage is real, perceived, or is simply being used by an attorney not qualified to practice estate planning, let alone design, prepare, and implement a revocable living trust agreement, as an excuse for not wanting his or her client to effect a revocable living trust as a substitute for a Will. The attorney may be hopeful that he or she will be called upon to probate the client's estate. Even attorneys not qualified to practice estate planning do know that a properly designed and correctly funded revocable living trust agreement can obviate the need for a court-supervised financial guardianship of a person's financial affairs during lifetime and eliminate the need for probate upon the estate owner's death.

Unfortunately, too many attorneys answer clients' questions not with responses based on the law but rather based on the fact that they are attorneys. Correct answers to questions are not based on what a person is but rather on the facts relevant to the questions. The answer to a question is not *right* or *wrong* solely on the basis of a person's profession. Rather, the answer must be founded in fact—not because the person answering the question is of a particular profession. Furthermore, what might be an alleged disadvantage of a revocable living trust to one person may not, in fact, be a real disadvantage to another person's situation.

Amendments Cannot Hide Original Trust Provisions

It has been alleged that trust amendments fail to conceal what was provided in the prior trust agreement.[1] The concern here is that a person who has been deleted as a beneficiary will know that they were previously a beneficiary because the original trust agreement reveals that fact. Or a beneficiary's share might be reduced from what was initially provided in the trust agreement. The notion is that it is easier and less expensive to make a new Will than a new revocable living trust.

This thinking is fallacious for at least two reasons. First, even if a Will is amended by a codicil, the original Will remains in effect. Secondly, the testator's legal capacity to effect a new Will may be questioned. If so, the entire Will may be declared void; whereas, if a codicil was effected, only that codicil may be declared void. A brief explanation in the amendment to the revocable living trust as to why a particular beneficiary's share is being altered can go a long way in defusing animosity or misunderstanding on the part of the beneficiary as to why his or her interest in the trust estate has been diminished.

In response to the allegation that trust amendments become unwieldy, so can codicils to a Will. As a rule of thumb, whenever a trustor effects four amendments to a revocable living trust agreement, a restatement of the entire living trust agreement should be prepared and executed. Generally, except for the deletion or addition of a personal representative, or other administrative changes, the trustor's original pour-over Will remains in full force and effect. This reduces or entirely eliminates the possibility of a trustor's legal capacity to make a Will being challenged.

This is an important consideration because, generally, a revocable living trust agreement standing alone is not considered to be a valid testamentary instrument for the disposition of a person's estate. This is because the execution of a revocable living trust usually does not conform to the requirements for the execution of Wills. However, most states have either adopted the Uniform Testamentary Additions to Trust Act or recognize the doctrine of incorporation by reference. Simply stated, the Uniform Testamentary Additions to Trusts Act provides that a valid devise or bequest may be made to the trustee of a trust, provided the trust is identified in the testator's Will and the terms of the trust are set forth in a written instrument. Such a trust instrument may be effected before or concurrently with the execution of the testator's Will or in the valid Will of a person who has predeceased the testator. Funding a revocable living trust agreement with a pour-over Will is discussed in Chapter 18, Power of Attorney and Pour-Over Will.

---

[1] Paul B. Sargent, *Facts and Fallacies of Living Trusts*, The Fifth Annual Philip E. Heckerling Institute on Estate Planning, University of Miami Law Center (1971): ¶ 71.203, 2-6 (hereafter Sargent, *Facts and Fallacies of Living Trusts.*)

Allocation of Receipts, Expenditures, Income, and Principal

If a revocable living trust is not correctly or completely funded, complex issues may arise between the trustor's probate estate and the trust estate under the revocable living trust as to the allocation of receipts, expenditures, income, and principal. Such issues can be mitigated initially by the careful design of the trust agreement in coordination with the trustor's Will and the manner in which the trustor determines to distribute property not otherwise disposed of under the revocable living trust agreement.

Apportionment of Taxes

Strict attention must be given to the matter of how taxes are to be paid on the value of property included in a person's *taxable* estate. In this regard, most Wills provide for the payment of taxes out of the residue of the decedent's estate. If part of the property comprising the decedent's gross estate passes to beneficiaries under the decedent's Will (probate estate) and to other beneficiaries outside the decedent's Will (nonprobate estate; e.g., by right of survivorship, by contract, to a beneficiary under a Totten trust, or under the provisions of a revocable living trust agreement), that part of the decedent's estate intended to pass to the beneficiaries under the decedent's Will can be decimated by the payment of taxes. In effect, the beneficiaries who were to receive part of the probate estate under the decedent's Will may receive much less than those beneficiaries receiving the decedent's nonprobate estate—all due to the noncoordination of the payment of taxes between the probate estate and nonprobate estate. This result can be avoided if the estate planning advisor takes seriously one's estate planning objectives when designing and coordinating the provisions of the pour-over Will and revocable living trust agreement.

Example

When Henry died, his Will named five individuals to share his probate estate. The value of Henry's gross estate was $1,120,000; of this amount, $420,000 was distributable under the terms of his Will (probate estate). The balance of his estate ($700,000) passed to Margaret (his live-in lady friend of more than twenty years) outside his Will by right of survivorship and by individual Totten trusts—a form of living trust (nonprobate estate). Henry directed in his Will that, ". . . my just debts and funeral expenses be promptly paid. I direct my Personal Representative to treat as an obligation of my estate and to pay, without any apportionment thereof other than that hereinafter specified, all estate, inheritance, or other death taxes or duties imposed and made payable by reason of my death . . . and, if any other person shall pay any such tax, my Personal Representative shall reimburse such person." The net effect of this language caused Henry's probate estate to bear the burden of all taxes, while Margaret received the lion's share of Henry's estate without being reduced by such taxes. Because neither Henry nor his attorney discussed the matter of the source of property from which the taxes were to be paid, it is reasonable to assume that Henry believed that the taxes would be charged against his entire *estate*—not just his *probate* estate. Like most people, Henry probably did not understand the difference between his *probate* estate and *nonprobate* estate and the role of each relative to the source of property for the payment of estate tax. It is interesting to note that Henry's attorney admitted that he didn't know anything about tax apportionment!

Consequently, the five individuals named as beneficiaries under Henry's Will received much less of his *probate* estate than they might have received had his Will provided for apportionment of taxes among the property passing both under (*probate* estate) and outside (*nonprobate* estate) of his Will. The same mistake is often made when a revocable living trust is used as a Will substitute but is not funded or is incorrectly funded. When an estate plan provides that property comprising the estate owner's gross estate is to be distributed under his or her Will, under his or her revocable living trust, by beneficiary designation in a contract, and by right of survivorship, and the estate owner wants all of his or her beneficiaries to share in the payment of taxes, then the appropriate tax apportionment language should be used in both the revocable living trust and Will (see files "APP0501.DOC" through "APP0504.DOC").[2]

Succession of Property Interests

With respect to trusts, the laws of most states do not address the issues concerning succession of property interests. In this regard, state statutes only provide for the distribution of property if a person dies with or without a Will. As a rule, similar statutory provisions do not apply with regard to trusts.

Divorce or Annulment of Marriage

If, after executing a Will, the testator is subsequently divorced or the marriage is annulled, the divorce or annulment revokes any disposition or appointment of property made by the Will to the former spouse,[3] unless otherwise provided in the Will or divorce decree.[4] It is not uncommon in such cases for state law to presume that the former spouse deceased the testator.[5]

Under a revocable living trust, if the trustor is subsequently divorced or the marriage is annulled, the divorce or annulment does not revoke any disposition or appointment of property made in the trust agreement to the former spouse. Thus, unless the trust agreement is amended after the trustor's divorce or annulment of the marriage, or the divorce decree addresses the rights of the former spouse under the trust agreement, the former spouse, even though divorced from the decedent trustor, remains a beneficiary of the trust agreement. Such a result, if not intended by the trustor, can wreak havoc on an otherwise well-designed estate plan.

The trustor may mitigate or entirely eliminate such a result by: amending the trust agreement following a divorce or annulment of marriage; or, in the initial design of the revocable living trust agreement, by specifically identifying his or her spouse by name, instead of generically referring to that person as "trustor's spouse," along with a statement to the effect that all references to trustor's spouse shall be to the person named and that, in the event of a divorce or annulment of the marriage, all provisions pertaining to said spouse are void; or by giving an attorney-in-fact under a durable power of attorney a limited power to amend the trust agreement with respect to substituting a new spouse for a previous spouse as the result of divorce, provided state law authorizes an attorney-in-fact to amend a revocable living trust agreement on behalf of the trustor.

Absent a provision in the revocable living trust agreement to the contrary, or the power in an attorney-in-fact under a durable power of attorney to amend a revocable living trust agreement on behalf of the trustor, a revocable living trust cannot be amended if the trustor becomes legally incapacitated. With this in mind, a former spouse could remain as a bene-

---

[2] "APP0501.DOC" through "APP0504.DOC" may be read in concert with "APP0201.DOC" through "APP0204.DOC").

[3] See, for example, Wyo. Stat. Ann. § 2-6-118 (Loislaw 2001); Mont. Code Ann. § 72-2-82 (Loislaw 2001); Or. Rev. Stat. § 112.315 (Loislaw 2001).

[4] See, for example, Md. Code § 4-105(4) (Loislaw 2001).

[5] See, for example, Or. Rev. Stat. § 112.315 (Loislaw 2001).

ficiary under the trust agreement, unless the former spouse's rights under the trust agreement were terminated by the court in granting the decree of marital dissolution or the court allows the revocable living trust to be partially or entirely revoked on petition by the incapacitated trustor's guardian. Of course, the value of property distributable to or continued in trust for the former surviving spouse does not qualify for the federal estate tax marital deduction in the decedent trustor's gross estate.

Amendment of Revocable Living Trust by Trustee

Most state statutes provide that, from the time a trust agreement is created until final distribution of the trust estate, a trustee has the power to perform, without court authorization, every act that a prudent person would perform for the purposes of the trust.

Ask Your Attorney

May a trustee be empowered to amend a revocable living trust agreement if the trustor becomes legally incapacitated?

Answer

Absent specific state law to the contrary, a trustee can be given the power to amend the trust agreement on behalf of the trustor.

In this regard, a disinterested trustee—that is, a trustee not subservient to the trustor within the meaning of a related or subordinate party under I.R.C. Section 672(c)—may be given the power to amend the trust agreement for specified purposes during the trustor's life. For example, if the trustor anticipates that a dissolution of his or her marriage could occur in the future because of present or previous marital discord, the trustor could empower the trustee to amend the trust agreement to delete a former spouse and redirect the distribution of the former spouse's share of the trust estate among the trustor's other beneficiaries. By including such a provision in the trust agreement, the trustor would not have to rely on the provisions of a divorce decree to eliminate the former spouse as a beneficiary of his or her revocable living trust. A similar provision could operate to permit the successor trustee to designate a new spouse of the trustor in a situation where the trustor remarries but becomes incapacitated before amending the trust agreement to include the new spouse as a beneficiary of the trust estate. To ensure that such a power in the successor trustee, who is also a beneficiary of the trust estate, is not interpreted as a general power of appointment, the trustor would be well advised to give such power to a disinterested trustee (the role of a disinterested trustee is discussed in Chapter 2, Framework of a Revocable Living Trust, § 2.4).

Control of Property by Former Spouses

Incidentally, a divorced individual can continue to benefit from the former deceased spouse's estate if property was owned during the marriage as joint tenants with right of survivorship and the former spouse's name is not removed from the deed. Upon the death of the first former spouse to die, the former surviving spouse is in legal title to the property by virtue of surviving the decedent. Such a result can be avoided if, at the time of the divorce, the decree of divorce provides that all property formerly owned as joint tenants with right of survivorship will be owned by the parties subsequent to the divorce as tenants in common. Under this ownership arrangement, each former spouse has control over the testamentary disposition of his or her undivided interest in the property. Such interest may be disposed of by Will or may be transferred to a revocable living trust. Likewise, with regard to life insurance on the lives of married individuals, if, subsequent to a divorce, a spouse whose life was insured dies, his or her former spouse, who was designated beneficiary of the life insurance proceeds, can still receive those proceeds if the decedent spouse did not change the beneficiary designation subsequent to the divorce and before the occurrence of his or her death. This same result can occur with other contract benefits.

Claim Period for Creditors

In most states, the period in which creditors have to file claims against the probate estate is limited by statute. As a general rule, no such limitation applies to the trust estate under a revocable living trust. Similarly, payment of creditor's claims against the probate estate is subject to a statutory hierarchy of priority, meaning that the availability of property for the support of a surviving spouse and children of the decedent has priority over the payment of creditors' claims. A decedent trustor's trust estate under a revocable living trust is not afforded this same protection.[6]

Furthermore, a creditor's claim against the probate estate may be disallowed or barred in its entirety if the claim is not filed within the statutory claim period. Absent probate of the decedent's Will, the certain elimination of creditors' claims against the trustor's trust estate under a revocable living trust is not available. However, on the one hand, this disadvantage may not be important, if the decedent's estate is not likely to be subject to creditors' claims. On the other hand, if the estate owner is at risk with respect to potential creditors' claims, then it may be advantageous to intentionally expose a portion of the estate to probate administration; in other words, be selective in the type and amount of property that would otherwise be transferred to the revocable living trust. Of course, the trustee could always admit the trust estate to a probate proceeding to toll the statute of limitations on creditors' claims.

Disposition of Tangible Personal Property

Listing items of tangible personal property to be distributed to beneficiaries under a revocable living trust agreement may not be practical. For example, if the trustor is a collector of, say, antiques or museum quality art objects, the trustor may not have determined the beneficiaries of such property at the time the trust agreement is effected. Such dispositions may be more appropriately made in a letter that is incorporated by reference into the trust agreement. By using a letter, the trustor is afforded the freedom of changing his or her mind without the necessity of effecting an amendment to the trust agreement.

Whether such a letter will be given legal effect depends on state law. Some state statutes require a separate writing identifying the disposition of tangible personal property. Usually, it is provided that a Will may refer to a written statement (e.g., a letter) or list to dispose of items of tangible personal property, other than money, not otherwise specifically disposed of by the Will. Tangible personal property is generally recognized as, but not limited to, household furniture and furnishings, other like home contents or of any vacation property, wearing apparel, jewelry, personal effects, books, art objects, collections, sporting and recreational equipment, stamp and coin collections, any automobile, equipment, machinery (including farm equipment, machinery, and implements), tools, and all other tangible personal property for personal use and purposes.

---

[6] *See* Clifton B. Kruse, Jr., "Revocable Trusts: Creditors' Rights After Settlor-debtor's Death," 7 *Probate & Property* 40 (Nov./Dec. 1993).

As a rule, to be considered evidence of one's intention, such a writing disposing of tangible personal property must describe the items and the identity of the recipients with reasonable certainty and be dated and signed. Whether a reference in a revocable living trust agreement to such a separate writing disposing of tangible personal property has legal effect depends on state law. Generally, such statutes provide that, "A will may refer to a written statement or list to dispose of items of tangible personal property not otherwise specifically disposed of by the will."[7] Even in the absence of statutory direction, it seems reasonable that, if a written statement regarding the disposition of tangible personal property is referred to in both a properly coordinated pour-over Will and revocable living trust agreement, such a written statement would be given legal effect.

Preserving Eligibility for Medicaid Benefits

Property cannot be sheltered in a revocable living trust in order to qualify for Medicaid benefits. Such a trust is considered a Medicaid qualifying trust, and the income and principal of the trust is considered a resource to the trustor (grantor) against which the trustor's eligibility for Medicaid benefits is measured.[8] The term *Medicaid qualifying trust* is a misnomer, in that it is not a trust wherein the property of the trust estate permits the trustor (grantor) to qualify for Medicaid benefits. Rather, it is just the opposite. A Medicaid qualifying trust is a trust, or similar device, established (other than by Will) by an individual (or an individual's spouse), under which the individual may be the beneficiary of all or part of the payments from the trust and the distribution of such payments is determined by one or more trustees who are permitted to exercise any discretion with respect to the distribution to the individual.[9] Apparently, if a Medicaid trust is established for an individual by another individual's Will, then the property comprising the trust estate may not be considered a resource to the beneficiary and may not be counted in determining the individual's eligibility for Medicaid benefits.[10]

If the trustor intends to provide for a supplemental needs trust for an incapacitated contingent beneficiary under a revocable living trust upon the trustor's death, consideration must be given to the definitions of *income* and *resources* under both state law and the Social Security Administration. To ensure the contingent beneficiary's continued eligibility for Medicaid, supplemental security income (SSI), and supplemental disability income (SDI) benefits, it is imperative that the assets of the supplemental needs trust not be used in any manner whatsoever which could be interpreted as being available to or for the beneficiary's support and maintenance. The words *support* and *maintenance* are almost synonymous with respect to their usage relative to one's eligibility for Medicaid, SSI, and SDI benefits. Even the term *supplemental needs* may be construed as support and maintenance. Hence, the special needs trust for the beneficiary should be a fully discretionary trust as to both income and principal distributions.[11] Moreover, in lieu of the term *supplemental needs*, it may be better to use the term *special needs*.

In this regard, distributions of income and principal from the trust for the beneficiary's special needs should be in the sole and absolute discretion of the trustee. The language,

---

[7] *See*, e.g., Mont. Code Ann. § 72-2-533 (Loislaw 2001).

[8] 42 USC § 1396a(k)(1).

[9] 42 USC § 1396a(k)(2).

[10] 42 USC § 1396a(k)(1).

[11] *See*, Clifton B. Kruse, Jr., "Medicaid Considerations for Lawyers Representing the Upper Crust," The Thirty-Third Annual Philip E. Heckerling Institute on Estate Planning. University of Miami Law Center (1999): Chapter 7, at ¶ 702.3, 7-29 (hereafter Kruse, Jr., "Medicaid Considerations for Lawyers").

"funds available from other sources," (see file "APP0201.DOC" Article VI (D) (1)) ▨ con-templates both federal and state benefits without saying so. The inclusion of the language, "to the extent sources of funds are otherwise available," should not cause the trustee to be compelled to pay or apply for the contingent beneficiary's benefit income or principal of the trust estate for food, shelter, routine medical care and drug expenses, clothing, reasonable and necessary transportation or motor vehicle expenses, utilities, household expenses, health and other ordinary and customary items needed for the beneficiary's maintenance[12] which might otherwise cause the beneficiary to be ineligible for government benefits.

Moreover, the discretion of the trustee to pay or apply for the benefit of the beneficiary income and principal should be expressed in discretionary terms and not as a direction on the part of the trustor. In this regard, "Trustee *may* pay or apply for the benefit of the beneficiary, . . . all or any part of the trust principal or income as the Trustee *may* in the Trustee's sole and absolute discretion find advisable to meet [the beneficiary's] special needs" (emphasis added) (see file "APP0201.DOC" Article VI (D) (2)), ▨ rather than a direction that the trustee must pay or apply income or principal for the benefit of the beneficiary. If the trustee is *directed* to pay or apply for the benefit of the beneficiary income or principal of the trust estate, such a direction may be interpreted as a legal obligation of the trustee to pay or apply income or principal for the benefit of the beneficiary. If the trustee is legally obligated to do something, then conceivably, the trustee can be compelled to make distributions of income or principal to or for the benefit of the beneficiary which, in turn, could compromise the purpose of the special needs trust and cause the beneficiary to be ineligible for government benefits. By using the discretionary term *may*, the trustee should not be legally compelled to perform an act that the trustee is not legally obligated to perform.[13]

The trustor's intention to create a purely discretionary special needs fund should be clearly stated in the special needs trust under the revocable living trust agreement so as not to create the impression that such fund is a substitute for funds available from other sources to provide for the beneficiary's special needs. The term *special needs* means those extraordinary things the special needs beneficiary cannot afford to purchase, activities in which the beneficiary cannot afford to participate, places that the beneficiary cannot visit, schooling and special equipment that the beneficiary cannot otherwise afford, cultural experiences that are beyond the beneficiary's means, companionship and social relationships that the beneficiary cannot afford—all due to the beneficiary's financial means and station of life. The term *special needs* includes extraordinary expenditures for the beneficiary's comfort above and beyond those which the beneficiary's station of life and financial means affords the beneficiary.

Moreover, the trustor should make it unequivocally clear that it is not trustor's intention to displace funds available from other sources that may otherwise be available to the beneficiary. The term *special needs* as used in the special needs trust under the revocable living trust agreement should not include food, shelter, routine medical care and drug expenses, clothing, reasonable and necessary transportation or motor vehicle expenses, utilities, household expenses, health and other ordinary and customary items needed for the beneficiary's maintenance[14] to the extent sources of funds are otherwise available (see file "APP0201.DOC" Article VI (D) (1)). ▨ Lastly, trustor should expressly provide that the special needs trust estate shall not be interpreted as, nor constitute, a legal life estate (see file "APP0201.DOC" Article VI (D) (3)). ▨

---

[12] *See* 20 C.F.R. § 404.366(a)(1) and (2) and (b).

[13] It is imperative that the trustor consults qualified legal counsel in these regards, especially, with respect to state law definitions of income and resources for Medicaid, SSI, and SDI eligibility.

[14] *See* 20 C.F.R. § 404.366(a)(1) and (2) and (b).

Environmental Liability

Under federal environmental laws, the trustee (defendant) of a revocable living trust may be liable for toxic clean-up costs associated with property transferred to the trust.[15] A *defendant* is not liable for such costs if the property is acquired under the terms of the decedent's Will.[16] However, with respect to a revocable living trust, the trustee is not liable for the clean-up costs if, at the time the defendant (trustee) acquired the facility, the trustee did not know and had no reason to know that any hazardous substance was disposed of on, in, or at the property.[17] To establish that the trustee (defendant) had no reason to know that a hazardous substance existed on the property, the trustee must have undertaken, at the time of acquiring the property, all appropriate inquiry into the previous ownership and uses of the property consistent with good commercial or customary practice in an effort to minimize liability.[18] If the trustor owns property that he or she suspects or knows is contaminated, legal title to the property should not be conveyed to the trustee of a revocable living trust. Instead, such property should be made a part of the trustor's probate estate so that it will pass to his or her beneficiary(ies) under the terms of the decedent's Will. By doing so, neither the personal representative nor the beneficiary may be liable for the cost of toxic clean-up.[19]

ALLEGED TAX DISADVANTAGES

When determining whether to convey legal title to certain property to the trustee of a revocable living trust, the reality of an alleged tax disadvantage must be taken into account. In other words, is the so-called disadvantage real or perceived? Furthermore, with respect to any one particular real disadvantage, the trustor must inquire about the likelihood of his or her estate ever really being affected by that alleged disadvantage. In this regard, the trustor must focus on the type of property being transferred to the trustee of the revocable living trust and how the trustor's estate planning objectives, if incorporated into the revocable living trust, might be impacted by any of the real or alleged tax disadvantages.[20]

Gifts Made within Three Years of Trustor's Death

Generally, the value of property gifted from a decedent trustor's revocable living trust made within three years of the decedent's death is not includable in the decedent trustor's gross estate, provided the trustor has retained no rights with respect to the transfers.[21] One must remember, though, this is not true for a transfer to a third party by the trustee of the incidents of ownership in a life insurance policy on the life of the trustor within three years of the insured trustor's death. Such a transfer by the trustee causes the value of the life insurance policy to be included in the decedent insured trustor's gross estate.[22]

---

[15] 42 USC § 9601(35)(A).

[16] 42 USC § 9601(35)(A)(iii).

[17] 42 USC § 9601(35)(A)(i).

[18] 42 USC § 9601(35)(B).

[19] *See* 42 USC § 9601(35)(A)(iii).

[20] Moy, 2, *A Practitioner's Guide to Estate Planning*, §29.07[B], at 29-56.

[21] I.R.C. § 2035(e).

[22] I.R.C. § 2035(a)(2).

Real Property Tax Exemptions

Homestead property tax exemptions for real property owned and used by a person may not be available if such property is titled in the name of a trustee of a revocable living trust. Likewise, if the legal title to property otherwise subject to a homestead exemption is conveyed to the trustee of a revocable living trust, the exemption may no longer be available as against the trustor's creditors. However, state law should be consulted to determine whether this issue is relevant to one's particular situation.[23]

Real Property Transfer Tax

Some states, individual counties, and other local taxing jurisdictions within a state may impose a tax on the transfer of real property. This tax is not exclusive to a revocable living trust. Generally, a transfer of real property means and includes every grant, sale, contract for sale, exchange, assignment, quitclaim, or other conveyance of ownership in or title to real property. Of course, exemptions usually apply to such a transfer tax. The transfer of real property to a revocable living trust may be exempt from the transfer tax if the selling price of the property is less than a certain statutory amount. The transfer tax may not apply if the transfer is considered a mere change in identity, form, place, or organization. The latter exception might apply where a husband and wife own real property as tenants by the entirety and convey title to the property to themselves as co-trustees of their joint revocable living trust or their respective separate revocable living trusts. Under this scenario, when the grantors (trustors) are the same in number and identity as the grantees (e.g., trustees), no change in identity occurs; and the transfer tax may not apply. Or a transfer of real property without consideration may be exempt from transfer tax. Such an exception would certainly apply to funding a revocable living trust because, as a rule, property is conveyed to a revocable living trust without consideration.

Furthermore, such transfer taxes may apply only to a *fee simple interest* in real property. When a titleholder has a fee simple estate (interest) in property, no other form of title right is held by anyone else. In the case of a revocable living trust, the trustee is in legal title to the property; and the beneficiary is in equitable title to the property. Since more than one person is in title to the property, the trustee holds less than an absolute fee simple interest in the property.

When the title to real property is conveyed to the trustee of a revocable living trust, the trustee has a *base fee estate*, which is less than a fee simple estate (interest) in the real property. In this regard, the trustor retains a beneficial, reversionary, and revocable interest in the trust estate property. Any local taxing jurisdiction that imposes a real property transfer tax on a *fee simple interest* should be challenged as to its authority to impose such tax on the conveyance of the title to real property to a revocable living trust wherein the trustee has a *base fee estate*.

Recommendation

In cases where this issue might arise, the following, as the case may require, should be inscribed in bold letters on every instrument (e.g., Bargain and Sale Deed, Warranty Deed, Grantor Deed (see, e.g., file "APP1001.DOC" Warranty Deed—Individual to Trustee)) ✍ effecting a conveyance of the title to real property to the trustee of a revocable living trust:

---

[23] Moy, 2, *A Practitioner's Guide to Estate Planning*, § 29.07[B][2], at 29-57.

1. **THIS AGREEMENT DOES NOT CONVEY A FEE SIMPLE INTEREST IN THE HEREIN DE-SCRIBED REAL PROPERTY AND IS NOT SUBJECT TO TRANSFER TAX UNDER _____ COUNTY (STATE) CODE SEC._____; or**

2. **INTRAFAMILY TRANSFER. NO MONETARY CONSIDERATION. NO TITLE SEARCH. THIS TRANSFER IS BEING MADE TO EFFECT AN ESTATE PLAN. GRANTOR IS TRUSTEE OF THE _____ REVOCABLE LIVING TRUST AGREEMENT CONVEYING PROPERTY HERSELF (HIMSELF) AS TRUSTEE OF THE RESTATEMENT OF THE _____ REVOCABLE LIVING TRUST AGREEMENT, DATED _____; or**

3. **INTRAFAMILY TRANSFER. NO MONETARY CONSIDERATION. NO TITLE SEARCH. THIS TRANSFER IS BEING MADE TO EFFECT AN ESTATE PLAN. GRANTOR IS SETTLOR (TRUSTOR) OF THE TRUST, TRUSTEE OF THE TRUST, AND PRIMARY BENEFICIARY.**

Revaluation of Real Property

Some states and local taxing jurisdictions may reappraise real property when a change of ownership occurs.

Ask Your Attorney

Will a transfer of real property to a revocable living trust cause a change in the assessed value of the property?

Answer

The answer to this question depends on state law or the law of the taxing jurisdiction. However, it is not uncommon for such a transfer to be exempt from reappraisal for purposes of local property taxes.

Further in this regard, the conveyance of legal title to real property to the trustee of a revocable living trust may not be regarded as a change in ownership if:

- The trustor-transferor is the primary beneficiary of the trust; provided, however, a change in ownership of trust property may be deemed to occur to the extent that persons other than the trustor-transferor are current beneficiaries of the trust; or

- The transferor is the trustor, and the trust is revocable by the trustor; provided, however, a change of ownership may occur at the time the revocable living trust becomes irrevocable, unless the trustor-transferor remains or becomes the primary beneficiary. Under this exception, the trust becomes irrevocable at the trustor's death; and it may be deemed irrevocable if the trustor becomes legally incapacitated. But, even in such instance, if the trustor is the primary beneficiary, then a change of ownership may not be deemed to occur; or

- The trustor-transferor retains reversionary rights over the property conveyed to the trustee, and the beneficial interests of persons other than the trustor-transferor do not exceed the duration of a certain period; or

- The taxing jurisdiction's exemption afforded interspousal transfers is applicable; provided, however, a change of ownership of trust property may occur to the extent that persons other than the trustor-transferor's spouse are beneficiaries of the trust; or

- The transfer is to a trust that results in the proportional interests of the beneficiaries in the property remaining the same before and after the transfer.

In most cases, the termination of a revocable living trust, or a portion of it, does not result in a change of ownership for purposes of reassessing the value of real property transferred to the trust when:

- Termination results in the distribution of trust property according to the terms of the trust to a person or entity who received a present interest (either use of or income from the property), causing a reappraisal when the trust was created or when it became irrevocable; provided, however, another change in ownership may occur when the remainder or reversionary interest becomes possessory, if the holder of that interest is a person or entity other than the present beneficiary; or
- Termination results from the trustor-transferor's exercise of the power of revocation, and the property is transferred by the trustee back to the trustor-transferor; or
- The trust did not exceed a certain statutory duration; and, on termination, the property reverts to the trustor-transferor; or
- The exemption afforded interspousal transfers is applicable; or
- Termination results in the transfer to the beneficiaries who receive the same proportional interests in the property as they held before the termination of the trust.

In view of the foregoing, the value of real property transferred to a revocable living trust may not be reappraised for real property tax purposes. Also, a higher assessed value should not be levied upon the property when it passes for the benefit of the survivor of married trustors. Conceivably, however, a higher assessed value could be levied in the future for reasons unrelated to a transfer of the title to a revocable living trust agreement. Those reasons could arise regardless of whether title to real property is conveyed to a revocable living trust or to another person or entity.

Reporting Income after Trustor's Death

A decedent's probate estate is permitted to select a fiscal year for reporting taxable income.[24] But a revocable living trust must use a calendar year.[25] Accordingly, a beneficiary cannot defer federal income tax on trust income after the trustor's death. This is because, in most cases, the taxpayer beneficiary and trust are both calendar-year taxpayers.[26] However, both a decedent's estate and a revocable living trust, which is primarily responsible for paying taxes, debts, and expenses of administration of the decedent's estate, are not required to pay estimated taxes for taxable years ending within two years of the decedent's death.[27]

Trustee Personally Liable for Payment of Estate Tax

The trustee of a revocable living trust (as well as a testamentary trust) and a personal representative under a decedent's Will are both personally liable for unpaid estate tax.[28] How-

---

[24] S. Rep. No. 99-313, 99th Cong., 2d Sess. 872, fn. 3 (1986).

[25] I.R.C. § 644(a).

[26] *See* I.R.C. § 662(c).

[27] I.R.C. § 6654(1)(2).

[28] I.R.C. § 6901; Treas. Reg. § 301.6901-1(b).

ever, both can be released from personal liability.[29] If the foregoing is a perceived disadvantage of using a revocable living trust to minimize federal estate tax, instead of using a Will, then it is erroneous, because the personal liability is the same for the trustee and the personal representative.[30]

Income Set Aside for Charity

As a general rule, a trust is denied a federal income tax deduction for gross income permanently set-aside for a qualified charitable organization.[31] Whether an amount has been permanently set-aside for a qualified charity depends upon the terms of the trust or the decedent's will.[32] However, if both the executor (if any) of the decedent's estate and the trustee of a qualified revocable trust (QRT) elect to have the revocable living trust treated as part of the decedent's estate for federal income tax purposes, such trust will be treated and taxed as part of the decedent's estate and not as a separate trust during the election period.[33] The decedent is the individual who was treated as the owner of the QRT under I.R.C. Section 676 on the date of that individual's death.[34]

Observation

For purposes of making the election, a person who has actual or constructive possession of property of the decedent is not an executor, unless that person is also appointed or qualified as an executor, administrator, or personal representative of the decedent's estate. If more that one jurisdiction has appointed an executor, the executor appointed in the domiciliary or primary proceeding is the executor of the related estate.[35] A related estate is the estate of the decedent (e.g., the trustor) who was treated as the owner of the QRT on the date of the decedent's death.[36]

The election period is the period of time during which an electing trust is treated and taxed as part of its related estate. An electing trust is a QRT for which a valid election under I.R.C. Section 645 has been made.[37] Once an I.R.C. Section 645 election has been made for the trust, the trust will be treated as an electing trust throughout the entire election period. The election period begins on the date of the decedent's death and terminates on the earlier of the day on which both the electing trust and related estate, if any, have distributed all of their assets, or the day before the applicable date. The election does not apply to suc-

---

[29] I.R.C. § 6905(a) and (c) and 2204(a) and (b). I.R.C. Sec. 2204(b) addresses the procedure a trustee must follow to be relieved of personal liability.

[30] I.R.C. § 2002; Treas. Reg. § 20.2002-1; Moy, 2, *A Practitioner's Guide to Estate Planning*, § 29.07[B][6] at 29-58.

[31] I.R.C. § 642(c)(2), (3); Treas. Reg. § 1.642(c)-2(b), (c).

[32] I.R.C. § 642(c)(2).

[33] I.R.C. § 645(a) (I.R.C. § 646 was renumbered as I.R.C. § 645 in the *Internal Revenue Service Restructuring and Reform Act of 1998*, Pub. L. No. 105-206, 105th Cong., 2d Sess. (22 July 1998), 112 Stat 685); Treas. Reg. § 1.645-1(a) and (b)(6) (December 24, 2002). *See* Edwin G. Fee, Jr., "Electing to Treat a Revocable Trust as Part of the Estate," 26 *Estate Planning* 118 (March/April 1999).

[34] Treas. Reg. § 1.645-1(b)(3) (December 24, 2002).

[35] Treas. Reg. § 1.645-1(b)(4) (December 24, 2002).

[36] Treas. Reg. § 1.645-1(b)(5) (December 24, 2002).

[37] Treas. Reg. § 1.645-1(b)(2) (December 24, 2002).

cessor trusts (trusts that are distributees under the trust instrument; e.g., qualified terminable interest property trust (QTIP), general power of appointment marital deduction trust, credit shelter trust, and so forth).[38] The rules for determining the duration of the election period are found in the treasury regulations.[39] This elective treatment is effective from the date of the decedent's death until two years after the decedent's death, if no federal estate tax return is required to be filed, or six months after the final determination of federal estate tax liability, if a federal estate tax return is required (*the applicable date*).[40]

The date of final determination of liability is the earliest of the following: (1) the date that is six months after the issuance by the IRS of an estate tax closing letter, unless a claim for refund with respect to the estate tax is filed within twelve months after the issuance of the letter; (2) the date of a final disposition of a claim for refund, as defined in the treasury regulations[41] that resolves the liability for the estate tax, unless suit is instituted within six months after a final disposition of the claim; (3) the date of execution of a settlement agreement with the IRS which determines the liability for the estate tax; (4) the date of issuance of a decision, judgment, decree, or other order by a proper court of jurisdiction resolving the liability for the estate tax, unless a notice of appeal or a petition for *certiorari* is filed within ninety days after the issuance of a decision, judgment, decree, or other order of a court; or (5) the date of expiration of the period of limitations for assessment of the estate tax provided in I.R.C. Section 6501.[42]

An electing trust and related estate are permitted to file a single, combined U.S. Fiduciary Income Tax Return (Form 1041). Nevertheless, the electing trust and related estate continue to be separate taxpayers for purposes of trust and estate administration (under Subtitle F of the Code, Procedure and Administration); and the fiduciaries of the electing trust and the fiduciaries of the related estate each continue to have responsibility for filing returns and paying the tax due for their respective entities, even though an I.R.C. Section 645 election has been made.[43] Thus, the executor must file a complete, accurate, and timely Form 1041 for the combined related estate and electing trust for each taxable year during the election period.[44] The trustee of the electing trust must provide the executor of the related estate with all the trust information necessary to permit the executor to file a complete, accurate, and timely Form 1041 for the combined electing trust and related estate for each taxable year during the election period.[45] The trustee and the executor must allocate the tax burden of the combined electing trust and related estate in a manner that reasonably reflects the respective tax obligations of the electing trust and related estate.[46] If the tax burden is not reasonably allocated, gifts may be deemed to have been made.[47] The trustee is responsible for ensuring that the electing trust's share of the tax burden is paid and the executor is responsible for ensuring that the related estate's share of the tax burden is timely paid.[48]

---

[38] Treas. Reg. § 1.645-1(f)(1) (December 24, 2002).

[39] *See* Treas. Reg. § 1.645-1(b)(6) and (f) (December 24, 2002).

[40] I.R.C. § 645(b)(2); Treas. Reg. § 1.645-1(f)(2)(i) and (ii) (December 24, 2002).

[41] Treas. Reg. § 1.645-1(f)(2)(iii) (December 24, 2002).

[42] Treas. Reg. § 1.645-1(f)(2)(iii) (December 24, 2002).

[43] T.D. 9032 67 F.R. 78371-78383, ¶ [20] (December 24, 2002).

[44] Treas. Reg. § 1.645-1(c)(1)(ii)(B) (December 24, 2002).

[45] Treas. Reg. § 1.645-1(c)(1)(ii)(A) (December 24, 2002).

[46] Treas. Reg. § 1.645-1(c)(1)(ii)(A)(3) and (B)(3) (December 24, 2002).

[47] T.D. 9032 67 F.R. 78371-78383, ¶ [20] (December 24, 2002).

[48] Treas. Reg. § 1.645-1(c)(1)(ii)(A)(4) and (B)(4) (December 24, 2002).

Making the Election

The election may be made whether or not an executor is appointed for the decedent's estate.[49] Once made, the election is irrevocable.[50] If there is an executor of the related estate, the trustees of each QRT joining in the election and the executor of the related estate make an election under I.R.C. Section 645 and Treasury Regulation Section 1.645-1(c) to treat each QRT joining in the election as part of the related estate by filing the election form to be provided by the IRS (Form 8855, "Election to Treat a Qualified Revocable Trust as Part of an Estate," should be available by July 1, 2003.[51]) for making the election properly completed[52] and signed under penalties of perjury, or in any other manner prescribed after December 24, 2002, by forms provided by the IRS, or by other published guidance for making the election. For the election to be valid, the election form must be filed not later than the time prescribed under I.R.C. Section 6072 for filing the Form 1041 for the first taxable year of the related estate (regardless of whether there is sufficient income to require the filing of that return). If an extension is granted for the filing of the Form 1041 for the first taxable year of the related estate, the election form will be timely filed if it is filed by the time prescribed for filing the Form 1041, including the extension granted with respect to the Form 1041.[53]

Observations

1. The due date for the Form 1041 filed for the taxable year ending with the date of the decedent's death is the fifteenth day of the fourth month (i.e., April 15) following the close of the twelve-month period that began with the first day of the decedent's last taxable year.[54]

2. With respect to an administrative trust under the revocable living trust which will continue for a period of time following the death of the decedent trustor to allow a winding-up of the affairs of the trust following the death of the trustor, such administrative trust is required to obtain a new taxpayer identification number (T.I.N.).[55]

3. If, following the death of the decedent trustor, the portion of the trust estate treated as owned by the decedent remains part of the original trust and the other portion (or portions) of the trust estate continues to be treated as owned by a grantor(s) or other person(s), the trust reports under the T.I.N. assigned to the trust prior to the decedent's death and the portion of the trust estate treated as owned by the decedent prior to the decedent's death (assuming the decedent's portion of the trust estate is not treated as terminating upon the decedent's death) continues to report under the T.I.N. used for reporting by the other portion (or portions) of the trust. For example, if a trust, reporting under Treasury Regulation Section 1.671-4(a), is treated as owned by three persons and one of them dies, the trust, including the portion of the trust no longer treated as owned by a grantor or other person, continues to report under the T.I.N. assigned to the trust prior to the death of that person.[56]

---

[49] T.D. 9032 67 F.R. 78371-78383, ¶ [17] (December 24, 2002).

[50] I.R.C. § 645(c); Treas. Reg. § 1.645-1(e)(1) (December 24, 2002).

[51] Treas. Reg. § 1.645-1(c)(1)(i) (December 24, 2002).

[52] Treas. Reg. § 1.645-1(c)(1)(ii) (December 24, 2002).

[53] Treas. Reg. § 1.645-1(c)(1)(i) (December 24, 2002).

[54] Treas. Reg. § 1.6072-1(a)(2) (December 24, 2002).

[55] Treas. Reg. § 301.6109-1(a)(3)(i)(A) (December 24, 2002).

[56] Treas. Reg. § 301.6109-1(a)(3)(i)(B) (December 24, 2002). *See* Treas. Reg. §1.671-4(a) regarding rules for filing the Form 1041 where only a portion of the trust estate is treated as owned by one or more persons.

If no executor is appointed for a related estate, an election to treat one or more QRTs of the decedent as one estate is made by the trustees of each QRT joining in the election by filing a properly completed election form, or in any other manner prescribed after December 24, 2002, by forms provided by the IRS, or by other published guidance for making the election. For the election to be valid, the election form must be filed not later than the time prescribed under I.R.C. Section 6072 for filing the Form 1041 for the first taxable year of the trust, taking into account the trustee's election to treat the trust as an estate under I.R.C. Section 645 (regardless of whether there is sufficient income to require the filing of that return). If an extension is granted for the filing of the Form 1041 for the first taxable year of the electing trust, the election form will be timely filed if it is filed by the time prescribed for filing the Form 1041, including the extension granted with respect to the filing of the Form 1041.[57] Estates and trusts of decedents dying *before* December 24, 2002, may follow the election procedures provided in the proposed Treasury regulations[58] or Revenue Procedure 98-13.[59] Finally, if there is more than one QRT, the election may be made for some or all of the QRTs. If no executor is appointed, one trustee must be appointed by the trustees of the electing trusts to file Forms 1041 for the combined electing trusts filing as an estate during the election period.[60]

Observation

If the executor of the related estate is not appointed until *after* the trustee has made an I.R.C. Section 645 election, the later appointed executor must consent to the I.R.C. Section 645 election for the election to be valid with respect to the related estate. Accordingly, in order for the election period to continue, a new Form 8855 must be filed by the trustee and the newly appointed executor within ninety days of the executor's appointment. If the executor does not agree to the election or a revised Form 8855 is not timely filed as required, the election period terminates the day before the appointment of the executor. If the IRS issues other guidance after December 24, 2002, for notifying the IRS of the executor's agreement to the election, the IRS must be notified in the manner provided in that guidance for the election period to continue.[61]

Qualified Revocable Trust.

A QRT is any trust (or portion thereof), which, on the date of decedent's death, was treated as owned by the decedent under I.R.C. Section 676 by reason of a power held by the decedent (determined without regard to any power or interest held by the decedent's spouse).[62] A trust that was treated as owned by the decedent under I.R.C. Section 676 by reason of a power that was exercisable by the decedent only with the approval or consent of a nonadverse party or with the approval or consent of the decedent's spouse is a QRT. A trust that was treated as owned by the decedent under I.R.C. Section 676 solely by reason of a power held by a nonadverse party or by reason of a power held by the decedent's spouse is not a QRT.[63] A trust qualifies as a QRT even if the trustor's power to revoke the trust lapses prior

---

[57] Treas. Reg. § 1.645-1(c)(2)(i) (December 24, 2002).

[58] REG-106542-98 65 F.R. 79015 (December 18, 2000); 2001-1 C.B. 473.

[59] Rev. Proc. 98-13, 1998-1 C.B. 370; T.D. 9032 67 F.R. 78371-78383, ¶ [39] (December 24, 2002).

[60] Treas. Reg. § 1.645-1(c)(3) (December 24, 2002).

[61] Treas. Reg. § 1.645-1(g)(1) (December 24, 2002).

[62] *See* I.R.C. § 672(e).

[63] Treas. Reg. § 1.645-1(b)(1) (December 24, 2002).

to the trustor's death as a result of the trustor's incapacity. The IRS and the Treasury Department believe that, if an agent or legal representative of the trustor can revoke the trust under state law during the trustor's incapacity, the trust will qualify as a QRT, even if the trustor is incapacitated on the date of the trustor's death.[64]

Income Tax Deduction

By making the election to treat the decedent trustor's revocable living trust part of the decedent trustor's estate, the trustee of the revocable living trust may take a federal income tax deduction for gross income set aside for a qualified charitable organization for all taxable years of the estate ending after the date of the trustor's death and before the applicable date.[65] The rule that allows both an estate and a trust (other than a simple trust) to deduct any amount of gross income, without limitation, which is actually paid during the tax year for a qualified charitable purpose did not change under the 1997 Act.[66]

Required Statement

Treasury Decision 9032[67] obsoletes Revenue Procedure 98-13.[68] Nevertheless, until Form 8855 is made available by the IRS, Revenue Procedure 98-13[69] may be relied upon regarding the content of the statement required to be attached to Form 1041[70] for purposes of the election to treat the assets of the decedent trustor's revocable living trust as part of the decedent trustor's estate for federal income tax purposes. The required statement must:[71]

- Identify the election as an election made under I.R.C. Sec. 645;[72]
- Contain the name, address, date of death, and T.I.N. of the decedent;[73]
- Contain the name, address, and T.I.N. of the QRT. If the revocable trust does not have a T.I.N. because the trustee was reporting trust income pursuant to the first alternative reporting method discussed under Tax Returns in Chapter 7, the trustee must obtain a T.I.N.,[74] unless a Form 1041 does not have to be filed for the trust for its taxable year ending after the date of the decedent's death because the following conditions are met: (a) the Form 1041 for the first taxable year of the decedent's estate is filed before the due date for filing a Form 1041 for the first taxable year of the trust ending after the date of the decedent's death; (b) items of income, deductions, and credits of the trust attributable to the decedent are reported under the first or second alternative

---

[64] T.D. 9032 67 F.R. 78371-78383, ¶ [14] (December 24, 2002).

[65] I.R.C. § 645(a).

[66] I.R.C. § 642(c)(1); Treas. Reg. § 1.642(c)-1(a); Moy, 2, *A Practitioner's Guide to Estate Planning*, § 29.07[B][7][b], at 29-59.

[67] T.D. 9032 67 F.R. 78371-78383, ¶s [43] and [44] (December 24, 2002).

[68] Rev. Proc. 98-13, 1998-1 C.B. 370; T.D. 9032 67 F.R. 78371-78383, ¶s [43] and [44] (December 24, 2002).

[69] Rev. Proc. 98-13, 1998-1 C.B. 370.

[70] T.D. 9032 67 F.R. 78371-78383, ¶ [39] (December 24, 2002).

[71] Rev. Proc. 98-13, 1998-1 C.B. 370, § 3.01.

[72] Section 6013(a)(1) of the *IRS Restructuring and Reform Act of 1998*, Pub. L. No. 105-206, 105th Cong., 2d Sess. (22 July 1998), 112 Stat. 685 redesignated I.R.C. § 646 as I.R.C. § 645, effective for estates of decedents dying after August 5, 1997. Section 1305(a) of the *Taxpayer Relief Act of 1997*, Pub. L. No. 105-34, 105th Cong., 2d Sess. (5 August 1997), 111 Stat. 788 added I.R.C. § 646, effective for estates of decedents dying after August 5, 1997. All references in Rev. Proc. 98-13, 1998-1 C.B. 370 are deemed to be references to I.R.C. § 645; Rev. Proc. 98-13, 1998-1 C.B. 370, § 3.01[1].

[73] Rev. Proc. 98-13, 1998-1 C.B. 370, § 3.01[2].

[74] Treas. Reg. § 1.645-1(d)(1) (December 24, 2002).

reporting methods discussed under Tax Returns in Chapter 7; and (c) the entire trust is a QRT.[75]

- Contain the name, address, and T.I.N. of the decedent's estate;[76]
- Provide a representation that, as of the date of the decedent's death, the trust for which the election is being made, or a portion of it, was treated under I.R.C. Section 676 as owned by the decedent of the estate referred to in I.R.C. Section 645(a) because the decedent could revoke the trust (determined without regard to I.R.C. Section 672(e));[77] and
- Be signed and dated by both executor or administrator of the decedent's estate and a trustee of the QRT.[78]

If more than one trustee or more than one executor is acting, only one must sign the required statement, unless otherwise required by the trust agreement or by local law. If there is no probate estate and, hence, no executor (or administrator), the election may still be made. In that case, a T.I.N. must still be obtained for the decedent's estate and only a trustee of the QRT must sign the required statement; however, the required statement must then include a representation that there is no executor or administrator and that neither an executor nor an administrator will be appointed.[79]

As a general rule, the original required statement must be attached to the Form 1041 filed for the decedent's estate for its first taxable year. In addition, unless the trustee of the trust is reporting under the first or second alternative reporting methods discussed under Tax Returns in Chapter 7, a copy of the required statement must be attached to a Form 1041 filed for the trust for the taxable year ending after the date of the decedent's death. The election is considered made when the original required statement is attached to the Form 1041 filed for the first taxable year of the decedent's estate, or when a copy of the required statement is attached to the Form 1041 filed for the trust, whichever occurs first. Once made, the election is effective from the date of the decedent's death.[80]

If there is no executor or administrator and neither one will be appointed (e.g., because the decedent died without a probate estate), a trustee of the QRT must sign every Form 1041 filed for the decedent's estate.[81] If a Form 1041 has already been filed for the trust for its taxable year ending after the date of the decedent's death without a copy of the required statement attached to the Form 1041, then the trust must file an amended Form 1041 and attach a copy of the required statement to the amended Form 1041. These procedures for electing to treat the assets of the decedent trustor's revocable living trust as part of his or her estate for federal income tax purposes apply to such elections made after August 5, 1997.[82]

Obtaining a Taxpayer Identification Number

Regardless of whether there is an executor for a related estate, and regardless of whether an I.R.C. Section 645 election will be made for the QRT, a T.I.N. must be obtained for the

---

[75] Rev. Proc. 98-13, 1998-1 C.B. 370, § 3.01[3].

[76] Rev. Proc. 98-13, 1998-1 C.B. 370, § 3.01[4].

[77] Rev. Proc. 98-13, 1998-1 C.B. 370, § 3.01[5].

[78] Rev. Proc. 98-13, 1998-1 C.B. 370, § 3.01[6].

[79] Rev. Proc. 98-13, 1998-1 C.B. 370, § 3.01[8].

[80] Rev. Proc. 98-13, 1998-1 C.B. 370, § 3.02[9].

[81] Rev. Proc. 98-13, 1998-1 C.B. 370, § 3.02[11].

[82] Rev. Proc. 98-13, 1998-1 C.B. 370, § 4[12]; Treas. Reg. § 1.651(a)-1(a).

QRT following the death of the decedent.[83] The trustee must furnish this T.I.N. to the payors of the QRT.[84]

If an I.R.C. Section 645 election *will be made* for a QRT, the executor of the related estate, if any, and the trustee of the QRT may treat the QRT as an electing trust from the date of the decedent's death until the due date for the I.R.C. Section 645 election. Accordingly, the trustee of the QRT is not required to file a Form 1041 for the QRT for the short taxable year beginning with the decedent's date of death and ending December 31 of that year. However, if a QRT is treated as an electing trust from the date of the decedent's death until the due date for the I.R.C. Section 645 election but a valid I.R.C. Section 645 election *is not made* for the QRT, the QRT will be subject to penalties and interest for failing to timely file a Form 1041 and pay the tax due.[85]

If the trustee of the QRT and the executor of the related estate, if any, *do not treat* the QRT as an electing trust, or if the trustee of the electing trust and the executor, if any, are uncertain whether an I.R.C. Section 645 election will be made for a QRT, the trustee of the QRT must file a Form 1041 for the short taxable year beginning with the date of the decedent's death and ending December 31 of that year (unless the QRT is not required to file a Form 1041 under I.R.C. Section 6012 for this period).[86]

If there is an executor and a valid I.R.C. Section 645 election is made for a QRT *after* a Form 1041 has been filed for the QRT, the trustee must amend the Form 1041. The QRT's items of income, deduction, and credit must be excluded from the amended Form 1041 filed and must be included on the Form 1041 filed for the first taxable year of the combined electing trust and related estate.[87] If there is *no executor* and a valid I.R.C. Section 645 election is made for a QRT *after* a Form 1041 has been filed for the QRT for the short taxable year beginning with the date of the decedent's death and ending December 31 of that year, the trustee must file an amended return for the QRT. The amended return must be filed consistent with the Treasury regulations[88] and must be filed by the due date of the Form 1041 for the QRT, taking into account the trustee's election under I.R.C. Section 645.[89]

Federal Income Tax Exemptions

The federal income tax exemption of a trust is smaller than that of an estate. An estate and a trust, like an individual, are allowed a personal exemption against taxable income. An estate is allowed a personal exemption of $600. For federal income tax purposes, trusts are either simple or complex. Neither term has anything to do with the seeming simplicity or complexity of the trust document. In other words, for trust income tax purposes, the words *simple* and *complex* are not applied in their everyday English usage. For purposes of trust income taxation, a simple trust is one that distributes only current income, is required to distribute current income, does not make charitable contributions, and is allowed a personal exemption of $300.[90] A complex trust is a trust that accumulates income, may or may not

---

[83] *See* Treas. Reg. § 301.6109-1(a)(3) (December 24, 2002).

[84] *See* Treas. Reg. § 301.6109-1(a)(5) (December 24, 2002) for the definition of payor; Treas. Reg. § 1.645-1(d)(1) (December 24, 2002).

[85] Treas. Reg. § 1.645-1(d)(2)(i) (December 24, 2002).

[86] Treas. Reg. § 1.645-1(d)(2)(ii)(A) (December 24, 2002).

[87] Treas. Reg. § 1.645-1(d)(2)(ii)(B)(1)(December 24, 2002).

[88] *See* Treas. Reg. § 1.645-1(e)(3) (December 24, 2002).

[89] Treas. Reg. § 1.645-1(d)(2)(ii)(B)(2) (December 24, 2002).

[90] I.R.C. § 642(b).

distribute income in the trustee's discretion, distributes principal, or makes charitable contributions, and is entitled to a $100 personal exemption.[91]

A trust may be a simple trust for one year and a complex trust for another year. Furthermore, a trust qualifies as a simple trust in a taxable year in which it is required to distribute all of its income currently and makes no other distributions, whether distributions of current income are, in fact, made. On the other hand, a trust is not a complex trust by reason of distributions of amounts other than income, unless such distributions are, in fact, made during the taxable year, whether they are required in that year.[92] A trust is always a complex trust in the year it terminates because it will distribute principal during its final taxable year.

Deduction for Losses

No federal income tax deduction is allowed with respect to any loss from the sale or exchange of property between the trustee and a beneficiary of the trust, because the trustee and a beneficiary of the trust are related taxpayers.[93] This rule also applies to testamentary trusts created under a decedent testator's Will and a trustor's revocable living trust.[94]

Personal Representative and Beneficiary Related Taxpayers

Under the 1997 Act,[95] the personal representative (executor/executrix) of an estate and a beneficiary of that estate are treated as related persons with respect to losses, expenses, and interest between related taxpayers, except in the case of a sale or exchange in satisfaction of a pecuniary bequest (i.e., a bequest or disposition of a fixed amount, for example, $126,000, and so forth).[96] Thus, in this limited way, the prior (before the 1997 Act) disadvantage of using a revocable living trust, in lieu of distributing an estate under a will, has been eliminated because the personal representative of an estate and the beneficiary of that estate are related taxpayers, just as the trustee of a trust and the beneficiary of the trust are related taxpayers.[97]

Overcoming Trustee and Beneficiary Related Taxpayer Disadvantage

The disadvantage of not being able to take a federal income tax deduction with respect to any loss from the sale or exchange of property between the trustee of a trust and a beneficiary of the trust still applies. This disadvantage of using a revocable living trust may be overcome, if the trustee, instead of distributing depreciated property to a beneficiary of the trust, were to sell such property to a person other than a beneficiary of the trust, take the appropriate deduction for the loss, and distribute the net proceeds from the sale of the property to the beneficiary of the trust.[98]

Stock Options

A stock option includes the right or privilege of an individual (optionee) to purchase, under no obligation, stock from a corporation (optionor) by virtue of the corporation's

---

[91] I.R.C. § 651(a); Treas. Reg. § 1.651(a)-1; I.R.C. § 661(a); Treas. Reg. § 1.661(a)(1); I.R.C. § 642(b).

[92] Treas. Reg. § 1.651(a)-1(b).

[93] I.R.C. § 267(a)(1), (b)(6).

[94] Moy, 2, *A Practitioner's Guide to Estate Planning*, §29.07[B][9], at 29-60.

[95] *The 1997 Act*, § 1308(a).

[96] I.R.C. § 267(b)(13).

[97] Moy, 2, *A Practitioner's Guide to Estate Planning*, §29.07[B][9][a], at 29-60.

[98] Ibid., §29.07[B][9][b], at 29-61.

offer at a stated price for a certain period of time.[99] No taxable gain is realized by the optionee when the option is exercised.[100]

Transfer of Option Ownership

This tax-free benefit only applies if the option is not transferable (other than by Will or by intestate distribution) by the optionee and is exercisable only by the optionee during the optionee's lifetime.[101] Accordingly, and as a general rule, an option that is transferred by the optionee during his or her lifetime or is exercisable during the optionee's lifetime by another person is not a tax-free transaction.[102] In this regard, *transfer* means the transfer of ownership of such share or the transfer of substantially all the rights of ownership.[103] However, a taxpayer who transfers interests in nonstatutory stock options and nonqualified deferred compensation to the taxpayer's former spouse, incident to divorce, is not required to include an amount in gross income upon the transfer. In addition, the former spouse of the taxpayer is required to include an amount in gross income when the former spouse exercises the stock options or when the deferred compensation is paid or made available to the former spouse. This rule does not apply to transfers of nonstatutory stock options, unfunded deferred compensation rights, or other future income rights to the extent such options or rights are nonvested at the time of transfer or to the extent that the transferor's rights to such income are subject to substantial contingencies at the time of the transfer.[104] With respect to a revocable living trust, if the trustor, as the optionee, conveys option rights to the trustee of a revocable living trust, the trustee cannot exercise the option income tax-free, even if the trustor is the trustee of the revocable living trust.

Transfer of Option by Will

The personal representative of the decedent's probate estate can exercise such an option income tax free.[105] Moreover, if the option itself, or the plan under which the option was granted, contains a provision permitting the optionee to designate the person who may exercise the option after his or her death, neither such provision, nor a designation pursuant to such provision, causes taxable gain to be realized upon exercise of the option.[106] This provision in the law allows the optionee to designate in his or her pour-over Will the trustee of a revocable living trust agreement to be the beneficiary of the option upon the death of the optionee and to exercise the option.

Passive Activity Losses

Any natural person[107] may offset losses from rental real property in which the taxpayer actively participates prior to his or her death up to a maximum of $25,000 annually against gross income.[108] This offset remains available to the decedent taxpayer's probate estate for up to two years following his or her death.[109]

---

[99] Treas. Reg. § 1.421-7(a)(1).

[100] I.R.C. § 421(a)(1).

[101] I.R.C. §§ 422(b)(5), 423(b)(9), and 424(b)(2); Treas. Reg. § 1.421-7(b)(2).

[102] Treas. Reg. § 1.421-7(b)(2).

[103] Treas. Reg. § 1.421-7(g).

[104] Rev. Rul. 2002-22, 2002-19 I.R.B. 849.

[105] I.R.C. §§ 422(b)(5), 423(b)(9) and 424(c)(1)(A); Treas. Reg. § 1.421-7(b)(2).

[106] Treas. Reg. § 1.421-7(b)(2).

[107] I.R.C. § 469(i)(1).

[108] I.R.C. § 469(i)(2).

[109] I.R.C. § 469(i)(4)(A).

Offset Available Under the 1997 Act

Under the 1997 Act, this offset is available to the trustee of a qualified revocable trust, if the trustee of the trust elects to have the revocable trust treated as part of the decedent's estate for federal income tax purposes[110] under the same rules that permit a trust to take a federal income tax deduction for gross income set aside for a qualified charitable organization.[111] Nevertheless, such losses still cannot be offset during the trustor's lifetime, if the legal title to the rental property is conveyed to the trustee of a revocable living trust, even if the trustor actively manages the property as trustee prior to the trustor's death.[112]

Amortization of Reforestation Expenditures

Similarly, under the 1997 Act, if the trustee elects to have a qualified revocable trust treated as part of the decedent's estate for federal income tax purposes, the trust can qualify for amortization of reforestation expenditures under I.R.C. Section 194(b)(4).[113] Thus, the rule that allows the benefit of a deduction for amortization of reforestation expenditures to the decedent's estate in the same manner as in the case of an individual[114] is extended to the trustee of a qualified revocable trust after the trustor's death.

However, a deduction for amortization of reforestation expenditures is still denied the trustor during lifetime when legal title to qualified timber property is conveyed to the trustee of a revocable living trust.[115] It is only after the trustor's death that the trustee is allowed an income tax deduction for amortization of reforestation expenditures on qualified timber property held in a revocable living trust[116] (i.e., poured-over into the decedent trustor's revocable living trust under the terms of the decedent's Will).

Small Business Corporation Stock

Generally, a loss on I.R.C. Section 1244 stock issued to an individual is treated as an ordinary income tax loss.[117] The term *section 1244 stock* means stock in a domestic small business corporation.[118] A small business corporation is a corporation if the aggregate amount of money and other property received by the corporation for stock, as a contribution to capital and as paid-in surplus, does not exceed $1 million.[119]

A corporation, trust, or estate is not entitled to ordinary loss treatment under I.R.C. Section 1244, regardless of how the stock was acquired. Similarly, an individual who acquires stock from a shareholder by purchase, gift, devise, or in any other manner is not en-

---

[110] I.R.C. § 645(a).

[111] I.R.C. § 645; *Taxpayer Relief Bill of 1997*, Conference Report and Statement of the Managers (H.Rep. 2014), as released on July 31, 1997, issued as CCH Special, Stand. Fed. Tax Rep. (CCH) Conf. Rep. 88 (August 4, 1997), at 71 (hereafter *Taxpayer Relief Bill of 1997*, Conference Report and Statement of the Managers (H. Pre. 2014)). *See* this Chapter 5 discussion under Income Set Aside for Charity, *supra*.

[112] I.R.C. § 469(i)(1).

[113] *Taxpayer Relief Bill of 1997*, Conf. Rep. and Statement of the Managers (H.Rep. 2014), at 71.

[114] I.R.C. § 194(b)(4).

[115] I.R.C. § 194(b)(3).

[116] *See* this Chapter 5 discussion under Income Set Aside for Charity, *supra*, for the rules pertaining to the election by trustee to treat a qualified revocable living trust as part of the decedent trustor's estate for federal income tax purposes.

[117] I.R.C. § 1244(a).

[118] I.R.C. § 1244(c)(1).

[119] I.R.C. § 1244(c)(3)(A).

titled to an ordinary loss under I.R.C. Section 1244 with respect to the stock.[120] Apparently, an ordinary income tax loss deduction on I.R.C. Section 1244 stock is not available to an individual (trustor) to whom such stock was issued, if he or she conveys legal title to the stock to the trustee of a revocable living trust. However, it is interesting to note that, if the individual to whom the stock was issued dies and bequeaths the stock to a beneficiary through the decedent's Will, that beneficiary is not entitled to the ordinary income tax loss deduction for that stock.[121] In effect, this means that the only individual entitled to the ordinary income tax loss deduction is the individual to whom the stock was originally issued. If a trustor, as the individual to whom the I.R.C. Section 1244 stock was originally issued, conveys legal title to such stock to the trustee of a revocable living trust, such a conveyance disqualifies the trustor from being entitled to the ordinary income tax loss deduction.[122] Of course, if the trustor does not anticipate ever realizing a loss on such stock, then no harm will be done if legal title to the stock is conveyed to the trustee of a revocable living trust.

LIMITATIONS OF A REVOCABLE LIVING TRUST

A revocable living trust is often referred to as a Will substitute, meaning, of course, that an individual's estate is distributed at death under the provisions of the revocable living trust agreement and not by the terms of his or her Will. Nevertheless, a Will is a critically important estate planning document that should always be coordinated and effected with the revocable living trust agreement (the importance and operation of a pour-over Will is discussed in Chapter 18). A revocable living trust has at least three major limitations:

1. The trustor cannot avoid income tax on the income generated from the trust estate.
2. The trust estate cannot be sheltered from the claims of the trustor's creditors.
3. The value of the trust estate cannot be excluded from the trustor's gross estate for purposes of the federal estate tax.

Avoidance of Federal Income Tax

A revocable living trust is a conduit through which all of the income, credits, and deductions attributable to the trust estate are those of the trustor. In other words, if the trustor is treated as the owner for the taxable year of all of the property comprising the trust estate because of his or her retained power to revoke the trust,[123] any income from such property is includable in the trustor's income for federal income tax purposes.[124] In this regard, the revocable living trust itself is not the taxpayer. All income is reported by the trustor on his or her Form 1040. As previously discussed in this chapter, only under certain circumstances is a Form 1041 required to be filed for the revocable living trust. Thus, because the revocable living trust is not the taxpayer, the trustor personally cannot avoid paying tax on the income generated by the property comprising the trust estate.

---

[120] Treas. Reg. § 1.1244(a)-1(b); I.R.C. § 1244(d)(4).

[121] Ibid.

[122] *See* Priv. Ltr. Rul. 9130003 (March 25, 1991); H. Rept. No. 1445, 95th Cong. 2d Sess., 1978-3 C.B. (Vol.1) 280.

[123] I.R.C. § 676(a).

[124] I.R.C. §§ 671, 676(a); Treas. Reg. §§ 1.671-1(a); 1.676(a)-1.

Exclude Value of Property From Trustor's Gross Estate

The gross estate includes the value of all property, real or personal, tangible or intangible, wherever situated.[125] Because the trustor of a revocable living trust retains the power to alter, amend, revoke, or terminate the trust agreement, the value of the property comprising the trust estate is included in the trustor's gross estate for purposes of the federal estate.[126] For this reason alone, it is critically important that the revocable living trust agreement provide schedules describing how property comprising the trust estate was titled before it was transferred to the revocable living trust (schedules of property are discussed in Chapter 2). This is important so that the property will retain is tax characteristics as to its inclusion in the trustor's gross estate for federal estate tax purposes.

As a general rule, the value of the property comprising the trust estate is eligible for the federal estate tax exemption amount. Remember, for federal estate tax purposes, a revocable living trust poses no particular advantage or disadvantage compared with a Will. All of the estate tax minimizing strategies available to the trustor as a testator (testatrix) under a Will are available under a revocable living trust for reducing or entirely eliminating federal estate tax on the value of the trustor's taxable trust estate. Moreover, through proper estate planning, the trustor can create within the revocable living trust subtrusts that can control the amount of a beneficiary's taxable estate while, at the same time, allowing the beneficiary the lifetime use, benefit, and enjoyment of the trust estate through the judicious exercise of general and limited powers of appointment (general and limited powers of appointment are discussed in Chapter 2).

The value of property comprising the decedent's gross estate is determined either at the date of death or the alternate valuation date.[127] When the alternate valuation date is selected, the property includable in the decedent's gross estate on his or her date of death is valued as of whichever of the following is applicable:[128]

- Any property distributed, sold, exchanged, or otherwise disposed of within six months after the decedent's death is valued as of the date of disposition.

- Any property not disposed of as described above is valued as of the date six months after the date of the decedent's death.

- Any property, interest, or estate that is effected by mere lapse of time is valued as of the date of the decedent's death.

Only one valuation date for the decedent's estate can be used. Regardless of whether the decedent's personal representative or trustee chooses to value the estate as of the date of the decedent's death or uses the alternate valuation date, all assets composing the gross estate must be valued as of the date chosen. The decedent's date of death cannot be used to value some of the decedent's property and the alternate valuation date to value other property.[129] The trust estate of a revocable living trust is not disqualified from using the alternate valuation date election.[130]

---

[125] I.R.C. §§ 2031(a) and 2033.

[126] I.R.C. §§ 2033, 2038(a)(1); Treas. Reg. §§ 20.2033-1(a) and 20.2038-1.

[127] I.R.C. §§ 2031(a) and 2032(a).

[128] I.R.C. § 2032(a); Treas. Reg. § 20.2032-1(a).

[129] Treas. Reg. § 20.2032-1(b)(2).

[130] I.R.C. §§ 2032(a) and 6018(a); Treas. Reg. § 20.2032-1(b)(1) and 20.2032-1(c)(2); Rev. Rul. 73-97, 1973-1 C.B. 404; Rev. Rul. 57-495, 1957-2 C.B. 616; Rev. Rul. 56-60, 1956-1 C.B. 443.

The alternate valuation date may be elected only if a Form 706 is required. Unless a Form 706 is required, the election is not effective.[131] Moreover, the election can only be made where the total value of all property in the decedent's gross estate, including the value of the trust estate under the revocable living trust, and the federal estate tax liability of the decedent's estate are both reduced.[132]

Protection of Assets From Trustor's Creditors

A revocable living trust agreement cannot legally protect the trustor's property from the claims of the trustor's past or future creditors. In this regard, the revocable living trust is not an asset protection trust. Certainly, a creditor might not think to inquire of a bank about whether the trustor has an account titled in the name of a trustee under a revocable living trust agreement. In this regard, a creditor might inquire of the trustor's bank if the trustor has an account titled in the trustor's individual name without thinking to ask if an account is titled in the trustor's name as trustee under a revocable living trust agreement. Similarly, a creditor may not consider that the trustor may have real property recorded in the trustor's name or the name of someone else as trustee under a revocable living trust agreement in the county wherein the trustor resides. In effect, this means that a creditor may be slowed down in obtaining information as to what the trustor owns; but, if the creditor is persistent and knowledgeable about revocable living trusts or suspicions that the debtor's property may be titled in the name of a trustee, sooner or later the creditor will prevail.

Of course, upon the death of the trustor, the trustor may direct assets composing the trust estate to continue in trust for the benefit of a contingent beneficiary(ies). The sub-trust(s) for a contingent beneficiary(ies) may contain spendthrift provisions, meaning that the assets of such trusts are protected from the imprudence of the beneficiary, as well as the claims of the beneficiary's creditors (see for example, file "APP0201.DOC" Article X (A) Spendthrift/Nonassignment).

---

[131] Treas. Reg. § 20.2032-1(b)(1); I.R.C. § 6018(a); Rev. Rul. 56-60, 1956-1 C.B. 443.

[132] I.R.C. § 2032(c).

Operation of a Revocable Living Trust and the Impact of Taxes

CHAPTER 6

Lifetime Operation of a Revocable Living Trust

LIFETIME CREATION OF A REVOCABLE LIVING TRUST

Many reasons exist for using a revocable living trust during lifetime.

Housekeeping Trust

The trustor may want the trust to act as a housekeeping trust. In this regard, the trust can relieve the trustor of the day-to-day responsibilities of property management. While the trustee is actively managing the trust estate, the trustor can still control the trust estate and benefit from its use.

Examples

1. Winifred, age eighty-nine, a resident of Oregon, owned real property in Minnesota and other investment property in Oregon. She developed a musculoskeletal degeneration of the spine; additionally, her hearing was severely impaired. Her mind was razor sharp, and she was perfectly capable of managing her financial affairs; but she was concerned for her personal and financial well-being in view of her advanced years and deteriorating physical condition. Consequently, Winifred created a *housekeeping*, or management, revocable living trust agreement in which she designated her son, Carl, as trustee. As trustee, Carl was responsible for his mother's financial affairs, paid her monthly bills, and provided her with physical care and financial advice.

   About a year after the revocable living trust was consummated, Winifred decided to make a major amendment to the trust agreement. One of her daughters had treated her unkindly, and Winifred decided that a change was needed in the distribution pattern of her trust estate upon her death. Because Winifred retained 100 percent control over the property comprising the trust estate, as well as the ability to amend the trust agreement, she was able to make an adjustment in the disposition provisions of the trust agreement. Upon her death a few months later, the titles to her real property in Minnesota and all of her investment property in Oregon were distributable to her beneficiaries without probate. This was because the legal titles to all of these properties were in the name of her son, Carl, as trustee of her revocable living trust agreement.

2. Alan is a retired barber. During his career as a barber, he skillfully acquired several residential and commercial rental properties. Several years ago, Alan decided that he would like to turn the management responsibility of his real properties over to his three daughters. However, he did not want to give up control of the properties. So Alan created a revocable living trust, wherein he named his three daughters as

co-trustees. In this manner, Alan retains 100 percent control over all of his property; but now he has the opportunity to begin coaching his three daughters in the management of his income-producing real properties. Alan's revocable living trust is providing just the right amount of *housekeeping* for both him and his wife, Stella.

Alan is happy; Stella is happy; and their three daughters are going to have a much easier job of managing their dad's property and taking care of their mother in the event of Alan's incapacity or death. If Alan becomes physically or mentally incapacitated, his daughters will know just what to do with regard to managing his financial affairs. Equally important, upon his death, no interruption will occur in the administration of Alan's estate because probate will not be required.

Control of Trustor's Property

Ask Your Attorney

With a revocable living trust, do I give up control of my property?

Answer

No. Whether the trustor does or does not serve as the trustee of the revocable living trust, the trustor retains 100 percent control of the property transferred to a revocable living trust. Thus, the trustor can amend, revoke, or terminate the trust, so long as the trustor possesses the legal capacity to do so. If the trustor becomes physically or mentally incapacitated, the successor trustee can assume the day-to-day management of the trust estate without the necessity of a court-appointed and supervised financial guardian.[1] In this regard, the revocable living trust can provide uninterrupted management of the trust estate during the trustor's lifetime and after the trustor's death. Thus, as previously discussed, humiliating, frustrating, and expensive financial guardianship proceedings can be avoided. Except for a durable power of attorney under certain state laws, mental incapacity can revoke a general power of attorney. Likewise, death revokes a durable general and special power of attorney. A properly designed and correctly funded revocable living trust agreement is not revoked by the trustor's incapacity or death.

Example

About two months after Lou and Marilyn effected their joint revocable living trust agreement, Lou suffered three massive strokes. His wife, Marilyn, as co-trustee, was able to continue managing their financial affairs, see to Lou's health care and financial needs, make investment decisions, pay bills, write checks, and conduct all of the financial activity that heretofore Lou had been doing before the strokes rendered him incapable of handling his own financial affairs. Because of the revocable living trust, the day-to-day management of Lou and Marilyn's financial affairs was not interrupted.

Withdrawal of Income and Principal from the Trust Estate

The trustor can withdraw income and principal from the trust estate during his or her lifetime without the consent of the trustee or any contingent beneficiary of the trust estate. The trustor, or any other person, can add property to the trust estate at any time—both before

---

[1] Moy, 2, *A Practitioner's Guide to Estate Planning*, § 29.04 [A] at 29-22.

and after the trustor's death. Similarly, if the trustor has effected either a durable general or special power of attorney, the trustor's attorney-in-fact can be empowered to convey title to property owned by the trustor to the trustee of the revocable living trust during the trustor's lifetime if the trustor becomes legally incapacitated. Such power in the attorney-in-fact may be critically important to the trustor to enable his or her revocable living trust to be funded, if, after the trust agreement is executed, but before the trustor can complete the funding process, the trustor becomes physically or mentally incapacitated, thereby rendering himself or herself incapable of completing the funding process. In such a situation, the attorney-in-fact can complete the funding process on behalf of the trustor.

Selling Trust Estate Assets

Ask Your Attorney

How easy or difficult will it be for me, as trustor, to sell property that is transferred to my revocable living trust?

Answer

About as easy as it would be if the trustor continued to own the property in his or her individual name.

In this regard, the trustor can direct the trustee to withdraw property from the trust estate. If the trustor wants to sell an asset, the trustee executes whatever instrument is required to effect a sale of the trust property. Even if the trustor does not intend to sell a particular asset comprising the trust estate but merely wants ownership of the asset retitled in his or her name, the trustee would still execute whatever instrument is required to achieve a reconveyance of the asset to the trustor. The proceeds of any property sold by the trustee are added to the trust estate for the trustor's use, benefit, and enjoyment.[2]

Examples

1. Assume that the trustor is the trustee of a revocable living trust. The trustor has conveyed the legal title to the trustor's home to himself or herself, as trustee of the revocable living trust agreement. The deed evidencing ownership of the property would read as follows:

   > Marian K. Wonderly, Trustee under the Marian K. Wonderly Revocable Living Trust Agreement, dated September 30, 2002.

   If the trustor determined to sell the property, the title company would require the trustee to execute a new deed in the trustee's name (Marian K. Wonderly) and sign off on the deed as Marian K. Wonderly, Trustee.

2. Assume that the trustor's daughter, Carol, is the trustee of her mother's revocable living trust. The mother, as trustor, has conveyed ownership of her stock portfolio, which is in a street name account with her stockbroker, to her daughter, Carol J. Fanning, Trustee. If the trustor determines to sell all or any one of the stocks in the portfolio, Carol, as trustee, would effect the sale not as the trustor's daughter but as trustee

---

[2] Ibid. § 29.04 [A], at 29-23.

under the trustor's (mother's) revocable living trust agreement. Accordingly, the stock brokerage firm would require Carol to consummate the sale as Carol J. Fanning, Trustee.

If real property comprising the trust estate is sold by the trustee, a title company will request evidence of the trustee's power to sell the property. Similarly, banks, transfer agents, and stock brokerage firms may have the same requirement with respect to a change in ownership of bank accounts and securities comprising the trust estate. In response to such a request, the trustee provides a Certificate of True Copy of the trust agreement (see file "APP0601.DOC"). This certification may be provided by the attorney who prepared the revocable living trust agreement, or the trustee may certify that the copy being presented is a true copy of the original trust agreement. Furthermore, it is not unusual for a title company, bank, transfer agent, or stock brokerage firm to request evidence that the person designated in the trust agreement is, in fact, serving as trustee. This assurance can be provided by the trustee effecting an Affidavit of Acting Trustee (see file "APP0602.DOC").

Appointment of Successor Trustee

Ask Your Attorney

What if I set-up a revocable living trust and decide that I want to name a different trustee, or maybe I want to change the distribution because of a family quarrel?

Answer

Even if a person other than the trustor is the trustee, the trustor can remove the trustee and appoint a successor trustee for any reason. Similarly, if a beneficiary falls out-of-favor with the trustor, the trustor can amend the trust agreement to replace that difficult or errant beneficiary (see example of Winifred, supra). This is true, provided the trustor has the legal capacity to make such an appointment.[3]

Revocable Living Trust As an Observation Center

Further in this regard, a revocable living trust can be used as an observation center. During the trustor's lifetime, the trustor can actually have the opportunity to witness his or her estate plan in action. In other words, the revocable living trust can provide the trustor the opportunity to observe how the trustee would probably manage the trust estate upon the trustor's death. If the trustor is not pleased by his or her observations, then changes can be made by correcting the trustee's management of the trust estate or, if necessary, by replacing the trustee. On the other hand, the trustee may be performing in a satisfactory manner; but other circumstances may develop within the trustor's family, thereby necessitating a change in trustee powers or other provisions of the trust agreement in order to more effectively deal with a particular situation.

Example

Ten years ago, Frances, age seventy-five, created a revocable living trust wherein she designated a bank as trustee. After the trust was executed, the only time Frances ever heard

---

[3] Ibid., § 29.04 [A] at 29-23.

from the trustee was when she received a twelve-page annual computerized report describing the property in her trust estate, along with a bill for $1,275. Frances never understood these reports. The trustee's lack of attention to her needs, in addition to discouraging her from amending the trust agreement to provide for her daughter in a particular manner, along with the trustee's impersonal nature, finally proved so unsatisfactory to Frances that she revoked the trust agreement in its entirety.

She withdrew the property that had been transferred to the trustee, paid the termination fee, and created a new revocable living trust, designating herself as trustee. She also named a successor individual trustee in the event of her incapacity or death. Presently, she is managing her financial affairs in a prudent and responsible manner, understands the extent of her property, and is otherwise in full and complete control of her financial affairs and very active social life. Even more importantly, she is very happy with her overall personal and financial situation.

Removal of Trustee

The rights and duties of a trustee are subject to any limitations imposed by the revocable trust agreement. In these regards, a trustee can be removed on the following grounds:

- If the trustee has committed a breach of trust.
- If the trustee is insolvent or otherwise unfit to administer the trust.
- If hostility or lack of cooperation among co-trustees impairs the administration of the trust estate.
- If the trustee fails or declines to act; or for other good cause.

Recall that a trust cannot fail for want of a trustee. A proper court of jurisdiction can appoint a successor trustee. Involving a court means retaining the services of an attorney to petition the court and engage the court in often time-consuming hearings on the merit of the petition and on the qualifications of those individuals nominated to act as trustee.

Beneficiaries Appoint Successor Trustee

In many cases, a more efficient and cost-effective way to appoint a successor trustee is to include a provision in the revocable trust agreement which allows a majority of those beneficiaries having a current interest in the income and principal of the trust estate to appoint a successor trustee. If only two beneficiaries of the trust estate are entitled to payments of income and principal or to a distributable share of the trust estate, their joint agreement can be required as to the appointment of a successor trustee. Those beneficiaries not of legal age or legal capacity would be represented by their guardian(s) (see, e.g., file "APP0201.DOC" Article II (E)). ▧ Appointment of the successor trustee is accomplished by the beneficiaries effecting an Appointment of Successor Trustee form (see file "APP0603.DOC"). ▧ The beneficiaries, in appointing a successor trustee, can also be empowered to designate the legal jurisdiction (situs) of the trust agreement itself.

Disagreement among Beneficiaries to Appoint Successor Trustee

Ask Your Attorney

What happens if the beneficiaries cannot agree on the selection and appointment of a successor trustee within a reasonable time period (e.g., not more than ninety days)?

Answer

In such an event, the revocable living trust agreement may provide that, if there are not more than two beneficiaries in interest of the trust estate, then a corporate successor trustee will be appointed by a panel of three independent nonbeneficiary arbitrators.

The two beneficiaries in interest will each select his or her own arbitrator and the two so selected arbitrators will designate the third arbitrator. The selection of the successor trustee, determined by the majority of the panel of arbitrators, will be respected and binding upon all the parties. If a successor trustee cannot be appointed by a majority of the beneficiaries or by a panel of three arbitrators within ninety days of a vacancy in the office of trustee of the trust agreement, then the revocable living trust agreement may provide that a successor corporate trustee be appointed by a proper court of jurisdiction. An alternate approach is simply to have a successor corporate trustee appointed by a proper court of jurisdiction; and such successor corporate trustee will administer the revocable living trust in the same manner and with the same rights and duties as those given to the individual trustees (see, e.g., file "APP0201.DOC" Article II (E) (2)) .

The instrument appointing the corporate successor trustee is signed and acknowledged by the successor trustee and a majority of the beneficiaries or the sole beneficiary in interest of the trust estate. It provides whether the successor trustee is to serve with or without bond and is attached to the revocable living trust agreement.

Revocable Living Trust for Trustor and Dependent

An older person with a dependent child may want to create a revocable living trust for their mutual benefit. Such a revocable living trust can provide lifetime financial protection for a parent; and, upon the parent's death, the trust can also manage the financial well-being of a dependent child. This application of a revocable living trust is especially useful in family situations where one parent may be deceased and the surviving parent is concerned about how his or her handicapped child will be cared for upon the parent's subsequent death.

Example

Hazel, age eighty-three, and her late husband, Walter, had only one child of their marriage; namely, Jill. Suffering from Downs Syndrome, Jill has been severely handicapped since birth and has been completely dependent upon her mother all of her life. Presently, Jill is fifty-seven years old. She is a delightful person with a witty sense of humor; but, like all of us, she has fears, frustrations, opinions, dreams, and desires. Unfortunately, though, Jill will always need someone to oversee her daily personal needs and to manage her financial affairs. As Hazel has grown older, she too recognizes her own frailties; and she is concerned not only for her own personal well-being and financial affairs but equally for Jill's welfare. Hazel's family situation is such that a guardianship proceeding for either Hazel or Jill, or both of them, would be devastating and could cause her family irreparable harm.

With these concerns and observations in mind, Hazel effected a revocable living trust agreement to alleviate these potential concerns and problems. The trust is designed so that Hazel, as trustor and trustee, has 100 percent control over Jill's and her own financial affairs. In the event of Hazel's physical or mental incapacity, provision is made for a successor trustee to provide for her care and financial well-being, as well as to provide for Jill's needs. Finally, upon Hazel's death, she has provided a plan for Jill's welfare and financial support. All of this will be accomplished without the necessity of humiliating and personally degrading guardianship hearings during either Hazel's or Jill's lifetime and without probate proceedings for Hazel's estate upon her death. Finally, upon Hazel's death, the trustee of the revocable living trust can provide Jill with the personal and financial continuity in her life which is so important for her peace of mind and well-being.

Disposition of Trust Estate upon Death of Trustor

Upon the trustor's death, he or she can direct disposition of the trust estate to anyone and in any manner he or she chooses, provided the manner chosen is not illegal, does not violate public policy, or is not an alienation of a surviving spouse's marital or creditor rights. The trustor may also make lifetime gifts of the trust estate. The trustor can realize all of the federal estate and gift tax benefits for his or her estate with a revocable living trust, just as he or she can by owning assets outside a revocable living trust but without a court-supervised financial guardianship during lifetime, probate at death, and the inability to control the disposition of survivorship and contract benefits (e.g., life insurance, retirement plan benefits, deferred compensation benefits, and so forth).[4]

Necessity of Revocable Living Trust for Trustor Who Has No Heirs

Ask Your Attorney

Because I have no living heirs, why would I want a revocable living trust?

Answer

One reason would certainly be to provide lifetime management of the trustor's property and financial affairs without the necessity of a court-appointed and court-supervised financial guardianship. A second reason may be to establish a living charitable remainder trust. The trustor may realize the following benefits from such a trust:

- *Lifetime income;*
- *A current charitable income tax deduction for the value of the remainder interest which passes to the charity upon the trustor's death;[5]*
- *The gift of the property in which the trustor retains an income interest is not subject to federal gift tax and does not use up any of the trustor's federal gift tax exemption; and*
- *The trustor's estate is entitled to a 100 percent federal charitable estate tax deduction for the value of the trust estate passing to a qualified charitable organization upon the trustor's death.[6]*

Ask Your Attorney

I have living heirs, but the value of my estate is less than the federal estate tax exemption amount. Why should I have a revocable living trust?

---

[4] Ibid.

[5] Treas. Reg. §§ 1.170(A)-6(b)(1) and (c); 1.664-2(d) and 1.664-3(d).

[6] I.R.C. § 2055(a) and (d).

A correctly funded revocable living trust agreement can provide the trustor lifetime management of the trustor's property and financial affairs without the necessity of a court-appointed and court-supervised financial guardianship. Upon the trustor's death, probate can be entirely avoided; and the trust estate can be distributed by the trustee to the trustor's beneficiaries more efficiently, with less delay, and at less financial and emotional expense.

Protection for Third Parties Dealing with the Trustee

A well-designed revocable living trust should provide protection for *third parties* dealing with the trustee. In this regard, inclusion of the following language in the revocable living trust agreement may be useful (see, e.g., file "APP0201.DOC" Article VIII (B) (2)):

(B) **Certain Limitations Concerning Trustees.** All authority exercisable . . . contained in this Trust Agreement:
  (1) **Delegation of Trust Administration.** A Trustee may delegate that individual Trustee.
  (2) **Third Persons.** With respect to a third person dealing with a Trustee or assisting a Trustee in the conduct of a transaction, the existence of trust powers and their proper exercise by the Trustee may be assumed without inquiry. The third person is not bound to inquire whether the Trustee has power to act or is properly exercising the power; and a third person, without actual knowledge that the Trustee is exceeding its powers or improperly exercising them, is fully protected in dealing with the Trustee as if the Trustee possessed and properly exercised the powers it purports to exercise. A third person is not bound to assure the proper application of trust estate assets paid or delivered to the Trustee.

TITLE TO PROPERTY VESTED IN TRUSTEE

Legal title to property conveyed to the trustee of a revocable living trust is vested in the trustee. Equitable title vests in the beneficiary of the revocable living trust. This means that the trustee is in legal title to the property for the exclusive use, benefit, and enjoyment of the beneficiary (beneficial title is in the name of the beneficiary).

Necessity to Amend Legal Documents
Conveying Property Title to Trustee

If the trustor-trustee becomes incapacitated or dies, does title to the property comprising the trust estate have to be retitled in the name of the successor trustee?

No.

Even though the trustor-trustee's name appears on the deed to real property or on bank accounts, securities, and other property comprising the trust estate, the instruments evidencing ownership by the trustee of property comprising the trust estate do not have to be redone to reflect that a successor trustee is acting as trustee of the trust estate. This is because the trust agreement provides that all rights, title, and interest in the trust estate shall immediately vest in the successor trustee at the time of appointment (see, e.g., file "APP0201.DOC" Article II (E) (3) and (C) (3)). The prior trustee, without warranty, transfers to the successor trustee the existing trust property. Therefore, the trust agreement itself is evidence that a successor trustee is in legal title to the trust estate property, even though the successor trustee's name does not actually appear on the instrument evidencing ownership.

Substantiating Authority of Successor Trustee

An acting trustee's duties and responsibilities may end because of death, incapacity, removal for cause by a proper court of jurisdiction, resignation, or for any other reason. Although a well-designed revocable living trust agreement provides for the succession of trustees, third parties dealing with the trustee may want the successor trustee's authority authenticated. A successor trustee's authority can be established by an Affidavit of Successor Trustee (General Application) (see file "APP0604.DOC").

This affidavit should name the revocable living trust that is the subject of the affidavit. It should describe any provisions of the trust agreement regarding the trustee's legal title to the trust estate and the authority granted to the initial and successor trustees. The affidavit should state why the successor trustee is acting as trustee, whether the trust agreement has been amended, and that it is in full force and effect. Attached to the affidavit should be those pages of the revocable living trust agreement naming the initial trustees creating the trust, trustees' powers, designation of successor trustee, and a copy of the signature page(s). A statement should be included to the effect that trust provisions not attached to the affidavit are of a personal and confidential nature because they set forth the disposition of the trust estate upon the trustor's death and do not modify the powers of the trustee.

Affidavit of Successor Trustee for Deceased Trustee

If a trustee succeeds as trustee due to the death of a trustee, a certified copy of the death certificate should be attached to an Affidavit of Successor Trustee (Death of Trustee) (see file "APP0605.DOC"). If a trustee succeeds as trustee due to the resignation of a trustee, a copy of the letter of resignation should be attached to the Affidavit of Successor Trustee (Resignation of Trustee) (see file "APP0606.DOC"). If a trustee succeeds because of a trustee's incapacity, a letter from the incapacitated trustee's doctor should be attached to the Affidavit of Successor Trustee (Incapacitated Trustee) (see file "APP0607.DOC"), verifying that the incapacitated trustee cannot perform the duties of trustee under the trust agreement.

TYPES OF REVOCABLE LIVING TRUSTS

A revocable living trust may be one of two forms: a joint revocable living trust agreement; or a single revocable living trust agreement. Generally, a joint revocable living trust is one trust document executed by husband and wife; but it could also be executed by unmarried partners. Each spouse or unmarried partner, as the case may be, is the trustor and trustee. A single revocable living trust can be executed by an unmarried individual, or each spouse can effect his or her own revocable living trust agreement. Regardless of whether a revocable living trust is a joint trust or a single trust, both may be one of three types: (1) standby holding title only revocable living trust; (2) management revocable living trust; or (3) a combination standby holding title and management revocable living trust.

Standby Holding Title Only Revocable Living Trust

Ask Your Attorney

Is it possible to have a revocable living trust agreement drawn up now but not become operational until I become incapacitated or die?

Answer

Yes.

In effect, whether the trustor acts as his or her own trustee or a third party is designated the initial trustee of a revocable living trust agreement, it has been said that a revocable living trust is a legal fiction much in the same way a subchapter S corporation is a legal fiction. In other words, while the trustor possesses the legal capacity to manage his or her affairs, the trustee really does nothing more than standby with respect to trustee duties and responsibilities under the revocable living trust agreement until, if ever, the trustee is called upon to administer or manage the trust estate for the benefit of the trustor, as primary beneficiary.

To accomplish the objective raised in the question, the trustor would create a standby holding title only revocable living trust. Such a revocable living trust is similar to that in file "APP0201.DOC," except that the language beginning with the second sentence in Article IV in file "APP0608.DOC" 📇 might be inserted at the end of the first sentence in Article III (A); and the language in Article V in file "APP0608.DOC" 📇 might be inserted following Article III Trust Property. A standby holding title only revocable living trust is created when the trustor is presently managing and handling the trustor's financial affairs in a prudent manner and contemplates doing so indefinitely. The trustor under such a trust retains absolute control over the management, use, benefit, and enjoyment of the trust estate—that is, the trustor's property, even though legal title to the property vests in the trustee. In effect, as previously mentioned, the trustee *stands by*, awaiting the trustor's direction with regard to the administration or management of the trust estate. If the trustor does not give the trustee any direction, the trustee will not take any action.

Trustor's Use and Benefit of Trust Estate

The trustor is entitled to receive and to devote to the trustor's own use and benefit all income of the standby trust estate. In addition, the trustor reserves the possession and use of the standby estate (principal) without payment of rent and without any accounting to the trustee (see, e.g., file "APP0201.DOC" Article IV (A), (B), and (C)). 📇 Moreover, the trustor has the exclusive powers and duties of management and custody of the standby estate.

Trustor as Nominee of Trustee

The trustor may act as nominee of the trustee for any standby property comprising the trust estate held by the trustee under the revocable living trust agreement (see, e.g., file "APP0201.DOC" Article IV (D)). 📇 When the trustor is acting as nominee for standby property comprising the trust estate, the trustor may receive directly any dividends, interest, income, or distributions of the standby property; and neither the trustor nor the trustee has any duty of accounting to the other or to any other person in regard to the standby property (see, e.g., file "APP0201.DOC" Article IV (D) (2)).

Written Direction of Trustor

If standby property is held by the trustee for safekeeping, the trustee will not sell, exchange, or otherwise dispose of such property except upon the trustor's written direction to the trustee. The trustee has no duty with respect to any such property delivered to it, except for its safekeeping; and the trustee is under no obligation to recommend a sale, exchange, or other investment action with respect to the property.

Trustee's Responsibility With Respect to Real Property

With respect to the legal title to real property conveyed to the trustee under a standby holding title only arrangement, the trustee does not assume and cannot be charged with responsibility for any liens or encumbrances on such property or for the sufficiency of the title to such property. The trustor retains possession and full management of such real property, including the right to collect rental income and to make and execute leases. Likewise, the trustor is responsible for the care, protection, maintenance and repair, collection of rents and profits, taxes, assessments and liens, mortgage payments, utility charges, and premiums for fire and other insurance as the trustor deems necessary or adequate to insure the real property against damage or loss; and the trustee has no duty in connection with these responsibilities.

Trustor's Obligations

The trustor has certain obligations regarding the property in a standby holding title only revocable living trust. In this regard, the trustor must protect, indemnify, and hold harmless the trustee against all liabilities, losses, expenses, and costs, including professional fees that may result directly or indirectly from the trustor's use, possession, management, or control of the standby property. In this regard, the trustee has, in addition to all powers conferred by law, a lien upon the income and principal of the entire trust estate for the payment of the foregoing items with the right to take possession of the trust estate property and to be reimbursed from the principal and income of the trust estate. Also, the trustee is not required to insure, pay taxes or assessments upon the trust estate, or otherwise protect such property. However, the trustee may carry insurance for the trustee's own protection at the expense of the trust estate in such amounts and form as the trustee believes appropriate (see, e.g., file "APP0201.DOC" Article III (A) (1) and (2)).

Furthermore, as regards standby holding title only property, the trustee is not required to comply with any direction from the trustor which may subject the trustee to liability. Nor is the trustee required to prosecute or defend any action, unless the trustor indemnifies the trustee accordingly (see, e.g., file "APP0201.DOC" Article III (A) (3)). Finally, the trustor is responsible for reporting income from the trust estate to the appropriate taxing authorities. The trustee is not responsible for including any such income in a Form 1041 or for the preparation of any other income tax returns with respect to any income received by the trustor in connection with the trust estate (see, e.g., file "APP0201.DOC" Article IV (E)).

Management Revocable Living Trust

When the trustor creates a management revocable living trust from the outset, as Winifred did in the above example, the trustor may do so because he or she is not interested in the day-to-day administration and management of the trustor's financial affairs. For example, the trustor may be physically but not mentally impaired, making it difficult to write, speak, hear, or otherwise function in a manner sufficient to handle the trustor's financial affairs prudently. For this reason, from the effective date of the trust agreement, the trustor may want the trustee to be responsible for handling and managing the trustor's financial affairs.

Except as may otherwise be specifically provided in the revocable living trust agreement, the trustee has full authority to utilize its best judgment in the management of the trust estate for the trustor's exclusive use, benefit, and enjoyment. It would not be unusual for the trustor to express in the trust agreement the trustor's confidence that the trustee will utilize the trustor's capabilities insofar as the same is possible and consistent with the conservation and proper management of the trust estate. In other words, so long as the trustor is capable of advising the trustee regarding the management of the trustor's financial affairs, the trustee will heed such advice, provided such advice is not detrimental to the trustor or is not illegal.

Combination Standby Holding Title Only and Management Revocable Living Trust

A combination standby holding title only and management revocable living trust is perhaps the most popular. In other words, the initial operation of the trust agreement is on a standby basis. That is to say, the trustor conveys to the trustee legal title to his or her property; but the trustee, in effect, *stands by*, awaiting direction or instructions from the trustor as to the administration and management of the trust estate. Of this author's eighteen clients who have died since 1979, only three of the eighteen activated the management provisions of their revocable living trusts before death. In other words, the successor trustee assumed the management of the trustor's financial affairs. Two of those eighteen clients, because of physical impairment, effected a management living trust agreement from the outset.

Trustor Acknowledges Possibility of Incapacity

When a trustor creates a combination standby holding title only and management revocable living trust agreement, he or she acknowledges that, with the adding of additional years, greater possibility exists that physical and mental breakdowns or emotional disorders, such as strokes, heart attacks, and so forth may render them incapable of properly managing and handling their financial affairs. With such acknowledgment in mind, the trust agreement provides that the trustee will assume the management of the trust estate at such time as the trustor: instructs the trustee in writing delivered to the trustee; or becomes incapacitated to the extent that trustor is unable to manage his or her financial affairs; or is deceased, whichever event first occurs. The foregoing example of Lou and Marilyn is illustrative of how the successor or co-trustee can assume the management of the incapacitated trustor's financial affairs.

Trustor Directs Trustee to Assume Management of Trust Estate

The trustor can direct the trustee to assume the active management of the trust estate. For example, suppose the trustor is injured in an accident or is suffering from an incurable disease yet the trustor is not mentally incapacitated but, due to the extent of the injury or illness, is concerned that he or she could lose the mental capacity to make decisions affecting the trustor's financial affairs. In such event, a letter can be prepared for the trustor's signature in which the trustor resigns as trustee and directs in writing (see, e.g., file "APP0201.DOC" Article II (C) (1) and (2)) the successor trustee designated in the revocable trust agreement to assume the duties as trustee under the trust agreement (see file "APP0609.DOC").

After the trustor has effected the letter directing the successor trustee to assume the duties of trustee, this person must add his or her signature to bank accounts, stock brokerage accounts, and any other accounts registered (titled) in the name of the revocable living trust agreement. The successor trustee can accomplish this by taking either the original or a photocopy of the letter signed by the trustor and acknowledged by a Notary Public, along with a copy of the revocable living trust agreement, to the institution where the account is held and requesting to have his or her signature added to the signature documents affecting that particular account. Along with the trust agreement, the successor trustee should present credible evidence as to his or her identity. The trust agreement establishes the fact that the trustor has designated this person as the successor trustee. The signed letter is evidence that the trustor has resigned as trustee and has directed the designated successor trustee to assume the active management of the trust estate.

Determining Mental Capacity of Trustor and Individual Trustee

Ask Your Attorney

What if I am incapacitated but cannot discern the nature or seriousness of my incapacity; will I have to submit myself to a guardianship proceeding?

Answer

If the revocable living trust agreement is properly designed, the answer is no. This potential eventuality should be taken into account when the trust agreement is designed.

Generally, a person recognizes that he or she might become unable to accurately discern a deterioration in health to the point where the successor trustee should step into the role of management. Likewise, most people would agree that whether a person is wholly or partially incapacitated is basically a medical determination. Judges are not qualified by medical training and experience to determine whether a person is physically or mentally capable of managing his or her personal and financial affairs. Judges make such decisions based on the advice and recommendations of doctors and others who are qualified to render such opinions as to a person's physical or mental condition.

Ask Your Attorney

With a revocable living trust agreement, who determines if I am, in fact, mentally incapacitated; and what protection do I have?

Answer

A well-designed revocable living trust agreement provides that a determination with respect to the trustor's (or individual trustee's) mental capacity is to be made by qualified doctors (see, e.g., file "APP0201.DOC" Article II (D)). ▨ Such a provision gives the trustor the same protection that is afforded the trustor in a guardianship proceeding but without the financial expense, emotional trauma and humiliation, and personal degradation that unfortunately can be associated with such a court-supervised proceeding.

Ask Your Attorney

With a revocable living trust, who has the final say as to whether I might be incapacitated?

Answer

A well-designed revocable living trust agreement should provide that such a determination be made by qualified, competent medical personnel.

With these realities in mind, the trustor does not want to experience a court-supervised financial guardianship proceeding for all of the reasons previously discussed. The trustor can provide in the revocable living trust agreement that the successor trustee assume the management of the trust estate upon the opinion and recommendation of competent medical advice. Moreover, keep in mind that, because of mental impairment, the trustor may not recognize his or her own incapacity.

In this regard, the revocable living trust agreement should provide that, if a difference of opinion develops between the trustor and the successor trustee as to the trustor's mental capacity or physical capability to function in the trustor's best interests, then two doctors will determine whether trustor is capable of managing trustor's affairs. One doctor will be trustor's primary care provider or, if none, the medical physician who is overseeing the general health of the trustor; and one doctor, to be referred by trustor's primary care provider or the medical physician who is overseeing the general health of the trustor, as the case may be, will be board certified in the specialty most closely associated with the alleged disability. Both doctors will personally examine the trustor. The opinion of the doctors with respect to the trustor's mental and/or physical capacity to manage trustor's own affairs will be respected and binding upon all the parties.

Similarly, if a difference of opinion develops between a successor individual trustee and any beneficiary as to the mental capacity or physical capability of the individual successor trustee to act as trustee, then the same provisions for the testing of the mental capacity or physical capability of the trustor will apply to determine the mental capacity or physical capability of the individual successor trustee. This provision in the trust agreement is a safe and effective way for the trustor and an individual trustee to avoid the humiliation and personal degradation of a competency hearing in a guardianship proceeding.

Trustor Resuming as Trustee

Ask Your Attorney

If I turn over the management of my financial affairs to my trustee, can I take back the management duties myself at a future time?

Answer

Yes, provided the trustor possesses the legal capacity to again act as trustee.

Certainly, if the trustor voluntarily resigns as trustee—not because of physical or mental incapacity—then the trustor can reactivate the standby holding title only provisions of the trust agreement. If, on the other hand, the trustor's inability to act as trustee was determined by doctors, as provided in the trust agreement, the same procedure can be used to determine whether the trustor (or individual trustee) should again act as trustee. If the trustor initially served as trustee, then the trustor should be able to again act as trustee, if the trustor is not incapacitated, as determined under the provisions of the trust agreement.

REVOCATION, TERMINATION, AND AMENDMENT OF A REVOCABLE LIVING TRUST

The trustor's retained power to revoke, terminate, and to amend the trust agreement during lifetime enables the trustor to retain control over his or her financial affairs and the property transferred to the trust without concern for how the trust estate and the trustor's financial affairs will be managed if the trustor becomes physically or mentally incapacitated.

Revocation and Termination During Trustor's Lifetime

Ask Your Attorney

I have a revocable living trust, and I don't like the way the disposition of my property is arranged in the event of my death. Can I get rid of my present revocable living trust; and, if so, how?

Answer

The trustor may either revoke the revocable living trust agreement in its entirety, terminate it, and replace it with a new revocable living trust agreement the way Frances did in the foregoing example or amend only those provisions of the present trust agreement which are not satisfactory.

Provided the trustor has the legal capacity, the revocable living trust agreement may be revoked in whole or in part by delivering a signed written instrument to that effect to the trustee (see, e.g., file "APP0201.DOC" Article V (A) and file "APP0207.DOC"). Upon notice of revocation, the trustee must within the period set forth in the trust agreement deliver to the trustor all of the property of the trust estate in the form of ownership (title or registration) designated by the trustor (see, e.g., file "APP0201.DOC" Article V (A) (1)). If the trustor revokes the trust agreement with respect to all or a major portion of the property comprising the trust estate, the trustee is entitled to retain sufficient property reasonably necessary to secure payment of liabilities lawfully incurred by the trustee in administering the trust estate, including trustee's fees that have been earned. However, the trustee need not withhold such property if the trustor indemnifies the trustee against loss and/or expense of overseeing the trust estate (see, e.g., file "APP0201.DOC" Article V (A) (3)). Finally, as a general rule, if the trustor does not revoke the trust agreement during the trustor's lifetime, then, upon the trustor's death, the trust agreement is irrevocable (see, e.g., file "APP0201.DOC" Article V (A)).

Subchapter S Corporation Stock

The trustee of a revocable living trust may own subchapter S corporation stock, provided the revocable living trust is a qualified subchapter S trust (funding a revocable living trust with subchapter S corporation stock is discussed in Chapter 12, Closely-Held Business Interests). Upon termination of the trust during the life of the current income beneficiary (e.g., trustor-beneficiary), the trust must be in compliance with I.R.C. Section 1361(d)(3)(A) and distribute all of the trust estate, including undistributed income, if any, to that beneficiary. Thus, the trust agreement must provide as follows: In compliance with I.R.C. Sec. 1361(d)(3)(A), upon the termination of the Trust Agreement during the life of Trustor, Trustee shall distribute all of the assets, including accrued, accumulated, and undistributed income, if any, composing the Trust Estate to the Trustor.

Lifetime Gifts of Property from Trust Estate

A well-designed revocable living trust empowers the trustor to make lifetime gifts of the trust estate. The trustor can direct the trustee to transfer assets of the trust estate to anyone the trustor chooses. If the trustor has a history of making gifts, the trustor may want to give the trustee the power to make gifts of the trust estate on the trustor's behalf if the trustor becomes incapacitated. Under present law, if the revocable living trust is properly designed, such a gift of assets from the trust estate by the trustee is not considered a relinquishment of the trustor's power to revoke the trust agreement with respect to the distributed property[7] or a transfer of an interest in property which would have been included in the trustor's gross estate if the trustor had retained the property. In other words, such gift is treated as a transfer made directly by the decedent trustor.[8]

Removing Property from the Revocable Living Trust

Ask Your Attorney

How do I remove property from my revocable living trust?

Answer

1. *If, as trustee, the trustor wants to sell the property, then the trustee conveys title to the new owner of the property.*

2. *If, as trustee, the trustor simply wants to remove the property from the trust and retitle (reregister) ownership of the property in the trustor's individual name, title is conveyed by the trustee to the trustor in the trustor's individual name.*

3. *If, as trustee, the trustor wants to remove the property from the trust and take title to the property with another person as joint tenants with right of survivorship (or other form of property ownership outside of the trust agreement), the trustee conveys title from the trustee to the trustor in the trustor's individual name. Then the trustor conveys title to the property in the trustor's individual name and the name of the other person as joint tenants with right of survivorship (or other form of property ownership, such as tenants in common or as community property).*

4. *If, as trustee, the trustor gifts property from the trust, then the trustor, as trustee, conveys title to the donee (new owner) of the property.*

Record-keeping of Property Removed from the Trust

Ask Your Attorney

What should I do if I sell or get rid of property once it has been transferred to my trustee?

Answer

Two methods are available.

1. *The description of the property on the applicable schedule attached at the end of the revocable living trust agreement can be deleted from the schedule by simply drawing a line through the description, dating the deletion, and making a notation regarding the disposition of the property; that is, "property sold; proceeds used to acquire (description of property acquired); or*

2. *A revised schedule can be created. If the deleted property is replaced with other property, a description of the replacement property can be added to the applicable schedule affecting that property.*

---

[7] I.R.C. § 2038(a)(1).
[8] I.R.C. § 2035(e).

Lifetime Amendment

For so long as the trustor possesses legal capacity, the trustor may amend the revocable living trust by a signed written instrument delivered to the trustee. Whether the trustor can delegate to an attorney-in-fact, under a durable power of attorney, the power to amend or revoke a revocable living trust agreement depends upon state law. Even if state law permits an attorney-in-fact to amend or revoke a revocable living trust agreement during the trustor's lifetime, thoughtful consideration should be given to granting such an awesome power under a power of attorney. If such a power is misplaced, the attorney-in-fact could wreak absolute havoc on a well-designed estate plan.

Amendments That Modify Trustee's Duties

The trustor cannot substantially increases the duties or liabilities of the trustee or change the trustee's compensation without the trustee's consent. Moreover, the trustee is not obligated to act under such an amendment, unless the trustee accepts it. Generally, an amendment becomes effective when it is signed by the trustor and at least one trustee. Changes that modify a trustee's duties, liabilities, or compensation are not effective until the amendment is signed by the affected trustee. If the trustee who is affected by the changes does not sign the amendment upon request, such refusal may constitute a resignation by that trustee.

Conveyance Documents Remain in Full Force and Effect

A well-designed revocable living trust agreement provides that, if amended, including substitution by a new trust, all references to the trustee in any documents conveying legal title to property to the trustee continue in full force and effect (see, e.g., "APP0201.DOC" Preamble, second paragraph). This provision can apply even if a new trustee is substituted for the initial or successor trustee. The purpose of this provision is to eliminate the need to execute new documents conveying legal title to property to the trustee. If a new trust replaces a trust that is revoked, the new trust should acknowledge its prior existence and declare that it replaces the revoked trust (see file "APP0610.DOC"). In this manner, the original conveyance documents are tied to the replacement trust and do not have to be replaced. Such a provision can eliminate unnecessary recording costs associated with conveying the title to real property to the trustee.

Signals That Alert Trustor to Amend Trust Agreement

Many of the same reasons to amend a Will apply to a revocable living trust:

- Trustor moves to another state (laws regarding trusts and the distribution of a person's property vary from state to state).
- Births, deaths, marriages, or divorces within the trustor's family.
- Changes in the tax laws; for example, TRA '76 and ERTA '81 were so revolutionary that every Will, revocable living trust, and buy-sell agreement should have been reviewed. In view of the Technical and Miscellaneous Revenue Act of 1988 (TAMRA '88),[9] the Wills and revocable living trusts of married individuals, where one spouse is a non-U.S. citizen, should be reviewed to be certain that, upon the death of the U.S. citizen spouse, his or her estate will qualify for the federal estate tax marital deduction for the value of property passing to the surviving non-U.S. citizen spouse, assuming that the decedent spouse wants his or her property passing to the surviving non-U.S. citizen spouse to qualify for the estate tax marital deduction.

---

[9] *Technical and Miscellaneous Revenue Act of 1988*, Pub. L. No. 100-647, 100th Cong., 2d Sess. (10 November 1988), 1988-3 C.B. 1 (hereafter TAMRA '88).

- Lifetime disposition of property in the revocable living trust; for example, provision may have been made for a beneficiary to receive a particular parcel of real property upon the trustor's death, but the trustor has sold the property (this is known as *ademption*).

- Changes in the value of trust estate property. Assume the trustor owns stock in two separate companies, CT&S and ESD. Both were of equal value when legal title to the securities was conveyed to the trustee. Upon the trustor's death, the trust agreement provides that the CT&S stock is to be distributed to one beneficiary and the ESD stock to another beneficiary. However, over the years, the CT&S stock has increased considerably in value; while the ESD stock has decreased in value. The result, though it is not the trustor's intention, is that one beneficiary will receive less than the other.

- Physical and mental capacity of trustor's beneficiaries. The trustor may want to change the amount and method by which the trust estate is distributable to a beneficiary who has become physically or mentally incapacitated since the trust agreement was effected.

- Changes in a beneficiary's financial circumstances. Perhaps a particular beneficiary has declared bankruptcy or has experienced a financial downturn, which may cause the trustor to feel differently about how much and in what manner the beneficiary should receive a share of the trustor's estate.

- In view of the 2001 Act, the trustor may need to revise the revocable living trust agreement to take advantage of the increased exemption amount or to revise distribution arrangements to a surviving spouse and children in view of the value of their respective estates.

Revocation and Amendment after Trustor's Death

Generally, upon the trustor's death, the revocable living trust becomes irrevocable. However, if a general power of appointment marital deduction trust is provided for the trustor's surviving spouse, the decedent trustor can give the surviving spouse the power to amend the marital deduction trust. Such a power of amendment would not be appropriate, though, where the trustee is directed to distribute the trust estate to a qualified terminable interest property (QTIP) trust. A power in the surviving spouse to amend the QTIP trust may cause the value of the property distributable to the trust from qualifying for the estate tax marital deduction in the estate of the decedent trustor spouse.[10] Likewise, the decedent trustor spouse should not give the surviving spouse a power to amend a credit shelter trust (nonmarital deduction trust; Trust B; by-pass trust). A power in the surviving spouse to amend such a nonmarital deduction trust may cause the value of the property comprising the trust estate to be included in the surviving spouse's gross estate upon his or her subsequent death.[11]

Amendments by Trustee after Trustor's Death

Because of ever-changing laws and their uncertain impact on persons' daily lives, the trustee can be empowered to amend a revocable trust living trust agreement after the trustor's death. If the trustee determines that the trust agreement is uncertain or incomplete in any respect or if subsequent legal developments or changes in federal and state laws render certain provisions of the trust agreement undesirable and unintended or obsolete as to its effectiveness in achieving the trustor's intentions, the trustee can effect amendments to the trust agreement to deal with these contingencies (see, e.g., "APP0201.DOC" Article V (C)). If a beneficiary

---

[10] *See* I.R.C. § 2056(b)(7)(B).
[11] *See* I.R.C. § 2041(b)(1).

is acting as a trustee, however, such a power in the trustee to amend the trust agreement must be carefully designed to avoid adverse tax consequence to the beneficiary. For example, it may be provided that the trustee can only amend the trust agreement to:

- Avoid court interpretation of language;
- Adjust trust provisions to follow laws affecting the federal income, estate, and gift tax treatment of the trust estate; and
- Modify the trustee's powers to administer the trust in order to carry out the purpose of the trust. As a rule, the trustee should not be given the power to amend the trust agreement in a way that affects the time, quality, or manner of a beneficiary's enjoyment of the trust estate or its income.

DAY-TO-DAY HANDLING OF THE TRUST ESTATE

The trustor's continued use, benefit, and enjoyment of property transferred to a revocable living trust does not change.

Bank Accounts

Bank checking, savings, and money market accounts are as accessible to the trustor under a revocable living trust as they were before being transferred to the trustee. A new account number and new checks are not required for existing accounts retitled in the trustor's name. Moreover, the trustor is not required to sign checks as *Trustee*. The trustee's name is not required to be imprinted on the checks. To the public at large, bank accounts continue to appear as though they are in the trustor's individual name. Although nothing precludes the trustor from having new checks issued to reflect the trustor's identity as trustee of a revocable living trust. What is important is that the bank's records reflect the fact that the bank account is titled in the name of the trustee of the revocable living trust.

Accommodation Accounts

Ask Your Attorney

As a convenience, I added my daughter's name to my checking account. If I title the checking account in my name, as trustee, can she still sign checks on my behalf?

Answer

Yes.

It is not uncommon for a trustor to have a bank account in his or her name with a child or other immediate family member. Most often, such an arrangement enables a family member to be listed on the account as an *accommodation* party to sign checks or to make deposits on behalf of the registered owner. Unless the revocable living trust agreement empowers the trustor, when acting as trustee, to nominate an accommodation party, most banks and other financial institutions are reluctant to allow such an accommodation party to operate when the account is titled in the name of a trustee. In Chapter 2, Framework of a Revocable Living Trust, a sample trust provision is provided wherein the trustor, when acting as trustee, may nominate another individual as a signatory on bank accounts (see Chapter 2, Framework of a Revocable Living Trust; Determining the Trustee of a Revocable Living Trust; Family Member as Trustee).

Observation

Some states do not permit a trustee to transfer its *office* (i.e., its duties and responsibilities) to another or delegate the entire administration of the trust to a co-trustee or to any other person. Unless otherwise specifically prohibited by state law or the trust agreement itself, this limitation does not prevent a trustee from delegating signature authority to any person.

Letter of Authorization From Trustee

Another approach that may be used to give an accommodation party signature authority on bank accounts is for the trustee to grant such authority in a letter to the financial institution (see file "APP0206.DOC"). Whether the financial institution will accept such an arrangement by letter outside the parameters of the revocable living trust agreement is problematical. As discussed in Chapter 2, Framework of a Revocable Living Trust, the better approach is to include in the revocable living trust agreement a provision that empowers the trustor, when acting as trustee, to nominate another individual as a signatory on bank accounts (see Chapter 2, Framework of a Revocable Living Trust; Determining the Trustee of a Revocable Living Trust; Family Member as Trustee).

Delegation of Signature Authority by Trustee

Similarly, a trustee who is not the trustor may want to delegate signature authority to someone in the trustee's absence. In such instance, the trustee may want to use a Delegation of Trustee Powers (see file "APP0611.DOC"). This instrument can be used by a trustee to delegate signature authority to another trustee or to any other person. The Delegation of Trustee Powers should be sufficient for that trustee or person to sign checks for accounts that are titled in the name of the trustee, provided the financial institution governing the account accepts the provision in the trust agreement that gives the trustee the power to delegate to another trustee or person any part or all of the trustee's powers.

Real Property

Funding a revocable living trust with real property is discussed in Chapter 10, Real Property Interests. Generally, dealing with real property as a trustee is not much different from holding title to real property as an individual. If the trustor-trustee sells the real property, the trustee effects the appropriate conveyance documents (see file "APP0612.DOC" Warranty Deed (Trustee to Buyer)).

Refinancing real property after title is conveyed to the trustee of a revocable living trust may be more troublesome than if the trustor held title to the property in his or her own name outside the trust, since most lending institutions are reluctant to finance real property that is in the name of a trustee of a revocable living trust. This minor inconvenience, however, can be overcome if the trustee reconveys title to the trustor for purposes of placing the title in the name of the party financially responsible for the loan. After the loan is made, the trustor reconveys title to the trustee and agrees to be responsible for the loan. Without exception, this author has not encountered a lending institution or title company objecting to this sequence of events in the loan-making process.

Securities

The process of buying, selling, and trading securities titled (registered) in the name of the trustee of a revocable living trust is really no different than if the trustor continued to own them in his or her name outside the trust agreement. Whenever securities compose the trust estate, the trustor's and trustee's signatures on the trust agreement should be both acknowledged by a Notary Public and guaranteed by a commercial bank officer or by an officer of a member firm of a major stock exchange. Signature guarantee enables the trustee to effect securities transactions with a broker-dealer or a transfer agent. Most of this author's clients choose to have their signatures guaranteed by an officer of a full-service bank where they have their checking accounts and where they are well known. Generally, a savings and loan company will not suffice. Powers that a trustee should have regarding securities are discussed in Chapter 3, Trustee's Powers, Duties, and Responsibilities.

Tangible Personal Property

Except for motor vehicles, watercraft, aircraft, and other types of vehicles requiring state licenses to operate, most tangible personal property is not evidenced by a certificate of title or form of ownership registration. The trustor can just as freely deal with such property as a trustor-trustee under a revocable living trust agreement as he or she could if such property were not transferred to a revocable living trust. For an example of the wording used to include tangible personal property not evidenced by a certificate of registration, title, or ownership in a revocable living trust, see file "APP0205.DOC" 📄 and discussion in Chapter 14, Tangible and Intangible Personal Property.

Closely-held Business Interests

Where permitted by state law, a trustee can own, terminate, and participate in the operation of any business enterprise, including a corporation, a sole proprietorship, a general or limited partnership, a family limited partnership (FLP), or a limited liability company (LLC). The manner in which the trustee effects purchases and sales of property comprising such business entities depends on state law, the provisions of the revocable living trust agreement itself, and the form in which the business is operating. Provided the trust agreement is properly designed in compliance with state law and takes into account the trustor's objectives with respect to his or her interest in a closely-held business, the trustor acting as trustee should not be confronted with any challenges with which he or she might otherwise have to contend if ownership of the closely-held business interest were held outside the revocable living trust. Nevertheless, this is an area where both real and perceived disadvantages do exist; so it is important that the trustor become familiar with the laws of his or her state pertaining to closely-held business interests owned by a trustee or consult an attorney who understands the issues confronting closely-held business owners.[12] Funding a revocable living trust with closely-held business interests is discussed in Chapter 12, Closely-held Business Interests.

COST OF CREATING AND OPERATING A REVOCABLE LIVING TRUST

Attorneys frequently advocate against using a revocable living trust because of the alleged expense in creating and operating it. Ben Feldman, perhaps the world's most successful life insurance salesman, once said: "Your estate represents a lifetime—your lifetime. If it was worth spending a lifetime to accumulate, it must be worth keeping. You didn't build it for the tax collector."[13] Keeping an estate together means investing part of what a person has

---

[12] See Julian S. Bush, *The Closely Held Business in the Revocable Trust: Advantages and Post-death Problems*, The Thirty-fourth Annual New York University Institute, (1976) at 1621 and Edwin T. Hood, John J. Mylan and Timothy P. O'Sullivan, *Closely Held Businesses in Estate Planning* 2d ed. (New York: Aspen Law & Business, 1998).

[13] Andrew H. Thomson, *The Feldman Method: The Words and Working Philosophy of the World's Greatest Insurance Salesman* (Lynbrook, New York: Farnsworth Publishing Company, Inc. 1969), at 166 (hereafter Thomson, *The Feldman Method*).

worked so hard to accumulate in order to keep together what has been created. Too often the cost of doing nothing is more than the cost of doing something! If one practitioner's fee to design and implement an estate plan, which might include a revocable living trust, seems high compared with a much lesser amount charged by another practitioner, just remember: the bitterness of paying for an improperly designed estate plan will remain long after the sweetness of low price is forgotten.

Cost of Creating a Revocable Living Trust

Ask Your Attorney

What is the cost of setting-up a revocable living trust agreement as opposed to what probate might cost without such a trust?

Answer

In most cases, probate will cost a decedent's estate more. Whereas, a revocable living trust may cost about $3,500, or possibly more, depending upon the complexity of the trustor's estate plan.

The monetary investment to create a well-designed and properly funded revocable living trust agreement, including the estate plan, pour-over Will, and all supplemental documents to correctly fund the trust can be relatively small and increase according to the type of assets composing the trustor's estate, the complexity of the trustor's distribution objectives, and the creativity required on the part of the estate planner to develop an estate plan to accomplish those objectives. The value (i.e., the *size* of a person's estate) should not influence the fee charged by the estate planner to design and develop an estate plan that meets the estate owner's planning objectives.

It is not uncommon for the cost of probate to be approximately 6 to 12 percent, or more, of the value of the decedent's probate estate; and that estimate does not take into account the amount that may have been expended on the decedent's behalf under a court-supervised guardianship before the decedent died. Unequivocally, this author's experience is that the cost of probate—not to mention the cost of a guardianship—can far exceed the cost of a well-designed estate plan that includes a well-designed and correctly funded revocable living trust.

The dollars expended to design, create, and implement an effective estate plan are a financial investment. If an estate owner expects to keep together what he or she has worked so hard during lifetime to create, then he or she should plan to invest a part of his or her estate to keep it intact in the event of physical or mental incapacity during lifetime and upon death. Part of that investment includes the skills of an experienced and knowledgeable attorney, accountant, and estate planning consultant advising the attorney and accountant, in the design, creation, and preparation of the legal documents necessary to implement an estate plan.

Cost to Convey Title to Property to Trustee

Fees imposed to record deeds for real property conveyed to the trustee of a revocable living trust vary from county-to-county throughout the United States. In addition, some counties impose a transfer tax when legal title to real property is conveyed from one person to another (see discussion in Chapter 5, Disadvantages, Reservations, and Limitations of a Revocable Living Trust and Chapter 10, Real Property Interests). Generally, conveyances of legal title to real property to the trustee of a revocable living trust are exempt from such county or local transfer taxes. Fees may be incurred when conveying legal title to tax-sheltered limited partnerships to a revocable living trust agreement. Usually, such fees are an administrative expense charged by the broker-dealer through whom the limited partnership is sold.

Trustee Fees

Ask Your Attorney

What do banks charge to be a trustee?

Answer

As a matter of policy, bank (or corporate) trustee fees are established by a schedule of services performed.

Maintenance or Acceptance Fees

Most banks charge a maintenance or acceptance fee to serve as a standby trustee of a revocable living trust. Of course, if the bank assumes the role of a managing trustee at the direction of the trustor, then the bank's regular schedule of trustee fees becomes operational. This is why most trustors designate themselves or a family member as trustee of a revocable living trust. In many cases, though, a bank or corporate trustee is designated in the revocable living trust agreement as the ultimate successor trustee to avoid the unnecessary expense of having a court appoint a successor trustee absent any provision in the trust agreement for the appointment of a successor trustee by the beneficiaries of the trustor's trust estate.

Managed Revocable Living Trust Accounts

With respect to managed trust accounts (management revocable living trust), some banks charge an annual fee on the value of stocks, bonds, or notes comprising the trust estate. On the first $1 million of value, the annual fee may be 1.5 percent; on the next $1 million, the annual fee may be 0.90 percent; and the annual fee on value over $2 million may be 0.65 percent. In many cases, a minimum annual fee is charged; for example, $3,750. Services included in this minimum annual fee may include: professional investment management on an ongoing basis; preparation of annual fiduciary income tax returns and tax information for trustors and beneficiaries; financial reporting that provides information to trustors on a periodic basis and meets legal requirements; custody and safekeeping of trust estate property; collection of income on trust estate property; and fulfillment of the trustor's estate plan in the event of incapacity or upon death.

Component Fees

Other banks may base their fees on components: base fee; a percentage of the market value of property under management; and hourly time charges. For example, for the management of cash, securities, common trust funds, and money market instruments, a bank may charge an annual fee of: first $1 million, 1.10 percent of market value; next $1 million, 0.75 percent of market value; next $3 million, 0.60 percent of market value; and over $5 million, the fee is negotiated. The annual fee charged for managing real property (exclusive of agricultural property), notes, mortgages, contracts, partnership interests, and miscellaneous personal property may be: first $1 million, 1.25 percent of market value; next $1 million, 1.00 percent of market value; next $3 million, 0.85 percent of market value; and over $5 million, the fee is negotiated, plus holding fees of $200 or more per year for each parcel of real property; $50 or more per year for each liability/installment obligation. With respect to agricultural property, the annual fees may be: 6 percent of gross income received, plus 0.60 percent of market value to $100,000 and 0.30 percent of market value in excess of $100,000. In addition, the bank may charge $100 or more per hour for the services of bank officers and $50 or more per hour for staff personnel. For example, time may be charged for opening and closing accounts, preparation of fiduciary income tax returns (with a certain minimum fee), filing of quarterly fiduciary estimated income tax payments (with a minimum annual fee), lease negotiations, real estate sales, management of closely-held business interests, managing unusual assets, litigation, and other administrative duties. In addition, the bank may charge for postage, insurance, long-distance telephone calls, security deliveries, mileage, photocopying, and so forth, as such expenses are incurred.

Fees Based on Categories of Services Performed

Banks may also charge fees according to categories of services performed; for example, managed accounts, nonmanaged accounts, managed real estate, and escrow services. For managed trust accounts (i.e., management revocable living trust agreement), the annual compensation may be calculated quarterly, as follows, with a minimum quarterly fee of $750. For investment management: 1.10 percent on first $500,000 of market value; 1.00 percent on next $500,000 of market value; 0.85 of 1.00 percent on next $1 million of market value; 0.75 of 1.00 percent on next $1 million of market value; and 0.60 of 1.00 percent on the balance. The base fee connected with administrative and accounting services for managed trust accounts may be $950. Extraordinary administrative time may be charged at $85 or more per hour. Charges for tax return preparation usually come under a separate schedule, as do real property transactions.

For nonmanaged trust accounts (i.e., standby holding title only revocable living trust), annual compensation is calculated quarterly with a minimum quarterly fee of about $750. A quarterly fee of 0.30 of 1 percent of market value may be charged for asset safekeeping services. Administrative and accounting services have a base fee of about $950, with about $30 to $50 charged for a purchase, sale, or transfer of trust estate property. Extraordinary administrative time may be billed at $85 or more per hour. Tax return preparation fees are usually outlined on a separate schedule.

An asset management fee of 1.25 percent of market value is not uncommon for managed real estate accounts. In addition, a title holding fee of $200 or more per property may be charged and $100 or more for each real estate note that is held in a real estate management account. Distributions, set-up, and hazardous waste inspection fees (commercial property only) are charged by the hour. A real property sales commission of 2 percent of the selling price may be charged, if the bank lists the property with a real estate broker; a 5 percent commission may be charged, if the bank lists the property itself. Lease negotiations on real property may be billed at 2 percent of revenue from the property.

Escrow Fees

With respect to escrow service, a fee of 0.30 of 1 percent or more of the market value of property annually, averaged monthly and collected quarterly, may be charged for asset safekeeping services. An annual base fee of $950 or more may be charged for administrative and accounting services. Miscellaneous receipts and disbursements may be billed at $5 or more per transaction. Purchases, sales, or transfers of assets may be charged at $30 or more per trade. An hourly rate of $85 or more may be charged for extraordinary administrative time. In addition, a minimum of $2,000 may be charged for each escrow and is held in the account as a deposit to be applied toward the charges outlined above.

Ask Your Attorney

Can I have a revocable living trust without having to pay annual fees to a trustee?

Answer

Yes, provided the trustee is not a bank, corporation, or other qualified financial institution. Remember, even if the trustor designates a bank, corporation, or other qualified financial institution as trustee of a standby holding title only revocable living trust, it will charge an annual maintenance or acceptance fee to serve as a standby trustee.

Compensating a Trustee

Ask Your Attorney

How is a trustee compensated?

Answer

Typically, the revocable living trust agreement provides that the trustee is entitled to reasonable compensation for services performed under the trust agreement [see, e.g., file "APP0201.DOC" Article VIII (G)]. Of course, if a bank (or corporate trustee) is designated trustee, reasonable compensation is determined by reference to the fee schedule used by the bank or corporate trustee at the time compensation is payable. A bank's schedule of fees may be used as a guide for compensating an individual trustee, even if the trustee is a family member.

Remember, though, fees paid to an individual trustee are subject to federal income tax upon receipt. Because of this, a family member who is also a beneficiary of the trust estate may prefer to receive his or her compensation in the form of a bequest that is not income taxable to the trustee-beneficiary. The following suggested language may be included in the revocable living trust agreement under the Article, Distribution of Trust Property On Death of Trustor (or, in a joint revocable living trust agreement, On Death of Trustors), to accomplish this preference:

(J) **Distribution of Residue: Real and Intangible Property.** As hereinbefore provided, upon the death of the Trustor [or Survivor Trustor], the remainder of the trust estate (except tangible personal property), including accrued, accumulated, and undistributed income, shall be distributed as follows:

(1) Specific Distributions.

(a) Trustee shall distribute to Trustors' granddaughter . . . for the benefit of Trustors' granddaughter.

(b) Trustee shall distribute the sum of fifty thousand and no one-hundredths dollars ($50,000.00), or ten percent of the value of Trustor's residuary trust estate, whichever amount is less, outright to Linda J. _____; or, in the event Linda does not survive Trustor, then, such distributable share of Trustor's residuary trust estate for Linda shall lapse; and, in lieu thereof, such distributable share shall be distributable by Trustee in equal shares to Paul, Robert and Margaret, as provided under this Article IX (J) (2). The herein distributable share to Linda is in lieu of all compensation or commissions to which she would otherwise be entitled as Personal Representative or Trustee.

Business Partners as Trustees

Occasionally, business partners may designate each other as trustees of their respective revocable living trusts. Under such circumstances, each trust agreement may provide that the trustee's compensation in his or her individual capacity as an owner in any business comprising the trust estate is completely separate from, and unrelated to, any compensation payable to the trustee. In this regard, if the trustee serves as an officer, director, or employee of the business, any salaries or other compensations paid to the trustee are in addition to, and not in lieu of, any fees received as a trustee. Inclusion in the revocable living trust agreement of the following suggested language may accomplish this objective:

(J) **Compensation of Trustee.** The Trustee shall be entitled to reasonable compensation for services rendered under this Trust Agreement. Trustee's compensation in his, her, its individual capacity as a participant in any business comprising an asset of the trust estate is completely separate from, and unrelated to, any compensation payable to the Trustee; and in this regard, Trustee is entitled to compensation as a participant in such business notwithstanding the fact that Trustee is entitled to reasonable compensation for service rendered under this Trust Agreement. If a corporate fiduciary is serving as Trustee, reasonable compensation shall be determined by reference to the fee schedule used by Trustee at the time such compensation is payable.

Observation/Recommendation

A significant part of the trustor's estate may consist of an interest in a closely-held business. If, at the time of the trustor's death, the trustor still owns an interest in the business or any entity that may have succeeded to the business, the trustor may want to authorize and empower (but not direct) the trustee, in the trustee's discretion, to continue such business for such period as the trustee determines. In such case, the trustor should expressly exonerate the trustee from any loss resulting from trustee's failure to diversify the assets of the trust estate. Likewise, the trustee should be authorized to invest additional property comprising the trust estate in the closely-held business, except to the extent that such investment would constitute nonproductive property comprising a trust, the property of which qualifies for the estate tax marital deduction in the trustor's trust estate.

Trustor's Spouse and Business Partner as Co-Trustees

Furthermore, a trustor's spouse may also own an interest in the same business as the decedent trustor. If the trustor's spouse and business partner act as co-trustees under the trustor's revocable living trust, the trustees should be authorized and empowered to act on behalf of any trust created under the trust agreement as to all matters relating to the business, despite the possibility that a conflict of interest might exist between the trust estate (or any trust created under the trust agreement or any beneficiary) and any one of the trustees. Accordingly, the trustees should be empowered to manage the business as they would have if they owned interests in the business in their own names and not as trustees. In this regard, they should be absolved from any liability to any beneficiary in connection with any action or omission taken in good faith with respect to the business. The following suggested language may be included in the article addressing Trustee Powers under the revocable living trust to accomplish this objective:

(B) **Discretionary Powers.** Without limiting the authority that the Trustee would otherwise have pursuant to law or pursuant to other provisions of this Trust Agreement, Trustee is hereby vested with the following discretionary powers that Trustee shall have until the final distribution of all assets in Trustee's hands:

(1) **Retain Assets.** To collect, hold and retain trust assets received from Trustor until, in the judgment of the Trustee, disposition of the assets should be made, independent of any requirement of diversification; and the assets may be retained even though they include an asset in which the Trustee is personally interested.

If, at the time of Trustor's death, Trustor shall own shares of stock of [name of business] or any entity that may have succeeded to its business, Trustor authorizes and empowers (but does not direct) Trustees, in their discretion, to continue such business for such period as Trustees, in their discretion, shall determine. Trustor realizes that a large portion of the assets of Trustor's trust estate or any trust created hereunder may be represented by Trustor's interest in [name of business] or any successor thereto, but Trustor expressly exonerates Trustees from any loss resulting from Trustee's failure to diversify the assets of Trustor's trust estate or any trust created hereunder. Trustees may invest additional assets of Trustor's estate or trust in [name of business], except to the extent prohibited under the provisions of Article VIII (E) (Provisions for Family Trust) and Article VIII (F) (Provisions for Marital Trust).

Trustor is aware that [name of Trustor's business associate or partner] and Trustor's spouse each have an interest in [name of business]. Trustor authorizes and empowers Trustees to act on behalf of any trust created hereunder as to all matters relating to [name of business], despite the possibility that there may be a conflict of interest between Trustor's trust estate, any trust created hereunder or any beneficiary hereunder and any one of the Trustees. Subject to the express provisions of this Trust Agreement, Trustees shall have the same power to manage the business of [name of business] as they would have if they owned its stock in their own rights and not as Trustees; and they shall be absolved from any liability to any beneficiary hereunder in connection with any action or omission taken in good faith with respect to the business of [name of business].

If Trustees shall serve as officers, directors, or employees of [name of business], any salaries or other compensation paid to any of them shall be in addition to, and not in lieu of, any fiduciary commissions or fees receivable by them.

Tax Reporting

As a general rule, all items of income, credit, and deduction are reported on the trustor's Form 1040. The exception is when a Form 1041 is required to be filed by the trustor because a person other than the trustor or the trustor's spouse is acting as trustee of the trust agreement during the trustor's lifetime (see discussion in Chapter 5, Disadvantages, Reservations, and Limitations of a Revocable Living Trust and Chapter 7, Federal Income Tax). No additional or unusual expense should be incurred by the trustor for the preparation of his or her Form 1040 because of the existence of the revocable living trust agreement.

TRUSTEE LIABILITY

Ask Your Attorney

What protection does my trustee have if someone sues my trust estate?

Answer

As a rule, the trustee cannot be sued personally for causes of action against the trust estate.

Claims of Trustor's Creditors

A trustee can be indemnified against the claims of the trustor's creditors or against anyone else, including a disgruntled beneficiary, who may sue the trust estate. Once, a trustor's attorney asked this author to act as successor trustee of the trustor's revocable living trust. Because of this author's familiarity with the client's family and the behavior of one of the trustor's adopted children, in particular, this author insisted on indemnification against personal expense in defending any actions that this individual or any other beneficiary might bring against the client's trust estate or against this author's actions as trustee. The attorney satisfied this request by including the following provision in an amendment to the revocable living trust agreement:

> (6) The Trustor is concerned that Pat B. _____ or other persons may attempt to take legal or other actions that may be inconsistent with the Trustor's intent as described herein and in documents referred to herein. The Trustor is also concerned that the successor Trustees may be unwilling to execute their duties out of concern for liability or claims asserted by third parties. In order to provide assurances to the successor Trustees, the successor Trustees are hereby indemnified and held harmless for all actions taken by them in good faith in the performance of their duties. The assets of all trusts created by the above Revocable Living Trust Agreement, as amended, shall be utilized to provide for the defense of such Trustees and the actions taken by them in good faith. Notwithstanding any of the provisions set forth in the above Revocable Living Trust Agreement, as amended, the successor Trustees may withhold distribution to beneficiaries after the death of the Trustor of such assets as the successor Trustees may determine to be necessary and appropriate, in the successor Trustee's sole judgment, to provide for the defense of all claims that may be asserted or threatened. After all such claims are resolved to the reasonable satisfaction of the successor Trustees, distribution may then go forward regarding such withheld assets.

Claims of Trustee's Creditors

Just as a trustee cannot be sued personally for causes of action against the trustor's trust estate, neither is the trust estate subject to the claims of the trustee's creditors. Many years ago, a trustor's daughter, who was acting as her mother's trustee, and the daughter's husband filed personal bankruptcy as the result of an IRS audit of their tax-sheltered investments. The IRS attached liens to all of their real property, including the trustor's real property that was titled in the name of her daughter as trustee of her mother's revocable living trust. Of course, the IRS attached this property in error; and, when informed of the mistake, the lien was immediately released. The daughter was not in legal title to the property in her individual name; she was in legal title to the property in a fiduciary capacity as trustee of her mother's revocable living trust. Therefore, this property was not available to the daughter to satisfy her creditors, including the IRS.

CHAPTER 7

FEDERAL INCOME TAX

GRANTOR TRUST RULES

A revocable living trust is a conduit through which all of the income, credits, and deductions attributable to the trust estate income belong to the trustor.[1] In this regard, the trust itself is not the taxpayer. Instead, all income, deductions, and credits are reported by the trustor on his or her U.S. Individual Income Tax Return (Form 1040).[2]

Trust Income, Deductions, and Credits

The general principle underlying the treatment of a revocable living trust as a conduit is that income of a trust over which the trustor has retained substantial dominion or control should be taxed to that person—not to the trust itself—or to the beneficiary to whom the income may be distributed.[3] An item of income, deduction, or credit included in computing the taxable income of the trustor is treated as if received by the trustor. For example, a charitable contribution made by the trustee of a revocable living trust which is attributed to the trustor is aggregated with the trustor's other charitable contributions to determine their deductibility.[4] Likewise, dividends received by a trust from sources outside the trust agreement which are attributed to the trustor are aggregated with the trustor's income from other sources to determine the trustor's total gross income.[5] The same is true for all other sources of income.

Trustor's Control of Trust Estate

Income of a trust is not included in computing the taxable income, deductions, and credits of a trustor solely on the grounds of the trustor's dominion and control over the trust.[6] However, this general rule does not apply in situations involving an assignment of future income, whether or not the assignment is to a revocable living trust. Thus, for example, a person who assigns his or her right to future income under an employment contract may be taxed on that income, even though the assignment is to a revocable living trust over which the assignor has retained none of the controls under the grantor trust rules.[7] Simi-

---

[1] I.R.C. § 671; Treas. Reg. § 1.671-1(a).

[2] Treas. Reg. § 1.671-4(b)(1) and (2).

[3] Treas. Reg. § 1.671-2(b).

[4] *See* I.R.C. § 170(b)(1)(A) flush language.

[5] Treas. Reg. § 1.671-2(c).

[6] I.R.C. § 671.

[7] I.R.C. §§ 671-679.

larly, a bondholder who assigns his or her right to interest may be taxed on interest payments, even though the assignment is to a revocable living trust not controlled by the assignor. Nor are the rules as to family partnerships affected by the provisions of the grantor trust rules, even though a partnership interest is held in a revocable living trust.[8]

Transfer and Leaseback Arrangement

Likewise, the grantor trust rules have no application in determining the right of a trustor to deductions for payments to a revocable living trust under a transfer and leaseback arrangement. Even though a trustor may not have dominion and control over the trust estate or its income, nevertheless the grantor trust rules do not prevent any person from being taxed on the income of a trust when it is used to discharge his or her legal obligation.[9] Such person is then treated as a beneficiary under I.R.C. Sections 641 through 669 or treated as an owner under I.R.C. Section 677 because the income is distributed for his or her benefit and not because of his or her dominion or control over the trust.[10]

Trustor as Owner of Trust Estate

The trustor is treated as the owner of the revocable living trust if:

- The trustor has retained a reversionary interest in the trust within specified time limits;[11]
- The trustor or a nonadverse party has certain powers over the beneficial interests under the trust;[12]
- Certain administrative powers over the trust exist under which the trustor can or does benefit;[13]
- The trustor or a nonadverse party has a power to revoke the trust or return the trust estate property to the trustor;[14] or
- The trustor or a nonadverse party has the power to distribute income to or for the benefit of the trustor or the trustor's spouse.[15]

An adverse party is any person having a substantial beneficial interest in a trust that would be adversely affected by the exercise or nonexercise of a power that he or she possesses respecting the trust. A person having a general power of appointment over the trust property has a beneficial interest in the trust estate.[16] A trustee is not an adverse party merely because of his or her interest as trustee. An interest is a substantial interest if its

---

[8] Treas. Reg. § 1.671-1(c).

[9] Treas. Reg. § 1.671-1(c); *see* I.R.C. § 662(a)(1) or (2), whichever is applicable, and Treas. Reg. § 1.662(a)-4.

[10] Treas. Reg. § 1.671-1(c).

[11] I.R.C. § 673(a).

[12] I.R.C. § 674(a); Treas. Reg. § 1.674(a)-1(a). An *adverse party* is any person having a substantial beneficial interest in the trust that would be adversely affected by the exercise or nonexercise of the power that such person possesses respecting the trust. A person having a general power of appointment over the trust property is deemed to have a beneficial interest in the trust (I.R.C. § 672(a)). A *nonadverse party* is any person who is not an adverse party (I.R.C. § 672(b)).

[13] I.R.C. § 675; Treas. Reg. § 1.675-1(a).

[14] I.R.C. § 676(a); Treas. Reg. § 1.676(a)-1.

[15] I.R.C. § 677(a); Treas. Reg. § 1.677(a)-1(a) and (b)(2).

[16] I.R.C. § 672(a); Treas. Reg. § 1.672(a)-1(a).

value in relation to the total value of the property subject to the power is not insignificant.[17] A nonadverse party is any person who is not an adverse party.[18]

Beneficiary as an Adverse Party

Ordinarily, a beneficiary is not an adverse party; but, if the beneficiary's right to share in the income or principal of a revocable living trust is limited to only a part, then, the beneficiary may be an adverse party only as to that part. Thus, if Al, Ben, Charlie, and Don are equal income beneficiaries of a revocable living trust, and the trustor can revoke the trust with Al's consent, the trustor is treated as the owner of a portion that represents three–fourths of the trust; and items of income, deduction, and credit attributable to that portion are included in determining the trustor's taxable income.[19]

The interest of a beneficiary entitled to ordinary income, as opposed to capital gain income, of a revocable living trust may or may not be adverse with respect to the exercise of a power over trust principal. Thus, if the income of a revocable living trust is payable to Al for life with a power (which is not a general power of appointment) in Al to appoint the principal to the trustor either during the trustor's life or by Will, Al's interest is adverse to the return of the principal to the trustor during Al's life but is not adverse to a return of the principal after Al's death. In other words, Al's interest is adverse as to ordinary income but is not adverse as to income allocable to principal. Therefore, assuming no other relevant facts exist, the trustor would not be taxed on the ordinary income of the trust under I.R.C. Sections 674, 676, or 677 but would be taxed under I.R.C. Section 677 on income allocable to principal (such as capital gains), since it may, in the discretion of a nonadverse party, be accumulated for future distribution to the trustor. Similarly, the interest of a contingent income beneficiary is adverse to a return of principal to the trustor before the termination of the trustor's interest but not to a return of principal after the termination of the trustor's interest.[20]

Remainderman as an Adverse Party

The interest of a remainderman[21] is adverse to the exercise of any power over the principal of a revocable living trust but not to the exercise of a power over any income interest preceding his or her remainder interest in the trust estate. For example, if the trustor creates a revocable living trust that provides for income to be distributed to Al for ten years and then for the principal to go to Pat, if then living, a power exercisable by Pat to revest principal in the trustor is a power exercisable by an adverse party; however, a power exercisable by Pat to distribute part or all of the ordinary income to the trustor may be a power exercisable by a nonadverse party (which would cause the ordinary income to be taxed to the trustor).[22]

BASIS AND HOLDING PERIOD OF TRUST PROPERTY

Trustor's Basis

As a general rule, the trustor's basis in property transferred to a revocable living trust is the same as it would be in the hands of the trustor. This basis is increased by the amount of gain or decreased by the amount of loss recognized to the trustor on such transfer under

---

[17] Treas. Reg. § 1.672(a)-1(a).

[18] I.R.C. § 672(b).

[19] Treas. Reg. § 1.672(a)-1(b).

[20] Treas. Reg. § 1.672(a)-1(c).

[21] A *remainderman* is an individual who is entitled to the remainder of an estate after a particular estate carved out of property has expired.

[22] Treas. Reg. § 1.672(a)-1(d).

the law applicable to the year in which the transfer was made.[23] In other words, the trustor's basis in property transferred to a revocable living trust is carried over to the trust. If the property is an investment made by the trustee (e.g., in the case of a sale by the trustee of property transferred by the trustor and the trustee reinvests the proceeds), the cost or other basis to the trustee is taken in lieu of the trustor's basis at the time the property was transferred to the revocable living trust.[24]

Donee's Basis in Property Gifted by Trustor

A donee's basis in property gifted by the trustor from a revocable living trust to the donee is the same as it would be in the hands of the trustor (donor). The same rule applies in determining loss, unless the basis is greater than the fair market value of the property at the time of the gift. In such case, the basis for determining loss is the fair market value at the time of the gift.[25]

Example

Doris (trustor) gifts to Ted (donee) income-producing property that has an adjusted basis of $100,000 at the date of the gift. The fair market value of the property at the date of the gift is $90,000. Ted later sells the property for $95,000. In such case, Ted realizes neither gain nor loss. The basis for determining loss is $90,000; therefore, Ted incurs no loss. Furthermore, Ted does not realize gain upon a sale of the property, since the basis for determining gain is $100,000.[26]

Furthermore, as a general rule, the donee's holding period for purposes of determining the maximum capital gain rate includes the trustor's (donor's) holding period.[27] If, in the previous example, gain or loss were an issue, Ted's holding period includes the period during which Doris (the trustor) held the property.

Basis of Trust Estate Upon Trustor's Death

Upon the trustor's death, assets composing the trust estate and includable in the decedent trustor's gross estate receive a new basis in the hands of the trustor's beneficiaries for federal income tax reporting purposes. The new basis is equal to the fair market value of the trust estate assets on the date of the decedent trustor's death, or, if elected, the alternate valuation date under I.R.C. Section 2032, or under the special use valuation provisions of I.R.C. Section 2032A.[28]

Community Property

With respect to community property transferred to a revocable living trust, neither the Code nor the Treasury Regulations provides specifically for the taxation of community property. However, one-half the value of community property is includable in the value of the gross estate of the first spouse to die.[29] Unlike property owned by spouses as joint tenants with right of survivorship (including tenants by the entirety with right of survivorship), the entire

---

[23] I.R.C. § 1015(b); Treas. Reg. § 1.1015-2(a)(1).

[24] Treas. Reg. § 1.1015-2(b).

[25] Treas. Reg. § 1.1015-1(a)(1); Moy, 2, *A Practitioner's Guide to Estate Planning*, § 29.05 [A][2] at 29-31.

[26] Treas. Reg. § 1.1015-1(a)(2).

[27] Treas. Reg. § 1.1223-1(b).

[28] I.R.C. §§ 1014(a), (d); Treas. Reg. § 1.1014-1(a).

[29] I.R.C. § 2033; Treas. Reg. § 20.2033-1.

value of community property (both spouse's respective vested one-half interests) receives a step-up (or step-down) in basis to the fair market value of the entire community property on the date of the first decedent spouse's death, or the alternate valuation date.[30] This rule applies even when the title to property classified as community property is conveyed to the trustee of a revocable living trust.

Spouse's Joint Property Rule

With respect to property owned by spouses as joint tenants with right of survivorship, under the *spouse's joint property rule*,[31] one-half the value of property owned as JTWROS by a husband and wife is includable in the value of the first decedent spouse's gross estate. One-half the value of such property receives a step-up (or step-down) in basis to the fair market value of the property on the date of the decedent spouse's death, or the alternate valuation date. The surviving spouse's basis is a carryover basis of his or her original cost or adjusted basis in his or her one-half share of the property owned as JTWROS.

Ask Your Attorney

If my spouse and I convey legal title to property we own as JTWROS to the trustee of our joint revocable living trust, does the spouse's joint property rule apply upon the death of the first of us to die?

Answer

Technically, no.

The *spouse's joint property rule* does not apply to the title to property conveyed to the trustee of a revocable living trust. This is because, once title to the property previously owned as JTWROS is conveyed to the trustee of the revocable living trust, the property is no longer considered owned by the spouses as JTWROS; and each spouse will then hold a beneficial undivided one-half interest as a tenant in common in the property. In effect, upon the first decedent spouse's death, only one-half the fair market value of the property on the date of the decedent spouse's death, or the alternate valuation date, will be included in the first decedent spouse's gross estate for federal estate tax purposes. Accordingly, only that one-half interest will receive a step-up (or step-down) in basis to the fair market value of the property on the date of the decedent spouse's death, or the alternate valuation date.[32]

Ask Your Attorney

With respect to the previous question, would the answer be the same if my spouse and I conveyed our respective one-half interests in property we owned as JTWROS to the trustee of our respective separate revocable living trusts?

Answer

Yes.

---

[30] I.R.C. § 1014(b)(6).

[31] I.R.C. § 2040(b)(1).

[32] Moy, 2, *A Practitioner's Guide to Estate Planning*, § 29.05 [A][3][b], at 29-33.

Pre-1977 Survivorship Property

Ask Your Attorney

Whether my spouse and I have a joint revocable living trust or each of us has our own separate revocable living trust, can each of us convey more than, or less than, our respective one-half interest in property owned as JTWROS to the trustee of our joint revocable living trust or respective separate revocable living trusts?

Answer

Yes.

For the estates of decedent spouses dying after 1981, the gross estate of the first spouse to die includes only one-half of the value of any and all property—real or personal (tangible or intangible)—owned by the decedent and his or her spouse as JTWROS (including tenants by the entirety), regardless of which spouse furnished the original consideration for the acquisition of the property and provided the decedent and his or her spouse are the only joint tenants.[33] However, the *spouse's joint property rule* does not apply to property acquired by spouses as JTWROS *before* 1977. It has been determined that, under the TRA '76, a spousal joint interest created before 1977 is specifically exempted from the *spouse's joint property rule*. Accordingly, if a husband and wife acquired property as JTWROS *before* 1977 and one of the spouses dies, 100 percent of the value of the property owned as JTWROS may be includable in the first decedent spouse's gross estate for federal estate tax purposes, except to the extent that the surviving spouse can prove contribution to the acquisition of the property.[34] In other words, the pre-ERTA '81 *consideration furnished test* rule under I.R.C. Section 2040(a) applies. This means that the amount of property owned by a husband and wife as JTWROS includable in the value of the estate of the first spouse to die will be proportionate to the consideration furnished by the first decedent spouse at the time the property was acquired. Absent evidence of such consideration, 100 percent of the value of such property is includable in the gross estate of the first spouse to die as provided under I.R.C. Section 2040(a).[35]

Holding Period

The holding period of any assets transferred to a revocable living trust is the same as the trustor's holding period. Capital gains and losses on property transferred to a revocable living trust belong to the trustor. Hence, the holding period for determining the character of the gain or loss is computed from the date the trustor acquired the property—not the date the property was transferred to the trust.[36]

---

[33] I.R.C. § 2040(b)(1); H. Rep. No. 97-201, 97th Cong., 1st Sess., 188 at 163 (1981), 1981-2 C.B. 352.

[34] *Gallenstein v. United States*, 975 F.2d 286 (6th Cir. 1992), *aff'g* 91-2 U.S. Tax Cas. (CCH) ¶ 60,088 (D.C. E.D. Ky. 1991); *Patten v. United States*, 116 F.3d 1029 (4th Cir. Va. 1997), *aff'g* 96-1 U.S. Tax Cas. (CCH) ¶ 60,231 (D.C. W.D. Va. 1996); *Anderson v. United States*, 96-1 U.S. Tax Cas. (CCH) ¶ 60,235 (D.C. Md. 1996); *Baszto v. United States*, 98-1 U.S. Tax Cas. (CCH) ¶ 60,305 (D.C. Florida 1998) [U.S. District court held that the effective date of the Economic Recovery Tax Act of 1981 did not control the application of I.R.C. § 2040(b)]; *Hahn v. Commissioner*, 110 T.C. 14 (1998). The IRS has acquiesced in *Hahn v. Commissioner*, Action on Decision CC-2001-006, October 19, 2001. Accordingly, the Service will no longer litigate that I.R.C. § 2040(b)(1) applies to joint interests created before January 1, 1977, where the deceased joint tenant died after December 31, 1981.

[35] Moy, 2, *A Practitioner's Guide to Estate Planning*, at § 29.05 [A][3][c], 29-33.

[36] Gen. Couns. Mem. 19347, 1938-1 C.B. 218, *declared obsolete on other grounds*, Rev. Rul. 73-209, 1973-1 C.B. 614; Moy, 2, *A Practitioner's Guide to Estate Planning*, § 29.05 [A][4], at 29-34.

Craig purchased publicly traded securities on September 5, 2002, and transferred them to a revocable living trust on December 10, 2002. The trust's holding period began on September 5, 2002, the same date on which Craig purchased the securities. The trust's holding period is the same as Craig's would have been if Craig had retained ownership of the securities in his individual name.

Upon the trustor's death, a new holding period for the property comprising the trust estate begins on the date the revocable living trust becomes irrevocable.[37] If such property is sold or otherwise disposed of by a person acquiring the property from the trustor within one year after the trustor's death, then such person is considered to have held such property for more than one year.[38]

Basis of Property Transferred within One Year of Death

Ask Your Attorney

I own low basis highly appreciated property. My spouse is in poor health and will probably predecease me. If I transfer the ownership of the property to my spouse, with the intent of receiving it back from my spouse upon his or her death, can I obtain a step-up in basis to fair market value of the property upon my spouse's date of death or the alternate valuation date?

Answer

Yes, provided the ill spouse does not die within one year after taking title to the property.

The general rule regarding fair market value as the basis of property acquired from a decedent does not apply to appreciated property acquired by a decedent by gift *within* one year of death.[39] If appreciated property is acquired by the decedent by gift during the one-year period ending on the date of the decedent's death and the property is acquired from the decedent by, or passes from the decedent to, the donor of such property, the basis of such property in the hands of the donor is the adjusted basis of the property in the hands of the decedent immediately before the death of the decedent.[40] This rule also applies when property is transferred to a revocable living trust.

---

[37] *Fifth Ave. Bank v. United States,* 41 F. Supp. 428 (Ct. Cl. 1941), *cert. denied,* 315 U.S. 820 (1942).

[38] I.R.C. § 1223(11); Moy, 2, *A Practitioner's Guide to Estate Planning,* § 29.05 [A][4], at 29-34.

[39] I.R.C. § 1014(c), (d) and (e).

[40] I.R.C. § 1014(e)(1). The legislative history underlying I.R.C. § 1014(e) expresses Congress's concern that, under the statutory scheme prior to enactment, an individual could transfer appreciated property to a family member immediately prior to the family member's death, anticipating that on the family member's death the individual would receive the property back (through bequest or devise) and obtain a step-up in basis to the fair market value of the property. Under such circumstances, the initial transfer to the decedent lacks substance because of the short period of time between the two transfers. Further, Congress recognized that the allowance of an unlimited estate tax marital deduction and the increase in the unified credit provided an even greater incentive for persons to plan such death-time transfers of appreciated property, because, in many cases, the provisions eliminated any estate and gift tax consequences with respect to the transfers (*See* H. Rep. No. 97-201, 97th Cong., 1st Sess. 188, 391 (1981), 1981-2 C.B. 352.).

Example

Marie died testate in June 1990. She was survived by her husband, Neville. One month prior to her death, she and Neville effected a revocable living trust (trust agreement). They placed all property owned by them into the trust agreement. The major portion of the property transferred to the revocable living trust was property owned by them as JTWROS. Some of the property was Neville's separate property.

Either Marie or Neville (trustors), acting alone and without the consent of the other, could revoke the revocable living trust during their joint lifetimes, in which case an undivided one-half interest in the trust estate would have been distributed by the trustee to each of Marie and Neville. Neither Marie nor Neville exercised the power to revoke the trust agreement. At the date of death of the first trustor to die, the trust agreement provided that the decedent trustor's one-half interest in the trust estate passed to the surviving trustor.

The trust agreement provided that the trustee pay the taxes, debts, and expenses of the first trustor to die from the trust estate but only if the trustee was notified to do so by the decedent trustor in a written document (other than in a Will) that had been signed and acknowledged in the form required for the recording of deeds in decedent trustor's state of domicile and delivered to the trustee during the trustor's lifetime. The surviving trustor's right to revoke the trust agreement was not affected during the lifetime of the trustor making the request. However, if the decedent trustor had made the request of the trustee and the surviving trustor had not elected to revoke the trust prior to the decedent trustor's death, then, at the time of the decedent trustor's death, the surviving trustor's powers to amend, revoke, and withdraw would be subject and subordinate to the trustee's duties to pay the taxes, debts, and expenses of the decedent trustor. At the date of Marie's death, neither she nor Neville had notified the trustee that the trustee was to make such payments.

Under I.R.C. Section 2041, Neville's one-half undivided interest in the trust estate was included in Marie's gross estate. Marie's one-half undivided interest in the trust estate was included under other Code sections. In this regard, I.R.C. Section 2041 provides that the gross estate includes the value of any property over which the decedent possessed a general power of appointment. Also, the gross estate includes the value of any property subject to a general power of appointment that the decedent released or exercised by a disposition of the power itself, which, if the property had been owned by the decedent, would be includable in the decedent's gross estate under I.R.C. Sections 2035 through 2038. Property acquired from the decedent includes property acquired through the exercise or nonexercise of a power of appointment, if the value of the property is included in the decedent's gross estate.[41]

In disallowing a step-up in basis for transfers made within one year of death, Congress clearly contemplated that a donor must relinquish actual dominion and control over the property for a full year prior to death. Unless the donor has relinquished actual dominion and control over the property and has done so for a sufficient period of time, the property cannot be properly characterized as being "acquired from the decedent," even if the property is included in the decedent's gross estate.[42] Neville (the donor) held dominion and control over the property throughout the year prior to Marie's death, since he could revoke the trust agreement at any time. It was only at Marie's death that the power to revoke the trust became ineffective. Because Neville never relinquished dominion and control over the property (and the property reverted back to Neville at Marie's death), the property was not acquired from Marie (the decedent) within the meaning of I.R.C. Section 1014(a) and (e), notwithstanding that it was includable in Marie's gross estate. Hence, the basis of the

---

[41] I.R.C. § 1014(b)(9).

[42] *See* H. Rep. No. 97-201, 97th Cong., 1st Sess. 188, 391 (1981), 1981-2 C.B. 352.

property in Neville's hands did not step-up to its fair market value at the date of Marie's death, as provided under I.R.C. Section 1014(a). Rather, the basis of the property in Neville's hands was Marie's adjusted basis in the property immediately before her death, as provided under I.R.C. Section 1014(e)(1).[43]

TRANSFERS OF PROPERTY BETWEEN SPOUSES

For federal income tax purposes, no gain or loss is recognized on a transfer of property from an individual to or in trust, including a revocable living trust, for the benefit of a spouse.[44] This rule applies regardless of whether the transfer is a gift, a sale, or exchange between spouses acting at arms' length[45] or whether the transfer is of property separately owned by the transferor or is a division (equal or unequal) of community property[46] or a division of property owned by the spouses as JTWROS.[47] The transferee is considered to have received the transferred property by gift; and, in all cases, the transferee's basis in the property is the transferor's adjusted basis in the property immediately before the transfer.[48] Even if the transfer is a bona fide sale, the transferee does not acquire a basis in the transferred property equal to the transferee's cost (the fair market value). This carryover-basis rule applies whether the adjusted basis of the transferred property is less than, equal to, or greater than, its fair market value at the time of transfer (or the value of any consideration provided by the transferee) and applies for purposes of determining loss, as well as gain, upon the subsequent disposition of the property by the transferee. Thus, this rule is different from the rule applied in I.R.C. Section 1015(a) for determining the basis of property acquired by gift.[49]

PROFESSIONAL FEES AND ADMINISTRATION EXPENSES

As a general rule, legal and other professional fees paid by the trustor for the actual preparation of the revocable living trust, pour-over Will, and supplemental documents necessary to fund the revocable living trust agreement are not deductible by the trustor for federal income tax purposes. However, professional fees paid by the trustee for tax advice (income, estate, and gift taxes), for expenses incurred for the production of income, or for the management, conservation, or maintenance of property held for the production of income with respect to property comprising the trust estate are deductible by the trustor for federal income tax purposes.[50]

Miscellaneous Deductions

Miscellaneous itemized deductions for any taxable year are allowed only to the extent that the aggregate of such deductions exceeds 2 percent of the trustor's adjusted gross income.[51] In this regard, the provision of the Code[52] regarding the determination of adjusted gross in-

---

[43] Tech. Adv. Mem. 9308002 (November 16, 1992).

[44] I.R.C. § 1041(a)(1).

[45] Treas. Reg. § 1.1041-1T(a) Q-2 and A-2.

[46] Treas. Reg. § 1.1041-1T(d) Q-10 and A-10.

[47] *See Arnes v. Commissioner*, 102 T.C. 522 (1994).

[48] I.R.C. § 1041(b).

[49] Treas. Reg. § 1.1041-1T(d) Q-11 and A-11.

[50] I.R.C. § 212; Treas. Reg. § 1.212-1(e).

[51] I.R.C. §§ 671 and 67(a); *Susan L. Bay v. Commissioner*, T.C. Memo 1998-411.

[52] I.R.C. Sec. 67(e)(1).

come of estates and trusts is not applicable because the trustor of a revocable living trust—rather than the trust—is the taxpayer.[53]

Trustee Fees

Trustee fees, if any, paid during the trustor's lifetime (e.g., trustee fees incurred under a management revocable living trust and the annual maintenance fee charged by a bank trustee with respect to a standby holding title only living trust) and administration expenses incurred in the operation of the revocable living trust are income tax deductible by the trustor to the extent that such fees exceed 2 percent of the trustor's adjusted gross income.[54]

Post-Death Administration Expenses

Administration expenses incurred by the revocable living trust after the trustor's death are deductible to the trust for federal income tax purposes, except to the extent they are allowed as federal estate tax deductions under I.R.C. Sections 2053 or 2054.[55]

SALE OF TRUST PROPERTY BETWEEN TRUSTOR AND TRUSTEE

Since a revocable living trust is a grantor trust and the Code provides that such a trust and the trustor (grantor) are one and the same for federal income tax purposes, one might assume that neither gain nor loss can be realized on sales between the trust and the trustor.

Ask Your Attorney

Can a taxable gain be realized on a sale of trust estate property by the trustee to the trustor or on a sale of property by the trustor to the trustee of the revocable living trust?

Answer

Yes—at least if the sales transaction takes place within the jurisdiction of the Second Circuit Court of Appeals.[56] However, a loss on such sales, even if realized, cannot be deducted by either the trustor or the trustee because the trustor and any trustee of the trust are considered related taxpayers.[57]

---

[53] I.R.C. § 671.

[54] I.R.C. § 671; Treas. Reg. § 1.671-2(c); *see Susan L. Bay v. Commissioner*, T.C. Memo 1998-411.

[55] Treas. Reg. § 1.212-1(i).

[56] *Rothstein v. United States*, 735 F.2d 704, 709-710 (2d Cir. 1984) (the states of Connecticut, New York, and Vermont are within the jurisdiction of the Second Circuit Court of Appeals.); *contra* Rev. Rul. 85-13, 1985-1 C.B. 184 (the IRS rejected *Rothstein* and ruled on facts identical to *Rothstein* that the revocable living trust and the trustor are one and the same, thus, in effect, making it impossible for a taxpayer to have meaningful dealings with himself or herself); Priv. Ltr. Rul. 9010065 (December 13, 1989); in keeping with its position in Rev. Rul. 85-13, the IRS ruled that, because the trustor was considered the owner of the revocable living trust, no gain or loss could be realized by either the taxpayer or the trusts as a result of the proposed transfer of partnership interests by the taxpayer to the trusts in exchange for cash and interests in other partnerships held by the trusts. The basis of each partnership interest exchanged is unaffected and neither the taxpayer nor the trusts could acquire a cost basis in such assets); *cf. Madorin v. Commissioner*, 84 T.C. 667 (1985) (the Tax Court seemed to adopt the Service's position in Rev. Rul. 85-13 but did not explicitly reject the position taken by the Second Circuit Court of Appeals in *Rothstein*).

[57] I.R.C. § 267(b)(4).

Ask Your Attorney

Can I purchase property from my revocable living trust using an installment sale and take an income tax deduction for the interest on the interest portion of the payments made to the trust?

Answer

Yes, taking into account the caveats discussed in the preceding answer and provided the deduction for the payment of interest is otherwise allowable under I.R.C. Section 163. Additionally, assuming the IRS does not challenge the transaction, the trustor may receive a basis in the property equal to the purchase price—the price at which the trustor purchases the property from the trust.[58] Similarly, if the trustee purchases the property from the trustor, the trust's new basis in the property is equal to the purchase price.

INSTALLMENT SALES AND INSTALLMENT OBLIGATIONS

The transfer to a revocable living trust of an installment obligation by the trustor who retains the right to revoke the trust and reacquire title to the trust estate property is not a disposition of such obligation within the meaning of I.R.C. Section 453(c).[59] This is because the trustor is considered the owner of the revocable living trust and, thus, as owner, must continue to report the income from the installment obligation in the same manner as before its transfer to the trust. Accordingly, no significant change takes place in the ownership of the installment obligation or the income therefrom; and, thus, no disposition of the installment obligation occurs which would otherwise cause gain or loss to be realized.[60] The same principle applies to the transfer of an installment obligation from the trustee of a revocable living trust back to the trustor.[61] Similarly, no disposition of any part of an installment obligation titled in the name of the trustee of a revocable living trust occurs if either or both trustors revoke a revocable living trust with respect to their one-half community property interests in such installment obligation.[62]

Distribution by Trustee of Unpaid Installment Obligation upon Trustor's Death

Upon the trustor's death, if the trustee distributes an unpaid installment obligation to the beneficiary of the revocable living trust, such a disposition accelerates the capital gains tax on the installment obligation to the trust. Capital gains on unpaid installment obligations distributed to a beneficiary at the termination of a trust are deductible by the trust and taxable to the beneficiary in the taxable year of distribution at the capital gains rate. The gain is the difference between the basis and the fair market value of the obligation at the time of distribution. The basis of the obligation is the excess of the face value of the obligation over an amount equal to the income reportable by the taxpayer if the obligation were satisfied

---

[58] *Rothstein v. United States*, 735 F.2d 704, 709 (2d Cir. 1984).

[59] Rev. Ruls. 74-613, 1974-2 C.B. 153; 76-100, 1976-1 C.B. 123; 67-70, 1967-1 C.B. 106.

[60] Rev. Rul. 76-100, 1976-1 C.B. 123.

[61] Ibid.

[62] Ibid.

in full.[63] It is the distribution of the installment obligation itself that triggers a taxable disposition. Evidently, so long as the installment obligation itself continues as part of the trust estate, no acceleration of income tax otherwise due will occur.[64]

Distribution of Installment Obligation in Which Trustor is Receiving Payments

Except as provided under I.R.C. Section 691, under I.R.C. Section 453(d) the distribution by the trustee of a revocable living trust of an installment obligation to a beneficiary of the trust in which the trustor was receiving installment payments is not a disposition of the installment obligation which causes gain or loss to be realized. Under I.R.C. Section 691, the installment obligation is considered income in respect of a decedent (IRD) to the extent of the face amount of the installment obligation over its basis in the hands of the decedent. Accordingly, the beneficiary is taxed on the distributive share of trust income derived from the decedent trustor's interest in the installment obligation.[65]

Trustee's Distribution of Installment Obligation Income

Regardless of whether an unpaid installment obligation or one from which the trustor was receiving installment payments is retained as part of the trust estate upon the trustor's death, the revocable living trust may or may not be taxed on the income. Of course, this will depend on whether the income is distributed to the beneficiary or retained by the trust. To avoid acceleration of the income tax due, the trustee may not want to distribute the installment obligation itself to a beneficiary but distribute only the income from it to the beneficiary.[66] Thus, the income from the installment obligation would be reported by the beneficiary in the same manner as it would have been reported if the trustor-obligee had lived and received the payment.[67]

SALE OF TRUSTOR'S PRINCIPAL RESIDENCE

The Code provides rules for the nonrecognition of gain on the involuntary conversion or sale of a taxpayer's principal residence.[68]

Involuntary Conversion

A taxpayer may avoid federal income tax on the gain from an involuntary conversion of his or her principal residence by destruction, theft, seizure, requisition, or condemnation. In this regard, when insurance proceeds or monies are received by the taxpayer, if those proceeds or monies are invested in a new principal residence within two years from the end of the taxable year in which the conversion occurred, the taxpayer is not taxed on the gain from the involuntary conversion.[69]

---

[63] Rev. Rul. 55-159, 1955-1 C.B. 391.

[64] Rev. Ruls. 55-159, 1955-1 C.B. 391 and 76-100, 1976-1 C.B. 123.

[65] Rev. Rul. 76-100, 1976-1 C.B. 123, 124.

[66] *Detroit Trust Co., Executor v. Commissioner*, 34 B.T.A. 586 (1936); Rev. Rul. 76-100, 1976-1 C.B. 123.

[67] I.R.C. § 691(a)(1), (3) and (4).

[68] I.R.C. §§ 1033 and 121.

[69] I.R.C. § 1033(a)(2).

Ask Your Attorney

If I convey the title to my principal residence to the trustee of a revocable living trust and the property is later involuntarily converted into money with which the trustee purchases replacement property, can I exclude the taxable gain, if any, from my income?

Answer

Yes. If the trustee purchases replacement property for the property that has been involuntarily converted into money within two years from the end of the taxable year in which the conversion occurred, the purchase can qualify the gain for nonrecognition of income.[70]

Principal Residence Exclusion

Under I.R.C. Section 121, up to $250,000 ($500,000 for a husband and wife who file a joint federal income tax return) may be excluded from gross income with respect to any sale or exchange of a taxpayer's principal residence.[71] To be eligible for the exclusion, a taxpayer must have owned the residence and occupied it as a principal residence for at least two of the five years prior to the sale or exchange.[72] Only one such sale or exchange every two years qualifies for the exclusion of gain from gross income.[73] A taxpayer who fails to meet these requirements by reason of a change of place of employment, health, or other unforeseen circumstances is able to exclude the fraction of the $250,000 ($500,000 if married filing a joint return) equal to the fraction of two years of which these requirements are met.[74]

Oftentimes, when a revocable living trust is created, the trustor is advised not to convey legal title to his or her principal residence to the trustee of the revocable living trust. This advice is usually given under the erroneous belief by many practitioners that such a conveyance will disqualify the trustor from taking advantage of the exclusion under I.R.C. Section 121.

Ask Your Attorney

Will a transfer of my principal residence to a revocable living trust disqualify me from taking advantage of the exclusion from gain on a sale of the property?[75]

Answer

No.

---

[70] Rev. Rul. 88-103, 1988-2 C.B. 304; Priv. Ltr. Ruls. 8729023 (April 17, 1987), 8609012 (November 26, 1985).

[71] I.R.C. § 121(b)(1), (2).

[72] I.R.C. § 121(a).

[73] I.R.C. § 121(b)(3).

[74] I.R.C. § 121(c)(2)(B), (c)(1).

[75] *See* Treas. Reg. § 1.121-3(a) and Treas. Reg. § 1.121-1(b) regarding the definition of *principal residence*.

If trustor conveys legal title to his or her principal residence to the trustee of a revocable living trust, the exclusion of gain from the sale of the trustor's principal residence under I.R.C. Section 121 is not lost upon the sale of the residence by the trustee. In several Private Letter Rulings,[76] the IRS has stated that its findings on the facts presented are subject to the taxpayer's ability ". . . to meet the age, ownership and use requirements of I.R.C. Sec[tion] 121." More importantly, all except two of the Private Letter Rulings on point[77] are supported by the Code and Revenue Rulings.[78]

The IRS has ruled favorably on the issue of a trustor using the exclusion of gain from the sale of a principal residence when his or her principal residence is transferred to the trustee of a revocable living trust in the following situations:

- Single trustor as trustee; one revocable living trust agreement;[79]
- Two trustors (e.g., husband and wife; or nonmarried individuals) as trustees; one revocable living trust agreement;[80]
- Two trustors (e.g., husband and wife); one revocable living trust agreement with one spouse as trustee; children designated as successor trustees;[81]
- One trustor; one revocable living trust agreement; and trustee who is not the trustor;[82]
- Two trustors (e.g., husband and wife); two revocable living trust agreements; each spouse acts as trustee of his or her own revocable living trust agreement. Property formerly owned as joint tenants with right of survivorship (including tenants by the entirety) is conveyed to each trust. The survivorship feature of the joint tenants with right of survivorship is severed.[83] Each spouse takes an undivided one-half interest in the property as a tenant in common. Each spouse conveys legal title to his/her undivided interest as tenant in common in the principal residence to the trustee of his/her

---

[76] Priv. Ltr. Ruls. 8006056 (November 16, 1979), 8007050 (November 23, 1979), 8313025 (December 23, 1982), 8549046 (September 11, 1985), 8239055 (June 29, 1982), 199912026 (December 23, 1998), and Rev. Ruls. 67-234, 1967-2 C.B. 78 and 67-235, 1967-2 C.B. 79. In Priv. Ltr. Rul. 8549046 the IRS again qualified its position with the same reasoning as in Priv. Ltr. Rul. 8313025 to the effect that the exclusion would be available if the trustor taxpayer did not become mentally incapacitated during the term of the trust.

[77] Ltr. Ruls. 8313025 (December 23, 1982) and 8549046 (September 11, 1985). The Service's position in Priv. Ltr. Ruls. 8313025 and 8549046 is erroneous, is not supported by the Code, case law and Revenue Rulings, and should not be confirmed by any court of law and should be ignored. Taxpayers should not fear that if they convey legal title to their principal residence to a revocable living trust and subsequently become mentally incapacitated that they will not be entitled to the exclusion from taxable gain upon a sale by the trustee of the property (*see* Doug H. Moy, "Revocable Living Trusts: Availability of One-Time Exclusion of Gain from Sale of Principal Residence in the Event Trustor Becomes Incompetent," 15 *Tax Management Estates, Gifts and Trusts Journal* 62 (March-April 1990) (hereafter Moy, "Revocable Living Trusts: Availability of One-Time Exclusion").

[78] I.R.C. §§ 121, 167, 676(a)(1); Treas. Reg. § 1.121-3(a); Treas. Reg. § 1.121-1(b); Rev. Ruls. 66-159, 1966-1 C.B. 162; 70-376, 1970-2 C.B. 164 (relating to I.R.C. § 1033).

[79] Priv. Ltr. Rul. 8006056 (November 16, 1979).

[80] Priv. Ltr. Rul. 8007050 (November 23, 1979).

[81] Priv. Ltr. Rul. 8313025 (December 23, 1982).

[82] Priv. Ltr. Rul. 8549046 (September 11, 1985).

[83] Severing the survivorship feature of joint tenants with right of survivorship is accomplished by the spouses conveying title in the property to themselves as tenants in common without right of survivorship. Each spouse may hold an undivided one-half interest in the property, or, any other percentage interest that may be appropriate with regard to their estate planning objectives.

respective revocable living trust. Upon a sale, each spouse may exclude up to $250,000 of the gain from his/her respective undivided one-half interest as tenant in common in the principal residence.[84]

- Two trustors (e.g., husband and wife); one revocable living trust with one spouse as trustee with children designated as successor trustees. In this situation, the IRS qualified its position compared with the second situation above by holding: "However, this ruling is strictly limited to the period of time which both you and B are alive, neither you [n]or B becomes subject to a judicial determination of incompetence, and you and B may fully exercise the power to revoke yours and B's respective interests in the trust."[85]

The IRS's position in the last situation above is erroneous, is not supported by the Code, case law and revenue rulings, should not be confirmed by any court of law[86] and should be ignored.

Observation

Except for Private Letter Ruling 199912026, the Revenue Rulings and Private Letter Rulings cited in the foregoing discussion were issued before the 1997 Act repealed I.R.C. Section 1034.[87] Nevertheless, these rulings are still valid as to the issue of whether a person may exclude the gain from income upon a sale of his or her principal residence when legal title to such property is conveyed to the trustee of a revocable living trust.

Issue of Mental Incapacity

Although the IRS stated in Private Letter Rulings 8313025 and 8549046 that, if the taxpayer (trustor) becomes mentally incapacitated after conveying legal title to his or her principal residence to the trustee of a revocable living trust, the exclusion may not be available to the taxpayer, a taxpayer should not be concerned about these rulings. Taxpayer should not fear that, if he or she conveys legal title to a principal residence to the trustee of a revocable living trust and subsequently becomes mentally incapacitated, he or she will not be entitled to the exclusion of gain from gross income upon a sale by the trustee of the property. In fact, if a taxpayer becomes physically or mentally incapable of self care and owns a home and occupies it as a principal residence for at least one of the five years prior to the sale or exchange, the taxpayer is treated as using such property as the taxpayer's principal residence during any time of the five-year period in which the taxpayer owns the property and resides in any facility (including a nursing home) licensed by a state or political subdivision to care for an individual in the taxpayer's condition.[88] This tacit recognition by Congress that a taxpayer may still benefit from the exclusion of gain from gross income, even if taxpayer is "mentally incapable of self-care," is further evidence that a person's mental incapacity, by itself, cannot deprive a person of the exclusion of gain from the sale of his or her

---

[84] The elements of this hypothetical scenario are suggested in Priv. Ltr. Rul. 8239055 (June 29, 1982) and Rev. Ruls. 67-234, 1967-2 C.B. 78 and 67-235, 1967-2 C.B. 79.

[85] Priv. Ltr. Rul. 8313025 (December 23, 1982); *see also* Priv. Ltr. Rul. 8549046 (September 11, 1985) (IRS again qualified its position with the same reasoning as in Priv. Ltr. Rul. 8313025).

[86] *See* Moy, "Revocable Living Trusts: Availability of One-Time Exclusion" for authoritative discussion as to why the Service's position is erroneous and should not be confirmed.

[87] *Taxpayer Relief Act of 1997*, Pub. L. 105-34, 105th Cong., 2d Sess. (1997), § 312(b).

[88] I.R.C. § 121(d)(7).

principal residence when legal title to such residence is conveyed to the trustee of a revocable living trust of which the taxpayer is the grantor (trustor) within the meaning of the grantor trust rules.[89]

With regard to the first four situations listed above, the IRS relied on I.R.C. Sections 676, 671, and Revenue Rulings 66-159[90] and 85-45[91] in support of its position. Code Section 676(a) provides, in part, that the trustor will be treated as the owner of any portion of a trust, whether or not he or she is treated as such owner under any other provision of I.R.C. Sections 671 through 679, where at any time the power to revest in the trustor title to such portion is exercisable by the trustor or a nonadverse party, or both.[92] Code Section 671 provides, in part, that, where the trustor is treated as the owner of any portion of the trust, there is included in computing the trustor's taxable income, deductions, and credits those items of income which are attributable to that portion of the trust, to the extent such items would be taken into account in computing the taxable income of an individual.[93]

Observation

With regard to Revenue Ruling 66-159,[94] the words "and the trust acquires new property, which is used by the grantor as his principal residence" imply that the exclusion under I.R.C. Section 121 is available to the trustor, even if the trustee acquires the property on behalf of the trustor. Of course, in such case, the trustor would have an equitable ownership interest in the trust property.

In Private Letter Ruling 8549046, the IRS included the following evidence in its holding:

Revenue Ruling 85-45[95] considers whether the beneficiary of a trust who is granted under the trust the unrestricted power to vest the entire trust corpus or trust income in any person, including herself, is entitled under section 121 of the Code to the exclusion from gross income of gain from the sale of a residence by the trust. The ruling holds that because the beneficiary had the sole power to vest the trust corpus or income therefrom in any person, the beneficiary is treated as the owner of the entire trust under section 678 of the Code and must, under section 671 of the Code, include items of income, deductions, and credits attributable to the trust in computing her taxable income and credits. Accordingly, the sale by the trust will be treated for federal income tax purposes as if made by the beneficiary.

Observation

In Revenue Ruling 85-45,[96] because "the beneficiary had the sole power to vest the trust corpus or income therefrom in any person" the beneficiary had a general power of appointment.

---

[89] I.R.C. §§ 671, 673(a), 674(a), 675, 676(a), and 677(a). *See* Moy, "Revocable Living Trusts: Availability of One-Time Exclusion."

[90] Rev. Rul. 66-159, 1966-1 C.B. 162.

[91] Rev. Rul. 85-45, 1985-1 C.B. 183.

[92] Priv. Ltr. Rul. 8549046 (September 11, 1985).

[93] Priv. Ltr. Ruls. 8006056 (November 16, 1979), 8007050 (November 23, 1979).

[94] Rev. Rul. 66-159, 1966-1 C.B. 162.

[95] Rev. Rul. 85-45, 1985-1 C.B. 183.

[96] Rev. Rul. 85-45, 1985-1 C.B. 183.

Residence Sold by Trustee

In Private Letter Ruling 200104005,[97] a husband and wife transferred their residence to a revocable living trust. The IRS ruled that, if a *trust* sells an individual's residence, the gain on the residence is taxable to the trust as owner of the residence and not to the individual beneficiary, except to the extent such individual is treated as owning a portion of the trust principal subject to a five-or-five power.[98] The trust was revocable by the husband and wife from the time that it was established until the death of the wife, at which time the trust was divided into two trusts—Trust A (e.g., general power of appointment marital deduction trust; QTIP trust; QDOT) and Trust B (e.g., credit shelter trust), each for the benefit of the decedent trustor's surviving spouse. To satisfy the maximum marital deduction formula provided for in the trust, Trust A, which remained revocable by the surviving spouse, was allocated all of the surviving spouse's interest in the community property estate, plus a portion of the decedent spouse's interest in the community property estate. The balance of the community property estate was allocated to Trust B, which is irrevocable, including 100 percent of the residence. The surviving spouse was given a five-or-five power in the assets constituting Trust B.

The Service ruled that, if the trustee of Trust B sells the residence, the gain on the residence would be taxable to Trust B as the owner of the trust estate and not to the surviving spouse, except to the extent that the surviving spouse is deemed the owner of a portion of the property pursuant to the surviving spouse's five-or-five power. Since the surviving spouse would be taxed on the gain from the sale of the residence, only to the extent of the surviving spouse's ownership pursuant to his or her five-or-five power in the residence, I.R.C. Section 121 only applies to the portion of the residence attributable to the five-or-five power.

Under the Service's reasoning in Private Letter Ruling 200104005, the surviving spouse would be denied the I.R.C. Section 121 exclusion because, in effect, the surviving spouse held only a life estate interest (i.e., a beneficial interest)—not a legal interest in the residence (the trustee held legal title to the residence—not the surviving spouse taxpayer). Thus, the surviving spouse taxpayer did not satisfy the ownership requirements under I.R.C. Section 121(a). Private Letter Ruling 200104005 is not in accord with Revenue Ruling 84-43,[99] which holds that a taxpayer may elect, under I.R.C. Section 121, to exclude from gross income up to $125,000 ($250,000 under present law) gain from the sale of taxpayer's *life estate* in taxpayer's principal residence. In reaching its conclusion, the IRS stated, "It is not necessary that the taxpayer own the entire fee interest in such residence." Furthermore, it is interesting to note that a taxpayer's ". . . bankruptcy estate succeeds to and takes into account the I.R.C. Section 121 exclusion with respect to the property transferred into the estate."[100]

Likewise, where the beneficiary of a revocable living trust does not have the power to vest the trust corpus or income therefrom in any person, the home sale exclusion is not available to the beneficiary. For example, assume that the taxpayer (beneficiary) presently

---

[97] Priv. Ltr. Rul. 200104005 (September 11, 2000).

[98] Property subject to a general power of appointment created after October 21, 1942, is includable in the gross estate of a decedent under I.R.C. § 2041(a)(2), even though the decedent does not have the power at the date of his or her death, if during his or her lifetime he or she exercised or released the power under circumstances such that, if the property subject to the power had been owned and transferred by the decedent, the property would be includable in the decedent's gross estate under I.R.C. § 2035, 2036, 2037, or 2038. Further, I.R.C. § 2041(b)(2) provides that the lapse of a power of appointment is considered to be a release of the power to the extent that the property that could have been appointed by exercise of the lapsed power exceeds the greater of (a) $5,000 or (b) 5 percent of the aggregate value, at the time of the lapse, of the assets out of which, or the proceeds of which, the exercise of the lapsed power could have been satisfied (Treas. Reg. § 20.2041-3(d)(1) and (3).

[99] Rev. Rul. 84-43, 1984-1 C.B. 27.

[100] Treas. Reg. § 1.1398-3(c).

lives in an assisted-living facility. Prior to entering the facility, the taxpayer lived in the residence for eighteen years. The taxpayer's mother established a revocable living trust in which the trustee holds base fee title to residence. Under the provisions of trust, the taxpayer is the income beneficiary of trust and does not have the power to vest the trust corpus or income therefrom in any person. At the time of the taxpayer's death, the trust estate vests in the taxpayer's children, who are over the age of twenty-one. The only asset of the revocable living trust is the residence, and it has not generated any income for taxpayer. The trustees plan to sell the residence and may rent it until its sale. The Service concluded that taxpayer is not the owner of any portion of the revocable living trust under I.R.C. Sections 671 through 678. Therefore, taxpayer is not considered the owner of the residence for purposes of satisfying the ownership requirements of I.R.C. Section 121.[101]

Property Sold by Trustee under 2001 Act

The 2001 Act added paragraph (9)(C) to I.R.C. Section 121(d), which provides that, for estates of decedents dying *after* December 31, 2009, the exclusion applies "to property sold by a *trust* which, immediately before the death of the decedent, was a qualified revocable trust [as defined in section 645(b)(1)] established by the decedent determined by taking into account the ownership and use by the decedent."[102] (Emphasis added) In this regard, the decedent's period of occupancy of the property as a principal residence can be added to an heir's (or beneficiary's) subsequent ownership and occupancy in determining whether the property was owned and occupied for two years as a principal residence, regardless of whether the residence was owned by such trust during the decedent's occupancy.[103] Presumably, a surviving spouse, as a life estate beneficiary of a credit shelter trust (including a QTIP trust or qualified domestic trust [QDOT]) created under the terms of a qualified revocable trust by the decedent spouse, will be eligible for the I.R.C. Section 121 exclusion subject to the occupancy requirement of I.R.C. Section 121(a).

Observations

1. I.R.C. Section 121(d)(9) provides that, "The exclusion under this section shall apply to property sold by— (A) the *estate* of a decedent, (B) any individual who acquired such property from the decedent (within the meaning of section 1022), and (C) a *trust* which, immediately before the death of the decedent, was a *qualified revocable trust* [as defined in section 645(b)(1)] established by the decedent." (Emphasis added) Notice that no provision is made for a *testamentary trust*. Presumably, the exclusion is not available to an individual taxpayer, as beneficiary of a testamentary life estate trust (i.e., a trust established by the decedent's will), except perhaps to the extent of the beneficiary's five-or-five power over the trust principal of which the principal residence is a part.[104] If this presumption is correct, then the revocable living trust clearly has an advantage over a testamentary trust of which any part or all of the decedent's principal residence is part of the trust estate.

2. Under the 2001 Act, after 2009, property passing to a general power of appointment marital deduction trust under I.R.C. Section 2056(b)(5) will not be eligible for additional basis increase in excess of $1.3 million up to the scheduled maximum $4.3 million amount for a surviving spouse. In this regard, only *qualified spousal property* will qualify

---

[101] Priv. Ltr. Rul. 200018021 (January 21, 2000).

[102] I.R.C. § 121(d)(9)(C), added by § 542(c) of the 2001 Act.

[103] Descriptions Contained in the Conference Committee Report on H.R. 1836, The Economic Growth and Tax Relief Reconciliation Bill of 2001, *Federal Estate and Gift Tax Reporter* (CCH) ¶ 29,056, at 44,157 (May 30, 2001) (hereafter Conference Committee Report on H.R. 1836).

[104] *See* Priv. Ltr. Rul. 200104005 (September 11, 2000).

for the additional $3 million basis adjustment. *Qualified spousal property* is *qualified terminable interest property,* as that term is defined for purposes of the QTIP trust.[105] Accordingly, it is unlikely that spouses will direct their respective interests in their principal residence to a general power of appointment marital deduction trust, because property allocated to such trust will not be eligible for additional basis increase for property acquired by a surviving spouse, even though such a trust would be a life estate trust for the surviving spouse.

Planning Strategy/Recommendation

Between now and 2010, upon the first decedent Trustor spouse's death, he or she may want to direct his or her interest in the principal residence to the surviving spouse's own revocable living trust so that such interest, together with the surviving spouse's interest, as trustor in his or her revocable living trust, becomes the surviving trustor spouse's entire interest in the principal residence in his or her revocable living trust. Under such an arrangement, the surviving spouse, as trustor of his or her revocable living trust agreement, may be eligible for maximum exclusion of gain from the sale of the principal residence.

UNITED STATES SAVINGS BONDS

Interest paid on U.S. Series EE savings bonds accumulates in the form of increment in value. The owner of such a bond may elect to report the annual incremental increase in value as income each year[106] or report the increase in redemption value in excess of the amount paid for the bond in gross income in the taxable year in which the bond is finally redeemed or in the taxable year of final maturity, whichever is earlier.[107] If the owner does not report the interest currently, disposition of the bonds before they are redeemed causes the accrued incremental value to be taxable to the owner in the year in which the disposition occurs.[108]

Ask Your Attorney

If I transfer ownership of a Series EE bond to the trustee of a revocable living trust, will I have to declare the accrued incremental value of the bond in my gross income for the year in which the bond is transferred to the trust?

Answer

No.

The IRS has addressed this question in revenue rulings and at least one private letter ruling. Revenue Ruling 58–2[109] deals with a taxpayer who established a revocable living

---

[105] I.R.C. § 1022(c)(3)(B), (5); I.R.C. § 2056(b)(7)(B).

[106] I.R.C. § 454(a).

[107] I.R.C. § 454(c).

[108] Treas. Reg. § 1.454-1(a)(1)(iii).

[109] Rev. Rul. 58-2, 1958-1 C.B. 236.

trust funded with Series E savings bonds previously owned by the taxpayer. Interest had accumulated on the bonds, but the taxpayer had not elected to report the accrued interest on the bonds currently. The revenue ruling holds that, since there was no disposition upon the transfer, the taxpayer did not realize the benefit of the interest at the time of the transfer to the revocable living trust. Accordingly, the taxpayer is not required to include in gross income the amount of interest accumulated to the date of transfer.

In Revenue Ruling 64–302,[110] a taxpayer exchanged, for a Series H bond, Series E savings bonds on which the interest had not been reported for federal income tax purposes and elected to continue to defer reporting the interest accumulated on the Series E bonds. The Series H bond was then reissued in the name of the trustee of a revocable living trust created by the taxpayer. The taxpayer was considered the owner of the trust because the income from the bond was held in the trust for future distribution to the trustor.[111] The revenue ruling holds that the reissuance of the Series H bond does not result, for federal income tax purposes, in a taxable event at the time of the reissuance. Accordingly, no interest is includable in the trustor's gross income until the Series H bond is disposed of, redeemed, or matures, whichever is earlier.

The issue presented in Private Letter Ruling 9009053[112] was whether the transfer to a revocable living trust of bonds owned solely by husband, solely by wife, and by husband or wife as co–owners, and the reissuance of the bonds into the name of the trustee of a revocable living trust, is a taxable event with respect to the accrued, unreported interest earned on the bonds before their transfer and reissuance in the name of the trustee. With respect to the bonds registered in the name of wife, payable on death to husband, or in the name of husband, payable on death to wife, their transfer to the revocable living trust owned by the husband and wife, as trustors, and reissuance in the name of the trustee is not a taxable event. Moreover, under the rationale of Revenue Rulings 58–2[113] and 64–302,[114] the transfer of Series E and EE bonds to a revocable living trust of which the taxpayer is considered the owner, and the reissuance of the bonds in the name of the trustee, will not standing alone result in a taxable event with respect to the unreported interest. In the present case, husband and wife were considered to own the entire revocable living trust under I.R.C. Sections 676(a) and 677(a). Therefore, with respect to the bonds registered in the names of husband or wife as co–owners, or wife or husband as co–owners, no taxable event occurs upon the transfer of such bonds to a revocable living trust and their reissuance in the name of the trustee.

QUALIFIED REPLACEMENT PROPERTY

The conveyance of legal title to a revocable living trust of qualified replacement property acquired with the proceeds from a sale of closely-held stock to an employee stock ownership plan (ESOP) does not result in taxable gain to the transferor-trustor. This is because, under I.R.C. Section 1042(e), such a transfer does not constitute a disposition of the replacement property. Similarly, the transfer of qualified replacement property between a revocable living trust and an irrevocable living trust is not treated as a disposition under I.R.C. Section 1042(e).[115] However, if the trustee disposes of any of the qualified

---

[110] Rev. Rul. 64-302, 1964-2 C.B. 170.
[111] I.R.C. Sec. 677(a)(2).
[112] Priv. Ltr. Rul. 9009053 (December 6, 1989).
[113] Rev. Rul. 58-2, 1958-1 C.B. 236.
[114] Rev. Rul. 64-302, 1964-2 C.B. 170.
[115] Priv. Ltr. Rul. 200239035 (April 19, 2002).

replacement property through the trust, such a disposition may result in the recognition of gain under I.R.C. Section 1042(e) to the extent of any gain realized on the disposition. Such gain most likely would be income taxable to the trustor and not to the trust, because a revocable living trust is a grantor trust under I.R.C. Sections 671 through 679. Transfers of qualified replacement property occurring as a result of the trustor's death do not result in recognition of gain.[116]

TAX RETURNS AND REPORTING METHODS

Ask Your Attorney

Am I required to file a separate income tax return for a revocable living trust?

Answer

Generally, no.

During the trustor's lifetime, all items of income, deduction, and credit from the revocable living trust are reported on the trustor's Form 1040 in accordance with its instructions.[117] Thus, as a general rule, the trustor (grantor) of a revocable living trust is not required to file a Form 1041.[118] Instead, the trustee may use alternative reporting methods.

Trust with Taxable Income or Gross Income of $600

If the revocable living trust has any taxable income or has gross income of $600 or more not otherwise reported by the trustor, regardless of the taxable income, or if any beneficiary of the trust is a nonresident alien, the trust must file Form 1041.[119] As a general rule, upon the trustor's death, a Form 1041 must be filed for any subtrusts created and funded under the revocable living trust, such as an administrative trust, general power of appointment marital deduction trust, QTIP trust, estate trust, QDOT, credit shelter trust, or any other trust that is irrevocable and funded with property distributable under the terms of the revocable living trust or which passes to the revocable living trust from any other source.[120]

Other Reporting Methods

The trustee has the option to file a Form 1041 with an attached statement of all items of income, deduction, and credits for the revocable living trust or use an alternative reporting method to report such items.[121] However, if the trustee elects not to file a Form 1041, the trustee's alternative reporting methods depend on whether the revocable living trust has more than one trustor (grantor). Regardless of the reporting method chosen, the trustee is not required to file any type of return with the IRS.[122]

---

[116] I.R.C. § 1042(e)(3)(B); Priv. Ltr. Rul. 9327080 (April 14, 1993).

[117] I.R.C. §§ 671, 676; Treas. Reg. § 1.676(a)-1. *See* Treas. Reg. § 1.671-4(b)(2)(ii)(A)(4), 1.671-4(b)(2)(ii)(B).

[118] Treas. Reg. § 1.671-4(a).

[119] I.R.C. § 6012(a)(4), (5).

[120] I.R.C. § 6012(a)(4).

[121] Treas. Reg. § 1.671-4(b)(1).

[122] Treas. Reg. § 1.671-4(b)(2)(ii)(B).

Revocable Living Trust with One Trustor

If the revocable living trust is owned by one trustor, the trustee may report items of income, deductions, and credits of the trust by using one of two reporting methods.

First Alternative Reporting Method

Under the first alternative reporting method, the trustee must furnish the trustor's name, taxpayer identification number (TIN) (trustor's Social Security Number), and address of the trust to all payors during the taxable year.[123] The term *payor* means any person who is required by any provision of the Code and Treasury Regulations to make any type of information return (including Form 1099 or Schedule K-1) with respect to the trust for the taxable year, including persons who make payments to the trust or who collect payments or otherwise act as middlemen on behalf of the trust. A broker, within the meaning of I.R.C. Section 6045, is considered a payor. A customer, within the meaning of I.R.C. Section 6045, is considered a payee.[124]

The trustee may not use the first alternative reporting method, unless the trustor provides the trustee with a complete Form W-9[125] and the trustee gives the name and TIN shown on that W-9 to all payors.[126] Unless the trustor is also the trustee or a co-trustee of the trust, the trustee must furnish the trustor with a statement that: (1) shows all items of income, deduction, and credit of the trust for the taxable year; (2) identifies the payor of each item of income; (3) provides the trustor with the information necessary to take the items into account in computing the trustor's taxable income; and (4) informs the trustor that the items of income, deduction, and credit and other information shown on the statement must be included in computing the taxable income and credits of the trustor on his or her income tax return.[127] The statement due date is the date specified by I.R.C. Section 6034A(a). The trustee must maintain a copy of the statement for three years from the due date.[128]

Second Alternative Reporting Method

Under the second alternative reporting method that the trustee may use for reporting items of income, deduction, and credit of the revocable living trust, the trustee must furnish the name, TIN, and address of the trust to all payors during the taxable year.[129] The TIN of the trust is the trustor's Social Security Number. If the trustor is acting as the trustee, then the address of the trust is the trustor's address.

Additional obligations are imposed on the trustee if the second alternative reporting method is used to report items of income, deduction, and credit of the revocable living trust. In this regard, the trustee must file with the IRS the appropriate Forms 1099, reporting the income or gross proceeds paid to the trust during the taxable year and showing the trust as the payor and the trustor, as the owner of the trust, as the payee. The trustee has the same obligations for filing the appropriate Forms 1099 as would a payor making reportable payments, except that the trustee must report each type of income in the aggregate and each item of gross proceeds separately.[130] The due date for the Forms 1099 is the same

---

[123] Treas. Reg. § 1.671-4(b)(2)(i)(A).
[124] Treas. Reg. § 1.671-4(b)(4).
[125] Treas. Reg. § 1.671-4(b)(1).
[126] Treas. Reg. § 1.671-4(e)(1).
[127] Treas. Reg. § 1.671-4(b)(2)(ii)(A).
[128] Treas. Reg. § 1.671-4(d).
[129] Treas. Reg. § 1.671-4(b)(2)(i)(B).
[130] Treas. Reg. § 1.671-4(b)(2)(iii)(A).

due date otherwise in effect for filing Forms 1099.[131] The amounts that must be included on any Forms 1099 do not include any amounts that are reportable by the payor on an information return other than Form 1099.

Trustor Not Acting as Trustee under Second Alternative Reporting Method

Under the second alternative reporting method, if the trustor is not acting as the trustee of the revocable living trust, the trustee must provide the trustor additional information. In this regard, the trustee must furnish the trustor a statement that: (1) shows all items of income, deduction, and credit of the trust for the taxable year; (2) provides the trustor with the information necessary to take the items of income, deduction, and credit into account in computing the trustor's taxable income; and (3) informs the trustor that the items of income, deduction, and credit and other information shown on the statement must be included in computing the trustor's taxable income and credits on the trustor's income tax return.[132] By furnishing the statement to the trustor, the trustee satisfies the obligation to furnish statements to recipients with respect to the Forms 1099 filed by the trustee.[133]

Revocable Living Trust with Two Trustors

If a revocable living trust is owned by two or more trustors (grantors) (e.g., a husband and wife who create a joint revocable living trust or unmarried partners), the trustee must furnish the name, TIN, and address of the trust to all payors for the taxable year.[134] In addition, the trustee must file with the IRS the appropriate Forms 1099, reporting the items of income paid to the trust by all payors during the taxable year attributable to the portion of the trust owned by each trustor and showing the trust as the payor and each trustor as the payee.[135] A joint revocable living trust, of which both the husband and wife are the trustors and file a joint Form 1040, is considered to be owned by one trustor (grantor).[136]

Evidently, whether one trustor is acting as trustee or both trustors are acting as co-trustees, or neither trustor is acting as trustee, the trustee must furnish each trustor a statement that:

- Shows all items of income, deduction, and credit of the trust for the taxable year attributable to the portion of the trust owned by each trustor;
- Provides each trustor with the information necessary to take the items of income, deduction, and credit into account in computing the trustor's taxable income; and
- Informs each trustor that the items of income, deduction, and credit and other information shown on the statement must be included in computing the trustor's taxable income and credits on the trustor's income tax return.[137]

Backup Withholding Requirements

If the Form W-9 required to be given to the trustee by the trustor indicates that the trustor is subject to backup withholding, the trustee must notify all payors of reportable interest and dividend payments of the requirement to backup withhold. If the Form W-9 indicates that the trustor is not subject to backup withholding, the trustee does not have to notify the

[131] Treas. Reg. § 1.671-4(c).
[132] Treas. Reg. § 1.671-4(b)(2)(iii)(B)(1).
[133] Treas. Reg. § 1.671-4(b)(2)(iii)(B)(2).
[134] Treas. Reg. § 1.671-4(b)(3)(i).
[135] Treas. Reg. § 1.671-4(b)(3)(ii)(A).
[136] Treas. Reg. § 1.671-4(b)(8).
[137] Treas. Reg. § 1.671-4(b)(3)(ii)(B)(1).

payors that backup withholding is not required. Since Form W-9 contains the address of the trustor and the trustee is required to furnish the address of the trust to all payors[138] and not the address of the trustor,[139] the trustee should not give the Form W-9, or a copy of it, to a payor. The trustee acts as the agent of the trustor for purposes of informing the payors of the requirement to backup withhold. Thus, a payor may rely on the name and TIN provided to the payor by the trustee and, if given, on the trustee's statement that the trustor is subject to backup withholding.[140] Whether a trustee is treated as a payor for purposes of backup withholding is determined under I.R.C. Section 3406.[141]

Changing Reporting Methods

A trustee's choice of alternative reporting methods may be changed at any time. If the trustee has filed a Form 1041 for any taxable year ending before January 1, 1996 (and has not filed a final Form 1041 pursuant to I.R.C. Section 1.671–4(b)(3)), or files a Form 1041 for any taxable year thereafter, the trustee must file a final Form 1041 for the taxable year that ends after January 1, 1995, and immediately precedes the first taxable year for which the trustee reports, using an alternative method, on the front of which form the trustee must write: "Pursuant to section 1.671–4(g), this is the final Form 1041 for this grantor trust."[142]

Example

> On January 3, 1994, Gerry, a U.S. citizen, created a revocable living trust of which he is the trustor (grantor) and his son, Frank, is the trustee. For tax years 1994 through 2001, Frank filed a Form 1041. On or before April 15, 2003, Frank files a Form 1041 with the IRS with an attached statement for the 2002 taxable year, showing the items of income, deduction, and credit of the trust. On the Form 1041, Frank states that, "Pursuant to section 1.671-4(g), this is the final Form 1041 for this grantor trust." Frank may now use one of the alternative reporting methods.[143]

A trustee may switch from reporting under one of the alternative reporting methods and choose instead to file a Form 1041. If the trustee reported under the first alternative reporting method and, therefore, furnished the name and TIN of the trustor to all payors, the trustee must furnish the name, TIN, and address of the trust to all payors for subsequent taxable years in which a Form 1041 is filed. If the trustee reported under the second alternative reporting method or under the method required for a revocable living trust with two trustors and, therefore, furnished the name and TIN of the trust to all payors, the trustee must indicate on each Annual Summary and Transmittal of U.S. Information Returns (Form 1096) for the final taxable year for which the trustee so reports that it is the final return of the trust.[144] A trustee for a revocable living trust with one trustor who chooses to file under the first alternative reporting method may later choose to file under the second alternative reporting method and vice versa.[145]

---

[138] Treas. Reg. § 1.671-4(b)(2)(i)(A).

[139] Treas. Reg. § 1.671-4(e)(1).

[140] Ibid.

[141] Treas. Reg. § 1.671-4(e)(2).

[142] Treas. Reg. § 1.671-4(g)(1).

[143] Treas. Reg. § 1.671-4(g)(4)(i).

[144] Treas. Reg. § 1.671-4(g)(2).

[145] Treas. Reg. § 1.671-4(g)(3).

Example

Frank, the trustee, reports using the second alternative reporting method and, therefore, furnishes the name, TIN, and address of the trust to all payors for the 2000 and 2001 taxable years. Frank chooses to file a Form 1041 for the 2002 taxable year. On each Form 1096 that Frank files for the 2002 taxable year, he indicates that it is the trust's final return. On or before April 15, 2003, Frank files with the IRS a Form 1041 with an attached statement, showing the items of income, deduction, and credit of the trust. On the Form 1041, Frank uses the same TIN that he used on the Forms 1041 and Forms 1099 he filed for previous taxable years.[146]

Trusts That Cannot Use Alternative Reporting Methods

The following trusts cannot use the alternative reporting methods discussed below but, rather, must file a Form 1041:[147]

- A common trust fund as defined in I.R.C. Section 584(a);
- A trust that has its legal jurisdiction (situs) or any of its assets located outside the United States;
- A trust that is a qualified subchapter S trust, as defined in I.R.C. Section 1361(d)(3);
- A trust all of which is treated as owned by one trustor (grantor) or one other person whose taxable year is a fiscal year;
- A trust all of which is treated as owned by one trustor (grantor) or one other person who is not a U.S. citizen; or
- A trust all of which is treated as owned by two or more trustors (grantors) or other persons—one of whom is not a U. S. citizen (e.g., husband and wife are the trustors, and one of the spouses is not a U.S. citizen).

Complete Form 1041 Not Required

The alleged disadvantage of filing a Form 1041 for the revocable living trust during the lifetime of the trustor is the additional expense of doing so. The truth is, it is not necessary to file a complete Form 1041. Instead, the Form 1041 becomes an information return and refers the IRS to the trustor taxpayer's Form 1040. In this regard, the following information is provided at the top of the return in the spaces provided:

- The calendar-year filing period of the trust;
- The *type of entity* box to be checked is *Grantor type trust*;
- Name of the trust; (e.g., Elizabeth A. Farnsworth Revocable Living Trust Agreement, dated August 23, 2002);
- Name of the trustee presently acting under the trust agreement;
- Trustee's address;
- Either the trustor's Social Security Number or, if applicable, the TIN of the trust; and
- Date the trust was created.

---

[146] Treas. Reg. § 1.671-4(g)(4)(ii).
[147] Treas. Reg. § 1.671-4(b)(6).

Across the front of the Form 1041, the following should be printed in large, bold letters:

**PLEASE SEE GRANTOR'S (TRUSTOR'S) FORM 1040
FOR THE SAME FILING PERIOD.**

The trustee signs and dates the Form 1041 and attaches it to the trustor's Form 1040.

Observation

The rules pertaining to the alternative reporting methods apply as well to persons treated as *owners* of revocable living trusts. The owner of a revocable living trust may not necessarily be the trustor (grantor).[148] With regard to the election under IRC Section 645 to have the revocable living trust treated as part of the decedent trustor's estate for federal income tax purposes, refer to the sections in Chapter 5 on "Disadvantages, Reservations, and Limitations of a Revocable Living Trust," "Alleged Tax Disadvantages," "Income Set Aside for Charity," Making the Election," and "Obtaining a Taxpayer Identification Number."

OBTAINING A TAXPAYER IDENTIFICATION NUMBER

It is not unusual for misinformed employees of banks, stock brokerage firms, transfer agents, credit unions, and other financial institutions to insist that a revocable living trust must have its own taxpayer identification number (TIN) or employer identification number (EIN).

When to Obtain Taxpayer Identification Number

If the first alternative reporting method[149] is used, the trustee need not obtain a TIN for the revocable living trust until either the first taxable year of the trust in which all of the trust is no longer owned by the trustor (e.g., at the trustor's death) or until the first taxable year of the trust for which the trustee no longer uses the first alternative reporting method.

Taxpayer Identification Number Required to File Form 1041

The trustee must obtain a TIN for the trust, as provided under Treasury Regulations Section 301.6109-1(d)(2), in order to file a Form 1041 under the second alternative reporting method or to file a Form 1041 for a single revocable living trust that has two or more trustors (e.g., husband and wife, as trustors; or domestic partners, as trustors).

Trustor's Social Security Number

In effect, unless the trustor is no longer the owner of the revocable living trust, or the trustee chooses not to use the first alternative reporting method, the trustor's Social Security Number is used as the TIN for the trust; and it is this number that the trustor gives to financial institutions (banks, stock brokerage firms, credit unions, and so forth) or transfer agents.[150]

---

[148] *See* I.R.C. § 678(a).

[149] See this Chapter 7 discussion under Tax Returns and Reporting Methods, *infra.*

[150] Treas. Reg. § 301.6109-1(a)(2)(i).

Payors

Any payor who is required to file an information return with respect to payments of income or proceeds to a revocable living trust must show on such return the name and TIN that the trustee provides the payor. Regardless of whether the trustee furnishes to the payor the name and TIN of the trustor (or other person treated as an owner of the revocable living trust) or the name and TIN of the revocable living trust, the payor must furnish a *statement to recipients* to the trustee of the revocable living trust, rather than to the trustor (or other person treated as the owner of the trust).[151]

Spouses as Co-trustors and Co-trustees

Ask Your Attorney

If spouses are each co-trustor and co-trustee of a joint revocable living trust and each spouse has separate investment accounts, the legal titles of which have been conveyed to them in their respective names as trustees and are listed on each respective schedule of assets, whose Social Security Number should be used as the TIN for the investment accounts titled in the spouses' names as co-trustees?

Answer

The ownership designation of separate investment accounts may either be titled in the spouses' names as co-trustees or in the name of the spouse as co-trustee of the investment account attributable to that spouse. The spouse to whom the investment account ownership is attributable would use his or her Social Security Number as the TIN for the investment account.

One should remember that, under the grantor trust rules,[152] any income from a revocable living trust is includable in the trustor's income for federal income tax purposes and is reported on the trustor's Form 1040.[153] If a husband and wife file a joint Form 1040, both spouses' respective Social Security numbers appear on the Form 1040. Thus, an investment account attributable to one spouse under a revocable living trust as that spouse's separate trust estate asset is identified by that spouse's Social Security Number on any forms required to be filed with the IRS.[154]

TAX YEAR

As a general rule, trusts are required to adopt a calendar-year tax year.[155] Since an individual taxpayer reports income based on a calendar-year tax year and a revocable living trust is created by an individual, the tax year of the revocable living trust is the same as the trustor's tax year. The IRS, however, has ruled that, where the trustor is treated as the owner of the entire trust estate (including the income) under I.R.C. Section 676(a) and re-

---

[151] Treas. Reg. § 301.6109-1(a)(2)(ii).

[152] I.R.C. §§ 671-678.

[153] I.R.C. § 671.

[154] *See* Treas. Reg. § 1.671-4(b)(3)(i).

[155] I.R.C. § 644(a).

ports income on a fiscal year, instead of a calendar year, the tax year of the revocable living trust is the same as the trustor's tax year. In other words, the trust can adopt the trustor's fiscal tax year.[156] If the trust has as its tax year a fiscal year, however, the trustee cannot use the alternative reporting methods[157] and may be required to file a Form 1041.[158]

STATE TAXES

The federal income tax concept of grantor trusts is recognized by most states. In this regard, whether a particular state's laws governing revocable living trusts are adopted legislatively or merely apply by reference to the taxpayer's federal gross, adjusted gross, or taxable income, the trustor should be treated as the owner of the revocable living trust for state income tax purposes.

Trust Situs

In some cases, the trustor might establish a revocable living trust under the jurisdiction of a state that is not the trustor's state of residency. In such cases, the state having legal jurisdiction over the trust may not recognize the grantor trust rules, thereby causing both the trustor and the trust to be taxed on trust income without any offsetting credits for the taxes paid by either the trustor or the trust.

Out-of-State Property

Conceivably, the same result could occur if the revocable living trust is created under the legal jurisdiction of the trustor's state of residency; but legal title to property situated in another state is conveyed to the trustee of the revocable living trust. The state having jurisdiction over the trust property may tax the trust on the income from that property. Likewise, the state having jurisdiction over the trust may recognize the grantor trust rules and tax the trustor on the income from the same property without any offsetting credits available to either the trustor or the trust for the taxes paid on the income from the property.

---

[156]Rev. Rul. 90-55, 1990-2 C.B. 161.

[157]See this Chapter 7 discussion under Tax Returns and Reporting Methods, Revocable Living Trust with One Trustor, and Revocable Living Trust with Two Trustors, *infra*.

[158]Treas. Reg. § 1.671-4(b)(6)(iv).

CHAPTER 8

Federal and State Transfer Taxes

FEDERAL ESTATE TAX

The U.S. Government imposes an indirect progressive estate tax on the privilege of transferring property upon one's death.[1] The property to be valued for estate tax purposes is that which the decedent actually transfers at death, rather than the interest held by the decedent before death or that held by the legatee (beneficiary) after death.[2] An estate tax credit (*applicable credit amount*) is allowed against the estate tax imposed by I.R.C. Section 2001 on the estate of every decedent who is a citizen or resident of the United States.[3] Because the estate tax is levied upon the happening of an event (death) and not on the tangible fruits of that event, it is an indirect tax. Furthermore, as an indirect tax, the U.S. Constitution does not prohibit Congress from imposing the estate tax. In fact, courts have upheld its constitutionality.[4] Furthermore, it has been held that the imposition of the estate tax is not a deprivation of equal protection under the law in violation of the U. S. Constitution.[5]

There exists a subtle dichotomy in the definition of the estate tax. On the one hand, the treasury regulations say that the estate tax is "neither a property tax nor an inheritance tax" but, rather, "is a tax imposed upon the transfer of the entire taxable estate and not upon any particular . . . distributive share." On the other hand, the treasury regulations say that the purpose of the federal estate tax is to tax the privilege of transferring the value of the estate owner's property at death.[6] In a way, this is all very interesting but quite academic. Not so academic, however, is the fact that, even though the estate tax is not levied on a particular asset or a beneficiary's distributive share, it generally is payable before the asset is distributed to a beneficiary.[7]

State law creates taxable legal interests and property rights in estates. The ultimate impact of the federal estate tax is controlled by state law. The federal estate tax is merely a tax imposed upon the *transfer of the value of property* at death; it does not control the method of distribution of that property to the decedent's beneficiary's or heirs.[8]

---

[1] *United States v. Manufacturers Natl. Bank of Detroit,* 363 U.S. 194, 198 (1960).

[2] *Propstra v. United States,* 680 F.2d 1248, 1250 (9th Cir. 1982); *see also Ahmanson Found. v. United States,* 674 F.2d 761, 769 (9th Cir. 1981); *Estate of Nowell v. Commissioner,* T.C. Memo 1999-15.

[3] I.R.C. § 2010(a).

[4] Treas. Reg. § 20.0-2(a) and 20.0-2(b)(2); *N.Y. Trust Co. (Purdy Est.) v. Eisner,* 256 U.S. 345, 65 L.Ed. 963 (1921); *Heitsch v. Kavanagh,* 200 F.2d 178 (6th Cir. 1952); Moy, 1, *A Practitioner's Guide to Estate Planning,* § 2.01, at 2-3.

[5] *Estate of Koester v. Commissioner,* T.C. Memo 2002–82.

[6] Treas. Reg. § 20.0-2(a) and 20.0-2(b)(2).

[7] Moy, 1, *A Practitioner's Guide to Estate Planning,* § 2.01, at 2-3.

Unified Gift and Estate Tax Rates

The federal estate tax is a progressive excise tax. Before 1977, two separate tax rate schedules applied to lifetime gifts and transfers of property at death. Congress viewed the two-tax-rate system as a way for people to avoid paying the higher tax on the real value of property at death. Furthermore, Congress viewed lifetime transfers as a tax-reducing vehicle afforded to only the wealthy and generally unavailable for those of small and moderate wealth. These estate owners generally want to retain their property until death to assure financial security during lifetime.[9]

Gift and Estate Tax Rates Consolidated

The Tax Reform Act of 1976 (TRA '76) consolidated the gift and estate tax rates to create a single unified transfer tax and credit system. This unified rate schedule provides progressive rates and applies to decedents dying after December 31, 1976, and to cumulative lifetime gifts made after that date. Under present law, the unified estate and gift tax rates for U.S. residents, U.S. citizens, and nonresident aliens (non-U.S. citizens not residents of the United States) start at 18 percent on the first $10,000 of taxable transfers and reach 49 percent on taxable transfers in excess of $2,500,000 in 2003.[10] Under the 2001 Act, from 2002 through 2009, the maximum federal estate tax rates and the exemption amount are shown in Exhibit 8.1.[11]

Applicable Exclusion Amount and Applicable Credit Amount under the 2001 Act

The 2001 Act phases in a new applicable exclusion amount and applicable credit amount, which is gradually increased to shelter $3.5 million of the value of property transferred at death from federal estate tax. The exemption, referred to as the *applicable exclusion amount*[12] (exemption amount), and the unified credit, referred to as the *applicable credit amount*[13] (unified credit), is $1,000,000 and $345,800, respectively, in 2003.[14] In the case of estates of decedents dying in calendar years after 2002 and before 2010, the tentative federal estate tax will be determined by using a table prescribed by the IRS (in lieu of using the table contained in I.R.C. Section 2001(c)(1) which will be the same table, except that the maximum rate of tax for any calendar year will be the rate discussed above; and the marginal federal estate tax brackets and the amounts setting forth the tax will be adjusted to the extent necessary to reflect the adjustments made by the reduction in the maximum federal estate tax rate).[15] Perhaps the most significant impact of the 2001 Act is the repeal of the federal estate and generation-skipping transfer tax after December 31, 2009.[16]

---

[8] Ibid.

[9] Ibid. § 2.01 [A], at 2-3.

[10] I.R.C. § 2001(c)(1).

[11] I.R.C. § 2001(c)(2); Moy, 1, *A Practitioner's Guide to Estate Planning*, § 2.01 [A], at 2-4.

[12] I.R.C. § 2010(c).

[13] I.R.C. § 2010(a).

[14] I.R.C. §§ 2001(c)(1), 2010(c).

[15] I.R.C. § 2001(c)(2)(A).

[16] I.R.C. §§ 2210(a); 2664 flush language and (d); Moy, 1, *A Practitioner's Guide to Estate Planning*, § 2.01 [A], at 2-5; for additional reading, *see* Sanford J. Schlesinger, "Estate and Gift Tax—Update 2001," *Estate Planning Review*, in 4 *Financial and Estate Planning* 1, Commerce Clearing House, Inc., Chicago, IL (January 22, 2002).

Exhibit 8.1   Maximum Federal Estate Tax Rates and Exemption Amounts 2002-2009

Calendar Year	Estate and GST Tax Deathtime Transfer	Highest Estate and Gift Tax Rates Exemption Amount
2002	$1 million	50 percent
2003	$1 million	49 percent
2004	$1.5 million	48 percent
2005	$1.5 million	47 percent
2006	$2 million	46 percent
2007	$2 million	45 percent
2008	$2 million	45 percent
2009	$3.5 million	45 percent
2010	N/A (taxes repealed)	top individual income tax rate

Reduction of Exemption Amount

The exemption amount is reduced (but not below zero) by the sum of: (1) the amount of decedent's taxable gifts (adjusted taxable gifts) made after December 31, 1976, which are not includable in the decedent's gross estate, and (2) the aggregate amount of the pre-TRA '76 $30,000 specific gift tax exemption allowed for gifts made by the decedent after September 8, 1976. In effect, the *exemption amount* is the reciprocal of the unified credit. The *exemption* is the amount of the gross estate exempt from (not subject to) federal estate tax or gift tax on lifetime gifts in excess of the gift tax annual exclusion amount or gift tax marital deduction. Conversely, the *unified credit* is a tax credit equivalent to the tax on the amount that is exempt from federal estate (or gift) tax and is subtracted from the tentative tax due (estate or gift tax). The applicable exclusion amount of the unified credit is not indexed for inflation.[17]

Active Members of U.S. Armed Forces

The federal estate tax is reduced for taxable estates of U.S. citizens or residents who are active members of the U.S. Armed Forces and who are killed in action while serving in a combat zone.[18] This provision also applies to active service members who die as a result of wounds, disease, or injury suffered while serving in a combat zone by reason of a hazard to which the service member was subjected as an incident of such service. In general, the effect of I.R.C. Section 2201 is to replace the federal estate tax that would otherwise be imposed with a federal estate tax equal to 125 percent of the maximum state death tax credit determined under I.R.C. Section 2011(b). Credits against the tax, including the unified credit of I.R.C. Section 2010 and the state death tax credit of I.R.C. Section 2011, then apply to reduce (or eliminate) the amount of the estate tax payable.

The reduction in federal estate tax under I.R.C. Section 2201 is equal in amount to the *additional estate tax* with respect to the estates of decedents dying before January 1, 2005. The *additional estate tax* is the difference between the federal estate tax imposed by I.R.C. Section 2001 and 125 percent of the maximum state death tax credit determined under I.R.C. Section 2011(b). With respect to the estates of decedents dying after December 31, 2004, I.R.C. Section 2201 provides that the *additional estate tax* is the difference between the federal estate tax imposed by I.R.C. Section 2001 and 125 percent of the maximum state death tax credit determined under I.R.C. section 2011(b) as in effect prior to its repeal by the 2001 Act.

---

[17] Moy, 1, *A Practitioner's Guide to Estate Planning*, § 2.01 [A], at 2-5.
[18] I.R.C. § 2201.

Victims of Terrorism

The Victims of Terrorism Tax Relief Act of 2001[19] generally treats individuals who die from wounds or injury incurred as a result of the terrorist attacks that occurred on September 11, 2001, or April 19, 1995, or as a result of illness incurred due to an attack involving anthrax which occurs on or after September 11, 2001, and before January 1, 2002, in the same manner as if they were active members of the U.S. Armed Forces killed in action while serving in a combat zone or dying as a result of wounds or injury suffered while serving in a combat zone for purposes of I.R.C. Section 2201.[20] Consequently, the estates of these individuals are eligible for the reduction in federal estate tax provided by I.R.C. Section 2201. The provision does not apply to any individual identified by the Attorney General to have been a participant or conspirator in any terrorist attack to which the provision applies, or a representative of such individual.[21]

The Terrorism Tax Relief Act also changes the general operation of I.R.C. Section 2201 as it applies to both the estates of service members who qualify for special estate tax treatment under present law and to the estates of individuals who qualify for the special treatment under provisions of the Act. In this regard, the federal estate tax is determined in the same manner for all estates that are eligible for federal estate tax reduction under I.R.C. Section 2201. In addition, the personal representative of an estate that is eligible for special estate tax treatment under I.R.C. Section 2201 may elect not to have I.R.C. Section 2201 apply to the estate. Thus, if an estate may receive more favorable treatment without the application of I.R.C. Section 2201 in the year of the decedent's death than it would under I.R.C. Section 2201, the personal representative may elect not to apply the provisions of I.R.C. Section 2201; and the estate tax owed (if any) would be determined pursuant to the generally applicable rules.[22]

As amended, I.R.C. Section 2201 no longer reduces federal estate tax by the amount of the *additional estate tax*. Instead, the federal estate tax liability of eligible estates is determined under I.R.C. Section 2001 (or I.R.C. Section 2101, in the case of decedents who were neither residents nor citizens of the United States), using a rate schedule that is equal to 125 percent of the present-law maximum state death tax credit amount.[23] This rate schedule is used to compute the tax under I.R.C. Section 2001(b) or Section 2101(b) (i.e., both the tentative tax under I.R.C. Section 2001(b)(1) and Section 2101(b) and the hypothetical gift tax under I.R.C. Section 2001(b)(2) are computed using this rate schedule). As a result of this provision, the estate tax is unified with the gift tax for purposes of I.R.C. Section 2201so that a single graduated (but reduced) rate schedule applies to transfers made by the individual at death, based upon the cumulative taxable transfers made both during lifetime and at death.[24]

In addition, while an alternative reduced rate table is provided for purposes of determining the tax under I.R.C. Section 2001(b) or Section 2101(b), the amount of the unified credit, nevertheless, is determined as if I.R.C. Section 2201 did not apply, based upon the unified credit as in effect on the date of death. For example, in the case of victims of the September 11, 2001, terrorist attack, the applicable unified credit amount under I.R.C. Section 2010(c) would be determined by reference to the actual I.R.C. Section 2001(c) rate table. A

---

[19] *Victims of Terrorism Tax Relief Act of 2001*, Pub. L. No. 107–134, 107th Cong., 1st Sess. (23 January 2002).

[20] I.R.C. §§ 2201(b)(2) and 692(d)(4).

[21] Joint Committee on Taxation's *Technical Explanation of H.R. 2884, The Victims of Terrorism Tax Relief Bill of 2001 (Final Version)*, Federal Estate and Gift Tax Reporter (CCH) I-44,185 (January 29, 2002) (hereafter *Technical Explanation of H.R. 2884*).

[22] *Technical Explanation of H.R. 2884*, at I-44,187.

[23] I.R.C. § 2201(c); *Technical Explanation of H.R. 2884*, at I-44,187.

[24] *Technical Explanation of H.R. 2884*, at I-44,187.

conforming amendment repeals I.R.C. Section 2011(d) because it no longer applies to taxpayers.[25]

The provisions of the Terrorism Tax Relief Act apply to estates of decedents dying on or after September 11, 2001, or, in the case of victims of the Oklahoma City terrorist attack, estates of decedents dying on or after April 19, 1995.[26] A special rule extends the period of limitations to permit the filing of a claim for refund resulting from these provisions until one year after the date of enactment (i.e., until January 23, 2003), if that period would otherwise have expired before that date.[27]

Determining Amount of Federal Estate Tax

The amount of the federal estate tax is determined by applying the unified rates to the sum of: (1) the amount of the taxable estate and (2) the amount of adjusted taxable gifts, less the tax payable on the value of lifetime gifts.[28] The phaseout of the graduated rates is repealed for estates of decedents dying after December 31, 2001.[29]

The decedent's date of death governs the laws applicable to the federal estate tax. All provisions affecting the computation of the federal estate tax must be those in effect at the time of the decedent's death—not those in effect at the time payment is due. Procedural questions (e.g., manner of making assessments or collecting taxes) are generally governed by the law in effect at the time of the procedure and not the date of death. Also, the date of death is important with regard to property owned by the decedent at death. For federal estate tax purposes, the date and time of the decedent's death are the standard time and date prevailing in the decedent's domicile in the United States at the instant of death. If a U.S. citizen dies in a foreign country that is the decedent's domicile, the date and time of death are the established day and time of such domicile at the instant of death—not the day and time of the place in the United States where the estate tax return must be filed.[30]

Citizenship and Residence

A person's citizenship and residence is important in determining the amount of the federal estate tax unified credit available to the decedent's estate. The unified credit applied against the federal estate tax is computed differently for estates of persons who are either citizens or residents of the United States than for persons who are nonresident aliens (not citizens of the United States). However, the same estate and gift tax rates applicable to U.S. citizens and residents apply to estates of nonresident aliens.[31] A *resident* decedent is a decedent who, at the time of his or her death, had his or her domicile in the United States. The term *United States*, as used in the estate tax treasury regulations, includes only the states and the District of Columbia. The term also includes the territories of Alaska and Hawaii prior to their admission as states.[32] A *nonresident* decedent is a decedent who, at the time of his or her death, had his or her domicile outside the United States under the principles set forth in Treasury Regulation Section 20.01(b)(1).[33]

---

[25] Ibid.

[26] I.R.C. § 2201(d)(1).

[27] I.R.C. § 2201(d)(2).

[28] I.R.C. § 2001(b).

[29] The 2001 Act, § 511(b), (f)(1); Moy, 1, *A Practitioner's Guide to Estate Planning*, § 2.01 [B], at 2-5.

[30] Rev. Rul. 74-424, 1974-2 C.B. 294, *modifying* Rev. Rul. 66-85, 1966-1 C.B. 213; Moy, 1, *A Practitioner's Guide to Estate Planning*, § 2.01 [B], at 2-5.

[31] I.R.C. § 2101(b).

[32] Treas. Reg. § 20.0-1(b)(1); I.R.C. § 7701(a)(9).

[33] Treas. Reg. § 20.0-1(b)(2). *See,* however, I.R.C. § 2202 with respect to missionaries in foreign service.

Observation

A child under the age of eighteen years born outside the United States who is in the legal and physical custody of an adoptive parent who is a citizen of the United States, whether by birth or naturalization, pursuant to a lawful admission for permanent residence, automatically becomes a citizen of the United States,[34] if the child satisfies the requirements applicable to adopted children under Section 101(b)(1) of the *Immigration and Nationality Act*.[35] In effect, a child under the age of eighteen years not a citizen of the United States, who is adopted by a U.S. citizen parent, *inherits* the parent's U.S. citizenship.

Citizen Residents of U.S. Possessions

The estate of a person who is a U.S. citizen by being a citizen of a U.S. possession or by birth or residence in that possession and who is a resident of a U.S. possession at the time of death is treated as the estate of a nonresident alien.[36]

Examples

1. Frank, whose parents were United States citizens by reason of their births in Boston, was born in the Virgin Islands on March 1, 1950. Frank died on June 23, 2001, while domiciled in the Virgin Islands. Frank is considered to have acquired his U.S. citizenship solely by reason of his birth in the Virgin Islands [section 306 of the Immigration and Nationality Act (66 Stat. 237, 8 U.S.C. 1406)].[37]

2. Antonio's father, Xavier, became a Puerto Rican citizen under the Foraker Act and a U.S. citizen under the Jones Act. Under the Foraker Act, all Spanish subjects who resided in Puerto Rico on April 11, 1899, and continued to reside there through April 12, 1900, and their children born subsequent thereto, who did not file a declaration of Spanish allegiance prior to April 11, 1900, were deemed to be citizens of Puerto Rico.[38] Under the *Jones Act*, United States citizenship was conferred to all persons who became citizens of Puerto Rico under the Foraker Act.[39] Therefore, Antonio, because he is the child of Xavier, derives his U.S. citizenship solely from being a citizen of a U.S. possession and is presently considered a *nonresident not a citizen of the United States* for purposes of applying I.R.C. Sections 2209 and 2501(c).[40]

Residents of U.S. possessions are entitled to a unified credit equal to the greater of (1) $13,000 or (2) that portion of $46,800 which the value of that part of the decedent's gross estate which at the time of the decedent's death is situated in the United States bears to the value of the decedent's entire gross estate wherever situated.[41] To the extent required

---

[34] Section 320(a), *Immigration and Nationality Act*, 8 U.S.C. 1431, as amended by § 101, *Child Citizenship Act of 2000*, Pub. L. No. 106-395, 106th Cong., 2d Sess. (31 October 2000) (hereafter *Child Citizenship Act of 2000*).

[35] Section 320(b) of the *Immigration and Nationality Act*, 8 U.S.C. 1431, as amended by § 101 *Child Citizenship Act of 2000*.

[36] I.R.C. § 2209; Treas. Reg. § 20.2209-1, examples (1) through (5).

[37] I.R.C. § 2209; Treas. Reg. § 20.2209-1, examples (1) through (5); Moy, 1, *A Practitioner's Guide to Estate Planning*, § 2.01 [D], at 2-6.

[38] Section 7 of the *Foraker Act*, 31 Stat. 77, 79 (1900) current version at 48 U.S.C. 733 (1988).

[39] Section 5 of the *Jones Act* (also known as the *Second Organic Act of Puerto Rico*), 39 Stat. 951, 953 (1917).

[40] Priv. Ltr. Rul. 200105048 (November 2, 2000).

[41] I.R.C. § 2102(c)(2); Moy, 1, *A Practitioner's Guide to Estate Planning*, § 2.01 [D], at 2-7.

under any treaty obligation of the United States, this credit is equal to the amount that bears the same ratio to the applicable credit amount in effect under I.R.C. Section 2010(c) for the calendar year that includes the date of death as the value of the part of the decedent's gross estate which at the time of death is situated in the United States bears to the value of the entire gross estate wherever situated.[42] Similarly, if a gift tax credit has been allowed under I.R.C. Section 2505 with respect to any lifetime gift made by the decedent, the estate tax unified credit is reduced by the gift tax credit allowed.[43]

Nonresident Aliens

In the case of a nonresident alien, only property situated in the U.S. is subject to the federal estate tax.[44] With respect to the issue of property situated in the United States, works of art loaned by a nonresident alien to museums located in the United States are not considered property within the United States for purposes of taxing estates of nonresident aliens. This is true, even when the art is purchased in the United States by a nonresident alien and immediately thereafter loaned to museums after the purchase. In this regard, the IRS acknowledges that the applicability of I.R.C. Section 2105(c) does not depend on the fulfillment of a useless act, such as exporting the items purchased and then importing them back into the United States.[45] Likewise, life insurance proceeds paid by a U.S.-based life insurance company on the life of a nonresident alien are not property situated within the United States.[46] The Service has ruled that a nonresident alien decedent's interest in a certificate of deposit held in trust is treated as non-U.S. situs property under I.R.C. Section 2105(b) excludable from the gross estate, even though the trust funds are held in a U.S. bank.[47] However, a short-term United States Treasury obligation held by a nonresident alien at death is includable in the nonresident alien's gross estate under I.R.C. Section 2104(c).[48]

Unified Credit Allowed Nonresident Alien

A unified credit of only $13,000 is allowed against a nonresident alien's estate tax on property situated in the United States. This unified credit amount exempts the first $60,000 in value of the nonresident alien's estate from federal estate tax.[49] This fixed dollar credit is allowed in order to eliminate the need to determine the nonresident alien's worldwide estate in order to calculate the unified credit.[50] However, if the nonresident alien's estate discloses worldwide assets and not just those situated in the United States, then the nonresident alien's estate is entitled to a unified credit of $46,800.[51]

Effect of Treaty on Unified Credit Allowed Nonresident Alien

When permitted by treaty, a nonresident alien's estate is allowed the unified credit allowed to a U.S. citizen for the calendar year that includes the date of death multiplied by the proportion of the total gross estate situated in the United States.[52] The proportional

---

[42] I.R.C. § 2102(c)(3)(A). *See also* Rev. Rul. 90-101, 1990-2 C.B. 315.

[43] I.R.C. § 2102(c)(3)(B).

[44] I.R.C. §§ 2103 and 2102(c)(3)(A).

[45] Priv. Ltr. Ruls. 9141014 (July 9, 1991) and 199922038 (March 3, 1999).

[46] I.R.C. § 2105(a).

[47] Rev. Rul. 82-193, 1982-2 C.B. 219 *clarifying* Rev. Rul. 69-596, 1969–2 C.B. 179.

[48] Tech. Adv. Mem. 9422001 (February 16, 1993); Moy, 1, *A Practitioner's Guide to Estate Planning,* § 2.01 [E], at 2-7.

[49] I.R.C. § 2102(c)(1).

[50] *Technical and Miscellaneous Revenue Act of 1988: Law and Explanation,* [Extra Edition No. 55], Standard Federal Tax Reports (CCH) Conf. Rep. 1258 (1988) (hereafter TAMRA '88 Law and Explanation).

[51] I.R.C. § 2102(c)(2).

[52] I.R.C. § 2102(c)(3)(A).

credit is allowed because, when a treaty is involved, the nonresident alien's worldwide estate is easily determinable.[53]

Unified Credit for Non-U.S. Citizen Who Is a Lawful Permanent Resident

If the non-U.S. citizen is a lawful permanent resident of the United States, then the unified credit allowed under I.R.C. Section 2010 is allowed to the estate of the non-U.S. citizen.[54] However, appropriate adjustments are made in the additional 5 percent rate imposed to reflect the actual credit allowed the nonresident alien. The additional 5 percent rate applies to the taxable transfers of a nonresident alien in excess of $10 million only to the extent necessary to phase out the benefit of the graduated rates and unified credit actually allowed, either by statute or by treaty.[55]

FEDERAL ESTATE TAX AND THE REVOCABLE LIVING TRUST

Federal estate tax cannot be avoided by conveying legal title to property to the trustee of a revocable living trust. The value of the trustor's interest in the trust estate is included in the decedent trustor's gross estate and is subject to federal estate tax.[56] The value of such property may be determined as of the trustor's date of death or the alternate valuation date.[57] Use of a revocable living trust does not cause the decedent trustor's trust estate to lose the alternate valuation date election.[58]

Ask Your Attorney

How much of my gross estate, including property in a revocable living trust, is exempt from federal estate tax?

Answer

Under present law, the value of property equal to the federal estate tax exemption amount included in the decedent trustor's revocable living trust is exempt from federal estate tax.

Estate Tax Minimizing Strategies

All of the federal estate tax minimizing strategies available to the decedent under a Will are likewise available to the trustor's interests in the trust estate under a revocable living trust. However, unlike a Will, under a correctly funded revocable living trust, the trustor can control the disposition of all property previously owned as JTWROS (including tenants by the entirety) and the value of property that would otherwise have passed to a named beneficiary by contract (e.g., individual and group life insurance, nonqualified deferred compensation, salary continuation, qualified retirement plan benefits, employee death benefits, and so forth) without the necessity of a probate proceeding. This same control is obtainable under a Will but only if property is titled (registered) in the estate owner's individual name and the beneficiary of the contract benefits is the testator's estate and not an individual.

---

[53] TAMRA '88 Law and Explanation, Conf. Rep. 1258.

[54] I.R.C. § 2001(a).

[55] I.R.C. § 2101(b) (under the 2001 Act, the phaseout of the graduated rates is repealed for estates of decedents dying *after* December 31, 2001).

[56] I.R.C. §§ 2031(a); 2033; 2038(a)(1); Treas. Reg. §§ 20.2033-1(a); 20.2038-1.

[57] I.R.C. §§ 2033; 2032(a).

[58] Treas. Reg. § 20.2032-1(b)(1), (c)(2); I.R.C. §§ 2032(a); 6018(a); Rev. Ruls. 73-97, 1973-1 C.B. 404; 57-495, 1957-2 C.B. 616; 56-60, 1956-1 C.B. 443.

Unfortunately, most Wills fail to operate as intended because the testator (or testatrix) continues to own property comprising his or her gross estate as JTWROS and designates individuals as beneficiaries of contract benefits. This failure of the Will to carry out a married testator's estate plan very often results in overqualification of the unlimited federal estate tax marital deduction in the estate of the first decedent spouse. In other words, the first decedent spouse's federal estate tax exemption amount is unnecessarily wasted because the value of too much property included in the first decedent spouse's gross estate passes to the surviving spouse, thereby qualifying for the unlimited estate tax marital deduction in the first decedent spouse's gross estate.

Estates of Married Persons

With respect to the trust estates of married persons, if their objective is to entirely eliminate or minimize, to the greatest extent possible, federal estate tax on the value of their combined estates, each spouse should provide for the maximum use of his or her federal estate tax exemption amount in a manner that does not cause the value of such property to be included in the surviving spouse's gross estate upon his or her subsequent death before utilizing the federal estate tax marital deduction. In effect, the value of property distributable to the surviving spouse which is sheltered from federal estate tax by the exemption amount should be distributable to a life estate trust (i.e., credit shelter trust; nonmarital deduction trust; or Trust B) under the revocable living trust for the lifetime benefit of the surviving spouse. Provided the life estate trust is properly designed, the value of the property comprising such a trust is not subject to federal estate tax upon the subsequent death of the surviving spouse.[59] By using this simple planning strategy under a revocable living trust, the combined taxable estate of a husband and wife having a value of two times the exemption amount in the year of the first decedent trustor spouse's death can pass to their beneficiaries entirely free of federal estate tax.

PERSON RESPONSIBLE FOR PAYMENT OF FEDERAL ESTATE TAX

The personal representative (executor; executrix) or administrator of the decedent's estate is personally liable for payment of the federal estate tax.[60] Generally speaking, the personal representative must pay the estate tax in full, in cash, within nine months from the date of

---

[59] See discussion in Chapter 16, Trust Planning for a Surviving Spouse.

[60] I.R.C. § 2002; *see*, *United States v. Elizabeth Bartlett*, 2002 TNT 53–17 (D.C. C.D. Ill. 1/19/2002) (court found decedent's surviving spouse under decedent's joint will liable both personally and as executor of decedent husband's estate for unpaid federal estate tax); *but see Little v. Commissioner*, 113 T.C. No. 31 (1999) (during administration of decedent's estate, the personal representative received information indicating possible income tax liabilities of the estate. The personal representative gave this information to the estate's lawyer, who erroneously and repeatedly advised the personal representative that the estate had no tax liabilities and advised the personal representative to make disbursements and distributions. The personal representative, acting in good faith, followed this advice and eventually closed the estate without paying the estate's income tax liabilities. The IRS determined that the personal representative was liable for the estate's unpaid income tax liabilities under 31 U.S.C. § 3713(b) (1994), which generally imposes personal liability on a fiduciary who pays others before paying claims of the United States. Liability under 31 U.S.C. § 3713(b) has been judicially limited to situations where a fiduciary knowingly disregards debts due to the United States. However, in this case, the court held that a fiduciary who reasonably and in good faith relies on an attorney's legal advice that there are no debts due to the United States before paying other claims has not knowingly disregarded debts of the United States. Accordingly, the personal representative was not liable for the income tax liabilities of the estate under 31 U.S.C. § 3713(b)).

the decedent's death.[61] The personal representative's liability is limited to (1) the smaller of the unpaid tax or (2) the debts paid ahead of the tax.[62] The word *debt* includes a beneficiary's distributive share of the estate. This means that the personal representative can also incur personal liability by distributing property to beneficiaries ahead of paying the estate tax and then end up owing any additional estate tax.[63] The personal representative can obtain an early discharge from personal liability by filing an application for discharge with the IRS.[64]

If no personal representative or administrator is appointed, qualified, and acting in the United States, any person (transferee) in actual or constructive possession of any property of the decedent is required to pay the entire estate tax to the extent of the value of the property. Generally, the transferee in possession of the property included in the value of the decedent's gross estate is personally liable for the tax to the extent of the value of the property.[65] A decedent's children were not held liable, though, for the estate tax due when their father, as fiduciary for their mother's estate, filed a fraudulent estate tax return for his wife's estate.[66] Presently, though, the Eighth and Eleventh Circuit Courts of Appeal are divided on the issue of whether the transferee's liability can exceed the value of the transferred property.[67] However, a surviving spouse who was not a personal representative of her decedent husband's estate and was not personally assessed for the estate tax due was not personally liable for the unpaid estate tax of her husband's estate as transferee of certain assets she received.[68]

---

[61] I.R.C. § 6075(a).

[62] I.R.C. § 6075(a); I.R.C. § 2002; Treas. Reg. § 20.2002-1; 31 U.S.C.S. § 192.

[63] Treas. Reg. § 20.2002-1; *Richard M. Baptiste v. Commissioner*, 94-2 U.S. Tax Cas. (CCH) ¶ 60,178 (11th Cir. 1994), *aff'g* T.C. Memo 1992-198 *and* T.C. Memo 1992-199 (final decision of Tax Court regarding estate tax imposed on a decedent's estate was *res judicata* for purposes of determining personal liability of a beneficiary of an insurance policy, the proceeds of which were includable in the decedent's gross estate, for unpaid taxes under I.R.C. § 6324(a)(2). In addition, the beneficiary's personal liability constituted a liability at law for purposes of I.R.C. § 6901(a)(1), thereby subjecting the beneficiary to the method of collection applicable in the case of transferred property); *United States v. Coppola, Jr.*, 85 F.3d 1015 (2d Cir. 1996); *United States v. Estate of Kime*, 950 F. Supp. 950 (D.C. D. Neb. Nov. 5, 1996); *D. Shawn Beckwith, Fiduciary v. Commissioner*, T.C. Memo 1995-20; *Huddleston v. Commissioner*, 75 AFTR2d ¶ 95-696 (5th Cir. 1995), *aff'g* T.C. Memo 1994-131; *see United States v. Elizabeth Bartlett*, 2002 TNT 53–17 (D.C. C.D. Ill. 1/19/2002) (court found decedent's surviving spouse under decedent's joint will liable both personally and as executor of decedent husband's estate for unpaid federal estate tax).

[64] I.R.C. § 2204; Moy, 1, *A Practitioner's Guide to Estate Planning*, § 2.01 [I], at 2-42.

[65] I.R.C. § 6324(a)(2); Treas. Reg. § 20.2002-1; *Fillman & First Interstate Bank v. United States*, 90-2 U.S. Tax Cas. (CCH) ¶ 60,041 (S.D. Iowa 1990); *Lee M. Bentley, et al. v. Commissioner*, T.C. Memo 1997-119; *Estate of Irene H. Govern v. Commissioner*, T.C. Memo 1996-434 (trustee personally liable for decedent's estate tax); *Estate of LeFever v. Commissioner*, 103 T.C. 525 (1994) (heirs cannot disavow special use valuation election and are liable for recapture of additional estate tax); *see also Frank Armstrong, III v. Commissioner*, 114 T.C. No. 5 (2000) (donees of gifts made by decedent includable in decedent's gross estate under I.R.C. § 2035(d)(3)(C) are transferees of property the value of which is treated as if included in decedent's gross estate pursuant to I.R.C. § 2035(d)(3)(C) and are, to the extent of the value of such property at the time of decedent's death, personally liable for unpaid estate taxes pursuant to I.R.C. § 6324(a)(2)).

[66] *In re H. Ulrich*, 88 AFTR2d ¶ 2001–5054 (DC La. Bankr. 2001).

[67] *Gabriel J. Baptiste v. Commissioner*, 29 F.3d 433 (8th Cir. 1994), *aff'g in part* and *rev'g in part* 100 T.C. 252 (1993) and *Richard M. Baptiste v. Commissioner*, 29 F.3d 1533 (11th Cir. 1994), *aff'g* T.C. Memo 1992-198 and T.C. Memo 1992-199.

[68] *Schneider v. United States*, 92-2 U.S. Tax Cas. (CCH) ¶ 60,119 (D.N.D. June 8, 1992); *Schneider v. United States*, 91-1 U.S. Tax Cas. (CCH) ¶ 60,068 (D.N.D. Apr. 10, 1991); Moy, 1, *A Practitioner's Guide to Estate Planning*, § 2.01 [I], at 2-42.

Ask Your Attorney

Is the payment of federal estate tax by the decedent's beneficiaries considered a gift by the beneficiaries for federal gift tax purposes?

Answer

Where the decedent's will does not express a clear intent as to which assets should bear the ultimate burden of the estate tax attributable to those assets, state apportionment law controls against such assets.[69] However, the IRS has ruled that the payment by beneficiaries of a pro rata share of the federal estate tax attributable to the inclusion of an IRA and a deferred income settlement option plan account (DISO) in the decedent's gross estate will not constitute gifts by the beneficiaries for federal gift tax purposes.[70]

The doctrine of equitable apportionment places the burden of the federal estate tax on the property that generates the tax and exonerates from the burden the property that does not generate the tax.[71] Thus, pursuant to the application of the doctrine of equitable apportionment under state law, the estate tax attributable to those assets must be paid from those assets. Accordingly, the payment by decedent's beneficiaries of a pro rata share of the federal estate tax attributable to the inclusion of assets in the decedent's gross estate does not constitute a gift by the beneficiaries for federal gift tax purposes.[72]

STATE DEATH TAX AND INHERITANCE TAXES

Generally, states may impose three types of death taxes on the value of property included in a decedent's gross estate, including the value of property in a revocable living trust: (1) estate tax; (2) inheritance tax; and (3) a pick-up tax equivalent to the federal state death tax credit[73] allowable against the federal estate tax. Some states impose an inheritance tax and not an estate tax, and some states impose both.

State Estate Tax

Like the federal estate tax, state estate tax is imposed on the net taxable value of property transferred at death. Many states recognize the same estate tax deductions, credits, and exemptions allowed by the federal government with regard to the federal estate tax. Not all states impose the same estate tax rates used to determine the federal estate tax.

State Inheritance Tax

Inheritance tax and estate tax are not the same. Inheritance tax is imposed on the value of property received by a beneficiary or heir (succession tax) upon the death of a person; whereas, an estate tax is imposed on the value of property transferred by a decedent to a beneficiary or heir. Theoretically, the beneficiary (or heir) pays the inheritance tax; and the decedent's estate pays the estate tax. However, in reality, the personal representative (or

---

[69] *See Carpenter v. Carpenter*, 267 S.W.2d 632, 642 (Sup. Ct. Mo. 1954); *Estate of Gangloff v. Borgers*, 743 S.W.2d 498, 502 (Mo. App. 1987); *Estate of Wahlin v. Bell*, 505 S.W.2d 99,103 (Mo. App. 1973).

[70] Priv. Ltr. Rul. 200027016 (April 4, 2000).

[71] *See Estate of Boder v. Albrecht Art Museum*, 850 S.W.2d 76, 78 (Sup. Ct. Mo. 1993).

[72] Priv. Ltr. Rul. 200027016 (April 4, 2000).

[73] I.R.C. § 2011.

trustee) generally pays the inheritance and estate tax on each beneficiary's respective share of the decedent's estate before such share is distributed to the beneficiary.

In some states, beneficiaries are classified as to their degrees of relationship to the decedent with the lower tax rates and larger exemptions assigned to closer relatives and the opposite for relatives further removed in their blood relationships to the decedent. Generally, in those states that do not classify beneficiaries, the inheritance tax is imposed at a flat percentage rate. Regardless of the manner in which the inheritance and estate tax is assessed, ultimately it is paid by the beneficiaries.

Credit for State Death Tax

The federal estate tax is reduced by any estate, inheritance, legacy, or succession tax actually paid to a state government on the value of any property included in the decedent's gross estate. This credit is known as the credit for state death tax.[74] Many states take advantage of the federal state death credit by collecting an estate tax equivalent to the maximum state death tax credit allowed. Hence, the state death tax credit is called the *pick-up* tax. The *pick-up* tax is not an additional tax cost to the decedent's estate. In effect, the state imposing the *pick-up* tax is sharing in revenue that the federal government would otherwise receive but for the allowance of the state death tax credit.

If federal estate tax is imposed on a decedent's estate, and the estate, inheritance, legacy, or succession tax payable to a state is less than the maximum state death tax credit allowed, a tax equal to the difference between the state inheritance tax and the maximum state death tax credit is imposed. If a decedent owns property in two or more states and the total of the taxes imposed by all of the states is less than the maximum state death tax credit allowed, the state of the decedent's residence may collect the difference between the total amount imposed and the maximum state death tax credit allowed against the federal estate tax.

Under the 2001 Act, from 2002 through 2004, the state death tax credit rate is, in effect, decreased from a maximum of 16 percent as follows: to 12 percent in 2002, to 8 percent in 2003, and to 4 percent in 2004. The amount of the maximum state death tax credit shown in the table in I.R.C. Section 2011(b) is reduced by 25 percent in 2002, 50 percent for the estates of decedents dying in 2003, and 75 percent for the estates of decedents dying in 2004 (see file APP0801.DOC).[75] The state death tax credit is repealed for estates of decedents dying after December 31, 2004.[76]

In 2005, after the state death tax credit is repealed, a deduction will be allowed for death taxes (e.g., any estate, inheritance, legacy, or succession taxes) actually paid to any state, the District of Columbia, or any foreign country[77] in respect of property included in the decedent's gross estate.[78] No deduction for a foreign death tax is allowed, unless the decrease in the federal estate tax imposed upon the decedent's estate which results from the deduction for foreign death tax will inure solely for the benefit of the public, charitable, or religious transferees described in I.R.C. Section 2055 or Section 2106(a)(2).[79] A deduction taken for foreign death taxes is a waiver of the right to claim a credit, against the federal estate tax, under a death tax convention with any foreign country for any tax or portion thereof in respect of which such deduction is taken.[80]

---

[74] Ibid.

[75] I.R.C. § 2011(b)(2); the 2001 Act, § 531(b).

[76] I.R.C. § 2011(g); Moy, 1, *A Practitioner's Guide to Estate Planning*, § 2.02 [C], at 2-68.

[77] I.R.C. § 2053(d)(1).

[78] I.R.C. § 2058(a).

[79] I.R.C. § 2053(d)(2).

[80] I.R.C. § 2053(d)(3)(A); *see* I.R.C. § 2014 for the effect of a deduction taken under I.R.C. § 2053(d) on the credit for foreign death taxes [I.R.C. § 2053(d)(3)(B)].

Observation

> For estates of decedents residing in those states not connected to the federal tax code, an amount of state death tax may still be imposed after repeal of the state death tax credit. The amount of state death tax imposed based on the federal state death tax credit in effect prior to its repeal will not be deductible against the federal estate tax. After repeal, the only amount that will be allowed as a deduction against the federal estate tax will be any estate, inheritance, legacy, or succession taxes actually paid to any state, the District of Columbia, or any foreign country[81] in respect of property included in the decedent's gross estate.[82]

FEDERAL GIFT TAX

A progressive excise tax is imposed by the U.S. Government on the value of lifetime transfers of property by individual citizens or residents of the United States.[83] The first federal gift tax was imposed by the Revenue Act of 1924. Repealed by the Revenue Act of 1926, the gift tax was reinstituted by the Revenue Act of 1932. With modifications, it has remained part of the Code ever since.[84]

Individual Donors

The gift tax applies only to individual donors making gifts; however, the donee may be an individual, partnership, corporation, foundation, trust, or any other person. The gift tax applies to a gratuitous transfer and is imposed on the value of the gift when it is made,[85] whether the transfer is in trust or otherwise, whether the gift is direct or indirect, and whether the property is real or personal, tangible or intangible.[86] Generally, the same rules used in determining the value of property for estate tax purposes are applied for the valuation of gifted property, except the alternate valuation date is not available in valuing lifetime gifts.[87]

Gifts Are Cumulative

The amount of the gift tax payable for any calendar year generally is determined by multiplying the applicable tax rate (from the unified rate schedule) by the cumulative lifetime taxable transfers made by the taxpayer and then subtracting any gift taxes payable for prior taxable periods. This amount is reduced by any available unified credit (and other applicable credits) to determine the gift tax liability for the taxable period. A donor cannot pay out-of-pocket the gift tax due until the unified credit against gift tax is used up.[88]

---

[81] I.R.C. § 2053(d)(1).

[82] I.R.C. § 2058(a).

[83] I.R.C. § 2501(a)(1); Treas. Reg. § 25.2511-2(a).

[84] Moy, 1, *A Practitioner's Guide to Estate Planning*, § 3.01, at 3-3. For additional discussion of the federal gift tax, see Chapter 1, Federal Gift Tax, Repeal of Federal Estate and Generation-Skipping Transfer Tax; Payment of Federal Gift Tax on Transfer of Property to Trust; and Federal Estate and Gift Tax Rates Reduced.

[85] Treas. Reg. § 25.2512(a).

[86] I.R.C. § 2511(a);

[87] I.R.C. § 2032(a).

[88] I.R.C. § 2505(a)(1); Rev. Rul. 79-398, 1979-2 C.B. 338; Rev. Rul. 81-223, 1981-1 C.B. 189.

The 2001 Act

As previously discussed,[89] the federal estate and generation-skipping transfer taxes are repealed for transfers after December 31, 2009.[90] However, the federal gift tax is not repealed; and the maximum federal gift tax exemption amount is $1 million in 2002 and thereafter.[91] After December 31, 2009, the top federal gift tax rate will be the top individual income tax rate (35 percent);[92] and, except as provided in treasury regulations, the transfer to a trust will be treated as a taxable gift, unless the trust is treated as wholly owned by the donor or the donor's spouse under the grantor trust provision of I.R.C. Sections 671 through 678 (e.g., a revocable living trust, a grantor retained annuity trust [GRAT], a grantor retained unitrust [GRUT], a personal residence trust [PRT], or a qualified personal residence trust [QPRT].[93]

Property Transferred to a Revocable Living Trust

The transfer of property to a revocable living trust is not a taxable event for gift tax purposes, and the property transferred to the trust is not subject to federal gift tax.[94]

Income Paid to a Beneficiary

Income from property comprising the trust estate of a revocable living trust paid to a beneficiary other than to the trustor or the trustor's spouse may constitute a taxable gift of the income by the trustor to the beneficiary.[95] In this regard, the gift tax annual exclusion may be applicable if the income paid is of a present interest and not accumulated as a future interest for the beneficiary. Likewise, to the extent the value of property comprising the trust

---

[89] *See* discussion in Chapter 1, The Economic Growth and Tax Relief Reconciliation Act of 2001.

[90] I.R.C. §§ 2210(a); 2664 flush language and (d).

[91] I.R.C. § 2505(a)(1); the 2001 Act, § 521(b), (e)(2).

[92] I.R.C. § 2502(a)(2).

[93] I.R.C. § 2511(c); Moy, 1, *A Practitioner's Guide to Estate Planning*, § 3.01, at 3-5.

[94] *Smith v. Shaughnessy*, 318 U.S. 176 (1943); Treas. Reg. §§ 25.2511-2(a); 25.2511-2(b), 25.2511-2(c); Priv. Ltr. Rul. 8940008 (June 29, 1989). *Cf.* Priv. Ltr. Rul. 9230021 (April 28, 1992) (trustor proposed to convey to a revocable living trust partnership interests that were subject to liabilities that exceeded the trustor's adjusted basis in the partnership interests. The IRS ruled: (1) that the transfer of the partnership interests was not taxable to the trustor under the rationale of Rev. Rul. 85-13, 1985-1 C.B. 184; and (2) that the adjusted basis and holding period of the property transferred to the trust is the same in the hands of the trustee as it was in the hands of the trustor prior to the transfer. In this case, the trustor was treated as the owner of the entire revocable living trust under I.R.C. § 674(a). Therefore, pursuant to Rev. Rul. 85-13, the trustor was considered as the owner of all the revocable living trust property for federal income tax purposes. Because, for federal income tax purposes, the trustor was treated as the owner of the partnership interests both before and after placing such interests into the revocable living trust, the IRS concluded that no "transfer of property" occurred for purposes of I.R.C. § 1041(a). Therefore, that section is inapplicable to this case. In addition, because no transfer of property occurred, I.R.C. § 1041(e), which is only applicable when a "transfer of property in trust" occurs, also does not apply to this case. [*See* Staff of the Joint Committee on Taxation, Explanation of Technical Corrections to the Tax Reform Act of 1984 and Other Recent Legislation, 99th Cong., 1st Sess. 119 (Comm. Print 1987), which states, "These rules [section 1041(e)] are not intended to apply where any gain will be taxed to the transferor under the grantor trust rules."] Because the trustor was treated as the owner of the partnership interests both before and after their transfer to the revocable living trust, the trustor's adjusted basis in, and the holding period of, the partnership interests remain the same.) Rev. Ruls. 54-537, 1954-2 C.B. 316, 54-538, 1954-2 C.B. 316.

[95] Treas. Reg. § 25.2511-2(f).

estate is gifted to a donee and does not qualify for the gift tax annual exclusion,[96] is not a qualified transfer,[97] does not qualify for the federal gift tax marital deduction,[98] and does not qualify for the federal charitable gift tax deduction,[99] such value is subject to federal gift tax. However, the same result would occur even if property was not transferred to a revocable living trust and gifts were made instead in the donor's individual name. Furthermore, consent by an income beneficiary, other than the trustor or the trustor's spouse, to a judicial early termination of a revocable living trust is a taxable gift event to the remainder beneficiaries.[100]

Property Transferred From Trustee to Trustor

Ask Your Attorney

If I direct my trustee to transfer back to me property comprising the trust estate, does such a transfer constitute a gift taxable event for purposes of the federal gift tax?

Answer

No.

If the trustor directs the trustee to transfer back to the trustor property that comprises the trust estate in the same form of ownership in which it was titled before its conveyance to the trustee, no federal gift taxable event occurs. This is because a gift is incomplete in every instance in which the trustor (donor) reserves the power to revest the beneficial title to property in himself or herself or where the donor's reserve power gives the donor the power to name new beneficiaries.[101] On the other hand, if the trustee transfers property from a revocable living trust to a beneficiary other than the trustor, such a transfer constitutes a completed transfer subject to federal gift tax.[102]

Survivorship Property Owned by Nonmarried Individuals

If property owned as JTWROS by nonmarried individuals is transferred to a revocable living trust, the surviving co-tenant may be subject to gift tax on that portion of the property which is considered to be the transfer of his or her original interest in the property to the revocable living trust.[103]

Survivorship Property Owned by Married Persons

In view of the unlimited gift tax marital deduction, if married trustors convey legal title to the trustee of a revocable living trust property that was owned as JTWROS before the trust was effected, the surviving co-tenant spouse will not be subject to federal gift tax on what

---

[96] I.R.C. § 2503(b).

[97] I.R.C. § 2503(e).

[98] I.R.C. § 2523.

[99] I.R.C. § 2522.

[100] Priv. Ltr. Rul. 9428032 (April 20, 1994). *See Wogman v. Wells Fargo Bank*, 267 F.2d 423 (Cal. App. 1954), *Estate of Gallimore v. Gallimore*, 222 P.2d 259 (Cal. App. 1950), *Estate of Bosch v. Commissioner*, 387 U.S. 456 (1967).

[101] Treas. Reg. § 25.2511–2(c); *see also* Tech. Adv. Mem. 9127008 (n.d.).

[102] Treas. Reg. §§ 25.2511-2(b) and 25.2511-2(f).

[103] Treas. Reg. § 25.2511-1(h)(5).

may have been considered by the spouses to be the transfer of the surviving spouse's original interest in the property transferred to the revocable living trust. Remember, the *spouse's joint property rule* determines the extent to which property owned as JTWROS (including tenants by the entirety) is included in the gross estate of the first decedent spouse. As a general rule, for married decedents who are both U.S. citizens dying after 1981, one-half the value of property owned by a husband and wife as JTWROS is includable in the gross estate of the first decedent spouse, regardless of which spouse furnished the original consideration for the acquisition of the property. This rule only applies when the spouses are the only joint owners as to their entire interest in the property.[104]

Married persons may find it advantageous to transfer property owned as JTWROS to a revocable living trust. With the revocable living trust serving as the repository of such property, the trustor can control the disposition of his or her respective interest in the property that was previously owned jointly—something that cannot be done if the property continues to be owned as JTWROS. This is because, upon the death of the first spouse (co-tenant) to die, the surviving co-tenant spouse has a vested interest in 100 percent of the property simply by surviving the decedent co-tenant. Accordingly, 100 percent of the value of the property is includable in the surviving spouse's gross estate upon his or her subsequent death.

Gift Tax Return

Ask Your Attorney

Do I have to file a federal gift tax return for property transferred to a revocable living trust?

Answer

No.

Generally, because the transfer of property to a revocable living trust is not subject to federal gift tax, the trustor is not required to file a Form 709.[105] However, if a person transfers property to himself or herself as trustee of a revocable living trust and retains no beneficial interest in the trust property and no power over the property, except fiduciary powers, the exercise or nonexercise of which is limited by a fixed or ascertainable standard, to change the beneficiaries of the transferred property, such person is considered to have made a completed gift; and the entire value of the transferred property is subject to the gift tax for which a Form 709 may be required.[106]

An inadvertent termination of a revocable living trust can result in unwanted federal gift tax. As a general rule, a state court's order approving a compromise agreement that reformation of a trust agreement rescinds the termination of a revocable living trust after the trust has terminated by its own terms during the life of the decedent is not effective for federal gift tax purposes to rescind the completed gift arising from the distribution of the trust estate to beneficiaries other than to the trustor at the time of the termination.[107] The courts have consistently held that judicial reformation cannot operate to change the federal tax consequences of a completed transaction.[108]

---

[104] I.R.C. § 2040(b)(1) and (2).

[105] *Smith v. Shaughnessy*, 318 U.S. 176 (1943); Treas. Reg. §§ 25.2511-2(a), (b), (c); I.R.C. § 6019.

[106] Treas. Reg. § 25.2511-2(g).

[107] Tech. Adv. Mem. 9127008 (n.d.).

[108] *See Van Den Wymelenberg v. United States*, 397 F.2d 443 (7th Cir. 1968).

Person Responsible for Payment of Gift Tax

Recall that the federal gift tax is not imposed upon the receipt of property by the donee; nor is it necessarily determined by the donee's enrichment or benefit from the gift. On the contrary, payment of the gift tax is the primary responsibility of the donor. The gift tax is an excise tax upon the donor's act of making the transfer. It is measured by the value of the property passing from the donor to the donee and is imposed, regardless of whether the identity of the donee is known or ascertainable at the time of the gift.[109]

Ask Your Attorney

As the donor of a gift, am I required to report the gift?

Answer

Apart from the requirements of a federal gift tax return and, as a general rule, except for gifts having an aggregate value in excess of the gift tax annual exclusion amount,[110] the donor does not report the gift on his or her income tax return; the donee does not report receipt of the gift on his or her income tax return; nor is the donee generally required to pay any income tax on the receipt of the gift property. However, the donee may be required to report any earnings from the gifted property (e.g., interest, dividends, rent, and so forth). Under present law, gift principal is income tax-free to the donee.[111]

Donor's Responsibility

Payment of the gift tax is the donor's responsibility. If the donor dies before the gift tax is paid, the decedent donor's personal representative (or administrator, if the decedent dies intestate) is responsible for payment of the gift tax from assets composing the decedent's estate. If the estate is without a qualified personal representative (or administrator), then the decedent's beneficiaries (or heirs) are responsible for payment of the unpaid gift tax to the extent of the value of their bequests, inheritances, devises, or distributive shares of the decedent donor's estate.[112]

Donee's Liability

During the donor's lifetime, if the gift tax is not paid when due, the donee is personally liable for the gift tax to the extent of the value of the gift.[113] The donee's liability for the gift tax is based on the value of the gift unreduced by the gift tax due.[114] Moreover, I.R.C. Section 6324(b) creates gift tax liability of donees personally at law and does not require that the IRS assert the liability against either the donor or the donee prior to the expiration of the three-year limitations period for assessment of gift tax against the donor.[115] As a general

---

[109] Treas. Reg. § 25.2512-2(a); Moy, 1, *A Practitioner's Guide to Estate Planning*, § 3.01 [C], at 3-23.

[110] I.R.C. § 6039F(a). With regard to large gifts received from foreign persons, refer to I.R.C. § 6039F(d); Rev. Proc. 99-42, 1999-46 I.R.B. 568.

[111] Moy, 1, *A Practitioner's Guide to Estate Planning*, § 3.01 [C], at 3-23.

[112] I.R.C. § 2502(c); Treas. Reg. §§ 25.2502-2; 25.2511-2(a); 25.6019-1(c); Moy, 1, *A Practitioner's Guide to Estate Planning*, § 3.01 [C][1], at 3-23.

[113] Treas. Reg. § 301.6324-1(b); *see Estate of Birnie M. Davenport v. Commissioner*, 84 AFTR2d ¶ 99–5037 (10th Cir. 1999), *aff'g* T.C. Memo 1997–390.

[114] *Ripley v. Commissioner*, 105 T.C. 358 (1995).

[115] *O'Neal v. Commissioner*, 102 T.C. 666 (1994).

rule, and as previously mentioned, the donee of any gift is not required to file any information return, gift tax return, or report the gift on an income tax return; however, the donee may be required to report on an income tax return any income generated by the gift. On the other hand, if the aggregate value of foreign gifts received by a United States person during any taxable year exceeds $10,000 (indexed for inflation),[116] such gift(s) must be reported on an Annual Return to Report Transactions with Foreign Trusts and Receipt of Certain Foreign Gifts (Form 3520).[117]

Gift Conditioned on Payment of Gift Tax by Donee

Sometimes the donor may not want to pay the gift tax. When a donor makes a gift on the condition that the donee pay the gift tax, the value of the gift is reduced by the amount of the gift tax paid by the donee, thereby resulting in a net gift.[118] However, if the donee's obligation to pay the gift tax is speculative and illusory, the net gift doctrine does not apply.[119]

Planning Strategy

If the donor is concerned about maximizing his or her exemption amount to offset gift tax on future gifts or to reduce federal estate tax at death, then the donor may want to make the gift subject to the condition that the donee pay the gift tax. Doing so results in a net gift by the donor, thereby reducing the taxable amount of the gift which shelters more of the donor's gift tax exemption amount.[120] Such a strategy may cause more of the decedent's estate tax exemption amount to be available to reduce any estate tax due upon the donor's death. In order for this strategy to operate successfully, the donor's timely filed gift tax return must reflect a reduction in the amount of the gift in the amount of gift tax paid by the donee. Accordingly, the gift tax attributable to the transfer of property may be deducted from the value of that property in arriving at the amount of the gift where it is shown, expressly or by implication from the circumstances surrounding the transfer, that the donor attached payment of the gift tax by the donee (or out of the transferred property) as a condition of the transfer. In such event, the resulting gift tax must, of course, actually be paid by the donee or from the subject property. The donee's personal check (money order or certified check purchased by the donee) or other evidence of payment by the donee, together with a notarized statement by the donor that the gift is made subject to the condition that the donee pay the gift tax, should be attached to the Form 709.

Donee Voluntarily Pays the Gift Tax

If the donor makes a gift and the donee *voluntarily* pays the gift tax from the property gifted, the entire value of the gift is subject to gift tax.[121] However, if the donee is obligated by the donor to pay the gift tax, the tax court views that requirement by the donor as a reserved interest by the donor in the gift property, which, in turn, reduces the value of the gift and the amount of gift tax due.[122] The IRS views the gift tax paid by the donee as consideration to the donor. Consequently, the value of the gift is the fair market value of the property gifted, less

---

[116] I.R.C. § 6039F(a).

[117] Moy, 1, *A Practitioner's Guide to Estate Planning*, § 3.01 [C][2], at 3-24.

[118] Ibid.

[119] *Estate of Frank Armstrong, Jr., v. United States*, 277 F.3d 490 (4th Cir. 2002), *aff'g* 87 AFTR2d ¶ 2001–447 (D.C. W.D. Virginia 2001).

[120] Rev. Rul. 71-232, 1971-1 C.B. 275.

[121] *Affelder v. Commissioner*, 7 T.C. 1190 (1946).

[122] *Harrison v. Commissioner*, 17 T.C. 1350 (1952); *Lingo v. Commissioner*, T.C. Memo 1954-31.

the amount of gift tax to be paid by the donee.[123] However, it is the donor's unified credit that must be used to determine the donee's gift tax liability.[124] If the gift tax paid by the donee on such a net gift made after March 3, 1981, exceeds the donor's adjusted basis in the property gifted, the excess is taxable income to the donor. Such a gift is treated as a sale by the donor for the amount of the gift tax.[125]

Agreement between Donor and Donee to Pay the Gift Tax

Ask Your Attorney

How is the gift tax computed if the gift is subject to an agreement between the donor and the donee which provides that the donee will pay the gift tax and any other tax, including interest and penalties that might be assessed as a result of the transfer?

Answer

Such interest and penalties may not be used to reduce the value of the taxable gift. Any delay in payment of the gift tax by the donee neutralizes the economic burden of the interest charged for the late payment. In determining the amount of the taxable gift, no interest for late payment of the tax may be subtracted from the value of the property transferred because the donee has had the use of the tax money from the time of the gift until the time of payment of the tax. Likewise, it would be contrary to public policy to reduce the taxable gift by the amount of any penalties that may be incurred because the donee's agreement to pay penalties was made in anticipation of a potential noncompliance with the gift tax law; namely, that the donor is responsible for payment of the gift tax.[126]

STATE GIFT TAX

Some states impose a gift tax on the value of property transferred during lifetime. Usually, the gift tax will be one of three types: (1) a tax imposed on the total cumulative taxable gifts, like the federal gift tax; (2) a tax imposed separately on the property transferred to each beneficiary. Generally, the beneficiaries are taxed according to their degrees of relationship

---

[123] Rev. Rul. 75-72, 1975-1 C.B. 310; *see* Priv. Ltr. Rul. 200122036 (March 1, 2001); *see also* Priv. Ltr. Rul. 200137022 (June 13, 2001) (gift taxes paid from renounced trust reduce value of gift by the gift taxes paid from the renounced trust); Priv. Ltr. Rul. 200044034 (August 8, 2000) (assignment by taxpayer's income interest in QTIP trust will be deemed a transfer of all of the property, other than the qualifying income interest, under I.R.C. § 2519. Pursuant to I.R.C. § 2207A(b), taxpayer has the right to recover from donees [taxpayer's daughters] the amount of the gift tax payable by taxpayer due to the deemed transfer. As a result, the transfer is treated as a net gift. The amount of the gift equals the value of the entire property in the QTIP trust subject to the qualifying income interest, determined on the date of disposition and reduced by the amount of gift taxes taxpayer has the right to recover from donees. Taxpayer's gift tax liability for her transfer of her qualifying income interest in the QTIP trust is determined under Treas. Reg. § 25.2511–2).

[124] Rev. Rul. 81-223, 1981-2 C.B. 189.

[125] *Diedrich v. Commissioner*, T.C. Memo 1979-441, *rev'd* 643 F.2d 499 (8th Cir. 1981), *aff'd* 457 U.S. 191 (S. Ct. 1982), *superseded by* statute as stated in *Davis v. Commissioner*, 746 F.2d 357; Moy, 1, *A Practitioner's Guide to Estate Planning*, § 3.01 [C][4], at 3-24.

[126] I.R.C. § 2502(c); Moy, 1, *A Practitioner's Guide to Estate Planning*, § 3.01 [C][5], at 3-25.

to the donor, with lower rates and larger exemptions for closer relatives; and (3) a flat rate tax on each gift as it is made, with applicable exemption and annual exclusion amounts taken into account.

State gift tax rates, exemptions, and exclusions may not be connected to federal law. For example, under present law, the federal gift tax annual exclusion is $10,000 for all gifts of a present interest per donee per calendar year.[127] However, some states provide a smaller gift tax annual exclusion. In such situations, state gift tax may be imposed on the difference. Also, some states do not provide a gift tax marital deduction.

GENERATION-SKIPPING TRANSFER TAX

The value of property in a revocable living trust transferred to a beneficiary who is two or more generations younger than the transferor is subject to the generation-skipping transfer (GST) tax.[128] Every individual transferor, including the trustor of a revocable living trust, is entitled to the maximum GST tax exemption.[129] Thus, if a husband and wife create a single joint revocable living trust agreement, each of them, as trustor, is entitled to the maximum GST tax exemption.[130]

---

[127] I.R.C. § 2503(b). The gift tax annual exclusion of $10,000 per donee is adjusted for inflation under I.R.C. § 2503(b)(2). The inflation-adjusted amount is published by the IRS as a Revenue Procedure at the end of the year preceding the year of adjustment. For the year 2003, the gift tax annual exclusion is $11,000.

[128] I.R.C. § 2613(a)(1).

[129] I.R.C. § 2631(a), (c).

[130] Moy, 2, *A Practitioner's Guide to Estate Planning*, § 29.06 [D], at 29-53. For a discussion of the generation-skipping transfer tax, see the sections on "Generation-Skipping Transfer Tax" "Repeal of Federal Estate and Generation-Skipping Transfer Tax," and "Federal Estate Tax Exemption Amount Increased" in Chapter 1.

Lifetime Funding of a Revocable Living Trust

CHAPTER 9

Overview of the Funding Process

FUNDING PROCESS

Recall from the discussion in Chapter 2, Framework of a Revocable Living Trust, that a revocable living trust itself does not own property; rather, the trustee is in legal title to property comprising the trust estate. A revocable living trust cannot operate unless the trustor conveys legal title to property to the trustee; or, upon the trustor's death, the decedent's personal representative under the decedent's pour-over Will conveys by court order the legal title to property comprising the decedent trustor's probate estate to the trustee of a revocable living trust; or the trust is designated beneficiary of contract benefits. This process of conveying legal title is known as *funding the trust*. In other words, legal title to property comprising the trust estate must be in the name of the trustee. This is what is meant by the expressions: *the trustee is in-title to the property*, or *the trust is funded*.

Ask Your Attorney

Do I have to put all of my assets into the revocable living trust?

Answer

No. However, only property (assets), the legal title to which has been properly conveyed to the trustee, is afforded protection under the trust agreement. Therefore, if the trustor intends to avoid a lifetime court-supervised financial guardianship of his or her financial affairs and probate of his or her estate upon death by utilizing a revocable living trust, then legal title to the trustor's property must be in the name of the trustee.

Importance of Funding Process

The process of funding a revocable living trust should be taken as seriously as the attention given by the trustor and his or her advisors to the design and development of the trustor's estate plan and the revocable living trust agreement. Whether the funding process is easy or difficult usually depends on the type of property being transferred to the trust agreement. Certainly, legal title to some kinds of property, such as qualified retirement plan benefits (including IRAs, Keogh plans, SEPs, and 401(k) plans), small business corporation stock (I.R.C. Sec. 1244), stock options, and rental property in which the trustor is entitled to passive activity losses, should not be conveyed to the trustee of a revocable living trust.[1]

---

[1] *See* discussion in Chapter 5, "Stock Options" and "Small Business Corporation Stock" sections.

Person Responsible for Funding

Following the execution of the revocable living trust agreement, the trustor should determine who is to be responsible for funding the trust agreement. The trustor, the trustor's attorney who designed and prepared the trust agreement, or any one of the trustor's other estate planning advisors may assist the trustor in transferring property to the trust agreement. Be assured that a lawyer's services are not necessarily required to fund a revocable living trust. However, do not misinterpret this to mean that a lawyer's services in funding a revocable living trust would not be helpful, especially if the trustor were to encounter difficulty in conveying legal title to a particular kind of asset to the trust agreement.

Generally speaking, if the trustor is capable of opening a bank account, stock brokerage account, or preparing a deed to real property, the trustor can fund a revocable living trust. The trustor should limit the number of people involved in funding the trust agreement. Practically speaking, either the trustor or the trustor's attorney should be solely responsible for funding the trust agreement. In this regard, to assist the trustor in conveying assets to the trust agreement, the trustor and his or her attorney should rely on the expertise of those persons most familiar and knowledgeable about certain kinds of property comprising the trustor's estate. If the trustor and his or her attorney agree that each will be responsible for transferring certain assets to the trust agreement, then both of them should also agree to provide each other with copies of the documents effecting such conveyances. The chapters that follow discuss how legal title to different kinds of property is conveyed to the trustee of a revocable living trust. With this information, the trustor can be in charge of the funding process.

Schedules Alone Insufficient

The inventory of the trustor's gross estate prepared by the estate planner in the design of the trustor's estate plan is used as a checklist when funding the revocable living trust agreement. The schedules attached to the trust agreement should include all of the property listed on the inventory, except those items that the trustor determines not to transfer to the trust.[2] Remember, though, listing property on the schedules alone is not sufficient to convey legal title to the property to the trustee. Just because items of property are listed on the schedules does not, in and of itself, mean that legal title to the property is in the name of the trustee. The most certain and absolute way to avoid probate of one's estate and a court-supervised financial guardianship of one's financial affairs is to convey during the trustor's lifetime the legal title to property to the trustee of the revocable living trust agreement. This is a rule of law that must be complied with to ensure recognition of the trustee's power and authority with respect to the property comprising the trust estate.[3] Alternative arrangements used to convey legal title to property to the trustee which may avoid probate of the property but will not avoid a financial guardianship of the property may include:

- A nominee arrangement that involves conveying legal title to property to an individual or entity that operates as an agent for the trustor. In a document separate from the revocable living trust, the nominee, as legal owner of the property, agrees to hold the property on behalf of the trust. This separate document is not disclosed. It is alleged that, under this arrangement, persons transacting business with the nominee are not aware of the existence of the revocable living trust.

- A separate document called a Joint Declaration of Trust Ownership, whereby, a husband and wife, acting as co-trustees of a joint revocable living trust agreement, or as

---

[2] *See* discussion regarding schedules in "Trust Property: Article III" section in Chapter 5.

[3] *Ballard v. McCoy*, 443 S.E.2d 146 (Va., 1994).

trustees of their respective individual revocable living trusts, own the property comprising the trust estate in their names as trustees as joint tenants with right of survivorship to avoid disclosure of the trust agreement.

- Designating the trustee as a beneficiary of a payable on death (POD) account.
- Post-mortem assignments in lieu of POD arrangements, whereby a separate document provides for an assignment of property to the revocable living trust after the trustor's death and
- Transfer on death (TOD) of securities. Under this arrangement, which is a form of securities registration recognized in only a few states, when securities are purchased, the trustee of the revocable living trust is designated the beneficiary of the securities. Because this arrangement is not recognized in all states, the trustor should consult with his or her attorney as to whether the trustor's state has adopted the Uniform Transfer on Death Security Registration Act or adheres to its provisions by statute.

PROPERTY TRANSFER PROCESS

Certain procedures should be followed to convey legal title to property to the trustee of a revocable living trust. Generally, these procedures are not complex; and, when carried out according to the discussion in this chapter and those that follow, operation of a revocable living trust as the trustor intended can be ensured.

Establishing Identity of Trust Agreement

The most important aspect of conveying legal title to property to the trustee of a revocable living trust is the legal identity of the trust agreement. When determining the name for a revocable living trust, three basic issues must be addressed: (1) legal sufficiency for title to property comprising the trust estate; (2) acceptability of the title to interested persons; and (3) adequacy of the description of the person in legal title to the property. Every properly designed revocable living trust contains four elements that, if used to describe the title holder of the property comprising the trust estate, should cover every question regarding legal sufficiency of title: (1) trustee's name; (2) a statement or acknowledgment that a trust has been created; (3) effective date of the trust; and (4) a statement or acknowledgment of contingent beneficiaries if the trustor and trustee are one and the same person (see discussion in Chapter 2, Framework of a Revocable Living Trust).

Example

EUGENE H. CURTIS and THERESA M. CURTIS, co-trustees
U/D/T dated January 15, 2003
F/B/O the Curtis Family[4]

Universally Accepted Wording

The wording used in the previous example satisfies the three legal requirements for the trust name and also uses the four elements that describe the title holder of the trust property. In the example, Eugene H. Curtis and Theresa M. Curtis are clearly designated as the

---

[4]This wording may be used to identify the trustees of a joint revocable living trust agreement or in the separate revocable living trusts of a husband and wife. With respect to the latter, spouses may serve as co-trustees of their respective separate revocable living trust agreements.

co-trustees of the trust agreement. The designation *U/D/T* (under declaration of trust) indicates that a trust has been declared; the date on which the trust was declared (January 15, 2003)[5] indicates the effective date of the trust; and the designation *F/B/O* (for and on behalf of; or for the benefit of) acknowledges the existence of contingent beneficiaries; namely, members of the Curtis family. The wording in the example is universally accepted by title companies, banks, savings and loan associations, credit unions, and transfer agents involved in the registration of securities.

Variations on Accepted Wording

The wording used in the previous example may vary among financial institutions. In other words, don't be surprised if the wording used on stock certificates, bank accounts, life insurance beneficiary designations, and so forth is not exactly the same as that shown. The following illustrates some of the variations in wording commonly used:

- MARILYN B. HILLARY TTEE
  7-1-96
  FBO HILLARY FAM
- MARILYN B. HILLARY, TR UA JUL 1 96
  THE HILLARY FAMILY
- MARILYN B. HILLARY TTEE
  FBO HILLARY FAMILY TRUST
  U/A DTD 7-1-96
- MARILYN B. HILLARY TR UA DTD 7/1/96
  FBO THE HILLARY FAMILY
- MARILYN B. HILLARY
  TR UA 7-1-96
- MARILYN B. HILLARY TR U/AGMT
  DTD 7/1/96 F/B/O THE HILLARY FAMILY

Importance of Date of Trust

Even though none of these descriptions is exactly the same as the one used in the previous example, nevertheless all of them adequately identify the revocable living trust and have legal sufficiency for title purposes. Do not accept any wording that does not evidence a date of the trust. Absent a date, satisfactory identification of a particular trust would be almost impossible. Similarly, in addition to the trustee's name, some evidence must be presented that the person named is, in fact, the trustee under the trust agreement. Therefore, the word *trustee*, or *co-trustee*, or the abbreviation TTEE, or TR, must appear in relation to the name of the person designated as the trustee. This is necessary to establish that the person named is serving in a fiduciary capacity and not in his or her capacity as an individual.

Procedure for Transferring Property to Trustee

Ask Your Attorney

How do I get all of my assets transferred to my revocable living trust agreement?

---

[5] *See* Chapter 2, "Preamble" section, for discussion of trust preamble.

Answer

The assets (property) themselves are not physically transferred to the revocable living trust agreement, nor are they necessarily physically given to the trustee. An asset is transferred to the trust agreement by effecting the appropriate document to convey legal title to the particular asset to the trustee of the trust agreement. In the chapters that follow, instructions are provided for transferring many different kinds of assets to a revocable living trust.

Ask Your Attorney

Is transferring property to a revocable living trust a complicated process?

Answer

As a general rule, the process of transferring property to a revocable living trust is not complicated. To date, this author can count on one hand the number of instances where transferring a particular asset to a revocable living trust was more difficult than initially anticipated.

Ask Your Attorney

Can property be transferred to the revocable living trust at the same time the trust is executed?

Answer

Generally, yes.

In most cases, tangible personal property (e.g., household furniture and furnishings, wearing apparel, jewelry and personal effects, books, art objects, collections, sporting and recreational equipment, any automobile, and so forth), interests in intangible personal property (e.g., mortgages, trust deeds, contracts, installment obligations, leases, royalties, patents, stocks and bonds, and so forth), and interests in real property can all be transferred to the revocable living trust immediately following execution of the trust agreement. Generally, in most cases, legal title to the trustor's interest in bank accounts, credit union accounts, brokerage accounts, annuities, and life insurance policies is transferred to the trustee of a revocable living trust following its execution. Transfer of these assets to the revocable living trust requires the completion of the financial institution's or insurance company's particular forms to effect conveyance of legal title to the trustee along with a copy of certain pages of the trust agreement.[6]

---

[6] *See* Chapter 2, "Is Recording a Revocable Living Trust Necessary" section, for discussion regarding the pages of the Trust Agreement to be provided financial institutions. *See also* Chapter 11, Chapter 13, and the section on "Retirement Plans, Life Insurance, and Annuities" in Chapter 15.

Conveying Legal Title to Trustee is a Three-Step Process

Conveying legal title to property to the trustee of a revocable living trust is a three-step process. The first step is to identify the kind of property to be transferred to the trust. The second step is to determine the appropriate document to use to convey legal title to that property to the trustee. For example, a warranty deed (grant deed or bargain and sale deed) generally is used to convey legal title to real property to the trustee. Assignment documents are used to convey interests in mortgages, trust deeds, contracts, installment obligations, leases, royalties, patents, and so forth to the trustee. Legal title to stocks and bonds to which the trustor physically holds the certificates is generally conveyed to the trustee by either endorsing the stock or bond certificate or by effecting an Assignment of Stock or Bond Power (see file "APP0901.DOC"). The third step is to create and execute the document of conveyance.

Conveying Legal Title to Real Property to Trustee

A fourth step may be necessary when transferring an interest in real property to a revocable living trust.[7] After the warranty deed (grant deed or bargain and sale deed) is executed, it should be recorded in the county wherein the real property is situated. Similarly, as a general rule, any document conveying an interest in a mortgage, trust deed, land sale contract, or lease should be recorded. The exception to this general rule applies when the previous instrument was not recorded. For example, if real property is leased to a tenant but the lease was not recorded, an assignment of the lease to the revocable living trust should not be recorded. In other words, a document involving property that has not been the subject of a previous recording should not be recorded. Also, unless otherwise required by local law, the revocable living trust agreement should not be recorded. In situations where recordation is required, usually, a carefully designed Memorandum of Trust (see files "APP0210.DOC" and "APP0211.DOC") or Trust Abstract or Certificate of Trust (see file "APP0212.DOC") will suffice. Such a Memorandum of Trust or Certificate of Trust ensures the trustor's privacy with respect to the confidential and detailed provisions of the revocable living trust agreement. Moreover, local law should always be consulted about the requirements for recording legal documents transferring property to a revocable living trust, such as deeds, assignments of contracts, assignments of leases, bills of sale, assignments of notes, and other conveyance documents.

Transferring Additional Property after Trust Initially Funded

Ask Your Attorney

How do I keep track of new investments or additional assets after I have already effected a revocable living trust?

Answer

By adding a description of the property to the appropriate schedule attached to the trust agreement or by executing a Trustee's Acceptance of Property Conveyed to Trust Agreement (Trustee's Acceptance) (see file "APP0902.DOC").

Ask Your Attorney

When I acquire new assets after the trust agreement is executed, how do I get these new assets into the revocable living trust?

---

[7] *See* additional discussion in Chapter 10.

Answer

By titling the newly acquired asset in the name of the trustee of the revocable living trust at the time the asset is acquired.

With respect to new assets acquired after the trust agreement has been executed and initially funded, the same process is used to convey legal title to the new assets to the trustee as was used for similar assets when the trust was initially funded. If additional monies are deposited into a bank account (credit union account or any other account into which regular deposits and withdrawals are made), no new documentation is required. Likewise, the same rule applies when new securities are acquired in a street name account; if the account itself is already titled (registered) in the name of the trustee of the revocable living trust, the individual securities in the account do not have to be titled (registered) in the name of the trustee of the revocable living trust. Only if a new account is opened (e.g., bank account, credit union account, street name account, and so forth) which is not already titled (registered) in the name of the trustee is it necessary to effect documentation titling (registering) the account in the name of the trustee.

REMOVING AND REPLACING TRUST ESTATE PROPERTY

At the risk of oversimplification, the process of removing trust estate property from the revocable living trust is the same as funding the trust but in reverse. Once property is removed from the revocable living trust, it may be replaced with like-kind property or entirely different property. The process of adding new property to replace property removed from the trust is the same as funding the trust initially. With respect to the matter of federal income tax, no gain or loss is recognized by the trustor or the revocable living trust on the transfer of property by the trustor to the trustee of the revocable living trust to fund the trust, on the transfer of any property from the trustee of the trust to the trustor, on the transfer of any property from the trustee of the trust to the trustor in payment of any annuity installments, or on the substitution by the trustor of property for property of the revocable living trust.[8]

Removing Property from a Revocable Living Trust

Ask Your Attorney

How do I remove property from my revocable living trust?

Answer

1. *If the trustee sells the property, then the trustee conveys legal title to the property to the new owner of the property.*

2. *If the trustor acting as the trustee (or disinterested trustee) simply wants to remove the property from the trust and retitle (reregister) ownership in the trustor's individual name, the trustee conveys legal title to the property from the trustee to the trustor in the trustor's individual name.*

3. *If the trustor acting as trustee (or disinterested trustee) wants to remove the property from the trust and take title to the property with another person as joint tenants with*

---

[8]Priv. Ltr. Ruls. 9519029 (February 10, 1995) and 9504021 (October 28, 1994); Rev. Rul. 85-13, 1985-1 C.B. 184.

right of survivorship, the trustee conveys legal title to the property from the trustee to the trustor in his or her individual name. Then, the trustor conveys legal title to the property in the trustor's individual name and the name of the other person as joint tenants with right of survivorship. The same procedure is used for establishing ownership as tenants in common or as community property.

4. *If the trustee wants to gift property comprising the trust estate on behalf of the trustor, then the trustee conveys legal title to the property to the donee (new owner) of the property.*

Ask Your Attorney

I have a revocable living trust; but, years ago, I got rid of many of my assets that were put into the trust. Should I have done something special, or what do I do now?

Answer

At the time the assets were removed from the trust estate, such removal might have been indicated on the schedules attached to the trust agreement. However, if a record of the removal of assets from the trust was not made, no harm has been done. Whether the trustor elects to continue under the same trust agreement or effect a new trust agreement, the trustor should inventory the assets composing the trustor's gross estate and effect the appropriate conveyance documents to transfer legal title to property to the trustee of the revocable living trust.

Ask Your Attorney

What should I do if I sell or get rid of property that has already been transferred to my trustee?

Answer

1. *The trustor can delete the property described on the applicable schedule attached to the end of the trust agreement by simply drawing a line through the description, dating the deletion, and making a notation regarding the disposition of the property; for example, "property sold; proceeds used to acquire (description of property acquired);" or*

2. *The trustor can create a revised schedule. If the deleted property is replaced with other property, a description of the replacement property can be added to the applicable schedule affecting that property.*

Ask Your Attorney

If I direct my trustee to transfer back to me property comprising the trust estate, does such a transfer constitute a gift taxable event for purposes of the federal gift tax?

Answer

No.

If the trustor directs the trustee to convey legal title to property that comprises the trust estate back to the trustor in the same form of ownership in which it was titled before its conveyance to the trustee, no federal gift taxable event occurs. This is because a gift is incomplete in every instance in which the trustor (donor) reserves the power to revest the beneficial title to property in himself or herself or where the donor's reserved power gives the donor the power to name new beneficiaries.[9] On the other hand, if the trustee conveys legal title to property comprising the trust estate to a beneficiary other than the trustor who did not initially transfer property to the revocable living trust, such a transfer constitutes a completed transfer subject to federal gift tax.[10]

Ask Your Attorney

Can the trustee sell or remove property from the trust estate without the trustor's consent?

Answer

No. For so long as the trustor possesses legal capacity and has not turned the management of the trust estate over to the successor trustee, the trustee must obtain the trustor's consent to sell, remove, or replace trust estate property (see, e.g., file "APP0201.DOC" Article IV (B)).

Adding Property to a Revocable Living Trust

Ask Your Attorney

How do I add new assets to a revocable living trust after I have already effected the trust agreement?

Answer

Title the asset in the name of the trustee of the revocable living trust and effect a Trustee's Acceptance (see file "APP0902.DOC").

Property (assets) may be added to the trust estate at any time by the trustor or any person during his or her lifetime or by testamentary transfer. However, the trustee has no duty, accountability, or responsibility to the trustor or to any other person with respect to property of which the trustee has no knowledge or notice, or which the trustee has not accepted, or which has not come into the trustee's possession and control. Therefore, when the trustor transfers additional property to the revocable living trust, a Trustee's Acceptance should be effected (see file "APP0902.DOC"). The applicable schedule to which the property has been added may be amended to reflect the addition of the property to the trust estate, or the Trustee's Acceptance form can serve as an addendum to the schedule. The efficient course of action is to amend the schedule to which the property has been

---

[9] Treas. Reg. § 25.2511-2(c); *see also* Tech. Adv. Mem. 9127008 (n.d.).

[10] Treas. Reg. §§ 25.2511-2(b) and 25.2511-2(f); *see* discussion in Chapter 8, "Property Transferred to a Revocable Living Trust" section.

added, rather than referring to individual Trustee's Acceptances to identify the property that has been added to the revocable living trust. Property listed on the schedules at the time the revocable living trust agreement is effected may be considered accepted by the trustee at that time, even though legal title to the property has not yet actually been conveyed to the trustee.

Bank Deposits

Ask Your Attorney

Do I have to complete a Trustee's Acceptance each time I deposit monies into an existing bank account (including credit union account, savings and loan account, and so forth) that is already titled in the name of my trustee?

Answer

No.

It is not the value of the account that determines whether it is included in the revocable living trust. The trustee need not be informed of deposits (or withdrawals) made to or from an existing account. A properly designed revocable living trust agreement should provide that deposits made from time-to-time into such an account constitutes transfers to the trustee. At any given time, the current balance in such an account determines the extent to which such account constitutes trust estate property. However, if the trustor removes funds from a bank account, terminates the account, and establishes a new account with the same or different financial institution, then, in such event, the trustor must be certain to title the new account in the name of the trustee, if the trustor wants the new account to be in his or her revocable living trust.[11]

Selling and Buying Securities

Ask Your Attorney

I have a street name account with my stock broker. If I sell a particular security comprising the account and purchase a new security, do I have to complete a Trustee's Acceptance with respect to the new security?

Answer

No.

In effect, the same rule applicable to deposits made to bank accounts applies to securities held in a *street name* brokerage account titled in the name of the trustee. In this regard, one advantage of a street name brokerage account is that a Trustee's Acceptance does not have to be completed each time a new security is added to the account. This is because the account itself, which holds the individual investments, is already titled in the name of the trustee of the revocable living trust. By contrast, if the trustor retains possession of the se-

---

[11] *See* discussion in Chapter 13.

curity certificate, then, each time the trustor acquires a new investment, the trustor must be certain to title it in the name of the trustee of the revocable living trust. Whether the trustor chooses a street name account to hold his or her investments or retains possession of the security certificates, such decision has no direct bearing on the trustee's power with respect to the investments. The real issue has to do with whether the trustor is more comfortable retaining possession of the security certificates instead of a brokerage firm retaining possession of the certificates in a street name account.

PRESERVING THE CHARACTER OF PROPERTY OWNERSHIP

Along with federal income and estate tax considerations, when a revocable living trust is used to distribute property at a person's death, special care must be exercised before death occurs to ascertain the character of the property owned by a husband and wife. In this regard, property held as community property, separate property, joint tenancy with right of survivorship, marital property (Wisconsin), and tenants in common before the trust is effected should be clearly identified before legal title to the property is conveyed to the trustee of the revocable living trust. If necessary, the spouses should effect acknowledged affidavits attesting to the form in which they held title to the property before it is conveyed to the trustee. Moreover, in order to avoid incorrect transfer and classification of an interest in community or separate property, a stock transfer agent may refuse to reregister ownership of securities in the name of another person, unless it can be determined whether the property is community or separate property.

Joint Tenants with Right of Survivorship

Whether married individuals use a joint revocable living trust or each spouse effects his or her own revocable living trust, funding a revocable living trust with property owned as JTWROS before the revocable living trust is effected can provide both tax and nontax estate planning benefits. It is beyond the scope of this book to discuss these advantages.[12] However, it is important to know the methods used to correctly convey legal title to property owned as JTWROS to a revocable living trust. Unless the survivorship feature is destroyed, property owned as JTWROS may pass to the surviving spouse (or other co-tenant) outside the revocable living trust upon the death of the first decedent spouse (or co-tenant). Such an event can wreak havoc on an otherwise well-designed estate plan.

Importance of State Law

State law must be consulted to determine the steps required to actually sever the survivorship feature. When in doubt about the best way to destroy the survivorship feature, create a tenancy in common without right of survivorship. With regard to real property owned by married individuals as JTWROS (including tenants by the entirety with right of survivorship), both spouses should join together in creating a deed wherein they convey legal title to the property to themselves as tenants in common without right of survivorship. That deed should be duly executed and recorded; then each spouse should effect a separate deed, wherein, each conveys legal title to his or her respective undivided one-half interest as a tenant in common to the trustee of either a joint revocable living trust or to each spouse's separate revocable living trust.

---

[12] For in-depth discussion of joint tenancy with right of survivorship, *see* Moy, 1, *A Practitioner's Guide to Estate Planning*, Chapter 5, at 5-3 through 5-61.

Preservation of Spouse's Joint Property Rule

Using this method, the spouse's joint property rule[13] is preserved. In effect, each spouse retains a 50 percent interest in the property that was formerly owned as JTWROS. The survivorship feature of the property formerly owned as JTWROS is effectively destroyed. Thus, upon the death of the first decedent spouse to die, his or her one-half (50 percent) interest in the property does not pass by right of survivorship to the surviving spouse. Accordingly, the decedent spouse can control the disposition of his or her one-half interest in the property. Such would not be true if the spouses had continued to own the property as JTWROS. By destroying the survivorship feature, the first decedent spouse can direct his or her one-half interest to an estate tax marital deduction trust (e.g., a qualified terminable interest property (QTIP) trust; general power of appointment marital deduction trust; Trust "A"; Estate Trust; or a qualified domestic trust [QDOT]); or a credit shelter trust (nonmarital deduction trust; Trust "B"). Even though the survivorship feature is destroyed, probate of the decedent spouse's one-half interest in the property, which, in effect, is a tenancy in common, is not required because legal title to the property was properly conveyed to the trustee of the revocable living trust during the trustor's lifetime.

Severing the Survivorship Feature of Property Owned as JTWROS

The survivorship feature of property owned as JTWROS can be destroyed in the revocable living trust agreement itself.[14] This may be accomplished by the spouses effecting a separate Tenancy Agreement to convert property that is owned as JTWROS to property owned as tenants in common, or it may also be accomplished by including the following language in a joint revocable living trust to describe the property that was owned as JTWROS before the revocable living trust was effected and which is listed on Schedule "A" (see, e.g., file "APP0204.DOC" Article III).

ARTICLE III

TRUST PROPERTY

(A) through (C).

(D) **Schedule "A" Property.** The property described in Schedule "A" is the Trustors' property that was owned by Trustors as joint tenants with right of survivorship and/or as tenants by the entirety with right of survivorship prior to the execution of this Trust Agreement. Such property shall retain its character only with respect to the determination of the proportionate value of such property to be included in the gross estate of the Decedent Trustor, as provided under I.R.C. Section 2040(b) and Oregon State law (or state of Trustor's domicile). By the conveyance of such property to this Trust Agreement, the survivorship feature of such property is hereby severed; and Trustors' interests in such property shall be undivided interests as tenants in common. This limitation shall terminate on the death of the Decedent Trustor. The initial Trustees shall have no more extensive power over such property than either of the Trustors would have had under Oregon State law (or state of Trustor's domicile).

If married persons effect separate revocable living trust agreements, then, before legal title to property that was owned as JTWROS by the spouses before the trusts were effected is conveyed to the trustee of each spouse's respective revocable living trust agreement, the sur-

---

[13] I.R.C. § 2040(b)(1).

[14] *See Black v. Commissioner*, 765 F.2d 862, 56 AFTR2d 85-6526, 85-2 U.S. Tax Cas. (CCH) ¶ 13,628 (9th Cir. 1985).

vivorship feature would be destroyed by the spouses conveying title in such property to themselves as tenants in common. Then, as previously discussed, each spouse would convey legal title to his or her undivided one-half interest (or any other percentage interest of ownership decided upon by the spouses when they convey title to themselves as tenants in common) in the property to the trustee of each spouse's respective revocable living trust agreement.

Community Property

Legal title to community property may be conveyed to the trustee of a revocable living trust without it losing its character as community property. However, if legal title to property classified as community property is not properly conveyed to the trustee of a revocable living trust, it can be inadvertently converted into the separate property of each spouse or as tenants in common. In this regard, both spouses must consent to the transfer of community property to the trustee of the revocable living trust. Married trustors should consult state statute to determine any particular requirements of the trustors' community property state as to the transfer of community property to a revocable living trust. Moreover, in the states of Washington, Idaho, and California, spouses can designate as quasi-community property certain separate property interests acquired while domiciled in a noncommunity property state.[15] The legal title to community property conveyed to the trustee of a revocable living trust retains its status as community property if the revocable living trust clearly establishes the following:[16]

- The married trustors intend that their community property will continue to be treated as community property after legal title to it is conveyed to the trustee of the revocable living trust;
- All income derived from the community property in the revocable living trust will be community property; and
- If the married trustors withdraw community property from the revocable living trust, the property will retain its community property status outside of the revocable living trust.

Planning Strategy

Married persons moving from a community property state to a noncommunity property state that recognizes the Community Property Rights at Death Act (CPRDA) (Alaska, Arkansas, Colorado, Connecticut, Hawaii, Kentucky, Michigan, Montana, New York, Oregon, Virginia, and Wyoming)[17] may benefit from continued recognition of their property as community property. That is because only one-half of the value of the first decedent spouse's interest in the community property is includable in his or her gross estate for purposes of the federal estate tax; yet, the entire value of the community property receives a step-up (or step-down) in basis to its fair market value at the date of death of the first decedent spouse, or the alternate valuation date.[18]

---

[15] For additional reading on the subject of quasi-community property, *see* Moy, 1, *A Practitioner's Guide to Estate Planning*, § 7.01[C] at 7-13.

[16] Rev. Rul. 66-283, 1966-2 C.B. 297; *see* discussion in Chapter 2, "Trust Property: Article III" section.

[17] Community Property Rights at Death Act (U.L.A.), § 62, 1991 supplement.

[18] For additional reading on this subject, *see* Gerald B. Treacy, Jr., "Planning to Preserve the Advantages of Community Property," 23 *Estate Planning* 24 (January 1996); Moy, 1, *A Practitioner's Guide to Estate Planning*, § 7.01[B][2], at 7-12.

Example

Evan and Cora were married in California where both were employed and resided for most of their married life. During their residency in California, they acquired several parcels of real property and other personal assets. Evan was employed by Standard Oil, and Cora was a school teacher in the California public school system. Upon retirement, both Evan and Cora received retirement benefits from their respective employer's qualified retirement plans.

In 2000, Evan and Cora sold their real property in California on real estate sales contracts and moved to Oregon. Any real or personal property they acquire in Oregon may be characterized as community property—not because Oregon is a community property state, but because the state of Oregon recognizes the Community Property Rights at Death Act (CPRDA). This is because their respective retirement income is community property derived from qualified plan benefits accrued while they were domiciled and employed in California. Likewise, the contract payments they receive from the sale of their real property in California may be considered community property. Similarly, if they apply any of the funds received from either or both of their qualified plan benefits or the payments from the sale of their real property in California for the purchase of real property in the state of Oregon, they may declare such property as community property.[19]

---

[19] Moy, 1, *A Practitioner's Guide to Estate Planning*, § 7.01[B][2], at 7-11.

CHAPTER 10

Real Property Interests

TITLE TO REAL PROPERTY CONVEYED TO TRUSTEE BY DEED

A trustor's interest in real property is transferred to a revocable living trust by deed. In this regard, one of four kinds of deeds may be used to convey legal title to real property to the trustee: Warranty Deed, Bargain and Sale Deed, Grant Deed (in California), or Quitclaim Deed. Before conveying the title to real property to the trustee of a revocable living trust, the following questions should be asked and answered:

1. Would local property tax exemptions be affected by a conveyance of the title to real property from the individual owner to the trustee?

2. Will real property insurance coverage be affected by the conveyance of the title to real property to the trustee? Apparently, a homeowner's policy can be issued if the trustor, trustee, or beneficiary occupies the premises. Thus, if a bank acts as trustee, a lapse in homeowner's insurance coverage would not result, provided the trustor or beneficiary under the trust occupied the premises.

3. How would any mortgages on the real property be affected by a conveyance of the title to the real property to the trustee; and, if the real property is encumbered with a mortgage, would such a transfer trigger a due-on-sale clause?

4. Will a new title insurance policy be required if the title to real property is conveyed to a trustee?

5. Would a state death tax exemption for the real property be affected by a conveyance of the title to the real property to the trustee?

6. Under local law (state, county, or city), would a transfer tax be imposed on the *selling price* of the property, the title of which is conveyed to the trustee?[1]

7. Would conveyance of the title to the real property to the trustee cause the trustor to be ineligible for the exclusion of gain from the sale of the trustor's principal residence if the trustee sells the real property?[2]

8. Would the trustor's interest in the real property conveyed to the trustee prohibit the exchange of the real property for other real property without recognition of gain or loss under I.R.C. Section 1031?[3]

---

[1] *See* discussion in this chapter, Local Transfer Tax.

[2] *See* discussion in "Sale of Trustor's Principal Residence" section, Chapter 7.

[3] *See* discussion in "Exchange of Real Property Held for Investment" section, this chapter.

9. Would real property, the title of which is conveyed to the trustee, used as a farm or in a trade or business, still qualify for special use valuation under I.R.C. Section 2032A?[4]

Kinds of Deeds

Warranty Deed

A warranty deed, sometimes called a general warranty deed, statutory warranty deed, or grant deed (in California), is a written instrument in which title to real property is conveyed by the property owner (the grantor) to the grantee (trustee); and the grantor (trustor) warrants and defends the title to the real property against any claim (see file "APP1001.DOC"). This is the best type of deed the trustee can receive from the trustor. It contains the following special covenants:

- The grantor (trustor) possesses *fee simple* title ownership in the real property;
- The real property is not encumbered, except as stated in the warranty deed;
- The grantor (trustor) will defend title to the property;
- The right of the grantee (trustee) to use the property without interference of possession.

Regardless of whether the trustor conveys title to real property from the trustor, as an individual, to himself or herself or to any third party, as trustee, a warranty deed is the best deed to use to ensure continuity of the chain of title. Some title companies may require that a warranty deed be used to maintain title insurance coverage when the title to real property is conveyed to a trustee of a revocable living trust. This is especially important if the trustee sells the property. A *warranty* in a warranty deed means that the grantor (trustor) guarantees to the grantee (trustee) that the grantee (trustee) is receiving clear title to the property, except for those exceptions disclosed on the public record. Such exceptions include easements, mortgages, and liens. If the property being conveyed to the trustee is subject to a mortgage, the following language should be included in the warranty deed: "Subject to Restrictive Covenants of Record and all liens and records of encumbrance." If the trustor has any reservations about using a warranty deed with respect to chain of title issues, then the trustor should request from a local title company a title search of the real property being transferred to the trustee before a warranty deed is effected.

Bargain and Sale Deed

A bargain and sale deed is a written instrument in which the grantor (trustor) conveys title and a known interest in the real property with no warranty expressed or implied (see file "APP1002.DOC").

Quitclaim Deed

A quitclaim deed is a written instrument generally used to release a questionable title right the grantor might hold in real property. This kind of deed does not warrant any title and is not used to convey a known title right (see file "APP1003.DOC"). It is true that a quitclaim deed may be used to convey title to real property to the trustee of a revocable living trust. However, such a deed is given with no "warranties," and the trustee cannot be guaranteed that it is receiving good title or that the trustor will defend the title to the property. It merely transfers the grantor's known interest in the property. If the trustor wants to en-

---

[4] *See* discussion in "Special Use Valuation for Farm and Business Real Property" section, this chapter.

sure the integrity of the chain of title to the real property being conveyed to the trustee of a revocable living trust, a quitclaim deed should not be used.

Requirements of a Valid Deed

Whether the trustor prepares the deed or hires a lawyer to prepare it, a valid, effective deed must:

- Be in written form;
- Contain an accurate and complete legal description of the real property conveyed;
- Have a grantee (trustee) capable of holding title to the real property;
- Have a conveyance clause (granting clause); and
- Be signed by the grantor (trustor). Generally, the grantor's (trustor's) signature must be acknowledged by a Notary Public.

Observation

Though not required, the deed should be dated. If the deed is not dated, delivery of the deed to the grantee (trustee) establishes the date. Also, *accuracy* is the watchword when preparing a valid, effective deed.

Requirements for Effective Deed

To be legally effective, a deed must:

- Be signed by the grantor (trustor) and acknowledgment of signature obtained before a Notary Public;
- Be sealed. A seal is a sign made to attest in the most formal manner the signing of the instrument. For this purpose, the expression used by the Notary Public, **"In Witness Whereof, I hereunto set my hand and official seal,"** *seals* the instrument; and
- Be delivered unconditionally. The final and absolute transfer of a deed from grantor (trustor) to grantee (trustee) can be accomplished by recording the deed, which serves as constructive notice to the world at large that a change in ownership of the real property has occurred; or by the grantee (trustee) taking physical possession of the real property, which serves as actual notice.

Recording Deeds

Ask Your Attorney

After effecting a deed wherein I have conveyed title to real property to the trustee of my revocable living trust, should I record the deed?

Answer

As a general rule, yes.

Recording a deed in the public records of the county (or township) where the property is situated informs the public about the property; for example, change of ownership or a lien affecting the title to the land. Deeds that may be recorded must be acknowledged in the presence of a Notary Public who is a disinterested party. In this regard, if the trustor's spouse is a Notary Public, he or she should not notarize his or her trustor spouse's signature. Usually, the cost of recording a deed is based on a flat fee for a one-page document, plus a certain amount for each additional printed page to be recorded.

Significance of Recordation

Unless a legitimate reason exists, such as a mortgagee exercising a due-on-sale clause in a mortgage, trust deed, or land sale contract, or the loss of a homestead exemption, the deed should be recorded. By doing so, all interested parties know who is in legal title to the real property. However, with respect to the issue of a due-on-sale clause, if the mortgagee or vendor-seller will not consent to a transfer of the title to the real property to the trustee, the trustor may be well-advised to deed the real property to the trustee and instruct the trustee not to record the deed until the indebtedness is satisfied or until after the trustor's death. If the trustor disposes of the real property during his or her lifetime, the unrecorded deed is reclaimed and destroyed. Moreover, it should be kept in mind that, if the deed is not recorded until after the trustor's death, probate may be required to *clear the title* to the real property from the decedent trustor to the trustee. Furthermore, if the deed is unrecorded during the trustor's lifetime and the trustor becomes incapacitated, the trustee may not have the legal authority under the trust agreement to manage the real property for the benefit of the trustor.

Beware the Advice of Lawyers Not to Record a Deed

Some lawyers advise against recording deeds that transfer title to real property to the trustee of a revocable living trust until after the trustor's death. A lawyer may try to convince the trustor that, if the deed is recorded, the trustor will also have to record a copy of the trust agreement. Generally, in those states requiring that the deed be accompanied by evidence of the trust agreement, a Memorandum of Trust will suffice (see files "APP0210.DOC," "APP0211.DOC," and "APP0212.DOC"). By recording a Memorandum of Trust, the trustor does not have to reveal the confidential terms of the revocable living trust agreement.

Real Property Owned as JTWROS

Beware lawyers who advise that the only way to convey title to real property owned as joint tenants with right of survivorship by married individuals is to not record the deed. Married individuals can convey title to real property owned as joint tenants with right of survivorship (including tenants by the entirety) to the trustee of a revocable living trust without losing the benefits of such form of property ownership. In principle, no tax difference exists between the severance of joint tenants with right of survivorship by conversion into separate individual ownership as tenants in common or individual ownership or severance by a transfer in trust.[5] So long as the trustor retains the right to revoke the trust, the joint tenancy, with respect to the co-tenants' respective interests in the jointly owned property, is not destroyed.[6] Accordingly, only the survivorship element of the joint tenancy is severed. If married trustors effect a joint revocable living trust agreement, then both spouse trustors should effect a single warranty deed wherein each spouse trustor conveys all of his or her respective interests in the real property owned as joint tenants with right of survivorship (including tenants by the entirety), as husband and wife, to themselves as co-

---

[5] *Estate of Carnall v. Commissioner*, 25 T.C. 654 (1955).
[6] *Estate of May v. Commissioner*, T.C.Memo 1978-20 (1978).

trustees of the revocable living trust, or to anyone else who is acting as the trustee (see file "APP1004.DOC").[7]

If, on the other hand, each spouse trustor has effected separate revocable living trust agreements, then transferring the spouse trustor's respective interests in real property owned as joint tenants with right of survivorship (including tenants by the entirety) to their separate revocable living trust agreements is a two-step process. The first step involves the creation of a single warranty deed wherein both spouse trustors convey their respective interests in the real property owned by them as joint tenants with right of survivorship (including tenants by the entirety), as husband and wife, to themselves as tenants in common (see file "APP1005.DOC"). This deed should be recorded. The second step involves the creation of a warranty deed by each spouse wherein each spouse conveys his or her undivided interest as a tenant in common to himself or herself as trustee of his or her revocable living trust or to whomever is acting as trustee (see files "APP1006.DOC" and "APP1007.DOC"). These deeds should be recorded.

Upon execution of these warranty deeds, each spouse's interest in real property formerly titled as joint tenants with right of survivorship (or as tenants by the entirety) is now in each spouse's revocable living trust. All of the estate tax benefits attributable to owning the property as joint tenants with right of survivorship continue, but now each spouse has control over his or her one-half interest in the property. In this regard, upon the death of the first spouse to die, his or her one-half interest in the property will not pass by right of survivorship to the surviving co-tenant spouse. Rather, under the provisions of the revocable living trust agreement, each spouse can direct the disposition of his or her interest in the property to trusts (e.g., general power of appointment marital deduction trust, qualified terminable interest property (QTIP) trust, Estate Trust, qualified domestic trust (QDOT), credit shelter trust, or trusts for children and other beneficiaries) created under the revocable living trust or outright free of the revocable living trust to any individual he or she chooses. This control over the disposition of the first decedent spouse's interest in the property allows the first decedent spouse to control the use of the federal estate tax exemption amount in his or her estate in relation to property qualifying for the unlimited federal estate tax marital deduction so that the first decedent spouse's federal estate tax exemption amount can be maximized to the fullest extent possible.

Observation

When spouses convey title to real property from themselves as joint tenants with right of survivorship to themselves as tenants in common, in effect, each spouse holds an undivided one-half interest in the real property. However, it may be that one spouse wants to hold an undivided interest that is greater or lesser than one-half (e.g., 75 percent, 25 percent, or some other percentage interest). Because of the federal unlimited gift tax marital deduction, such an unequal division can be effected between married individuals without the imposition of federal gift tax on the conveyance from the spouse with the smaller interest to the spouse who ends up with the larger interest. Be certain, though, to determine if state law imposes a gift tax on such unequal transfers between spouses.

Recording Fees

Another argument advanced for not recording the deed is the immediate avoidance of recording fees. However, these fees are nominal relative to the total investment for the design of an effective estate plan. Moreover, the cost of obtaining a court-supervised financial

---

[7] For additional discussion, *see* "Joint Tenants With Right of Survivorship" section in Chapter 9.

guardianship, compared with the total investment of effecting a revocable living trust and properly funding it, including the nominal recording fees associated with deeds, is so much greater that it makes the argument of not recording deeds ridiculous.

Unrecorded Deed

Ask Your Attorney

Is a deed that I do not intend to record prepared any differently than a deed that will be recorded?

Answer

No.

An unrecorded deed includes the same information as a recorded deed, but the former is not recorded until the trustor's incapacity or death. As a general rule, delivery of a deed to the grantee is necessary to convey title; and recording the deed is evidence of delivery.[8] Nevertheless, mere possession of an unrecorded deed by the grantee (trustee) may be sufficient to establish that delivery was completed during the grantor's (trustor's) lifetime.[9] In other words, after execution of the deed, some evidence must exist that the trustee received the deed (see file "APP1008.DOC").

An advantage to not recording the deed is that, if the trustor decides to dispose of the property during his or her lifetime, either by sale, exchange, or gift, the unrecorded deed can be returned to the trustor and destroyed without the necessity of effecting a new deed. Presumably, the trustor would retain the deed issued previous to the deed conveying title to the trustee, thereby rendering unnecessary the need to effect a retitling of the real property into the trustor's name. In the event of the trustor's physical disability, mental incapacity, or death, the deed can be recorded, thereby obviating the need for a court-supervised financial guardianship of the trustor's financial affairs or a probate of the trustor's estate upon death. Remember, though, this technique only operates in those states that recognize the validity of unrecorded deeds.

In some states, unrecorded deeds are not valid. A disadvantage of using the unrecorded deed technique in such states is that, if the deed is recorded subsequent to physical disability, mental incapacity, or death, the trustee's authority to manage the property under the terms of the revocable living trust agreement may not be recognized because conveyance of the title to the real property to the trustee of the revocable living trust occurred after the fact. Usually, when a deed is recorded, it is date- and time-stamped, thereby making it impossible to say that the deed was recorded before the trustor decedent's death when his or her death, in fact, occurred at a time earlier than the date and time stamped on the deed. When in doubt about whether a deed is valid if not recorded, record the deed. The minor inconvenience, if any, and the nominal cost of recording the deed is insignificant to the potential cost of not having the title to the real property correctly conveyed to the trustee.

---

[8] 23 AmJur2d, Deeds 137.

[9] William L. Schmidt, Jr., "How to Fund a Revocable Living Trust Correctly," 20 *Estate Planning* 67, 69 (March/April 1993).

State and County Law

Ask Your Attorney

Must I hire a lawyer to prepare a deed to convey title to real property to the trustee of a revocable living trust?

Answer

No, not as a general rule. However, state law must be consulted and carefully followed in the preparation, execution, and recording of deeds.

State and county law should always be consulted before the preparation of a deed. It is not unusual to encounter special requirements with respect to what must be included in a deed before it will be accepted for recording. For example, in the state of Maryland, a fee-simple deed, mortgage, or deed of trust recorded in the counties of Montgomery, Prince George's, and Washington must "bear a certification of an attorney at law that the instrument has been prepared by an attorney or under an attorney's supervision, or a certification that the instrument was prepared by one of the parties named in the instrument."[10] Every deed recorded in Prince George's County, Maryland, must "contain a reference to the election district in which the property described in the deed is located."[11] Every deed or other instrument recorded in Talbot County, Maryland, must "have written, typed, or printed on its back, to be readily visible when folded for filing in the appropriate drawer or file, the name of every party to the deed or other instrument and the nature or character of the instrument."[12] In North Carolina, if the title to real property is transferred to a trustee, and if the trustee is given the express power to "sell, encumber or deal with the land in any manner, such power shall be noted upon the [deed] by the term 'with power to sell' or 'with power to encumber,' or by other apt words."[13] Under at least one state's statutes, unless the trustee's authority to deal with real property is expressed in the conveyance instrument, the words "trustee" or "as trustee," following the grantee's name, are given no effect as to the trustee's powers under the trust; and the assumption is that the grantee, as an individual, has unlimited power with respect to the real property.[14]

When state law imposes such a requirement, a warranty deed, with a Memorandum of Trust attached to it, should be effected and recorded. The warranty deed should include a reference to the Memorandum of Trust (see file "APP1009.DOC") that includes the following provision (see file "APP0210.DOC"):

> Powers of Trustee: Under the terms of the Trust Agreement, my Trustee is given the powers granted a Trustee under the Powers of Trustee as provided under _____ State law, including the right to sell, exchange, assign, lease, encumber, or otherwise alienate all or any part of the trust estate, including real property comprising the trust estate in any manner, on such terms as my Trustee shall determine.

---

[10] Md. Ann. Code Title 2, § 3-104(f)(1) (2002).

[11] Md. Ann. Code Title 2, § 3-104(f)(2) (2002).

[12] Md. Ann. Code Title 2, § 3-104(f)(3) (2002).

[13] N.C. Gen. Stat. § 43-42 (2001).

[14] Mont. Code Ann. § 70-21-307 (2002).

Where to Find State Statutes

Most public libraries have a copy of their state's statutes. State statutes are also available on-line.[15] By referring to the index of the state statutes under "deeds," "real property," "real property conveyances," or similar listing, the state's particular recording requirements and deed contents of the state or county in which the real property is situated can be found. When in doubt about the particular state or county requirements for recording a deed, telephone the recorder's office of the county wherein the real property is situated and inquire as to the requirements. In any event, an attorney should know what special language, if any, or special requirements the state in which the real property is situated imposes in a deed that conveys the title to real property to the trustee of a revocable living trust.

Local Transfer Tax

Because, among personnel in county recording offices, no standard degree of knowledge exists concerning the operation of a revocable living trust, recording clerks do not always immediately recognize whether the title to real property being conveyed to the trustee is exempt from local transfer taxes. Hence, the following information should be included on the first page of every deed transferring title to real property to the trustee of a revocable living trust:

> INTRA FAMILY TRANSFER. NO MONETARY CONSIDERATION. NO TITLE SEARCH. THIS TRANSFER IS BEING MADE TO EFFECT AN ESTATE PLAN. GRANTOR IS SETTLOR (TRUSTOR) OF THE _____ TRUST, TRUSTEE OF THE TRUST, AND PRIMARY BENEFICIARY.

Immediately following this statement, the grantor's (trustor's) name and address should be provided. Next, the grantee's (trustee's) name and address should be given. Then direction should be given that, after the deed is recorded, it should be returned to the trustee at the address provided. Finally, the following statement should be included:

> UNTIL A CHANGE IS REQUESTED, ALL TAX STATEMENTS SHALL BE SENT TO THE FOLLOWING ADDRESS: (name and address of person responsible for payment of real property taxes) (see file "APP1001.DOC").

Evidence of Title

Ask Your Attorney

Will a new title insurance policy be required if the title to real property is transferred to the trustee of a revocable living trust?

Answer

Generally, no.

---

[15]On-line at http://www.findlaw.com/11stategov/md/laws.html. In this citation, "md" is for the state of Maryland. Use the U.S. Postal Service abbreviation for the state to be searched; for example, "or" for Oregon; "mt" for Montana, "nc" for North Carolina, and so forth. At each cite, search references for "laws," "statutes," or "Code."

Title Insurance

State law provides certain formalities that must be complied with to secure title to the rightful owner of real property. If these formalities are not observed and complied with, the conveyance of title to real property to the trustee of a revocable living trust may be defective. A title insurance policy insures the owner of property against defect or failure of title, except for certain printed exceptions in the policy. No definite rule seems to exist regarding whether a new title insurance policy should be issued when title to real property is conveyed to the trustee of a revocable living trust. However, if the trustee sells real property comprising the trust estate, the purchaser will want to be assured that the trustee, as seller, holds good title to the property being conveyed. This is why use of a warranty deed is preferred over a bargain and sale deed when title to real property is conveyed to the trustee of a revocable living trust. Accordingly, a title insurance policy will be provided to the purchaser by the trustee as seller of the real property. When in doubt about whether a new title insurance policy should be obtained when the title to real property is initially conveyed to the trustee of a revocable living trust, inquire of a local title company or an attorney.

Verification of Trustee's Interest in the Real Property

Even though title to real property comprising the trust estate is in the name of the trustee, as evidenced by a warranty deed (or bargain and sale deed), when the trustee sells the real property, the title company may require evidence of the trust agreement and that it is still in effect. In these regards, the title company wants substantiation that the person named as trustee is authorized to deal with the real property and has the power to do so under the terms of the trust agreement. As part of the closing process when real property owned by the trustee of a revocable living trust is sold, the title company may request a copy of the trust agreement. In most cases, title officers are not interested in reviewing the entire trust agreement. Rather, they want to review only those provisions of the trust agreement which establish its existence (the preamble, designation of successor trustees, trustee powers, and the signature pages). In other words, the title company wants verification that the trustee is in legal title to the real property and has the legal power to sell or otherwise deal with the property.

Verification of Successor Trustee

Occasionally, the name of the trustee appearing on the deed is not the same as the trustee who is selling the real property. The original trustee may have resigned or died. In such case, the title company may require verification of the successor trustee's appointment and authority under the trust agreement (see file "APP1010.DOC"). 🖾 Or, in the absence of an executed Affidavit of Successor Trustee (see files "APP0604.DOC" through "APP0607 .DOC") 🖾, if the trustee resigned as a consequence of physical disability or mental incapacity, the title company may require a letter from the former trustee's physician to that effect; or, if the trustee is not acting as a result of death, a certified copy of the death certificate may have to be submitted to the title company. If the trustee simply resigned, then the title company may require a statement from the former trustee to that effect. Use and execution of the appropriate Affidavit of Successor Trustee, when the successor trustee assumes the duties as acting trustee, can alleviate unnecessary paperwork and delay in the closing of a real property transaction.

REAL PROPERTY SUBJECT TO INDEBTEDNESS

Ask Your Attorney

Can the title to "mortgaged" real property be conveyed to the trustee of a revocable living trust?

Answer

Yes. The title to real property that is the subject of a trust deed, mortgage, or land sale contract can be conveyed to the trustee of a revocable living trust.

Due-on-Sale Clause

A mortgage, trust deed, or land sale contract should be carefully reviewed to determine the existence of due-on-sale or due-on-transfer provisions that could trigger acceleration of the outstanding indebtedness on the real property. The term *due-on-sale clause* means a contract provision that authorizes a lender, at its option, to declare due and payable sums secured by the lender's security instrument, if all or any part of the property, or an interest therein, securing the real property loan is sold or transferred without the lender's prior written consent. Following are typical due-on-sale provisions found in a mortgage, trust deed, and land sale contract.

Mortgage

"Due on Sale Consent by Lender. Lender may, at its option, declare immediately due and payable all sums secured by this mortgage upon the sale or transfer, without the lender's prior written consent, of all or any part of the real property, or any interest in the real property. A 'sale or transfer' means the conveyance of real property or any right, title, or interest therein; whether legal or equitable; whether voluntary or involuntary; whether by outright sale, deed, installment sale contract, land contract, contract for deed, leasehold interest with a term greater than three (3) years, lease-option contract, or by sale, assignment, or transfer of any beneficial interest in or to any land trust holding title to the real property or by any other method of conveyance of real property interest. If any grantor is a corporation or partnership, transfer also includes any change in ownership of more than 25 percent of the voting stock or partnership interests, as the case may be, of grantor. However, this option shall not be exercised by lender if such exercise is prohibited by federal law or by Oregon law."[16]

Trust Deed

"Transfer of the Property or a Beneficial Interest in Borrower. If all or any part of the property or any interest in it is sold or transferred (or if a beneficial interest in borrower is sold or transferred and borrower is not a natural person) without lender's prior written consent, lender may, at its option, require immediate payment in full of all sums secured by this security instrument. However, this option shall not be exercised by lender if exercise is prohibited by federal law as of the date of this security instrument."

Land Sale Contract

"The entire unpaid balance of principal and accrued but unpaid interest shall become immediately due in the event purchaser assigns, sells, or transfers this contract or any interest in the property without seller's prior written consent."

Federal Law

With respect to a real property loan secured by a lien on residential real property, federal law provides that a lender may not exercise a due-on-sale clause when the title to residen-

---

[16]Laser Pro™ Ver. 3.10a(c) 1993 CFI Bankers Service Group, Inc. All rights reserved.

tial real property is conveyed to the trustee of a revocable living trust in which the borrower is and remains a beneficiary; and such conveyance does not relate to a transfer of rights of occupancy in the property.[17] Therefore, if the trustor transfers the title to his or her principal residence or vacation home to the trustee of a revocable living trust and the trustor is the beneficiary of the revocable living trust, the lender cannot accelerate the loan secured by the real property. Regardless of federal law, the trustor would be well advised to inform the lender in writing of the proposed conveyance of the title to real property subject to a loan to the trustee of his or her revocable living trust (see file "APP1011.DOC"). A copy of the operative pages of the revocable living trust agreement evidencing the identity of the trustor, trustee, beneficiaries, and powers of the trustee should accompany the letter to the lender. Consent of the lender should be obtained to convey the title to the real property to the trustee before the deed is recorded. Except for the refusal by a credit union, this author has never had a lender deny a trustor's request to convey title to real property subject to a loan to the trustee of the trustor's revocable living trust. A warranty deed is used to convey the trustor's interest in the real property to the trustee of the trustor's revocable living trust, subject to the indebtedness. (see file "APP1001.DOC").

Planning Strategy

When real property is subject to indebtedness under either a mortgage or trust deed, be certain to describe in the following manner the instrument in the warranty deed:

The said property is free from encumbrances except for that certain Deed of Trust recorded August 21, 1980, in Book 3267, Pages 220-225, of the records of

_____ County, State of _____ .

The trustor should enclose with the letter to the lender a copy of the proposed warranty deed so the lender can see that the trustor intends to convey title to the real property to the trustee of a revocable living trust, subject to the mortgage or trust deed.

Veterans Administration Financed Real Property

Real property subject to a loan obtained through a state office of the Department of Veteran's Affairs can be transferred to a revocable living trust. A letter from trustors to the Oregon Department of Veterans Affairs inquiring whether a conveyance of the title to trustors' principal residence to themselves as co-trustees of their revocable living trust, financed through the Department of Veteran's Affairs, would trigger the due-on-sale clause drew no response. After repeated inquiries to the Department of Veterans Affairs went unanswered, trustors effected a warranty deed, conveying title to their principal residence to themselves as co-trustees of their revocable living trust, and recorded the deed. Eventually, a representative of the Department of Veterans Affairs contacted trustors by telephone and informed them that their request to convey the title to their principal residence to themselves as co-trustees of their revocable living trust had been approved. Of course, the warranty deed mentioned the fact that the real property was "subject to restrictive covenants of record and all liens and records of encumbrance."

---

[17] Garn-St. Germain Depository Institutions Act of 1982, 12 U.S.C.A. § 1701j-3(d)(8) (1983).

FEDERAL TAX ISSUES

The federal income tax issues affecting a transfer of the title to the trustor's principal residence to the trustee of a revocable living trust are discussed in Chapter 7, Federal Income Tax. These issues include: (1) the exclusion of gain from sale of principal residence (I.R.C. Section 121); and (2) involuntary conversions of real property (I.R.C. Section 1033). In this chapter, the subject of exchanges of real property held for investment (I.R.C. Section 1031), transfers of certain farm real property (I.R.C. Section 1040), and real property for which special use valuation is elected (I.R.C. Section 2032A) are discussed.

Exchange of Real Property Held for Investment

As a general rule, the conveyance of title to real property to the trustee of a revocable living trust does not prevent such property from qualifying for a tax-free exchange under I.R.C. Section 1031. The Code provides that no gain or loss is recognized on the exchange of property held for productive use in a trade or business or for investment if such property is exchanged solely for property of like kind which is to be held either for productive use in a trade or business or for investment.[18] However, this general rule does not apply to the exchange of specified types of property,[19] such as certificates of trust or beneficial interests in trusts.[20] For these purposes, the term *trust*, as used in the Code, refers to an arrangement created by a Will or by a revocable living (*inter vivos*) declaration, whereby trustees take title to property for the purpose of protecting or conserving it for the beneficiaries under the ordinary rules applied in chancery or probate courts. Generally, an *arrangement* is treated as a trust under the Code if it can be shown that the purpose of the arrangement is to vest in trustees responsibility for the protection and conservation of property for beneficiaries who cannot share in the discharge of this responsibility.[21]

In a revocable living trust, the trustee holds legal title to the trust estate property for the benefit of the trustor. The trustor is not issued certificates of beneficial interest in the trust estate property.[22] Rather, the trustor continues to hold beneficial title to the underlying property of the trust estate; for example, real property, securities, bank accounts, life insurance, annuities, tangible personal property, and intangible personal property. In effect, the trustor retains beneficial ownership of the trust estate property for federal income tax purposes.

Accordingly, provided the requirements of I.R.C. Section 1031 are otherwise satisfied and the following conditions are satisfied in the trust agreement, real property comprising the trust estate may be exchanged for other real property without recognition of gain or loss:[23]

- The trustee holds title to the real property;
- The beneficiary, or a designee of the beneficiary (e.g., attorney-in-fact under a power of attorney), has the exclusive right to direct or control the trustee in dealing with the title to the property; and

---

[18] I.R.C. § 1031(a)(1).

[19] I.R.C. § 1031(a)(2).

[20] I.R.C. § 1031(a)(2)(E).

[21] Treas. Reg. § 301.7701-4(a).

[22] The matter of certificates of beneficial interest (CBI) not being issued with respect to the trustor's beneficial interest in the trust estate under a revocable living trust is not to be confused with CBIs or units of beneficial interest (UBI) that are commonly issued for the irrevocable living Family Estate Trust, also known as a *pure, constitutional,* or *equity* trust—all of which are abusive trust tax shelters. The IRS has undertaken a nationally coordinated enforcement initiative to address abusive trust schemes—the National Compliance Strategy, Fiduciary and Special Projects (Notice 97-24, 1997-16 I.R.B. 6).

[23] Rev. Rul. 92-105, 1992-2 C.B. 204.

- The beneficiary has the exclusive control of the management of the property (e.g., standby holding title only revocable living trust agreement or combination standby holding title only and management trust agreement), the exclusive right to the earnings and proceeds from the property, and the obligation to pay any taxes and liabilities relating to the property.

Transfer of Certain Farm Real Property

If the personal representative of a decedent's estate transfers to a qualified heir[24] any real property used as a farm or in a trade or business,[25] with respect to which special use valuation is elected under I.R.C. Section 2032A, then the gain on such transfer is recognized to the estate only to the extent that, on the date of such transfer, the fair market value of such property exceeds the value of the property for purposes of determining the federal estate tax determined without regard to the special use valuation election.[26] A similar rule applies where the trustee of a trust (any portion of which is included in the decedent's gross estate) transfers property with respect to which the special use valuation election is made.[27] The basis of such property is its basis immediately before the transfer increased by the amount of the gain recognized to the estate or trust on the transfer.[28]

Special Use Valuation for Farm and Business Real Property

Generally, the value of property included in a decedent's gross estate is its fair market value. Often, with respect to real property, fair market value is determined by analyzing the highest and best use for the property. Under I.R.C. Section 2032A, real property included in the decedent's gross estate may be valued based on its "qualified use" in farming or other trade or business use.[29] In some cases, the special use value may be considerably lower than the so-called fair market value based upon highest and best use. In cases where this is true, the decedent's federal estate tax liability may be significantly reduced.[30]

Real property may qualify for the I.R.C. Section 2032A special use valuation election if:

- The decedent was a U.S. citizen or resident at the time of death;[31]

- The real property is located in the United States;[32]

- The real property was, on the date of the decedent's death, used by the decedent or by a member of the decedent's family either (a) as a farm or (b) in a trade or business;[33]

- Fifty percent or more of the adjusted value of the decedent's gross estate consists of the adjusted value of real or personal property that (a) was being used by the

---

[24] I.R.C. § 2032A(e)(1).

[25] I.R.C. § 2032A(b)(2).

[26] I.R.C. § 1040(a).

[27] I.R.C. § 1040(b).

[28] I.R.C. § 1040(c).

[29] I.R.C. § 2032A(a)(1)(B), (b)(1) and (2); Treas. Reg. § 20.2032A-3(a).

[30] For an in-depth discussion of special use valuation, *see* Moy, 1, *A Practitioner's Guide to Estate Planning*, § 10.03.

[31] I.R.C. § 2032A(a)(1).

[32] I.R.C. § 2032A(b)(1).

[33] I.R.C. § 2032A(b)(1) and (2).

decedent or a family member as a farm or in a business on the date of the decedent's death and (b) was acquired from or passed from the decedent to a qualified heir;[34]

- Twenty-five percent or more of the adjusted value of the decedent's gross estate consists of the adjusted value of real property that (a) was acquired from or passed from the decedent to a qualified heir and (b) the decedent or a member of the decedent's family owned and used as a farm or in a business for a total of at least five years during the eight-year period ending on the date of the decedent's death;[35]

- For a total of at least five years during the eight-year period ending on the date of the decedent's death, (a) such real property was owned by the decedent or a member of the decedent's family and was used as a farm or in a business; and (b) there was material participation by the decedent or a member of the his or her family in the operation of the farm or other business;[36] and

- The real property is designated in the written agreement signed by each person in being who has an interest (whether or not in possession) in any property designated in such agreement consenting to recapture of estate tax that the personal representative of the decedent's estate must file with the federal estate tax return in connection with the election..[37]

Making the Special Use Valuation Election

The special use valuation election is made on the Form 706.[38] The election may be made on a late-filed Form 706, provided it is the first Form 706 filed.[39] Once the election is made, it is irrevocable. In making the election, the personal representative must attach to the estate tax return (Form 706) a notice of election and an agreement to special use valuation signed by all parties with an interest in the property (whether or not in possession of the property).[40] A detailed list of the information that must be included in the notice of election is outlined in the treasury regulations.[41]

Recapture of Federal Estate Tax

A recapture of the federal estate tax that would have been imposed in the decedent's estate but for the special use valuation election is imposed on qualified heirs who breach the conditions of the special use valuation election. In this regard, if, within ten years (fifteen years for individuals dying before 1982)[42] after the decedent's death and before the death of the qualified heir, (1) the qualified heir disposes of any interest in qualified property (other than by a disposition to a member of his or her family)[43] or (2) the qualified heir ceases to

---

[34] I.R.C. § 2032A(b)(1)(A); *contra Thompson v. Commissioner*, 864 F.2d 1128 (4th Cir. 1989), *rev'g* 89 T.C. 619 (1987) (concluding that all of the concurrent interests in a given parcel of real property need not pass to only qualified heirs in order to sustain the special use valuation election). *See* H. rept. 94-1380 (1976), 1976-3 C.B. (Vol. 3) 735, 761. *See also McAlpine v. Commissioner*, 96 T.C. 134 (1991) (an election of special use valuation and the recapture agreement signed by all interested parties were valid and that petitioner was entitled to use the special valuation in computing the estate tax due).

[35] I.R.C. § 2032A(b)(1)(B).

[36] I.R.C. § 2032A(b)(1)(B) and (C); *Brockman v. Commissioner*, 903 F.2d 518 (7th Cir. 1990).

[37] I.R.C. § 2032A(b)(1)(D), (c) and (d)(2).

[38] I.R.C. § 2032A(d)(1); *see* Rev. Proc. 92-85, 1992-2 C.B. 69.

[39] Temp. Treas. Reg. § 22.0(b).

[40] I.R.C. § 2032A(a)(1)(B); (d); (d)(2); Treas. Reg. § 20.2032A-8(a)(3); 20.2032A-8(c)(1).

[41] Treas. Reg. § 20.2032A-8(a)(3).

[42] I.R.C. § 2032A(c)(1).

[43] Priv. Ltr. Rul. 9642055 (July 24, 1996).

use for the qualified use the qualified property that was acquired (or passed) from the decedent, then an additional estate tax is imposed.[44] The recapture tax is designed to recoup the special tax savings inappropriately enjoyed by the qualified heir when the heir elected the special use valuation.[45]

Ask Your Attorney

I am a beneficiary of real property, the value of which was determined in the decedent's estate under the special use valuation provisions of I.R.C. Section 2032A. If I convey title to my interest in this real property to the trustee of a revocable living trust within ten years after the decedent's death and before my death, will such a conveyance trigger a recapture of the federal estate that would have been imposed if special use valuation of the real property had not been elected?

Answer

No.

The conveyance of title to qualified use property to the trustee of a revocable living trust is not a taxable disposition for purposes of I.R.C. Section 2032A(c) provided that: (1) the trustor (taxpayer), as trustee of the revocable living trust, and the trustor, in the capacity as beneficiary of the trust, enter into a recapture agreement to be fully liable for any additional estate tax that may be imposed under I.R.C. Section 2032A(c); and (2) the trustee of the revocable living trust continues to use the specially valued property in its qualified use. Further, if the trustor should die during the ten-year recapture period, the transfer of the property on the trustor's death will not be considered a taxable disposition for purposes of I.R.C. Section 2032A(c), provided that the property has either remained in the revocable living trust or is distributed to the trustor before his or her death.[46]

---

[44] I.R.C. § 2032A(c)(1); *see also* Priv. Ltr. Rul. 9340035 (July 7, 1993) (sale by decedent's cousins of property, for which special use valuation was elected in decedent's estate, to one of cousin's sons and his wife did not constitute disposition or cessation of qualified use); Priv. Ltr. Rul. 9333002 (April 20, 1993) (foreclosure on property that has been specially valued under I.R.C. § 2032A is neither a disposition within the meaning of I.R.C. § 2032A(c)(1)(A) nor an involuntary conversion within the meaning of I.R.C. § 2032A(h)(3)(A) when, during foreclosure proceedings, qualified heir continuously uses property in qualified use and repurchases property in proceedings; *Stovall v. Commissioner*, 101 T.C. 140 (1993). In *Stovall* a qualified heir received from the decedent's estate farm property qualifying for special use valuation under I.R.C. § 2032A. Within fifteen years of the decedent's death [I.R.C. § 2032A(c)(1) before amendment by ERTA '81, § 421(c)(1)(A)], the heir leased the qualified real property to a co-heir under a cash rental arrangement. Within the fifteen-year period following the decedent's death, the IRS issued a questionnaire to the heir inquiring about the rental agreement, which the heir answered and returned to the IRS, disclosing the cash rental of the qualified property. The court held: (1) the heir's cash rental of qualified property constituted a cessation of qualified use resulting in liability for additional federal estate tax under I.R.C. § 2032A(c)(2)(A) with respect to the qualified property; (2) in the absence of regulations, the questionnaire filed by the heir with the IRS disclosing the cash rental arrangement of the qualified real property constituted notification to the IRS under I.R.C. § 2032A(f) of the cessation of qualified use and commenced the period of limitations on assessment and collection; and (3) because the notices of deficiency were issued more than three years after the date the IRS received notification of the cessation of qualified use, the IRS was barred from assessing and collecting additional federal estate tax.

[45] *Williamson v. Commissioner*, 974 F.2d 1525 (9th Cir. 1992), *aff'g* 93 T.C. 242 (1989).

[46] Priv. Ltr. Rul. 9519015 (February 7, 1995).

Would the sale of qualified real property by the trustee of a living trust to a qualified heir, or a member of the qualified heir's family, be a recapture event?

No.

As a general rule, the sale of qualified use property by the trustee to a qualified heir, or a member of the qualified heir's family, is not a recapture event, provided the purchaser signs the required recapture agreement.[47] Accordingly, an individual who stands merely as a potential purchaser of the qualified use real property need not sign the recapture agreement as a condition for making the initial special use valuation election. If, in fact, the individual purchases the property, his or her signature would be required at that time as a condition for avoiding the recapture tax.[48]

Availability of Special Use Valuation upon Death of Trustor

If I convey the title to my farm real property to the trustee of my revocable living trust, will the property be eligible for special use valuation under I.R.C. Section 2032A in the event of my death?

Assuming that the farm real property includable in the trustor's gross estate otherwise satisfies the requirements of I.R.C. Section 2032A, conveyance of the title to farm real property to the trustee of a revocable living trust will not cause loss of the special use valuation election under I.R.C. Section 2032A.

One of the requirements to elect special use valuation is that the real property valued under I.R.C. Section 2032A must pass from the decedent to a qualified heir or be acquired from the decedent by a qualified heir. The real property may be owned directly or indirectly through ownership of an interest in a corporation, a partnership, or a trust. Where the ownership is indirect because of a corporation, partnership, or sole proprietorship, the decedent's interest must also qualify under the tests of I.R.C. Section 6166(b)(1) as an interest in a closely-held business on the date of the decedent's death.[49] An interest in a closely-held business includes: (1) an interest in a sole proprietorship; (2) an interest as a partner in a partnership where either twenty percent or more of the total capital interest in the partnership is included in the decedent's gross estate or such partnership has forty-five or fewer partners; or (3) an interest in a corporation where 20 percent or more of the value of the voting stock of the corporation is included in the decedent's gross estate or such corporation has forty-five or fewer shareholders.[50]

---

[47] I.R.C. § 2032A(d)(2); *see* I.R.C. § 2032A(c)(1)(A) and 2032A(e)(1).

[48] Tech. Adv. Mem. 9228005 (March 31, 1992).

[49] Treas. Reg. § 20.2032A-3(b)(1).

[50] I.R.C. § 6166(b)(1).

Real property in a revocable living trust can qualify for special use valuation. To the extent that the qualified heir has a present interest in the real property comprising the trust estate, for which special use valuation has been elected, such property is deemed to have passed from the decedent to the qualified heir.[51] An unrestricted right to immediate use, possession, or enjoyment of property or the income from the property, such as a life estate or term certain, is a present interest.[52] However, as a general rule, if the trustee has the discretion to fund trusts under the revocable living trust agreement with real property used as a farm or in a business, such real property is not eligible for special use valuation or for consideration in determining whether the 50 percent and 25 percent threshold requirements[53] are satisfied.[54] Moreover, if the trustee is authorized to exercise discretion in withholding payments of income to the beneficiary and add such income to the principal of the trust estate, the beneficiary's interest in the real property is not a present interest; and the real property is not considered as having passed to a qualified heir.[55] Therefore, the real property is not qualified real property. Accordingly, any property (or portion thereof) in which a qualified heir does not have a present interest is not eligible for special use valuation under I.R.C. Sec. 2032A.[56]

On the other hand, these rules may not apply to a surviving spouse who is the beneficiary of a trust comprised of real property used as a farm or in a business. For purposes of the federal estate tax marital deduction, a surviving spouse must be entitled to all the income of property held in a trust for the lifetime benefit of the surviving spouse. This is true even though the spouse is not entitled to the income from the decedent spouse's estate assets for the period before distribution of those assets by the personal representative, unless the personal representative is, by the terms of the decedent's will, authorized or directed to delay the distribution beyond the period reasonably required for administration of the decedent's estate.[57] The mere administrative power to withhold distributions from the trust until full and final satisfaction of all taxes does not result in the failure to satisfy the present interest requirement of I.R.C. Section 2032A. The IRS acknowledges that a contrary conclusion would disqualify most estates and trusts from special use valuation treatment, a result that Congress did not intend. Interestingly, the IRS asserts "[e]ven assuming, arguendo, that the discretionary power to withhold trust distributions results in failure to satisfy the present interest requirement, special use value should be, nevertheless, allowable under section 2032A(g) of the Code."[58]

SPECIAL KINDS OF REAL PROPERTY

Cooperative Apartments

Cooperative apartments of a cooperative housing corporation consist of dwelling units in a multi-dwelling complex in which each owner has an interest in the entire complex and a lease of his or her own apartment, though not ownership of the real property, as in the case of a condominium. In a cooperative apartment arrangement, a person owns stock in the cooperative and not a direct undivided interest in the underlying real property itself. Each

---

[51] S. Rept. No. 94-1236, 94th Cong., 2d Sess. (1976), Vol. 3 1976-3 C.B. 807, 960.

[52] Treas. Reg. § 25.2503-3(b).

[53] I.R.C. § 2032A(b)(1)(A) and (b)(1)(B).

[54] Tech. Adv. Mem. 8244001 (January 14, 1981).

[55] Treas. Reg. § 20.2032A-3(b).

[56] Tech. Adv. Mem. 8244001 (January 14, 1981).

[57] Treas. Reg. § 20.2056(b)-5(f)(9).

[58] Tech. Adv. Mem. 8532007 (April 22, 1985).

stockholder is entitled to occupy for dwelling purposes a particular house, or an apartment in a building, owned or leased by a cooperative housing corporation, for a specified term of years.

Income Tax Deduction to Tenant-Stockholder

A cooperative housing corporation is denied favorable income tax treatment when less than 80 percent of its gross income is derived from tenant-stockholders.[59] A tenant-stockholder is allowed an income tax deduction for amounts paid or accrued to a cooperative housing corporation to the extent such amounts represent the tenant-stockholder's proportionate share of (1) real estate taxes allowed as a deduction to the corporation (2) certain interest allowable as a deduction to the corporation under I.R.C. Section 163 which is paid or incurred by the corporation on its contracted indebtedness.[60] The term *tenant-stockholder* means a person who is a stockholder in a cooperative housing corporation.[61] For taxable years beginning before January 1, 1987, tenant-stockholders include only individuals, certain lending institutions, and certain persons from whom the cooperative housing corporation has acquired the apartments or houses (or leaseholds thereon).[62]

Conveyance of Tenant-Stockholder's Interest to Trustee

Ask Your Attorney

If I convey my interest as a tenant-stockholder in a cooperative housing corporation to the trustee of my revocable living trust, will I lose the income tax deductions otherwise allowed to me?

Answer

No.

The term *tenant-stockholder* means a person who is a stockholder in a cooperative housing corporation.[63] The term *person* includes an individual; a corporation; a partnership; a trust or estate; a joint-stock company; an association; or a syndicate, group, pool, joint venture, or other unincorporated organization or group. Such term also includes a guardian; committee; trustee; executor; administrator; trustee in bankruptcy; receiver; assignee for the benefit of creditors; conservator; or any person acting in a fiduciary capacity.[64] In effect, I.R.C. Section 671 provides that the revocable living trust acts as a conduit through which its income flows to the trustor and is taxed to the trustor.[65] Where the trustor is the owner of the entire trust estate, the trustor is the owner of stock in a cooperative housing corporation conveyed to the trustee of a revocable living trust, even if the trustor is not acting as the trustee. Accordingly, even though the trustee would be in legal title to the trustor's interest as a ten-

---

[59] I.R.C. § 216(b)(1)(D); Treas. Reg. § 1.216-1(e)(4).

[60] I.R.C. § 216(a).

[61] I.R.C. § 216(b)(2).

[62] Treas. Reg. § 1.216-1(f).

[63] I.R.C. § 216(b)(2).

[64] Treas. Reg. § 301.7701-1(a).

[65] *See* discussion in Chapter 7.

ant-stockholder, the trustor—not the trustee—is the tenant-stockholder; and the amount paid by the trustee under the proprietary lease to the corporation is considered derived from the trustee for purposes of determining whether 80 percent or more of the gross income of the cooperative housing corporation is derived from tenant-stockholders.[66]

Gifting Stock in a Cooperative Housing Corporation

Ask Your Attorney

Can the trustor or trustee gift to a donee stock in a cooperative housing corporation held in a revocable living trust?

Answer

Yes.[67]

Trustor Residing in Cooperative Apartment

Ask Your Attorney

If the trustor is not the trustee, does the trustor, as tenant-stockholder, have to live in the cooperative apartment of which the trustee is the lessee?

Answer

No.

Each stockholder of a cooperative corporation, whether the stockholder qualifies as a tenant-stockholder, must be entitled to occupy for dwelling purposes an apartment in a building or a unit in a housing development owned or leased by such corporation. The stockholder (i.e., trustor) is not required to occupy the premises. The right, as against the corporation, to occupy the premises is sufficient. Such right must be conferred on each stockholder solely by reasons of his or her ownership of stock in the corporation. That is, the stock must entitle the owner thereof either to occupy the premises or to a lease of the premises. The fact that the right to continue to occupy the premises is dependent upon the payment of charges to the corporation in the nature of rentals or assessments is immaterial. For taxable years beginning after December 31, 1986, the fact that, by agreement with the cooperative housing corporation, a person or his or her nominee may not occupy the house or apartment without the prior approval of such corporation will not be taken into account in any case where:

- A person acquires stock of the cooperative housing corporation by operation of law, by inheritance, or by foreclosure (or by instrument in lieu of foreclosure);
- A person other than an individual acquires stock in the cooperative housing corporation; and

---

[66] Rev. Rul. 71-294, 1971-2 C.B. 16.

[67] *See* Treas. Reg. § 1.216-1(h), Example (1).

- The person from whom the corporation has acquired the apartments or houses (or leaseholds therein) acquires any stock of the cooperative housing corporation from the corporation not later than one year after the date on which the apartments or houses (or leaseholds therein) are transferred to the corporation by such person.[68]

Action to be Taken to Convey Tenant-Stockholder's Interest to Trustee

Before conveying an interest as a tenant-stockholder in cooperative housing corporation stock to the trustee of a revocable living trust, the trustor should do the following:

- Obtain approval from the cooperative housing corporation's board of directors or appropriate officer (see file "APP1012.DOC").
- Carefully review the stock certificate(s) for any restrictions (legends) regarding transferring the stock;
- Carefully review the lease agreement for restrictions on assignment.

Conveyance Forms

Upon granting approval for the conveyance of the tenant-stockholder's interest in the cooperative housing corporation stock to the trustee of a revocable living trust, the corporation may provide the trustor with the required forms to effect such a conveyance. If forms are not provided, then the tenant-stockholder's interest in the stock may be conveyed to the trustee in one of two ways:

1. By endorsing the stock certificate to the trustee, using the following wording as an example: Eugene H. Curtis and Theresa M. Curtis, co-trustees; U/D/T dated January 15, 2003; F/B/O the Curtis Family; or
2. By effecting an Assignment of Stock Power (see file "APP0901.DOC").

Lease Agreement

The lease agreement entered into by and between the lessor and lessee (presumably the tenant-stockholder trustor) should be assigned to the trustee of the revocable living trust. For this purpose, an Assignment of Cooperative Housing Corporation Lease may be used (see file "APP1013.DOC"). The purpose of this assignment of lease is to ensure that, if the trustor becomes physically disabled or mentally incapacitated during the term of the lease, the trustee can manage the lease under the terms of the revocable living trust for the benefit of the trustor.

Condominiums

A condominium is an estate in real property consisting of an undivided interest in common in the real property together with a separate interest in space in a building on the real property. The building may be for residential, industrial, or commercial purposes and consist of an apartment, office, or store.[69] A condominium management association may require the approval of the board of directors or an officer of the association to any conveyance of the condominium owner's interest in the real property to the trustee of a revocable living trust

---

[68] Treas. Reg. § 1.216-1(e)(2).
[69] Black, *Black's Law Dictionary*, at 267.

(see file "APP1014.DOC"). In this regard, the primary interest of the condominium management association is that an individual actually occupy the condominium unit whenever a residential condominium is involved. Upon granting approval for the conveyance of the condominium owner's interest in the condominium to the trustee of a revocable living trust, the condominium management association may provide the trustor with the required forms to effect such a conveyance. If forms are not provided, then the trustor's interest in the condominium real property may be conveyed to the trustee by effecting a warranty deed (see file "APP1015.DOC"). Always check the Declarations and Bylaws of the Condominium Association to ascertain any limitations regarding the conveyance of an owner's interest in a condominium.

Time-Shares

A time-share is a unit of ownership in real property. Use of the real property is divided into interval time periods during which the owner has the exclusive right to occupy the property. The interval time periods are usually divided into weeks. The interval time period may be for the same one or two weeks each year or on a reservation basis in common with other lessees. Most time-shares are either an apartment occupancy lease or time-share ownership.

Apartment Occupancy Lease

Under this time-share arrangement, the owner simply has the right to occupy any unit among the vacation apartments as an apartment occupancy leasehold interest with an interval time period of, say, fourteen days on a reservation basis in common with other lessees for a predetermined number of years. Under such an arrangement, the owner of the time share is not guaranteed occupancy of a certain vacation apartment from one year to the next; and the owner's time-share interest may or may not consist of an interest in real property. If the ownership interest is not an undivided interest in the real property, then it is a time-share by contract. The owner's time-share interest is conveyed to the trustee of a revocable living trust by effecting an Assignment of Time-Share Ownership Agreement (or Assignment of Condominium Ownership Agreement) (see file "APP1016.DOC") or Assignment of Leasehold (see file "APP1017.DOC"). A copy of the lease or contract should be attached to the Assignment.

Time-Share Ownership

Under this time-share arrangement, the owner holds an undivided interest in the real property and the exclusive right to occupy a certain apartment or condominium unit for a specified interval time period (interval unit) each year. If the time-share ownership entitles the owner to an undivided interest in the real property comprising the occupancy of dwellings, then the trustor would effect a warranty deed to convey his or her interest in the time-share to the trustee of a revocable living trust (see file "APP1018.DOC").

Assignment Clause

It is not unusual for a lease agreement or a time-share ownership agreement to include an assignment clause. Such a clause provides that the lessee may not assign the lease, either in whole or in part, to any third person unless the consent of the lessor is first obtained for such assignment in writing. Provision is also made that such consent will not be unreasonably withheld. A transfer charge may be made for redrawing the lease and books of account. In view of such a provision, the trustor should obtain the written consent of the lessor before actually conveying his or her ownership interest in a time-share to the trustee of a revocable living trust (see file "APP1019.DOC").

Observations

1. It is not uncommon for more than one married couple to own a time-share interest together. The *spouse's joint property rule* determines the extent to which property owned as JTWROS (or as tenants by the entirety) is included in the gross estate of the first decedent spouse. As a general rule, for married decedents who are both U.S. citizens dying after 1981, one-half the value of property owned by a husband and wife as JTWROS (or as tenants by the entirety), regardless of which spouse furnished the original consideration for the acquisition of the property, is included in the gross estate of the first decedent spouse. This rule only applies when the spouses are the only joint owners as to their entire interest in the property.[70]

   A three-way joint ownership of property among a husband and wife and a third party may not be eligible for the federal estate tax marital deduction[71] and the 50 percent treatment as to the value of the property owned as JTWROS includable in the gross estate of the first decedent spouse.[72] For example, suppose two married couples own a time-share as follows: Tom and Betty, as JTWROS; and Rich and Evelyn, as JTWROS. Because Betty and Tom or Rich and Evelyn, respectively, are not the only joint tenants, does this mean that the federal estate tax marital deduction is not available to the estate of the first decedent spouse of each couple and that the spouse's joint property rule does not apply to either couple? No, because Tom and Betty and Rich and Evelyn are the only joint owners as to their respective entire interest in the property.

2. A situation might exist where the trustor owns an undivided interest in the real property and the exclusive right to occupy a certain apartment unit for a specified interval time period (interval unit) each year. The trustor's right to occupy a certain apartment or condominium unit may exist by contract. In such a case, the trustor would effect a warranty deed to convey his or her undivided interest in the time-share real property to the trustee of a revocable living trust and an Assignment of Time-Share Ownership Agreement (see file "APP1016.DOC") (or Assignment of Condominium Ownership Agreement) to convey the trustor's interest in the interval time period to the trustee of a revocable living trust. In other words, it would be necessary to effect both documents in order to convey all of the trustor's interests in the time-share arrangement to the trustee of his or her revocable living trust.

Income-Producing Real Property

If the trustor owns real property that produces income, the title to such real property can be conveyed to the trustee of a revocable living trust by effecting a warranty deed. If the income from the real property is governed by a rental or lease agreement and the trustor wants the agreement to be in the name of the trustee of the revocable living trust, then an Assignment of Lease to the trustee must be effected (see file "APP1020.DOC").

Even though title to the rental real property is conveyed to the trustee by warranty deed, if the lease agreement itself is not in the name of the trustee, then it does not come under the

---

[70] I.R.C. § 2040(b)(1) and (2). *See* discussion in "Spouse's Joint Property Rule" section, Chapter 7, and "Estates of Married Persons" section, Chapter 8.

[71] *See Jeschke v. United States*, 814 F.2d 568 (10th Cir. 1987), *aff'g* 84-1 U.S. Tax Cas. (CCH) ¶ 13,562 (D. Kan., 1984); *Jackson v. United States*, 376 U.S. 503 (1964). For an in-depth analysis of the issue of three-way property ownership as JTWROS, *see* Doug H. Moy, "Joint Ownership of Property: Two's Company, But Is Three a Crowd?" 39 *National Public Accountant* 16-19; 34-37 (Jan. 1994).

[72] I.R.C. § 2040(b)(2)(B).

protection of the revocable living trust. If the trustor becomes physically disabled or mentally incapacitated, the lease agreement may be subject to a court-supervised financial guardianship. Furthermore, upon the trustor's death, if the trustee is not in title to the lease agreement, the payments under the lease agreement may be included in the decedent trustor's probate estate. After the lease has been assigned to the trustee of the trustor's revocable living trust, tenants should make their checks payable to the trustee, even if the trustor is acting as the trustee. If the trustor is the trustee, the rental payments should not be made to the trustor in his or her individual name but, rather, in the trustor's name as trustee.

Out-of-State Real Property

Real property titled in an individual's name may be included in the decedent's probate estate in the state in which the real property is situate. Likewise, in the event of the trustor's physical disability or mental incapacity, a court-supervised financial guardianship proceeding with respect to the real property may have to be commenced in the county wherein the real property is situate. Out-of-state probate proceedings (ancillary probate proceedings) can be avoided when title to such real property is conveyed to the trustee of a revocable living trust. The law of the state in which the real property is situate must be reviewed as to deed content and recording requirements.

Ask Your Attorney

Must the legal jurisdiction (situs) of a revocable living trust be in the state in which the real property is situate, even though I do not reside in that state?

Answer

No.

Easements

An easement is the interest that one person has in the land of another. For example, a person may have the right of vehicular passage and pedestrian traffic over, across, and along all of a certain parcel of land belonging to another person. Generally, such an easement is defined in the landowner's deed to the real property. The person entitled to the easement can convey his or her right in the easement to the trustee of a revocable living trust by effecting an Assignment of Easement (see file "APP1021.DOC").

Dwellings on Leased Land

A dwelling on leased land may be considered tangible personal property—not real property. For example, the United States Department of Agriculture, through the United States Forest Service, issues Special Use Permits authorizing the construction of dwellings on federally owned land. Usually, such dwellings are vacation homes. A trustor can convey his or her interest in the Special Use Permit to the trustee of a revocable living trust with the approval of the Forest Service officer by whom the permit was given, or his or her successor, subject to such conditions as may be imposed at the time of transfer. In this regard, the Forest Service conducts an inspection of the dwelling and real property upon which it is located. Generally, the District Office of the National Forest Service, wherein the dwelling is located, will require the following before a new permit is issued:

- A copy of the document showing the change of ownership;
- Completion of Request for Termination/Application;
- Completion of Transfer Maintenance Agreement, which assures that the new owners will complete maintenance items by the scheduled due date on the inspection report; and
- Payment of the transfer fee.

Approval of the appropriate district officer of the U.S. Forest Service should be obtained before the trustor conveys his or her interest in the dwelling to the trustee of a revocable living trust (see file "APP1022.DOC"). 🖳 The trustor's interest in the Special Use Permit may be conveyed to the trustee of a revocable living trust by effecting an Assignment of Special Use Permit (see file "APP1023.DOC"). 🖳 The trustor's interest in the dwelling itself may be conveyed to the trustee of a revocable living trust by effecting an Assignment of Recreation Dwelling on U.S. Forest Service Land (see file "APP1024.DOC"). 🖳 Copies of both documents should be provided the District Office of the U.S. Forest Service having jurisdiction of the Special Use Permit.

Ask Your Attorney

My mountain cabin is located on U.S. Forest Service land for which I have a Special Use Permit issued in the name of the trustee of my revocable living trust. Can I sell the cabin; and, if so, how do I do this?

Answer

Yes, the trustee of the revocable living trust can sell the cabin; and the Special Use Permit can be reissued in the name of the buyer. The same process used to convey the trustor's interest in the Special Use Permit to the trustee of a revocable living trust is followed to transfer the trustor's interest in the Special Use Permit to the new owner. If the cabin (dwelling) is sold to the buyer on a contract, the trustee would sell the cabin under a Contract—Personal Property U.S. Forest Service Land (see file "APP1025.DOC"). 🖳

OTHER REAL PROPERTY INTERESTS

Trust Deed

In some states, a trust deed is used in place of a mortgage. Under a trust deed, the grantor conveys to a trustee a conditional title in the real property to secure the repayment of a sum of money or the performance of other conditions for the benefit of the beneficiary. The grantor is the person who holds fee title, actually borrows the money, and is the giver of the trust deed. The trustee is the person who holds conditional title for the benefit of the beneficiary lender who holds a naked title. In most states, only a title company, bank, savings and loan association, or an attorney can act as the trustee under a trust deed. The beneficiary is the lender under the trust deed. Usually, a demand note, promissory note, or installment note is used with a trust deed. Though the trust deed is recorded, the note itself is not recorded.

The beneficiary's beneficial interest in the trust deed, together with the notes, moneys, and obligations described or referred to in the trust deed, including interest, can be conveyed to the trustee of a revocable living trust by effecting an Assignment of Trust Deed by Beneficiary or Beneficiary's Successor in Interest (see file "APP1026.DOC"). This assignment should be recorded. As a rule, the beneficiary does not have to obtain approval of the trustee (e.g., the title company) to convey his or her beneficial interest in the trust deed to the trustee of a revocable living trust. Upon receipt of the original note marked "paid" and delivery of the trust deed to the trustee, along with a request from the beneficiary for reconveyance, the trustee under the trust deed effects a Trust Deed of Reconveyance, which reconveys the conditional title given the trustee at the inception of the trust deed. The beneficiary's interest in the trust deed is then extinguished. Also, the beneficiary's interest in the note secured by the trust deed must be conveyed to the trustee of the revocable living trust (see file "APP1027.DOC"). The grantor of a trust deed may also convey his or her interest in the real property to the trustee of a revocable living trust by obtaining approval of the trustee of the trust deed and the beneficiary.[73]

Observation

The Assignment of Installment Note (see file "APP1027.DOC") may be modified to be an Assignment of Demand Note or Assignment of Promissory Note simply by changing the name of the note being assigned.

Mortgage

A mortgage is an interest in land created by a written instrument providing security for the performance of an obligation or the payment of a debt. The mortgagor is the person borrowing money and is the one who gives the mortgage lien as security for the loan. The mortgagee is the lender who receives the lien. The lender (mortgagee) may convey its interest in the mortgage to the trustee of a revocable living trust by effecting an Assignment of Mortgage (see file "APP1028.DOC"). If the original mortgage was recorded, the Assignment of Mortgage should also be recorded. Upon satisfaction of the mortgage by the mortgagor, the trustee of the revocable living trust effects a Satisfaction of Mortgage or Full Mortgage Release (see file "APP1029.DOC").

Land Sale Contract

When real property is sold under a land sale contract, the seller (vendor) retains the deed until the buyer (vendee), who retains equitable title in the real property, has satisfied the terms of the contract. If the trustor is the vendor selling real property under a land sale contract, the trustor's interest in both the contract and the real property can be conveyed to the trustee of a revocable living trust by effecting an Assignment of Land Sale Contract (see file "APP1030.DOC"). If the trustor is the vendee purchasing real property under a land sale contract, upon obtaining the consent of the vendor, the trustor's interest in the contract can be conveyed to the trustee of a revocable living trust by effecting an Assignment of Land Sale Contract (see file "APP1031.DOC"). Whether the trustor is the vendor-seller or the vendee-buyer, if the original land sale contract was recorded, the Assignment of Land Sale Contract should also be recorded.

The assignment must contain a full and accurate legal description of the real property or a reference to the real property as it is described in the original land sale contract. The

---

[73]*See* discussion in "Due-on-Sale Clause" section, this chapter, regarding real property subject to indebtedness).

terms of the land sale contract can be incorporated by reference into the assignment, or a copy of the land sale contract can be attached to the assignment. As already mentioned, the land sale contract may contain a due-on-sale clause. When in doubt as to the effect of such a clause in the contract, the trustor's attorney should review it and advise the trustor on how to proceed with respect to obtaining the seller's consent to convey the vendee's interest in the underlying real property subject to the contract to the trustee of the trustor's revocable living trust. If, on the other hand, the trustor is not uncertain about the meaning of the due-on-sale clause, he or she should obtain the consent of the seller to convey the trustor's interest, as buyer under the contract, to the trustee of the trustor's revocable living trust (see file "APP1032.DOC").

Leases

Generally, a lease is a written contract that gives a person possession and use of real property for a determined period of time. The lessor (landlord) is the person who holds title to the real property and gives the right to use and occupancy to the lessee (tenant). The lessee (tenant) is the person to whom possession of the property has been given for a specific rental and time. The interest of a tenant under a lease is called a leasehold. As the holder of a leasehold interest, the lessee has the right to assign the lease, the right to sublease the real property, and the beneficial right to occupancy of the property. However, the approval of the lessor may be required for the lessee to assign the lease to a third party. Assuming consent of the lessor is obtained, the lessee may convey his or her interest in the lease to the trustee of a revocable living trust by effecting an Assignment of Leasehold (see file "APP1017.DOC"). The lessor can convey his or her interest in the lease to the trustee of a revocable living trust by effecting an Assignment of Lease (see file "APP1020.DOC").

CHAPTER 11

Publicly-Traded Securities and U.S. Government Obligations

STOCKS

Legal title to registered publicly-traded stocks, bonds, mutual funds, and limited partnerships is conveyed to the trustee of a revocable living trust by requesting either the transfer agent or stockbroker to effect a change in ownership.

Transfer Agent

If the trustor physically possesses stock certificates not registered in a brokerage account, then the transfer agent should be requested to retitle the securities in the name of the trustee of the revocable living trust. Generally, the name of the transfer agent is on the front of the stock certificate and may be identified as *transfer agent* or as *registrar*. If the stock certificate is several years old, time and expense may be saved by telephoning the transfer agent identified on the stock certificate to determine if that transfer agent still handles a particular company's stock. If the transfer agent cannot be located, a local stockbroker may know who the transfer agent is for a particular company's stock.

Transfer Agent's Procedure

Usually, the transfer agent has a prescribed format and procedure for transferring legal title of securities to the trustee of a revocable living trust. The trustor should request from the transfer agent the necessary forms and requirements to reregister the security in the name of the trustee of a revocable living trust (see file "APP1101.DOC"). The transfer agent will respond with a list of instructions.

Submit Original Stock Certificate

Generally, the transfer agent will require that the original stock certificate representing shares of the subject company be submitted with the registered owner's signature on the endorsed stock certificate guaranteed by a commercial bank or by a stockbroker who is a member of a national securities exchange. The *endorsement* or stock power is found on the backside of the stock certificate (see file "APP1102.DOC"). A signature acknowledgment by a Notary Public or by an officer of a savings and loan association does not satisfy the signature guarantee requirement. The trustor's signature should be on file at the place where the guarantee is obtained.

Conveying Title to Multiple Stock Certificates

If legal title to many stock certificates representing a particular company is to be conveyed to the trustee of a revocable living trust, a single Assignment of Stock or Bond Power may be effected for all of the shares the trustor owns in a particular company (see file "APP0901.DOC"). All of the certificates representing ownership of stock in a particular company, along with the single executed Assignment of Stock or Bond Power, are submitted to the transfer agent for reregistration in the name of the trustee of the revocable living trust.

Letter of Instruction

In addition to providing the original stock certificates properly endorsed, or an Assignment of Stock or Bond Power, the transfer agent will request a letter of instruction stating the name of the revocable living trust, date of the trust, name and address of the trustee, and the taxpayer identification number to be used for the revocable living trust (see files "APP1103.DOC," "APP1104.DOC," and "APP1105.DOC"). This information, along with the original stock certificate(s), may be sent to the transfer agent through the U.S. Postal Service by registered mail, return receipt requested. The trustor should retain a photocopy of the letter of instruction and both sides of the endorsed stock certificates. Also, it is a good idea to include the return receipt number in the letter so as to *tie* the letter to the receipt.

Copy of Trust Agreement

Though not common, the transfer agent may request a complete copy of the revocable living trust agreement. The trustor should steadfastly resist providing the transfer agent a complete copy of the revocable living trust agreement for one simple and irrefutable reason—the provisions addressing the disposition of the trust estate upon the death of the trustor are no one's business except the trustor and members of his or her immediate family, assuming of course, that the trustor wishes to share these provisions with his or her immediate family members. Nevertheless, if pressed to provide a copy of the trust agreement, the trustor should submit either a Memorandum of Trust (see file "APP0210.DOC") or the following specific pages of the revocable living trust agreement evidencing existence of the trust:

- First page (Preamble) of the trust agreement identifying the trustor;
- Pages naming the original and successor trustees;
- Pages describing the trustee's powers, specifically those pertaining to options, calls, puts, and margin accounts;
- Signature pages showing the signatures of trustor(s) and trustee(s) to evidence that the trust has, in fact, been effected; and
- Pages evidencing that the signatures of the trustor(s) and trustee(s) have been notarized. Though not often required, it is a good idea to have these same signatures guaranteed.

Other Pages of the Trust Agreement

In some cases, other pages of the revocable living trust agreement may be requested by the transfer agent (e.g., those pages enumerating the trustor's right to revoke and amend the trust agreement). If a transfer agent insists on receiving a complete copy of the trust agreement, under no circumstances should the trustor provide a copy of the trust provisions describing distribution of the trust estate upon the trustor's death. This is a private personal matter and is probably one of the reasons why the trustor effected a revocable living trust in the first place; namely, to ensure privacy in the administration of his or her affairs in the event of incapacity and/or upon death. Moreover, the trustor should not be required to submit to anyone to whom the trustor would not otherwise provide his or her personal financial statement a copy of the schedules of property comprising the trust estate which are attached to the revocable living trust agreement.

Stockbroker Account

An account into which all of the trustor's securities are held with a stockbroker can be established in the name of the trustee of the revocable living trust. Such an account is popularly known as a *street name account*. If the trustor establishes a street name account, he or she should be certain to request from the stockbroker a detailed receipt of all certificates deposited into the account. Generally, the broker retains physical possession of the certificates; and the trustor's only evidence of beneficial ownership is the account statement listing the securities and their value. If giving up physical possession of the stock certificates is disquieting to the trustor, the stockbroker will most likely allow the trustor to retain possession of the certificates after the account has been opened. If the trustor already has a street name account, the stockbroker or account representative can be directed in writing to retitle the account into the name of the trustee of the trustor's revocable living trust (see file "APP1106.DOC").

Advantage of Street Name Account

One advantage of a street name account is that a Trustee's Acceptance (see file "APP0902.DOC") does not have to be completed each time a new security is added to the account. This is because the account itself, which holds the individual investments (securities), is already titled in the name of the trustee of the revocable living trust. In contrast, if the trustor retains possession of the security certificate, then each time the trustor acquires a new investment, the new security must be titled in the name of the trustee of the revocable living trust. Whether the trustor chooses a street name account to hold his or her securities or retains physical possession of the security certificates has no direct bearing on the trustee's power with respect to the securities. The real issue has to do with whether the trustor is more comfortable retaining physical possession of the security certificates instead of a brokerage firm retaining possession of the certificates in a street name account.

Opening a Street Name Account in the Name of Trustee

When a street name account is opened, the broker will require evidence of the existence of the revocable living trust agreement. In this regard, the trustor has three options:

1. Provide the stockbroker with a Memorandum of Trust;
2. Provide the stockbroker with specific pages of the revocable living trust agreement (see discussion in this regard relative to using a transfer agent to retitle securities in the name of the trustee of a revocable living trust); or
3. Provide the stockbroker with a copy of the revocable living trust agreement, excepting the trust provisions describing the disposition of the trust estate upon the trustor's death and the schedules of property comprising the trust estate attached to the trust agreement.

Most stockbrokers require more than a Memorandum of Trust as evidence that a legal trust exists for the purpose of the trustee holding title to securities. Many stockbrokers will accept the trust pages discussed above with respect to transfer agents. However, overall, both the trustor and his or her stockbroker will be better served if the stockbroker has a nearly complete copy of the trust agreement in the trustor's account file.

BONDS

Registered Bonds

Legal title to registered publicly-traded bonds of which the trustor holds physical possession of the certificates can be conveyed to the trustee of a revocable living trust in the same manner as publicly-traded stocks. Such a conveyance is accomplished by effecting the endorsement on the backside of the bond and submitting the bond to the transfer agent listed on the face of the bond (see file "APP1102.DOC"). When endorsing the bond, the trustor should be certain to have his or her signature guaranteed in the same manner as he or she would for publicly-traded stocks.

Bearer Bonds

Legal title to bearer bonds can be conveyed to the trustee of a revocable living trust. A bearer bond is a bond that is not registered and is identified on its face by the wording "pay to the bearer," or "pay to the bearer or, if this Bond be registered as hereinafter provided, to the registered owner." The person (bearer) in possession of the bond can buy, sell, or otherwise negotiate the bond. In this sense, bearer bonds are like cash. The value of bearer bonds is includable in the decedent bearer's gross estate.[1] Failure to include the value of bearer bonds in the gross estate may constitute fraud[2] or invite imposition by the IRS of valuation misstatement penalties.[3]

Safekeeping Bearer Bonds that Cannot be Reregistered

If a bearer bond cannot be reregistered, it may be assigned to the trustee of a revocable living trust. An Assignment of Bearer Bonds (see file "APP1107.DOC") can be effected to assign bearer bonds to the trustee. However, such an assignment does not retitle the bonds in the name of the trustee on the books of the issuer. Hence, the Assignment should be attached to the bonds; and the bonds should be held in a safe deposit box (or other secured place) with the identity and location of the safe deposit box included on the appropriate schedule of assets attached to the revocable living trust agreement. At best, this creates a paper trail to the bonds so that the trustor's beneficiaries will know that the trustee is the "bearer" of the bonds.

Ask Your Attorney

If the trustee of my revocable living trust is deemed the "bearer" of the bonds either because the bonds are titled in the name of the trustee or because the bonds were assigned to the trustee, would the value of the bonds be included in the trustee's gross estate upon his or her death?

Answer

No. Like all other assets titled in the name of the trustee or assigned to the trustee, the trustee is in title to the bonds only as a fiduciary and does not hold equitable or beneficial title to the bonds. In other words, it is not the trustee's property (asset) to be transferred

---

[1] I.R.C. § 2031(a).

[2] I.R.C. § 6663(a).

[3] I.R.C. § 6662(b), (c), and (g).

to the trustor's beneficiaries under the terms of the revocable living trust agreement. Accordingly, the bonds are not included in the value of the trustee's gross estate, even though the bonds are "bearer" bonds.

Why Bearer Bonds Should Be Registered in Name of Trustee

Because it is foolhardy to exclude the value of bearer bonds from one's gross estate, if the bond provides for registration, it makes good sense to register an existing bearer bond in the name of the trustee of a revocable living trust. Such registration enables the trustee to manage the bonds for the lifetime benefit of the trustor. Moreover, upon the trustor's death, probate of the bonds may be avoided; and the bonds can be distributable to the trustor's beneficiaries as provided under the terms of the revocable living trust agreement. Registration of the bonds in the name of the trustee of a revocable living trust can be accomplished in the same manner as retitling publicly-traded stocks and registered bonds in the name of the trustee. In this regard, if a bond power is provided on the bond, the bond certificate(s) may be endorsed; or, if a bond power is not provided, an Assignment of Stock or Bond Power (see file "APP0901.DOC") can be used. Upon completion of the endorsement or execution of the bond power, the bond(s) should be sent to the transfer agent (sometimes listed on the bearer bond as the "trustee") through the U.S. Postal Service by registered mail, return receipt requested. The trustor should retain a photocopy of the letter of instruction and both sides of the endorsed bond.

RESTRICTED SECURITIES

Several terms are used in the securities industry to denote restrictions imposed on the resale and transfer of certain securities. The term frequently used to describe these securities is *restricted securities*; but they are sometimes referred to as *unregistered securities, investment letter stock, control stock,* or *private placement stock.* Frequently, these terms are used interchangeably. They all indicate that these particular securities cannot lawfully be distributed to the general public until a registration statement relating to the corporation underlying the securities has been filed and has also become effective under the rules promulgated and enforced by the United States Securities & Exchange Commission (SEC) pursuant to the federal securities laws.[4]

Restricted Securities Defined

Restricted securities are defined by the SEC under Rule 144, as "securities acquired directly or indirectly from the issuer thereof, or from an affiliate of such issuer, in a transaction or chain of transactions not involving any public offering."[5] Unregistered securities are those securities with respect to which a registration statement, providing full disclosure by the issuing corporation, has not been filed with the SEC pursuant to the Securities Act of 1933. The registration statement is a condition precedent to a public distribution of securities in interstate commerce and is aimed at providing the prospective investor with a factual basis for sound judgment in making investment decisions.[6] Investment letter stock and letter stock are shares of stock which have been issued by a corporation without the benefit of filing a registration statement with the SEC. Such stock is subject to resale and transfer restrictions set forth in a letter agreement requested by the issuer and signed by the buyer of

---

[4]Rev. Rul. 77-287, 1977-2 C.B. 319, Sec. 3.02.

[5]Rev. Rul. 77-287, 1977-2 C.B. 319, Sec. 3.02(a).

[6]Rev. Rul. 77-287, 1977-2 C.B. 319, Sec. 3.02(b).

the stock when the stock is delivered. Such stock may be found in the hands of either individual investors or institutional investors.[7]

Control Stock

The term *control stock* indicates that the shares of stock have been held or are being held by an officer, director, or other person close to the management of the corporation. These persons are subject to certain requirements pursuant to SEC rules upon resale of shares they own in such corporations.[8] Private placement stock is stock that has been placed with an institution or other investor who will presumably hold it for a long period and ultimately arrange to have the stock registered, if it is to be offered to the general public. Such stock may or may not be subject to a letter agreement. Private placements of stock are exempted from the registration and prospectus provisions of the Securities Act of 1933.[9]

Exempt Securities

Some securities may be classified as exempt. Exempted securities are classes of securities which are expressly excluded from the registration provisions of the Securities Act of 1933 and the distribution provisions of the Securities Exchange Act of 1934.[10] Similarly, exempted transactions are certain sales or distributions of securities which do not involve a public offering and are excluded from the registration and prospectus provisions of the Securities Act of 1933 and distribution provisions of the Securities Exchange Act of 1934. The exempted status makes it unnecessary for issuers of securities to go through the registration process.[11] If the trustor owns restricted or exempt securities, he or she should check with the corporate secretary of the company whose stock the trustor owns to determine what, if any, restrictions may be imposed on the stock with respect to conveying legal title of the stock to the trustee of a revocable living trust.

MUTUAL FUND ACCOUNTS

Legal title to a mutual fund account can be conveyed to the trustee of a revocable living trust by requesting the company representing the mutual fund to reregister the trustor's account in the name of the trustee of the trustor's revocable living trust (see file "APP1108.DOC"). For married individuals who have effected a joint revocable living trust, the following example may be followed with respect to the registration format: EUGENE H. CURTIS and THERESA M. CURTIS, co-trustees; U/D/T dated January 15, 2003; F/B/O the Curtis Family. The registration format for a single revocable living trust should read as follows: EUGENE H. CURTIS, Trustee; U/D/T dated January 15, 2003; F/B/O the Curtis Family. If the trustor acquired the mutual fund through a broker, that person should be able to assist in reregistering the ownership of the mutual fund in the name of the trustee of the trustor's revocable living trust. Whether the company representing the mutual fund or the trustor's broker assists in the reregistration process, the trustor may be required to provide the same evidence of the revocable living trust as the trustor would for the retitling of stock certificates. In addition, the trustor may be required to have his or her signature guaranteed on any forms used to effect the change of ownership.

---

[7] Rev. Rul. 77-287, 1977-2 C.B. 319, Sec. 3.02(c).

[8] Rev. Rul. 77-287, 1977-2 C.B. 319, Sec. 3.02(d).

[9] Rev. Rul. 77-287, 1977-2 C.B. 319, Sec. 3.02(e).

[10] Rev. Rul. 77-287, 1977-2 C.B. 319, Sec. 3.02(f).

[11] Rev. Rul. 77-287, 1977-2 C.B. 319, Sec. 3.02(g).

INVESTMENT LIMITED PARTNERSHIPS

Before the trustor attempts to convey title in an investment limited partnership (e.g., a leasing program) to the trustee of his or her revocable living trust, the documentation evidencing the partnership interest should be reviewed to determine what restrictions, if any, have been placed on the transfer of ownership. As a rule, written permission of the general partner will be required before a change of ownership can be effected (see file "APP1109.DOC"). When requesting the general partner's written permission, the trustor should include in a letter an Assignment of Limited Partnership Interest (see file "APP1110.DOC"). This Assignment informs the general partner of the trustor's intent to transfer ownership of his or her limited partnership interest to the trustee of his or her revocable living trust and also provides the general partner's consent for the trustor to do so.

Documents to Effect

In addition to obtaining the general partner's consent to convey ownership of a limited partnership to the trustee of a revocable living trust, the general partner may provide the trustor the following documents to be executed and returned to the general partner:

- Assignment and Assumption Agreements;
- An executed copy of the Subscription Agreement completed by the trustee (assignee).

Along with the aforementioned documents, the general partner may request the trustor to return the original Certificate of Ownership previously issued to the trustor as the investor. Also, most investment-limited partnerships impose a fee to cover all administrative and legal costs incurred in the transfer. As a rule, the *admission* of the new registration becomes effective as stated in the Assumption and Subscription Agreements upon receipt by the general partner of the completed aforementioned documents.

Conveyance of Investment Limited Partnership to Trustee

Conveyance to Trustee of Spouse's Revocable Living Trust

Ask Your Attorney

If I convey ownership of my interest in an investment limited partnership to the trustee of my revocable living trust, at a later time can I then transfer such interest to the trustee of my spouse's revocable living trust without adverse income tax consequences?

Answer

Yes.

A spouse can convey, either as an individual or as a trustee of a revocable living trust, his or her interest in an investment partnership to the trustee of the other spouse's revocable living trust without incurring gain or loss.[12] Even if the transferor spouse is not the trustee of his or her revocable living trust, if the trustor spouse has the power to revoke the

---

[12] I.R.C. § 1041(a); Treas. Reg. § 1.1041-1T(d), Q and A-12.

trust, no gain or loss is incurred on such a transfer. This is true even if the transferor spouse's liabilities in the partnerships exceed his or her adjusted basis in those partnerships.[13]

Grantor Trust Rules With Respect to Investment Limited Partnership

Under I.R.C. Section 671, if a grantor (trustor) is treated as the owner of any portion of a trust under I.R.C. Sections 673 through 679 (the grantor trust rules), then, in computing the grantor's taxable income and credits, the grantor must include the items of income, deductions, and credits of the trust attributable to the portion of the trust considered owned by the grantor to the extent those items would be taken into account in computing the taxable income or credits of an individual. Under I.R.C. Section 676, the grantor is treated as the owner of any portion of a trust if the grantor or a nonadverse party, or both, has a power to revest title to that portion in the grantor. If a grantor is treated as the owner of an entire trust, the grantor is considered as owner of the trust assets for federal income tax purposes.[14]

No Gain or Loss on Transfer of Property to Spouse

Code Section 1041(a) provides that no gain or loss is recognized on a transfer of property from an individual to (or in trust for the benefit of) a spouse.[15] This rule applies regardless of whether the transfer is a gift, a sale, or an exchange between spouses acting at arm's length.[16] Code Section 1041(b) provides that, in the case of any transfer of property described in I.R.C. Section 1041(a), the property is treated as acquired by the transferee by gift; and the basis of the transferee in the property is the adjusted basis of the transferor. In this regard, the transferee of property under I.R.C. Section 1041 recognizes no gain or loss upon receipt of the transferred property. In all cases, the basis of the transferred property in the hands of the transferee is the adjusted basis of such property in the hands of the transferor immediately before the transfer. Even if the transfer is a bona fide sale, the transferee does not acquire a basis in the transferred property equal to the transferee's cost (the fair market value). This carryover basis rule applies whether the adjusted basis of the transferred property is less than, equal to, or greater than its fair market value at the time of transfer (or the value of any consideration provided by the transferee) and applies for purposes of determining loss, as well as gain, upon the subsequent disposition of the property by the transferee. Thus, this rule is different from the rule applied in I.R.C. Section 1015(a) for determining the basis of property acquired by gift.[17]

Property Subject to Liabilities

The nonrecognition and basis rules apply even if the transferred property is subject to liabilities that exceed the adjusted basis of the property.[18]

Example

Assume husband owns property having a fair market value of $10,000 and an adjusted basis of $1,000. In contemplation of making a transfer of this property incident to a divorce from his wife, husband borrows $5,000 from a bank, using the property as security for the borrowing. Husband then transfers the property to wife, and wife assumes or takes the prop-

---

[13] Priv. Ltr. Rul. 8644012 (July 31, 1986).

[14] *See* Rev. Rul. 85-13, 1985-1 C.B. 184.

[15] Treas. Reg. § 1.1041-1T, Q and A-1 and § 1.1041-1T(d), Q and A-10.

[16] Treas. Reg. § 1.1041-1T(a), Q and A-2.

[17] Treas. Reg. § 1.1041-1T(d), Q and A-11.

[18] Treas. Reg. § 1.1041-1T(d), Q and A-12.

erty subject to the liability to pay the $5,000 debt. Under I.R.C. Section 1041, husband recognizes no gain or loss upon the transfer of the property; and the adjusted basis of the property in the hands of wife is $1,000.

Conveyance of Trustor's Investment Partnership Interest to Trustee Governed by I.R.C. Section 1041

Under I.R.C. Section 676, if each spouse has the power to revoke all of his or her revocable living trust, then, as trustor, for federal income tax purposes, he or she is treated as the owner of all of his or her revocable living trust. Therefore, the transfer of an investment partnership interest by either a husband or wife, either individually or as trustee of his or her revocable living trust, to the trustee of the other spouse's revocable living trust is a transfer from one spouse to the other spouse for purposes of I.R.C. Section 1041. Because the transfers of the investment partnership interests are transfers of property, they are governed by the nonrecognition rules of I.R.C. Section 1041 and the temporary regulations thereunder. Accordingly, the basis of the transferee spouse in the partnership interests, either as an individual taxpayer or as a trustee of such spouse's revocable living trust, is the adjusted basis of the transferor, as grantor, trustee, and/or individual taxpayer.[19]

U.S. GOVERNMENT OBLIGATIONS

U.S. Savings Bonds

The ownership of Series E, Series EE, Series H, and Series HH U.S. savings bonds can be conveyed to the trustee of a revocable living trust without the incremental value (accrued interest) being taxed to the owner at the time of the transfer.[20] If U.S. savings bonds are registered in the names of "A" or "B," as co-owners, no taxable event occurs upon the transfer (reissuance) of the bonds to the trustee of a revocable living trust and their reissuance in the name of the trustee.[21] Likewise, if U.S. savings bonds are registered in the name of "A" payable on death to "B," no income taxable event occurs when the bonds are transferred to the trustee of a revocable living trust and reissued in the name of the trustee.[22]

U.S. savings bonds must be reissued to convey ownership to the trustee of a revocable living trust. To convey ownership of U.S. savings bonds to the trustee of a revocable living trust, Department of the Treasury Bureau of the Public Debt Form PDF 1851 (Request to Reissue United States Savings Bonds to a Personal Trust) is used. When necessary, use Continuation Sheet for Listing Securities Form PDF 3500. It is important to have the latest revised form(s) available. The instructions on the form(s) should be carefully followed, and the trustor's (owner's) signature must be *certified* (guaranteed) in the same manner as for reregistering ownership of publicly-traded securities. The completed forms and bonds, together with any other appropriate forms and evidence, should be sent to the Savings Bond Processing Site nearest the trustor. The addresses of the five Savings Bond Processing Sites are listed on the form PDF 1851. When mailed, they should be sent by registered mail.

These forms can be obtained by U.S. Postal Service in about one week from the Federal Reserve Bank of Kansas City, Omaha Branch, 2201 Farnam Street, Omaha, NE 68102-1218, P.O. Box 3958, Omaha, NE 68103-0958, telephone (800) 333-2919, or 1(800) 722-2678, or (402) 221-5500. Or the forms can be obtained on-line at *http://www.publicdebt.treas.gov.*

---

[19] I.R.C. § 1041(b)(2); Treas. Reg. § 1.1041-1T(d), Q and A-11.

[20] Priv. Ltr. Rul. 7826024 (March 28, 1978); Rev. Ruls. 58-2, 1958-1 C.B. 236; 64-302, 1964-2 C.B. 170. *See* discussion in Chapter 7, United States Savings Bonds.

[21] Priv. Ltr. Rul. 9009053 (December 6, 1989).

[22] Rev. Rul. 70-428, 1970-2 C.B. 5; Priv. Ltr. Rul. 9009053 (December 6, 1989).

This is the Bureau of the Public Debt on-line website. Once at the site, click on "Forms;" then click on "Savings Bond Forms Ordering" or "Securities Forms Treasury Direct." The forms can be downloaded using Adobe Acrobat Software. This software can be downloaded free-of-charge from the Bureau of Public Debt website. The forms may also be obtained by sending an e-mail to: IS-MAB@bpd.treas.gov. The trustor should include his or her mailing address and a daytime telephone number and a list of the requested forms.

Book-Entry U.S. Treasury Bills

When conveying ownership of book-entry U.S. treasury bills to the trustee of a revocable living trust, Department of the Treasury Bureau of the Public Debt Form PDF 5179 (Security Transfer Request—Treasury Direct) or Form PDF 5182 (New Account Request—Treasury Direct) is used. Signature guarantee is required on Form PDF 5179 in the same manner as for reregistering ownership of publicly-traded securities. Signature guarantee is not required on Form PDF 5182. If U.S. treasury bills are held in a Treasury Direct account, Form PDF 5179 is used to convey ownership to the trustee of a revocable living trust and is submitted to the trustor's Treasury Direct office. The Treasury Direct address is found on the trustor's Treasury Direct Statement of Account or on the web (www.treasurydirect.gov). The form must be received at least ten business days in advance of: the maturity date of the security to ensure processing; and an interest payment date for the security to ensure processing prior to that date. If U.S. treasury bills are held in *definitive form* (actual physical possession), then Form PDF 5182 is submitted along with the treasury bills, to request that a Treasury Direct account be established in the name of the trustee of a revocable living trust. Form PDF 5182 and the treasury bills may be sent directly to one of three Treasury Direct offices listed on the form by registered mail. Assistance may be obtained by calling 1(800) 722-2678. Form PDF 5182 may be used to establish a Treasury Direct account. The instructions to Forms PDF 5179 and PDF 5182 must be read and followed carefully.

U.S. Treasury Notes and Bonds

Ownership of U.S. treasury notes and bonds may be conveyed to the trustee of a revocable living trust in a manner similar to that of publicly-traded securities. Each note or bond must be endorsed on the back of the certificate by the registered owner, and his or her signature must be guaranteed in the same way as for publicly-traded securities. Form PDF 5182 (New Account Request—Treasury Direct) must accompany the endorsed certificate(s).[23] If U.S. treasury notes or bonds are held in a Treasury Direct account, Form PDF 5179 (Security Transfer Request—Treasury Direct) is used to convey account ownership to the trustee of a revocable living trust.[24]

Flower Bonds

So-called *flower bonds* are marketable U.S. Treasury certificates, Treasury notes, or Treasury bills that can be redeemed by a decedent's personal representative at par value plus accrued interest to pay federal estate taxes. The only issue of *flower bonds* outstanding is the

---

[23] *See* discussion *infra* under Book-Entry U.S. Treasury Bills for information on where to submit Form PDF 5182.

[24] *See* discussion *infra* regarding Book-Entry U.S. Treasury Bills for information on the signature guarantee requirement on form PDF 5179 and where to submit Form PDF 5179.

$3\frac{1}{2}$ percent bonds of 1998 which have matured, the ownership of which cannot now be changed; that is to say, since the bonds have matured, the ownership of them cannot be conveyed to the trustee of a revocable living trust. According to a spokesperson in the Bureau of Public Debt, no new bonds have been issued to replace flower bonds.

To be eligible for redemption to pay federal estate tax, the flower bonds must be owned by the decedent at the time of his or her death (not acquired after the decedent's death) and be part of the decedent's gross estate.[25] These bonds are included in the decedent's gross estate at par value, even if the market value is less than par.[26] If the market value is greater than par, they are included in the gross estate at the mean between the highest and lowest quoted selling prices.[27] The gross estate includes the par value of flower bonds which could have been applied toward a part of the estate tax, even if they are not used to pay the estate tax and are sold on the market at less than par value.[28] Flower bonds in excess of the amount that may be applied are included in the gross estate at their market value.[29] Upon the trustor's death, if bearer flower bonds in denominations of less than $5,000 are included as part of the decedent trustor's trust estate, they may be redeemed by submitting the bonds with a Form W-9. If the bond is more than $5,000, then, Form PDF 1071 must be submitted with the bond. The bond(s) should be sent by registered mail to the Bureau of Public Debt, Definitive Section, P.O. Box 426, Parkersburg, WV 26106.

Flower bonds titled in the name of the trustee of a revocable living trust prior to their maturity may be redeemed to pay federal estate tax if:[30]

- The trust actually terminated in favor of the decedent's estate; in other words, the property comprising the trust estate pours over or is distributable to the decedent trustor's estate; or

- If the trustee is required to pay the decedent's federal estate tax under the terms of the trust instrument or otherwise; or

- To the extent the debts of the decedent's estate, including costs of administration, state inheritance, and federal estate taxes, exceed the assets of the decedent's estate without regard to the trust estate.

No transactions involving changes of ownership of the bonds may be conducted after an owner's death without affecting the eligibility of the bonds for redemption at par for

---

[25] 31 C.F.R. § 306.28(b) (1993); Treas. Reg. § 20.6151-1(c); Tech. Adv. Mem. 9235003 (May 20, 1992).

[26] Treas. Reg. §§ 20.6151-1(c), 301.6312-1(a) and 301.6312-2; Rev. Rul. 69-489, 1969-2 C.B. 172.

[27] *Banker's Trust Company v. United States*, 284 F.2d 537, 538 (2d Cir. 1960); Rev. Ruls. 69-489, 1969-2 C.B. 172 and 81-228, 1981-2 C.B. 171.

[28] *Estate of Simmie v. Commissioner*, 632 F.2d 93 (9th Cir. 1980), *aff'g* 69 T.C. 890 (1978); Rev. Rul. 81-228, 1981-2 C.B. 171.

[29] IRS Pub. 448 (1992) Federal Estate and Gift Taxes 11; Tech. Adv. Mem. 9235003 (May 20, 1992) where IRS held that for purposes of valuing flower bonds for inclusion in the gross estate of a decedent, the bonds must be included at the higher of par value (plus accrued interest) or the mean between the highest and lowest selling price on the valuation date (plus accrued interest) to the extent of the final estate tax liability determined. Bonds in excess of that amount are valued at the mean between the highest and lowest selling price on the valuation date (i.e., market value); *contra Estate of Fried v. Commissioner*, 54 T.C. 805 (1970), *aff'd* 445 F.2d 979 (2d Cir. 1971), *cert. denied* 404 U.S. 1016 (1972); *Estate of Simmie v. Commissioner*, 632 F.2d 93 (9th Cir. 1980), *aff'g* 69 T.C. 890 (1978). Both *Fried* and *Simmie* hold that the value of bonds in excess of the final estate tax liability is valued at par.

[30] 31 C.F.R. § 306.28(b)(iii) (1993).

payment of the federal estate tax. Transactions involving no changes of ownership that may be conducted without affecting eligibility are:[31]

- Exchange of bonds for those of lower denominations where the bonds exceed the amount of the tax and are not in the lowest authorized denominations;
- Exchange of registered bonds for coupon bonds;
- Exchange of coupon bonds for bonds registered in the names of the representatives of the decedent's estate;
- Transfer of bonds from the owner or his or her nominee to the names of the representatives of the owner's estate; and
- Purchase by or for the account of any owner prior to his or her death, held in book-entry form, and thereafter converted to definitive bonds.

Where an estate includes eligible treasury bonds but pays its estate tax in cash, the estate can get back its cash payment to the extent it redeems eligible treasury bonds before the estate is distributed or within two years from the time the tax was paid, whichever occurs earlier. Except in the case of redemption by substitution, the effective redemption date is the date the payment is made.[32] In the case of redemption by substitution, the date of payment is the date the estate tax was paid other than by use of eligible treasury bonds.[33] All inquiries with respect to the redemption of flower bonds should made to the Bureau of the Public Debt, telephone (304) 480-7936, 8:30 A.M. to 4:30 P.M. Eastern Standard Time.

---

[31] 31 C.F.R. § 306.28(c).

[32] Rev. Proc. 69-18, 1969-2 C.B. 300, Sec. 6; Rev. Rul. 76-312, 1976-2 C.B. 262; *see* Rev. Rul. 69-489, 1969-2 C.B. 172.

[33] Rev. Proc. 69-18, 1969-2 C.B. 300, Sec. 7; *see* Rev. Rul. 69-489, 1969-2 C.B. 172.

CHAPTER 12

Closely-Held Business Interests

TRUSTOR'S BUSINESS INTERESTS

Most closely-held businesses are operated as proprietorships, corporations, or partnerships. A partnership may also include a limited liability company. The Code prescribes certain categories, or classes, into which various organizations fall for purposes of taxation. These categories, or classes, include associations (which are taxable as corporations), partnerships, and trusts. The tests, or standards, that are applied in determining the classification of an organization (whether it is an association, a partnership, a trust, or other taxable entity) are determined under the Code.[1]

Importance of Local Law

Even though the classes into which organizations are placed for purposes of taxation are determined under the Code, a particular organization might be classified as a trust under the law of one state and a corporation under the law of another state. However, for purposes of the Code, this organization would be uniformly classed as a trust, an association (and, therefore, taxable as a corporation), or some other entity, depending upon its nature under the classification standards of the Code. Similarly, the term *partnership* is not limited to the common-law meaning of partnership but is broader in its scope and includes groups not commonly called partnerships.[2] The term *corporation* is not limited to the artificial entity usually known as a corporation but includes also an association, a trust classed as an association because of its nature or its activities, a joint-stock company, and an insurance company. Although it is the Code, rather than local law, which establishes the tests or standards that are applied in determining the classification in which an organization belongs, local law governs in determining whether the legal relationships that have been established in the formation of an organization are such that the standards are met. Thus, it is local law that must be applied in determining such matters as the legal relationships of the members of the organization among themselves and with the public at large and the interests of the members of the organization in its assets.[3]

---

[1] Treas. Reg. § 301.7701-(b); Treas. Reg. §§ 301.7701-2 to 301.7701-4 set forth these tests, or standards, which are applied in determining whether an organization is an association (see Treas. Reg. § 301.7701-2), a partnership (see Treas. Reg. § 301.7701-3), or a trust (see Treas. Reg. § 301.7701-4).

[2] Treas. Reg. §§ 301.7701-1(c), 1.761-1 and 301.7701-3.

[3] Treas. Reg. § 301.7701-1(c).

Associations

The term *association* refers to an organization whose characteristics require it to be classified for purposes of taxation as a corporation, rather than as another type of organization, such as a partnership or a trust. Several characteristics, when taken together, distinguish a corporation from other organizations. These are:[4]

- Associates;
- An objective to carry on business and divide the gains therefrom;
- Continuity of life;
- Centralization of management;
- Liability for corporate debts limited to corporate property; and
- Free transferability of interests.

Whether a particular organization is classified as an association must be determined by taking into account the presence or absence of each of these corporate characteristics. The presence or absence of these characteristics depends upon the facts in each individual case. In this regard, no centralization of continuing exclusive authority to make management decisions exists, unless the managers of a business have sole authority to make such decisions. For example, in the case of a corporation or a trust, the concentration of management powers in a board of directors or trustees effectively prevents a stockholder or a trust beneficiary, simply because such person is a stockholder or beneficiary, from binding the corporation or the trust by his or her acts.[5] In addition to these major characteristics, other factors may be found in some cases that may be significant in classifying an organization as an association, a partnership, or a trust. An organization is treated as an association if the corporate characteristics are such that the organization more nearly resembles a corporation than a partnership or trust.[6]

Absence of Characteristics

Because associates and an objective to carry on business for joint profit are essential characteristics of all organizations engaged in business for profit (other than the so-called one-man corporation and the sole proprietorship), the absence of either of these essential characteristics causes an arrangement among co-owners of property for the development of such property for the separate profit of each not to be classified as an association. Some of the major characteristics of a corporation are common to trusts and corporations, and others are common to partnerships and corporations. Characteristics common to trusts and corporations are not material in attempting to distinguish between a trust and an association, and characteristics common to partnerships and corporations are not material in attempting to distinguish between an association and a partnership. For example, since centralization of management, continuity of life, free transferability of interests, and limited liability are generally common to trusts and corporations, the determination of whether a trust that has such characteristics is to be treated for tax purposes as a trust or as an association depends on whether associates and an objective to carry on business and divide the gains therefrom exist. On the other hand, since associates and an objective to carry on business and divide the gains therefrom are generally common to both corporations and part-

---

[4] Treas. Reg. § 301.7701-2(a)(1).
[5] Treas. Reg. § 301.7701-2(c)(4).
[6] Treas. Reg. § 301.7701-2(a)(1); *see Morrissey et al. v. Commissioner*, 296 U.S. 344 (1935).

nerships, the determination of whether an organization that has such characteristics is to be treated for tax purposes as a partnership or as an association depends on whether centralization of management, continuity of life, free transferability of interests, and limited liability exists.[7]

Unincorporated Organization

An unincorporated organization is not classified as an association, unless such organization has more corporate characteristics than noncorporate characteristics. In determining whether an organization has more corporate characteristics than noncorporate characteristics, all characteristics common to both types of organizations are to be considered. For example, if a limited partnership has centralized management and free transferability of interests but lacks continuity of life and limited liability, and if the limited partnership has no other characteristics that are significant in determining its classification, such limited partnership is not classified as an association. Although the limited partnership also has associates and an objective to carry on business and divide the gains therefrom, these characteristics are not considered because they are common to both corporations and partnerships.[8]

Trusts

In general, the term *trust*, as used in the Code, refers to an arrangement created either by a Will or by a lifetime (inter vivos) declaration, whereby trustees take title to property for the purpose of protecting or conserving it for the beneficiaries under the ordinary rules applied in chancery or probate courts. Usually, the beneficiaries of such a trust do no more than accept the benefits thereof and are not the voluntary planners or creators of the trust arrangement. However, the beneficiaries of such a trust may be the persons who create it; and it is recognized as a trust under the Code if it was created for the purpose of protecting or conserving the trust property for beneficiaries who stand in the same relation to the trust as they would if the trust had been created by others for them. As a rule, an arrangement is treated as a trust under the Code if the purpose of the arrangement is to vest in trustees responsibility for the protection and conservation of property for beneficiaries who cannot share in the discharge of this responsibility and, therefore, are not associates in a joint enterprise for the conduct of business for profit.[9]

Other arrangements are known as trusts because the legal title to property is conveyed to trustees for the benefit of beneficiaries but are not classified as trusts for purposes of the Code because they are not arrangements to protect or conserve the property for the beneficiaries. These trusts, which are often known as business or commercial trusts, generally are created by the beneficiaries simply as a device to carry on a profit-making business that normally would be carried on through business organizations classified under the Code as corporations or partnerships. However, that the trust estate property is not supplied by the beneficiaries is not sufficient reason in itself for classifying the arrangement as an ordinary trust, rather than as an association or partnership. Although any organization is technically cast in the trust form by conveying title to property to trustees for the benefit of persons designated as beneficiaries; it does not change the real character of the organization if the organization more nearly resembles an association or a partnership than a trust.[10]

---

[7] Treas. Reg. § 301.7701-2(a)(2).

[8] Treas. Reg. § 301.7701-2(a)(3).

[9] Treas. Reg. § 301.7701-4(a).

[10] Treas. Reg. § 301.7701-4(b).

Revocable Living Trust Not Classified as an Association

It is important that title to the trustor's business interests conveyed to the trustee of a revocable living trust does not cause the trust to be classified as an association taxed as a corporation. In other words, the revocable living trust should not replace the existing business entity. A typical, properly designed revocable living trust does not become the entity that operates a closely-held business. Rather, the trustor only conveys legal title to the trustor's interest in the business to the trustee; and the trustor retains a beneficial or equitable interest in the closely-held business interest that is part of the trustor's trust estate.

Unless prohibited by state law, when the trustor is also the trustee of a revocable living trust, in effect, the trustor has the same control in the business interest as he or she would have if such interest continued to be owned by the trustor in his or her individual name outside of the revocable living trust. Similarly, if the trustor is not the trustee, and the trustee is operating under a standby holding title only revocable living trust for the trustor's benefit, the trustor still controls the interest that he or she *owns* in the business entity. Upon the trustor's death, the interest held by the trustor in a business entity can be distributed by the trustee outright to a beneficiary, continue in trust for a beneficiary, or be divided and distributed outright to one beneficiary and continued in trust for another beneficiary. Of course, the distribution of one's interest in a closely-held business upon death, or the management of one's interest in such business in the event of incapacity, may be controlled by a buy-sell agreement coordinated with the distribution provisions of a revocable living trust.

Trustee Power to Operate Business Entity

Whether the trustor presently owns an interest in a business entity, a properly designed revocable living trust empowers the trustee to continue or participate in the operation of any business. Such a power is essential to maximize the trustee's ability to invest trust estate property upon the trustor's death for the trustor's beneficiaries. Typical powers in the trustee to continue or participate in the operation of any business may include the following and would be included in the Article of the revocable living trust addressing Trustee Powers:

Business Participation. To terminate or to continue or participate in the operation of any business enterprise, including a corporation, a sole proprietorship, or a general or limited partnership; and to effect any form of incorporation, dissolution, liquidation, reorganization, or other change in the form of the business enterprise, or to lend money or make a capital contribution to any such business enterprise; to participate in any plan of reorganization, specifically including recapitalization, including (name of trustor's business interest), or any entity that may have succeeded to its business, or any other corporation electing Subchapter S corporation status, the stock of which may comprise the trust estate; and to transfer or deposit any stock or other securities of said corporation or other Subchapter S corporation; and to accept and retain new stock or other securities, pursuant to any such plan; and to exercise all voting and other rights pertaining to such property, including, without limitation, the right to enter into any shareholder agreements.

Engage in Partnership. To continue as or become a limited partner in any partnership.

Business Personnel. To elect or employ directors, officers, employees, partners, or agents of any business and to compensate such persons, whether or not any such person is a trustee, director, officer, partner, or agent of a trustee or beneficiary of the trust.

Retention of Closely-Held Business Interest. To retain any real estate interests, closely-held securities, or affiliated companies or business interests, including shares of stock in a Subchapter S corporation, regardless of lack of diversification, risk, or nonproductivity, except as provided under Article IX (F) (Provisions for Marital QTIP Trust) Article IX (G) (Provisions of [general power of appointment marital deduction trust]), as long as it deems advisable; and to sell or dispose of such interests only after careful consideration and after determining that sale or disposition is, in the existing circumstances, in the best interests of the trust estate or its beneficiaries.

SOLE PROPRIETOR

A person is a sole proprietor if he or she is self-employed and is the sole owner of an unincorporated business.

Conveyance of Sole Proprietorship Assets to Trustee

Because the assets of a sole proprietorship are owned by the sole proprietor (e.g., trustor) as an individual and not as a separate legal business entity, title to each asset or group of assets constituting the sole proprietorship must be conveyed to the trustee of the revocable living trust. Depending on the type of asset comprising the sole proprietorship, the appropriate instrument of conveyance, as discussed throughout this book, would be used to convey legal title of the asset to the trustee of the revocable living trust.

Self-Declared Nominee Arrangement

One commentator has suggested that a trustor sole proprietor might create a self-declared nominee arrangement in which proprietorship assets listed on an attached schedule are declared to be held for the benefit, and on behalf, of the trust. A nominee partnership might also be formed to hold the assets as agent for the sole proprietor.[11]

Assignment of Assets

Title to assets used in a sole proprietorship may be conveyed to the trustee of a revocable living trust individually or they may be grouped together and conveyed by category in an Assignment of Sole Proprietorship Assets to Trustee (see file "APP1201.DOC"). Such assets may be assigned to the trustee of a revocable living trust after the trustor acquires them, or they can be titled in the name of the trustee at the time of acquisition. When conveying title to assets of a sole proprietorship to the trustee of a revocable living trust, a record should be maintained with respect to business assets and personal assets. This is important because, if a business operated as a sole proprietorship is sold, the trustor will actually be selling all the individual assets of the business.

Classification of Assets for Income Tax Purposes

To determine whether the gain or loss on the sale of an asset is capital gain or loss or ordinary gain or loss, the trustor must classify the assets sold into one of the following three categories:

1. Capital assets;
2. Real property and depreciable property used in the business and held for more than one year[12] (this includes amortizable I.R.C. Section 197 intangibles); and

---

[11] L. William Schmidt, Jr., "How to Fund a Revocable Living Trust Correctly," 20 *Estate Planning* 67, 73 (March/April 1993).

[12] I.R.C. § 1222(3) and (4).

3. Other property—for example, stock-in-trade, inventory, or property used in the business and held one year or less.[13]

Accounts and Notes Receivable

Accounts and notes receivable acquired in the ordinary course of business for services rendered or from the sale of stock-in-trade are not capital assets and are classified in category 3. Accounts receivable should be assigned to the trustee of a revocable living trust as a separate group of assets. By assigning the accounts receivable to the trustee, if the trustor becomes physically disabled or mentally incapacitated, the trustee can be empowered to manage the receivables for the trustor's benefit. In addition, if accounts receivable are pledged or are used as a security interest, the trustor needs to obtain the holder's permission to convey title to the accounts to the trustee of a revocable living trust. Upon conveying the accounts receivable to the trustee, a new Uniform Commercial Code Financing Statement should be completed and filed evidencing the conveyance of the accounts receivable or other assets to the trustee of the revocable living trust.

Installment Notes

Installment notes from the sale of stock-in-trade are classified in category 3.

Merchandise Inventories

Merchandise inventories are not capital assets and belong in category 3.

Land and Leaseholds

Land and leaseholds used in business are not capital assets. If they are held for more than one year, they belong in category 2; and, if they are held one year or less, they belong in category 3.

Buildings, Machinery, Furniture, and Fixtures

Buildings, machinery, furniture, and fixtures that are used in business are not capital assets. They are classified in category 2, if held for more than one year, and in category 3, if held for one year or less.

Patents

Patents used in business should ordinarily be classified in category 2, if held more than one year, and in category 3, if held one year or less. If the trustor is the inventor (or if the trustor is entitled to the same treatment as the inventor) and the trustor sells all substantial rights to patent property or a patent, or an undivided interest in all such rights, to a person other than a related person, the sale is treated as a sale of a long-term capital asset and is included in category 1.

Copyrights

Copyrights used in business should be classified in category 2, if held more than one year, and in category 3, if held one year or less. However, if the trustor sells a copyright that he or she created, or if a copyright is sold which gets its basis from the person who created the property, it should not be classified in category 2. Instead, it should be classified in category 3.

---

[13]I.R.C. § 1222(1) and (2).

Registration of Sole Proprietorship Name

Most states require that a business operating as a sole proprietorship in a name other than the sole proprietor be registered. Whether the sole proprietorship must conduct its business in the name of the revocable living trust to which its assets have been transferred is a matter of state law. If the sole proprietorship is conducted in the name of the revocable living trust, third parties dealing with the sole proprietorship may require evidence that the trustee is empowered to conduct the business of the sole proprietorship. In this regard, either a Memorandum of Trust (see file "APP0210.DOC") or Certificate of Trust (see file "APP0212.DOC") may be used to provide such evidence. As previously mentioned, a properly designed revocable living trust empowers the trustee to continue or participate in the operation of any business.

Fiduciary Income Tax Return (Form 1041)

Ask Your Attorney

If I convey title to assets used in my sole proprietorship to the trustee of my revocable living trust, even if I am the trustee, am I required to file a Form 1041 for the trust?

Answer

No. The trustor would report income derived from the sole proprietorship on his or her Form 1040.[14]

Ask Your Attorney

If I convey title to assets used in my sole proprietorship to the trustee of my revocable living trust, even if I am the trustee, and operate my business in the name of the trust, am I required to file a Form 1041 for the trust?

Answer

No. Income derived from the sole proprietorship is reported on the trustor's Form 1040.[15]

Planning Strategy

If the trustor is a sole proprietor and an immediate member of the trustor's family (e.g., spouse, child, or sibling) is qualified, interested, and capable of continuing the business if the trustor becomes incapacitated or dies, the trustor may want to consider designating that person as the successor trustee of his or her revocable living trust. By designating this person as successor trustee, continuity of business ownership and management can be provided for the trustor and those members of the trustor's family who are dependent on the income generated by the sole proprietorship. A buy-sell agreement could be effected with the successor trustee to be funded with life insurance to enable the successor trustee to purchase the business from the trustor's trust estate upon the trustor's death.

---

[14] *See* discussion in "Grantor Trust Rules" section, Chapter 7, pertaining to taxation of trust income.

[15] *See* discussion in "Grantor Trust Rules" section, Chapter 7, pertaining to taxation of trust income.

CORPORATIONS

Conveyance of Stock Ownership to Trustee

Ownership of stock in a closely-held corporation can be conveyed to the trustee of a revocable living trust in one of two ways: (1) by the title holder endorsing the stock power on the back of the stock certificate in the same manner as endorsing the stock power on a stock certificate for a publicly-traded corporation; or (2) effecting a stock power separate from the stock certificate itself. Oftentimes, with closely-held corporate stock, it is more practical to assign ownership of such stock to the trustee of a revocable living trust by using an Assignment of Stock Power (see file "APP1202.DOC"). 🔳 If the trustor revokes the revocable living trust or determines to withdraw the stock from the revocable living trust, new stock certificates do not have to be issued.

Stock Restrictions

Before conveying title of closely-held corporate stock to the trustee of a revocable living trust, the trustor should be certain to verify the existence of any restrictions on the transferability of the stock. Such restrictions may be inscribed on the stock certificates, or they may be found in a buy-sell agreement or in the bylaws of the corporation. If restrictions on the transfer of the stock exist, permission must be obtained from the appropriate corporate officer before conveying title to the stock to the trustee of a revocable living trust.

Buy-Sell Agreement

A buy-sell agreement (stock redemption or shareholders' agreement) should provide for ownership of stock in a closely-held corporation by the trustee of a revocable living trust. Likewise, if an existing buy-sell agreement does not provide for ownership of such stock by the trustee of a living trust, the agreement should be modified accordingly.

Ask Your Attorney

Would a modification to our corporation's buy-sell agreement to allow the trustee of a revocable living trust to own stock in our corporation trigger the special valuation rules under I.R.C. Section 2703?

Answer

No.

A buy-sell agreement is a legal instrument the purpose of which is to provide for the future transfer of ownership and control of a closely-held business while *pegging* the value of the owner's interest in the business for purposes of the federal estate tax upon the owner's death.[16] Under such an agreement, the business owner's estate agrees to sell the decedent business owner's interest; and either the business itself (redemption agreement, in the case of a corporation, or an entity agreement, in the case of a partnership) or the surviving owners themselves (cross-purchase agreement) agree to purchase the decedent

---

[16] *See* James D. Fife, "Structuring Buy-Sell Agreements to Fix Estate Tax Value," 22 *Estate Planning* 67 (March/April 1995); Linda M. Johnson and Brian R. Greenstein, "Using Buy-Sell Agreements to Establish the Value of a Closely Held Business," 81 *Journal of Taxation* 362 (Dec. 1994).

owner's interest in the business at a fixed or previously agreed upon formula or option price. Such an agreement should not be viewed as a device to *freeze* the value of corporate stock. The word *freeze* elicits unwanted scrutiny by the IRS, and the concept of *freezing* the value of business assets for federal estate and gift tax purposes is probably about as dead as the dinosaurs. Instead, such an agreement should be viewed as a means for ensuring corporate and management continuity, employee security, and for restricting sales of the stock to persons outside the trustor's immediate family.[17]

Restriction Upon Sale or Transfer of Property

A restriction upon the sale or transfer of property (e.g., a business interest) can effectively reduce the fair market value of the property subject to the agreement conferring the restriction. To combat the existence of options or contracts to purchase which may affect the value of stock for purposes of the federal estate tax, Congress enacted I.R.C. Section 2703. The general rule under I.R.C. Section 2703 is that the value of any property is determined without regard to: any option, agreement, or other right to acquire or use the property at a price less than fair market value of the property (without regard to such option, agreement, or right); or any restriction on the right to sell or use such property.[18] However, the general rule does not apply to any option, agreement, right, or restriction that meets each of the following requirements:[19]

- It is a bona fide business arrangement;
- It is not a device to transfer such property to members of the decedent's family for less than full and adequate consideration in money or money's worth;[20]
- Its terms are comparable to similar arrangements entered into by persons in an arm's-length transaction.

Agreements Affected by Special Valuation Rules

The special valuation rules governing buy-sell agreements apply to agreements, options, rights, or restrictions entered into or granted *after* October 8, 1990. The same rules apply to agreements, options, rights, or restrictions that are substantially modified after October 8, 1990, even though the original agreement, option, rights, or restrictions were entered into or granted *before* October 9, 1990.[21] A right or restriction that is substantially modified after October 8, 1990, is treated as a right or restriction created on the date of the modification. Any discretionary modification of a right or restriction, whether or not authorized by the terms of the agreement, which results in other than a *de minimis* change to the quality, value, or timing of the rights of any party with respect to property that is subject to the right or restriction is a substantial modification.[22]

---

[17] Moy, 1, *A Practitioner's Guide to Estate Planning*, § 12.02, at 12-16; *see* S. Tobisman, "Estate and Gift Tax Considerations in Buy-Sell Agreements," 35 *U.S. California Tax Institute* ¶ 2700 (1983); Staff of Joint Committee on Taxation, *Federal Tax Consequences of Estate Freezes: In Anticipation of Hearing Held by the House Ways and Means Committee*, 101st Cong., 2d Sess. (April 24, 1990), Federal Estate and Gift Tax Reporter (CCH), at 15,227 (hereafter *Federal Tax Consequences of Estate Freezes*).

[18] I.R.C. § 2703(a).

[19] I.R.C. § 2703(b).

[20] Treas. Reg. § 20.2031-2(h); *Federal Tax Consequences of Estate Freezes*, at 15,225.

[21] RRA '90, § 11602(e)(1)(A)(ii); Louis A. Mezzullo, "New Estate Freeze Rules Replacing 2036(c) Expand Planning Potential," 74 *Journal of Taxation* 4, 10 (January 1991); *see* Priv. Ltr. Ruls. 9151045 (September 26, 1991), 9248026 (September 1, 1992) substituted for 9226063 (March 31, 1992), 9226051 (March 30, 1992).

[22] Treas. Reg. § 25.2703-1(c)(1).

Substantial Modification

A substantial modification does not include a discretionary modification of an agreement conferring a right or restriction, if the modification does not change the right or restriction.[23] Provided the title to stock to be conveyed to the trustee of a revocable living trust does not result in other than a *de minimis* change to the quality, value, or timing of the rights of the shareholders or with respect to the stock of the corporation, such a conveyance is not a substantial modification of the original buy-sell agreement (or to the articles of incorporation or bylaws) which would cause I.R.C. Section 2703 to be applicable to such transfer.[24]

S CORPORATIONS

An eligible domestic corporation can avoid double taxation (once to the corporation and again to the shareholders) by electing to be treated as an S corporation under the rules of subchapter S of the Code.[25] In this way, the S corporation passes its items of income, loss, deduction, and credits through to its shareholders to be included on their separate returns.[26]

Trusts That Can Be S Corporation Shareholders

The following trusts, other than foreign trusts, can be shareholders of an S corporation:

- A trust that is treated as entirely owned by an individual who is a U.S. citizen or resident (e.g., a revocable living trust).[27] The deemed owner (usually the trustor)—not the trustee—is treated as the shareholder.[28]

- A trust (e.g., a revocable living trust) in effect immediately before the owner's[29] death and which continues in existence after the owner's death may continue to be an S corporation shareholder for stock held by the trust at the time of the owner's death. Such a trust is valid only for a period of sixty days, beginning on the date of the owner's death. However, if the entire principal of the trust is included in the owner's gross estate, the sixty-day period becomes a two-year period.[30] A trust is considered to continue in existence if the trust continues to hold the stock of the S corporation during the period of administration of the decedent's estate or if, after the period of administration, the trust continues to hold the stock pursuant to the terms of the Will or the trust agreement.[31] If the trust consists of community property, and the decedent's community property interest in the trust is includable in the decedent's gross estate for purposes of the federal estate tax, then the entire trust estate will be deemed includable in the decedent's gross estate. Further, for the purpose of determining whether the entire trust estate is includable in the gross estate of the deemed owner, if the decedent's spouse was treated as an owner of a portion of the trust

---

[23] Treas. Reg. Sec. 25.2703-1(c)(2)(ii).

[24] *See* Priv. Ltr. Rul. 9417007 (January 13, 1994).

[25] I.R.C. § 1362(a).

[26] I.R.C. § 1363(a) and (b).

[27] I.R.C. § 1361(c)(2)(A)(i); Treas. Reg. § 1.1361-1(h)(1)(i).

[28] I.R.C. § 1361(c)(2)(A) and 1361(c)(2)(B)(i).

[29] *See* I.R.C. § 678(a) (the *owner* of a revocable living trust does not necessarily have to be the trustor [grantor] of the trust).

[30] I.R.C. § 1361(c)(2)(A)(ii); Treas. Reg. § 1.1361-1(h)(1)(ii).

[31] *See* Treas. Reg. §1.641(b)-3 for rules concerning the termination of estates and trusts for federal income tax purposes.

under the grantor trust rules immediately before the decedent's death, the surviving spouse's portion is disregarded. The owner's estate is treated as the shareholder.[32]

- Any trust to which S corporation stock is transferred under the terms of a Will—but only for sixty days, beginning with the day the stock was transferred to the trust.[33] The estate of the person leaving the Will is treated as the shareholder.[34]
- A trust created primarily to exercise the voting power of S corporation stock transferred to it.[35] Each beneficiary of such a trust is treated as a shareholder.[36]
- A qualified subchapter S trust (QSST) under which the beneficiary makes an election under I.R.C. Section 1361(d)(2).[37]

Observation

A foreign trust, within the meaning of the Code,[38] even if it qualifies as a grantor trust, cannot be a shareholder of an S corporation.[39]

Qualified Subchapter S Trust

Ask Your Attorney

My company operates as an S corporation, and I want to convey title to my stock in the corporation to the trustee of my revocable living trust. Does my revocable living trust have to be specially designed in order for the trust to be a shareholder of my S corporation?

Answer

Yes.

In order for the trustor of a revocable living trust to be an eligible shareholder in an S corporation during the trustor's lifetime, it must be a grantor trust (within the meaning of I.R.C. Sections 671 through 678) that is owned by an individual who is a citizen or resident of the United States.[40] The owner of the revocable living trust, generally the trustor, is the shareholder of the S corporation stock conveyed to the trustee.[41] Upon the trustor's death, the revocable living trust can continue as an eligible shareholder in an S corporation for a

---

[32] I.R.C. § 1361(c)(2)(B)(ii).

[33] I.R.C. § 1361(c)(2)(A)(iii); Treas. Reg. § 1.1361-1(h)(iv).

[34] I.R.C. § 1361(c)(2)(B)(iii).

[35] I.R.C. § 1361(c)(2)(A)(iv); Treas. Reg. § 1.1361-1(h)(v).

[36] I.R.C. § 1361(c)(2)(B)(iv).

[37] I.R.C. § 1361(d)(1); Treas. Reg. § 1.1361-1(h)(1)(iii).

[38] I.R.C. § 7701(a)(31).

[39] Treas. Reg. § 1.1361-1(h)(2).

[40] I.R.C. § 1361(c)(2)(A)(i).

[41] I.R.C. § 1361(c)(2)(B)(i); *see* I.R.C. § 678(a) which provides that "A person other than the grantor [i.e., the trustor] shall be treated as the owner of any portion of a trust with respect to which: (1) such person has a power exercisable solely by himself [or herself] to vest the corpus or the income therefrom in himself [or herself], or (2) such person has previously partially released or otherwise modified such a power and after the release or modification retains such control as would, within the principles of sections 671 to 677, inclusive, subject a grantor of a trust to treatment as the owner thereof."

period extending beyond two years[42] from the trustor's date of death only if it adheres to the requirements of a qualified subchapter S trust (QSST).[43] The beneficiary of a QSST is the owner of that portion of the trust estate that consists of stock in an S corporation.[44] The terms of a QSST require that:

- During the *life* of the current income beneficiary, there can be only one income beneficiary of the trust;[45]

- Any trust estate principal (i.e., corpus) distributed during the *life* of the current income beneficiary may be distributed only to such beneficiary; [46]

- The income interest of the current income beneficiary in the trust shall terminate on the earlier of such beneficiary's death or the termination of the trust;[47]

- Upon the termination of the trust during the *life* of the current income beneficiary, the trust shall distribute all of its assets to such beneficiary;[48] and

- All of the income (within the meaning of I.R.C. Section 643(b)) of which is distributed (or required to be distributed) currently to one individual who is a citizen or resident of the United States.[49]

Unless otherwise provided under local law or the terms of the trust, income of the trust includes distributions to the trust from the S corporation for the taxable year in question but does not include the trust's pro rata share of the S corporation's items of income, loss, deduction, or credit determined under I.R.C. Section 1366.[50] If, under the terms of the trust, income is not required to be distributed currently, the trustee may elect under I.R.C. Section 663(b) to consider a distribution made in the first sixty-five days of a taxable year as made on the last day of the preceding taxable year.[51] The income distribution requirement must be satisfied for the taxable year of the trust or for that part of the trust's taxable year during which it holds S corporation stock.[52]

Husband and Wife Beneficiaries of a Joint Revocable Living Trust

If a husband and wife are income beneficiaries of a joint revocable living trust, file a joint income tax return, and each is a U.S. citizen or resident, both are treated as one income beneficiary for purposes of a QSST. If a husband and wife are treated as one income beneficiary, both must join in any action required of them as an income beneficiary of the trust. For example, each spouse must sign the QSST election, continue to be a U.S. citizen or resident, and continue to file joint income tax returns for the entire period that the QSST election is in effect.[53]

---

[42] I.R.C. § 1361(d)(3)(A)(i).

[43] I.R.C. § 1361(d)(3).

[44] I.R.C. § 1361(d)(1)(B).

[45] I.R.C. § 1361(d)(3)(A)(i); Treas. Reg. § 1.1361-1(j)(1)(ii)(A).

[46] I.R.C. § 1361(d)(3)(A)(ii); Treas. Reg. § 1.1361-1(j)(1)(ii)(B).

[47] I.R.C. § 1361(d)(3)(A)(iii); Treas. Reg. § 1.1361-1(j)(1)(ii)(C).

[48] I.R.C. § 1361(d)(3)(A)(iv); Treas. Reg. § 1.1361-1(j)(1)(ii)(D).

[49] I.R.C. § 1361(d)(3)(A)(i); § 1361(d)(3)(B); Treas. Reg. § 1.1361-1(j)(1)(i).

[50] *See* Treas. Reg. §§ 1.651(a)-2(a) and 1.663(b)-1(a) for rules relating to the determination of whether all of the income of a trust is distributed (or is required to be distributed) currently.

[51] *See* I.R.C. § 663(b) and Treas. Reg. § 1.663(b)-2 for rules on the time and manner for making the election.

[52] Treas. Reg. § 1.1361-1(j)(1)(i).

[53] Treas. Reg. § 1.1361-1(j)(2)(i).

Trust Instrument and Local Law

The determination of whether the terms of a revocable living trust (or testamentary trust) meet all of the requirements of a QSST depends upon the terms of the trust instrument and applicable local law. For example, if the trust provides for one income beneficiary but, under local law, the trust is considered to have two income beneficiaries, then both beneficiaries are considered the income beneficiaries of the trust.[54] If, under local law, a distribution to the income beneficiary is in satisfaction of the trustor's legal obligation of support to that income beneficiary, the trust does not qualify as a QSST as of the date of distribution because, under I.R.C. Section 677(b), if income is distributed, the trustor is treated as the owner of the ordinary income portion of the trust; or, if trust principal is distributed, the trustor is treated as a beneficiary under I.R.C. Section 662.[55]

Example

Fran creates a trust for the benefit of her minor child, Gretchen. Under the terms of the trust, all income is payable to Gretchen until the trust terminates on the earlier of Gretchen's attaining age thirty-five or Gretchen's death. Upon the termination of the trust, all principal must be distributed to Gretchen or Gretchen's estate. The trust includes all of the provisions that would otherwise qualify it as a QSST but does not preclude the trustee from making income distributions to Gretchen which will be in satisfaction of Fran's legal obligation to support Gretchen. Under the applicable local law, distributions of trust income to Gretchen satisfy Fran's legal obligation to support Gretchen. If the trustee distributes income to Gretchen in satisfaction of Fran's legal obligation to support Gretchen, the trust does not qualify as a QSST because Fran is treated as the owner of the ordinary income portion of the trust. Further, the trust is not a grantor trust because the trust is subject to tax on the income allocable to principal.[56]

If, under the terms of the trust, a person (including the income beneficiary) has a special power to appoint, during the life of the income beneficiary, trust income or principal to any person other than the current income beneficiary, the trust does not qualify as a QSST. However, if the power of appointment results in the trustor being treated as the owner of the entire trust under the grantor trust rules, the trust may be a permitted shareholder of an S corporation.[57]

Separate Share Rule

A substantially separate and independent share of a trust, within the meaning of I.R.C. Section 663(c), is treated as a separate trust for purposes of a QSST.[58] For a separate share that holds S corporation stock to qualify as a QSST, the terms of the trust applicable to that separate share must meet the QSST requirements.[59]

---

[54] Treas. Reg. § 1.1361-1(j)(2)(ii)(A).

[55] *See* Treas. Reg. §§ 1.677(b)-1 for rules on the treatment of trusts for support and 1.662(a)-4 for rules concerning amounts used in discharge of a legal obligation; Treas. Reg. § 1.1361-1(j)(2)(ii)(B).

[56] Treas. Reg. § 1.1361-1(j)(2)(ii)(C).

[57] I.R.C. § 1361(c)(2)(A)(i); Treas. Reg. § 1.1361-1(h)(1)(i) and 1.1361-1(j)(2)(iii).

[58] I.R.C. § 1361(d)(3) flush language. *See* I.R.C. § 663(c).

[59] Treas. Reg. § 1.1361-1(j)(3).

QTIP Trust

If property, including S corporation stock or stock of a corporation that intends to make an S election, is conveyed to the trustee of a revocable living trust and an election is made to treat all or a portion of such property as QTIP under I.R.C. Section 2056(b)(7), the income beneficiary may make the QSST election if the trust qualifies as a QSST.[60] However, if property is conveyed to the trustee of a living QTIP trust,[61] the income beneficiary may not make a QSST election, even if the trust qualifies as a QSST because the trustor is treated as the owner of the income portion of the trust under I.R.C. Section 677. In addition, if property is transferred to a living QTIP trust, the trust does not qualify as a QSST, unless, under the terms of the QTIP trust, the trustor is treated as the owner of the entire trust under the grantor trust rules.[62] If the trustor ceases to be the income beneficiary's spouse, the trust may qualify as a QSST if it otherwise qualifies as a QSST.[63]

Qualified Subchapter S Trust Election

A QSST election must be made separately with respect to each corporation whose stock is held by the trust.[64] If title to S corporation stock is conveyed to the trustee of a revocable living trust, the QSST election must be made within the sixteen-day-and-two-month grace period, beginning on the day that the stock is transferred to the trust.[65] Once made, the election can only be revoked with the consent of the secretary of the treasury (Secretary).[66] The QSST election does not itself constitute an election as to the status of the corporation; the corporation must make the election provided by I.R.C. Section 1362(a) to be an S corporation. Until the effective date of a corporation's S election, the beneficiary is not treated as the owner of the stock of the corporation for purposes of I.R.C. Section 678.[67]

Current Income Beneficiary Makes the Election

The current income beneficiary of the trust must make the election by signing and filing with the service center with which the corporation files its income tax return the applicable form or a statement that:[68]

- Contains the name, address, and taxpayer identification number of the current income beneficiary, the trust, and the corporation;
- Identifies the election as an election made under I.R.C. Section 1361(d)(2);
- Specifies the date on which the election is to become effective (not earlier than fifteen days and two months before the date on which the election is filed);
- Specifies the date (or dates) on which the stock of the corporation was transferred to the trust; and

---

[60] Treas. Reg. § 1.1361-1(j)(4).

[61] I.R.C. § 2523(f). For additional reading on the use of a lifetime QTIP trust, *see* Moy, 2, *A Practitioner's Guide to Estate Planning*, § 24.02[B][1].

[62] I.R.C. §§ 671 to 677.

[63] Treas. Reg. § 1.1361-1(j)(4).

[64] I.R.C. § 1361(d)(2)(B)(i).

[65] I.R.C. § 1361(d)(2)(D); Treas. Reg. § 1.1361-1(j)(6)(iii)(A) and § 1.1361-1(j)(6)(iii)(B).

[66] I.R.C. § 1361(d)(2)(C).

[67] Treas. Reg. § 1.1361-1(j)(6)(i).

[68] Treas. Reg. § 1.1361-1(j)(6)(ii).

- Provides all information and representations necessary to show that, under the terms of trust and applicable local law: (a) during the life of the current income beneficiary, there will be only one income beneficiary of the trust (if husband and wife are beneficiaries, that they will file joint returns and that both are U.S. residents or citizens);[69] (b) any principal distributed during the life of the current income beneficiary may be distributed only to that beneficiary;[70] (c) the current income beneficiary's income interest in the trust will terminate on the earlier of the beneficiary's death or upon termination of the trust;[71] and (d) upon the termination of the trust during the life of such income beneficiary, the trust will distribute all its assets to such beneficiary.[72]

- The trust is required to distribute all of its income currently, or the trustee will distribute all of its income currently if not so required by the terms of the trust.[73]

- No distribution of trust estate income or principal by the trust will be in satisfaction of the grantor's legal obligation to support or maintain the income beneficiary.[74]

Revocable Living Trust Ceases to Be a Grantor Trust

If a revocable living trust ceases to be a grantor trust but also satisfies the requirements of a QSST, the QSST election must be filed within the sixteen-day-and-two-month period, beginning on the date on which the trust ceases to be a grantor trust. If the estate of the trust owner is treated as the shareholder, the QSST election may be filed at any time but no later than the end of the sixteen-day-and-two-month period, beginning on the date on which the estate of the trust owner ceases to be treated as a shareholder.[75] If a corporation's S election terminates because of a late QSST election, the corporation may request inadvertent termination relief under I.R.C. Section 1362(f).[76]

Trustor Not Current Income Beneficiary

If the trustor is treated as the owner of all or a portion of a grantor trust that consists of S corporation stock, and the current income beneficiary is not the trustor, the current income beneficiary may not make the QSST election, even if the trust is a QSST. However, if the current income beneficiary (or beneficiaries who are husband and wife, if both spouses are U.S. citizens or residents and file a joint income tax return) of a trust is treated as the owner of all or a portion of the trust consisting of S corporation stock, the current income beneficiary (or beneficiaries who are husband and wife, if both spouses are U.S. citizens or residents and file a joint income tax return) may make the QSST election.[77]

Income Beneficiary Is Shareholder

The income beneficiary who makes the QSST election and is treated as the owner of that portion of the trust that consists of S corporation stock is treated as the S corporation

---

[69] Treas. Reg. § 1.1361-1(j)(6)(ii)(E)(1)(i).

[70] Treas. Reg. § 1.1361-1(j)(6)(ii)(E)(1)(ii).

[71] Treas. Reg. § 1.1361-1(j)(6)(ii)(E)(1)(iii).

[72] Treas. Reg. § 1.1361-1(j)(6)(ii)(E)(1)(iv).

[73] Treas. Reg. § 1.1361-1(j)(6)(ii)(E)(2).

[74] Treas. Reg. § 1.1361-1(j)(6)(ii)(E)(3).

[75] Treas. Reg. § 1.1361-1(j)(6)(iii)(C).

[76] *See* Treas. Reg. § 1.1362-4 for rules concerning inadvertent terminations; Treas. Reg. § 1.1361-1(j)(6)(iii)(D).

[77] Treas. Reg. § 1.1361-1(j)(6)(iv); *see* Treas. Reg. § 1.1361-1(k)(1), Example 8.

shareholder.[78] If, upon the death of an income beneficiary, the trust continues in existence, continues to hold S corporation stock but no longer satisfies the QSST requirements, and is not a grantor trust, then, as of the date of the income beneficiary's death, the income beneficiary's estate is treated as the shareholder of the S corporation with respect to which the income beneficiary made the QSST election. The income beneficiary's estate ordinarily ceases to be treated as the shareholder upon the earlier of the transfer of that stock by the trust or the expiration of the sixty-day period beginning on the day of the income beneficiary's death. However, if the entire principal of the trust is includable in the income beneficiary's gross estate, his or her estate ceases to be treated as the shareholder upon the earlier of the transfer of that stock by the trust or the expiration of the two-year period beginning on the day of the income beneficiary's death. For the purpose of determining whether the entire trust principal is includable in the income beneficiary's gross estate, any community property interest in the trust held by the income beneficiary's spouse which arises by reason of applicable state law is disregarded. During the period that the income beneficiary's estate is treated as the S corporation shareholder, the trust is also treated as the shareholder. If, after the sixty-day period or the two-year period, if applicable, the trust continues to hold S corporation stock, the corporation's S election terminates. If the termination is inadvertent, the corporation may request relief under I.R.C. Section 1362(f).[79]

Coordination with Grantor Trust Rules

Under a QSST, the income beneficiary is treated as the owner of that portion of the trust that consists of the stock of an S corporation for which the QSST election was made. However, an income beneficiary who is deemed an owner only because he or she elected to have the trust treated as a QSST is not treated as the owner of the S corporation stock in determining and attributing the federal income tax consequences of a disposition of the stock by the trustee of the QSST. For example, if the trustee of the QSST sells the S corporation stock, the QSST terminates as to the stock; and any gain or loss recognized on the sale is attributable to the trust—not to the income beneficiary. Similarly, if the trustee of a QSST distributes its S corporation stock to the income beneficiary, the QSST election terminates as to the distributed stock; and the consequences of the distribution are determined by reference to the status of the trust apart from the income beneficiary's terminating ownership status under I.R.C. Sections 678 and 1361(d)(1). The tax treatment of assets composing the QSST, other than the S corporation stock, are governed by I.R.C. Sections 641 through 668, except as otherwise provided under I.R.C. Sections 671 through 678.[80]

Successive Income Beneficiary

If the income beneficiary of a QSST who made a QSST election dies, each successive income beneficiary of that trust is treated as consenting to the election, unless a successive income beneficiary affirmatively refuses to consent to the election.[81] For this purpose, the term *successive income beneficiary* includes a beneficiary of a trust whose interest is a separate share within the meaning of I.R.C. Section 663(c) but does not include any beneficiary of a trust that is created upon the death of the income beneficiary of the QSST and which is a new trust under local law.[82]

---

[78] Treas. Reg. § 1.1361-1(j)(7)(i).

[79] Treas. Reg. § 1.1361-1(j)(7)(ii).

[80] Treas. Reg. § 1.1361-1(j)(8).

[81] I.R.C. § 1361(d)(2)(B)(ii).

[82] Treas. Reg. § 1.1361-1(j)(9)(i).

Examples

1. Shares of stock in an S corporation are held by Trust A, a QSST for which a QSST election was made. Brad is the sole income beneficiary of Trust A. On Brad's death, under the terms of Trust A, Janice and Kelley become the current income beneficiaries of Trust A. Janice and Kelley each hold a separate and independent share of Trust A within the meaning of I.R.C. Section 663(c). Janice and Kelley are successive income beneficiaries of Trust A, and they are treated as consenting to Brad's QSST election.[83]

2. Assume the same facts as in Example 1, except that, on Brad's death, under the terms of Trust A and local law, Trust A terminates; and the principal is to be divided equally and held in newly created Trust B and Trust C. The sole income beneficiaries of Trust B and Trust C are Janice and Kelley, respectively. Because Trust A terminated, Janice and Kelley are not successive income beneficiaries of Trust A. Janice and Kelley must make QSST elections for their respective trusts to qualify as QSSTs, if they qualify. The result is the same whether or not the trustee of Trusts B and C is the same as the trustee of Trust A.[84]

Affirmative Refusal to Consent

Upon the death of the income beneficiary, if the successive income beneficiary does not want to consent to the QSST election, he or she must affirmatively refuse to consent to the election.[85] A successive income beneficiary of a QSST must make an affirmative refusal to consent by signing and filing with the service center where the corporation files its income tax return a statement that:[86]

- Contains the name, address, and taxpayer identification number of the successive income beneficiary, the trust, and the corporation for which the election was made;
- Identifies the refusal as an affirmative refusal to consent under I.R.C. Section 1361(d)(2); and
- Sets forth the date on which the successive income beneficiary became the income beneficiary.

The affirmative refusal to consent must be filed within fifteen days and two months after the date on which the successive income beneficiary becomes the income beneficiary. The affirmative refusal to consent is effective as of the date on which the successive income beneficiary becomes the current income beneficiary.[87]

Revocation of QSST Election

A QSST election may be revoked only with the consent of the Secretary.[88] A revocation cannot be granted when its purpose is the avoidance of federal income tax when the taxable year is closed. The application for consent to revoke the election must be submitted to the

---

[83] Treas. Reg. § 1.1361-1(j)(9)(ii), Example 1.

[84] Treas. Reg. § 1.1361-1(j)(9)(ii), Example 2.

[85] I.R.C. § 1361(d)(2)(B)(ii).

[86] I.R.C. § 1361(d)(2)(B)(ii); Treas. Reg. § 1.1361-1(j)(10)(i).

[87] Treas. Reg. § 1.1361-1(j)(10)(ii).

[88] I.R.C. § 1361(d)(2)(C).

IRS in the form of a letter ruling request under the appropriate revenue procedure. The application must be signed by the current income beneficiary and must:[89]

- Contain the name, address, and taxpayer identification number of the current income beneficiary, the trust, and the corporation with respect to which the QSST election was made;
- Identify the election being revoked as an election made under I.R.C. Section 1361(d)(2); and
- Explain why the current income beneficiary seeks to revoke the QSST election, and indicate that the beneficiary understands the consequences of the revocation.

Ask Your Attorney

Is the process of conveying title to S corporation stock to the trustee of a revocable living trust by endorsing the stock certificate or effecting a separate stock power the same as conveying title to the stock in a regular corporation to the trustee of a revocable living trust?

Answer

Yes.

PROFESSIONAL CORPORATIONS

Under the Code, a professional corporation is a corporation in which 95 percent or more of the activities of the corporation involve the performance of services in the fields of health, law, engineering, architecture, accounting, actuarial science, veterinary services, performing arts, and consulting;[90] and at least 95 percent or more of the value of its stock is held by employees or their estates or beneficiaries.[91] Generally, most states require that holders of the majority of each class of shares of a professional corporation entitled to vote be persons who are licensed or authorized within the state to render one or more of the professional services for which the corporation is organized.

State Law Governs Whether Trustee Can Own Stock in Professional Corporation

Whether the trustee of a revocable living trust can be an eligible shareholder in a professional corporation is a matter of state law. In many cases, the shareholder of a professional corporation may sell or transfer shares only in a manner that leaves the corporation in compliance with state law. Moreover, upon a shareholder's death, his or her shares must be disposed according to any agreement between the shareholder and the corporation or the remaining shareholders. As a general rule, if the deceased shareholder was the only shareholder of the professional corporation at the time of his or her death, the corporation must cease providing professional services as of the date of the deceased shareholder's death, unless the corporation has retained the services of an individual licensed or authorized within the state to render the professional service for which the corporation is organized.

---

[89] Treas. Reg. § 1.1361-1(j)(11).
[90] I.R.C. § 448(d)(2)(A); Treas. Reg. § 1.448-1T(e)(4)(i).
[91] I.R.C. § 448(d)(2)(B); Treas. Reg. § 1.448-1T(e)(5)(i).

Usually, within a certain period, the deceased shareholder's shares must be sold to a person or persons who are licensed or otherwise authorized in the state to render the professional service.

Ineligible Trustee

The trustee of a revocable living trust who is not licensed to render the professional service for which the professional corporation is organized may be an eligible shareholder but may not be permitted to vote the shares. Whether the trustee can vote the shares may not be the critical test as to the trustee's legal ownership of the shares. If the trustee is in legal title to the shares (i.e., is the legal shareholder of record), then all of the benefits of avoiding a court-supervised financial guardianship during the trustor's lifetime and probate of the decedent trustor's estate at his or her death may be realized.

Ineligible Trustee Gives Proxy to Licensed Shareholder

It is not uncommon for an unlicensed person to give a licensed member of the same corporation, or an attorney licensed to practice law in the state, a proxy to vote the shares of a professional corporation. If the trustee of the revocable living trust is not licensed to render the service for which the professional corporation is organized, the trustee can give a proxy to vote the shares to a shareholder of the same corporation who is licensed or authorized within the state to render such professional services. Of course, if the successor trustee named in the revocable living trust is licensed to render the professional services for which the trustor is licensed to render, then the successor trustee should be able to vote the shares of which the trustee is in legal title.

Planning Strategy

If the trustor is a licensed professional and operates his or her practice as a professional corporation, the revocable living trust should be designed in compliance with state law regarding the ownership of shares by a nonlicensed person in a professional corporation. Or the trustor may determine to designate a licensed person to be a co-trustee of the revocable living trust with another individual who is not a licensed professional. The revocable living trust agreement can provide that the licensed co-trustee will be in legal title to the shares in the professional corporation and will have exclusive authority under the trust agreement to deal with those shares, including the power to vote the shares. The other co-trustee can be responsible for all other property comprising the trust estate. In this regard, the trustor's attorney or estate planning consultant should carefully review the laws of the trustor's state pertaining to professional corporations, as well as the bylaws of the professional corporation, to provide the successor trustee(s) maximum advantage as to the holding of title to shares in a professional corporation. In this regard, it is critically important that the trustee be given the power to vote a security in person or by general or limited proxy.

Ask Your Attorney

Aside from the restrictions that may be imposed by state law on the conveyance of the title to stock in a professional corporation to the trustee of a revocable living trust, is the process of conveying title to professional corporation stock to the trustee of a revocable living trust by endorsing the stock certificate or effecting a separate stock power the same as conveying title to the stock in a regular corporation to the trustee of a revocable living trust?

Answer

Yes.

PARTNERSHIPS

A partnership is the relationship between two or more persons who join together to carry on a trade or business. Each person contributes money, property, labor, or skill; and each expects to share in the profits and losses of the partnership. If spouses carry on a business together and share in the profits and losses, they may be partners whether or not they have a formal partnership agreement.

General and Limited Partnerships

Partnerships may be general or limited. In a general partnership, all partners assume full financial responsibility for the business affairs of the partnership. This means that each partner is personally liable for each other's actions affecting the partnership. A limited partnership includes both general and limited partners. As a rule, a limited partner has no voice in the management of the partnership. A limited partner's personal liability for debts of the partnership is limited to his or her investment in the partnership. A partner who takes an active role in the management of the partnership is subject to the same rules applying to a general partnership.

Absent state statute, case law, or a restriction in the partnership agreement, the trustor's interests in a general and limited partnership can be conveyed to the trustee of a revocable living trust. Under a revocable living trust, when the trustor transfers his or her general or limited partnership interest in a partnership to the trustee of a revocable living trust, the trustor continues to be treated as the partner for federal income tax purposes.[92] A general partnership interest is conveyed to the trustee of a revocable living trust by effecting an Assignment of General Partnership Interest to Trustee (see file "APP1203.DOC"). A limited partnership interest can be conveyed to the trustee by effecting an Assignment of Limited Partnership Interest to Trustee (see file "APP1110.DOC").

Family Limited Partnerships

Members of a family can be partners in a partnership. Members of a family limited partnership include only spouses, ancestors, and lineal descendants, or any trust for their primary benefit. Family members are recognized as partners only if the following requirements are met:

- If capital is a material income-producing factor, they acquired their capital interest in a bona fide transaction (even if by gift or purchase from another family member), actually own the partnership interest, and actually control the interest; or
- If capital is not a material income-producing factor, they must have joined together in good faith to conduct a business. In addition, they must have agreed that contributions of each entitle them to a share in the profits. Some capital or service must be provided by each partner.

---

[92] I.R.C. §§ 7701(a)(2) and 671; Treas. Reg. § 1.704-1(e)(2)(vii).

Capital as Material Income-Producing Factor

In a family partnership, capital is a material income-producing factor if a substantial part of the gross income of the business comes from the use of capital. Capital is ordinarily an income-producing factor if the operation of the business requires substantial inventories or investments in plant, machinery, or equipment. In general, capital is not a material income-producing factor if the income of the business consists principally of fees, commissions, or other compensation for personal services performed by members of employees of the partnership.[93]

Trustee as Limited Partner

The trustee of a revocable living trust may be recognized as a partner of a family limited partnership for income tax purposes under the general principles relating to family partnerships as applied to the particular facts of the trust-partnership arrangement. A trustee who is unrelated to and independent of the trustor, and who participates as a partner and receives distribution of the income distributable to the trust, is recognized as the legal owner of the partnership interest held in trust, unless the trustor retains controls inconsistent with such ownership. However, if the trustor is the trustee, or if the trustee is amenable to the trustor's control, the provisions of the trust instrument (particularly, as to whether the trustee is subject to the responsibilities of a fiduciary), the provisions of the partnership agreement and the conduct of the parties must all be taken into account in determining whether the trustee in a fiduciary capacity has become the real owner of the partnership interest. Where the trustor is the trustee, the trust may be recognized as a partner only if the trustor, in his or her participation in the affairs of the partnership, actively represents and protects the interests of the beneficiaries in accordance with the obligations of a fiduciary and does not subordinate such interests to the interests of the trustor. Furthermore, if the trustor is the trustee, the following factors are given particular consideration:[94]

- Whether the trust is recognized as a partner in business dealings with customers and creditors; and
- Whether, if any amount of the partnership income is not properly retained for the reasonable needs of the business, the trust's share of such amount is distributed to the trust annually and paid to the beneficiaries or reinvested with regard solely to the interests of the beneficiaries.

Limited Liability Company

Generally, for federal income tax purposes, a limited liability company (LLC) is classified as a partnership—not a corporation.[95] Neither the members nor managers of a limited liability company are personally liable for the debts, judgments, liabilities, or obligations of the company.[96] Absent state statute, a restriction in the articles of organization, or a restriction in a buy-sell agreement prohibiting the transfer of a partner's interest in the limited liability company to the trustee of a revocable living trust, the trustor's interests in a limited liability company can be conveyed to the trustee of a revocable living trust by effecting an Assignment of Interest in a Limited Liability Company to Trustee (see file "APP1204.DOC").

---

[93] Treas. Reg. § 1.704-1(e)(1)(iv).

[94] Treas. Reg. § 1.704-1(e)(2)(vii).

[95] Rev. Rul. 88-76, 1988-2 C.B. 360.

[96] *See*, e.g.,Wyo. Stat. § 17-15-113 (2002). It may be said that the State of Wyoming is the *father* of the limited liability company concept.

PROFESSIONAL PARTNERSHIPS

State Law

Most often, professional partnerships are operated as general partnerships. Just like professional corporations, most states require that the general partners be persons who are licensed or authorized within the state to render one or more of the professional services for which the partnership is organized. Whether the trustee of a revocable living trust can hold legal title to a general partner's interest in a professional partnership is a matter of state law. Generally, a general partner of a professional partnership can assign his or her partnership interest only in a manner that leaves the partnership in compliance with state law. Moreover, upon a partner's death, his or her partnership interest must either: (a) be sold to the remaining partners, the partnership entity, a licensed professional whom the remaining partners are willing to admit to the partnership; or (b) the partnership interest simply dies with the partner. All of the rules for winding up the affairs of a deceased general partner's interest in a nonprofessional partnership are applicable in a professional partnership.

Buy-Sell Agreement

It is not uncommon for a professional partnership to have a buy-sell agreement that restricts the transfer of a partner's interest in the partnership. Before conveying an interest in a professional partnership to the trustee of a revocable living trust, the trustor must first determine the existence of any such restrictions. Whether such restrictions apply specifically to the transfer of a general partner's interest in a professional partnership to the trustee of a revocable living trust may be readily determined by reviewing the partnership agreement. If such a restriction does exist, then the partners may want to effect an amendment to the articles of partnership and to any buy-sell agreement affecting the partnership. Absent state statute or a restriction in the articles of partnership prohibiting the conveyance of a partner's interest in the professional partnership to the trustee of a revocable living trust, the trustor's partnership interest can be conveyed to the trustee of a revocable living trust by effecting an Assignment of General Partnership Interest to Trustee (see file "APP1203.DOC").

SPECIAL TAX BENEFITS FOR CLOSELY-HELD BUSINESSES

The Code provides special estate tax provisions for closely-held business interests. The benefits of installment payment of federal estate tax, stock redemptions to pay death taxes, special use valuation of real property used in farming or business,[97] and the family-owned business interest estate tax deduction all can be used, even if the trustor's closely-held business interest is conveyed to the trustee of a revocable living trust.

Deferral and Installment Payment of Federal Estate Tax

If the trustor's gross estate includes an interest in a closely-held business, the trustor's personal representative (executor; executrix) may be able to elect to pay part of the federal estate tax in installments. For the estate to qualify for the election, the decedent must have been a U.S. citizen or resident at the time of death.[98] The maximum amount that can be paid in installments is that part of the federal estate tax which is attributable to the closely-held business. This amount is the value of the interest which is included in the gross estate and

---

[97] *See* discussion in "Special Use Valuation for Farm and Business Real Property," section, Chapter 10.
[98] I.R.C. § 6166(a)(1).

which meets the percentage requirement.[99] For example, if 50 percent of the adjusted gross estate is attributable to the closely-held business amount, the personal representative of the decedent trustor's estate could elect to make installment payments on up to 50 percent of the federal estate tax.

Requirements to Qualify for Deferral and Installment Payments

To qualify for installment payments, the value of an interest in a closely-held business which is included in the gross estate must be more than (exceed) 35 percent (the percentage requirement) of the adjusted gross estate[100] (the value of the gross estate reduced by the sum of the amounts allowable as a deduction under I.R.C. Sections 2053 or 2054; [i.e., expenses, indebtedness, taxes, and losses]).[101] Interest in two or more closely-held businesses is treated as an interest in a single closely-held business if at least 20 percent of the total value of each business is included in the gross estate. For this purpose, an interest in a closely-held business which represents the surviving spouse's interest in property held by the decedent and the surviving spouse as community property or as joint tenants with right of survivorship, tenants by the entirety, or tenants in common is treated as having been included in the value of the decedent's gross estate.[102]

Passive Activity Assets

The value of any interest in a closely-held business does not include the value of that part of the interest that is attributable to passive assets held by that business.[103] This only applies in determining the closely-held business amount and whether the more than 35-percent requirement is met.[104] A passive asset is any asset not used in carrying on a trade or business. Stock in another corporation is a passive asset, unless the stock is treated as held by the decedent because of the election to treat holding company stock as business-company stock and the stock qualified under the percentage requirement. If a corporation owns at least 20 percent in value of the voting stock of another corporation, or the other corporation had no more than forty-five shareholders (fifteen shareholders for estates of decedents dying prior to 2002), and at least 80 percent of the value of the assets of each of these corporations is attributable to assets used in carrying on a trade or business, then these corporations are treated as one corporation; and the stock held is not treated as a passive asset. Stock held in the other corporation is not taken into account in determining the 80-percent requirement.[105]

---

[99] I.R.C. § 6166(a)(2).

[100] I.R.C. § 6166(a)(1).

[101] I.R.C. § 6166(b)(6).

[102] I.R.C. § 6166(c).

[103] For an in-depth analysis of oil and gas royalty interests included in the value of a decedent's closely held business with regard to the issue of installment payment of federal estate tax under I.R.C. § 6166, *see* Doug H. Moy, "Deferring the Payment of Federal Estate Tax Under I.R.C. § 6166 in View of TAM 9214010," 18 *Tax Management Estates, Gifts and Trusts Journal* 107 (July/August 1993). In Tech. Adv. Mem. 9214010 (December 23, 1991) the decedent actually used the monies received as oil and gas royalties, not just the interest on them, in her closely held business of raising cattle and breeding and training cutting horses; yet the IRS denied the present value of the oil and gas reserves ($465,375), from which the royalties were derived, as an interest in decedent's closely held business for purposes of installment payment of the federal estate tax under I.R.C. § 6166 attributable to the present value of the oil and gas reserves included in decedent's gross estate.

[104] I.R.C. § 6166(b)(9)(A).

[105] I.R.C. § 6166(b)(9)(B).

Interest in a Closely-Held Business Defined

For purposes of making installment payments, an interest in a closely-held business means:[106]

- An interest as a proprietor in a trade or business carried on as a proprietorship;[107]
- An interest as a partner in a partnership carrying on a trade or business if 20 percent or more of the total capital interest was included in the gross estate of the decedent or the partnership had no more than forty-five partners (fifteen partners for estates of decedents dying prior to 2002);[108]
- Stock in a corporation carrying on a trade or business if 20 percent or more of the voting stock of this corporation is included in the gross estate of the decedent or the corporation had no more than forty-five shareholders (fifteen shareholders for estates of decedents dying prior to 2002).[109]

Decedent's Interest in Closely-Held Business Determined Immediately before Death

The determination of whether the decedent owned an interest in a closely-held business for purposes of installment payment of the federal estate tax is made as of the time immediately before the decedent's death.[110] Property owned directly or indirectly by or for a corporation, partnership, estate, or trust is treated as owned proportionately by or for its shareholders, partners, or beneficiaries. However, with trusts, only beneficiaries with present interests are considered.[111] A present interest means that the beneficiaries have a present right to the trust income.

Deferred Payment of Principal

Under the installment method, the trustor's personal representative may elect to defer the payment of principal (the estate tax)—but not interest—for up to five years from the original due date for paying the estate tax.[112] After the first installment of estate tax is paid, the personal representative must pay the remaining installments annually by the date one year after the due date of the preceding installment.[113] There can be no more than ten installment payments.[114] Interest on the unpaid portion of the estate tax is not deferred and must be paid annually. Interest must be paid at the same time and as a part of each installment payment of the tax.[115] Under the 2001 Act, estates that entered into an installment payment arrangement prior to the repeal of the federal estate tax (i.e., before 2010) will continue to make their payments past the date for repeal (i.e., December 31, 2009).[116]

---

[106] I.R.C. § 6166(b)(1).

[107] I.R.C. § 6166(b)(1)(A).

[108] I.R.C. § 6166(b)(1)(B).

[109] I.R.C. § 6166(b)(1)(C).

[110] I.R.C. § 6166(b)(2)(A).

[111] I.R.C. § 6166(b)(2)(C).

[112] I.R.C. § 6166(f)(1).

[113] I.R.C. § 6166(a)(3).

[114] I.R.C. § 6166(a)(1).

[115] I.R.C. § 6166(f)(2).

[116] H.R. Rep. No. 107-37, at 85 (2001) (both House Ways and Means Committee Report accompanying the Death Tax Elimination bill of 2001 [H.R. Rep. No. 107-37, at 85] and the Senate Finance Committee Report accompanying the Restoring Earnings to Lift Individuals and Empower Families [RELIEF] of 2001 [S. Rep. No. 107-30] provide that certain tax benefits extending past the date for repeal of the estate tax will continue to past the date repeal of the estate tax becomes effective. In this regard, "The conference agreement [H.R. Conf. Rep. No. 107-84] follows the Senate amendment . . ."). However, with the single exception of distributions from qualified domestic trusts, nowhere in the 2001 Act does language address the continued applicability of such provisions following repeal of the federal estate tax. Moy, 1, *A Practitioner's Guide to Estate Planning*, § 2.01[J][4], at 2-51.

Special Interest Rate

If the decedent trustor's personal representative elects to make installment payments of the estate tax attributable to the value of a closely-held business included in the decedent trustor's gross estate, a special interest rate applies. A 2 percent interest rate is imposed on the amount of deferred estate tax attributable to the first $1 million in taxable value of the closely-held business (i.e., *the lesser of* the amount of the tentative tax which would be determined under the rate schedule set forth in I.R.C. Section 2001(c) if the amount with respect to which such tentative tax is to be computed were the sum of $1,000,000 and the applicable exclusion amount in effect under I.R.C. Section 2010(c), reduced by the applicable credit amount in effect under I.R.C. Section 2010(c), or the amount of the estate tax imposed which is extended as provided in I.R.C. Section 6166).[117] In the case of estates of decedents dying after 1998, the $1 million threshold is indexed for inflation in multiples of $10,000.[118] For the year 2003, the dollar amount used to determine the value of closely-held business interests eligible for the special low interest rate for deferred payment of federal estate tax is $1,120,000.[119] The balance of the deferred estate tax in excess of $1,120,000 is subject to interest at 45 percent of the underpayment rate under I.R.C. Section 6621 (the federal short-term rate, plus three percentage points).[120] The interest paid on estate taxes deferred under I.R.C. Section 6166 is not deductible for estate or income tax purposes.[121]

For the estate of any decedent dying before January 1, 1998, with respect to which the decedent's personal representative elected to defer the payment of estate tax under I.R.C. Section 6166, the personal representative may make a one-time election to use the lower interest rate (i.e., 2 percent instead of 4 percent) and forego the interest deduction for installments due after the date of the election. However, such estates do not receive the benefit of the increase in the amount eligible (e.g., $1,120,000) for the 2 percent interest rate (i.e., only the amount that was previously eligible for the 4 percent rate would be eligible for the 2 percent rate).[122] The maximum amount of the federal estate tax subject to the 4 percent interest rate prior to the 1997 Act was the lesser of:[123]

- $345,800 (the estate tax on $1 million) reduced by the amount of the allowable unified credit; or

- The amount of the estate tax which is attributable to the closely-held business and which is payable in installments.

Ask Your Attorney

If I convey title to my interest in a closely-held business to the trustee of a revocable living trust, can my estate still qualify for deferral and installment payment of the federal estate tax attributable to the value of my interest in the closely-held business?

---

[117] I.R.C. § 6601(j)(2).

[118] I.R.C. § 6601(j)(3).

[119] Rev. Proc. 2002-70, 2002-46 I.R.B. 1 at .31. The inflation-adjusted rates are published by the IRS in November or December of the year preceding the year the adjustments are to become effective.

[120] I.R.C. § 6601(j)(1)(B); Moy, 1, *A Practitioner's Guide to Estate Planning*, § 2.01[J][4], at 2-51.

[121] I.R.C. §§ 2053(c)(1)(D) and 163(k).

[122] Taxpayer Relief Bill of 1997, Conference Report and Statement of Managers (H.R. 2014), as released on July 31, 1997, issued as a CCH Special, Standard Federal Tax Reports (CCH) Conf. Rep., 88 (August 4, 1997); the 1997 Act, § 503(d)(2).

[123] I.R.C. § 6601(j)(2) before amendment by the 1997 Act, § 503(a).

Answer

Yes. The tax status of the beneficial owner of a closely-held business interest conveyed to the trustee of a revocable living trust is no different than outright ownership of the closely-held business interest for purposes of deferral and installment payment of the federal estate tax under I.R.C. Section 6166.[124]

Stock Redemptions to Pay Death Taxes

If stock that is included in a decedent's gross estate is redeemed, the distribution is exempt from dividend treatment under certain circumstances. The distribution in redemption of the stock is treated as an exchange and results in capital gain if the stock was held as a capital asset at the time of the exchange.[125] The amount that qualifies for exchange treatment is limited to the sum of:[126]

- The estate, inheritance, legacy, and succession taxes (including any interest collected as part of these taxes) imposed because of a decedent's death; and
- The amount of funeral and administration expenses allowable as deductions to the estate.

Eligibility for I.R.C. Section 303 Stock Redemption

To be eligible for an I.R.C. Section 303 stock redemption, the value of the closely-held stock includable in the decedent's gross estate must *exceed* 35 percent of the value of the adjusted gross estate.[127] Stock of two or more corporations may be combined to satisfy the 35 percent requirement, provided at least 20 percent in value of the outstanding stock of each corporation is included in determining the value of the decedent's gross estate. If the 20 percent requirement is satisfied, the stock of two or more corporations is treated as the stock of a single corporation.[128] In applying the 20-percent test, a surviving spouse's interest in stock held by the decedent and the surviving spouse as community property or as joint tenants with right of survivorship, tenants by the entirety, or tenants in common is treated as included in the decedent's gross estate.[129]

Eligibility of Closely-Held Stock Conveyed to Trustee for I.R.C. Section 303 Stock Redemption

Ask Your Attorney

If I convey title to my interest in a closely-held business to the trustee of a revocable living trust and such business interest otherwise qualifies for a redemption to pay death taxes, will the fact that the title to such business interest is in the name of the trustee render the value of the business interest includable in my gross estate ineligible for the redemption to pay death taxes, funeral, and administration expenses?

---

[124] Priv. Ltr. Rul. 9311031 (December 18, 1992; *see also* Priv. Ltr. Ruls. 9202017 (October 10, 1991), 9116009 (January 15, 1991), 8813047 (January 4, 1988), 8741076 (July 17, 1987), and 8621030 (February 20, 1986)) (wherein closely-held business interests conveyed to the trustee of living trusts before the decedents' deaths otherwise qualified for deferred and installment payment of estate tax under I.R.C. § 6166).

[125] I.R.C. §§ 303(a) and 302(a) and (b); Treas. Reg. § 1.303-3(a).

[126] I.R.C. § 303(a).

[127] I.R.C. § 303(b)(2)(A).

[128] Moy, 1, *A Practitioner's Guide to Estate Planning*, § 2.01[J][5], at 2-61.

[129] I.R.C. § 303(b)(2)(B).

Answer

No.[130]

Although the redeemed stock must be included in determining the decedent's gross estate,[131] the stock need not be owned by the decedent's estate in order to qualify for exchange treatment. Thus, a qualifying redemption may be made of stock included in the gross estate because it was property over which the decedent had a general power of appointment, which the decedent has previously transferred subject to retained dispositive powers (e.g., to the trustee of a revocable living trust) or which was held by the decedent as a joint tenant.[132] Exchange treatment applies to the distribution only to the extent that the interest of a shareholder is reduced directly or through a binding obligation to contribute toward the payment of the death taxes, funeral, and administrative expenses.[133]

Stock Transferred Within Three Years of Death

Under present law, the value of gifts made within three years of death may be includable in the value of the gross estate for certain limited purposes. One of these purposes is to determine if the decedent's gross estate qualifies for an I.R.C. Section 303 stock redemption. The purpose of including the value of such gifts in the gross estate is to prevent the making of gifts in order to make the closely-held stock represent 35 percent of the value of the adjusted gross estate. In order for the decedent's estate to qualify for an I.R.C. Section 303 stock redemption, more than 35 percent of the adjusted gross estate must consist of the decedent's interest in the closely-held business *both before and after* inclusion in the value of the gross estate of property transfers made within three years of the decedent's death.[134]

This rule applies to *any property* gifted—not just closely-held business interests. Consequently, such gifts could result in the decedent's estate being disqualified from using an I.R.C. Section 303 stock redemption while such gifts cannot result in qualifying the decedent's estate for the election. Consequently, if a trustor's estate may qualify for an I.R.C. Section 303 stock redemption, care must be exercised in implementing lifetime gifting programs.[135]

Ask Your Attorney

In view of the rule regarding the transfer of stock in a closely-held corporation within three years of death, does this rule include a transfer of the title in such stock to the trustee of a revocable living trust within three years of the trustor's death?

Answer

No. As a general rule, the conveyance of title to property to the trustee of a revocable living trust is not a gift-taxable event.[136] Hence, such stock is not precluded from otherwise qualifying for a stock redemption under I.R.C. Section 303.[137]

---

[130] Treas. Reg. § 1.303-2(f); Priv. Ltr. Ruls. 8813047 (January 4, 1988) and 8621030 (February 20, 1986).

[131] I.R.C. § 303(a).

[132] Treas. Reg. § 1.303-2(a), (b), and (f).

[133] I.R.C. § 303(b)(3).

[134] Moy, 1, *A Practitioner's Guide to Estate Planning*, § 2.01[J][5][a], at 2-61.

[135] Ibid.

[136] *See* discussion in Chapter Eight 8, "Federal Gift Tax" section.

[137] I.R.C. § 2035(e); see Rev. Rul. 84-76, 1984-1 C.B. 91.

Family-Owned Business Interest Deduction

The 1997 Act added I.R.C. Section 2033A, which provided an exclusion from the gross estate equal to the lesser of: (1) the adjusted value of the decedent's qualified family-owned business interests or (2) the excess of $1.3 million over the exemption amount in effect at the time of the decedent's death. The *IRS Restructuring and Reform Act of 1998* redesignated I.R.C. Section 2033A as I.R.C. Section 2057,[138] making the exclusion a deduction.[139]

Qualified Family-Owned Business Interests

Qualified family-owned business interests are the interests that are included in determining the value of the gross estate and are acquired by any qualified heir from, or passed to any qualified heir from, the decedent within the meaning of I.R.C. Section 2032A(e)(9).[140]

A qualified family-owned business interest is defined as any interest in a trade or business, regardless of the form in which it is held; (i.e., sole proprietorship, regular C corporation, S corporation, general partnership, limited partnership, family limited partnership, limited liability company, limited liability partnership) with a principal place of business in the United States[141] and meeting the following ownership requirements: (a) at least 50 percent by one family; (b) at least 70 percent by two families; or (c) at least 90 percent by three families, provided that the decedent's family owns at least 30 percent of the trade or business. A decedent is treated as engaged in a trade or business if any member of the decedent's family is engaged in such trade or business.[142] The ownership requirements must be satisfied both in terms of vote and value. In other words, the requisite ownership must be measured against both: the total combined voting power of all classes of stock entitled to vote; and the value of all classes of stock.[143] With respect to a partnership, the requisite ownership is determined by the ownership of the appropriate percentage of the capital interests in the partnership.[144]

Eligible Estates

In effect, for purposes of the federal estate tax, the value of the decedent's taxable estate is determined by deducting from the value of the gross estate the adjusted value of the qualified family-owned business interests of the decedent.[145] The personal representative of the decedent's estate can elect to deduct the adjusted value of a qualified family-owned busi-

---

[138] *IRS Restructuring and Reform Act of 1998*, § 6007(b)(1)(A).

[139] For additional reading, *see* Shannon E. O'Brien, "Estate Tax Treatment of Family-owned Businesses: The Evolution of Internal Revenue Code Section 2057," 67 University of Missouri-Kansas Law Review 495 (1999); Moy, 2, *A Practitioner's Guide to Estate Planning*, § 22.01, at 22-3.

[140] I.R.C. § 2057(b)(2); Moy, 2, *A Practitioner's Guide to Estate Planning*, § 22.02[B][1], at 22-6.

[141] I.R.C. § 2057(e)(2)(A).

[142] I.R.C. § 2057(e)(1).

[143] I.R.C. § 2057(e)(3)(A)(i).

[144] I.R.C. § 2057(e)(3)(A)(ii); Moy, 2, *A Practitioner's Guide to Estate Planning*, § 22.03[A], at 22-8.

[145] I.R.C. § 2057(a)(1); for additional reading see Stanley M. Burnstein, "Family-owned Business Deduction is Enhanced by Balance Sheet Planning," 25 *Estate Planning* 348 (Oct. 1998); Sebastian V. Grassi, Jr., "Drafting for the Family-owned Business Deduction," 90 *Journal of Taxation* 358 (June 1999); Gary L. Maydew, "The Qualified Family-owned Business Interest Deduction: RRA 98 Clears Up Some of the Confusion," in 3 *Financial and Estate Planning* (Commerce Clearing House, Inc) ¶ 31,981, at 26,535; Jerry A. Kasner, "After the Estate Tax Family Business Deduction, What Next?" 2 *One Disc Weekly Tax Review* 1, (Tax Analysts Oct. 27, 2000).

ness interest (QFOBI) up to a maximum of $675,000.[146] This deduction, together with an exemption amount of $625,000,[147] allows the decedent's estate to, in effect, *exempt* a total of $1.3 million from federal estate tax. Unlike use of the unlimited estate tax marital deduction, which includes the decedent's available exemption amount, the estate tax deduction for a QFOBI is limited to $675,000 but may be combined with the decedent's exemption amount up to a limit of $625,000. However, the maximum amount of the QFOBI estate tax deduction and the exemption amount are coordinated so that, as the exemption amount increases, the estate is able to take full advantage of the maximum estate tax benefit available. In this regard, if the gross estate includes less than $675,000 of QFOBIs, the applicable exemption amount increases on a dollar-for-dollar basis (but not above the amount that would apply to the estate without regard to I.R.C. Section 2057) up to the applicable exemption amount generally available for the year of the decedent's death.[148] In 2004, the qualified family-owned business interest deduction is repealed.[149]

Ask Your Attorney

If I convey title to my interest(s) in a family-owned business to the trustee of a revocable living trust of which I am the trustor, trustee, and primary beneficiary, will the family-owned business deduction still be available to my estate?

Answer

Yes. Assuming that all requirements to take the family-owned business interest deduction are satisfied, conveyance of the trustor's ownership interest in a family-owned business, as that term is defined under I.R.C. Section 2057(b)(2), to the trustee of a revocable living trust does not cause loss to the trustor's estate of the family-owned business interest deduction under I.R.C. Section 2057. The answer is the same even if the trustor does not act as the trustee of the revocable living trust.

---

[146] I.R.C. § 2057(a)(2).

[147] I.R.C. § 2057(a)(3)(A).

[148] I.R.C. § 2057(a)(3)(B).

[149] I.R.C. § 2057(j); Moy, 2, *A Practitioner's Guide to Estate Planning*, § 22.02[A], at 22-4.

CHAPTER 13

Accounts in Banks, Savings Associations, and Credit Unions

DAY-TO-DAY OPERATION

The title to accounts in banks, savings associations, and credit unions, including money market accounts and certificates of deposit, can be conveyed to the trustee of a revocable living trust. A trustor's checking, savings, and money market accounts are just as accessible to the trustor under a revocable living trust agreement as they were before title to them was conveyed to the trustee. Regardless of whether the trustor presently owns bank accounts in his or her own individual name or as joint tenants with right of survivorship with the trustor's spouse or a member of the trustor's immediate family (e.g., a son or daughter; niece or nephew; sister or brother) or an unrelated party (e.g., domestic partner), title to the trustor's bank accounts should be conveyed to the trustee of the trustor's revocable living trust. Even if the trustor maintains a minimum balance each month in the account, it should be in the name of the trustee of the trustor's revocable living trust. The biggest disadvantage of continuing to hold title to a bank account as joint tenants with right of survivorship, in lieu of conveying title to the account to the trustee of a revocable living trust, is that, if either or both co-tenants become incapacitated, a proper court of jurisdiction may appoint a guardian (or conservator) to oversee both the incapacitated and nonincapacitated co-tenant's interest in the account.[1] Upon the death of the first co-tenant to die, the surviving co-tenant's interest in the account may be subject to probate upon his or her subsequent death. The same result can occur if the trustor continues to own a bank account in his or her own individual name or as a tenant in common.

Observation/Recommendation

A trustor should not allow an attorney to convince him or her to not convey the title to a bank account to the trustee of a revocable living trust because the account balance is less than the maximum allowed for personal property under the small estate statute of the trustor's state.[2] As time passes, the balance in the account, when added together with all of the trustor's other tangible and intangible property, may exceed the dollar limit under a small estate statute, thereby, causing the funds in the bank account to be subject to a formal probate proceeding upon the trustor's death or to a court-supervised financial guardianship during the trustor's lifetime.

---

[1] 39 Am Jur2d, Guardian and Ward, §§ 73 and 78.

[2] *See* discussion this chapter under Credit Unions.

New Bank Account Not Required

Ask Your Attorney

If I convey the title to my existing bank account to the trustee of a revocable living trust, do I have to open a new bank account in the name of the trustee?

Answer

No; generally, when title to a bank checking account is conveyed to the trustee of a revocable living trust, a new account number and new checks are not required.

Signature Requirement on Checks

Ask Your Attorney

If I am the trustee of my revocable living trust, do I have to sign my name as trustee each time I write a check?

Answer

No; the trustor is not required to sign checks as trustee.

Trustee's Name Imprint On Checks

The trustor is not required to imprint the name of the revocable living trust or the trustee's name on the checks. To the public at large, the trustor's bank accounts continue to appear as they have always appeared; that is, in the trustor's name as an individual person—not in the name of the trustor-trustee as trustor-trustee of a revocable living trust. On the other hand, nothing precludes the trustor from having new checks issued to reflect his or her identity as trustee of the trustor's revocable living trust. What is important is that the bank's records reflect that the bank account is registered (titled) in the name of the trustee of the revocable living trust agreement.

Writing Checks When Trustor Is Not the Trustee

Ask Your Attorney

If I am not the trustee, can I still write checks on the account that is titled in the name of the trustee?

Answer

Yes.

If the revocable living trust has been properly designed, the trustor may act as a nominee of the trustee. In this regard, the trustor may establish a joint bank account with the trustee. Deposits made from time-to-time into such an account constitute transfers of funds to the trustee. As a nominee of the trustee with respect to the account, the trustor is not considered a co-owner. The trustor may, however, write checks or make withdrawals from the account without the cosignature of the trustee. The writing of such checks by the trustor constitutes withdrawals of funds from the trust estate, and the trustee has no further interest in or duty with regard to the amounts withdrawn.

Family Member's Name on Checking Account With Trustor

Ask Your Attorney

As a convenience, I added my daughter's name to my checking account. If I retitle the checking account in my name as trustee of my revocable living trust, can she still sign checks on my behalf?

Answer

Yes.

Trustor Nominates Accommodation Party

It is not uncommon for a trustor to have a bank account in his or her name with a child or other immediate family member. Most often, such an arrangement enables a family member to be listed on the account as an accommodation party to sign checks or to make deposits on behalf of the registered owner. Unless the revocable living trust agreement empowers the trustor, when acting as trustee, to nominate an accommodation party, most banks and other financial institutions are reluctant to allow such an accommodation party to operate when the account is titled in the name of a trustee. In Chapter 2,[3] a sample trust provision is provided wherein the trustor, when acting as trustee, may nominate another individual as a signatory on bank accounts.

Observation

Some states do not permit a trustee to transfer its responsibilities to another or delegate the entire administration of the trust to a co-trustee or to any other person.[4] Unless otherwise specifically prohibited by state law or the trust agreement itself, this limitation does not prevent a trustee from delegating signature authority to any person.

Letter of Authority

Another approach that may be used to give an accommodation party signature authority on bank accounts is for the trustor to grant such authority, and the trustee and accommodation party to accept such authority, in a letter to the financial institution (see file "APP0206.DOC"). 📄 Whether the financial institution will accept such an arrangement by letter outside the parameters of the revocable living trust agreement is problematical.

---

[3] *See* "Family Members as Trustees" section, Chapter 2.

[4] *See, e.g.,* Wyo. Stat. § 4-8-104 (2002), except as provided under § 4-9-109, Delegation of Investment and Management Functions; Mont. Code Ann. § 72-34-113(1) (2001); Idaho Code § 68-107 (2001), except as provided under Chapter 14, Title 26, Idaho Code; Utah Code Ann. § 75-7-403 (2002), except as provided under § 7-5-14 or subsection 75-7-302(12); Haw. Rev. Stat. § 554A-4 (2002).

The better approach is to include in the revocable living trust agreement a provision that empowers the trustor, when acting as trustee, to nominate another individual as a signatory on bank accounts.[5]

Delegation of Signature Authority in Trustee's Absence

Similarly, a trustee who is not the trustor may want to delegate signature authority to someone in the trustee's absence. In such instance, the trustee may want to use a Delegation of Trustee Powers (see file "APP0611.DOC"). This instrument can be used by a trustee to delegate signature authority to another trustee or to any other person. The Delegation of Trustee Powers should be sufficient for that trustee or person to sign checks for accounts that are titled in the name of the trustee, provided the financial institution governing the account accepts the provision in the trust agreement which gives the trustee the power to delegate to another trustee or person any part or all of the trustee's powers.

RETITLING ACCOUNTS

Single Trustor

If the trustor is a single person and is both the trustor and trustee of his or her revocable living trust, bank accounts should be titled in the trustor's name as trustee using the following format:

> Eugene H. Curtis, Trustee under the Eugene H. Curtis Revocable Living Trust Agreement, dated February 15, 2003.

Married Trustors

For married trustors wherein both spouses are trustors and trustees under a joint revocable living trust agreement, all bank accounts presently owned as joint tenants with right of survivorship should be titled in the trustors' names as co-trustees of their joint revocable living trust, using the following format:

> Eugene H. Curtis and Theresa M. Curtis, co-Trustees under the Curtis Family Revocable Living Trust Agreement, dated February 15, 2003

Married Trustors with Joint and Individually-Owned Bank Accounts

For married trustors wherein both spouses are trustors and trustees under a joint revocable living trust agreement but, in addition to accounts owned as joint tenants with right of survivorship, one or both trustors also have accounts titled in their own individual names, then each trustor's respective account would be titled using the following format and list that particular account on the appropriate schedule attached at the end of the trust agreement:[6]

> Eugene H. Curtis, co-Trustee under the Curtis Family Revocable Living Trust Agreement, dated February 15, 2003 , or

---

[5] *See* discussion in "Family Members as Trustees" section, Chapter 2.

[6] *See* "Trust Property: Article III" section in Chapter 2 for discussion regarding schedules.

Theresa M. Curtis, co-Trustee under the Curtis Family Revocable Living Trust Agreement, dated February 15, 2003

Married Trustors with Separate Revocable Living Trusts

For married trustors with separate revocable living trusts of which each trustor-spouse, respectively, is the trustee and both trustor-spouses want access to the funds in the account previously titled as JTWROS, then the account should be titled in the trustor's names as trustees of the trusts as tenants in common:

Eugene H. Curtis, Trustee under the Eugene H. Curtis Revocable Living Trust Agreement, dated February 15, **or** Theresa M. Curtis, Trustee under the Theresa M. Curtis Revocable Living Trust Agreement, dated February 15, 2003.

(It would not be unusual for the bank to add the language "as tenants in common".)

Universal Title Wording

Most banks and credit unions recognize a universal wording format to retitle accounts in the name of the trustee of a revocable living trust; for example:

- One trustor; single trust: Eugene H. Curtis, Trustee U/D/T (*Under Declaration of Trust*), dated February 15, 2003;
- Married trustors; joint trust: Eugene H. Curtis **or** Theresa M. Curtis, co-Trustees U/D/T (*Under Declaration of Trust*), dated February 15, 2003;
- Married trustors; joint trust; separate accounts: Eugene H. Curtis, co-Trustee U/D/T (*Under Declaration of Trust*), dated February 15, 2003, **or** Theresa M. Curtis, co-Trustee, U/D/T (*Under Declaration of Trust*), dated February 15, 2003;
- Married trustors; two separate trusts, but both spouses want access to one account: Eugene H. Curtis, Trustee U/D/T (*Under Declaration of Trust*), dated February 15, 2003, **or** Theresa M. Curtis, Trustee U/D/T (*Under Declaration of Trust*), dated February 15, 2003.

Observations

1. In all of the foregoing registration formats, the trustor is not listed as trustee; only the trustee's name shows as the legal title holder to the property conveyed to the trustee of the revocable living trust. Even if the trustor is the trustee of the revocable living trust, the legal title to the property comprising the trust estate is titled in the trustor's name as trustee—not as trustor. This is because the trustee—not the trustor—is in legal title to the trust estate property. If the trustor is not the trustee, then the trustee's name is listed as the legal owner of the property comprising the trust estate. Unless the trustor is operating as a nominee of the trustee, the trustor's name is only revealed in the revocable living trust agreement itself.

2. In all the preceding registration formats except the first, the alternate *or* is used in place of the conjunction *and*. Use of the conjunction *and* causes bankers angst because they view the word *and* as requiring the signatures of all account owners on checks, withdrawals, and so forth. By using the word *or*, either account owner can write checks and make withdrawals from the account without the other account owner's signature.

COMMUNICATING WITH BANK EMPLOYEES

Initiating Retitling Process

Because of the proliferation of revocable living trusts, bank personnel have become more at-
tuned and knowledgeable about them. One way to initiate the process of retitling a bank account in the name of the trustee of a revocable living trust is to write a letter to the bank
requesting the appropriate forms and signature cards for effecting the change of ownership.

Single Person

If the trustor is a single person (or a married person with a separate trust) and is both the
trustor and trustee of a revocable living trust and wants to retitle a bank account in the
trustee's name under a revocable living trust, the Bank Letter Single may be used (see file
"APP1301.DOC").

Married Trustors With Joint Revocable Living Trust

If the trustors are married, have a joint revocable living trust, wherein both spouses are co-
trustors and co-trustees, and the trustors want to retitle a bank account in both spouses'
names as co-trustees, the Bank Letter Joint may be used (see file "APP1302.DOC").

Married Trustors With Separate Revocable Living Trusts

If the trustors are married but each trustor-spouse has his or her own revocable living trust
of which each trustor-spouse, respectively, is the trustee and both trustor-spouses want access to the funds in the account, the Bank Letter Tenants in Common may be used (see file
"APP1303.DOC").

Visit the Bank in Person

The better way to initiate the process of retitling a bank account in the name of the trustee
of a revocable living trust is to visit the bank in person. However, never assume that the
personal banking representative behind the desk understands the operation of a revocable
living trust. Upon entering the bank with the objective of conveying the title to bank accounts to the trustee of a revocable living trust, the trustor's experience in accomplishing
this objective will be directly related to the trustor's own level of knowledge and the manner in which the trustor presents himself or herself. In this regard, the trustor should take
charge of the retitling of ownership process from beginning to completion. Moreover, as a
matter of practice, the trustor's attorney or estate planner should accompany the trustor to
the bank to familiarize the trustor with the retitling process.

In order to be in charge of the retitling of ownership process, the trustor needs a tract
to follow. By exuding confidence in the trustor's mission, he or she will be viewed by bank
personnel as someone who knows what he or she is doing; and the trustor is not as apt to
falter in responding to questions asked of the trustor about the revocable living trust. Following is a suggested track to use when approaching bank personnel for the purpose of
retitling bank accounts into the name of the trustee of a revocable living trust:

> Hello, my name is _____ (or my name is _____ , and I would like
> you to meet my wife (or husband)_____). Recently, I (we) effected a revo-
> cable living trust agreement. I (we) am (are) the trustor(s), trustee(s), and the primary
> beneficiary(ies) of the trust; and I (we) want to retitle the ownership of my (our) check-
> ing account into my (our) name(s) as trustee(s) of my (our) revocable living trust agree-
> ment. I (we) have prepared the ownership wording for you to use in retitling the
> account and also have copies of the appropriate pages of the revocable living trust
> which I (we) know you require for your bank records.

Observation

On October 26, 2001, President Bush signed into law the USA Patriot Act.[7] Title III of the Act captioned "International Money Laundering Abatement and Anti-terrorist Financing Act of 2001" adds several new provisions to the Bank Secrecy Act (BSA), 31 U.S.C. 5311, and so forth. These provisions are intended to facilitate the prevention, detection, and prosecution of international money laundering and the financing of terrorism. Section 326 of the Act adds a new subsection (1) to 31 U.S.C. 5318 which requires the Secretary to prescribe regulations setting forth minimum standards for financial institutions which relate to the identification and verification of any person who applies to open an account.[8] In effect, financial institutions are required to implement reasonable procedures to verify the identity of any person seeking to open an account or to be a signatory on any account to the extent reasonable and practicable; to maintain records of the information used to verify the person's identity; and determine whether the person appears on any lists of known or suspected terrorists or terrorist organizations provided to the financial institution by any government agency. The proposed regulation applies to banks, savings associations, and credit unions. Financial institutions may describe these new policies to bank customers as "Know Your Customer" policies.

A *customer* means any person seeking to open a *new* account. *Customer* includes both individuals and other persons such as corporations, partnerships, and trusts. In addition, any person seeking to open an account at a bank, on or after the effective date of the final rule, will be a *customer*, regardless of whether that person already has an account at the bank. *Customer* is also defined to include any signatory on an account.[9] *Person* includes not only individuals, but also *trusts* and estates.[10] In other words, if the trustor is not the trustee of a revocable living trust, the trustee must prove his or her identity to the financial institution. Similarly, if the trustor is the trustee and wants to add to the account another person (e.g., a son, daughter, other immediate family member, or unrelated individual) as a co-trustee under the revocable living trust agreement, the identity of the person to be added (the signatory) to the account must be proven to the financial institution.

Though preferred by financial institutions, it is not necessary that a person appear in person to open a new account, retitle an existing account, or add a signatory to an existing account. Thus, when an account is opened for a customer who is not physically present (e.g., by telephone, by mail, and over the Internet), a bank is permitted to use other methods of verification.[11]

Recognition of the Trust Agreement

Ask Your Attorney

With regard to the suggested wording for retitling ownership of bank accounts or certificates of deposit in the name of the trustee of a revocable living trust, does this mean that such an account or asset is now under the terms of the trust?

---

[7] *USA Patriot Act*, Pub. L. No. 107-56, 115 Stat. 272 (26 October 2001).

[8] The proposed regulations are in 31 C.F.R. 103 and are reproduced in 67 Federal Register 48290-48299, Tuesday, July 23, 2002.

[9] Prop. Treas. Reg. § 103.121(a)(3), 67 Fed. Reg. 48292 (2002).

[10] Prop. Treas. Reg. § 103.121(a)(5), 67 Fed. Reg. 48292 (2002).

[11] Prop. Treas. Reg. § 103.121(b)(2)(ii)(B), 67 Fed. Reg. 48293 (2002).

Answer

Yes and no. Yes, in the fact that the trustee under the trust agreement holds legal title to the bank account; no, in respect to whether the bank's internal policy will honor the authority of the trustee under the trust agreement. If the trustor becomes physically disabled or mentally incapacitated, the bank may require evidence of a financial guardianship for the trustor having been appointed by a proper court of jurisdiction. Upon the trustor's death, the bank may require letters testamentary from the probate court.

Durable Power of Attorney

Of course, these are the very legal actions that the trustor wants to avoid and why a revocable living trust was effected in the first place. Two lifetime solutions exist to overcome these unnecessary legal actions. One solution is for the trustor to effect a durable power of attorney (general or special) designating the successor trustee to act as the trustor's attorney-in-fact. Many banks and other financial institutions will accept a durable power of attorney, authorizing the holder of the power to act on behalf of the grantor of the power. In some cases, though, a financial institution may require a certification to be attached to the power of attorney to the effect that it is a true and correct copy of the original power of attorney and that the power of attorney is still in full force and effect, has not been revoked, and the maker is alive as of the date of the certification. Of course, if the power of attorney is being used with regard to securities transactions, the holder of the power must have had his or her signature on the certificate guaranteed. It is also a good idea for the trustor, as the maker of the power of attorney, to have his or her signature guaranteed.

Observation

Remember, a durable power of attorney is only as effective as it is specific with regard to the powers granted to the attorney-in-fact. Therefore, forethought and thoroughness should be exercised in the design of the power of attorney.

Incapacity to be Determined by Doctors

The second and most effective solution to overcome the unnecessary legal action of a court-supervised financial guardianship is to include a provision in the revocable living trust that the question of whether the trustor possesses requisite mental capacity will be determined by doctors and not by a court of law.[12] Such a provision eliminates the need for a court-supervised financial guardianship because the trustee occupies that role under the revocable living trust agreement. Remember, though, upon the trustor's death, a durable power of attorney is not operative in the hands of the attorney-in-fact for administering the financial affairs of the decedent principal's estate. In this regard, the bank or other financial institution may request letters testamentary from the probate court having jurisdiction over the decedent trustor's estate. If legal title to the asset in question has been correctly conveyed to the trustee of the revocable living trust and the trust agreement is effective and operational at the death of the trustor, letters testamentary are not required for the bank to deal with the account in question. Generally, it is sufficient to show the bank a certified copy of the revocable living trust agreement, or the original revocable living trust agreement, or a Certificate of Trust (see file "APP0212.DOC") along with an acknowledged statement by the trustee that the revocable living trust agreement has not been amended, altered, or

---

[12] *See* discussion in "Initial and Successor Trustees: Article II" section, Chapter 2.

revoked (see file "APP0602.DOC," Affidavit of Acting Trustee), 🖾 is in full force and effect to evidence the fact that the trustee holds legal title to the bank account (certificate of deposit, and so forth), and that letters testamentary are not required.

Taxpayer Identification Number

The bank employee will inquire of the trustor as to the taxpayer identification number for the revocable living trust. The trustor should respond by saying: "My Social Security Number is to be used as the TIN (or, if married trustors have effected a joint revocable living trust, each trustor-spouse should give the bank employee his or her Social Security Number). It is not unusual for misinformed employees of banks, savings associations, and credit unions to insist that a revocable living trust must have its own TIN. Treasury regulations specifically provide that: "A grantor trust described in I.R.C. Reg. § 1.671-4(b) shall not obtain an employer identification number until such time as the trust is no longer described in I.R.C. Reg. § 1.671-4(b)." Instead, the trustor must furnish his or her Social Security Number to payers of income; and payees must report income as if paid to the trustor—not the trust.[13]

Evidence of the Revocable Living Trust Agreement

Ask Your Attorney

Just how private is my revocable living trust agreement; must the bank read it before my account can be retitled?

Answer

A revocable living trust is only as private as the trustor makes it.

Trust Documentation to Provide Bank

Though not a common request by bank personnel, the trustor may be asked to provide a *complete* copy of the revocable living trust. It is the exception, rather than the rule, for a bank's attorneys to request a complete copy of the trust agreement. The legal staff of the bank is only interested in knowing that a legal trust has been effected and that the trustee is empowered to hold legal title to the bank account. If the trustor is asked to do so, he or she should submit either selected pages of the trust agreement or a copy of the revocable living trust agreement, excepting the trust provisions describing the disposition of the trust estate upon the trustor's death and the schedules of property comprising the trust estate which are attached to the trust agreement. In most cases, however, the following specific pages of the trust agreement will be accepted as evidence of its existence:

1. First page (Preamble) of the trust agreement identifying the trustor, trustee, primary and contingent beneficiaries;
2. Pages naming the initial and successor trustees;
3. Pages describing the trustee's powers, specifically, those pertaining to bank accounts;

---

[13] Treas. Reg. § 301.6109-1(a)(2).

4. Signature pages showing the signatures of trustor(s) and trustee(s) to evidence that the trust has, in fact, been effected; and

5. Pages evidencing that the signatures of the trustor(s) and trustee(s) have been notarized.

Miscellaneous Trust Documentation to Provide Bank

In some cases, other pages of the revocable living trust may be requested by the bank's legal staff (e.g., those pages evidencing the trustor's right to revoke and amend the trust agreement). If the bank's legal staff insists on receiving a complete copy of the trust agreement, under no circumstances should the trustor provide a copy of the trust provisions describing disposition of the trust estate upon the trustor's death. Moreover, the trustor should not be required to submit to anyone to whom the trustor would not otherwise provide his or her personal financial statement a copy of the schedules of property comprising the trust estate which are attached to the trust agreement.

Recommendation

If bank personnel insist on reviewing a complete copy of the revocable living trust agreement, the trustor should request that the original document be returned to the trustor after the account has been retitled in the name of the trustee and that only copies of the specific pages listed above be retained by the bank. In lieu of submitting an entire copy of the revocable living trust agreement or even selected pages as discussed above, the trustor could submit to the bank a Certificate of Trust (see file "APP0212.DOC") , provided such a Certificate of Trust is recognized by the legal jurisdiction (e.g., state) wherein the bank account is located.

CREDIT UNIONS

Unfortunately, not all credit unions allow accounts to be titled in the name of the trustee of a revocable living trust. In such case, if the trustor is married, he or she may want to title the account as joint tenants with right of survivorship or under some type of beneficiary designation acceptable to the credit union (e.g., payable on death [POD] or transfer on death [TOD]). Whether the trustor is married or single, if title to the account is not conveyed to the trustee of a revocable living trust, then it is imperative that the trustor effect a durable power of attorney that specifically empowers the attorney-in-fact to deal with credit union accounts. At least, under a durable power of attorney, an unnecessary court-supervised financial guardianship of the account can be avoided if the trustor becomes legally incapacitated.

Upon the trustor's death, under the small estate statutes of most states, a formal probate proceeding may not be necessary to convey ownership of the account to the trustee of a revocable living trust agreement under the terms of the decedent's pour-over Will. For example, if the fair market value of the decedent's probate estate is $140,000 or less and consists of tangible personal property having a fair market value of $50,000 or less, or real property having a fair market value of $90,000 or less, or a combination of tangible personal property and real property not exceeding $50,000 or $90,000, respectively,[14] the decedent's personal representative can file an affidavit, along with a copy of the decedent's Will, pay

---

[14] *See, e.g.,* Or. Rev. Stat. § 114.515(2) (Loislaw 2001).

a modest filing fee, and, within a statutory period (e.g., 30 days), distribute the account to the trustee of the revocable living trust.

CERTIFICATES OF DEPOSIT

Title to a certificate of deposit (CD) is conveyed to the trustee of a revocable living trust by reissuing the CD. However, before conveying title to a CD to the trustee of a revocable living trust, the trustor should inquire of the bank that issued the CD whether a penalty for withdrawal prior to maturity may be assessed. Even though the trustor's Social Security Number is the Taxpayer Identification Number of the trustor's revocable living trust, a change in ownership of the CD to the trustee of a revocable living trust prior to its maturity may be considered a withdrawal event that causes a penalty to be imposed. Obviously, the best time to convey title of the CD to the trustee of a revocable living trust is when the CD matures and a new CD can be issued in the name of the trustee.

Assignment of CD to Trustee Before Maturity Date

The maturity date of a CD may not coincide with the trustor's time frame for funding his or her revocable living trust. The trustor may be concerned that, in the event of physical disability or mental incapacity, a financial guardian may be appointed to manage a CD that is not in the trustor's revocable living trust. This concern can be alleviated with an Assignment of Certificate of Deposit Contract (see file "APP1304.DOC"). Even though the trustee may not be in evidence as the title holder on the face of the certificate, nevertheless the assignment evidences the trustor's intention and direction that the CD comprise the trust estate and, for all purposes, is to be administered by the trustee of the trustor's revocable living trust. If the CD has not matured and the trustor has received assurances from the bank that it cannot be reregistered on the face of the certificate until its maturity date, then the trustor can effect the Assignment of Certificate of Deposit Contract and either take it to the bank in person or mail it to the bank, along with a cover letter of instruction (see file "APP1305.DOC").

Initiating Change of Ownership for Matured CD

On the other hand, if the CD has matured and the trustor wants the bank to retitle it in the name of the trustee of the trustor's revocable living trust, the trustor can initiate the change of ownership process either by going to the bank in person to complete the required forms or by directing the bank in writing to effect the change of ownership to the trustee and mail to the trustor the required forms for his or her signature (see file "APP1306.DOC"). Whether the trustor goes to the bank in person or directs the bank in writing to effect a change in the ownership of a CD, the bank will require the same evidence of the existence of the revocable living trust as required for conveying the title to any other bank account to the trustee of a revocable living trust and the trustor's identity in view of the bank's federal mandate to know its customer.

FEDERAL DEPOSIT INSURANCE CORPORATION COVERAGE FOR ACCOUNTS IN REVOCABLE LIVING TRUSTS

The Federal Deposit Insurance Corporation (FDIC) insures deposits in some, but not all, banks and savings associations. Any person or entity can have FDIC insurance on a deposit. A depositor does not have to be a U.S. citizen or even a resident of the United States.

Federal Deposit Insurance protects only deposits payable in the United States. Deposits that are only payable overseas and not in the United States are not insured.

Revocable living trust documents can be many pages in length and vary greatly in their terms with a single term making a big difference in the amount of insurance coverage permitted. For this reason, it is difficult to make quick and easy statements about how accounts in revocable living trusts are insured. It is possible, however, to say that, if a depositor holds only one revocable living trust account in a bank or savings association, and no other kinds of accounts in that institution, the trust account will be insured for at least $100,000. However, under certain circumstances, such a trust account might be insured for far more than $100,000. Further, if the depositor (e.g., trustor) who set up the trust also holds individually owned funds in the same bank or savings association, under certain circumstances, the trust account might be insured separately from the individually owned funds of the trustor and for far more than $100,000.[15]

Qualifying Beneficiaries of a Revocable Living Trust

The separate insurance coverage of revocable living trust accounts is dependent upon the trustor's intention that, upon the trustor's death, the funds in the account "shall belong" to the trustor's spouse, children, grandchildren, parents, brothers or sisters; that is, *qualifying beneficiaries*.[16] This requirement does not necessarily mean that the funds must be distributed outright to the beneficiary upon the trustor's death. However, it does mean that the beneficiary must have a vested interest in his or her share of the trust funds (i.e., insured bank account) upon the trustor's death. Revocable living trust documents, however, frequently contain one or more contingencies that make it impossible for the beneficiary to have a vested interest in the trust. These are referred to as *defeating contingencies*. When a defeating contingency exists, the trust funds are insured as if they were the individually owned funds of the trustor.[17]

Examples

1. Mr. Jones has $100,000 in an individually owned bank account and $150,000 in the same bank in a revocable living trust account subject to a defeating contingency. The FDIC would treat the $150,000 as if it were the individually owned funds of Mr. Jones. The $150,000 would be added to the $100,000 for a total of $250,000, and Mr. Jones would be insured for only $100,000.[18]

2. Ruth establishes an account payable upon death to her nephew. The account would be insured as a single ownership account owned by Ruth.[19]

---

[15] Federal Deposit Insurance Corporation. *FDIC Legal Division Staff's Guidelines on the Insurance of Revocable Trust Accounts Including Living Trusts*. Memorandum dated April 1, 1999, issued as attachment to FDIC Financial Institution Letter (FIL)-4-2002 Re: Deposit Insurance Coverage of Revocable Trust Accounts (hereafter FDIC Guidelines), at 1.

[16] 12 C.F.R. 330.10(a) (1999). *Child* includes a biological child, adopted child, and stepchild of the owner. *Grandchild* includes a biological child, adopted child, and stepchild of any of the owner's children. *Parent* includes a biological parent, adoptive parents, and stepparents of the owner. *Brother* includes a full brother, half brother, brother through adoption, and stepbrother. *Sister* includes a full sister, half sister, sister through adoption, and stepsister [12 C.F.R. 330.10(e) (1999)].

[17] FDIC Guidelines, at 1; 12 C.F.R. 330.10(c) (1999).

[18] FDIC Guidelines, at 1.

[19] 12 C.F.R. 330.10(c) (1999).

3. Similarly, if Ben establishes an account payable upon his death to his wife, son and nephew (a nonqualifying beneficiary), two-thirds of the account balance would be eligible for POD coverage up to $200,000 corresponding to the two qualifying beneficiaries (i.e., Ben's wife and son). The amount corresponding to the nonqualifying beneficiary (i.e., the nephew) would be deemed to be owned by Ben in his single ownership capacity and insured accordingly.[20]

Conditions for FDIC Insurance Coverage

For purposes of obtaining FDIC insurance coverage for an account in the name of a trustee of a revocable living trust, it is important to remember that a revocable living trust account is an account owned by an individual—the trustor who establishes the trust or someone other than the trustor who is considered the owner under the grantor trust rules[21]—which shows an intention that the funds in the trust will belong to a designated beneficiary upon the account owner's death. In order to qualify for the special insurance coverage provided to revocable living trust accounts under the regulations,[22] the following two conditions must be met upon the death of the last trustor to die (e.g., married trustors under a joint revocable living trust agreement; nonmarried trustors under a joint revocable living trust). The same conditions would apply to a single trustor under a single revocable living trust:[23]

1. There must be one or more qualifying beneficiaries to benefit from the trust; that is, one or more of the beneficiaries upon the death of the last trustor to die must be the spouse, child, grandchild, parent, or sibling of a trustor; and

2. A qualifying beneficiary, at the death of the last trustor to die, must have a vested or noncontingent interest in the trust (such that the funds might be said to *belong* to the beneficiary). This "vested or noncontingent interest" for revocable living trusts is defined far differently from the "vested or noncontingent interest" irrevocable trust eligibility for FDIC insurance coverage and should not be confused with the FDIC definition of an irrevocable trust.

First Condition

The first condition—that, upon the death of the last trustor to die, there must be one or more qualifying beneficiaries of a trustor to benefit from the trust—is not difficult to satisfy. The separate insurance coverage of revocable living trust accounts is dependent upon a showing by the trustor that, at his or her death, the funds in the account "shall belong" to the trustor's spouse, child, grandchild, parent, brother or sister.[24]

Second Condition

The second condition, however—that a qualifying beneficiary must have a vested or noncontingent interest in the trust—is much more difficult to satisfy. The FDIC defines a *vested interest* in the context of a revocable living trust as:[25]

1. An interest to which no defeating contingency is attached; and

---

[20] Ibid.

[21] *See* I.R.C. §§ 671, 678, and 679.

[22] *See* 12 C.F.R. 330.10 (1999).

[23] FDIC Guidelines, at 5.

[24] FDIC Guidelines, at 5; 12 C.F.R. 330.10(a) and (b) (1999).

[25] FDIC Guidelines, at 5.

2. An interest where the person holding it has already been born and his or her identity ascertained upon the death of the last trustor to die (or upon the earlier default of the insured depository institution); and

3. An interest where, no later than upon the death of the last trustor to die, the trustee is instructed to set-aside a share of the trust principal for this particular beneficiary (even if that share might later change in size, for example, when another grandchild of the trustor is born after the death of the last trustor to die but before the funds are scheduled to be finally distributed; note, however, that this grandchild, because he or she was born after the death of the last trustor, would not be considered a qualifying beneficiary because of requirement (2)); and

4. An interest where the beneficiary either receives an outright distribution of his or her share of the trust estate upon the death of the last trustor to die or can invade the principal of his or her share to an unlimited extent at his or her demand from that time on or where the beneficiary will eventually take his or her share outright, provided that he or she survives for a given number of years or to a certain age, or, if he or she does not so survive, provided that his or her share in the trust will pass to his or her estate or his or her heirs at his or her death.

Married Trustors: Joint Revocable Living Trust

Assuming that a revocable living trust fulfills all of the above requirements, the following example shows how an account holding the funds of that trust would be insured.

Example

Davis and Libby, husband and wife, acting as co-trustors, establish a joint revocable living trust for the benefit of the survivor of them and their four children. Upon the death of the first of Davis or Libby to die, the revocable living trust is divided into a general power of appointment marital deduction trust (marital trust)[26] for the surviving spouse and a credit shelter trust (i.e., family trust; bypass trust) for their children. The revocable living trust defines how much of each spouse's estate is to be allocated to each of these subtrusts and provides that the surviving spouse will be able to invade the principal of the marital trust to an unlimited extent during his or her lifetime and, if he or she wishes, to dispose of the remainder (if any) of the marital trust by his or her Last Will (i.e., by exercising a general power of appointment). The revocable living trust also provides that, upon the death of the last of Davis or Libby to die, the trustee is to set aside a share of the family trust for each of their children then living. Each child is to receive his or her share outright when he or she attains the age of twenty-one years. If a child dies before attaining age twenty-one, his or her share of the trust estate is distributable to his or her estate or heirs.[27]

FDIC Insurance Coverage for Joint Revocable Living Trust

In determining the amount of FDIC insurance coverage available to a joint revocable living trust, it is important to remember that the amount of insurance coverage can change according to who is alive when the bank or savings association fails and according to whether the trust then in operation is a revocable or irrevocable trust. In this regard, upon the death of the last trustor to die, the joint revocable living trust becomes irrevocable. With respect to the trust established by Davis and Libby in the above example, while both Davis and

---

[26] *See* I.R.C. § 2056(b)(5).

[27] FDIC Guidelines, at 6.

Libby are alive, the trust is revocable.[28] Similarly, that part of the joint revocable living trust governing the surviving spouse's separate interest in the trust estate would continue to be revocable. Only the marital trust and the credit shelter trust would be irrevocable upon the first decedent trustor-spouse's death.

Accordingly, upon the death of Davis or Libby, the funds belonging to one or more of their four children (i.e., qualifying beneficiaries) will be insured in the amount of up to $100,000 in the aggregate as to each such named qualifying beneficiary, separately, from any other accounts of the owner or the beneficiaries.[29] Since, upon the death of the last of Davis or Libby to die, their four children are the qualifying beneficiaries, if the depository institution should fail while both Davis and Libby are alive, the trust would be insured for a maximum amount equal to:

$$\text{the number of trustors then living (2)} \times \text{the number of qualifying} \\ \text{beneficiaries then living (4)} \times \$100{,}000 = \$800{,}000^{30}$$

However, where a husband and wife establish a joint revocable living trust account, naming themselves as the sole beneficiaries of the trust, such account will not be insured as described above but will instead be insured in accordance with the joint account provisions of the FDIC regulations.[31] With respect to joint accounts, whether owned as JTWROS, as tenants in common, or as tenants by the entirety, each such account is insured separately from any individually owned deposit accounts maintained by the co-owners. For example, if Casey has an account titled in his own name and also is a joint owner of a qualifying joint account, Casey's interest in the joint account would be insured separately from the account titled in his individual name. Qualifying joint accounts in the names of both husband and wife which are comprised of community property funds are added together and insured up to $200,000, separately, from any funds deposited into accounts in their respective individual names.[32]

Observation

It is not likely that a husband and wife would create a joint revocable living trust naming themselves as the sole beneficiaries. As discussed in Chapter 2, Framework of a Revocable Living Trust,[33] in order for a revocable living trust to be legally valid and effective, a trustor-trustee should not be the sole beneficiary of the trust agreement. This is because, under common law, legal title and equitable title in the property conveyed to the trust would merge; and the trust would no longer exist.[34] If such a merger occurred, a declaration of trust would have no legal effect, unless a beneficiary other than the person (trustor-trustee) in legal title to the trust estate is in existence at the time of the trustor-trustee-beneficiary's death. Whenever the trustor is also the trustee and the primary beneficiary of a revocable living trust, a contingent beneficiary must be designated to succeed to the primary beneficiary's equitable interest in the trust estate.

---

[28] Ibid.

[29] 12 C.F.R. 330.10(a) (1999).

[30] 12 C.F.R. 330.10(d) (1999); FDIC Guidelines, at 6.

[31] 12 C.F.R. 330.10(d) and (f) (1999). *See* 12 C.F.R. 330.9 (1999).

[32] 12 C.F.R. 330.9(a) (1999).

[33] "Components of a Revocable Living Trusts, Preamble, Beneficiary" section, Chapter 2.

[34] *Blades v. Norfolk S. Ry.*, 224 N.C. 32, 29 S.E. 141, 151 (1944).

Death of First Spouse to Die

In the example of Davis and Libby, upon the death of the first of Davis or Libby to die, the trust remains revocable (because the surviving spouse still has the power to revoke it but only as to that part of the trust governing the surviving trustor-spouse's separate property interests in the trust estate); and the rules for revocable living trusts continue to apply. Once again, in the case of Davis and Libby, the qualifying beneficiaries who will have a vested interest in the trust estate upon the death of the last of Davis or Libby to die are their four children. Thus, if the depository institution should fail when the surviving trustor is alive, the revocable living trust would be insured for a maximum amount equal to the number of:

$$\text{trustors then living (1)} \times \text{the number of qualifying beneficiaries then living (4)} \times \$100{,}000 = \$400{,}000$$

Upon the subsequent death of the surviving spouse, the revocable living trust usually becomes irrevocable (because, usually, only the trustors have the power to revoke the trust; and, once they have died, that power is gone).[35]

Rules for Revocable Living Trust That Becomes Irrevocable Upon Death of Trustor

Because, upon the death of the last of Davis or Libby to die, the trust becomes irrevocable, the rules for irrevocable trusts apply. Under the rules for irrevocable trusts, in order for a beneficiary's interest to receive separate insurance coverage, the beneficiary need not be only the spouse, child, grandchild, parent, or sibling of the trustor. Instead, the rule for irrevocable trusts adds together all of the *noncontingent trust interests* of the same beneficiary which are created by the same trustor (in one or more irrevocable trusts) and insures that beneficiary's total interest that is derived from that trustor for up to $100,000 with such coverage remaining separate from that provided for other accounts maintained by the trustors, trustees, or beneficiaries of the irrevocable trust (or trusts) at the same insured depository institution. In addition, each trust interest in any irrevocable trust established by two or more trustors is deemed to be derived from each trustor pro rata to his or her actual contribution to the trust. All interests of an irrevocable trust which are deemed to be contingent are added together and insured for up to $100,000, separately, from the coverage for noncontingent interests. The FDIC defines a *noncontingent trust interest* as it applies to irrevocable trusts as a trust interest capable of determination without evaluation of contingencies, except for those covered by the present worth or life expectancy tables of the Code.[36]

Defeating Contingencies

In order for a revocable living trust to be covered by FDIC insurance, the trust must provide that at least one qualifying beneficiary will have a vested interest in the trust estate upon the death of the last trustor to die. One of the requirements of a vested interest is that there is no condition attached to it that would render it contingent.[37]

The Effect of a Defeating Contingency

One Trustor; One Revocable Living Trust

Assume that a trustor establishes a revocable living trust for his or her spouse and three children. Upon the trustor's death, should the trustor's spouse survive the trustor, the trust

---

[35] FDIC Guidelines, at 6.

[36] FDIC Guidelines, at 7; *see* 12 C.F.R. 330.13 (1999); 12 C.F.R. 330.1(1) (1999).

[37] FDIC Guidelines, at 7.

is divided into a marital trust for the surviving spouse and a family trust for the children. The revocable living trust defines how much is to be allocated to the marital trust and provides that, upon the trustor's death, the family trust is to be divided into equal shares for his or her children then living and immediately distributed outright to those children. However, the trust also provides that, if the trustor's probate estate should prove insufficient to pay for all of the legacies the trustor makes in his or her Last Will, the trustor's personal representative can require that the trustee use the funds in the family trust to pay for those legacies. This clause in the trust has the effect of making the children's interests contingent and, thus, ineligible for the special insurance coverage provided by the FDIC regulations.[38] As a result, those funds attributable to the children's interests would be insured like the trustor's individually owned funds; that is, they would be aggregated with any individually owned funds held by the trustor in the same institution, and the entire amount would be insured for up to $100,000. If the trustor holds no individually owned funds in that institution, those funds attributable to the children's interests would still be added together and insured for up to $100,000.[39]

Beneficiary Must Survive Trustor

Another *defeating contingency* occurs when the revocable living trust provides that a beneficiary must survive the trustor for a given period of time before the beneficiary's trust share is established. However, a requirement that the beneficiary must survive the trustor "for a single moment" before the beneficiary's trust share is established is not a defeating contingency. Assume that a trustor establishes a very simple trust for his or her spouse. Upon the trustor's death, the trustor wants everything in the trust to be distributed to his or her spouse outright but only if the spouse survives the trustor for nine months. As a result of this condition, the surviving spouse's interest in the trust is only contingent, since he or she will have a vested interest in the trust only if he or she survives the trustor-spouse for nine months.[40]

Observation

Requiring the surviving spouse to survive for nine months would cause loss of the unlimited estate tax marital deduction in the decedent trustor-spouse's gross estate for the value of the account passing to the surviving spouse.[41] Only a period of six months or less is permitted.[42]

Once an interest is vested, however, it is permissible to provide that a beneficiary will not receive an outright distribution of the funds until he or she attains a certain age or until he or she has survived for a given amount of time (e.g., until a child has attained the age of majority). Delaying the outright distribution of funds in this way does not prevent a qualifying beneficiary with a vested interest from receiving FDIC insurance coverage, provided that, if such a beneficiary does not survive for the given amount of time or reach the given age, the trust provides that his or her share will be distributable to his or her estate or heirs.[43]

---

[38] *See* 12 C.F.R. 330.10 (1999).

[39] FDIC Guidelines, at 7.

[40] Ibid.

[41] I.R.C. § 2056(b)(3).

[42] I.R.C. § 2056(b)(3)(A).

[43] FDIC Guidelines, at 7.

Trustee's Discretion to Distribute Income and Principal

A *defeating contingency* arises when a beneficiary's receipt of trust estate income and/or principal occurs only at the discretion of the trustee (where the beneficiary is not the trustee). In such case, because the beneficiary has no right to the funds, the nonexercise of the trustee's discretion may cause the beneficiary never to receive trust income and/or principal. Likewise, where the beneficiary is to receive payments only once he or she has satisfied a particular condition (e.g., received a college degree, or married, or upon some other condition), each of these conditions is a contingency that will defeat the FDIC insurance coverage of the beneficiary's trust estate interest.[44]

Nondefeating Contingencies

Some contingencies do not defeat the separate insurability of a beneficiary's revocable living trust estate interest. For instance, a condition that the beneficiary must survive the trustor for only a moment in order to benefit from the trust; a condition that inheritance, estate and other death taxes, last illness and funeral expenses, the decedent's debts and administrative expenses relating to the trustor's estate must be paid from the trust; a condition that attorney's fees, accountant's fees, and other expenses of operating the trust must be paid from the trust; and a condition that the marital trust (or family trust) will not be formed unless a spouse (or issue) survives the trustor for only a moment (e.g., a common disaster clause)—all of these conditions are expected provisions in a revocable living trust and can be included without being held to prevent the beneficiary from having a vested interest in the trust, provided the beneficiary does have a vested interest.[45]

Designating Qualifying and Nonqualifying Beneficiaries of a Revocable Living Trust

A trustor may create a revocable living trust that provides for qualifying and nonqualifying beneficiaries to receive the trust estate upon the death of the trustor. Such a trust may be established by married persons, each having his or her own separate trust, or by a trustor not married having his or her own revocable living trust, or by married trustors creating a joint revocable living trust. Assume that married persons establish a joint revocable living trust and fund it with $400,000 in an account in a depository institution for their son and their nephew. In such case, their son is a qualifying beneficiary; but their nephew is not. Unless stated otherwise in the revocable living trust, it is presumed that the husband and wife have contributed equal sums to the trust and that the beneficiaries will share equally in it. This means that the husband is viewed as having contributed $100,000 for the benefit of his son and $100,000 for the benefit of his nephew and that the wife is viewed as having contributed the same amounts for each beneficiary. Since the nephew is not a qualifying beneficiary, the $100,000 representing his beneficial interest derived from the husband will be combined with any individually owned funds of the husband which are held in the same institution; and the total amount will be insured for up to only $100,000. If the husband holds no individually owned funds in that institution, the nephew's beneficial interest derived from the husband will still be insured for up to $100,000. In the same way, the $100,000 representing the nephew's beneficial interest derived from the wife will be combined with any individually owned funds of the wife and insured in the aggregate to $100,000. As to the remaining amounts—the $100,000 held by the husband for the benefit of his son and the $100,000 held by the wife for the benefit of this same son—each amount

---

[44] Ibid.
[45] Ibid.

will be separately insured for up to the maximum amount of $100,000, or a total of $200,000 in insurance coverage for their son's interest in the trust.[46]

Married Trustors; Joint Revocable Living Trust; Trustors Sole Beneficiaries

Though unusual, a husband and wife may establish a joint revocable living trust under which they are the sole beneficiaries or the trust is established for the benefit of only one of them.[47] In this case, where the husband and wife are co-trustees and co-primary beneficiaries, and where the trust estate is distributable to the survivor trustor (primary beneficiary) upon the death of the first co-trustor to die, the FDIC considers this trust the equivalent of a joint account with right of survivorship. Therefore, while both trustor-spouses are alive, the account will be insured in accordance with the rules of the FDIC governing joint accounts up to a maximum of $200,000 (in aggregation with any other joint accounts owned by the husband and/or wife at the same depository institution).[48] This rule applies to trusts in the form of (1) husband (H) and wife (W) in trust for H and W; (2) H and W in trust for H; and (3) H and W in trust for W.[49]

However, a trust in the form of H in trust for W or W in trust for H is still eligible for FDIC insurance coverage, provided that the other requirements of FDIC regulations are met.[50] Thus, a simple POD account in the form of H in trust for W would be separately insured for up to $100,000; and a similar POD account in the form of W in trust for H would also be separately insured for up to $100,000, for a total of $200,000 of insurance coverage.[51]

DEPOSITS TO EXISTING ACCOUNTS

Ask Your Attorney

Each time I make a deposit of funds into a savings or checking account that is already titled in the name of the trustee of my revocable living trust, am I required to effect registration forms to add the additional funds to my trust?

Answer

No.

A bank account that is already registered in the name of the trustee of a revocable living trust operates much like a street name account with a stockbroker for securities. In this regard, each time the trustor makes a deposit of funds into the bank account, it is not necessary to register the deposit in the name of the trustee. This is because the account itself, which holds the funds deposited into it, is already titled in the name of the trustee of the revocable living trust.

---

[46] FDIC Guidelines, at 8.

[47] *See* discussion in "Observation" subsection of "FDIC Insurance Coverage for Joint Revocable Living Trust" section, this chapter.

[48] *See* discussion in "FDIC Insurance Coverage for Joint Revocable Living Trust" section, this chapter.

[49] FDIC Guidelines, at 8.

[50] *See* section 12 C.F.R. 333.10 (1999).

[51] FDIC Guidelines, at 8.

CHAPTER 14

Tangible and Intangible Personal Property

CLASSIFICATION OF TANGIBLE PERSONAL PROPERTY

Tangible Personal Property

Most people don't think of household furniture, fixtures and furnishings, wearing apparel, jewelry, personal effects, books, art objects, collections (e.g., stamp, coin, buttons, dolls, and so forth), sporting and recreational equipment, automobiles, equipment, machinery, tools, and all other property for personal use as tangible personal property. Yet, that is exactly what these items are. Tangible personal property is property that has physical form, is capable of being touched, seen, held, and is capable of being apprehensible by our minds.[1]

Intangible Personal Property

Intangible personal property is distinguished from tangible personal property in that it does not have a physical form that can be seen, touched, or held. For example, a contract, mortgage, trust deed, lease, securities, notes receivable, bank accounts, money market funds, certificates of deposit, or other assets that do not have physical form are considered intangible personal property. Such property is not apprehensible to our minds in the same way as is tangible personal property.

Gross Estate, Probate Estate and Nonprobate Estate

The value of tangible and intangible personal property is includable in a decedent's gross estate for federal estate tax purposes.[2] This property may also be included in a decedent's probate estate or nonprobate estate. Moreover, tangible and intangible personal property may be subject to a court-supervised financial guardianship during a person's lifetime.

Ownership of Tangible Personal Property

With these realities in mind, the ownership of all of a trustor's tangible personal property and most intangible personal property should be conveyed to the trustee of the trustor's revocable living trust. The ownership of tangible personal property may be evidenced by a certificate of ownership or registered title of ownership. Generally, whenever the ownership of tangible personal property is evidenced by a registered title, such registration is filed with the state that licenses the use of such property or a branch of the federal govern-

---

[1] Black, *Black's Law Dictionary*, at 1305.
[2] I.R.C. § 2031(a).

ment (e.g., airplanes and boats). Also, when the ownership of tangible personal property is evidenced by a certificate of ownership, such ownership may be registered with a state agency or a private organization. For example, a cattle brand may be registered with the General Recorder of Marks and Brands of the state in which the brand is registered.[3] An animal, such as a dog, may be registered with the American Kennel Club, in which case the owner of the animal is listed on the Registration Certificate. To record a transfer of the ownership of the dog in the records of the American Kennel Club, the owner must complete the transfer form on the backside of the Registration Certificate. Signatures of both the present owner and the new owner are required.

Regardless of the documentation evidencing title of ownership to an item of tangible personal property, the instructions pertaining to a transfer of ownership must be carefully followed. If the trustor is in doubt about how to transfer the ownership of an item of tangible personal property to the trustee of his or her revocable living trust when evidenced by a written document of ownership, inquiry should be made of the organization, agency, or appropriate authority issuing the instrument of ownership. The price of a telephone call or postage stamp to mail a letter or the time spent to send an e-mail may be the ounce of prevention necessary to avoid a pound of headache. On the other hand, many items of tangible personal property exist without any written documentation of ownership; for example, jewelry, art objects, hobby collections, and so forth, are just a few items that come to mind.

TITLE TO TANGIBLE PERSONAL PROPERTY

Title to tangible personal property is usually evidenced by a written instrument. For example, ownership of an automobile is usually evidenced by a title and registration filed with the state in which the vehicle is licensed. Motor homes, mobile homes, motorcycles, boats, boat trailers, airplanes, snowmobiles, and myriad other types of tangible personal property may require federal and/or state registration of title evidencing ownership. The title to all of these items of tangible personal property may be conveyed to the trustee of a revocable living trust.

Motor Vehicles

Ask Your Attorney

How is title to a motor vehicle conveyed to the trustee of a revocable living trust?

Answer

By completing an application for title and registration wherein the trustee of the revocable living trust is listed as the owner of the automobile.

Probate of Motor Vehicles

The title to a motor vehicle (e.g., automobile, motor home, motorcycle, and so forth), exclusive of nonlicensed off-the-road motor vehicles, which, as a rule, do not require registration, is evidenced by a certificate of title and registration. Before the trustor requests the requisite forms to convey title to a motor vehicle to the trustee of his or her revocable living trust, the trustor should inquire of his or her state's motor vehicle division whether probate of a motor vehicle titled in the trustor's individual name is necessary in the trustor's

---

[3] *See* e.g., Mont. Code Ann. § 81-3-101 (2001).

state of residence. If not, the trustor may determine not to convey the title to, say, his or her automobile, to the trustee of the trustor's revocable living trust. The trustor should beware, though, that, if the automobile is not titled in the name of the trustee of the trustor's revocable living trust, and absent a well-designed durable power of attorney, if the trustor becomes legally incapacitated during lifetime, a court-supervised financial guardianship may be necessary to manage or dispose of an automobile registered in the trustor's individual name, rather than in the name of the trustee of the trustor's revocable living trust.

Conveying Title of Motor Vehicle to Trustee

Generally, title to a registered motor vehicle can be conveyed to the trustee of a revocable living trust in one of two ways:

1. By completing the application for a new title on the backside of the original certificate of title; or
2. By requesting from the motor vehicles division of the state in which the vehicle is registered an application for title and registration or similar form.

Completing Application for Title and Registration

When completing an application for title and registration, the trustor must be certain to answer all questions completely and provide all information requested. Also, the trustor must be certain to name any security interest holder in the vehicle. Moreover, the trustor may be well advised to inform the security interest holder of the trustor's intention to convey the title to the vehicle to the trustee of the trustor's revocable living trust and obtain the security interest holder's consent to such a conveyance of title.

Registration Formats

Where it asks on the application for the name of the owner in which the title is to be registered, the following formats can be used to register the title to an automobile in the name of the trustee of a revocable living trust:

1. If the trustor is a single person and is both the trustor and trustee of his or her revocable living trust, the following format should be used: Eugene H. Curtis, Trustee under the Eugene H. Curtis Revocable Living Trust Agreement, dated February 15, 2003.
2. If the trustor is married, has a joint revocable living trust wherein both spouses are trustors and trustees, the following format should be used: Eugene H. Curtis and Theresa M. Curtis, co-Trustees under the Curtis Family Revocable Living Trust Agreement, dated February 15, 2003.
3. If the trustor is married, has a joint revocable living trust wherein both spouses are trustors and trustees, but each spouse has an automobile titled in his or her respective individual name, then the trustors would title their respective automobiles using the following format and identify that automobile on the appropriate schedule attached at the end of the trust agreement:[4] Eugene H. Curtis, co-Trustee under the Curtis Family Revocable Living Trust Agreement, dated February 15, 2003; or Theresa M. Curtis, co-Trustee under the Curtis Family Revocable Living Trust Agreement, dated February 15, 2003.
4. If the trustor is married but each spouse has a separate revocable living trust of which each spouse, respectively, is the trustee, and both spouses want ownership of

---

[4] *See* discussion in "Trust Property: Article III" section, Chapter 2.

an automobile that the spouses had owned with right of survivorship before effecting their respective revocable living trusts, then the spouses should apply for title to the automobile in their names as trustees of their respective trusts as tenants in common: Eugene H. Curtis, Trustee under the Eugene H. Curtis Revocable Living Trust Agreement, dated February 15, 2003 *and* Theresa M. Curtis, Trustee under the Theresa M. Curtis Revocable Living Trust Agreement, dated February 15, 2003. (It would not be unusual for a state department of motor vehicles to request the language "as tenants in common" be added to the above wording.)

Observation

The foregoing examples of title format can be used for any registered item of tangible personal property.

Registration Fee

In most cases, a registration fee is charged to retitle a motor vehicle. Some states may impose an excise tax on the value of the motor vehicle when a change in title is effected. Also, some states impose an additional charge if the application is not submitted to the motor vehicles division within a certain number of days from the date the application is signed. Whether the trustor must submit the application to the motor vehicles division in person or may mail it is a matter of state law. Regardless of a particular state's law in this regard, the trustor may be better served by delivering the application in person to the nearest branch of the motor vehicles division office.

Informing Automobile Insurance Company

Finally, the trustor should be certain to consult with a representative of his or her automobile insurance company to advise the insurance company that the title to the motor vehicle has been registered in the name of the trustee of a revocable living trust, even if the trustor is the trustee of the revocable living trust.

Beware Advice of Attorney to Not Convey Motor Vehicle Title to Trustee

A trustor should not be surprised if his or her attorney advises against conveying title to an automobile to the trustee of a revocable living trust. Absent state statute or case law prohibiting such a conveyance, an attorney may, nevertheless, argue that a state's small estate statute can obviate the need to convey ownership of the automobile to the trustee of a revocable living trust. The fallacy in such advise is that the small estate statutes of most states limit the dollar amount of tangible personal property which can be distributed from the decedent's probate estate without a formal probate proceeding (e.g., $50,000 in the State of Oregon).[5] Given the price of automobiles today, together with the value of other items of tangible personal property which may comprise the trustor's gross estate, such as the value of funds in bank accounts, and so forth, the statutory minimum amount may be easily exceeded. Therefore, it seems only prudent to convey the title to an automobile to the trustee of a revocable living trust.

Airplanes

Under federal law, it is unlawful to operate or navigate in the United States any civil aircraft eligible for registration that is not registered with the Federal Aviation Administration (FAA).[6] An aircraft may be registered only by and in the legal name of its owner.[7]

---

[5] *See* discussion in "Credit Unions" section, Chapter 13; *See also e.g.,* Or. Rev. Stat. § 114.515(2) (Loislaw 2001).

Ask Your Attorney

Can the trustee of a revocable living trust hold legal title to an aircraft?

Answer

Yes.

An individual, partnership, or a corporation may hold legal title to an aircraft as trustee of a revocable living trust.[8] To register an aircraft in the name of the trustee of a revocable living trust, the trustor should send a check or money order in the amount of five dollars (U.S. funds) made payable to the United States Treasury, along with the completed AC Form 8050-1, Aircraft Registration Application, and Bill of Sale signed in ink from the last registered owner (i.e., either from the previous owner who is not the trustor or from the trustor in his or her individual name to the trustee) to the FAA Aircraft Registration Branch. Use of an original Aircraft Registration Application, AC Form 8050-1, is required. Photocopied or computer-generated copies of this form are not acceptable for the registration of an aircraft. Aircraft Registration Applications may be obtained from the Aircraft Registration branch or the trustor's local FAA Flight Standards District Office. The applicant's physical location or physical address must be shown on the application if a post office box is entered as the mailing address. A trustee who holds legal title to an aircraft in trust must comply with the following requirements:[9]

1. Each trustee must be either a U.S. citizen or a resident alien.
2. The trustee must submit a certified true copy of the complete revocable living trust agreement to the FAA. The certificate of aircraft registration is issued to a single applicant as trustee or to several trustees jointly as co-trustees.
3. The trustee must submit an Affidavit of Acting Trustee for Aircraft Registration to the FAA to the effect that each beneficiary under the trust, including each person whose security interest in the aircraft is incorporated in the trust, is either a U.S. citizen or a resident alien (see file "APP1401.DOC"). 🖫 If any beneficiary under the trust, including a person whose security interest in the aircraft is incorporated in the trust, is not a U.S. citizen or resident alien, an affidavit from each trustee stating the trustee is not aware of any reason, situation, or relationship as a result of those persons who together would have more than 25 percent of the aggregate power to influence or limit the exercise of the trustee's authority.

According to FAA instructions, a "certified true copy" of the revocable living trust agreement must be a complete copy of the original, including all terms, signatures, and dates, to which is attached a signed statement that the copy has been compared with the original and that it is a true copy. The copy must be legible, reproducible, and printed on paper permanent in nature. The application, Affidavit of Acting Trustee for Aircraft Registration, and the copy of the revocable living trust agreement may either be mailed to the Federal Aviation Administration Aircraft Registry, Department of Transportation, P.O. Box 25504, Oklahoma City, OK 73125-0504, telephone (405) 954-3116 or delivered in person to the Registry at 6425 S. Denning, Registry Building, Room 118, Oklahoma City, OK 73169-6937, telephone (405) 954-4206; Fax: (405) 954-3548 and (405) 954-8068.

---

[6] 49 U.S.C. § 1401(a) (1988); 14 C.F.R. § 47.3(b)(1) (1979).

[7] 14 C.F.R. § 47.5(b) (1979).

[8] *See* 14 C.F.R. 47.7(c) (1979).

[9] 14 C.F.R. § 47.7(c) (1979).

Observations

1. The copy of the revocable living trust agreement submitted with the application can be returned to the applicant after it has been reviewed by a member of the FAA legal staff. A sample transmittal letter, requesting that the trust agreement not be made a matter of public record and that, upon completion of counsel's review of the trust agreement and issuance of the certificate of registration, the complete trust agreement be returned to the applicant, is provided in this book (see file "APP1402.DOC").

2. The trustor should be certain to effect and submit a change of ownership application with the trustor's state aeronautics division when title to an airplane is conveyed to the trustee of a revocable living trust. This application can be found on the backside of the title or certificate of registration issued by the state aeronautics division (see files "APP1403.DOC," "APP1404.DOC," and "APP1405.DOC").

3. Any one of the trustee registration formats previously discussed in this chapter may be used to convey the title to an airplane to the trustee of a revocable living trust.

Boats

Boat Size

The documentation required to convey ownership of a boat to the trustee of a revocable living trust depends on the size of the boat. Generally, if a boat is less than five net tons, it is ineligible to be documented with the U.S. Coast Guard.[10] Net tonnage is a measure of a vessel's volume. It should not be confused with the vessel's weight, which may also be expressed in tons. Most vessels more than twenty-five feet in length will measure five net tons or more. For information about how tonnage is determined, including a web-based interactive form that calculates tonnage, visit the U.S. Coast Guard Marine Safety Center's web site at the Marine Safety Center's Tonnage Page at *http://www.uscg.mil*.

U.S. Coast Guard Supplied Documents

For boats that are required to be documented,[11] the U.S. Coast Guard will provide the trustor with a package of documents that can be used to convey the title to an eligible vessel to the trustee of a revocable living trust. All trustees and all beneficiaries with an enforceable interest in the revocable living trust must certify that they are U.S. citizens and that they are eligible to document vessels. A list naming all trustees and beneficiaries with an enforceable interest under the trust must be attached to the Application for Initial Issue, Exchange, or Replacement of Certificate of Documentation; Redocumentation (Application for Documentation) (Department of Transportation U.S. Coast Guard Form CG-1258 (Rev. 9-97)). A Builder's Certification and First Transfer of Title form (Department of Transportation U.S. Coast Guard Form CG-1261 (Rev. 9-92)) and a Bill of Sale (Department of Transportation U.S. Coast Guard Form CG-1340 (Rev. 9-92)) must also be completed and attached to the Application for Documentation. All of these forms are available from the U.S. Department of Transportation, United States Coast Guard, National Vessel Documentation Center, 792 T J Jackson Drive, Falling Waters, WV 25419-9502. The forms may be requested in writing or by telephoning toll-free 1 (800) 799-8362 or (304) 271-2400 to request mail delivery of the forms

---

[10] 46 U.S.C. § 12102(a) (2002).

[11] Vessels of five net tons or more used in fishing activities on navigable waters of the U.S., or in the Exclusive Economic Zone (EEZ), or used in coastwise trade must be documented, unless the vessel is exempt from documentation. Coastwise trade is generally defined as the transportation of merchandise or passengers between points in the U.S. or the EEZ. In addition, towboats operating between points in the U.S. or EEZ or between the EEZ and points in the U.S. and dredges operating in the U.S. or the EEZ must be documented.

by leaving an address to which the forms may be mailed; or, to receive the forms instantaneously by "FAX on demand," telephone (304) 271-2405 *from a FAX telephone*; or the documentation forms may be downloaded at *http://www.uscg.mil/hq/gm/vdoc/genpub.htm*.

Vessel Subject to a Mortgage

If the trustor's vessel is subject to a mortgage, before the title to the vessel can be conveyed to the trustee of a revocable living trust (or any other owner), either a Satisfaction/Release of Mortgage or Claim of Lien (see file "APP1406.DOC") 📰 or Consent of the Mortgagee (Optional Application for Filing) (Department of Transportation U.S. Coast Guard Form CG-5542 (Rev. 9-92)) must be presented with the Application for Documentation. All of the properly completed forms should be mailed to the above address, along with a letter requesting that the legal title to the vessel be conveyed to the trustee of the trustor's revocable living trust (see file "APP1407.DOC"). 📰 Upon receipt of the requisite forms and existing certificate of documentation, if applicable, a new certificate of documentation will be issued evidencing the name of the trustee of the trustor's revocable living trust as the legal title holder to the vessel.

Other Boats

Most other boats are registered with a state marine board or agency, and the conveyance of title of such boats to the trustee of a revocable living trust is accomplished in a manner similar to retitling an automobile. In this regard, a certificate of title for a boat usually includes an application for new title or an endorsement section on the backside of the certificate of title. By following the instructions on the certificate of title, the title to the boat can be conveyed to the trustee of a revocable living trust.

Manufactured and Mobile Homes

Manufactured Home

Generally, a manufactured home is delivered on wheels to the real property upon which it is to be affixed. Usually, the wheels are removed for installation. Whether a manufactured home is deemed real property once it becomes fixed to the land or remains tangible personal property is a matter of state law. If it is deemed real property, then title to the home is conveyed to the trustee of a revocable living trust by deed. On the other hand, if the manufactured home retains its character as tangible personal property, then ownership may be conveyed to the trustee of a revocable living trust by an Assignment of Manufactured Home. Such an Assignment is prepared like any other Assignment of an untitled interest in tangible personal property. A complete description of the home should be included in the Assignment, and the legal description of the land upon which it is affixed should also be included. If the trustor is in doubt about the law governing such homes, inquiry should be made of local, county, and state offices regarding building codes and regulations pertaining to manufactured homes.

Mobile Home

A traditional mobile home usually remains on its wheels and is not affixed to the land. In many states, the ownership of a mobile home is evidenced by a title and registration filed with the state department of motor vehicles. A conveyance of ownership to the trustee of a revocable living trust is accomplished in the same manner as retitling an automobile.

UNTITLED TANGIBLE PERSONAL PROPERTY

Ownership of some types of tangible personal property may not be evidenced by a title of registration or a certificate of ownership.

Ask Your Attorney

How is ownership of untitled tangible personal property conveyed to the trustee of a revocable living trust?

Answer

The ownership of such property is conveyed to the trustee of a revocable living trust by effecting an Assignment of Tangible Personal Property.

This Assignment can be a general assignment wherein all of the trustor's tangible personal property is categorized (see files "APP1408.DOC" and "APP1409.DOC"). By categorizing all tangible personal property, the trustor does not have to list each and every item of such property the trustor owns. On the other hand, it may be advisable to effect a separate Assignment of Tangible Personal Property for items of significant monetary or sentimental value (e.g., art objects, jewelry, equipment, machinery, and tools, collections, and so forth) (see files "APP1410.DOC" and "APP1411.DOC").

Ask Your Attorney

Except for tangible personal property that I may want to separately assign to the trustee of my revocable living trust, do I have to effect an assignment each and every time I purchase an item of personal property?

Answer

No. The general assignments in the Appendices cover "all other items of tangible personal property for personal use which I (we) now own, have an interest in, or which I (we) may own, acquire, or have an interest in, in the future."

Observation

When the trustor assigns ownership of a specific item of tangible personal property to the trustee of a revocable living trust, it is important to provide a complete, accurate, and detailed description of the property so that it is clearly identifiable by the trustee and beneficiaries of the revocable living trust.

TITLED INTANGIBLE PERSONAL PROPERTY

The ownership of intangible personal property may be titled or untitled (i.e., registered or unregistered). Conveyance of an ownership interest in titled intangible personal property is accomplished by assignment or by completion of the requisite form of a particular state or federal government agency.

Copyrights, Trademarks, and Patents

Copyrights, trademarks, and patents are examples of titled intangible personal property rights, the ownership of which may be conveyed to the trustee of a revocable living trust.

Copyright

A copyright gives a person protection for an artistic or literary work. The ownership of a copyright, including any of the exclusive rights comprised in a copyright, may be transferred in whole or in part by any means of conveyance to the trustee of a revocable living trust.[12] A transfer of copyright ownership to the trustee of a revocable living trust is not valid unless an instrument of conveyance, or a note or memorandum of the transfer is in writing and signed by the owner of the rights conveyed or such owner's duly authorized agent.[13] Thus, if the trustor is legally incapacitated but has appointed an attorney-in-fact under a durable power of attorney, and the power of attorney provides that the attorney-in-fact can convey ownership of the principal's (trustor's) property to the trustee of a revocable living trust, the attorney-in-fact can convey the trustor's interest in a copyright to the trustee of a revocable living trust. A certificate of acknowledgment is not required for the validity of a transfer to the trustee but is prima facie evidence of the transfer, if:[14]

- In the case of a transfer effected in the United States, the certificate is issued by a person authorized to administer oaths (e.g., a Notary Public) within the United States; or
- In the case of a transfer effected in a foreign country, the certificate is issued by a diplomatic or consular officer of the United States or by a person authorized to administer oaths whose authority is proved by a certificate of such an officer.

An Assignment of Copyright to Trustee of a Revocable Living Trust should be used to convey ownership of a copyright to the trustee of a revocable living trust (see file "APP1412.DOC"). The Assignment should be submitted to the Register of Copyrights, Library of Congress, Washington, D.C. 20559 to be recorded.[15] Upon receipt of the Assignment and the requisite fee, the Register of Copyrights will record the Assignment and return it to the trustee with a certificate of recordation.[16]

Trademark

A trademark may be a word, symbol, design, or combination word and design, a slogan, or even a distinctive sound that identifies and distinguishes the goods or services of one party from those of another. If used to identify a service, a trademark can be called a service mark. Like a copyright, a federal registration is not needed for a trademark in order for a trademark to have protection; and a trademark may be used without obtaining a registration. However, certain federal statutory remedies against infringements are not available to the owner if a copyright or trademark is not registered.

Ownership of a trademark can be conveyed to the trustee of a revocable living trust by filing for recordation with the U.S. Department of Commerce, Patent and Trademark Office, Washington, D.C. 20231, together with the requisite fee, an Assignment of Trademark to Trustee of a Revocable Living Trust (see file "APP1413.DOC").

Patent

A patent gives protection for an invention. Ownership of a patent can be conveyed to the trustee of a revocable living trust by filing for recordation with the U.S. Department of Commerce, Patent and Trademark Office, Washington, D.C. 20231, together with the

---

[12] 17 U.S.C. § 201(d) (1988).
[13] 17 U.S.C. § 204(a) (1988).
[14] 17 U.S.C. § 204(b) (1988).
[15] 17 U.S.C. § 205(a) (1988).
[16] 17 U.S.C. § 205(b) (1988).

requisite fee, an Assignment of Patent to Trustee of a Revocable Living Trust (see file "APP1414.DOC").

Judgments

The value of a court-ordered judgment, awarded before the decedent's death, is included in the decedent's gross estate.[17] The trustor's interest in a judgment can be conveyed to the trustee of a revocable living trust by effecting an Assignment of Judgment to Trustee of a Revocable Living Trust and recording it in the county where the judgment was entered. The following information should be included in the Assignment (see file "APP1415 .DOC"):[18]

- Title of the cause;
- Name of the court in which the judgment was rendered;
- Date of the judgment;
- Name and address of the judgment debtor;
- Amount of the judgment;
- Rate of interest to which the judgment is subject or amount of interest due; and
- A statement as to whether any payments have been made on the judgment and, if so, when and in what amounts.

Oil and Gas Interests

An ownership interest in nonpublicly-traded oil and gas leases on federal government lands can be conveyed to the trustee of a revocable living trust. This can be accomplished by requesting from the U.S. Department of the Interior, Bureau of Land Management (BLM), a current Assignment of Record Title Interest in a Lease for Oil and Gas or Geothermal Resources form. Approval by the BLM of an assignment of record title to 100 percent of a portion of the leased lands creates separate leases of the retained and the assigned portions but does not change the terms and conditions of the lease anniversary date for purposes of payment of annual rental. A separate assignment form must be used for each lease assigned to the trustee of a revocable living trust. The completed assignment should be filed in the appropriate BLM office.

UNTITLED INTANGIBLE PERSONAL PROPERTY

Ownership of untitled intangible personal property may be evidenced by an instrument of ownership (e.g., promissory note, publishing contract, and so forth), or there may be no written instrument of ownership (e.g., crop retains, undocumented loans, and so forth).

Promissory Notes, Demand Notes, and Installment Notes

Ownership interest in a promissory note, demand note, or installment note representing funds that the trustor has loaned to an individual or entity can be conveyed to the trustee

---

[17] I.R.C. § 2031(a). See *Estate of Lennon v. Commissioner*, T.C. Memo 1991-360 (August 5, 1991) re valuation of judgments for federal estate tax purposes.
[18] Treas. Reg. § 20.6018-3(c)(5).

of a revocable living trust. The instrument used to effect such a conveyance is an Assignment (see files "APP1416.DOC," "APP1417.DOC," and "APP1027.DOC").

Undocumented Loans

It is not uncommon for a person to loan friends and family members money and not require the borrower to sign a note. The lender's ownership interest in such undocumented loans can be conveyed to the trustee of a revocable living trust by an Assignment of Loans to Family and Friends Not Evidenced by a Written Note (see file "APP1418.DOC").

Royalties under a Publishing Contract

The engagement of an author by a publisher is considered a personal relationship. Thus, under most publishing contracts or agreements, the rights granted to the author are not assignable; nor may the obligations imposed be delegated without the prior written consent of the publisher. However, the author usually is permitted to assign any royalties due the author without the publisher's consent. Nevertheless, if the trustor is an author, before effecting an assignment of the trustor's interests under a publishing contract to the trustee of a revocable living trust, the trustor would be well advised to obtain the publisher's permission to do so (see file "APP1419.DOC"). Once the trustor has obtained the consent, then he or she can effect an Assignment of Author's Interest in Publishing Contract to the trustee of his or her revocable living trust (see file "APP1420.DOC").

Crop Retains

Oftentimes, farmers belong to growers cooperatives (co-op) to which they either sell their crops or grow certain crops for the co-op. As a rule, when the co-op buys the farmer's crop, a certain percentage of the purchase price is held by the co-op in the form of *crop retains* from five to seven years before being distributed to the farmer. Accordingly, the value of these retains is included in the decedent farmer's gross estate, even though the farmer may not have actually received the retains.[19] Incidentally, the value of such crop retains is considered income in respect of a decedent.[20] Since such retains generally are not evidenced by a certificate of ownership, about the only way to register them in the name of the trustee of a revocable living trust is to direct the co-op in writing to do so (see file "APP1421.DOC").

MISCELLANEOUS INTANGIBLE PERSONAL PROPERTY

In addition to publicly-traded securities and U.S. Government obligations, closely-held business interests, bank accounts, retirement plan benefits, life insurance and annuities, and the kinds of intangible personal property discussed in this chapter, the trustor may own other kinds of intangible personal property. As a general rule, the title to such property may be conveyed to the trustee of a revocable living trust by the trustor assigning his or her interest in the asset to the trustee. In all cases, general assignment language should be used in the assignment instrument. When designing such an assignment, it is important to include a complete, accurate, and detailed description of the property so that it is clearly identifiable by the trustee and beneficiaries of the revocable living trust. The sample

---

[19] I.R.C. § 2031(a).
[20] I.R.C. § 691(c)(1)(A).

assignments included in this book are by no means exhaustive, but they are representative of a wide array of intangible personal property that may be transferred to the trustee of a revocable living trust.

SAFE DEPOSIT BOX

Ownership of Safe Deposit Box

If the trustor rents a safe deposit box in a financial institution, the rental agreement should be in the name of the trustee of the trustor's revocable living trust. An existing rental agreement can be amended to list the trustee as the *owner* of the safe deposit box. If, for some reason, the existing rental agreement cannot be amended, a new rental agreement may be effected wherein the trustee is listed as the renter of the box. A successor trustee should also be listed on the rental agreement, should the succession of trustees under the trust agreement be insufficient to permit a successor trustee access to the box if the initial trustee becomes legally incapacitated or dies. If the trustor is not the trustee of his or her revocable living trust, then the trustor's signature should be added to the rental agreement as an authorized deputy of the trustee. As an authorized deputy of the trustee, the trustor can access the safe deposit box without the trustee being present.

Value of Contents Included in Gross Estate

The value of the contents of a safe deposit box is included in the estate of the person who is in title to the property items in the box. Nevertheless, IRS estate tax examiners require proof of ownership for purposes of excluding such items from a decedent's gross estate. In this regard, IRS estate tax examiners are admonished:

> that possession of property carries with it a presumption of ownership, and this presumption is not overcome by a bare allegation to the effect that other people claim the property. In other words, the burden of proof is upon the claimants to show that they are the actual owners of property in the possession of the decedent.[21]

Ask Your Attorney

If the trustor is not the trustee of his or her revocable living trust, does this mean that the value of the contents of a trustor's safe deposit box will be included in the trustee's gross estate, if the trustee predeceases the trustor?

Answer

No, not as a general rule. The value of the contents of the safe deposit box would not necessarily be included in the trustee's gross estate to the extent it can be shown that the contents of the safe deposit are, in fact, the property of the trustor—not the trustee. The trustee would only be holding title to the box in a fiduciary capacity for the benefit of the trustor.

---

[21] Commerce Clearing House, ed. *Audit Technique Handbook for Estate Tax Examiners* (IRM 4350). In *Audit* Vol. II of *Internal Revenue Manual* (IRM) § 333(6). 3 vols. Commerce Clearing House, Inc., December 16, 1987 (hereafter IRM 4350).

Cash in a Safe Deposit Box

When cash is found in the decedent's safe deposit box, it must be included in the gross estate, unless the decedent's personal representative or trustee can prove clearly that such cash belonged to someone else. The problem cases for IRS estate tax examiners usually involve loose cash in a safe deposit box claimed by a member of the decedent's family or funds contained in envelopes (sealed or unsealed) with the name of an individual written thereon by the decedent. The claimant usually alleges a gift by the decedent or a deposit of funds to be held in the box by the decedent as a favor to the owner. Usually, to resolve any uncertainty the IRS estate tax examiner might have as to the rightful ownership of the loose cash, he or she will request sworn affidavits from all interested parties.[22] Obviously, a claimant is in a much better position if the personal representative, trustee, or attorney for either, can testify that, prior to the opening of the safe deposit box, it was known that the property in question was owned by the claimant and not the decedent.[23] Finally, if the trustor keeps large sums of cash in a safe deposit box, and the trustee of his or her revocable living trust is in title as the renter of the safe deposit box, then, if the trustor becomes legally incapacitated, the trustee can access these monies for the trustor's benefit without a proper court of jurisdiction having to appoint a court-supervised financial guardian of the monies.

Observation

> If the cash in the envelope exceeds in value the gift tax annual exclusion amount, the trustor should be careful about alleging that the cash was a gift from the decedent to the trustor; the IRS estate tax examiner might inquire as to whether a United States Gift (and Generation-Skipping Transfer) Tax Return (Form 709) was filed by the decedent.

---

[22] IRM 4350 § 830(3).
[23] IRM 4350 § 830(4).

CHAPTER 15

Qualified and Nonqualified Retirement Plans

QUALIFIED RETIREMENT PLANS

Qualified retirement benefits are those provided by employer-sponsored plans satisfying the requirements of I.R.C. Section 401. Such plans include stock bonus, pension, or profit-sharing plans, including 401(k) plans, which are for the exclusive benefit of employees or their beneficiaries.[1] With respect to the minimum distribution requirement for qualified plan benefits,[2] all stock bonus, pension, and profit-sharing plans qualified under I.R.C. Section 401(a) and annuity contracts described in I.R.C. Section 403(a) are subject to the required minimum distribution rules.[3] Under I.R.C. Section 403(b)(10), annuity contracts or custodial accounts described in I.R.C. Section 403(b) are subject to required minimum distribution rules.[4] Under I.R.C. Section 408(a)(6) and 408(b)(3), IRAs (including, for some purposes, Roth IRAs under section 408A) are subject to the required minimum distribution rules.[5] Finally, under I.R.C. Section 457(d)(2), certain deferred compensation plans for employees of tax-exempt organizations or state and local government employees are subject to required minimum distribution rules.[6]

It is not the purpose of this chapter to discuss the complex requirements of qualified retirement plan benefits or the intricate income tax issues relative to the selection of beneficiaries of plan benefits. Instead, the focus in this chapter is on whether the trustee of a revocable living trust can be the owner and beneficiary of the trustor's qualified plan benefits.

Most private qualified retirement plans in the United States are trust fund plans wherein the trust agreement is between the employer and a trustee. In effect, the employer is the *trustor* of the qualified retirement benefit plan trust; and the employee, who is the participant in the retirement plan, is the *beneficiary*. The employee is not the owner of any portion of a qualified retirement plan trust.[7] Nevertheless, the present value of the qualified

---

[1] I.R.C. § 401(a).

[2] I.R.C. § 401(a)(9), and Treas. Reg. §§ 1.401(a)(9)-1 and 1.401(a)(9)-2 through 1.401(a)(9)-9 (April 17, 2002).

[3] *See* Treas. Reg. § 1.401(a)(9)-1 and §§1.401(a)(9)-2 through 1.401(a)(9)-9 (April 17, 2002) for the distribution rules applicable to these plans.

[4] *See* Treas. Reg. §1.403(b)-3 for the distribution rules applicable to these annuity contracts or custodial accounts.

[5] *See* Treas. Reg. §1.408-8 (April 17, 2002) for the distribution rules applicable to individual retirement plans and Treas. Reg. §1.408A-6 for the distribution rules applicable to Roth IRAs under I.R.C. § 408A.

[6] Treas. Reg. § 1.401(a)(9)-1, A-1 (April 17, 2002).

[7] I.R.C. § 402(b)(3).

plan benefit may be included in the decedent employee's gross estate for purposes of the federal estate tax.[8] Thus, the trustee holds legal title to the retirement fund assets; and the employee holds a beneficial or equitable interest in the retirement plan benefits.[9] Notwithstanding that the employer is the *trustor* for purposes of a qualified plan benefit trust, in this chapter, the employee is the trustor for purposes of a revocable living trust.

VALUE OF QUALIFIED RETIREMENT PLANS INCLUDED IN GROSS ESTATE

As a general rule, the value of qualified retirement plan benefits is included in the decedent employee's gross estate.[10] Whether the value of qualified retirement plan benefits is included in the value of the decedent employee's probate estate is determined by the identity of the designated beneficiary. If the decedent employee's estate is the designated beneficiary of such benefits, those benefits may be subject to probate; whereas, if the same benefits are payable to the trustee of a revocable living trust (or to any other individual), probate may be avoided. Furthermore, if an employee designates his or her estate beneficiary of qualified plan benefits, then, for purposes of the required minimum distributions under I.R.C. Section 401(a)(9), as set forth in the Treasury Regulations,[11] the employee will be treated as having no designated beneficiary.[12]

TRUSTEE AS OWNER OF QUALIFIED RETIREMENT PLANS

About the only real reason why an employee would want to know if the trustee of a revocable living trust can be the owner of his or her qualified retirement plan benefits during the employee's lifetime is so, if the employee becomes physically disabled or mentally incapacitated and cannot elect the form of benefit payout when he or she retires or designate the beneficiary of the retirement plan benefit upon the employee's death, the trustee may do so on the employee's behalf.

Ask Your Attorney

Can the trustee of a revocable living trust be in legal title to an employee's interest in qualified retirement plan benefits?

Answer

No.

A revocable living trust is not a *qualified trust* within the meaning of I.R.C. Section 401(a).[13] Therefore, the trustee of a revocable living trust cannot be the legal owner of an

---

[8] I.R.C. § 2039(a).

[9] *See* Treas. Reg. § 1.402(b)-1(d)(2).

[10] I.R.C. § 2039(a).

[11] Treas. Reg. §§ 1.401(a)(9)-1 through 1.401(a)(9)-9 (April 17, 2002).

[12] Treas. Reg. § 1.401(a)(9)-4, A-3 (April 17, 2002).

[13] I.R.C. § 402(c)(8)(A).

employee's qualified retirement plan benefits, even if the employee is the trustee of his or her own revocable living trust.[14] Moreover, conveyance of the employee's interest in the qualified retirement plan to the trustee of a revocable living trust would be in violation of the requirement that a qualified trust must not permit the assignment or alienation of the plan benefits.[15] The transfer of an employee's interest in a qualified retirement plan benefit to the trustee of a revocable living trust would constitute a *prohibited transaction*.[16] As a prohibited transaction, such a transfer may subject the fair market value of the employee's entire interest in the plan to income tax in the year in which the prohibited transaction occurs.[17]

TRUSTEE AS BENEFICIARY OF QUALIFIED RETIREMENT PLANS

The trustee of a revocable living trust can be named beneficiary of a decedent employee's qualified retirement plan benefit. In this regard, the beneficiaries of the revocable living trust (and not the trust itself) will be treated as the designated beneficiaries of the employee under the qualified plan for purposes of determining the required minimum distributions under I.R.C. Section 401(a)(9).[18] The Code defines the term *qualified retirement plan* to include IRAs, among other types of retirement plans.[19] Rules similar to those governing the distributions from qualified plans governed by I.R.C. Section 401(a)(9) apply to distributions from IRAs.[20] For purposes of required minimum distributions from a qualified plan, the term *designated beneficiary* means any individual designated as the beneficiary by the employee.[21] Accordingly, the trustee of a revocable living trust may also be the named beneficiary of a trustor's IRA.

Requirements to Name Trustee as Beneficiary

As a general rule, only an individual may be a designated beneficiary of an employee's qualified plan benefit.[22] A person's estate cannot be a designated beneficiary because it is not an individual.[23] Similarly, a revocable living trust itself may not be the designated beneficiary, even though the trust is named as a beneficiary. However, if certain requirements are met, required minimum distributions made to the trustee of a revocable living trust are treated as paid to the beneficiaries of the trust with respect to the trust's interest in the employee's qualified plan. All beneficiaries of the revocable living trust, with respect to the trust's interest in the employee's qualified plan, are treated as designated beneficiaries of the employee under the plan for purposes of determining the required minimum distributions under I.R.C. Section 401(a)(9).[24] The requirements that must be met are:[25]

---

[14] I.R.C. §§ 401(a), 401(a)(2), 401(a)(13)(A), 402(b)(3), and 4975(c)(1)(D) and (e)(2)(A); Treas. Reg. § 1.401-1(a)(3).

[15] I.R.C. § 401(a)(13)(A).

[16] I.R.C. § 4975(c)(1)(D) and (E), 4975(e)(2)(A), and 4975(e)(2)(G)(iii).

[17] *See* Treas. Reg. § 53.4941(e)-1(b)(2)(ii).

[18] I.R.C. § 401(a)(9)(E); Treas. Reg. § 1.401(a)(9)-4, A-5(a) (April 17, 2002).

[19] I.R.C. § 4974(c).

[20] I.R.C. § 408(a)(6).

[21] I.R.C. § 401(a)(9)(E).

[22] Treas. Reg. § 1.401(a)(9)-4, A-1 and A-3 (April 17, 2002).

[23] Treas. Reg. § 1.401(a)(9)-4, A-3 (April 17, 2002).

[24] Treas. Reg. § 1.401(a)(9)-4, A-5(a) (April 17, 2002).

[25] Treas. Reg. § 1.401(a)(9)-4, A-5(b) (April 17, 2002).

- The revocable living trust is a valid trust under state law, or would be, but for the fact that there is no corpus.
- The trust is irrevocable, or will, by its terms, become irrevocable, upon the death of the employee.
- The beneficiaries of the revocable living trust who are beneficiaries with respect to the trust's interest in the employee's benefit are identifiable from the trust instrument.
- The employee provides the required documentation to the plan administrator.

Documentation Required for Distributions Commencing before Employee's Death

In order to satisfy the documentation requirement for distributions required under I.R.C. Section 401(a)(9) commencing before the employee's death, the employee must either:

1. Provide to the plan administrator a copy of the revocable living trust instrument and agree that, if the trust is amended at any time in the future, the employee will, within a reasonable time, provide to the plan administrator a copy of each such amendment;[26] or

2. Provide to the plan administrator a list of all beneficiaries of the trust (including contingent and remaindermen beneficiaries with a description of the conditions on their entitlement sufficient to establish that the spouse is the sole beneficiary) for purposes of I.R.C. Section 401(a)(9). In addition, the employee must certify that, to the best of the employee's knowledge, this list is correct and complete and that (a) the trust is valid under state law; (b) the trust is irrevocable, or will, by its terms, become irrevocable, upon the death of the employee; and (c) the beneficiaries of the trust who are beneficiaries with respect to the trust's interest in the employee's benefit are identifiable from the trust instrument. Furthermore, the employee agrees to provide the plan administrator corrected certifications to the extent that an amendment to the trust changes any information previously certified and agrees to provide a copy of the trust to the plan administrator upon demand.[27]

Documentation Required for Distributions Commencing after Employee's Death

In order to satisfy the documentation requirement for required distributions commencing after the employee's death, by October 31 of the calendar year immediately following the calendar year in which the employee died, the trustee of the trust must either:

1. Provide the plan administrator with a final list of all beneficiaries of the trust (including contingent and remaindermen beneficiaries with a description of the conditions on their entitlement) as of September 30 of the calendar year following the calendar year of the employee's death; certify that, to the best of the trustee's knowledge, this list is correct and complete and that the following are satisfied as of the date of the employee's death: (a) the trust is valid under state law; (b) the trust is irrevocable, or will, by its terms, become irrevocable, upon the death of the employee;

---

[26] Treas. Reg. § 1.401(a)(9)-4, A-6(a)(1) (April 17, 2002).
[27] Treas. Reg. § 1.401(a)(9)-4, A-6(a)(2) (April 17, 2002).

and (c) the beneficiaries of the trust who are beneficiaries with respect to the trust's interest in the employee's benefit are identifiable from the trust instrument. In addition, the trustee must agree to provide a copy of the trust to the plan administrator upon demand;[28] or

2. Provide the plan administrator with a copy of the actual trust document for the trust that is named as a beneficiary of the employee under the plan as of the employee's date of death.[29]

Observation

If a trust fails to satisfy the rule[30] permitting the beneficiaries of the trust, and not the trust itself, to be treated as the employee's designated beneficiaries solely because the trust documentation was not provided to the plan administrator by October 31 of the calendar year following the calendar year in which the employee died, and such documentation is provided to the plan administrator by October 31, 2003, the beneficiaries of the trust will be treated as designated beneficiaries of the employee under the plan for purposes of determining the required minimum distributions under I.R.C. Section 401(a)(9).[31]

Relief for Discrepancy between Trust and Employee Certifications

If required minimum distributions are determined based on the information provided to the plan administrator in certifications or the trust itself, a plan will not fail to satisfy the minimum required distributions merely because the actual terms of the trust are inconsistent with the information in those certifications or the trust previously provided to the plan administrator. This is true only if the plan administrator reasonably relied on the information provided and the minimum required distributions for calendar years after the calendar year in which the discrepancy is discovered are determined based on the actual terms of the trust. For purposes of determining the amount of the excise tax under I.R.C. Section 4974, the required minimum distribution is determined for any year based on the actual terms of the trust in effect during the year.[32]

Irrevocable Subtrusts

With respect to the requirement that the revocable living trust must be irrevocable, if, upon the trustor's death, a subtrust (e.g., a qualified terminable interest property (QTIP) trust, general power of appointment marital deduction trust, credit shelter trust, and so forth) of the revocable living trust which receives the distribution from the qualified plan is irrevocable, then the revocable living trust itself satisfies the requirement that it is irrevocable.[33] Regarding the third requirement, a designated beneficiary need not be specified by name in the plan or by the employee in order to be a designated beneficiary, so long as the indi-

---

[28] Treas. Reg. § 1.401(a)(9)-4, A-6(b)(1) (April 17, 2002).

[29] Treas. Reg. § 1.401(a)(9)-4, A-6(b)(2) (April 17, 2002).

[30] Treas. Reg. § 1.401(a)(9)-4, A-5 (April 17, 2002).

[31] Treas. Reg. § 1.401(a)(9)-1, A-2(c) (April 17, 2002).

[32] Treas. Reg. § 1.401(a)(9)-4, A-6(c) (April 17, 2002).

[33] Treas. Reg. § 1.401(a)(9)-4, A-5(b)(2) (April 17, 2002); see Priv. Ltr. Ruls. 9012009 (November 6, 1989), 9037048 (June 20, 1990), and 9119067 (February 14, 1991).

vidual who is to be the beneficiary is identifiable under the plan as of the employee's required beginning date or as of the date of the employee's death.[34] In other words, it is sufficient that the identity of the revocable living trust itself is identifiable under the plan.[35] Furthermore, the trust may identify beneficiaries as a class, rather than by name. In such case, the members of a class of beneficiaries capable of expansion or contraction will be treated as being identifiable if it is possible to identify the class member with the shortest life expectancy.[36]

Except as provided in the Treasury Regulations,[37] the employee's designated beneficiary is determined based on the beneficiaries designated as of the date of the employee's death who remain beneficiaries as of September 30 of the calendar year following the calendar year of the employee's death. Consequently, except as provided in Treasury Regulations,[38] any person who was a beneficiary as of the date of the employee's death, but is not a beneficiary as of that September 30 (e.g., because the person receives the entire benefit to which the person is entitled before that September 30), is not taken into account in determining the employee's designated beneficiary for purposes of determining the distribution period for minimum required distributions after the employee's death. Accordingly, if a person disclaims entitlement to the employee's benefit, pursuant to a disclaimer that satisfies I.R.C. Section 2518 by that September 30, thereby allowing other beneficiaries to receive the benefit in lieu of that person, the disclaiming person is not taken into account in determining the employee's designated beneficiary.[39]

EMPLOYEE DIES BEFORE COMMENCEMENT OF DISTRIBUTIONS

Ask Your Attorney

I am a single person. If the trustee of my revocable living trust is the beneficiary of my qualified plan benefits and I die before distributions commence from the plan, can those distributions be made to the designated successor beneficiary of the revocable living trust based on the successor beneficiary's life expectancy?

Answer

Yes.

Generally, the Code requires that the employee's *interest* in a qualified plan be distributed beginning not later than the required beginning date over the life of such employee or over the lives of such employee and a designated beneficiary (or over a period not extending beyond the life expectancy of such employee or the life expectancy of such employee and a designated beneficiary).[40] In order to satisfy the life expectancy rule, if the named beneficiary is the trustee of the decedent employee's revocable living trust, distributions must commence to the designated beneficiary(ies) under the trust on or before the end of

---

[34] Treas. Reg. § 1.401(a)(9)-4, A-4(a) (April 17, 2002).

[35] *See* Treas. Reg. § 1.401(a)(9)-4, A-5(a) (April 17, 2002).

[36] Treas. Reg. § 1.401(a)(9)-4, A-1 (April 17, 2002).

[37] Treas. Reg. § 1.401(a)(9)-4, A-4(b) and §1.401(a)(9)-6T (April 17, 2002).

[38] Treas. Reg. § 1.401(a)(9)-6T (April 17, 2002).

[39] Treas. Reg. § 1.401(a)(9)-4, A-4(a) (April 17, 2002).

[40] I.R.C. § 401(a)(9)(A)(ii) and § 401(a)(9)(B)(iii); Treas. Reg. § 1.401(a)(9)-3, A-1(a) (April 17, 2002).

the calendar year immediately following the calendar year in which the employee died.[41] The designated beneficiary's remaining life expectancy is determined using the beneficiary's age as of the beneficiary's birthday in the calendar year immediately following the calendar year of the employee's death. In subsequent calendar years, the applicable distribution period is reduced by one for each calendar year that has elapsed after the calendar year immediately following the calendar year of the employee's death.[42]

If the qualified plan benefits are payable to multiple designated beneficiaries under the decedent employee trustor's revocable living trust, then the designated beneficiary with the shortest life expectancy will be the designated beneficiary for purposes of determining the applicable distribution period.[43] However, the separate account rules[44] are not available to beneficiaries of a trust with respect to the trust's interest in the employee's benefit.[45] If the beneficiary of the revocable living trust named as beneficiary of the employee's interest is another trust (e.g., a QTIP trust, general power of appointment marital deduction trust, credit shelter trust, irrevocable life insurance trust, and so forth) the beneficiaries of the other trust will be treated as being designated as beneficiaries of the first trust and, thus having been designated by the employee under the plan for purposes of determining the distribution period, provided that the requirements of the Treasury Regulations[46] are satisfied with respect to such other trust in addition to the trust named as beneficiary.[47]

EMPLOYEE DIES AFTER COMMENCEMENT OF DISTRIBUTIONS

Ask Your Attorney

If the trustee of my revocable living trust is named beneficiary of my qualified plan benefits and I die after distributions commence from the plan but before my entire interest in the plan is distributed to me, can those distributions be made to the successor beneficiary of the revocable living trust based on the successor beneficiary's life expectancy?

Answer

No.

If distribution of the employee's interest has begun and the employee dies before his or her entire interest has been distributed to him or her, the remaining portion of such interest must be distributed at least as rapidly as under the distribution method being used as of the date of the employee's death.[48] The amount required to be distributed for each distribution calendar year following the calendar year of the employee's death generally de-

---

[41] Treas. Reg. § 1.401(a)(9)-3, A-3(a) (April 17, 2002).

[42] Treas. Reg. § 1.401(a)(9)-5, A-5(c)(1) (April 17, 2002); Priv. Ltr. Rul. 9012009 (November 6, 1989). Life expectancies for purposes of determining required minimum distributions under I.R.C. Section 401(a)(9) must be computed using the Single Life Table in Treas. Reg. § 1.401(a)(9)-9, A-1 and the Joint and Last Survivor Table in Treas. Reg. § 1.401(a)(9)-9, A-3 (Treas. Reg. § 1.401(a)(9)-5, A-6) (April 17, 2002).

[43] Treas. Reg. § 1.401(a)(9)-5, A-7(a)(1) (April 17, 2002).

[44] Treas. Reg. § 1.401(a)(9)-8, A-2 (April 17, 2002).

[45] Treas. Reg. § 1.401(a)(9)-4, A-5(c) (April 17, 2002).

[46] Treas. Reg. § 1.401(a)(9)-4, A-5(b) (April 17, 2002).

[47] Treas. Reg. § 1.401(a)(9)-4, A-5(d) (April 17, 2002).

[48] I.R.C. § 401(a)(9)(B)(i); Treas. Reg. § 1.401(a)(9)-2, A-5 (April 17, 2002).

pends on whether a distribution is in the form of distributions from an individual account under a defined contribution plan or annuity payments under a defined benefit plan. The Treasury Regulations[49] describe the method of determining the required minimum distribution in accordance with the Code[50] from an individual account. The Treasury Regulations[51] also describe the method of determining the required minimum distributions with respect to annuity payments from a defined benefit plan or an annuity contract.[52] In effect, if the employee elected to receive distributions over his or her life expectancy, then, such distributions will continue to the trustee of the revocable living trust for the benefit of the successor beneficiary based on the life expectancy of the employee (trustor).[53]

Contingent and Successor Beneficiaries

The attorney, in designing a revocable living trust of which the trustee is to be named beneficiary of the employee trustor's qualified retirement plan benefit, must use caution in the manner in which the beneficiary's entitlement to the interests in the trust are defined (i.e., how the benefits are to be paid to the beneficiary(ies)) and in the design of the trust (i.e., any subtrust) which will receive the qualified plan benefits.[54] If a beneficiary is considered a *contingent* beneficiary, rather than a *successor* beneficiary, because such beneficiary's entitlement to an employee's benefit after the employee's death is a *contingent right*, such contingent beneficiary is, nevertheless, considered to be a beneficiary for purposes of determining whether a person other than an individual is designated as a beneficiary (which would result in the employee being treated as having no designated beneficiary)[55] under the rules for determining which designated beneficiary has the shortest life expectancy.[56]

Example

Trustor established IRA accounts at a bank and named the trustee of her revocable living trust beneficiary of the IRA accounts. Upon trustor's death, the primary beneficiaries of the trust are trustor's two minor grandchildren. If either such beneficiary should die before attaining the age of thirty years, the entire amount of the IRAs will be distributed to the

---

[49] Treas. Reg. § 1.401(a)(9)-5 (April 17, 2002).

[50] I.R.C. § 401(a)(9)(B)(i).

[51] Treas. Reg. § 1.401(a)(9)-6T (April 17, 2002).

[52] Treas. Reg. § 1.401(a)(9)-2, A-5 (April 17, 2002).

[53] I.R.C. § 401(a)(9)(B)(ii); Priv. Ltr. Rul. 9119067 (February 14, 1991).

[54] *See* Thomas W. Houghton and Harvey B. Wallace II, "Using Trusts Effectively in Retirement Planning, Part II: Planning and Drafting Suggestions," 16 *Probate & Property* 34 (November/December 2002) (hereafter Houghton and Wallace II, "Using Trusts Effectively in Retirement Planning, Part II") for an excellent discussion of the issues involved in naming the trustee of a trust the beneficiary of qualified plan benefits, whether such trust be a revocable living trust or a testamentary trust, and examples of beneficiary form designations and suggested provisions for conduit and nonconduit subtrusts. For additional reading, *see* Chris Cline, "They're Finally Here! IRA and Qualified Plan Distribution Rules Under the Final Regulations," 27 *Tax Management Estates, Gifts and Trusts Journal* 190 (July-August 2002); Lee A. Snow, "Final IRA Distribution Regulations Offer New Planning Opportunities," in 3 *Financial and Estate Planning*, Commerce Clearing House, Inc., Chicago, Ill., ¶ 32,441, at 27,335; Clark M. Blackman II and Karen S. Gerstner, "Estate Planning: Should a Trust be the Beneficiary of Your IRA?" 24 *American Association of Individual Investors Journal* 31 (October 2002).

[55] *See* Treas. Reg. § 1.401(a)(9)-4, A-3 (April 17, 2002).

[56] Treas. Reg. § 1.401(a)(9)-5, A-7(b) (April 17, 2002).

other beneficiary. However, if both such beneficiaries die before the age of thirty years, the trust, in its entirety, will be distributed to contingent beneficiaries who are much older. As of December 31[57] of the year following trustor's death, the oldest contingent beneficiary named in the trust was sixty-seven and was born July 21, 1933. The IRS ruled that the required minimum distributions from the IRA accounts must be based on the life expectancy of the oldest beneficiary, including contingent beneficiaries, named in the trust—not the oldest life expectancy of trustor's two minor grandchildren who are the primary beneficiaries of the trust.[58]

On the other hand, the Treasury Regulations provide that a person will not be considered a beneficiary for purposes of determining who is the beneficiary with the shortest life expectancy, or whether a person who is not an individual is a beneficiary, merely because the person could become the *successor* to the interest of one of the employee's beneficiaries after that beneficiary's death. However, this rule does not apply to a person who has any right (including a contingent right) to an employee's benefit beyond being a mere potential successor to the interest of one of the employee's beneficiaries upon that beneficiary's death. Thus, for example, if the first beneficiary has a right to all income with respect to an employee's individual account during that beneficiary's life and a second beneficiary has a right to the principal but only after the death of the first income beneficiary (any portion of the principal distributed during the life of the first income beneficiary to be held in trust until that first beneficiary's death), both beneficiaries must be taken into account in determining the beneficiary with the shortest life expectancy and whether only individuals are beneficiaries.[59] If the individual beneficiary whose life expectancy is being used to calculate the distribution period dies after September 30 of the calendar year following the calendar year of the employee's death, such beneficiary's remaining life expectancy will be used to determine the distribution period without regard to the life expectancy of the subsequent beneficiary.[60] However, if a subtrust under the revocable living trust is a *conduit* or *pass-through* trust that requires that all trust proceeds, or at least the required minimum distributions from the employee's qualified plan be distributed to the subtrust by year-end, then the life expectancy of any contingent beneficiary(ies) will not be considered.[61]

Examples

1. Full-Time Employment, Inc. (Employer) maintains a defined contribution plan (Plan). Faris (Employee), an employee of Employer, died in 2003 at the age of fifty-five, survived by spouse, Kayelle, who was fifty years old. Prior to Faris's death, Employer had established an account balance for Faris in Plan. Faris's account balance is invested only in productive assets. Faris named the trustee of his revocable living trust (Trust) as the beneficiary of all amounts payable from his account in Plan after his death. A copy of the

---

[57] Prop. Treas. Reg. § 1.401(a)(9)-1 Q&A, C-3 provided that the exception provided in I.R.C. § 401(a)(9)(B)(iii) would be satisfied if the distributions to a nonspouse beneficiary commenced on or before December 31 of the calendar year immediately following the year in which the employee dies. This same rule applies under the Treasury Regulations finalized April 17, 2002 [Treas. Reg. § 1.401(a)(9)-3, A-3(a) [April 17, 2002]).

[58] Priv. Ltr. Rul. 200228025 (April 18, 2002) (note that this private letter ruling was dated one day after the final treasury regulations became effective; namely, April 17, 2002).

[59] Treas. Reg. § 1.401(a)(9)-5, A-7(c)(1) (April 17, 2002).

[60] Treas. Reg. § 1.401(a)(9)-5, A-7(c)(2) (April 17, 2002).

[61] Treas. Reg. § 1.401(a)(9)-5, A-7(c) Examples 1 and 2.

Trust and a list of the trust beneficiaries were provided to the plan administrator of Plan by October 31 of the calendar year following the calendar year of Faris's death. As of the date of Faris's death, the Trust was irrevocable and was a valid trust under the laws of the state of Faris's domicile. Faris's account balance in Plan was includable in Faris's gross estate under I.R.C. Section 2039.

Under the terms of the Trust, all trust income is payable annually to Kayelle, and no one has the power to appoint Trust principal to any person other than Kayelle. Faris's children, who are all younger than Kayelle, are the sole remainder beneficiaries of the Trust. No other person has a beneficial interest in the Trust. Under the terms of the Trust, Kayelle has the power, exercisable annually, to compel the trustee to withdraw from Faris's account balance in the Plan an amount equal to the income earned on the assets held in Faris's account in the Plan during the calendar year and to distribute that amount through the Trust to Kayelle. The Plan contains no prohibition on withdrawal from Faris's account of amounts in excess of the annual required minimum distributions under I.R.C. Section 401(a)(9). In accordance with the terms of the Plan, the trustee of the Trust elects, in order to satisfy I.R.C. Section 401(a)(9), to receive annual required minimum distributions using the life expectancy rule in I.R.C. Section 401(a)(9)(B)(iii) for distributions over a distribution period equal to Kayelle's life expectancy. If Kayelle exercises the withdrawal power, the trustee must withdraw from Faris's account under the Plan the greater of the amount of income earned in the account during the calendar year or the required minimum distribution. However, under the terms of the Trust, and applicable state law, only the portion of the Plan distribution received by the trustee equal to the income earned by Faris's account in the Plan is required to be distributed to Kayelle (along with any other trust income).

Because some amounts distributed from Faris' account in the Plan to the Trust may be accumulated in the Trust during Kayelle's lifetime for the benefit of Faris's children, as remaindermen beneficiaries of the Trust, even though access to those amounts are delayed until after Kayelle's death, Faris's children are *contingent beneficiaries* of Faris's account in the Plan in addition to Kayelle; and Kayelle is not the sole designated beneficiary of Faris's account. Thus, the designated beneficiary used to determine the distribution period from Faris's account in the Plan is the beneficiary with the shortest life expectancy. Kayelle's life expectancy is the shortest of all the potential beneficiaries of the Trust's interest in Faris's account in the Plan (including remainder beneficiaries). Thus, the distribution period for purposes of I.R.C. Section 401(a)(9)(B)(iii) is Kayelle's life expectancy. Because Kayelle is not the sole designated beneficiary of the Trust's interest in Faris's account in the Plan, the special rule in I.R.C. Section 401(a)(9)(B)(iv) is not available; and the annual required minimum distributions from the account to the Trust must begin no later than the end of the calendar year immediately following the calendar year of Faris's death.[62]

2. The facts are the same as Example 1, except that the Trust provides that all amounts distributed from Faris's account in the Plan to the trustee while Kayelle is alive will be paid directly to Kayelle upon receipt by the trustee of the Trust.

In this case, Kayelle is the sole designated beneficiary of Faris's account in the Plan for purposes of determining the designated beneficiary under I.R.C. Section 401(a)(9)(B)(iii) and (iv). No amounts distributed from Faris's account in the Plan to the Trust are accumulated in the Trust during Kayelle's lifetime for the benefit of any other beneficiary. Therefore, the residuary beneficiaries (i.e., Faris's children) of the Trust are mere potential successors to Kayelle's interest in the Plan. Because Kayelle is the sole beneficiary of the Trust's interest in Faris's account in the Plan, the annual required minimum

---

[62] Treas. Reg. § 1.401(a)(9)-5, A-7(c)(3) Example 1 (April 17, 2002).

distributions from Faris's account to the Trust must begin no later than the end of the calendar year in which Faris would have attained age 70½, rather than the calendar year immediately following the calendar year of Faris's death.[63]

Observations

1. The foregoing example illustrates the importance of the attorney having a thorough understanding of his or her client's wishes with respect to whether income distributed from the qualified plan may be accumulated by the trustee. Whether such income may be accumulated or must be distributed to the designated beneficiary determines whether the remainder beneficiaries are regarded as *contingent beneficiaries* or *successor beneficiaries*. If the remainder beneficiaries are considered *successor beneficiaries*, then the designated beneficiary may be entitled to defer distribution of the required minimum distributions until the end of the calendar year in which the decedent employee would have attained age 70½ but for his or her death.

2. The distinction, then, between a *contingent* beneficiary and a *successor* beneficiary for purposes of determining the beneficiary with the shortest life expectancy seems to be in whether the primary beneficiary (e.g., Kayelle in the above examples) is entitled to all of the proceeds (i.e., both principal and income) of the decedent employee trustor's qualified retirement plan benefit. Under such circumstances, the remainder beneficiaries (e.g., Faris's children) would be considered *successor* beneficiaries—not *contingent* beneficiaries. Apparently, based on the above examples, if any part of the decedent employee trustor's qualified retirement plan benefit may be accumulated for remainder beneficiaries, then, the beneficiary with the shortest life expectancy of all the beneficiaries is the measuring life for determining minimum required distributions. Under such circumstance, the remainder beneficiaries (e.g., Faris's children) would be considered *contingent* beneficiaries—not *successor* beneficiaries. Thus, it is important that the attorney designing the revocable living trust understand this distinction and be able to explain it to the trustor so as to be able to maximize deferment of income tax on the distributions from qualified retirement plan benefits.

Naming Trustee Beneficiary when Trustor Is Married

Ask Your Attorney

I am married, and I'm a participant in my employer's qualified retirement plan. Can I name the trustee of my revocable living trust as beneficiary of the plan distributions in the event of my death?

Answer

Yes.

However, in this regard, if the trustor's spouse is presently designated beneficiary of the trustor's qualified retirement plan, then his or her consent may be required in order for the trustor to designate the trustee of his or her revocable living trust beneficiary of qualified plan distributions. Likewise, if the trustor is married and has just become a participant

---

[63] Treas. Reg. § 1.401(a)(9)-5, A-7(c)(3) Example 2 (April 17, 2002).

in a qualified retirement plan but has not named a beneficiary, the trustor's spouse's consent may be required to designate the trustee of the trustor's revocable living trust beneficiary of the qualified plan.[64] This rule applies even if the trustor's spouse is the trustee of the trustor's revocable living trust. This rule does not apply to nonqualified retirement plan benefits and IRAs.

TAX-FREE ROLLOVER OF DECEDENT TRUSTOR'S QUALIFIED PLAN BENEFIT BY SURVIVING SPOUSE

Ask Your Attorney

If I designate the trustee of my revocable living trust beneficiary of my qualified retirement plan, can my surviving spouse effect a tax-free rollover of the benefit to an IRA?

Answer

As a general rule, yes.[65]

Ask Your Attorney

Can the trustee of a revocable living trust, on behalf of a surviving spouse, effect a tax-free rollover of his or her decedent spouse employee's qualified plan or IRA?

Answer

As a general rule, no.[66]

However, in Private Letter Rulings,[67] the IRS has held that the co-trustee of a revocable living trust who was the decedent employee's spouse can effect a tax-free rollover of his or her decedent spouse's IRA into his or her own IRA, even though the trustee of the revocable living trust is named beneficiary of the decedent employee's IRA. In each case, however, the decedent employee's surviving spouse was the sole beneficiary of the revocable living trust with respect to the decedent employee's IRA. According to the Service, because the surviving spouse would ultimately acquire the IRA proceeds "from and by reason of the death of [his or] her [spouse]," the IRA would not be an inherited IRA defined in I.R.C. Section 408(d)(3)(C)(ii). In accordance with the Treasury Regulations, the Service determined that the decedent employee's spouse is to be treated as the IRA payee and beneficiary under I.R.C. Section 408(d)(1) and 408(d)(3). Thus, the surviving spouse may

---

[64] I.R.C. § 417(a)(2); Treas. Reg. § 1.417(e)-1(b)(1) (July 19, 2000).

[65] Priv. Ltr. Ruls. 8928082 (April 24, 1989), 8927042 (April 11, 1989) (relative to surviving spouse's community property interest in decedent spouse's qualified retirement plan benefit payable to the trustee of a revocable living trust); 200242044 (July 23, 2002) and 200245055 (n.d.) (both of these Priv. Ltr. Ruls. were issued after Treas. Reg. § 1.408-8, A-5(a) became effective on April 17, 2002).

[66] Treas. Reg. § 1.402(c)-2, A-12(b) (April 21, 2000); I.R.C. § 402(c)(4); Treas. Reg. § 1.408-8, A-5(a) (April 17, 2002).

[67] Priv. Ltr. Ruls. 200242044 (July 23, 2002) and 200245055 (n.d.).

elect to treat the IRA proceeds as his or her own and roll them over into his or her own IRA, even though the proceeds were received initially by the surviving spouse as co-trustee of the decedent employee's revocable living trust.[68]

Surviving Spouse Must Be Sole Beneficiary

As a general rule, only a surviving spouse can effect a tax-free rollover of a decedent spouse's qualified retirement plan benefit into an IRA (eligible retirement plan) by reason of the decedent spouse's death.[69] The trustee of a revocable living trust may be named beneficiary of a lump-sum distribution from a qualified retirement plan, and the decedent employee's surviving spouse may be entitled to effect a tax-free rollover of the distribution.[70] However, when naming the trustee of a revocable living trust beneficiary of a lump-sum distribution, special attention must be directed to what control, if any, the surviving spouse has over income distributions of the revocable living trust and the manner in which the surviving spouse, as a beneficiary of the revocable living trust, is entitled to the lump-sum distribution.[71]

In this regard, if the surviving spouse is the sole beneficiary of the revocable living trust that receives the decedent spouse's lump-sum distribution from the qualified retirement plan and, pursuant to the terms of the revocable living trust, retains control over the distribution of the trust income, the surviving spouse can effect a tax-free rollover of the lump-sum distribution to his or her own IRA.[72] In such a situation, if the lump-sum distribution received by the trustee of the revocable living trust, as a result of the decedent spouse's death, is distributed from the trust to the surviving spouse and, thereafter, contributed by the surviving spouse to his or her rollover IRA all within sixty days following the date of the distribution from the decedent spouse's qualified plan, then the surviving spouse is deemed to have effected a tax-free rollover of the lump-sum distribution.[73]

Surviving Spouse as Trustee

It is beneficial if the surviving spouse is the successor trustee of the decedent spouse's revocable living trust. If the decedent spouse has named the trustee of his or her revocable living trust beneficiary of qualified plan proceeds, and his or her surviving spouse is not the trustee of the decedent spouse's revocable living trust and cannot become a trustee under its provisions or cannot have any authority to allocate assets between or among subtrusts created under the revocable living trust for the benefit of the surviving spouse, then the distribution of the qualified retirement plan proceeds to the revocable living trust may not be considered paid to the surviving spouse. Accordingly, such a distribution may be includable in the surviving spouse's gross income.[74] In this regard, I.R.C. Section 402(c)(9) requires that a qualified plan distribution be made to a surviving spouse.

---

[68] Priv. Ltr. Rul. 200242044 (July 23, 2002).

[69] I.R.C. § 402(c)(4) and (9); Treas. Reg. § 1.402(c)-2, A-12(a) and (b) (April 21, 2000); Treas. Reg. § 1.408-8, A-5(a) (April 17, 2002).

[70] Priv. Ltr. Ruls. 8928082 (April 24, 1989), 8927042 (April 11, 1989), 200242044 (July 23, 2002), and 200245055 (n.d.).

[71] *See* Priv. Ltr. Rul. 9232041 (May 15, 1992).

[72] Priv. Ltr. Ruls. 200242044 (July 23, 2002), 200245055 (n.d.), and 9232041 (May 15, 1992) (defined-benefit pension plan).

[73] Priv. Ltr. Ruls. 200245055 (n.d.), 200242044 (July 23, 2002), 9232041 (May 15, 1992) (defined-benefit pension plan), 8928082 (April 24, 1989) and 8927042 (April 11, 1989).

[74] Priv. Ltr. Ruls. 9303031 (October 29, 1992) and 9145041 (August 16, 1991).

Qualified Plan Benefit Passing through a Third Party

Generally, if a decedent's qualified plan or annuity contract assets pass through a third party (e.g., an estate or a trust) and are then distributed to the decedent's surviving spouse, such spouse is treated as acquiring them from the third party and not from the decedent. Thus, under such circumstances, a surviving spouse would not be eligible to rollover either the qualified plan or annuity contract proceeds into his or her own IRA. However, where neither the trustee nor the decedent's personal representative has any discretion as to the allocation of assets to a trust for the benefit of the surviving spouse, and the surviving spouse can appoint those trust assets to himself or herself, such assets are eligible to be transferred via a trustee-to-trustee transfer to an IRA maintained in the name of the surviving spouse.[75] Moreover, the Service acknowledges the reality that, if the surviving spouse is the sole beneficiary of the qualified plan under a revocable living trust, then the surviving spouse receives "from and by reason of the death of [his or] her [spouse]" the qualified plan benefit and "may elect to treat those [qualified plan benefits or] IRA proceeds as [his or] her own and roll them over into [his or] her own IRA.[76]

Observation

The distribution of only a portion of a lump-sum distribution from a qualified plan to the decedent employee's surviving spouse precludes the surviving spouse from effecting a tax-free rollover of the undistributed qualified plan proceeds. Accordingly, such proceeds are includable in the surviving spouse's gross income.[77] Thus, the surviving spouse is precluded from effecting a tax-free rollover of a portion of a lump-sum distribution from a qualified plan payable to the trustee of a revocable living trust.

Financial Security for Surviving Spouse

For a variety of reasons, a surviving spouse may not want the responsibility of managing the decedent spouse's assets, including qualified plan benefits. Naming the trustee of a revocable living trust beneficiary of qualified plans and IRAs can protect the surviving spouse's use and enjoyment of those distributions and eliminate the need for a court-supervised financial guardianship if he or she is physically disabled or mentally incapacitated at the time of the trustor's death or thereafter. If the trustor or his or her attorney or tax adviser is uncertain whether the trustee of the trustor's revocable living trust or the trustor's surviving spouse should be named beneficiary of qualified plans and IRAs, then the safest choice is to name the trustor's spouse as the beneficiary.

Of course, the trustor can provide a fallback position in the revocable living trust agreement by using disclaimers. One of two approaches may be used:[78]

1. Designate the employee trustor's spouse or the marital deduction trust as the primary beneficiary of the qualified plan and IRA benefits and provide that, if the spouse predeceases the employee trustor or to the extent that the spouse (or the trustee of the revocable living trust) disclaims the benefits, the benefits will pass to the credit shelter trust as the successor beneficiary; or

[75] Priv. Ltr. Rul. 9533042 (May 25, 1995).
[76] Priv. Ltr. Rul. 200242044 (July 23, 2002).
[77] Priv. Ltr. Rul. 9145041 (August 16, 1991).
[78] Houghton and Wallace II, "Using Trusts Effectively in Estate Planning, Part II," at 38.

2. Designate the credit shelter trust under the employee trustor's revocable living trust as primary beneficiary and provide that, to the extent the trustee of the revocable living trust disclaims the benefits, the benefits will pass to the surviving spouse (or to a subaccount of the marital deduction trust that the trustee may, in turn, disclaim in favor of the surviving spouse) as successor beneficiary. The exercise of such a disclaimer by the trustee with the qualified plan benefits passing directly to the surviving spouse, and not to a subaccount of the marital deduction trust, would enable the trustor's surviving spouse to effect a tax-free rollover of the decedent trustor's retirement plan benefits into his or her own IRA, thus enabling the surviving spouse to defer the income taxation of the benefits until the surviving spouse's required beginning date. This would also permit the surviving spouse to name his or her children or a credit shelter trust under his or her own revocable living trust for the children as beneficiaries upon the subsequent death of the surviving spouse, further extending the required minimum distributions over the life expectancy of the oldest child.[79]

Observation

The surviving spouse may be the trustee of the marital deduction and/or credit shelter trust.[80] The trustor can obtain from his or her employer or retirement plan administrator the requisite beneficiary forms to name the trustee of his or her revocable living trust beneficiary of the qualified retirement plan. The beneficiary forms will need to be customized to mirror the provisions of the marital deduction and credit shelter trusts so that the plan administrator or trustee or custodian of the IRA will be informed as to the manner in which distributions from the qualified plans are to be made to the trustee of the revocable living trust.[81]

Recommendation

Even though the trustee of a revocable living trust may be named beneficiary of qualified plans and IRAs for a designated beneficiary, the trustor should carefully review all available beneficiary options before naming the trustee of a revocable living trust beneficiary of such benefits. The Treasury Regulations that became effective April 17, 2002,[82] are unnecessarily complex. Hopefully, the IRS will provide additional guidance, either in the form of amendments to these regulations or temporary regulations, to assist practitioners in advising qualified plan participants on how to proceed with respect to naming the trustee of a revocable living trust beneficiary of qualified plans and IRAs. Since this continues to be an evolving area of the law, it is important that qualified plan participants consult with their attorney and tax adviser to know the most recent changes proposed or finalized by the IRS; *caution* is the watchword in these regards.

---

[79] Houghton and Wallace II, "Using Trusts Effectively in Estate Planning, Part II," at 36.

[80] For a discussion of the surviving spouse acting as the trustee of the credit shelter trust, *see* Moy, 2, *A Practitioner's Guide to Estate Planning*, § 28.06[C], at 28-88 through 28-90.

[81] *See* Houghton and Wallace II, "Using Trusts Effectively in Estate Planning, Part II," at 39-41 for sample beneficiary designation provisions.

[82] Treas. Reg. §§ 1.401(a)(9)-1 through 1.401(a)(9)-9 (April 17, 2002) and 1.408-8 (April 17, 2002).

TRUSTEE AS INTERMEDIARY PAYEE OF QUALIFIED RETIREMENT PLAN

A recurring concern of individuals with respect to qualified retirement plans is how to exercise *ownership* rights if they become physically disabled or mentally incapacitated. Except for empowering an attorney-in-fact under a durable power of attorney to stand in one's shoes in such matters, the only other available option is for the trustee of a revocable living trust to be in-title to such benefits. However, in this regard, the trustee of a revocable living trust cannot be the legal owner of qualified retirement plans, even if the employee participant is the trustee of his or her own revocable living trust;[83] but this does not necessarily preclude the trustee from being an intermediary payee of such benefits upon the employee trustor attaining his or her required beginning date. However, during the trustor's employment, he or she would have to rely on the authority of his or her attorney-in-fact under a durable power of attorney to make decisions affecting such benefits (i.e., electing the form of benefit payout and selecting the designated beneficiary to receive the benefit(s) upon the employee participant's death) if the employee trustor were to become physically disabled or mentally incapacitated.

Avoiding Court-Supervised Financial Guardianship

Ask Your Attorney

Upon my retirement, can I name the trustee of my revocable living trust the intermediary payee of my qualified retirement plan benefits?

Answer

Unfortunately, the Code, Treasury Regulations, Revenue Rulings, and IRS Letter Rulings do not seem to directly answer this question. Furthermore, the term intermediary payee *is not defined in the Code.*

One reason a trustor might want to name the trustee of his or her revocable living trust the intermediary payee of his or her qualified retirement plan upon the trustor attaining his or her required beginning date is to avoid a court-supervised financial guardianship of the benefits if he or she were to become physically disabled or mentally incapacitated. Inherent in this question is the issue of whether the trustor can effect a tax-free rollover of a lump-sum distribution from a qualified plan benefit or IRA[84] if the trustee of a revocable living trust is involved as an intermediary payee. Certainly, the trustor's identity as the primary beneficiary under the revocable living trust and distributee of the qualified plan benefits, within the meaning of I.R.C. Section 402, should not be called into question. Though the Code, Treasury Regulations, and Private Letter Rulings do not specifically address this issue, nevertheless they do lend support to a *yes* response to the previous question.

Distributions from Employee's Qualified Retirement Plan

Apparently, no restriction exists which would prevent the trustor from naming the trustee of his or her revocable living trust as the intermediary payee of distributions from his or her

---

[83] I.R.C. §§ 401(a), 401(a)(2), 401(a)(13)(A), 401(c)(8)(A), 402(b)(3), and 4975(c)(1)(D) and (e)(2)(A); Treas. Reg. § 1.401-1(a)(3).

[84] I.R.C. § 402(f)(2).

qualified retirement plan upon the trustor attaining his or her required beginning date. The Code specifically provides that a qualified trust must distribute the employee's entire interest in the qualified retirement plan to such employee not later than the required beginning date,[85] or "beginning not later than the required beginning date … over the life of such employee or over the lives of such employee and a designated beneficiary (or over a period not extending beyond the life expectancy of such employee or the life expectancy of such employee and a designated beneficiary)."[86] This rule can be applied to the trustor under a revocable living trust who elects to receive distributions from a qualified retirement plan based on his or her life expectancy and, upon death, directs such distributions to be made to the trustee of a revocable living trust over the trustor's life expectancy (had the trustor survived) for the benefit of the beneficiary of the trust.[87]

Income from Qualified Retirement Plan Taxable to Distributee

Code Section 402 provides generally that the amount actually distributed to any distributee by a qualified retirement plan "shall be taxable" to the distributee in the year in which the amount is distributed as provided under I.R.C. Section 72.[88] With respect to a revocable living trust, if the employee trustor is the primary beneficiary and is to receive, under the terms of the trust agreement, all trust estate income and distributions of principal (i.e., a *conduit trust*), and the trustee is required by the terms of the trust agreement to distribute income to or for the benefit of the trustor, then the trustor should, within the meaning of I.R.C. Section 402, be considered the distributee who is taxable on the receipt of qualified retirement plan proceeds.[89] Since a revocable living trust acts as a conduit through which all items of income, deductions, and credits against the tax of the trust are attributable to the trustor,[90] the proceeds of a qualified retirement plan payable to the trustee of a revocable living trust for the benefit of the employee trustor pass through the trustee to the trustor.[91] Similarly, because distributions from a qualified retirement plan which a trustor receives based on his or her life expectancy and which are distributed to the trustee of a revocable living trust upon the trustor's death can continue to be distributed to the trustee over the trustor's life expectancy (had the trustor survived) for the benefit of the beneficiary of the trust, such distributions should also be allowed to the employee trustor under the provisions of the revocable living trust during his or her lifetime as an intermediary payee.[92]

Distributee Other than Employee or Employee's Spouse

Both the Code and the Treasury Regulations provide that a *distributee* other than the employee or the employee's surviving spouse cannot effect an eligible tax-free rollover distribution to an eligible retirement plan.[93] The operative word is *distributee*. In this regard and

---

[85] I.R.C. § 401(a)(9)(A)(i). The term *required beginning date* means April 1 of the calendar year following the later of (a) the calendar year in which the employee attains age $70\frac{1}{2}$; or (b) the calendar year in which the employee retires (I.R.C. § 401(a)(9)(C)(i)). The rule under (b) does not apply except as provided in I.R.C. § 409(d) in the case of an employee who is a 5-percent owner (as defined in I.R.C. § 416 with respect to the plan year ending in the calendar year in which the employee attains age $70\frac{1}{2}$, or for purposes of I.R.C. § 408(a)(6) or (b)(3)) (I.R.C. § 401(a)(9)(C)(ii)).

[86] I.R.C. § 401(a)(9)(A)(ii).

[87] Priv. Ltr. Rul. 9119067 (February 14, 1991).

[88] I.R.C. § 402(a); Priv. Ltr. Rul. 9145041 (August 16, 1991).

[89] I.R.C. §§ 677(a) and 72(s)(4), (6), and (7); Priv. Ltr. Rul. 9145041 (August 16, 1991).

[90] I.R.C. § 671.

[91] Priv. Ltr. Ruls. 9533042 (May 25, 1995) and 9303031 (October 29, 1992).

[92] Priv. Ltr. Rul. 9119067 (February 14, 1991).

with respect to a tax-free rollover of a lump-sum distribution from a qualified retirement plan to an eligible retirement plan (IRA), if the employee trustor—not the trustee—is considered the distributee, as primary beneficiary under his or her revocable living trust, then the trustee should be able to effect an eligible rollover distribution on behalf of the employee trustor. This is no different than if the employee's attorney-in-fact, under a durable power of attorney, effected the rollover on behalf of the employee. The real issue is the identity of the recipient of the qualified retirement plan benefits; if that person is the employee, then the trustee should be able to effect a tax-free rollover because the rollover is for the employee trustor's benefit, or his or her beneficiaries.[94] Even if the employee trustor directs a lump-sum distribution be made to the trustee of a revocable living trust and the trustee subsequently, on behalf of the trustor, transfers any portion of the eligible rollover distribution proceeds to an eligible retirement plan, such distribution should not be included in the trustor's gross income for the taxable year in which the proceeds were paid.[95]

Surviving Spouse Acting as Trustee

In further support of this argument, a surviving spouse of a decedent employee, acting as the successor trustee of the decedent spouse's revocable living trust, can effect a tax-free rollover of the deceased spouse's lump-sum distribution from a qualified retirement plan to an eligible retirement plan for the benefit of the surviving spouse.[96] Similarly, if the trustee does not have the discretionary power to allocate trust estate property consisting of a lump-sum distribution from a qualified retirement plan to a trust for the benefit of the surviving spouse, and the surviving spouse can appoint those trust assets to himself or herself, then the surviving spouse should be able to effect a tax-free rollover of the deceased spouse's lump-sum distribution to an eligible retirement plan.[97] Therefore, it follows that, if the employee trustor is the trustee of his or her revocable living trust, then he or she should be considered the distributee for purposes of receiving qualified retirement plan benefits for the exclusive benefit of the employee or the employee's beneficiaries within the meaning of I.R.C. Sections 401(a) and 402(a).

Observation

The word *trust*, as used in the language, "a trust shall not constitute a qualified trust unless the plan provides . . . ," relative to qualified retirement plans, does not pertain to a revocable living trust. In other words, many qualified retirement plans are trust arrangements; and, if the plan is to operate as a trust, certain requirements must be fulfilled for the plan to be a qualified retirement plan within the meaning of I.R.C. Section 401. Thus, with respect to qualified retirement plan benefits, when the Code and Treasury Regulations speak of distributions by a trust, this means a trust described in I.R.C. Section 401(a) which is exempt under I.R.C. Section 501(a) for the taxable year of the trust in which the distribution is made—not distributions from a revocable living trust.

---

[93] I.R.C. § 402(c)(4) and (9); Treas. Reg. § 1.402(c)-2, A-3(a) and A-12(a) (April 21, 2000); Treas. Reg. § 1.408-8, A-5 (April 17, 2002).

[94] *See* Rev. Rul. 72-241, 1972-1 C.B. 108 (it is held that any settlement option of a qualified plan [other than an option contemplated in Rev. Rul. 72-240, 1972-1 C.B. 108] will meet the requirement of Treas. Reg. § 1.401-1(b)(1) that benefits payable to the beneficiary of an employee must be incidental to the primary purpose of distributing accumulated funds to the employee, if it contains certain provisions, whereby the present value of the payments to be made to the participant is more than 50 percent of the present value of the total payments to be made to the participant and his or her beneficiaries).

[95] I.R.C. § 402(a); Treas. Reg. § 1.402(c)-2, A-11 (April 21, 2000); Priv. Ltr. Rul. 9145041 (August 16, 1991).

[96] Priv. Ltr. Ruls. 200245055 (n.d.), 200242044 (July 23, 2002), and 8928082 (April 24, 1989).

[97] Priv. Ltr. Rul. 9533042 (May 25, 1995).

U.S. GOVERNMENT/CIVIL SERVICE RETIREMENT PLANS

U.S. Government retirement plans generally are required to satisfy the same requirements imposed upon private employer-sponsored qualified retirement plans. Minor differences in benefits may exist among the myriad departments and agencies; but, for the most part, the estate planning rules regarding inclusion of the value of qualified retirement plan benefits in the decedent-employee's gross estate and the distribution of benefits are similar to those of private employer-sponsored qualified retirement plans. Thus, the same restrictions and planning opportunities as apply to private employer-sponsored qualified retirement plans, with respect to the trustee of a revocable living trust, should apply to government retirement plans.

RAILROAD RETIREMENT

Benefits paid under the Railroad Retirement Act of 1974 fall into two categories. These categories are treated differently for income tax purposes. Rules similar to those under I.R.C. Section 401 are used to determine whether a retirement plan provided by a railroad employer, whose employees are entitled to benefits under the Railroad Retirement Act of 1974, is a qualified retirement plan. Such rules take into account the employer-derived portion of the employees' tier-two Railroad Retirement benefits and any supplemental annuity under the Railroad Retirement Act of 1974.[98]

Tier-One Railroad Retirement Benefits

The first category is the amount of tier-one Railroad Retirement benefits which equals the Social Security benefit that a railroad employee or beneficiary would have been entitled to receive under the Social Security system. This part of the tier-one benefit is the *social security equivalent benefit* (SSEB), and it is treated for federal income tax purposes like Social Security benefits. For more information on the SSEB part of tier-one benefits, see Form RRB-1099 instructions, Payments by the Railroad Retirement Board, and IRS Publication 915, Social Security and Equivalent Railroad Retirement Benefits (Rev. 2001).

Tier-Two Railroad Retirement Benefits

The second category contains the remainder of the tier-one benefits, called the *nonsocial security equivalent benefit* (NSSEB). It also contains any tier-two benefits, vested dual benefits, and supplemental annuity benefits. For income tax purposes, this amount is treated as an amount received from a qualified retirement plan. These amounts are reported on Form RRB-1099-R, Annuities or Pensions by the Railroad Retirement Board.

Railroad Retirement Benefits Payable to Trustee

Because retirement plans for railroad employees entitled to benefits under the Railroad Retirement Act of 1974 must meet the requirements under I.R.C. Section 401, rules similar to those set forth in I.R.C. Section 401, as they apply to private employer-sponsored qualified retirement plans, must be followed. Therefore, the trustee of a revocable living trust cannot be the legal owner of railroad retirement plan benefits, even if the employee is the trustee of his or her own revocable living trust. However, like private employer-sponsored qualified retirement plans and IRAs, the trustee of a revocable living trust should not be restricted from being named beneficiary of such plan proceeds. Whether the trustee can be an intermediary payee of Railroad Retirement plan benefits should be no more uncertain than

---

[98] I.R.C. § 401(l)(6).

with respect to private-employer sponsored qualified retirement plan benefits. Similarly, the rules regarding a tax-free rollover of a lump-sum distribution from a Railroad Retirement plan payable to the trustee of a revocable living trust, by the decedent-employee's surviving spouse, to an eligible retirement plan should apply.

OTHER RETIREMENT PLANS

In addition to qualified retirement plans that satisfy the requirements of I.R.C. Section 401, other retirement plans are available to the estate owner. These include retirement plans sponsored by tax-exempt organizations (e.g., tax-sheltered annuities [TSAs]), Keogh or H.R.-10 plans for the self-employed, and IRAs. In its own way, each of these retirement plans is *qualified*. However, they are not qualified in the same way that qualified retirement plans are qualified under I.R.C. Section 401. Nevertheless, these other retirement plans must satisfy certain requirements in order to receive favorable income tax treatment.

Tax-Exempt Organization Retirement Plans

An employee of certain tax-exempt organizations may be eligible to purchase a tax-sheltered annuity (TSA) (or tax-deferred annuity [TDA]) as part of his or her employment benefits package. Such organizations include colleges, universities, public schools, hospitals, charitable and religious organizations, certain scientific institutions, and so forth.[99] These benefits are generally provided by the employer for the employee by reducing the employee's salary. The salary reduction amount is used to purchase an endowment contract or annuity from a life insurance company.[100] The value of the annuity proceeds, plus the appreciation of the proceeds, accumulates income-tax-free for the benefit of the employee.[101] The value of the TSA is includable in the decedent employee's gross estate for federal estate tax purposes.[102]

The trustee of a revocable living trust cannot be the legal owner of tax-sheltered annuities for the same reasons the trustee cannot be the legal owner of an employee's qualified retirement plan. With regard to distributions from TSAs, the trustor should follow the general rules that apply to distributions from qualified retirement plans. Likewise, the rules applicable to the tax-free rollover of a lump-sum distribution from a qualified retirement plan apply to a tax-free rollover of a lump-sum distribution from a TSA.[103] In this regard, the trustee of a revocable living trust can be named the beneficiary of a TSA; and a decedent employee's surviving spouse can effect a tax-free rollover of a lump-sum distribution from a TSA to an eligible retirement plan, even if the surviving spouse is the successor trustee and beneficiary of the revocable living trust created by the decedent spouse trustor.[104] Lastly, the same considerations relative to the trustee of a revocable living trust acting as an intermediary payee of lifetime distributions from a qualified retirement plan should also apply to a TSA.

Keogh (HR-10) Retirement Plans

Many businesses operate as sole proprietorships. Oftentimes, the business owner will adopt for both the business owner and his or her employees a retirement plan known as a Keogh plan. Keogh plans extend to the self-employed, within the meaning of I.R.C. Section

---

[99] I.R.C. §§ 501(c)(3), 170(b)(1)(A)(ii).

[100] I.R.C. § 403(b)(1)(A).

[101] I.R.C. § 403(b)(1).

[102] I.R.C. § 2039(a).

[103] Treas. Reg. § 1.403(b)-2, A-1 (April 21, 2000).

[104] Priv. Ltr. Rul. 9034067 (May 31, 1990).

401, tax benefits similar to those available to employees under qualified retirement plans. Annual contributions to the plan (up to a certain amount) are income-tax deductible to the employer. The estate planning considerations for the inclusion of the value of such benefits in the decedent-employee's gross estate and distributions from such plans are the same as for qualified retirement plans. This means that the trustee of a revocable living trust cannot be the legal owner of Keogh plan benefits, even if the employee is the trustee of his or her own revocable living trust. However, like private employer-sponsored qualified retirement plans benefits, the trustee of a revocable living trust should not be restricted from being named beneficiary of such plan proceeds. The same considerations relative to the trustee of a revocable living trust acting as an intermediary payee of lifetime distributions from a qualified retirement plan should also apply to a Keogh plan.

Individual Retirement Accounts (IRAs)

The term *individual retirement account* means a trust created or organized in the United States for the exclusive benefit of an individual or his or her beneficiaries which meets certain requirements as provided under I.R.C. Section 408.[105] Nothing in I.R.C. Section 408 requires that such an individual be employed or that the allowable contributions to an IRA be derived from earned income. As a general rule, an individual, whether or not already covered by a qualified retirement plan, may establish an IRA and set aside a certain percentage of annual income in an individual retirement trust or custodial account. The *Tax Reform Act of 1986* effected changes pertaining to contributions allowed an individual relative to his or her annual income if he or she is already covered by a qualified retirement plan.[106]

Value of IRA Included in Gross Estate

The value of an IRA is includable in the decedent IRA owner's gross estate for federal estate tax purposes whether the decedent's beneficiary is his or her estate or another beneficiary. To the extent the value of the IRA included in the decedent's gross estate qualifies for the federal estate tax marital deduction or charitable deductions or is sheltered by the federal estate tax exemption amount, it is not subject to federal estate tax.

QTIP Trust Election for IRA

The decedent's executor (personal representative) may elect to treat an IRA and a QTIP trust as qualified terminable interest property, if the trustee of the testamentary trust (or revocable living trust) is named beneficiary of the decedent's IRA and the surviving spouse can compel the trustee to withdraw from the IRA the required minimum distribution (i.e., all of the proceeds—both principal and income—of the decedent's IRA)[107] at least annually and to distribute that amount to the surviving spouse.[108]

---

[105] I.R.C. § 408(a).

[106] I.R.C. § 219(g).

[107] *See* Treas. Reg. § 1.401(a)(9)-5, A-7(c)(3), Example 2 (April 17, 2002) and discussion in this chapter, *Contingent* and *Successor* Beneficiaries; Houghton and Wallace II, "Using Trusts Effectively in Estate Planning, Part II," at 41 for sample "Trust Provision For Conduit Subtrusts" ("Retirement Benefit Conduit Subtrust").

[108] *See* Rev. Rul. 2000-2, 2000-3 I.R.B. 305 *obsoleting* Rev. Rul. 89-89, 1989-2 C.B. 231 to be read in conjunction with Treas. Reg. §§ 1.401(a)(9)-1, 1.401(a)(9)-4, and 1.401(a)(9)-5 (April 17, 2002). For additional reading with respect to the estate tax marital deduction in relation to qualified plan benefits and IRAs, *see* M. Read Moore, "Interaction of the Estate Tax Marital Deduction and Qualified Plan and IRA Benefits," 23 *Estate Planning* 86 (February 1996); Dr. Ralph Switzer, Jr. and Daniel A. Pollock, "Using a QTIP Trust to Extend the Life of an IRA," 21 *Tax Management Estates, Gifts and Trusts Journal* 95 (March-April 1996); Moy, 2, *A Practitioner's Guide to Estate Planning*, § 28.04[D], at 28-44.

Trustee as Owner of IRA

The trustor should not convey ownership of his or her IRA to the trustee of a revocable living trust. An IRA is for the exclusive benefit of an individual or his or her beneficiaries.[109] Hence, the trustee of a revocable living trust cannot be the legal owner of the trustor's IRA.[110] Even if the trustor is the trustee of his or her revocable living trust, designating the trustee as the legal owner of an IRA constitutes a prohibited transaction.[111] Consequently, the trustor's IRA would cease to be an individual retirement account as of the first day of the taxable year in which title to the IRA is conveyed to the trustee, even if the trustor and the trustee are one and the same person. If the IRA ceases to be an IRA, then distribution in an amount equal to the fair market value of all assets in the account as of the first day of the taxable year is deemed to have occurred.[112]

Trustee as Beneficiary of IRA

The trustee of a revocable living trust may be named beneficiary of a trustor's IRA. The same rules applicable to required minimum distributions and a tax-free rollover of a lump-sum distribution from a qualified retirement plan under I.R.C. Section 401 apply to proceeds of an IRA distributed to the trustee of a revocable living trust for the benefit of the decedent's beneficiaries and surviving spouse. The same considerations relative to the trustee of a revocable living trust acting as an intermediary payee of lifetime distributions from a qualified retirement plan should also apply to an IRA when the individual for whom the IRA is established commences withdrawals from the account.

NONQUALIFIED RETIREMENT PLANS

Nonqualified retirement plans do not have to meet the same rigid requirements of the Code as do qualified retirement plans. Because most nonqualified retirement plans have transferable death benefits, they are generally includable in the value of the decedent employee's gross estate for federal estate tax purposes. Hence, it is important to coordinate the value of such benefits with selecting the right beneficiary to receive the nonqualified retirement plan proceeds in order to minimize federal estate and income taxes.

Nonqualified Deferred Compensation

Nonqualified deferred compensation plans have enjoyed varying degrees of popularity over the years. As executive *perks*, they have been popular devices to reduce income taxes for high-salaried corporate employees. Usually, a highly compensated employee negotiates with his or her employer to defer part of his or her salary until retirement or some other mutually agreed-upon time.

Various revenue rulings have considered the federal income tax consequences of nonqualified deferred compensation arrangements. In general, these rulings hold that, if the deferral agreement is consummated before the employee earns the compensation and the deferred salary is not secured with notes or any other form of security interest or placed in

---

[109] I.R.C. § 408(a).

[110] I.R.C. § 4975(c)(1)(D) and (e)(2)(A).

[111] I.R.C. § 408(e)(2).

[112] I.R.C. § 408(e)(2)(B).

a trust[113] or escrow account only for the exclusive benefit of the employee[114] to the exclusion of the employer's general creditors,[115] then the compensation that is deferred is not subject to federal income tax under the economic benefit doctrine until it is actually received by the employee, the employee's estate (or trust estate, in the case of a revocable living trust), or designated beneficiary.[116] However, an employee does not receive income as a result of the employer's purchase of a life insurance contract to provide a source of funds for nonqualified deferred compensation because the insurance contract is the employer's asset subject to the claims of the employer's creditors.[117]

Trustee as Owner of Nonqualified Deferred Compensation

Ask Your Attorney

Can the trustee of my revocable living trust, even if I am the trustee, be the legal owner of my nonqualified deferred compensation?

Answer

No.

An employee cannot have a preferred claim on or any beneficial ownership interest in any assets of a nonqualified deferred compensation arrangement. Any rights secured under such a plan are mere unsecured contractual rights. Furthermore, the participant employee's right to any benefit payments under a nonqualified deferred compensation plan may not be anticipated, alienated, sold, transferred, assigned, pledged, encumbered, attached, or garnished.[118] Therefore, the trustee of a revocable living trust cannot be the legal owner of the trustor's participating interest in a nonqualified deferred compensation arrangement.

---

[113] *But see, e.g.,* Priv. Ltr. Ruls. 9536027 (June 15, 1995) (employer created a series of irrevocable grantor trusts of which its subsidiaries were deemed the owners for purposes of establishing deferred compensation arrangements for employees of the subsidiaries); 8907034 (November 21, 1988) (adoption of a deferred compensation plan together with the establishment and settlement of a trust to discharge corporation's obligations under the plan, and the earnings on those assets, will not result in current recognition of income by the participants under the constructive receipt or the economic benefit doctrine); 8834052 (May 27, 1988) (in effect, same holding as in 8834052); and 8841023 (July 9, 1988) (payments by corporation under a deferred compensation plan to an irrevocable trust established by the participant will be includable in the participant employee's gross income in the year paid, pursuant to I.R.C. §§ 83(a) and 451(a)).

[114] *Sproull v. Commissioner,* 16 T.C. 244 (1951), *aff'd per curiam,* 194 F.2d 541 (6th Cir. 1952); Rev. Rul. 60-31, Situation 4, 1960-1 C.B. 174; Priv. Ltr. Ruls. 8907034 (November 21, 1988) and 8834052 (May 27, 1988).

[115] Rev. Rul. 60-31, Situations 1-3, 1960-1 C.B. 174; *see also* Rev. Rul. 69-650, 1969-2 C.B. 106 (the portion of the employee's salary deferred in accordance with the terms of the employee's employment contract is not includable in income in the year earned. The amount deferred is includable in the gross income of the recipient in the later taxable year(s) in which it is actually received by or otherwise made available to him, whichever is earlier); and Rev. Rul. 69-649, 1969-2 C.B. 106 (incentive bonus award to the employee, which is deferred under a supplementary retirement plan, is not includable in income in the year earned).

[116] I.R.C. § 451(a); Treas. Reg. § 1.451-2(a); Priv. Ltr. Rul. 8834052 (May 27, 1988).

[117] Rev. Ruls. 72-25, 1972-1 C.B. 127 and 68-99, 1968-1 C.B. 193; Priv. Ltr. Rul. 8834052 (May 27, 1988).

[118] I.R.C. § 83(a); Priv. Ltr. Ruls. 9536027 (June 15, 1995) and 8834052 (May 27, 1988).

Nonqualified Deferred Compensation Payments Deposited Into Account in Name of Trustee

Ask Your Attorney

Since the trustee of a revocable living trust cannot be the legal owner of my nonqualified deferred compensation, is there any way to protect the distributions from my nonqualified deferred compensation plan as they are made to me from a court-supervised financial guardianship if I become physically disabled or mentally incapacitated?

Answer

Yes.

As the trustor receives each distribution from the nonqualified deferred compensation plan, whether it be monthly, quarterly, semi-annually, or annually, he or she can deposit them into an account (e.g., bank account, brokerage account, and so forth) that is titled in the name of the trustee of the trustor's revocable living trust. Once these funds are deposited into an account owned by the trustee, the trustee has the power to manage the funds for the trustor's benefit as provided under the provisions of the revocable living trust agreement. If the trustor becomes physically disabled or mentally incapacitated after receiving a distribution, an attorney-in-fact, under a properly designed durable power of attorney, can deposit the funds into an account titled in the name of the trustee of the trustor's revocable living trust. Upon the trustor's receipt of the funds, such income no longer constitutes nonqualified deferred compensation and is fully income taxable to the employee for whom the income was initially deferred (e.g., the trustor).[119]

Value of Nonqualified Deferred Compensation Included in Gross Estate

For federal estate tax purposes, the present value of nonqualified deferred compensation remaining unpaid upon the employee's death and received by the decedent employee's estate or beneficiary is includable in his or her gross estate.[120] Nonqualified deferred

---

[119] I.R.C. §§ 83(a) and 451(a); Treas. Reg. § 1.451-2(a).

[120] I.R.C. § 2039(a); *Estate of Wadewitz v. Commissioner*, 339 F.2d 980 (7th Cir. 1964); Tech. Adv. Mem. 9002002 (September 26, 1989) (alternate valuation date). The present value of the deferred compensation payments included in the decedent employee's gross estate is determined by reference to the appropriate applicable federal interest rate (AFR) for the month in which the employee died and to Table B, column (2) (Annuity) opposite the number of years the employee was entitled to receive the deferred compensation (e.g., five years, ten years, and so forth) found in United States Internal Revenue Service, Treasury Department, Bureau of Internal Revenue, *Actuarial Values Book Aleph*, Publication 1457 (7-1999), U.S. Government Printing Office, Washington, D.C., 1999, Catalog Number 63854M (hereafter IRS Publication 1457 (7-1999)). For example, Martha was entitled, at the date of her death (December 5, 2002), to deferred compensation payments of $50,000 per year for five years, or a total of $250,000. The present value of these payments includable in Martha's gross estate is $111,295 ($25,000 x 4.4518 (annuity factor based on AFR of 4.0% for month of December 2002) = $111,295 (IRS Publication 1457, Table B(4.0), annuity factor of 4.4518, opposite five years, at 720. If IRS Publication 1457 is not available, the annuity factor may be calculated by following the instructions in Treas. Reg. § 20.2031-7(d)(2)(iv)); Moy, 1, *A Practitioner's Guide to Estate Planning*, § 17.07[A], at 17-80.

compensation paid after the decedent employee's death is taxed as IRD.[121] Furthermore, a person who is required to include IRD in gross income may be entitled to an income tax deduction for that portion of the estate tax imposed upon the decedent's estate which is attributable to the inclusion of the IRD in the value of the decedent's gross estate.[122]

Observation

Nonqualified deferred compensation is distinguished from salary continuation arrangements. Salary continuation involves the employer's agreement to pay the employee's salary to a named beneficiary (e.g., the employee's spouse) for a certain number of years following the decedent employee's death. In cases where the employee does not retain any rights or benefits in the salary continuation arrangement during his or her lifetime in an attempt to exclude the value of the salary payments from the gross estate (i.e., by designating an irrevocable beneficiary), the IRS had contended that the employee makes a completed gift of the contractual benefits to the beneficiary upon the employee's death.[123] However, the IRS has acknowledged that its position in this issue is inconsistent with that taken by the U.S. Tax Court in *Estate of DiMarco v. Commissioner*.[124]

Federal Estate and Income Tax Savings

Upon the employee's death, federal estate and income tax savings can be realized by selecting the right beneficiary to receive the employee's nonqualified deferred compensation. Federal estate tax savings can be obtained if the nonqualified deferred compensation passes to the employee's spouse in a manner qualifying it for the estate tax marital deduction. The payments will be includable in the surviving spouse's gross income upon receipt.

Ordinarily, because nonqualified deferred compensation payments are considered income in respect of a decedent (IRD), the beneficiary would be entitled to an income tax deduction for that portion of the federal estate tax imposed upon the decedent employee's estate which is attributable to the inclusion of the IRD in the value of the decedent employee's gross estate. However, the decedent employee's surviving spouse is not entitled to such an income tax deduction if the nonqualified deferred compensation qualifies for the estate tax marital deduction in the decedent employee spouse's gross estate. This is because the value of the nonqualified deferred compensation would not be part of the decedent employee spouse's *taxable* estate. Therefore, none of the resulting estate tax (if any) payable on the value of the decedent's taxable estate would be attributable to the inclusion of the nonqualified deferred compensation in the value of his or her gross estate.

---

[121] I.R.C. § 691(a)(1) and (c)(1); Treas. Reg. § 1.691(c)-1(a).

[122] I.R.C. § 691(c)(1)(A); Treas. Reg. § 1.691(c)-1(a).

[123] Rev. Rul. 81-31, 1981-1 C.B. 388.

[124] Rev. Rul. 92-68, 1992-2 C.B. 257, revoking Rev. Rul. 81-31, 1981-1 C.B. 475. In this regard, the IRS has reconsidered Rev. Rul. 81-31, 1981-1 C.B. 475, in view of the Tax Court's opinion in *Estate of DiMarco v. Commissioner*, 87 T.C. 653 (1986), *acq. in result* 1990-2 C.B. 1. Rev. Rul. 81-31 held that a decedent made a gift of the value of a death benefit passing to the decedent's surviving spouse and that the gift became complete in the calendar quarter in which the decedent dies, at which time the amount of the gift first became susceptible of valuation. The ruling is inconsistent with the result in *DiMarco*. Hence, Rev. Rul. 81-31 is revoked.

Trustee as Beneficiary of Nonqualified Deferred Compensation

The trustee of a revocable living trust can be named beneficiary of the trustor's nonquali-fied deferred compensation.[125] By naming the trustee of the trustor's revocable living trust beneficiary of the trustor's nonqualified deferred compensation, at least two benefits can be realized:

1. Avoidance of probate of the nonqualified deferred compensation amounts distrib-uted; and
2. Control over the distribution of the nonqualified deferred compensation for the benefit of the trustor's surviving spouse.

By this control, the nonqualified deferred compensation can intentionally be made to not qualify for the estate tax marital deduction in the trustor's gross estate. This is accom-plished by providing in the revocable living trust that nonqualified deferred compensation will be distributable to a credit shelter trust (family trust; nonmarital deduction trust; Trust B) for the lifetime benefit of the trustor's surviving spouse. If the trustor has already des-ignated his or her spouse as beneficiary of the trustor's nonqualified deferred compensa-tion, and such designation is irrevocable, then the trustor should include a disclaimer provision in his or her revocable living trust to the effect that any property disclaimed by the trustor's surviving spouse, whether passing under the terms of the revocable living trust or outside the revocable living trust, will be distributable to the credit shelter trust for the lifetime benefit of the trustor's surviving spouse. If the surviving spouse effects a qual-ified disclaimer,[126] the value of the property so disclaimed will not qualify for the estate tax marital deduction in the decedent trustor's gross estate. Rather, the value of the disclaimed property will be includable in the trustor's taxable estate. Thus, the surviving spouse may then be entitled to the income tax deduction for the estate tax attributable to the value of the nonqualified deferred compensation included in the trustor's gross estate.

Contractual Employer Death Benefits

Contractual death benefits provided by employers are different than nonqualified deferred compensation but, like nonqualified deferred compensation, are not part of a qualified re-tirement plan. Most often, a contractual death benefit provides that, upon the employee's death while employed, the employer promises to pay the employee's surviving spouse (or other designated beneficiary, such as the trustee of a revocable living trust) certain amounts. Usually, these *certain amounts* are tied to the employee's annual salary and may provide annual death benefits equivalent to salary of two or three years. If these payments are made to the employee's designated beneficiary while he or she is employed and by reason of the employee's death, they are includable in the value of the employee's gross estate for federal

---

[125] *See* Rev. Ruls. 69-650, 1969-2 C.B. 106 (if the employee should die prior to receiving the total amount credited to his account, the entire balance remaining is to be promptly paid to his or her legal representative); 69-649, 1969-2 C.B. 106 (in the case of death, the awards are payable to the employee's designated beneficiary); and 60-31, 1960-1 C.B. 174 (upon the employee's death prior to the employee's receipt in full of the balance in the account, the remaining balance is distributable to the employee's personal representative), modified by Rev. Rul. 64-279, 1964-2 C.B. 121, modified by Rev. Rul. 70-435, 1970-2 C.B. 100; Priv. Ltr. Rul. 8834052 (May 27, 1988) (benefits payable under a nonqualified deferred compensation plan and from the trust will be includable in the gross in-come of a participant or beneficiary for the taxable year that benefits are paid or made available, whichever is earlier).

[126] I.R.C. § 2518.

estate tax purposes.[127] Provided the death benefits pass to the employee's surviving spouse in a qualified manner, they should qualify for the estate tax marital deduction.

Contractual Employer Death Benefits Included in Beneficiary's Gross Income

The payment of contractual employer benefits by the employer to the employee's designated beneficiary is included in the beneficiary's gross income. If the death benefit is funded with life insurance, the proceeds paid by reason of the employee's death may be received by the beneficiary entirely free of federal income tax.[128]

Employee Designates Beneficiary

Although contractual employer death benefits are owned by the employer—not the employee—nevertheless, the employee often retains the right to designate a beneficiary of his or her choice to receive the death benefits. It is this power to designate the beneficiary of the death benefits which causes the value of the death benefits to be includable in the decedent employee's gross estate for purposes of the federal estate tax. Unfortunately, unless the employer is willing to omit this right at the time the employment agreement is being negotiated, the value of the death benefits is includable in the employee's gross estate.

Trustee as Owner and Beneficiary of Contractual Employer Death Benefits

Since the employer owns the death benefits, the trustee of a revocable living trust cannot be the legal owner of them. However, the employee can name the trustee of a revocable living trust beneficiary of the benefits upon the employee's death. If the employment agreement permits the employee to change the beneficiary from time to time, then the employee should be certain to effect a well-designed durable power of attorney that empowers the attorney-in-fact to designate a beneficiary of the death benefits if the employee cannot because of physical disability or mental incapacity.

Voluntary Employer Death Benefits

Of all the possible employer-provided death benefits, voluntary employer death benefits are perhaps the most difficult to evaluate for estate planning purposes. This is because the payments are made voluntarily by the employer and cannot be ascertained with any certainty. When the trustor is faced with this type of benefit, he or she should inquire of his or her employer if similar benefits have been paid to employee's beneficiaries in the past so the trustor can understand the employer's position with regard to such benefits. Since voluntary employer death benefits are owned by the employer, the trustee of a revocable living trust probably cannot be the legal owner of such benefits.

Value of Voluntary Employer Death Benefits Included in Gross Estate

If a voluntary employer death benefit is paid by the trustor's employer, it may or may not be includable in the value of the trustor's gross estate. Both the IRS and the courts have adhered to the rule that such benefits are includable in the value of the decedent employee's gross estate if it can be shown that the benefit was receivable by any beneficiary by reason

---

[127] I.R.C. § 2033; Treas. Reg. § 20.2033-1(a); I.R.C. § 2036(a); Treas. Reg. § 20.2036-1(a); I.R.C. § 2037; Treas. Reg. § 20.2037-1(a)(2); I.R.C. § 2038; Treas. Reg. § 20.2038-1(a); I.R.C. § 2039(a); Treas. Reg. § 20.2039-1(a) and (b)(1)(ii).

[128] I.R.C. § 101(a)(1).

of surviving the decedent under any form of contract or agreement.[129] On the other hand, the IRS says that the value of an employee's voluntary payment to the employee's surviving spouse is not includable in the value of the decedent employee's gross estate if it was not paid under a contract or agreement.[130]

Conversely, even if the voluntary employer death benefit is not paid under a contract or agreement, the IRS has included the value of voluntary employer death benefits in the decedent employee's gross estate where it has been shown that the employer previously and consistently paid an annuity or other such payments to the employee's beneficiary.[131] The IRS has also been inconsistent in its position by agreeing with a U.S. Tax Court decision that such benefits are not includable in the value of the decedent's gross estate, even where the employer follows a practice of paying death benefits subject to its own discretion.[132]

Trustee as Beneficiary of Voluntary Employer Death Benefits

Regardless of whether a voluntary employer death benefit is includable in the value of the trustor's gross estate, the benefit may be includable in the gross income of the designated beneficiary. If the trustee of a revocable living trust is designated beneficiary, the benefit is included in the gross income of the beneficiary, provided the trustee is required to distribute all trust income currently to the beneficiary. Whether the payment is included in the beneficiary's gross income depends on whether the payment is considered a gift from the employer to the employee trustor's beneficiary or whether the payment represents compensation to the employee. The former is not income taxable to the beneficiary; whereas, the latter is income taxable to the beneficiary.

Recommendations[133]

1. If the trustor is in doubt about whether a voluntary employer death benefit would be includable in the value of his or her gross estate, the trustor should insist that the estate planner include the projected value. This is a good example of where, in the estate planning process, it is to the trustor's advantage to be aware of the worst case scenario.
2. Even if the voluntary employer death benefit is not includable in the value of the trustor's gross estate, it should be planned for inclusion in the surviving beneficiary's gross estate. In this case, the value of the payment, unless gifted during the beneficiary's lifetime or disposed of by some other means, would be includable as an asset in the surviving beneficiary's gross estate.

---

[129] I.R.C. § 2039(a); Treas. Reg. § 20.2039-1(a) and (b)(ii); *Estate of Bahen v. United States,* 305 F.2d 827 (Ct.Cl. 1962); *Neely v. United States,* 613 F.2d 802 (Ct.Cl. 1980).

[130] Treas. Reg. § 20.2039-1(b)(2) Example (4).

[131] Treas. Reg. § 20.2039-1(b)(2) Example (4); Priv. Ltr. Ruls. 8005011 (October 29, 1979) and 7851010 (September 8, 1978).

[132] *Estate of Barr v. Commissioner,* 40 T.C. 227 (1963); *but see Gray, Executor v. United States,* 278 F.Supp. 281 (D.N.J. 1967).

[133] Moy, 1, *A Practitioner's Guide to Estate Planning,* § 17.07[C], at 17-86.

CHAPTER 16

Life Insurance and Annuities

LIFE INSURANCE

Under the Code, *insurance* means life insurance of every description, including whole life policies, term life insurance, group life insurance, limited pay life insurance, double indemnity, travel and accident life insurance, endowment contracts (before being paid-up), no-fault auto life insurance, and death benefits paid by fraternal beneficial societies operating under the lodge system.[1] The term *life insurance* does not include:

- Premium refunds in the event of suicide;
- No-risk, single premium policies combining annuities and life insurance; and
- Certain employer-provided survivorship benefits.[2]

Life Insurance Creates Liquidity

The first purpose of life insurance is to offset the economic loss that results from death during a person's productive years and to take care of the money needs that continue no matter when death occurs.[3] With a piece of paper (life insurance application), a drop of ink (signature of the insured-applicant), and a few pennies on the dollar (premium), a person can create an instant estate worth thousands or millions of dollars upon the death of the insured. These discounted dollars, or dollars for pennies apiece, can provide a valuable source of liquidity in an estate to satisfy clearance (expenses of administration) and transfer costs (federal estate and state death taxes).

Need for Cash

Even estates of the wealthiest decedents oftentimes lack sufficient liquid assets with which to satisfy clearance and transfer costs. Because of this, personal representatives or trustees have to sell assets, oftentimes under forced sale conditions and perhaps in an unfavorable market climate, to obtain necessary cash. Life insurance can be effective in providing needed cash so that other estate assets do not have to be liquidated. In any event, whatever life insurance is available at death, it should be considered before all other assets as a good source of funds to satisfy clearance and transfer costs and cash bequests.

---

[1] Treas. Reg. § 20.2042-1(a)(1)(ii); Rev. Rul. 83-44, 1983-1 C.B. 6.

[2] *Estate of Anthony DiMarco v. Commissioner*, 87 T.C. 39 (1986). In *DiMarco* the court held that Rev. Rul. 81-31, 1981-1 C.B. 475, is inconsistent with the Code.

[3] The Life Underwriter Training Council, *Life Underwriter Training Council Course: The Life Insurance Saleman*, 25th ed., 7 vols. (City and State unknown), The Life Underwriter Training Council (1971), Vol. 1, at 16.

Ownership and Beneficiary Designation

Moreover, the issue of policy ownership and beneficiary designation of existing insurance contracts and new policies about to be acquired should be carefully coordinated with the insured's overall estate planning goals and objectives. Whenever possible and practical, life insurance proceeds should not be made subject to federal estate and state death taxes. Life insurance proceeds of significant amounts should not be included in the insured decedent's gross estate. The ownership and beneficiary designations of life insurance policies should be arranged to exclude such proceeds from the insured decedent's gross estate. Similarly, such proceeds should not be subject to estate tax in the beneficiary's resulting estate. If the trustee of a revocable living trust is the legal owner of a life insurance policy insuring the trustor's life, then, upon the death of the insured trustor, the value of the life insurance proceeds is includable in the trustor's gross estate.[4]

Federal Estate Taxation of Life Insurance

A common belief is that life insurance proceeds payable to a surviving spouse or to a beneficiary other than the decedent's estate are not includable in the value of the decedent's gross estate. As a general rule, such life insurance proceeds are not includable in the decedent's *probate estate*. The gross estate includes the value of life insurance proceeds, together with any accumulated or postmortem dividends, on the insured decedent's life if the proceeds:

- Are receivable by the decedent's probate or trust estate;
- Are receivable by another person for the benefit of the decedent's probate or trust estate; or
- Are not receivable by or for the benefit of the decedent's estate but the insured decedent possessed an incident of ownership in the life insurance policy.[5]

Transfer of Ownership

If the insured decedent did not possess an incident of ownership in the life insurance policy at the time of his or her death or did not transfer ownership of the insurance policy to another person within three years of death, no part of the insurance proceeds is includable in the insured decedent's gross estate under I.R.C. Section 2042.[6] If the life insurance proceeds are not paid in a lump sum but are distributed to the beneficiary in deferred payments, the value includable in the insured decedent's gross estate is the amount used by the insurance company as the cost of the installment benefits. If the insured decedent had obtained a loan against the insurance policy from the insurer, the balance of the loan and any accrued interest is subtracted from the value of the death proceeds, and only the net value is included in the decedent's gross estate for federal estate tax purposes.[7]

Trustee as Owner and Beneficiary

If the trustor who is the insured under a life insurance policy intends not to exclude the value of a life insurance policy from his or her gross estate for federal estate tax purposes, then the trustee of the trustor's revocable living trust should be the legal owner and beneficiary of the policy. Before conveying the ownership of a life insurance policy to the trustee

---

[4] I.R.C. §§ 2035(a)(2) and 2038(a)(1).
[5] I.R.C. § 2042; Treas. Reg. § 20.2042-1(a)(1).
[6] Treas. Reg. § 20.2042-1(c)(1).
[7] I.R.C. § 2053(a)(4).

of a revocable living trust, the trustor should check state statute to determine what effect, if any, such a conveyance might have on the exemption of the life insurance proceeds upon the insured trustor's death from state inheritance or estate taxes. By conveying the ownership of a life insurance policy to the trustee of a revocable living trust, if the insured trustor becomes physically disabled or mentally incapacitated, the trustee can exercise all the incidents of ownership in the life insurance policy on the trustor's behalf under the provisions of the living trust agreement. If the trustee of the revocable living trust is the beneficiary of the life insurance proceeds upon the trustor's death, such proceeds can be used to satisfy clearance and transfer costs, fund specific cash bequests, fund marital deduction trusts (qualified terminable interest property (QTIP), general power of appointment marital deduction trusts, and estate trusts), and fund credit shelter trusts under the revocable living trust.

Incident of Ownership

The term *incident of ownership* refers to the right of the insured, or the insured's estate, to the economic benefits of a life insurance policy. In general, an incident of ownership includes the power to:[8]

- Change the beneficiary;
- Surrender or cancel the policy;
- Assign the policy or revoke an assignment. The IRS has ruled that the insured's retained right to repurchase an assigned life insurance policy constitutes an incident of ownership.[9]
- Pledge the policy as security for a loan;
- Obtain a loan against the surrender value of the policy; or
- Elect settlement options for the insurance proceeds.

Elect Settlement Options and Power to Change Beneficial Ownership

A power in the insured decedent to select settlement options is not specifically mentioned as an incident of ownership in either the Code or the Treasury Regulations.[10] However, a power in the insured "to change the beneficial ownership in the policy or its proceeds, or the time and manner of enjoyment thereof" is an incident of ownership.[11] The incidents of ownership held by a corporation or partnership (including a limited liability company or limited liability partnership) in a life insurance policy on the life of a sole or controlling shareholder (or general partner) may be attributable to the insured.[12] The meaning of incident of ownership is not limited to ownership of a life insurance policy in the technical legal sense.[13] Such right may be either expressed or implied, and local law may control in determining the insured's rights in the policy.

Observations/Recommendations

1. If the trustor owns a life insurance policy on the life of his or her spouse, the trustor should not transfer the ownership of such a life insurance contract to the trustee of a re-

---

[8] Treas. Reg. § 20.2042-1(c)(2).

[9] Tech. Adv. Mem. 9128008 (March 29, 1991).

[10] I.R.C. § 2042; Treas. Reg. § 20.2042-1(c)(4).

[11] Treas. Reg. § 20.2042-1(c)(4).

[12] Treas. Reg. § 20.2042-1(c)(2) and (6).

[13] Treas. Reg. § 20.2042-1(c)(2).

vocable living trust if the *insured* spouse is a present or successor trustee of the revocable living trust. In such a case, the *insured* spouse is deemed to have an incident of ownership in the life insurance contract on the *insured* decedent's life where the incident of owner-ship is held in a fiduciary capacity (i.e., as a trustee or personal representative).[14]

2. The trustee of a revocable living trust should not be the beneficiary of a life insurance contract, insuring the life of the trustor, which is owned by the trustor's spouse or other third party, because the trustor's right to amend the revocable living trust could be con-strued as an indirect right to change the beneficiary of the contract that has been made payable to the trustee of the revocable living trust.[15]

Conveying Ownership of Life Insurance Policy to Trustee

The trustor can convey the ownership of a life insurance policy (whether the trustor is the insured or is presently the owner of a policy insuring the life of another individual) to the trustee of a revocable living trust and designate the trustee beneficiary of the proceeds by requesting a change of ownership and beneficiary designation form from the insurance company (see file "APP1601.DOC"). 🖼 Some life insurance companies have two different forms—one for change of ownership and one for change of beneficiary, while others com-bine both in a single form. In the request letter, the trustor should be certain to mention that the new owner and beneficiary are to be the trustee of a revocable living trust. This is im-portant because some insurance companies use a separate form when the policy is owned by a trustee or when the trustee is designated beneficiary of the life insurance proceeds.

Like other financial institutions, no universal standard seems to exist among life in-surance companies with respect to the wording used for designating the trustee of a revo-cable living trust as the owner or beneficiary of a life insurance contract. Nevertheless, as for any other property conveyed to the trustee, the same admonitions apply with respect to the sufficiency of legal title in the wording used to designate the trustee the legal owner of the life insurance contract.

Single Trustor

If the trustor is a single person and is both the trustor and trustee of his or her revocable liv-ing trust, the ownership of the life insurance contract should be titled in the trustor's name as trustee using the following format:

> Eugene H. Curtis, Trustee, or any successor trustee, under the Eugene H. Curtis Revo-cable Living Trust Agreement, dated February 15, 2003.

Married Trustors: Joint Revocable Living Trust

If the trustor is married, has a joint revocable living trust wherein both spouses are trustors and trustees, then the ownership of life insurance contracts insuring the trustors' respective individual lives should be titled in the trustors' names as co-trustees of the joint revocable living trust, using either of the two following formats; and the policies should be listed on the appropriate schedule attached at the end of the trust agreement:[16]

> 1. Eugene H. Curtis and Theresa M. Curtis, co-Trustees, or any successor trustee, under the Curtis Family Revocable Living Trust Agreement, dated February 15, 2003; or

---

[14] Treas. Reg. § 20.2042-1(c)(4); *Rose v. United States,* 511 F.2d 259 (5th Cir. 1975); *Terriberry v. United States,* 517 F.2d 285 (5th Cir. 1975).

[15] *Margrave v. Commissioner,* 71 T.C. 13 (1978); Treas. Reg. § 20.2042-1(c)(4).

[16] *See* discussion in "Trust Property: Article III" section, Chapter 2.

2. Eugene H. Curtis, co-Trustee, or any successor trustee, under the Curtis Family Revocable Living Trust Agreement, dated February 15, 2003; (for a policy owned by Eugene on his life); or

Theresa M. Curtis, co-Trustee, or any successor trustee, under the Curtis Family Revocable Living Trust Agreement, dated February 15, 2003 (for a policy owned by Theresa on her life).

Observation

The option (1) format above can be used for a *second-to-die* or *first-to-die* life insurance contract that insures the lives of both spouses under a single contract. The option (2) format above may be used in situations where a husband and wife have different successor trustees for their respective trust estates under the joint revocable living trust agreement.

Married Trustors; Separate Revocable Living Trusts

If the trustors are married and each spouse has his or her own separate revocable living trust of which each spouse, respectively, is the trustee, and both spouses want access to each other's life insurance contracts, then the trustors should title the life insurance contracts in their names as trustees of the trusts as tenants in common:

Eugene H. Curtis, Trustee under the Eugene H. Curtis Revocable Living Trust Agreement, dated February 15, 2003, **and** Theresa M. Curtis, Trustee under the Theresa M. Curtis Revocable Living Trust Agreement, dated February 15, 2003.

(It would not be unusual for the life insurance company to add the language "as tenants in common.")

Observation

Most insurance companies recognize and accept the same universal-wording format accepted by banks and credit unions to designate the trustee of a revocable living trust as owner of a life insurance policy.[17]

Trustee as Beneficiary

Since no universal format exists among life insurance companies with respect to the wording used for designating the trustee of a revocable living trust beneficiary of a life insurance contract, the trustor should anticipate inconsistency in this regard. Unless the insurance company provides specific wording in the instructions to the change of beneficiary form to use in designating the trustee beneficiary, the following wording should be universally acceptable:

(*name of trustee*), trustee, or any successor trustee, under the (*name of trust*) Revocable Living Trust Agreement, dated (*date trust was effected*), and supplements or amendments thereto, if said trust agreement shall then be in force and, if not, to the personal representative(s), administrator(s), or assign(s) of the insured (or policy owner).

---

[17] *See* discussion in Chapter 13.

Observation

If the trustor is the trustee of his or her revocable living trust, the trustor does not name himself or herself, as trustee, as the beneficiary of the life insurance contract; the trustor can't because the trustor will be deceased when the insurance company pays the proceeds of the contract insuring the trustor's life. Hence, the successor trustee under the revocable living trust is named. On the other hand, if the trustor conveys ownership of a life insurance contract insuring the life of another individual to his or her revocable living trust, then the trustor can name himself or herself trustee as the beneficiary of the life insurance proceeds.

Change of Successor Trustee

Ask Your Attorney

If I change the successor trustee under my revocable living trust agreement, or effect a restatement of the entire trust agreement because of major amendments to the original trust agreement, do I have to effect a new change of ownership or beneficiary form with the life insurance company?

Answer

No.

The language, *"or any successor trustee,"* takes into account such changes to the original trust agreement. Also, a properly designed restatement of the original revocable living trust agreement should include the following language in the preamble:

Reference to the "Trustee" in this Trust Agreement, in any amendment to this Trust Agreement and in any writings conveying, transferring, or assigning property to this Trust Agreement, whether prior to, contemporaneously herewith, or after the execution of this Restatement of (*name of trust*) Revocable Living Trust Agreement, shall remain in full force and effect notwithstanding anything to the contrary and shall be deemed a reference to whomever is serving as Trustee—whether the initial, alternate, successor, or substitute Trustee. Provided further, all property or interests in property conveyed to this Trust prior to the execution of this Restatement shall continue as part of the trust estate; and it shall not be necessary to reconvey such property to the Trustee of the Restatement of the (*name of trust*) Revocable Living Trust Agreement.

United States Government Life Insurance

National Service Life Insurance

An insured veteran may not assign ownership of his or her National Service Life Insurance (NSLI) policy or divest himself or herself of its ownership.[18] Therefore, the trustee of a

---

[18] Instructions to Veterans Administration Form 29-336 (June 1982) superseded by Form 29-336 (Aug. 2000). This prohibition against assignment or divesture of ownership does not appear in the instructions on Form 29-336 (Aug. 2000). However, such prohibition is evidenced on VA Form 29-538 (Feb. 1990—latest revised edition) "Assignment—Government Life Insurance Benefits." In this regard, "an assignment [of National Service Life Insurance] may be made only in favor of the insured's widow, widower, child, father, mother, grandfather, grandmother, brother or sister."

revocable living trust cannot be the legal owner of such life insurance. However, the trustee of a revocable living trust can be designated beneficiary of National Service Life Insurance. This is accomplished by requesting from the Department of Veterans Affairs Form 29-336 (Aug. 2000) Designation of Beneficiary Government Life Insurance. This form is available in pdf format online at: http://www.insurance.va.gov/inForceGliSite/forms/forms.htm. The form may be completed online or can be downloaded. It can then be printed with the entries already completed. The completed form should be mailed to the address shown on the form. Under "Remarks" (item 5.) on Form 29-336, the insured trustor should print or type the following:

> I acknowledge that the Veterans Administration has no liability to see to the application of the proceeds of Government Life Insurance by the Trustee to the fulfillment of the purpose of the Trust.

The following wording should be used on Form 29-336 to designate the trustee of a revocable living trust as the "principal" beneficiary of the life insurance contract:

> (*name of trustee*), trustee, or any successor trustee, under the (*name of trust*) Revocable Living Trust Agreement, dated (*date trust was effected*), and supplements or amendments thereto, if said trust agreement shall then be in force, and, if not, to the personal representative(s), administrator(s), or assign(s) of the insured.

Federal Employee's Group Life Insurance

If the trustor is employed by the U.S. Government, the trustee of a revocable living trust cannot be the legal owner of the government employee's group life insurance. In this regard, "An assignment may be made only in favor of the insured's widow, widower, child, grandchild, parent, brother, sister, uncle, aunt, nephew, niece, brother-in-law, or sister-in-law."[19] However, the trustee of the trustor's revocable living trust can be named beneficiary of Federal Employee's Group Life Insurance. Form SF 2823 (Rev. April 2001) Designation of Beneficiary Federal Employee's Group Life Insurance (FEGLI) Program (Beneficiary Designation) is used for this purpose. This form is available in pdf format at: http://www.opm.gov/insure/life/. Most life insurance companies prefer change of beneficiary forms to be filled-out in the handwriting (printed) of the owner of the insurance contract or the insurance agent. However, the U.S. Office of Personnel Management (OPM), of which the Office of Federal Employees' Group Life Insurance is solely responsible for the administration of the life insurance program and the payment of claims, admonishes anyone completing Form SF 2823 that erasures and cross-outs are not to appear on the form. In such case, a new form should be completed. Moreover, "Erasures, cross-outs and alterations cause delay in the payment of benefits and may make the entire designation invalid."[20] On Form SF 2823, if the employee trustor has previously named a beneficiary and is requesting to name the trustee of his or her revocable living trust beneficiary, then the designation should state, "Cancel Prior Designation(s)." The Office of Federal Employees' Group Life Insurance is not responsible for the application or disposition of the proceeds of the Federal Employees' Group Life Insurance by the trustee, and the receipt by the trustee of the proceeds is a full discharge of the liability of the Office of Federal Employees' Group Life Insurance. Furthermore, when designating the trustee of a revocable living trust as beneficiary, the following wording is recommended:

---

[19] VA Form 29-538 "Assignment—Government Life Insurance Benefits" (Feb. 1990—latest revised version).

[20] Instructions to Form SF 2823, page 2 (Aug. 2000).

Trustee(s) or Successor Trustee(s) as provided in the (*name of trust*) Agreement dated (*effective date of trust*), if valid. Otherwise to: (*name of beneficiary other than trust*).

In order for a trustee beneficiary designation to be valid, the "Inter Vivos Trustee Designation" form (see file "APP1602.DOC") must be attached to the Designation of Beneficiary Federal Employee's Group Life Insurance (FEGLI) Program form. When completing the Designation of Beneficiary Federal Employee's Group Life Insurance (FEGLI) Program form, the insured trustor should include "See Attached" in the space for the designation of the beneficiary. The completed Beneficiary Designation form, together with the attached Inter Vivos Trustee Designation form, should be mailed to the address shown in the instructions to the Beneficiary Designation form. According to the OPM, while it is not absolutely necessary to use the OPM-established formats (i.e., the Inter Vivos Trustee Designation form), the following information must be included for the trustee beneficiary designation to be valid:

- A statement that the FEGLI death benefit is to be paid to the trustee or successor trustee; and
- Name and date of the trust (for revocable living trusts).

Group Term Life Insurance

The value of group term life insurance provided by an employer may be included in the insured decedent employee's gross estate. This is true if the insured decedent employee can:[21]

- Change the beneficiary of the policy;
- Terminate the policy;
- Prevent the employer's cancellation of the policy by purchasing the policy; or
- Select a settlement option for the policy proceeds.

Cancellation of Group Policy by Employer

Cancellation of a group term life insurance policy by the employer because of the insured employee's voluntary termination of employment does not constitute an incident of ownership in the employee.[22]

Employee's Right to Convert Group Term Life Insurance

The insured employee's right to convert group term life insurance to an individual policy upon termination of employment is not an incident of ownership.[23] However, if the insured employee converts a group term life insurance policy to an individual policy and such policy is issued to a trustee (as owner and beneficiary) of an *irrevocable* trust created by another person and the insured dies within three years of making the conversion, the conversion right is an incident of ownership.[24]

---

[21] I.R.C. § 2042; Treas. Reg. § 20.2042-1(c)(2).

[22] *Estate of Smead v. Commissioner*, 78 T.C. 43 (1982); Rev. Rul. 72-307, 1972-1 C.B. 307.

[23] Rev. Rul. 84-130, 1984-2 C.B. 194; Prior to Rev. Rul. 84-130, the IRS ruled in Rev. Rul. 72-307, 1972-1 C.B. 307 that an employee's power to cancel group term life insurance by terminating employment was not an incident of ownership when the conversion privilege and insurance coverage both cease at the termination of employment.

[24] Tech. Adv. Mem. 9141007 (June 19, 1991). For additional discussion of Tech Adv. Mem. 9141007, *see* Moy, 1, *A Practitioner's Guide to Estate Planning*, § 18.02[B][9], at 18-32 through 18-36.

Excluding Value of Group Term Life Insurance from Gross Estate

The value of group term life insurance may be excluded from the insured employee decedent's gross estate. This can be accomplished if:[25]

- The master group policy and state law permit the insured employee to make an absolute assignment of all the insured's incidents of ownership in the insurance policy, including any privilege of converting the insurance to an individual policy upon termination of employment; and
- The insured irrevocably assigns all incidents of ownership, including any conversion privilege, to the new owner of the policy. If either the master group policy or state law prohibits the assignment of the insured's conversion privilege, the proceeds of the policy are includable in the insured's gross estate, regardless of any effort by the insured to assign the conversion privilege. Even if the insured makes an effective assignment of all incidents of ownership in the policy, the proceeds may, nevertheless, be includable in the insured's gross estate if the assignment occurs within three years of the insured's death.[26]

Trustee as Owner

If the insured trustor's employer provides group term life insurance and the trustor does not intend to remove the value of the proceeds from his or her gross estate for federal estate tax purposes, then the trustor may want to convey ownership of the policy to the trustee of his or her revocable living trust agreement. The reasons for doing this are the same as those with regard to conveying the ownership of an individual life insurance contract to the trustee of a revocable living trust. However, whether the insured trustor can convey the ownership of the group life insurance to the trustee of a revocable living trust depends on the provisions of the master group policy and state law. If such a conveyance can be effected, it is accomplished in a manner similar to conveying the ownership of an individual life insurance contract to the trustee of a revocable living trust, except that the requisite forms would be obtained from the employer. The same trustee ownership-wording format used for an individual life insurance contract is used for group life insurance.

Trustee as Beneficiary

Certainly, the trustee of a revocable living trust can be designated beneficiary of group life insurance proceeds. The same reasons and benefits relative to designating the trustee of a revocable living trust beneficiary of an individual life insurance contract apply to group life insurance. The requisite forms for designating the trustee of a revocable living trust beneficiary of group life insurance would be obtained from the employer. The same beneficiary wording used for an individual life insurance contract is used for group life insurance.

ANNUITIES

Annuities are either commercial or private. A commercial annuity is a contract entered into by and between an insurance company and the individual annuitant. The annuitant pays

[25] Rev. Rul. 69-54, 1969-1 C.B. 221.

[26] For additional reading, *see* Lee Slavutin, MD, CPC, CLU, "Planning Strategies with Group-Term Life Insurance: Interview with Lee Slavutin, MD, CPC, CLU," interview by editors of Commerce Clearing House, Inc., *Estate Planning Review*, in 3 *Financial and Estate Planning*, issue 445 (June 18, 1998) 41; Stephen J. Krass and Cynthia L. Alicia, "Estate Planning for Group-term Life Insurance," in 3 *Financial and Estate Planning* ¶ 29,101 (CCH); Bradley E. S. Fogel, "Using Life Insurance Trusts to Hold Group Term Life Insurance," 1997 *Probate & Property* 30 (September/October 1997).

money (a premium) to an insurance company in exchange for the insurance company's promise (annuity contract or policy) to pay the annuitant a fixed sum (annuity) monthly, quarter-annually, semi-annually, or annually for the annuitant's lifetime or for a certain number of years (period). A private annuity is a similar arrangement but is an agreement by and between an individual (the annuitant) and a private person (e.g., another private individual, a charitable organization, a family member, or a trust or corporation). Regardless of whether the annuity is commercial or private, each annuity payment is, in part, a return of the annuitant's investment (capital), which is not income taxable to the annuitant and, in part, the income (interest) earned on the unliquidated principal (investment), which is income taxable to the annuitant.[27]

Commercial Annuities

Commercial annuities are either purchased with a single premium or by annual premiums over a period of years (fixed period). The annual premium payments may be divided into monthly, quarter-annual, or semi-annual payments. In addition, the annuity payments can commence immediately or at some time after the annuity contract is purchased. Thus, a single premium immediate life annuity is paid by a single payment (premium); and the payments begin immediately to the annuitant. Conversely, single premium deferred life annuities are also available. As the name suggests, the annuity is paid in a single payment. However, the income benefit to the annuitant does not begin immediately; rather, it is deferred to a future beginning date. Finally, an annual premium deferred life annuity is also available.[28]

Trustee as Owner

Unless the annuity contract itself or the plan of which the annuity is a part prohibits the trustee of a revocable living trust from being the legal owner of the contract, the trustee should be the legal owner of the annuity. As a general rule, the Code provides that, if an annuity contract is held by a person who is not a natural person (e.g., a trustee), the contract is not treated as an annuity contract. Therefore, the income on the contract for any taxable year of the annuitant is treated as ordinary income received or accrued by the owner during the taxable year. However, the Code further provides that, if a trust or other entity holds the annuity contract as an agent for a natural person, the foregoing rule does not apply.[29] The legislative history of I.R.C. Section 72(u) shows that Congress intended, where a nonnatural person (e.g., a corporation or trust) is a nominal owner of an annuity but the beneficial owner (trustor) is a natural person, the annuity is treated as held by a natural person.[30] This rule also applies if the trust is irrevocable. If the trustor is the annuitant, by designating the trustee of his or her revocable living trust the legal owner of the annuity contract, the annuity payments to the trustor during his or her lifetime can be administered by the trustee if the trustor becomes physically disabled or mentally incapacitated.

Federal Income Tax

With respect to the issue of income tax, if the trustee of a revocable living trust is the legal owner of the annuity contract, the primary annuitant is treated as the holder of the contract.

---

[27] S.S. Huebner and Kenneth Black, Jr., *Life Insurance*, Appleton-Century-Crofts, Educational Division, Meredith Corporation, New York, NY (8th ed. 1972), at 118 (hereafter Huebner and Black, *Life Insurance*); Moy, 1, *A Practitioner's Guide to Estate Planning*, § 17.01[C], at 17-6; I.R.C. § 72(b).

[28] Moy, 1, *A Practitioner's Guide to Estate Planning*, § 17.01[C], at 17-1.

[29] I.R.C. § 72(u)(1).

[30] H.R. Conf. Rep. 841, 99th Cong., 2d Sess. II-401-402 (1986), 1986-3 (Vol. 4) C.B. 1, 401-402; Priv. Ltr. Rul. 9120024 (February 20, 1991).

The term *primary annuitant* means the individual, whose life events are of primary importance in affecting the timing or amount of the payout under the contract.[31] In other words, if the trustor is the annuitant, then, for purposes of federal income tax, the trustor is the *individual* whose life measures the annuity payments—not the trustee.

Starting Date and Expected Annuity Return

Most property is conveyed to the trustee of a revocable living trust for no consideration. In the case of an annuity, the legal title of which is conveyed to the trustee of a revocable living trust, the annuity starting date and the expected return under the contract are determined as though the transfer to the trustee did not occur.[32] All premiums or other consideration paid by the trustee or deemed to have been paid by the trustor-annuitant for the annuity are considered paid by the trustor. In determining the trustee's investment in the annuity contract, the trustee's aggregate amount of premiums or other consideration paid is reduced by all amounts either received or deemed to have been received by the trustee or the trustor before the annuity starting date or before the date on which an amount is first received as an annuity, whichever is the later, to the extent that such amounts were excludable from the trustor's gross income under the applicable income tax law at the time of receipt.[33]

Trustee as Beneficiary

The trustee of a revocable living trust can be the beneficiary of the annuity to receive the undistributed annuity payments upon the annuitant's death.[34] The reasons discussed for designating the trustee of a revocable living trust beneficiary of life insurance proceeds also apply to designating the trustee beneficiary of annuity payments. The requisite forms to convey the ownership of an annuity to the trustee of a revocable living trust and to designate the trustee beneficiary of the annuity may be obtained by requesting them from the insurance company. If the trustor were to become physically disabled or mentally incapacitated in the interim before receiving the forms to effect the changes, the letters themselves requesting the forms may be sufficient for the insurance company to effect the changes without the necessity of their forms being executed (see files "APP1603.DOC" and "APP1604.DOC").

Private Annuity

Everyday it becomes more challenging to eliminate or minimize federal estate tax on a large estate. As the value of the estate increases, it becomes increasingly more difficult to transfer significant amounts of property over a short period without using up any of the federal estate tax exemption amount. Using the exemption amount to minimize gift taxes is similar to the process of purchasing life insurance; namely, neither should be done until the need is identified and other available solutions are examined and tested. Aside from making charitable gifts, utilizing the gift tax annual exclusion and qualified transfers, utilizing the gift tax marital deduction, creating a grantor retained annuity or unitrust, or creating a qualified personal residence trust, just about all of the other available transfer techniques (which are beyond the scope of this book) require financial participation by the transferee (e.g., family limited partnership, limited liability company, and so forth). Moreover, some transfer strategies are quite sophisticated and may not be suitable to the nature

---

[31] I.R.C. § 72(s)(6).
[32] Treas. Reg. §§ 1.72-10(b) and 1.72-4(b).
[33] Treas. Reg. § 1.72-10(b).
[34] I.R.C. § 72(s)(4).

of the trustor's property, to his or her philosophy, or to the trustor's ability to comprehend and understand the consequences of the planning strategy.[35]

Private Annuity Defined

A private annuity is an agreement between two persons, neither of who is an insurance company. The transferor (annuitant) transfers complete ownership of property to the transferee (obligor of the payments to the transferor-annuitant). The transferee promises to make periodic payments to the transferor for a certain period or for the transferor's lifetime or for the lifetime of his or her spouse (joint and survivor annuity). Accordingly, a private annuity may be one of two types:[36]

1. Single life annuity in which payments cease at the death of the annuitant and the value of the annuity that would have been paid to the annuitant is not included in the decedent annuitant's gross estate for federal estate tax purposes; and

2. Joint and survivor annuity in which payments continue until the death of the last survivor (e.g., husband and wife).

Satisfying Different Financial Needs

A private annuity may satisfy several different financial needs. A person may want to transfer a large asset out of his or her estate to another family member in order to eliminate or greatly reduce potential federal estate tax. Or a private annuity may be used to convert nonincome-producing property into income-producing property. Or a fixed retirement income can be obtained by using a private annuity. Or a person may own a low-basis, highly appreciated asset that he or she would like to sell so that the proceeds could be invested in a commercial annuity. However, the owner of the asset realizes that substantial income tax must be recognized on the gain if the asset is sold and that payment of the resulting taxes will reduce the amount of the proceeds available to invest in the annuity. Rather than sell the asset, a better solution may be to effect a private annuity. A private annuity would enable the owner of the asset to defer the taxable gain over a number of years. Finally, an estate owner who is a major shareholder in a closely-held family-owned business but does not have a retirement plan for himself or herself or his or her employees may effect a sale of such interest in the business to key employees or a family member under a private annuity arrangement that can provide the shareholder with lifetime retirement income and possible federal estate tax savings.[37]

Trustee as Owner

The Trustee of a revocable living trust can be the legal owner of a private annuity whether it is a single life annuity or a joint and survivor annuity. As with a commercial annuity, the trustor-annuitant—not the trustee—is the measuring life for purposes of the annuity payments. The trustor can convey the ownership of a private annuity to the trustee of a revocable living trust by effecting an Assignment of Private Annuity (see file "APP1605.DOC"). After the trustor has conveyed ownership of the annuity to the trustee, the trustor should inform the transferee that future annuity payments are to be made payable to the trustee (see file "APP1606.DOC"). Of course, if the trustor is the trustee, the trustor would simply deposit the payments into a bank account already titled in the trustor's name as trustee. Likewise, if the trustor is not the trustee, the trustee would deposit the payments into a bank account (an account of which the trustor presumably is able to write checks) titled in the name of the trustee, unless the trustor is physically disabled or mentally

---

[35] Moy, 1, *A Practitioner's Guide to Estate Planning*, § 17.04, at 17-22.

[36] Ibid., § 17.04[A], at 17-23.

[37] Ibid.

incapacitated, in which case the trustee would apply the payments for the trustor's benefit, as provided under the revocable living trust agreement.

Trustee as Beneficiary

The trustee of a revocable living trust does not need to be designated beneficiary of the private annuity payments. With a single life annuity, upon the trustor-annuitant's death, the annuity payments terminate. With a joint and survivor annuity, upon the death of the first annuitant to die, the survivor annuitant will continue to receive the annuity payments under the terms of the private annuity agreement. Upon the subsequent death of the surviving annuitant, most private annuity agreements provide that the annuity payments terminate. Therefore, the revocable living trust does not need to be designated beneficiary.

Lottery Annuity

Winning a large state lottery can make a person an instant millionaire and create interesting estate planning challenges. A lottery annuity is the receipt of a fixed annual payment of money for a certain number of years. Regardless of whether such an annuity is underwritten by a life insurance company or is self-funded by the state sponsoring the lottery, it is established for a certain number of years. Typically, when a life insurance company is involved, the state pays the insurance company a sum of money to purchase a term-certain annuity, which is used to fund the prize paid to the lottery winner. For example, Martin, who had won $2 million in the Oregon State lottery, elected to receive his prize in the form of an annuity. The Oregon Lottery funded this $2 million prize by purchasing from a life insurance company a nineteen-year annuity certain for a payment of $1,202,257. Martin receives $100,000 annually net of federal income tax for nineteen years; he received the first installment of $100,000 outright in cash.

Annuitant's Estate as Beneficiary

Martin had already received six annual annuity payments when his accountant referred him to this author for estate planning consultation. When the annuity contract was consummated, Martin had directed the Oregon Lottery to designate his estate as the beneficiary of the lottery annuity upon his death. Martin already had a substantial estate before he won the lottery, and his primary estate planning objectives were to protect himself from an unnecessary court-supervised financial guardianship if he were to become physically and/or mentally incapacitated and to avoid probate of his estate upon his death. Martin's attorney recommended that he effect a revocable living trust to be the beneficiary of his remaining lottery annuity payments.

Owner of Lottery Annuity

The owner of Martin's lottery annuity contract is the Oregon State Lottery, and Martin is the annuitant. Under Oregon law, payment of any lottery prize may be paid according to the terms of a deceased prizewinner's signed beneficiary designation form filed with the Oregon Lottery Commission.[38] Martin decided to change the beneficiary designation of his lottery annuity from his estate to the trustee of his revocable living trust. The requisite "Beneficiary Designation" change form used by the life insurance company was duly executed and signed by a representative of the Oregon Lottery, naming the trustee, or any successor trustee, of Martin's revocable living trust as the beneficiary of his lottery annuity. This change of beneficiary designation eliminates a probate of the remaining lottery annuity proceeds upon Martin's death.

---

[38] Or. Rev. Stat. § 461.250(7)(a)(A) (Loislaw 2001).

Assignment of Annuitant's Interest in Lottery Annuity to Trustee

The next step was for Martin, as the annuitant, to assign his interest in the lottery annuity to himself as trustee of his revocable living trust agreement (see file "APP1607.DOC").[39] 🖾 Under Oregon law, a lottery winner may assign the prize to a person designated pursuant to an appropriate judicial order of the Circuit Court for the county in which the assignor resides or in which the headquarters of the Oregon State Lottery Commission are located.[40] Unresolved was the issue of whether a lottery annuity could be assigned to the trustee of a revocable living trust.

In an earlier case involving husband and wife winners of the Oregon Lottery, upon presenting their winning ticket for payment, the winners directed payments be made to themselves as co-trustees of their revocable living trust. In other words, the revocable living trust had already been effected; and the first annual payment was to be made to the trustee. In this case, the Oregon Attorney General's office opined that the Oregon Lottery may make payment of lottery prize amounts directly to the trustee of a revocable living trust of which the prize winner is the settlor (trustor), trustee, and one of the trust beneficiaries. In that case, the Assistant Attorney General opined that:

> the [Oregon] Lottery may make payment of a Lottery prize to the winner, with the winner designated as the trustee of a living trust. The prize in that instance literally complies with the constitutional and statutory requirement that the prizes be paid to "adult persons." In this case, the only difference in the prize payment check would be that the payees' status as the trustees of revocable living trusts would be recognized on the face of the prize payment checks.
>
> Moreover, the Lottery's implementing statutes suggest that corporate persons may be Lottery players to whom prizes may be paid. ORS 461.010(5) defines a lottery game as "any procedure authorized by the commission whereby prizes are distributed among persons who have paid, or unconditionally agreed to pay, for tickets or shares which provide the opportunity to win such prizes." That definition is immediately followed by the definition of "person" in ORS 461.010(6): "Person" means any natural person or corporation, *trust*, association, partnership, joint venture, subsidiary or other business entity. [Emphasis added]
>
> In this case, the payment will be made directly to an "adult person," albeit, one identified as the trustee of a revocable living trust. Therefore, the proposed payee designation does not pose the risk of payment of a prize to a minor. *See* ORS 461.250(2).[41] Moreover, because the check makes payment directly to the true winner, whose [sic] is a natural person, the check cannot reasonably be construed as an assignment *of the right* to a prize, which may be accomplished only by a court order. [Emphasis in original] *See* ORS 461.250(7)(a). The issuance of such a prize payment check also is consistent with the prize payment requirements of OAR [Oregon Administrative Rules] 177-10-70.[42]

---

[39] Or. Rev. Stat. § 461.253(4)(a) (Loislaw 2001).

[40] Or. Rev. Stat. § 461.250(7)(a)(B) and 461.253(l) (Loislaw 2001).

[41] *See* Or. Rev. Stat. § 461.250(2) (Loislaw 2001) which states, "No prize shall be paid to any person under 18 years of age."

[42] Assistant Attorney General of the State of Oregon, Oregon Department of Justice, to the Contract Officer Oregon State Lottery, Memorandum, 16 May 1997, Salem, Oregon, cited with permission (hereafter Memorandum). The Memorandum contains the following disclaimer: "This Memorandum constitutes advice that is given exclusively to the Oregon State Lottery and is solely for the use of the Oregon State Lottery. No person may use or is entitled to rely on the advice in this memorandum, and it neither contains nor may be construed as containing any advice concerning the applicability of any tax laws to any person or entity."

This earlier case is distinguishable from Martin's situation in that he had already received six annual annuity payments and wanted to assign future annual annuity payments to himself as trustee of his revocable living trust. The purpose of effecting such an assignment was to eliminate a court-supervised financial guardianship of his interest, as the annuitant, in the lottery annuity if he were to become physically or mentally incapacitated, which, in Martin's case, was a real possibility in view of his medical history of cancer.

Imposition of State Income Tax upon Assignment of Annuitant's Interest in Lottery Annuity to Trustee

Further unresolved was the issue of whether the State of Oregon would impose income tax on the remaining value of the lottery annuity, if it were assigned to the trustee of a revocable living trust. With respect to prizes resulting from lottery tickets purchased before January 1, 1998, the value of such prizes were exempt from Oregon state income tax. In this regard, Oregon law provided that "[n]o state or local taxes shall be imposed upon the sale of lottery tickets or shares of the state lottery . . . or any prize awarded by the state lottery, . . ." Today, Oregon law provides that a prize that is greater than $600 shall be subject to Oregon State income tax.[43] Before Martin's attorney proceeded with a petition to the Circuit Court (see file "APP1608.DOC") 🖾 seeking an order to effect an assignment of Martin's interest in his lottery annuity to himself as the trustee of his revocable living trust, Martin's attorney directed this author to request in writing declaratory rulings from the Oregon Department of Revenue on the unresolved issues. Declaratory rulings are to Oregon state income tax issues what private letter rulings issued by the IRS are to federal income tax issues. This author wrote the issues in the context in which they should be confirmed by the Oregon Department of Revenue. Accordingly, the issues relative to an assignment by Martin of his interest in the lottery annuity to himself as trustee of his revocable living trust were presented to the Oregon Department of Revenue as follows:[44]

- An assignment by taxpayer, approved by an appropriate judicial order, of his interest in the lottery annuity policy to himself as trustee of his revocable living trust (trust) does not subject the annual lottery annuity payments to State of Oregon income tax upon taxpayer's receipt of said payments as the sole primary income beneficiary of the trust.

- An assignment by taxpayer, approved by an appropriate judicial order, of taxpayer's interest in the lottery annuity policy to himself as trustee of the trust does not subject the annual lottery annuity payments to State of Oregon income tax in the event taxpayer becomes legally incapacitated (whether such incapacity is determined under the provisions of the trust or by a court of competent jurisdiction) and said payments are payable to or for the benefit of taxpayer, as sole primary income beneficiary of the trust, by the successor trustee, as provided under the trust.

- Upon the death of taxpayer, receipt by the successor trustee of the trust, as designated beneficiary of the annual lottery annuity payments, does not subject such payments to State of Oregon income tax.

- Receipt by the contingent beneficiaries of the trust of their proportionate share of the annual lottery annuity payments does not subject such beneficiary(ies) to State of Oregon income tax on their respective proportionate shares of the annual lottery annuity payment.

---

[43] Or. Rev. Stat. § 461.560(1) (Loislaw 2001).

[44] Doug H. Moy to Oregon Department of Revenue, 23 May 1997, Lake Oswego, OR.

- Whether a sale (assignment) by taxpayer of taxpayer's entire interest in the lottery annuity policy, approved by an appropriate judicial order, subjects taxpayer to State of Oregon income tax on the present value of said policy in the year of sale (assignment).

Observation

The request for the Declaratory Rulings was made with respect to the Oregon State income tax issues *before* prizes greater than $600 were subject to Oregon State income tax.

Oregon Department of Revenue Declaratory Rulings

The Oregon Department of Revenue issued declaratory rulings in the affirmative, thereby supporting this author's position on the unresolved issues presented. (Upon receiving the favorable declaratory rulings, this author assisted Martin's attorney in the preparation of the Petition for Order Assigning Lottery Payments (see file "APP1608.DOC"), which was filed with the Circuit Court of the State of Oregon and which subsequently was granted by the Circuit Court's Order Directing Lottery Prize Payments to the trustee of Martin's revocable living trust. First, the Department of Revenue addressed issue number five. It determined that an assignment of a taxpayer's rights to receive future lottery payments in exchange for compensation constitutes a sale of those rights, and the taxpayer is taxed on the gain from that sale. The gain on the sale is the difference between the amount realized and the adjusted basis of the rights assigned. Since the rights have no basis, the amount realized is fully taxable.[45]

Moreover, it is the position of the Oregon Department of Revenue that the assignment by Martin of his lottery winnings to a revocable living trust for no compensation is not a taxable transaction. This remains the case even when the revocable living trust becomes irrevocable at the trustor's death and the trust and/or beneficiaries become responsible for reporting the lottery proceeds for federal income tax purposes.[46] Since Martin won the prize as the result of a lottery ticket purchased before January 1, 1998, the contingent beneficiaries of Martin's revocable living trust do not include in gross income for Oregon state income tax purposes the value of their proportionate shares of the lottery annuity payments upon Martin's death. However, all net prizes valued at more than $600 paid as a result of lottery tickets purchased after January 1, 1998, are subject to a State of Oregon income tax rate of 8 percent.[47] Thus, lottery annuity payments attributable to lottery winnings of over $600 as a result of tickets purchased after January 1, 1998, are included in gross income of contingent beneficiaries for State of Oregon income tax purposes.

Furthermore, with respect to prizes won as the result of a lottery ticket purchased before January 1, 1998, it is the opinion of the Oregon Department of Revenue that the assignment of future lottery proceeds to the trustee of a revocable living trust does not subject the annual lottery payments to Oregon income tax.[48] In this regard, "the transfer to the revocable living trust of the taxpayer's rights to the lottery proceeds constitutes a gratuitous transfer. It is the Department's opinion that only an assignment representing a sale of those

---

[45] Gary Friesen, Manager, Corporation and Estate Section, Business Division, Oregon Department of Revenue to Thomas P. Joseph, Jr., Attorney at Law, 8 July 1997, Salem, Oregon, at 1 (hereafter Letter).

[46] Letter, at 2.

[47] Or. Rev. Stat. § 461.560(1) and 316.194(1) (Loislaw 2001). A lottery prize payment made to a trust is not subject to the withholding of tax at the rate of 8 percent by the Oregon State Lottery Commission.

[48] However, after January 1, 1998, all lottery tickets purchased which produce a prize valued at more than $600 are subject to State of Oregon income tax of 8 percent (Or. Rev. Stat. §§ 461.560(1) and 316.194 (Loislaw 2001)).

rights is taxable by Oregon." As pointed out by the Department of Revenue, a revocable living trust under the grantor trust rules (I.R.C. Sections 671-677) is ignored for tax purposes. The taxpayer reports all income, deductions, and credits on his or her personal income tax return as if the taxpayer owns the trust assets personally. The Department of Revenue concluded its opinion by stating, "Since the assignment of the taxpayer's rights in the Lottery Annuity Policy is not, for tax purposes, a completed transaction due to the taxpayer's power to revoke the trust, the taxpayer remains exempt from Oregon tax on the lottery proceeds that he is required to report for federal purposes."[49] Even though the State of Oregon views the transfer to the trustee of a revocable living trust of the taxpayer's rights to the lottery proceeds as a gratuitous transfer, the present value of the lottery annuity is not subject to federal gift tax because of the trustor's right to revoke the trust; that is, a completed gift does not occur.

Federal Income Taxation of Annuitant's Interest in Lottery Annuity Assigned to Trustee

In addition to the issue of state income tax, federal income taxation of an annuity assigned to the trustee of a revocable living trust must also be addressed. In this regard, the question is whether the annuity payments received by the trustor, as primary beneficiary of the revocable living trust, are income taxable to the trustor at the trustor's individual income tax rates or are income taxable under the tax rates for trusts. Under an assignment of the annual lottery payments to the trustee of Martin's revocable living trust, the trustee of the trust would not be in legal title to the lottery annuity; rather, the Oregon State Lottery continues as the legal title holder of the lottery annuity policy. Furthermore, under I.R.C. Section 72(s)(6)(A), if the holder of the annuity contract is not an individual, the primary annuitant is treated as the holder of the contract (the Oregon State Lottery is not an individual). Under I.R.C. Section 72(s)(6)(B), the term *primary annuitant* means the individual, the events in the life of whom are of primary importance in affecting the timing or amount of the payout under the annuity contract. Clearly, Martin is the individual, the events in the life of whom are of primary importance in affecting the timing or amount of the payout under the annuity contract.

In addition, as a general rule, I.R.C. Section 72(u)(1) provides that, if any annuity contract is held by a person who is not a natural person (e.g., a trustee; Oregon State Lottery), the income on the contract for any taxable year of the policyholder is treated as ordinary income received or accrued by the owner during such taxable year (however, the Oregon State Lottery is not the annuitant; therefore, the income is not received by it). For this purpose, holding by a trust or other entity as an agent for a natural person is not taken into account.[50] The IRS has stated that, "No federal court has yet addressed when a trust is acting as an agent for a natural person within the meaning of section 72(u)(1)."[51] However, for the *natural person* rule to apply, the trustee must be in legal title to the annuity.[52] With respect

---

[49] Letter, at 2.

[50] I.R.C. § 72(u)(1).

[51] Priv. Ltr. Rul. 9639057 (June 24, 1996). *See also* Priv. Ltr. Rul. 200018046 (February 8, 2000) (group annuity contract held by a trust is held for a natural person within the meaning of I.R.C. § 72(u)); Priv. Ltr. Rul. 199933033 (May 25, 1999) (annuity contract held by irrevocable grantor trust is considered owned by a natural person for purposes of I.R.C. § 72(u)); Priv. Ltr. Rul. 199905015 (November 5, 19[9]8) (three annuity contracts held in trust are considered owned by natural persons for purposes of I.R.C. § 72(u)).

[52] *See* Priv. Ltr. Rul. 9204010 (October 10, 1991) (annuity contract owned by trustee is considered owned by a natural person for purposes of I.R.C. § 72(u)(1)); Priv. Ltr. Rul. 9204014 (October 24, 1991) (same holding as in Priv. Ltr. Rul. 9204010).

to Martin, the trustee of his revocable living trust is not in legal title to the lottery annuity; the Oregon State Lottery continues as the legal titleholder of the Lottery Annuity Policy. As an assignee, the trustee of the revocable living trust holds only an equitable interest in the Lottery Annuity for the benefit of Martin, as primary beneficiary, who possesses a beneficial interest in the lottery annuity under the provisions of the revocable living trust. In this regard, it makes no difference whether Martin or a third party is the trustee of the revocable living trust.

Finally, and perhaps most importantly, the rules with respect to the treatment of annuity contracts not held by natural persons do not apply if the annuity at issue is an immediate annuity.[53] In this regard, the term *immediate annuity* means an annuity that is purchased with a single premium or annuity consideration, the annuity starting date of which commences no later than one year from the date of the purchase of the annuity, and which provides for a series of substantially equal periodic payments (to be made not less frequently than annually) during the annuity period.[54]

A lottery annuity is characterized as an immediate annuity. Generally, even if the first lottery payment is given to the winner in cash (as in Martin's case), Martin's first annual payment under the lottery annuity began not later than one year from the date of the purchase of the annuity. Thus, for federal income tax purposes, all income from the annual lottery annuity payments, if assigned to the trustee of a revocable living trust, continue to be reported by the trustor on the trustor's Form 1040. Similarly, at least in the state of Oregon, since taxpayers are not subject to State of Oregon income tax on the annual lottery annuity payments, resulting from lottery tickets purchased *before* January 1, 1998, neither is the trustor subject to State of Oregon income tax on receipt of the annual lottery annuity payments assigned to the trustee of a revocable living trust agreement.[55]

State Taxation of Lottery Payments to Incapacitated Trustor

With respect to prizes won as the result of a lottery ticket purchased *before* January 1, 1998, the Oregon Department of Revenue did not specifically address the issue of how the annual lottery annuity payments are taxed to the trustor if he or she becomes legally incapacitated. For federal income tax purposes, whether or not the trustor becomes legally incapacitated, all income from the annual lottery annuity payments assigned to the trustee of a revocable living trust continue to be reported by the trustor on Form 1040. In this regard, a trustor's legal incapacity does not change his or her status as the owner of a revocable living trust under the grantor trust rules.

The Code does not define the word *owner*. Generally, the word *owner* must be interpreted in its context and according to the circumstances in which it is used.[56] In the strictest sense, the word *owner* means legal owner; however, it may also include any person with a beneficial interest in property.[57] In addition, ownership may be an equitable interest in property.[58] Recall that, in a trust, the beneficiary has an equitable interest; and the trustee holds

---

[53] I.R.C. § 72(u)(3)(E) and (4); Rev. Rul. 92-95, 1992-2 C.B. 43 (an immediate annuity is excepted from the provisions of I.R.C. § 72(u) because of the relative absence of opportunity for tax benefits attributable to the deferral of income on the annuity contract).

[54] I.R.C. § 72(u)(4).

[55] After January 1, 1998, all lottery tickets purchased that produce a prize valued at more than $600 are subject to a State of Oregon income tax rate of 8 percent (Or. Rev. Stat. §§ 461.560(1) and 316.194 (Loislaw 2001)).

[56] *Warren v. Borawski*, 37 A.2d 364, 365, 366, 130 Conn. 676; *General Realty Impt. Co. v. City of New Haven*, 50 A.2d 59, 61, 133 Conn. 238.

[57] *Siemer v. Schuermann Bldg. & Realty Co.*, 381 S.W.2d 821, 826 (Mo.).

[58] *In re Freeman's Heirs at Law*, 128 S.E. 404, 408, 189 N.C. 790.

a legal interest in the trust property (trust estate).[59] Of course, the trustor of a revocable living trust, as primary lifetime beneficiary of the trust, possesses an equitable ownership interest in the property conveyed to the trustee. Thus, for purposes of I.R.C. Sections 671-677, the trustor's ownership of the trust estate is an equitable interest—not a legal interest.

Code Section 671 does not provide that, in order for the grantor (trustor), rather than the trust, to be the taxpayer, the trustor must be both trustor and trustee; nor does it provide that the trustor must have a legal (fee simple) interest in the trust. In fact, I.R.C. Sections 673-677 provide that the grantor (trustor) is treated as the owner of any portion of a trust in respect of which the grantor has a reversionary interest in either the corpus or the income therefrom, or the beneficial enjoyment of the corpus or the income therefrom is subject to a power of disposition, exercisable by the grantor or a nonadverse party, or both, without the approval or consent of any adverse party.[60] Accordingly, where the trustor (taxpayer) is the primary lifetime beneficiary of the revocable living trust, if the trustor (taxpayer) becomes legally incapacitated, does the trustor now hold an ownership interest less than an equitable interest in the trust estate? The answer is no. This is because the trustor (taxpayer), as the lifetime beneficiary of the revocable living trust, continues to hold an equitable ownership interest in the trust estate.

Therefore, for the trustor to be the *owner* under I.R.C. Sections 671-677 means that the trustor holds an equitable ownership interest in the trust estate. An individual who is otherwise required to file an income tax return and pay income taxes is not excused from doing so merely because he or she is incompetent or incapacitated.[61] In such case, a taxpayer may have an agent make the return if the taxpayer is unable to do so.[62] Consequently, for federal income tax purposes, physical or mental incapacity does not excuse the taxpayer from reporting annual lottery annuity payments assigned to the trustee of a revocable living trust on the trustor's Form 1040.

The inability of the trustor (taxpayer) due to physical or mental incapacity to revoke the revocable living trust does not deny the trustor (taxpayer) the income tax benefits afforded by I.R.C. Section 671. Code Section 671 does not provide that, in order for the grantor (trustor) to be treated as the owner of a trust under the grantor trust rules, the grantor must qualify under each section of I.R.C. Sections 671-677. Thus, even if the trustor (taxpayer) could not "fully exercise the power to revoke" the revocable living trust under I.R.C. Section 676(a) because of physical or mental incapacity, so long as the trustor is treated as the owner of any portion of the revocable living trust under I.R.C. Sections 671-677, the trustor continues to report the annual lottery annuity payments on Form 1040, even if the Form 1040 is prepared by the trustor's (taxpayer's) agent.[63] Therefore, if a trustor (taxpayer) is not presently subject to State of Oregon income tax on the annual lottery annuity payments, then trustor (taxpayer) is not subject to State of Oregon income tax on the annual lottery annuity payments paid to or on behalf of trustor (taxpayer) by the successor trustee of the revocable living trust if the trustor (taxpayer) becomes physically and/or mentally incapacitated, whether determined under the provisions of the revocable living trust or by a proper court of jurisdiction.

---

[59] *Restatement (Second) of Trusts* § 2(f); *see* discussion in "Definition of a Revocable Living Trust" and "Components of a Revocable Living Trust" sections in Chapter 2.

[60] I.R.C. §§ 673(a); 674(a); 675(1); 676(a) and 677(a).

[61] I.R.C. § 6012(a)(1)(A) and (b)(2).

[62] Treas. Reg. § 1.6012-1(a)(5).

[63] For additional arguments supporting the position that the trustor of a revocable living trust is still the taxpayer even if incapacitated, *see* Moy, "Revocable Living Trusts: Availability of One-Time Exclusion."

Importance of State Law

Whether a lottery winner may assign a prize to the trustee of a revocable living trust depends on state law. In Oregon, the Oregon State Lottery collects a nonrefundable processing fee of $500 for each assignee when the copy of the petition is served on the Oregon Lottery Commission.[64] In addition to this processing fee, attorney's fees are involved in the preparation, filing, and defense, if necessary, of a petition to assign a lottery annuity to the trustee of a revocable living trust. In Oregon, these expenses can be avoided if, before a name of the owner of the ticket is imprinted or placed upon a lottery ticket in the area designated for *name*, the lottery winner directs the Oregon State Lottery to make the prize payment checks payable to the trustee of a revocable living trust or to a bank or investment account titled in the name of the trustee of such a trust. Similarly, if the lottery winner chooses a lottery annuity, the trustee may be designated the payee of the annual lottery annuity payments at the time application for the lottery annuity is made.

---

[64] Or. Rev. Stat. § 461.253(2) (Loislaw 2001).

PART IV

Supporting Documents

CHAPTER 17

Power of Attorney and Pour-Over Will

COORDINATING A DURABLE POWER OF ATTORNEY WITH A REVOCABLE LIVING TRUST

A power of attorney is a written document wherein one person, called the *principal*, appoints another person as his or her *attorney-in-fact* (agent) with the authority to perform certain specified acts on behalf of the principal. The person acting as the attorney-in-fact is not the same as a duly licensed attorney at law;[1] although, a practicing or nonpracticing attorney may serve as the principal's attorney-in-fact under a power of attorney. The authority granted under a power of attorney may either be general or specific or a combination of both. In effect, a power of attorney is an extension of the principal's abilities to perform certain acts that the principal would otherwise perform if he or she chose to do so or were capable of performing.

Durable Power of Attorney

A durable power of attorney authorizes the attorney-in-fact to perform certain acts beyond the principal's physical or mental incapacity to do so.[2] As a rule, if a power of attorney is a durable power of attorney, it will contain the words, "This power of attorney shall not be affected by subsequent disability or incapacity of the principal, or lapse of time;" or "This power of attorney shall become effective upon the disability or incapacity of the principal" (a so-called springing durable power of attorney) or similar words. In other words, the power of attorney expresses the principal's intention that the authority conferred upon the attorney-in-fact is exercisable regardless of the principal's subsequent physical or mental incapacity.[3]

Durable General Power of Attorney

A durable general power of attorney is perhaps one of the most important and valuable legal documents a person can effect; while, at the same time, it can be the most dangerous. In regard to the latter, with a durable general power of attorney, the principal gives the attorney-in-fact the key to the front door of the principal's estate. In effect, the attorney-in-fact can do just about anything he or she wants to do with respect to the principal's property. Because a durable general power of attorney gives the attorney-in-fact such awesome power over the principal's financial affairs, the principal cannot afford to have this authority and power abused. For this reason alone, it is absolutely imperative that the

---

[1] 3 Am Jur2d, Agency, § 23.
[2] 3 Am Jur2d, Agency, § 28.
[3] Uniform Durable Power of Attorney Act, § 1, 8A U.L.A. 89 (1991).

honesty, integrity, and trustworthiness of the person chosen to be the principal's attorney-in-fact be beyond reproach. If the trustor is the trustee of his or her revocable living trust, a good choice for the trustor's attorney-in-fact would be the successor trustee of the trustor's revocable living trust. If the trustor has enough confidence and trust in that person to be the successor trustee of his or her revocable living trust, the same confidence and trust should extend to that person being empowered to act as the trustor's attorney-in-fact.

Durable Special Power of Attorney

If the trustor is genuinely concerned about giving someone a durable general power of attorney but wants to empower his or her attorney-in-fact with the authority to convey title to his or her property to the trustee of a revocable living trust if the trustor becomes physically disabled or mentally incapacitated, then the trustor should effect a durable special power of attorney (see file "APP1701.DOC"). The trustor must be absolutely certain that the durable special power of attorney he or she effects complies with state law for a durable power of attorney. Under a durable special power of attorney, the attorney-in-fact is authorized to perform only those actions specifically provided. In this regard, as the principal, the trustor can specifically authorize his or her attorney-in-fact to only effect legal documents and carry out actions necessary to convey title to the trustor's property to the trustee of a revocable living trust. Thus, the attorney-in-fact is prohibited from otherwise dealing with the trustor's property. Such a power of attorney can give the trustor the assurance needed that, if he or she becomes physically disabled or mentally incapacitated following the execution of his or her revocable living trust and before it is completely funded, the attorney-in-fact can complete the funding process on behalf of the trustor.

Elimination of Court-Appointed Financial Guardian

A carefully designed and properly executed durable power of attorney can obviate the need for a court-appointed guardianship of the principal's financial affairs. Similarly, along with a qualified durable power of attorney for health care (directive to physicians), an attorney-in-fact can be authorized to oversee the principal's personal care, including making health care-related decisions. All fifty states, plus the District of Columbia, provide by statute for the use of the durable power of attorney. Unfortunately, though, the laws among the states are not uniform as to the requirements of a durable power of attorney. Therefore, strict adherence to state law is strongly advised with respect to the powers that may be granted to the attorney-in-fact.

State Law Governs Powers of Attorney

Federal law does not govern powers of attorney. Such powers are governed either by common law or state statute.[4] Generally, the validity of the durable power of attorney is determined under the laws of the state where the document was effected.

Example

Bob, the principal, is a legal resident of Oregon. Bob gives his son, Chris (the attorney-in-fact), a durable power of attorney. Chris is a legal resident of the state of Washington. The durable power of attorney is effected in the state of Oregon. Chris takes the original durable power of attorney to his home in Washington State and places the document in

---

[4]Francis J. Collin, Jr., John J. Lombard, Jr., Albert L. Moses, editor, and Harley J. Spitler, *Drafting the Durable Power of Attorney A Systems Approach*, 2d ed. (Colorado Springs, Colorado: Shepard's McGraw-Hill, 1987), at 18 (hereafter Collin, Jr., *Drafting the Durable Power of Attorney*).

safekeeping. The validity of the durable power of attorney is determined by Oregon state law—not the law of Washington State.[5]

However, the validity of the acts performed by the attorney-in-fact is governed by the law of the state where the agent acts.[6] In this regard, the state where the agent acts has the most significant relationship to the parties and the transaction.

Example

Using the same facts as in the previous example, Bob executes a durable power of attorney for health care under the law of the state of Oregon, naming Chris as his attorney-in-fact. Bob is injured in an automobile accident in Nevada and placed on life support in a Nevada hospital. Chris's authority under the durable power of attorney to make health care decisions for Bob is governed by Nevada state law—not Oregon state law.[7]

Management of Principal's Property

A primary advantage of a durable power of attorney is that the attorney-in-fact can control and manage the principal's property before, during, and after the principal's physical or mental incapacity without the necessity of a court-supervised financial guardian. The extent to which the durable power of attorney document will carry out the principal's objectives depends on the credibility of the instrument in the minds of third parties who may rely on the authority of the agent. Generally, the more specific the agent's authority, the greater likelihood that third parties will be willing to accept the agent's authority. Furthermore, the principal should be as specific as possible regarding the post-incapacity acts conferred upon the agent.

Agents Accountability to Guardian and Principal

Under a durable power of attorney, if appointment of a guardian for the principal is necessary, the attorney-in-fact is accountable to both the guardian and the principal. The guardian has the same power to revoke or amend the power of attorney that the principal would have had if he or she were not incapacitated.[8] A durable power of attorney may be considered an instrument in writing under which the principal may nominate a guardian of his or her personal and financial affairs.[9]

Death of Principal and Attorney-in-Fact

Like a guardianship, a durable power of attorney cannot serve as a bridge between the lifetime and post-death management of the principal's financial affairs; nor can it operate in lieu of a court-supervised proceeding to administer the principal's probate estate. This is because the principal's death terminates the agent's authority. Consequently, any act performed by the agent subsequent to the principal's death will not affect the principal's estate.[10] Similarly, the death of the attorney-in-fact revokes a durable power of attorney. Likewise, the death of one joint agent revokes the power of attorney as to the surviving agent.[11]

---

[5] Collin, Jr., *Drafting the Durable Power of Attorney*, at 18.

[6] Ibid., at 18-19.

[7] Ibid., at 19.

[8] 3 Am Jur2d, Agency, § 58.

[9] *See* 3 Am Jur2d, Agency, § 58.

[10] 3 Am Jur2d, Agency, § 55.

[11] 3 Am Jur2d, Agency, § 57.

Ask Your Attorney

If I effect a revocable living trust, is a power of attorney still necessary?

Answer

Both a durable power of attorney and a durable power of attorney for health care, along with a revocable living trust, should be part of every trustor's estate plan. On the one hand, a revocable living trust is a superior alternative to a durable power of attorney. Legally, the trustee under a revocable living trust agreement does not have the authority to provide for the trustor's personal care like an attorney-in-fact does under a durable power of attorney for health care. On the other hand, the ideal arrangement is for the successor trustee to also be the trustor's attorney-in-fact under both a durable power of attorney and a durable power of attorney for health care.

Successor Trustee as Attorney-in-Fact

Designating the successor trustee of a revocable living trust agreement as the trustor's attorney-in-fact under a durable power of attorney can be invaluable for at least two reasons. First, not all durable powers of attorney are universally accepted by banks, stock brokerage firms, transfer agents, and other financial institutions. Oftentimes, a revocable living trust agreement is more likely to be accepted by financial institutions and other third parties because legal title to trust property is actually in the name of the trustee; legal title to property of which an attorney-in-fact has control under a durable power of attorney is not in the name of the attorney-in-fact. Furthermore, a revocable living trust is a traditional legal arrangement; and the law governing trusts is better established than the law governing durable powers of attorney.

Secondly, under a durable power of attorney, the principal can authorize his or her attorney-in-fact to complete important phases of the principal's estate plan which otherwise may go unfinished as the result of the physical or mental incapacity of the principal. For example, if the trustor becomes incapacitated after having effected a revocable living trust agreement but before the trustor has conveyed legal title to property to the trustee, the durable power of attorney can authorize the attorney-in-fact to effect the legal documents necessary to convey legal title to the property to the trustee. Similarly, such authority in the agent may be invaluable to convey legal title to the trustee of property that the trustor may *inherit* after the onset of physical or mental incapacity. Furthermore, the trustor could empower his or her attorney-in-fact to name the trustee of the trustor's revocable living trust as beneficiary of certain qualified and nonqualified retirement plans or name the trustee beneficiary of certain life insurance contracts insuring the trustor's life or the life of someone else.

Moreover, the attorney-in-fact should be given the authority to execute deeds in order to convey the trustor's interest in real property to the trustee of a revocable living trust and to effect stock transfers or assignments to the trustee. In addition, if permitted under local law, the trustor may want to authorize his or her attorney-in-fact to amend the trustor's revocable living trust. Whether an attorney-in-fact can create and effect a revocable living trust is a matter of state law to determine. However, an attorney-in-fact cannot make a Last Will for a testator.

Choosing between a Revocable Living Trust and a Durable Power of Attorney

Does the foregoing suggest that one must choose between the use of a revocable living trust or a durable power of attorney? The answer is unequivocally *no!* In fact, a revocable living trust agreement and a durable power of attorney, as well as a durable power of attorney for health care, are remarkably compatible estate planning documents that, when properly designed and effected in concert, can provide for a practical and foolproof estate plan. The most significant reason for this unique compatibility is that the agent under the durable power of attorney can be authorized to perform acts that the principal would perform if not for the principal's incapacity or temporary unavailability. In this regard, under the durable power of attorney, the principal extends his or her ability to the attorney-in-fact to complete important phases of the principal's estate plan which may otherwise go unfinished in the event the principal becomes incapacitated.

Thus, every revocable living trust agreement should be accompanied by either a durable general power of attorney or a durable special power of attorney. A revocable living trust cannot achieve all of its purposes if it is not properly funded; and it cannot be funded until after it is effected. Absent a durable power of attorney, if the trustor becomes physically disabled or mentally incapacitated following the execution of the revocable living trust agreement, to the extent rendering the trustor incapable of funding the trust, then title to the trustor's property cannot be conveyed to the trustee. Under a durable power of attorney, the trustor can authorize his or her attorney-in-fact to effect the necessary conveyances to the trustee of his or her revocable living trust.

Observation/Recommendation

Provision should be made in the durable power of attorney for the activation of the power of attorney if the principal goes missing. Furthermore, provision should also be made for a successor attorney-in-fact if the designated attorney-in-fact likewise goes missing.

POUR-OVER WILL

Ask Your Attorney

If I have a properly designed and funded revocable living trust, do I still need a Last Will?

Answer

Unequivocally, yes!

Every revocable living trust should be accompanied by a pour-over Will. The trustor should beware the attorney who advises the trustor that it is not necessary to have a Last Will coordinated with the revocable living trust. In fact, any attorney who would make such a recommendation is not qualified to design, prepare, or implement a revocable living trust.

Generally, a pour-over Will serves as a testamentary backup to a revocable living trust. A pour-over Will does exactly what the term implies; it pours property from either a Last Will or trust into another Last Will or trust to be managed by the fiduciaries under the terms of the other instrument. Only property owned by a person in his or her individual name or which is payable to his or her estate can pour-over under the pour-over Will to the trustee of a revocable living trust. Property owned as joint tenants with right of survivorship (including tenants by the entirety) cannot pour-over to the trustee of a revocable living trust upon the trustor's death.[12]

---

[12] For additional reading, *see* Robert J. Lynn, "Problems With Pour-over Wills," 47 *Ohio State Law Journal* 47 (1986); with regard to the issues confronting persons who hold title to property as JTWROS, *see* "Property Received by Right of Survivorship" section in Chapter 1 and Moy, 1, *A Practitioner's Guide to Estate Planning*, Chapter 5, Joint Tenancy With Right of Survivorship.

Examples

1. In her will, Zella gives her residuary estate in equal shares to her sister, Laura, her brother, Earl, and her sister, Ina Mae, or their respective surviving children by right of representation. "Except, however, as regards the share of my residuary estate for my brother, Earl, I give, devise, and bequeath said share to Robert E. E_____ and Darlene G. Q_____, as Trustees, under a Revocable Living Trust Agreement executed by my brother, Earl L. E_____, and his wife, Opal F. E_____, as Trustors, dated April 4, 1994. Said share shall be the sole and separate property of my brother, Earl, and shall be added to Schedule "B" of said Trust Agreement as the sole and separate property of Earl L. E_____. If said Revocable Living Trust Agreement is revoked either before or after the date of my death, I give, devise, and bequeath the share for my brother, Earl, unto him outright if he shall survive me, or in equal shares to his surviving children, or, if only one of them survives, all to the survivor of them."

2. In her pour-over will, Ruth gives her residuary estate "to the Trustee then acting under that certain Declaration of Trust known as the Ruth F._____ Revocable Living Trust Agreement, dated August 15, 1995, wherein I am the Trustor; and I direct that such residue shall be added to and co-mingled with the Trust property of such Revocable Living Trust Agreement and shall be held, administered, and distributed in accordance with the terms, conditions, and fiduciary powers of said Trust, including any amendments made thereto before my death (whether made before or after the execution of this Will), it being my intention not to create a separate testamentary trust nor to subject such Revocable Living Trust Agreement to the jurisdiction of the Probate Court. If for any reason such distribution of my estate is ineffective, then I give such residue to E. Hugh_____, Jr., or his successor or successors, as Trustee, to be held in a Testamentary Trust in accordance with the terms conditions and fiduciary powers of the hereinbefore described Trust, including any amendments made thereto before my death (whether made before or after the execution of this Will), which provisions are hereby incorporated by reference herein and made part hereof. If, in accordance with the provisions of the Trust, any portion thereof is distributable free of the Trust, then such portion shall be paid directly to the recipient entitled thereto by my Personal Representative."

3. In his will, Edward gives his residuary estate "to the National Bank of Commerce of Seattle, a national banking association, with its principal office in Seattle, Washington, or its successors, in trust, nevertheless, to be added to that certain trust established by the testator and pursuant to that certain Life Insurance Trust Agreement, dated June 6, 1996, which agreement covers not only all insurance policies and the proceeds thereof from time to time dedicated to said trust or delivered to said Trustee for incorporation in said trust, but also all property of whatsoever kind and wheresoever situated, which from time to time may be devised . . . to said Trustee . . . for the purpose of said trust."

Revocable Living Trust Not a Last Will

Technically and legally, a revocable living trust is not a Last Will and Testament. Oftentimes, a revocable living trust is referred to as a Will substitute; but it is not a Last Will. As a rule, an unfunded revocable living trust, standing alone, is not considered a valid testamentary instrument for the disposition of an individual's estate. This is because such trusts usually do not conform to the requirements for the execution of Wills. In this regard, the trustor may insist of his or her attorney that the trustor's revocable living trust be effected with the same formalities as a Last Will, if, for no other reason than to provide additional efficacy to the execution of the trust. Most states, however, have either adopted either the Uniform Testamentary Additions to Trusts Act or recognize the doctrine of *incorporation by reference.*[13] Simply stated, the Uniform Testamentary Additions to Trusts Act provides that a valid devise or bequest may be made to the trustee of a trust, provided the trust is identified in the testator's Last Will, the terms of the trust are set forth in a written instrument, and the instrument is executed with requirements similar to those for executing a Last Will. Such a trust instrument may be effected before or concurrently with the execution of the testator's Last Will or in the valid Last Will of a person who has predeceased the testator.

Doctrine of Independent Significance

Those states that do not recognize either the Uniform Testamentary Additions to Trusts Act or the doctrine of *incorporation by reference* generally will uphold the provisions of a pour-over Will distributing property to the trustee of a revocable living trust under the doctrine of *independent significance.* In effect, this doctrine holds that an act or document is said to have independent legal significance so as to carry out the wishes of the testator or decedent if it is not executed solely to avoid the requirements of a Last Will. Accordingly, what may appear to be a testamentary disposition without observing the requirements of local law regarding Wills may be given effect.[14] Regardless of whether the doctrine of *incorporation by reference* rule or the doctrine of *independent significance* rule is followed, the pour-over Will, when used and properly coordinated with a revocable living trust agreement, gives such a trust legal effect for disposing of a trustor's assets upon his or her death.

Purposes of Pour-Over Will

A properly designed pour-over Will may accomplish a variety of purposes:

Coordination of Asset Disposition

A pour-over Will provides coordination of the disposition of the trustor's assets under the terms of a revocable living trust agreement, whether those assets are disposed of under his or her Last Will or legal title is conveyed to the trustee of the revocable living trust agreement during the trustor's lifetime and are held, managed, or distributed by the trust upon the trustor's death.

Coordinated Disposition of Inherited Property

Another important purpose of the pour-over Will is to coordinate the disposition of any inherited property the trustor may receive before death but which, because of death, the trustor did not convey legal title to such property to the trustee of his or her revocable living trust. Thus, the disposition of such property may be coordinated with the disposition of the trustor's other trust estate assets. Absent a pour-over Will, such inherited property would probably be distributed according to the laws of intestate distribution. The pattern of intestate distribution for the disposition of such assets may not be the same as for the trustor's assets under the terms of his or her revocable trust agreement.

---

[13] *See Clark v. Greenhalge,* 41 Mass. 410, 582 N.E.2d 949 (1991); *Matter of Estate of Norton,* 330 N.C. 378, 410 S.E.2d 484 (1991); *Matter of Estate of Sneed,* 953 P.2d 1111 (Okla., 1998) (doctrine of incorporation by reference used to make revocable living trust part of decedent's will); *In re Scmitt's Will,* 187 Misc. 409, 61 NYS2d 569 (Surr. Ct., Westch Co.) *appeal dismissed* 63 NYS2d 215 (2d Dept., 1946); *Matter of Fowles,* 222 N.Y. 222 (1918); *Matter of Andrest,* 96 Misc. 389, 160 NYS 505 (Surr. Ct., Fulton Co. 1916); *In re Will of Hall,* 59 Misc.2d 881, 300 NYS2d 813 (Surr. West., 1969) (all regarding problems associated with doctrine of incorporation by reference in New York State); *In re Estate of McGabee,* 550 So.2d 83 (Fla. Dist. Ct. App., 1989) (provisions of paper attached to will were incorporated by reference into will).

[14] Black, *Black's Law Dictionary,* at 693.

Failure by Trustor to Convey Title to Assets to Trustee during Trustor's Lifetime

If, during the trustor's lifetime, he or she forgets to convey a particular asset to the trustee of his or her revocable living trust after it is executed and initially funded, then, following the trustor's death, such property may be poured-over to the trustee of the trustor's revocable living trust under the terms of the pour-over Will.

Trustor's Revocation of Revocable Living Trust

A properly designed and executed pour-over Will is important because the trustor might revoke the revocable living trust during his or her lifetime, thereby canceling what would otherwise be the trustor's only *testamentary* plan of estate distribution. Absent a valid Last Will to effect property distributions upon the trustor's death, the trustor may be considered to have died intestate. In such case, the trustor's estate would be distributed according to state statute regarding intestate succession.

Probate

Whether the property distributable to the trustee of the trustor's revocable living trust under a pour-over Will is subject to probate depends on the provisions of the small estate statutes of the trustor's domicile or state of residency. Even if such property falls outside the small estate statutory dollar amount passing under the terms of the trustor's pour-over Will or does not satisfy other statutory requirements and must be probated before it can be conveyed to the trustee of the trustor's revocable living trust, it can still be administered and distributed by the trustee under the terms of the revocable living trust agreement. Absent the pour-over Will, such property may be distributable by a court-appointed administrator and be subject to the laws of intestate succession under the law of the trustor's domicile or state of residency.

Recognizing a Pour-Over Will

Generally, a pour-over Will looks like and contains all the provisions of a regular Last Will with at least one exception. Aside from specific distributions of tangible personal property, no provisions are made for specific distributions of the testator's residuary estate (assets remaining after all taxes, debts, and the costs of administering the testator's estate have been satisfied). Typically, the testator declares that the remainder of his or her probate estate is to be given "to the Trustee then acting under that certain Declaration of Trust known as the (*name of the trustor's trust*) Family Revocable Living Trust Agreement, dated (*effective date of the trust*)," or similar language. Thus, the trustee of the revocable living trust actually distributes the trust estate to the trustor's beneficiaries as provided under the trust agreement.

If the terms of the revocable living trust are incorporated by reference into the pour-over Will, even if the trustor revokes the revocable living trust agreement, the terms of the trust would still be followed upon the trustor's death to distribute his or her estate. This would occur even though the revocable living trust may lose its independent significance and have no validity standing by itself. This is because the law of succession abhors intestate distribution of a testator's estate if it can be clearly shown that the testator intended otherwise.[15] With this in mind, if the trustor revokes his or her living trust agreement, and whether the trustor effects a replacement revocable living trust agreement, he or she should be certain to review his or her current pour-over Will to determine if it should be revoked or amended.

---

[15] *In re Estate of Baer*, 446 So.2d 1128 (Fla. Dist. Ct. App. 1984); Uniform Probate Code § 2-512, 8 *Uniform Laws Annotated* (1995).

A typical pour-over Will provision may read as follows:[16]

ARTICLE III

STATEMENT OF INTENTION

It is my intention to dispose of all of my property at the time of my death which I have right to dispose of by Will, including any real, tangible and intangible personal property, wheresoever situated, and any property over which I have power of appointment, which I may own at my death.

ARTICLE IV

DISPOSITION OF RESIDUE

(A) **Declaration of Trust.** I give, devise and bequeath all of the rest, residue, and remainder of my estate, of every type and description and wherever situated, including property over which I have power to appoint, to the Trustee then acting under that certain Declaration of Trust known as the (*name of trust*) Revocable Living Trust Agreement, dated September 1, 2000, and any amendments thereto, between myself, (*name of trustor*), as Trustor and (*name of trustee*), as Trustee. I direct that such residue shall be added to and co-mingled with the Trust property of said Revocable Living Trust and shall be held, administered, and distributed in accordance with the terms, conditions, and fiduciary powers of said Trust, including any amendments made thereto before my death (whether made before or after the execution of this Last Will)—it being my intention not to create a separate or testamentary trust nor to subject such Trust to the jurisdiction of the Probate Court. If, for any reason, such distribution of my estate is ineffective, then I give such residue to (*name of successor trustee*), or his or her successor or successors, as Trustee (*or as co-trustees*), to be held in a testamentary trust in accordance with the terms, conditions, and fiduciary powers of the hereinbefore described Trust, including any amendments made before my death (whether made before or after the execution of this Last Will), which provisions are hereby incorporated herein by reference and made part hereof. If, in accordance with the provisions of the Trust, any portion thereof is distributable free of the Trust, then such portion shall be paid directly to the recipient entitled thereto by my Personal Representative.

(B) **Tangible Personal Property.** If I have deposited with my Personal Representative written instructions concerning disposition of my tangible personal property, the distribution shall be made in accordance therewith. If I have not deposited such instructions, I have every confidence that my [*name of beneficiary(ies)*] and the Trustee of the (*name of beneficiary*) Special Needs Trust under the (*name of trustor*) Revocable Living Trust Agreement, dated September 1, 2000, will be able to make such distributions fairly; and, if any question arises as to a particular item, then the decision of my Personal Representative shall be conclusive.

Observation

The names of the testator's beneficiaries may be the testator's children, grandchildren, nephews, nieces, and so forth. In the above example, testator directed that her tangible personal property be distributed among her children and the trustee of the Special Needs

---

[16]For sample pour-over Wills, *see* files "APP0501.DOC" (Pour-Over Will of Single Testator); "APP0502.DOC" (Pour-Over Will of Husband); "APP0503.DOC" (Pour-Over Will of Wife); and "APP0504.DOC" (Pour-Over Wills of Husband and Wife to accompany Joint Revocable Living Trust).

Trust under her Revocable Living Trust Agreement for the benefit of her handicapped grandson (see file "APP0501.DOC" for the complete pour-over Will of this testator).

Determining When to Review a Last Will

Whenever the trustor has reason to amend his or her revocable living trust, a review of the trustor's pour-over Will should also be conducted to be certain that the provisions under the pour-over Will are coordinated with the changes made in his or her revocable living trust. Furthermore, the happening or nonhappening of certain events in the trustor's life may necessitate a complete review of the trustor's overall estate plan which, of course, would include a review of his or her revocable living trust and accompanying pour-over Will. In the examples of events[17] listed below which may necessitate a review of the trustor's Last Will, though technically the person who makes a Last Will is called the *testator* (if the maker of the Last Will is a man) or *testatrix* (if the maker of the Last Will is a woman), in this discussion, the maker of the Last Will is referred to as the trustor.

A Move to Another State

Laws regarding Wills and the disposition of a person's property vary from state to state. Adherence to state law is important.

Births, Deaths, Marriages, or Divorces within the Trustor's Family

As a general rule, the laws of most states look for after-born children (i.e., children born after the trustor executes his or her Last Will but later neglects to amend the Last Will to include the after-born child(ren)). In some cases, some children of the decedent trustor can be disinherited; and the after-born child may be entitled to a disproportionate share of the decedent trustor's probate estate at the expense of the trustor's other children.[18] For this reason, it is critically important for the trustor to periodically review his or her Last Will with respect to the issue of after-born children.

Changes in the Tax Laws

With the enactment of the 2001 Act and future federal tax legislation, trustors should consult their attorneys and tax advisers to determine what impact such legislation might have on their estate plans and, in particular, their Last Wills and revocable living trusts.

Lifetime Disposition of Assets Mentioned in a Last Will

For example, the trustor may provide in his or her Will for a beneficiary to receive a particular parcel of real estate; but he or she may later sell the same property. This is known as ademption.

Changes in the Value of Assets

Assume the trustor owns stock in two separate companies—GT&S and TPI. Both are of equal value when the trustor's Last Will is first established, so the trustor leaves the GT&S stock to one beneficiary and the TPI stock to another. Later, the GT&S stock increases considerably in value; while the TPI stock decreases in value. The result, though it is not the trustor's intention, is that one beneficiary will receive less than the other.

---

[17] Moy, 2, *A Practitioner's Guide to Estate Planning*, § 30.06, at 30-68; for additional reading, *see* Stephen R. Leimberg and Charles K. Plotnick, "How to Review a Will," 34 *Practical Lawyer* 13 (Sept. 1988).

[18] *Estate of Newman*, 451 NYS2d 637 (N.Y. Surr. 1982).

Physical Condition of the Trustor's Beneficiaries and Trustor

The trustor may want to change the amount of and method by which he or she leaves assets to a beneficiary who has become ill or physically or mentally incapacitated since the trustor's Last Will was executed. In addition, a trustor whose health has deteriorated may change his or her estate plan to begin a gift-giving program to maximize the gift tax annual exclusion or to make gifts to charitable organizations in order to minimize the impact of federal estate tax upon the trustor's death.

Changes in a Beneficiary's Financial Circumstances

Perhaps a particular beneficiary has become bankrupt or has experienced some other adverse financial situation that may cause the trustor to feel differently about what this beneficiary should receive from his or her estate and how the beneficiary should receive it.

Failure to Have a Last Will

Obviously, the aforementioned events are only a few of the most common which should prompt the trustor to review his or her pour-over Will and overall estate plan. If the trustor does not have a pour-over Will, or if his or her present pour-over Will does not accurately reflect his or her current circumstances, some or all of the trustor's estate may go to the wrong people—or to the right people but in the wrong manner. As a result, unnecessary federal estate and state death taxes could take a heavy toll on the amount trustor's beneficiaries receive. Additionally, lengthy, bitter, and costly legal disputes could waste much of the assets in the trustor's estate and leave the trustor's family irrevocably split emotionally. By taking positive action and maintaining an up-to-date pour-over Will, the trustor can keep these and other unwanted possibilities from ever becoming reality for his or her beneficiaries. An outdated pour-over Will can cause just as many problems as having no Last Will at all![19]

Codicils

Some of the foregoing described events may require the trustor to have an entirely new pour-over Will written and executed; whereas, other events may only necessitate an amendment to his or her existing pour-over Will. The trustor can amend his or her pour-over Will by executing a *codicil* (see file "APP1702.DOC" 📄) with all of the formalities of the will itself.

Trust Failure

In the case *In re Estate of Rose*, failure by the decedent's surviving spouse to execute a codicil to her pour-over Will resulted in the failure of a new trust because the first trust had been revoked, thereby leaving nothing into which the decedent's pour-over Will could pour. The second trust could not be used to show an ambiguity because extrinsic evidence is admissible only after an ambiguity is shown.[20]

As a rule, the trustor should only use a codicil to make minor changes to his or her pour-over Will. Care should be exercised when the attorney prepares the codicil so as not to effect an unintended revocation of provisions in the pour-over Will. If the trustor's mental capacity to execute a new pour-over Will is suspect, the trustor may be well advised to execute a codicil and leave the original pour-over Will alone. This approach may avoid the

[19] Moy, 2, *A Practitioner's Guide to Estate Planning*, § 30.06, at 30-70.
[20] *In re Estate of Rose*, 772 S.W.2d 887 (Mo. Ct. App. 1989).

possibility of questions being raised as to testamentary capacity, as well as the validity of the appointment of the personal representative and as to the exercise of various powers and directions contained in the original pour-over Will. On the other hand, if the trustor is in full possession of his or her faculties and wishes to effect substantial changes regarding the disposition of his or her estate, the trustor should consider executing an entirely new pour-over Will.[21]

Reasons to Effect a New Pour-Over Will

Many reasons may exist why trustor should effect a new pour-over Will—not the least of which may involve a beneficiary included under the original pour-over Will but excluded from the new pour-over Will. Similarly, the trustor may choose to gift less to a particular beneficiary under a new pour-over Will than the same beneficiary would receive under the original pour-over Will. If a codicil was executed to effect such changes, the affected beneficiaries may feel offended upon a reading of the original pour-over Will and subsequently challenge the validity of the new provisions.[22] In addition, under the original pour-over Will, the trustee under the trustor's revocable living trust may be the same individual or corporate trustee or independent trust company that is named personal representative under the trustor's pour-over Will. If the trustor amends the revocable living trust agreement to replace the initial or successor trustee, then the trustor may or may not want to designate the new initial or successor trustee personal representative under his or her pour-over Will. If such a change is desirable, then the trustor should effect a codicil to his or her pour-over Will to that effect.

Overuse of Codicils

Finally, the relative ease with which codicils may be created and added to pour-over Wills often leads to an overuse of this method of amending or updating estate plans. The addition of numerous codicils to a pour-over Will may lead to inconsistencies and misinterpretations of the entire original pour-over Will. If the trustor wishes to effect major changes in his or her existing pour-over Will as a result of his or her estate planner's recommendations, and assuming the trustor's testamentary capacity is not uncertain, the trustor should have an entirely new pour-over Will designed, prepared, and executed.[23]

---

[21] Moy, 2, *A Practitioner's Guide to Estate Planning*, § 30.06[A], at 30-70.
[22] Ibid., at 30-71.
[23] Ibid

Bibliography

PRIMARY SOURCES

Alaska. *Alaska Statute* (Loislaw 2001).

3 *American Jurisprudence2d* (Am.Jur.2d), Agency, §§ 23, 28, 55, 57, 58.

23 *American Jurisprudence2d* (AmJur2d), Deeds 137.

39 *American Jurisprudence2d* (Am.Jur.2d), Guardian and Ward, §§ 1, 18, 20, 24, 27, 29, 30, 46, 48, 62, 64, 73, 78, 111.

76 *American Jurisprudence2d* (Am.Jur.2d), Trusts, §§ 35, 62.

American Law Institute. *Restatement (Second) of Trusts* (1959) (hereafter *Restatement (Second) of Trusts*).

Assistant Attorney General of the State of Oregon, Oregon Department of Justice, to the Contract Officer Oregon State Lottery, memorandum, 16 May 1997, Salem, Oregon, cited with permission (hereafter Memorandum).

Child Citizenship Act of 2000, Pub. L. No. 106-395, 106th Cong., 2d sess., 31 October 2000 (hereafter *Child Citizenship Act of 2000*).

Colorado. *Colorado Revised Statutes.* (Bradford Publishing Co., 2001).

Commerce Clearing House, ed. *Audit Technique Handbook for Estate Tax Examiners* (IRM 4350). In *Audit* Vol. II of *Internal Revenue Manual* (IRM). 3 vols. Chicago: Commerce Clearing House, Inc., 1987 (hereafter IRM 4350).

Commerce Clearing House, ed. *Explanation of Tax Reform Act of 1986.* In *Federal Tax Guide Reports.* Chicago: Commerce Clearing House, Inc., 1986 (hereafter *Explanation of Tax Reform Act of 1986*).

Commerce Clearing House, ed. *IRS Letter Rulings Reports.* Chicago: Commerce Clearing House, Inc., 1977.

Commerce Clearing House, ed. *Revenue Reconciliation Act of 1990 (H.R. 5835) Law and Explanation.* In *Standard Federal Tax Reports.* Chicago: Commerce Clearing House, Inc., 1990.

Commerce Clearing House, ed. *Tax Court Memorandum Decisions.* Chicago: Commerce Clearing House, Inc., 1946.

Commerce Clearing House, ed. *Tax Reform Bill of 1986 (H.R. 3838) Statement of the Managers filed 9/18/86.* In *Standard Federal Tax Reports,* two parts. Chicago: Commerce Clearing House, Inc., 1986.

Commerce Clearing House, ed. *Technical and Miscellaneous Revenue Act of 1988: Law and Explanation.* In *Standard Federal Tax Reports.* Chicago: Commerce Clearing House, Inc., 1988.

Commerce Clearing House, ed., *2001 Tax Legislation: Law, Explanation and Analysis (Economic Growth and Tax Relief Reconciliation Act of 2001).* Chicago: Commerce Clearing House, Inc., 2001 (hereafter CCH, *2001 Tax Legislation: Law, Explanation and Analysis*).

Commerce Clearing House, ed. *U.S. Tax Cases*. Chicago: Commerce Clearing House, Inc., 1938.

89 *Corpus Juris Secundum* (C.J.S.) 841.

Descriptions Contained in the Conference Committee Report on H.R. 1836, The Economic Growth and Tax Relief Reconciliation Bill of 2001, Fed. Est. & Gift Tax Rep. (CCH) ¶ 29,056 (30 May 2001) (hereafter *Conference Committee Report on H.R. 1836*).

The Economic Growth and Tax Relief Reconciliation Act of 2001, Pub. L. No. 107-16, 107th Cong., 1st sess. (7 June 2001) (hereafter "the 2001 Act").

Economic Growth and Tax Relief Reconciliation Bill 2001 (H.R.. 1836), Descriptions Contained in the Conference Committee Report on H.R. 1836, the Economic Growth and Tax Relief Reconciliation Bill of 2001, as released on 30 May 2001, Fed. Est. & Gift Tax Rep. (CCH), ¶ 29,056 (hereafter *Conference Committee Report on H.R. 1836*).

Economic Recovery Tax Act of 1981, Pub. L. No. 97-34, 97th Cong., 1st sess. (1981), 1981-2 C.B. 256 (hereafter ERTA '81).

Federal Deposit Insurance Corporation. *FDIC Legal Division Staff's Guidelines on the Insurance of Revocable Trust Accounts Including Living Trusts*. Memorandum dated 1 April 1999, issued as attachment to FDIC Financial Institution Letter (FIL)-4-2002 Re: Deposit Insurance Coverage of Revocable Trust Accounts (hereafter FDIC Guidelines).

Friesen, Gary, manager. Corporation and Estate Section, Business Division, Oregon Department of Revenue to Thomas P. Joseph, Jr., Attorney-at-Law, 8 July 1997, Salem, Oregon (hereafter Letter).

Garn-St. Germain Depository Institutions Act of 1982, 12 U.S.C.A. § 1701j-3(d)(8) (1983).

Hawaii. *Hawaii Revised Statutes*. 2002.

Idaho. *General Laws of Idaho Annotated*. Indianapolis-New York: The Bobs Merrill Company, Inc. 1979. [Idaho Code (Bobs-Merrill 2001)].

Immigration and Nationality Act, Section 320(a). 8 U.S.C. 1431, as amended by Section 101, *Child Citizenship Act of 2000*, Pub. L. No. 106-395, 106th Cong., 2d sess., 31 October 2000 (hereafter *Child Citizenship Act of 2000*).

Internal Revenue Service Restructuring and Reform Act of 1998, Pub. L. No. 105-206, 105th Cong., 2d sess., 22 July 1998, 112 Stat 685 (hereafter *IRS Restructuring and Reform Act of 1998*).

Joint Committee on Taxation's *Technical Explanation of H.R. 2884, The Victims of Terrorism Tax Relief Bill of 2001 (Final Version)*, Fed. Est. & Gift Tax Rep. (CCH) I-44, 185 (29 January 2002) (hereafter *Technical Explanation of H.R. 2884*).

Maryland. *Maryland Annotated Code*. (2002).

Montana. *Montana Code Annotated*. (2001).

Moy, Doug H., to Oregon Department of Revenue, 23 May 1997, Lake Oswego, OR.

North Carolina. *North Carolina General Statutes*. (2001).

Omnibus Budget Reconciliation Act of 1990, Pub. L. No. 101-508, 101st Cong., 2d sess., 5 November 1990, 1991-2 C.B.481.

Oregon. *Oregon Revised Statutes* (ORS) (2001).

Research Institute of America. *Revenue Act and Pension Protection Act of 1987. Conference Bill and Report*. In *Federal Tax Coordinator 2d*. Special Edition No. 1 6 January 1988. New York: Research Institute of America, Inc., 1988.

Revenue Reconciliation Act of 1990 (H.R. 5835) Law and Explanation [Extra Edition No. 48], Stand. Fed. Tax Rep. (CCH) (hereafter RRA '90 Law and Explanation).

Revenue Reconciliation Act of 1990 in *Omnibus Budget Reconciliation Act of 1990*. Pub. L. No. 101-508, 101st Cong., 2d sess., 1990, 1991-2 C.B. 481 (hereafter RRA '90).

Staff of the Joint Committee on Taxation. *Explanation of Technical Corrections to the Tax Reform Act of 1984 and Other Recent Legislation*, 99th Cong., 1st sess. 119 (Comm. Print 1987).

Staff of Joint Committee on Taxation. *Federal Tax Consequences of Estate Freezes: In Anticipation of Hearing Held by the House Ways and Means Committee*, 101st Cong., 2d sess., 24

April 1990. In *Federal Estate and Gift Tax Reports*. Chicago: Commerce Clearing House, Inc., 1990 (hereafter *Federal Tax Consequences of Estate Freezes*).

Tax Reform Act of 1976. Pub. L. 94-455, 94th Cong., 2d sess., 24 October 1976, 1976-3 (Vol. 1) C.B. 1.

Tax Reform Act of 1984. Pub. L. 98-369, 98th Cong., 2d sess., 18 July 1984, 1984-3 C.B. 1.

Tax Reform Act of 1986. Pub. L. No. 99-514, 99th Cong., 2d sess., 22 October 1986, 1986-3 C.B. 1 (hereafter TRA '86).

Taxpayer Relief Act of 1997. Pub. L. No. 105-34, 105th Cong., 1st sess., 1997, 111 Stat. 788 (hereafter "the 1997 Act").

Taxpayer Relief Bill of 1997, Conference Report and Statement of Managers (H.R. 2014), as released on 31 July 1997, issued as a CCH Special, Stand. Fed. Tax Rep. (CCH) Conf. Rep., 88 (4 August 1997).

Technical and Miscellaneous Revenue Act of 1988. Pub. L. No. 100-647, 100th Cong., 2d sess., 10 November 1988, 1988-3 C.B. 1 (hereafter TAMRA '88).

Technical and Miscellaneous Revenue Act of 1988: Law and Explanation, [Extra Edition No. 55], Stand. Fed. Tax Rep. (CCH) Conf. Rep. 1258 (1988) (hereafter TAMRA '88 Law and Explanation).

Uniform Durable Power of Attorney Act. 8A Uniform Laws Annotated 89 (West 1991).

Uniform Laws Annotated. St. Paul, MN: West Publishing Company, 1976, 1983, 1991, 1995.

Uniform Probate Code § 2-512. 8 Uniform Laws Annotated (1995).

Uniform Testamentary Additions to Trust Act. 8A Uniform Laws Annotated 603 (West 1983).

United States. *Code of Federal Regulations*. The Office of the Federal Register National Archives and Records Administration. 1999.

United States. *Code of Federal Tax Regulations*. St. Paul, MN: West Publishing Company, 1954.

United States. *Reports of the Tax Court of the United States*. Washington, D.C.: U.S. Government Printing Office, 1943.

United States. *Reports of the United States Board of Tax Appeals*. Washington, D.C.: U.S. Government Printing Office, 1926.

United States. *United States Code*.

United States Code. *Internal Revenue Code of 1986*. St. Paul, MN: West Publishing Company, 1986.

U.S. Congress. House. H. Rep. No. 97-201, 97th Cong., 1st sess., 188 (1981), 1981-2 C.B. 352.

U.S. Congress. House. H.R. Conf. Rep. 841, 99th Cong., 2d sess., II-401-402 (1986), 1986-3 (Vol. 4) C.B. 1.

U.S. Congress. House. H.R. Rep. No. 107-37, 107th Cong., 1st sess., 85 (2001).

U.S. Congress. Senate. S. Rep. No. 94-1236, 94th Cong., 2d sess., 1976, 1976-3 (Vol. 3) C.B. 807.

U.S. Congress. Senate. S. Rep. No. 99-313, 99th Cong., 2d sess., 872 (1986).

U.S. Congress. Senate. S. Rep. No. 107-30, 107th Cong., 1st sess., 2001.

United States Internal Revenue Service. Treasury Department. Bureau of Internal Revenue. *Actuarial Values Book Aleph. Publication 1457* (7-1999). Washington, D.C.: U.S. Government Printing Office, 1999. Catalog Number 63854M (hereafter IRS Publication 1457 [7-1999]).

United States Internal Revenue Service. Treasury Department. Bureau of Internal Revenue. *Cumulative Bulletin*, 1919 to present. Washington, D.C.: U.S. Government Printing Office, 1922.

United States Internal Revenue Service. Treasury Department. Bureau of Internal Revenue. *Statistics of Income Bulletin*, Projections, Winter 2001-2002, Publication 1136 (Rev. 2-2002), Russell Gieman, Chief, Projections and Forecasting Group, Internal Revenue Service, Table 1—Number of Returns Filed, or to be Filed, With the Internal Revenue Service, Calendar Years 2000-2008 (hereafter IRS, *Statistics of Income Bulletin*, Winter 2001-2002, Publication 1136 (Rev. 2-2002), Table 1).

USA Patriot Act, Pub. L. No. 107-56, 115 Stat. 272 (26 October 2001).

Utah. *Utah Code Annotated*. 2002.

Victims of Terrorism Tax Relief Act of 2001, Pub. L. No. 107-134, 107th Cong., 1st sess., 23 January 2002.

Wisconsin. *Wisconsin Statute Annotated* (Loislaw 2001).

Wyoming. *Wyoming Statutes*. 2002.

ARTICLES AND PERIODICALS

Aucutt, Ronald D. "An A-to-Z 'To Do' List Following EGTRRA." *Estate Planning* 28 (December 2001): 606.

Begleiter, Martin D. "Anti-contest Clauses: When You Care Enough to Send the Final Threat." *Arizona State Law Journal* 26 (1994): 629.

Blackman, Clark M., II, and Karen S. Gerstner. "Estate Planning: Should a Trust be the Beneficiary of Your IRA?" *American Association of Individual Investors Journal* 24 (October 2002): 31.

Blattmachr, Jonathan G. "Are You Using the Wrong Tax Apportionment Clause?" *Probate & Property* 3 (November/December 1989): 23.

———. "Tax Apportionment: The Most Important Clause in Many Wills." *American Law Institute–American Bar Association Course Materials Journal* 14 (Dec. 1989): 107.

Blattmachr, Jonathan G., and Lauren Y. Detzel. "Estate Planning Changes in the 2001 Tax Act—More Than You Can Count." *Journal of Taxation* 95 (August 2001): 74.

Blattmachr, Jonathan G., Georgiana J. Slade, and Bridget J. Crawford. "Selected Estate Planning Strategies for Persons With Less Than $3 Million." *Estate Planning* 26 (July 1999): 243.

Burnstein, Stanley M. "Family-owned Business Deduction is Enhanced by Balance Sheet Planning." *Estate Planning* 25 (October 1998): 348.

Bush, Julian S. *The Closely Held Business in the Revocable Trust: Advantages and Post-death Problems*. The Thirty-fourth Annual New York University Institute (1976): 1621.

Carroll, John L., and Brian K. Carroll. "Avoiding the Will Contest." *Property & Probate* 8 (May/June 1994): 61.

Cline, Chris. "They're Finally Here! IRA and Qualified Plan Distribution Rules Under the Final Regulations." *Tax Management Estates, Gifts and Trusts Journal* 27 (July-August 2002): 190.

Cline, Christopher P., and Marcia L. Jory. "The Uniform Prudent Investor Act: Trust Drafting and Administration." *Estate Planning* 26 (December 1999): 451.

Commerce Clearing House. "Carryover Basis Redux." *Estate Planning Review* in *Financial and Estate Planning* 4. Commerce Clearing House, Inc., Chicago (June 22, 2001): 50.

Commerce Clearing House Tax Advisory Board. "The Changing Practice of Tax Law for Lawyers and Accountants." *Taxes* 72 (April 1994): 190, 207 (hereafter CCH Tax Advisory Board, "Practice of Tax Law for Lawyers and Accountants").

Dobris, Joel C. "New Forms of Private Trusts for the Twenty-first Century—Principal and Income." *Real Property, Probate & Trust Journal* 31 (1996): 1.

Fee, Edwin G., Jr. "Electing to Treat a Revocable Trust as Part of the Estate." *Estate Planning* 26 (March/April 1999): 118.

Fife, James D. "Structuring Buy-Sell Agreements to Fix Estate Tax Value." *Estate Planning* 22 (March/April 1995): 67.

Fogel, Bradley E. S. "Using Life Insurance Trusts to Hold Group Term Life Insurance." *Probate & Property* 11 (September/October 1997): 30.

Frees, David. "Marketing Estate Planning After The 2001 Act: Interview With David Frees," interview by editors of Commerce Clearing House, Inc. *Estate Planning Review* in 4 *Financial and Estate Planning*, issue 521 (August 20, 2001): 89.

Grassi, Sebastian V., Jr. "Drafting for the Family-owned Business Deduction." *Journal of Taxation* 90 (June 1999): 358.

Gulecas, James F., and Alan S. Gassman. "The Economic Growth and Tax Relief Reconciliation Act of 2001: Practical Estate Planning." *Practical Tax Lawyer* 15 (Summer 2001): 35.

Horn, Jerold. "Prudent Investor Rule, Modern Portfolio Theory, and Private Trusts: Drafting and Administration Including the Give-me-five Unitrust." *Real Property, Probate & Trust Journal* 33 (Spring 1998): 1.

Houghton, Thomas W., and Harvey B. Wallace, II. "Using Trusts Effectively in Retirement Planning, Part II: Planning and Drafting Suggestions. *Probate & Property* 16 (November/December 2002): 34 (hereafter Houghton and Wallace II, "Using Trusts Effectively in Retirement Planning, Part II").

Johanson, Stanley M. "The Use of Tax-saving Clauses in Drafting Wills & Trusts." *The Fifteenth Annual Philip E. Heckerling Institute on Estate Planning*, University of Miami Law Center (1981): Chapter 21.

Johnson, Linda M., and Brian R. Greenstein. "Using Buy-Sell Agreements to Establish the Value of a Closely Held Business." *Journal of Taxation* 81 (December 1994): 362.

Kasner, Jerry A. "After the Estate Tax Family Business Deduction, What Next?" *One Disc Weekly Tax Review* 2 (Tax Analysts Oct. 27, 2000): 1.

Keister, David W., and William J. McCarthy, Jr. "1997 Principal and Income Act Reflects Modern Trust Investing." *Estate Planning* 26 (March/April 1999): 99.

Kess, Sidney, and Lee Slavutin. "Planning Techniques and Tips: Important Considerations in Drafting the Will." *Estate Planning Review* in 4 *Financial and Estate Planning*. Commerce Clearing House, Inc., Chicago (19 July 2001): 60.

Kiziah, Trent S. "Estate Tax Apportionment: '"Except as Otherwise Directed.'" *Florida Bar Journal* 64 (Nov. 1990): 52.

Krass, Stephen J., and Cynthia L. Alicia. "Estate Planning for Group-term Life Insurance," in 3 *Financial and Estate Planning*. Commerce Clearing House, Inc., Chicago: ¶ 29,101 .

Kruse, Clifton B., Jr. "Medicaid Considerations for Lawyers Representing the Upper Crust." *The Thirty-Third Annual Philip E. Heckerling Institute on Estate Planning*, University of Miami Law Center 7 (1999): Chapter 7 (hereafter Kruse, Jr., "Medicaid Considerations for Lawyers").

———. "Revocable Trusts: Creditors' Rights After Settlor-debtor's Death." *Probate & Property* 7 (November/December 1993): 40.

Leimberg, Stephen R., and Charles K. Plotnick. "How to Review a Will." *Practical Lawyer* 34 (September 1988): 13.

Lynn, Robert J. "Problems With Pour-over Wills." *Ohio State Law Journal* 47 (1986): 47.

Marcovici, Philip, Teresa Lewis, Marnin J. Michaels, Victoria A. Dalmas and Christine Hsieh-Kammerlander. "New U.S. Tax Act: Dramatic Consequences for Estate, Gift, GST Regime in the Foreign Context: Part 1." *Estate Planner's Alert* 26 (September 2001): 2, Part 2 (October 2001): 2, in Research Institute of America *Estate Planning & Taxation Coordinator*.

Maydew, Gary L. "The Qualified Family-owned Business Interest Deduction: RRA 98 Clears Up Some of the Confusion," in 3 *Financial and Estate Planning*. Commerce Clearing House, Inc., Chicago: ¶ 31,981.

Mezzullo, Louis A. "New Estate Freeze Rules Replacing 2036(c) Expand Planning Potential." *Journal of Taxation* 74 (January 1991): 4.

Moore, M. Read. "Interaction of the Estate Tax Marital Deduction and Qualified Plan and IRA Benefits." *Estate Planning* 23 (February 1996): 86.

Moy, Doug H. "Deferring the Payment of Federal Estate Tax Under I.R.C. § 6166 in View of TAM 9214010." *Tax Management Estates, Gifts and Trusts Journal* 18 (July/August 1993): 107.

————. "Joint Ownership of Property: Two's Company, but Is Three a Crowd?" *National Public Accountant* 39 (Jan. 1994): 16-19, 34-37.

————. "Revocable Living Trusts: Availability of One-Time Exclusion of Gain from Sale of Principal Residence in the Event Trustor Becomes Incompetent." *Tax Management Estates, Gifts and Trusts Journal* 15 (March-April 1990): 62 (hereafter Moy, "Revocable Living Trusts: Availability of One-Time Exclusion").

Newlin, Charles F., and Andrea C. Chomakos. "The 2001 Tax Act: Uncharted Waters for Estate Planners." *Probate & Property* 15 (September-October 2001): 32.

Northern Trust Company. "The Economic Growth and Tax Relief Reconciliation Act of 2001," in 3 *Financial and Estate Planning*, Commerce Clearing House, Inc., Chicago: ¶ 32,351.

O'Brien, Shannon E. "Estate Tax Treatment of Family-owned Businesses: The Evolution of Internal Revenue Code Section 2057." *University of Missouri-Kansas Law Review* 67 (1999): 495.

Plaine, Lloyd Leva. "The Proposed Generation-Skipping Transfer Tax in the House-Passed Tax Reform Bill." *Tax Management Estates, Gifts and Trust Journal* 11 (May-June 1986): 63 (hereafter Plaine, "The Proposed Generation-Skipping Transfer Tax").

Sargent, Paul B. "Facts and Fallacies of Living Trusts." *The Fifth Annual Philip E. Heckerling Institute on Estate Planning*, University of Miami Law Center 7 (1971): ¶ 71,203 (hereafter Sargent, "Facts and Fallacies of Living Trusts.")

Schlesinger, Sanford J. "Estate and Gift Tax—Update 2001." *Estate Planning Review*, in 4 *Financial and Estate Planning*. Commerce Clearing House, Inc., Chicago (22 January 2002): 1.

Schmidt, William L., Jr. "How to Fund a Revocable Living Trust Correctly." *Estate Planning* 20 (March-April 1993): 67.

Slade, Georgiana J. "The Beneficiary as Trustee: A Pandora's Box." *Tax Management Estates, Gifts and Trusts Journal* 19 (November-December 1994): 197.

Slavutin, Lee, MD, CPC, CLU. "Planning Strategies with Group-Term Life Insurance: Interview with Lee Slavutin, MD, CPC, CLU, interview by editors of Commerce Clearing House, Inc. *Estate Planning Review*, in 3 *Financial and Estate Planning*, issue 445 (June 18, 1998): 41.

Snow, Lee A. "Final IRA Distribution Regulations Offer New Planning Opportunities," in 3 *Financial and Estate Planning*, Commerce Clearing House, Inc., Chicago, Ill.: ¶ 32,441.

Solberg, T. "Buy-Sell Agreements Can Freeze Asset Values and in Some Cases Make Them Disappear." *Taxes* 59 (July 1981): 437.

Soled, Jay A., and Dena L. Wolf. "Rev. Rul. 92-26: An Inspiration from Ponce de Leon." *Tax Management Estates, Gifts and Trusts Journal* 17 (September-October 1992): 151.

Sommerfeld, Nicholas U. "Techniques That Can Help Professionals Develop A More Successful Practice." *Estate Planning* 10 (November 1983): 330.

Spacapan, Edward Jr. "2001 Tax Act Substantially Improve Retirement and Savings Plans." *Estate Planning* 29 (January 2002): 16.

Switzer, Dr. Ralph, Jr. and Daniel A. Pollock. "Using a QTIP Trust to Extend the Life of an IRA" *Tax Management Estates, Gifts and Trusts Journal* 21 (March-April 1996): 95.

Tobisman, S. "Estate and Gift Tax Considerations in Buy-Sell Agreements." *U.S. California Tax Institute* 35 (1983): ¶ 2,700.

Treacy, Gerald B., Jr. "Planning to Preserve the Advantages of Community Property." *Estate Planning* 23 (January 1996): 24.

Wolf, Robert B. "Total Return Trusts—Can Your Clients Afford Anything Less?" *Real Property, Probate & Trust Journal* 33 (Spring 1998): 131.

BOOKS, MONOGRAPHS, AND TAX SERVICE PUBLICATIONS

Adams, Roy M. *Practical Estate Planning—The Routine and the Unexpected*, Sponsored by The Salvation Army, Wells Fargo Private Client Service, and Oregon Public Broadcasting, Tuesday, 24 September 2002, Oregon Public Broadcasting, Portland, Oregon (hereafter Adams, *Practical Estate Planning*).

Black, Henry Campbell M.A. *Black's Law Dictionary*, 5th ed. St. Paul, MN: West Publishing Co., 1979 (hereafter Black, *Black's Law Dictionary*).

Collin, Francis J., Jr., John J. Lombard, Jr., Albert L. Moses, editor, and Harley J. Spitler. *Drafting the Durable Power of Attorney A Systems Approach*, 2d ed. Colorado Springs, CO: Shepard's McGraw-Hill, 1987 (hereafter Collin, Jr., *Drafting the Durable Power of Attorney*).

Dacey, Norman F. *How to Avoid Probate*. New York: Crown Publishers, 1965.

Hood, Edwin T., John J. Mylan, and Timothy P. O'Sullivan. *Closely Held Businesses in Estate Planning*, 2d ed. New York: Aspen Law & Business, 1998.

Huebner, S.S., and Kenneth Black, Jr. *Life Insurance*, 8th ed. New York: Appleton-Century-Crofts, Educational Division, Meredith Corporation, 1972 (hereafter Huebner and Black, *Life Insurance*).

The Life Underwriter Training Council. *Life Underwriter Training Council Course: The Life Insurance Salesman*, 25th ed. 7 vols. (n.p.): The Life Underwriter Training Council, 1971.

Kraut, Jayson, ed. *American Jurisprudence Second Edition*. Rochester, NY: The Lawyer's Co-operative Publishing Company; San Francisco, California: Bancroft-Whitney, 1976.

Laser Pro™ Ver. 3.10a(c). (n.p.): CFI Bankers Service Group, Inc. All rights reserved, 1993.

Moy, Doug H. *A Practitioner's Guide to Estate Planning: Guidance and Planning Strategies*, 2 vols. New York: Aspen Publishers, Inc., 2002 (hereafter Moy, *A Practitioner's Guide to Estate Planning*).

Scott, Austin Wakeman. *Scott On Trusts*, 3d ed. Boston, MA: Little, Brown, 1967 and Supp. 1987 (hereafter *Scott on Trusts*).

Thomson, Andrew H. *The Feldman Method: The Words and Working Philosophy of the World's Greatest Insurance Salesman*. Lynbrook, NY: Farnsworth Publishing Company, Inc., 1969 (hereafter Thomson, *The Feldman Method*).

Train, John, and Thomas A. Melfe. *Investing and Managing Trusts Under the New Prudent Investor Rule*. Harvard Business School Press, 1999.

Turner, George M., M.S., J.D. *Revocable Trusts*. Colorado Springs, CO: Shepard's/McGraw-Hill, 1983 (hereafter Turner, *Revocable Trusts*).

Index